IMAGE DATABASES

IMAGE DATABASES

Search and Retrieval of Digital Imagery

Edited by

Vittorio Castelli
Lawrence D. Bergman
IBM T.J. Watson Research Center

JOHN WILEY & SONS, INC.

This book is printed on acid-free paper. ♾

Published simultaneously in Canada.

For ordering and customer service, call 1-800-CALL-WILEY.

Library of Congress Cataloging-in-Publication Data Is Available

ISBN 0-471-32116-8

Printed in the United States of America.

10 9 8 7 6 5 4 3 2 1

To Susan, for her loving support of this work—Vittorio

To family and friends, who made this all possible—Larry

CONTENTS

CONTRIBUTORS

Lawrence D. Bergman, IBM T.J. Watson Research Center, 30 Saw Mill River Rd., Hawthorne, NY 10532

Vittorio Castelli, IBM T.J. Watson Research Center, P.O. Box 128, Yorktown Heights, NY 10598

Kaushik Chakrabarti, University of California at Irvine, Information & Computer Science, 444 Computer Science Building, Irvine, CA 92697-3425

Shih-Fu Chang, Columbia University, Department of Electrical Engineering, S.W. Mudd Building, Room 1312, New York, NY 10027

Carlo Colombo, Università Di Firenze, Dipartimento di Sistemi E Informatica, Via Santa Marta 3, 1-50139 Firenze, Italy

Alberto Del Bimbo, Università di Firenze, Dipartimento di Sistemi E Informatica, Via Santa Marta 3, 1-50139 Firenze, Italy

Christos Faloutsos, Carnegie Mellon University, Department of Computer Science, Wean Hall, Pittsburgh, PA 15213-3891

Sheila S. Hemami, Cornell University, School of Electrical Engineering, 332 Rhodes Hall, Ithaca, NY 14853

Alejandro Jaimes, Columbia University, Department of Electrical Engineering, 500 West 120th Street, S.W. Mudd Bldg., Room 1312, New York, NY 10027

Benjamin B. Kimia, Brown University, Department of Engineering, Barus and Holley 320, Box D, Providence, RI 02912

C.-C. Jay Kuo, University of Southern California, Department of Electrical Engineering Systems, MC2564, Los Angeles, CA 90089-2564

Ying Li, University of Southern California, Department of Electrical Engineering-Systems, EEB 400, Los Angeles, CA 90089

Wei-Ying Ma, Microsoft Research China, Beijing, China

B.S. Manjunath, University of California at Santa Barbara, Department of Electrical and Computer Engineering, Santa Barbara, CA 93106-9560

Sharad Mehrotra, University of California at Irvine, Information & Computer Science, 444 Computer Science Building, Irvine, CA 92697-3425

Michael Ortega-Binderberger, University of Illinois, Department of Computer Science, Urbana-Champaign, IL

Sethuraman Panchanathan, Arizona State University, Department of Computer Sciences and Engineering, P.O. Box 875406, Tempe, AZ 85287-5406

Jeffrey W. Percival, University of Wisconsin, Space Astronomy Laboratory, 6295 Chamberlain Hall, 1150 University Avenue, Madison, WI 53706

H.K. Ramapriyan, Earth Science Data and Information System Project, Code 423 NASA, Goddard Space Flight Center, Greenbelt, MD 20771

Prashant Shenoy, University of Massachusetts, Department of Computer Science, Amherst, MA 01003-4610

John R. Smith, IBM T.J. Watson Research Center, 30 Saw Mill River Road, Hawthorne, NY 10532

Kent Soo Hoo, Jr., University of California at San Francisco, Radiology, Box 0628, 505 Parnassus Avenue, San Francisco, CA 94143-0628

Peter Tilke, Schlumberger–Doll Research Center, Old Quarry Rd, Ridgefield, CT 06877

Harrick M. Vin, University of Texas at Austin, Department of Computer Sciences, Taylor Hall 2.124, Austin, TX 78750

Xia Sharon Wan, 1704 Automation Parkway, San Jose, CA 95131

Stephen Wong, University of California at San Francisco, Radiology, P.O.Box 0628, 505 Parnassus Avenue, San Francisco, CA 94143-0628

PREFACE

Image databases pose new and challenging problems to the research community. Over the past 40 years, database technology has matured with the development of relational databases, object-relational databases, and object-oriented databases. Extensions to these databases have been developed to handle nontraditional data types, such as images, video, audio, and maps. The core functionalities of classical databases, however, are tailored toward simple data types and do not extend gracefully to nonstructured information.

As the amount of digital imagery grows, techniques that are specifically tailored to such data types need to be developed and more widely deployed. Over the last few years, standardization efforts have taken place in fields such as medicine, geographic information systems, and video in parallel with the development of large digital archives. Search and indexing technology has developed over the same time frame, leading to a wide variety of research prototypes and ad-hoc commercial solutions for searching imagery, video, and other multimedia types. There still is a lack, however, of large commercial systems that integrate existing techniques for storage, indexing, and retrieval of image databases.

In this volume, we present the state of the art of a number of disciplines that converge in image database technology. We motivate the volume by presenting selected applications, including photographic, remotely sensed, petroleum, and medical imagery.

The technology section is divided into two main areas: a portion on storage and one on retrieval. We start with a chapter on system architecture, detailing hierarchical storage management schemes, the role of caching, storage layout issues, and architectural trade-offs. This is followed by a chapter on applications of traditional databases to indexing image repositories, with emphasis on data modeling and organization. Image compression is an integral part of image storage management, and we devote a chapter to the topic, describing the fundamental concepts, reviewing and comparing the main existing standards, outlining nonstandard compression techniques, and discussing evaluation and trade-offs in selecting appropriate methods. Since delivery of imagery over limited bandwidth channels is a universal problem, we include a chapter describing the transmission of imagery in digital format, including techniques such as progressive transmission.

The second half of the technology section describes search and retrieval techniques. We begin with an overview of the area. Low-level image features, such as color, texture, and shape, are typically used to index image archives, and we devote a chapter to each of these. This is followed by a chapter on indexing techniques for spatial queries, range queries, similarity, and nearest-neighbor queries. The next chapter discusses the use of multiple abstraction levels and compressed or transformed images for improving search efficiency. The last chapter addresses the automatic extraction of semantic information from imagery.

This book is intended for several audiences. It can be used as a textbook for a graduate-level course on image databases, as it provides a wide range of introductory material and extensive bibliographies that are appropriate for directing further reading. It is also a valuable reference for developers and researchers in the field, as well as an introduction for IT professionals who need to further their understanding of the discipline.

IMAGE DATABASES

1 Digital Imagery: Fundamentals

VITTORIO CASTELLI
IBM T.J. Watson Research Center, Yorktown Heights, New York
LAWRENCE D. BERGMAN
IBM T.J. Watson Research Center, Hawthorne, New York

1.1 DIGITAL IMAGERY

Digital images have a predominant position among multimedia data types. Unlike video and audio, which are mostly used by the entertainment and news industry, images are central to a wide variety of fields ranging from art history to medicine, including astronomy, oil exploration, and weather forecasting. Digital imagery plays a valuable role in numerous human activities, such as law enforcement, agriculture and forestry management, earth science, urban planning, as well as sports, newscasting, and entertainment.

This chapter provides an overview of the topics covered in this book. We first describe several applications of digital imagery, some of which are covered in Chapters 2 to 5. The main technological factors that support the management and exchange of digital imagery, namely, acquisition, storage (Chapter 6), database management (Chapter 7), compression (Chapter 8), and transmission (Chapter 9) are then discussed.

Finally, a section has been devoted to content-based retrieval, a large class of techniques specifically designed for retrieving images and video. Chapters 10 to 17 cover these topics in detail.

1.2 APPLICATIONS OF DIGITAL IMAGES

Applications of digital imagery are continually developing. In this section, some of the major ones have been reviewed and the enabling economical and technological factors have been discussed briefly.

1.2.1 Visible Imagery

Photographic images are increasingly being acquired, stored, and transmitted in digital format. Their applications range from personal use to media and advertising, education, art, and even research in the humanities.

Image Databases: Search and Retrieval of Digital Imagery, Edited by Vittorio Castelli and Lawrence D. Bergman.
ISBN 0-471-32116-8

In the consumer market, digital cameras are slowly replacing traditional film-based cameras. The characteristics of devices for acquiring, displaying, and printing digital images are improving while their prices are decreasing. The resolution and color fidelity of digital cameras and desktop scanners are improving. Advancements in storage technology make it possible to store large number of pictures in digital cameras before uploading them to a personal computer. Inexpensive color printers can produce good quality reproductions of digital photographs. Digital images are also easy to share and disseminate: they can be posted on personal web sites or sent via e-mail to distant friends and relatives at no cost.

The advertisement and the media industries maintain large collection of images and need systems to store, archive, browse, and search them by content.

Museums and art galleries are increasingly relying on digital libraries to organize and promote their collections [1], and advertise special exhibits. These digital libraries, accessible via the Internet, provide an excellent source of material for the education sector and, in particular, for K-12.

A novel and extremely important application of digital libraries is to organize collections of rare and fragile documents. These documents are usually kept in highly controlled environments, characterized by low light and precise temperature and humidity levels. Only scholars can gain access to such documents, usually for a very limited time to minimize the risk of damage. Technology is changing this scenario: complex professional scanners have been developed that have very good color fidelity and depth (42-bit color or more) as well as high resolution. These scanners can capture the finest details, even those invisible without the aid of a magnifying lens, without risk to the original documents. The resulting digital images can be safely distributed to a wide audience across the Internet, allowing scholars to study otherwise inaccessible documents.

1.2.2 Remotely Sensed Images

One of the earliest application areas of digital imagery was remote sensing. Numerous satellites continuously monitor the surface of the earth. The majority of them measure the reflectance of the surface of the earth or atmospheric layers. Others measure thermal emission in the far-infrared and near-microwave portion of the spectrum, while yet others use synthetic-aperture radars and measure both reflectance and travel time (hence elevation). Some instruments acquire measurements in a single portion of the spectrum; others simultaneously acquire images in several spectral bands; finally, some radiometers acquire measurements in tens or hundreds of narrow spectral bands. Geostationary satellites on a high equatorial orbit are well suited to acquire low-resolution images of large portions of the earth's surface (where each pixel corresponds to tens of square miles), and are typically used for weather prediction. Nongeostationary satellites are usually on a polar orbit — their position relative to the ground depends both on their orbital motion and on the rotation of the earth. Lower-orbiting satellites typically acquire higher-resolution images but require more revolutions to cover the entire surface of the earth. Satellites used for environmental monitoring usually produce low-resolution images, where each pixel corresponds to surface areas on the order of square kilometers. Other commercial satellites have higher resolution. The Landsat TM instrument has a resolution of about 30 m on the ground, and the latest generation of commercial instruments have resolutions of 1 to 3 m. Satellites for military applications have even higher resolution.

The sheer volume of satellite-produced imagery, on the order of hundreds of gigabytes a day, makes acquisition, preparation, storage, indexing, retrieval, and distribution of the data very difficult.

The diverse community of users often combine remotely sensed images with different types of data, including geographic or demographic information, ground-station observations, and photographs taken from planes. The resulting need for data fusion and interoperability poses further challenges to database and application developers.

1.2.3 Medical Images

Images are used in medicine for both diagnostic and educational purposes. Radiology departments produce the vast majority of medical images, while anatomic photographs and histological microphotographs account for a small fraction of the overall data volume.

Radiological images capture physical properties of the body, such as opacity to X rays (radiographies and CT scans), reflectance to ultrasounds, concentration of water or other chemicals (MRI), and distribution of elements within organs (PET). Medical images can be used to investigate anatomic features (e.g., broken bones or tumors) and physiological functions (e.g., imbalances in the activity of specific organs).

The availability of high-quality, high-resolution displays of sensors with better characteristics (sensitivity, quantum efficiency, etc.) than photographic film, of fast interconnection networks, and of inexpensive secondary and tertiary storage are driving radiology departments toward entirely digital, filmless environments, wherein image databases play a central role.

The main challenges faced by medical image databases are integration with the hospital work flow and interoperability.

1.2.4 Geologic Images

Oil companies are among the main producers and consumers of digital imagery. Oil exploration often starts with seismic surveys, in which large geologic formations are imaged by generating sound waves and measuring how they are reflected at the interface between different strata. Seismic surveys produce data that is processed into two- or three-dimensional imagery.

Data are also routinely acquired during drilling operation. Measurements of physical properties of the rock surrounding the well bore are measured with special-purpose imaging tools, either during drilling or afterwards. Some instruments measure aggregate properties of the surrounding rock and produce a single measurement every sampling interval; others have arrays of sensors that take localized measurements along the circumference of the well bore. The former measures are usually displayed as one-dimensional signals and the latter measures are displayed as (long and thin) images.

Sections of rock (core) are also selectively removed from the bottom of the well, prepared, and photographed for further analysis. Visible-light or infrared-light microphotographs of core sections are often used to assess structural properties of the rock, and a scanning electron microscope is occasionally used to produce images at even higher magnification.

Image databases designed for the oil industry face the challenges of large data volumes, a wide diversity of data formats, and the need to combine data from multiple sources (data fusion) for the purpose of analysis.

1.2.5 Biometric Identification

Images are widely used for personal-identification purposes. In particular, fingerprints have long been used in law enforcement and are becoming increasingly popular for access control to secure information and identity. checks during firearm sales. Some technologies, such as face recognition, are still in the research domain, while others, such as retinal scan matching, have very specialized applications and are not widespread.

Fingerprinting has traditionally been a labor-intensive manual task performed by highly skilled workers. However, the same technological factors that have enabled the development of digital libraries, and the availability of inkless fingerprint scanners, have made it possible to create digital fingerprint archives[2,3].

Fingerprint verification (to determine if two fingerprints are from the same finger), identification (retrieving archived fingerprints that match the one given), and classification (assigning a fingerprint to a predefined class) all rely on the positions of distinctive characteristics of the fingerprint called *minutiae*. Typical minutiae are the points where a ridge bifurcates or where a ridge terminates. Fingerprint collections are searched by matching the presence and relative positions of minutiae. Facial matching procedures operate similarly — extracting essential features and then matching them against pre-extracted features from images in the database.

The main challenges in constructing biometric databases are the reliable extraction of minutiae and the matching strategy. Matching, in particular, is difficult: it must rely on rotation- and translation-invariant algorithms, it must be robust to missing and spurious data (the extraction algorithm might fail to identify relevant features or might extract nonexistent features, especially if the image quality is poor), and it must account for distortions due to lighting and positioning. The development of efficient indexing methods that satisfy these requirements is still an open research problem.

1.2.6 Astronomical Imagery

Astronomers acquire data in all regions of the electromagnetic spectrum. Although the atmosphere blocks most high-energy waves (UV, X- rays and γ-

rays), as well as large portions of the infrared and lower-frequency waves, it has large transparency windows that allowed the development of visible-light and radio wave astronomy. High-energy astronomy is possible using instruments mounted on high-altitude planes or orbiting satellites. Radio telescopes acquire signals in the long-wave, short-wave and microwave ranges, and are used to produce two-dimensional maps, often displayed as images.

Traditionally, astronomy has heavily relied on plate-based photography for infrared, visual, and ultraviolet studies (in astronomy, glass plates are used instead of photographic film). Long exposures (of up to tens of hours) make it possible to capture objects that are one to two orders of magnitude too dim to be detected by the human eye through the same instrument.

Photographic plates are not the ideal detectors — they are expensive and fragile, often have small defects that can hide important information, are not very sensitive to light, lose sensitivity during exposure, and their reproduction for distribution is labor-intensive. Their main benefits are large size and high resolution.

Starting from the mid-1980s, sensors that acquire images in digital format have become more and more widely used. In particular, charge-coupled devices (CCD) have found widespread application in astronomy. High-resolution sensor arrays, with responses that go beyond the visible spectrum are now commonly available. These instruments are extremely sensitive — when coupled with photomultipliers, they can almost detect the arrival of individual photons. Images that used to require hours of exposure can now be produced in minutes or less. Additionally, techniques exist to digitally reduce the inherent electrical noise of the sensor, further enhancing the quality of the image. Since the images are produced directly in digital format, a photograph is often acquired by collecting a sequence of short-exposure snapshots and combining them digitally. Image-processing techniques exist to compensate for atmospheric turbulence and for inaccuracies in telescope movement. Solid-state devices are also the detectors of choice for orbiting telescopes.

Digital libraries that organize the wealth of astronomical information are growing continuously and are increasingly providing support for communities beyond professional astronomers and astrophysicists, including school systems and amateur astronomers.

1.2.7 Document Management

Digital imagery plays an increasingly important role in traditional office management. Although we are far from the "paperless office" that many have envisioned, more and more information is being stored digitally, much of it in the form of imagery.

Perhaps the best case in point is archiving of cancelled checks. This information in the past was stored on microfilm — a medium that was difficult to manage. Moving this information to digital storage has resulted in enhanced ease of access and reduced storage volume. The savings are even more dramatic when digital imagery is used to replace paper records.

Although many documents can be very efficiently compressed by using optical character recognition (OCR) to convert them into text, for many applications the format of the original document is best retained using two-dimensional images.

Challenges in document management include automated scanning technology, automated indexing for rapid retrieval, and managing the imagery within the context of traditional database management systems.

1.2.8 Catalogs

Perhaps the most evident role of digital imagery to end consumers is on-line catalogs. Rapidly replacing traditional print catalogs, on-line catalogs often run to hundreds of pages with large volumes of color imagery. These applications range from simple display of small thumbnails to advanced facilities that allow high-resolution pan and zoom, and even manipulation of three-dimensional models.

The requirements for digital catalogs include support for multiresolution storage and transmission, rapid retrieval, and integration with traditional database facilities.

1.3 TECHNOLOGICAL FACTORS

1.3.1 Acquisition and Compression

In the past decade, high-quality digital image acquisition systems have become increasingly available. They range from devices for personal use, such as inexpensive high-definition color scanners and cameras, to professional scanners with extremely precise color calibration (used to image art and rare document collections), to complex medical instruments such as digital mammography and digital radiology sensor arrays.

Compression is an essential technique for the management of large image collections. Compression techniques belong to one of two classes. Lossless compression algorithms ensure that the original image is exactly reconstructed from the compressed data. Lossy algorithms only allow reconstruction of an approximation of the original data. Lossless schemes usually reduce the data volume by a factor of 2 or 3 at best, whereas lossy schemes can reduce the storage requirement by a factor of 10 without introducing visually appreciable distortions.

In addition to its role in reducing the storage requirements for digital archives (and the associated enhancements in availability), compression plays an important role in transmission of imagery. In particular, progressive transmission techniques enable browsing of large image collections that would otherwise be inaccessible.

Numerous standards for representing, compressing, storing, and manipulating digital imagery have been developed and are widely employed by the producers of computer software and hardware. The existence of these standards significantly simplifies a variety of tasks related to digital imagery management.

1.3.2 Storage and Database Support

Recent advances in computer hardware have made storage of large collections of digital imagery both convenient and inexpensive. The capacity of moderately priced hard drives has increased 10 times over the past four years. Redundant arrays of inexpensive disks (RAIDs) provide fast, fault-tolerant, and high-capacity storage solutions at low cost. Optical and magneto-optical disks offer high capacity and random access capability and are well suited for large robotic tertiary storage systems. The cost of write-once CD-ROMs is below 1 dollar per gigabyte when they are bought in bulk, making archival storage available at unprecedented levels.

Modern technology also provides the fault-tolerance required in many application areas. High-capacity media with long shelf life allow storage of medical images for periods of several years, as mandated by law. In oil exploration, images acquired over a long period of time can help in modeling the evolution of a reservoir and in determining the best exploitation policies. Loss-resilient disk-placement techniques and compression algorithms can produce high-quality approximations of the original images even in the presence of hardware faults (e.g., while a faulty disk is being replaced and its contents are being recovered from a backup tape). These technologies are essential in some applications, such as medicine, where the user must be allowed to retrieve a large part of an image even during system faults.

Numerous software advances have enabled guarantees of high-quality service to users accessing large image repositories. At the operating system level, software policies exist to optimally place images on disk and multiresolution images across multiple disks in order to minimize response time. Strategies to distribute imagery across hierarchical storage management systems exist, and, together with caching and batching policies, allow the efficient management of very large collections.

At the middleware level, database technology advancements have been made to support image repositories. Object-relational databases can store image files as binary large objects (BLOBs) and allow application developers to define new data types (user-defined data types — UDTs) and methods to manipulate them (user-defined functions — UDFs).

1.3.3 Transmission and Display

The explosion of the Internet has facilitated the distribution and sharing of digital imagery and has fostered new fields, such as teleconsultation in medicine, which were unthinkable just two decades ago. Numerous techniques have been developed to transmit digital images. *Progressive transmission* methods are particularly interesting. They allow the receiver to display a lossy version of the image, possibly at low resolution, shortly after the transmission begins, with improvements in quality as more data is received. Because of these techniques, the user can decide whether the image is of interest and terminate the transmission if necessary, without having to wait for the entire data file.

Advances in display technology are providing affordable solutions for specialized fields such as medicine, where extremely high-resolution (2,000 × 2,000 pixels or more), high-contrast, large dynamic range (12 bits or more for gray scale images), very limited geometric distortion, and small footprint displays are necessary.

1.4 INDEXING LARGE COLLECTION OF DIGITAL IMAGES

A large body of research has been devoted to developing mechanisms for efficiently retrieving images from a collection. By nature, images contain unstructured information, which makes the search task extremely difficult. A typical query on a financial database would ask for all the checks written on a specific account and cleared during the last statement period; a typical query on a database of photographic images could request all images containing a red Ferrari F50. The former operation is rather simple: all the transaction records in the database contain the desired information (date, type, account, amount) and the database management system is built to efficiently execute it. The latter operation is a formidable task, unless all the images in the repository have been manually annotated.

The unstructured information contained within images is difficult to capture automatically. Techniques that seek to index this unstructured visual information are grouped under the collective name of *content-based retrieval.*

1.4.1 Content-Based Retrieval of Images

In content-based retrieval [4], the user describes the desired content in terms of visual features, and the system retrieves images that best match the description. Content-based retrieval is therefore a type of retrieval by similarity.

Image content can be defined at different levels of abstraction [5–7]. At the lowest level, an image is a collection of pixels. Pixel-level content is rarely used in retrieval tasks. It is however, important, in very specific applications, for example, in identifying ground control points used to georegister remotely sensed images or anatomic details used for coregistering medical images from different modalities.

The raw data can be processed to produce numeric descriptors capturing specific visual characteristics called *features*. The most important features for image databases are color, texture, and shape. Features can be extracted from entire images describing global visual characteristics or from portions of images describing local characteristics. In general, a feature-level representation of an image requires significantly less space than the image itself.

The next abstraction level describes the semantics. A semantic-level characterization of photographic images is an extremely complex task, and this field is characterized by countless open problems. However, in numerous scientific disciplines, semantic content can be inferred from the lower abstraction levels. For example, it is possible to deduce the type of land cover using spectral information from satellite images [8]; similarly, color, texture, and ancillary one-dimensional measurements can be used to determine the composition of geologic strata imaged for oil exploration purposes.

At the highest level, images are often accompanied by metadata. Metadata may contain information that cannot be obtained directly from the image, as well as an actual description of the image content. For example, medical images (Chapter 4) stored for clinical purposes are accompanied by a radiological report, detailing their relevant characteristics.

It is often natural to describe image content in terms of objects, which can be defined at one or more abstraction levels. It is often very difficult to identify objects in photographic images; however, scientific data is often more amenable to automatic object extraction. For example, a bone section in an MRI scan is a very dark connected area (feature level), a forest in a remotely sensed image is a connected area covered by evergreen or deciduous trees (semantic level), and so on.

To support content-based retrieval at any of the abstraction levels, appropriate quantities that describe the characteristics of interest must be defined, algorithms to extract these quantities from images must be devised, similarity measures to support the retrieval must be selected, and indexing techniques to efficiently search large collection of data must be adopted.

1.4.2 Multidimensional Indexing

Content-based retrieval relies heavily on similarity search over high-dimensional spaces. More specifically, image features such as color or texture are represented using multidimensional descriptors that may have tens or hundreds of components.

The search task can be made significantly more efficient by relying on multidimensional indexing structures. There are a large variety of multidimensional indexing methods, which differ in the type of queries they support and the dimensionality of the space where they are advantageous.

Most existing database management systems (DBMS) do not support multidimensional indexes, and those that do support them usually offer a very limited selection of such methods. Active research is being conducted on how to provide mechanisms in the DBMS that would allow users to incorporate the multidimensional indexing structures of choice into the search engine.

1.5 OVERVIEW OF THE BOOK

The chapters that follow are divided into three parts. The first part analyzes different application areas for digital imagery. Each chapter analyzes the characteristics of the data and their use, describes the requirements for image databases, and outlines current research issues. Chapter 2 describes several applications of visible imagery, including art collections and trademarks. Chapter 3 is devoted to databases of remotely sensed images. Chapter 4 analyzes the different types of medical images, discusses standardization efforts, and describes the structure of work flow–integrated medical image databases. Chapter 5 describes the different types of data used in oil exploration, the corresponding acquisition and processing procedures, and their individual and combined uses. This chapter also describes data and metadata formats, as well as emerging standards for interoperability between acquisition, transmission, storage, and retrieval systems.

The second part of the book discusses the major enabling technologies for image repositories. Chapter 6 describes storage architectures for managing multimedia collections. Chapter 7 discusses support for image and multimedia types in database management systems. Chapter 8 is an overview of image compression, and Chapter 9 describes the transmission of digital imagery.

The third part of the book is devoted to organizing, searching, and retrieving images. Chapter 10 introduces the concept of content-based search. Chapters 11, 12 and 13 discuss how to represent image content using low-level features (color, texture and shape, respectively) and how to perform feature-based similarity search. Feature-based search is very expensive if the image repository is large, and the use of multidimensional indexing structures and appropriate search strategies significantly improves the response time. Chapter 14 discusses multidimensional indexing structures and their application to multimedia database indexing, and Chapter 15 describes retrieval strategies that efficiently prune the search space. Chapter 16 discusses how to advantageously use properties of compression algorithms to index images. Chapter 17 covers image retrieval using semantic content.

REFERENCES

1. F. Mintzer. Developing digital libraries of cultural content for Internet access. *IEEE Commun. Mag.* **37**(1), 72–78 (1999).
2. A.K. Jain, H. Lin, and R. Bolle. On-line fingerprint verification. *IEEE Trans. Pattern Anal. Machine Intell.* **19**(4), 302–314 (1997).
3. A.K. Jain, H. Lin, S. Pankanti, and R. Bolle. An identity-authentication system using fingerprints. *Proc. IEEE* **85**(9), 1365–1388 (1997).
4. W. Niblack et al., The QBIC Project: querying images by content using color, texture, and shape, *Proc. SPIE, Storage and Retrieval for Image and Video Databases*, **1908**, 173–187 (1993).
5. L.D. Bergman, V. Castelli, C.-S. Li, and J.R. Smith. SPIRE, a digital library for scientific information, *Special Issue of IJODL, "in the tradition of Alexandrian Scholars"* **3**(1), 85–99 (2000).
6. C.-S. Li, P.S. Yu, and V. Castelli. MALM, a framework for mining sequence databases at multiple abstraction levels, *Proceedings of the 7th International conference on Information and Knowledge Management CIKM'98*, Bethesda, Md. USA, 3–7 1998 pp. 267–272.
7. V. Castelli et al., Progressive search and retrieval in large image archives, *IBM J. Res. Dev.* **42**(2), 253–268 (1998).
8. V. Castelli, C.-S. Li, J.J. Turek, and I. Kontoyiannis, Progressive classification in the compressed domain for large EOS satellite databases. *Proc. IEEE ICASSP'96* **4**, 2201–2204 (1996).

2 Visible Image Retrieval

CARLO COLOMBO and ALBERTO DEL BIMBO
Universitá di Firenze, Firenze, Italy

2.1 INTRODUCTION

The emergence of multimedia, the availability of large digital archives, and the rapid growth of the World Wide Web (WWW) have recently attracted research efforts in providing tools for effective retrieval of image data based on their content (*content-based image retrieval*, CBIR). The relevance of CBIR for many applications, ranging from art galleries and museum archives to pictures and photographs, medical and geographic databases, criminal investigations, intellectual properties and trademarks, and fashion and interior design, make this research field one of the fastest growing in information technology. Yet, after a decade of intensive research, CBIR technologies, except perhaps for very specialized areas such as crime prevention, medical diagnosis, or fashion design, have had a limited impact on real-world applications. For instance, recent attempts to enhance text-based search engines on the WWW with CBIR options highlight both an increasing interest in the use of digital imagery and the current limitations of general-purpose image search facilities.

This chapter reviews applications and research themes in *visible image retrieval* (VisIR), that is, retrieval by content of heterogeneous collections of single images generated with visible spectrum technologies. It is generally agreed that a key design challenge in the field is how to reduce the semantic gap between user expectation and system support, especially in nonprofessional applications. Recently, the interest in sophisticated image analysis and recognition techniques as a way to enhance the built-in intelligence of systems has been greatly reduced in favor of new models of human perception and advanced human–computer interaction tools aimed at exploiting the user's intelligence and understanding of the retrieval task at hand. A careful image domain and retrieval task analysis is also of great importance to ensure that queries are formulated at a semantic level, appropriate for a specific application. A number of examples encompassing different semantic levels and application contexts,

Image Databases: Search and Retrieval of Digital Imagery, Edited by Vittorio Castelli and Lawrence D. Bergman.
ISBN 0-471-32116-8

including retrieval of trademarks and of art images, are presented and discussed, providing insight into the state of the art of content-based image retrieval systems and techniques.

2.2 IMAGE RETRIEVAL AND ITS APPLICATIONS

This section includes a critical discussion of the main limitations affecting current CBIR systems, followed by a taxonomy of VisIR systems and applications from the perspective of semantic requirements.

2.2.1 Current Limitations of Content-Based Image Retrieval

Semantic Gap. Because of the huge amount of heterogeneous information in modern digital archives, a common requirement for modern CBIR systems is that visual content annotation should be automatic. This gives rise to a *semantic gap* (namely, a discrepancy between the query a user ideally *would* and the one which he actually *could* submit to an information retrieval system), limiting the effectiveness of image retrieval systems.

As an example of semantic gap in text-based retrieval, consider the task of extracting humorous sentences from a digital archive including books by Mark Twain: this is simply impossible to ask from a standard textual, syntactic database system. However, the same system will accept queries such as "find me all the sentences including the word 'steamboat' " without problems. Consider now submitting this last query (maybe using an example picture) to a current State of the art, automatically annotated image retrieval system including pictures from illustrated books of the nineteenth century: the system response is not likely to consist of a set of steamboat images. Current automatic annotations of visual content are, in fact, based on raw image properties, and all retrieved images will look like the example image with respect to their color, texture, and so on. We can therefore conclude that the semantic gap is wider for images than for text; this is because, unlike text, images cannot be regarded as a syntactically structured collection of words, each with a well-defined semantics. The word "steamboat" stands for a thousand possible images of steamboats but, unfortunately, current visual recognition technology is very far from providing textual annotation — for example, of steamboat, river, crowd, and so forth — of pictorial content.

First-generation CBIR systems were based on manual and textual annotation to represent image content, thus exhibiting less-evident semantic gaps than modern, automatic CBIR approaches. Manual and textual annotation proved to work reasonably well, for example, for newspaper photographic archives. However, this technique can only be applied to small data volumes and, to be truly effective, annotation must be limited to very narrow visual domains (e.g., photographs of buildings or of celebrities, etc.). Moreover, in some cases, textually annotating visual content can be a hard job (think, for example, of nonfigurative graphic objects, such as trademarks). Note that the reverse of the sentence mentioned earlier seems equally true, namely, the image of a steamboat stands for a thousand words. Increasing the semantic level by manual intervention is also known to introduce subjectivity in the content classification process (going back to Mark Twain's example, one would hardly agree with the choice of humorous sentences made by the annotator). This can be a serious limitation because of the difficulty of anticipating the queries that future users will actually submit.

The foregoing discussion provides insight into the semantic gap problem and suggests ways to solve it. Explicitly, *(1)* the notion of "information content" is extremely vague and ambiguous, as it reflects a subjective interpretation of data: there is no such thing as an objective annotation of information content, especially at a semantic level; *(2)* modern CBIR systems are, nevertheless, required to operate in an automatic way and as close as possible to the one users are expected to refer to in their queries at a semantic level; *(3)* gaps between system and user semantics are partially due to the nature of the information being searched and partially due to the manner in which a CBIR system operates; *(4)* to bridge the semantic gap, extreme care should be devoted to the manner in which CBIR systems internally represent visual information and externally interact with the users.

Recognition Versus Similarity Retrieval. In the last few years, a number of CBIR systems using image-recognition technologies proved reliable enough for professional applications in industrial automation, biomedicine, social security, and so forth. Face-recognition systems are now widely used for biometric authentication and crime prevention [1]; similarly, automatic image-based detection of tumor cells in tissues is being used to support medical diagnosis and prevention [2].

However, there is much more to image retrieval than simple *recognition*. In particular, the fundamental role that human factors play in all phases of a CBIR project — from development to use — has been largely neglected in the CBIR literature. In fact, CBIR has long been considered only a subbranch of consolidated disciplines such as pattern recognition, computer vision, and even artificial intelligence, in which interaction with a user plays a secondary role. To overcome some of the current limitations of CBIR, metrics, performance measures, and retrieval strategies that incorporate an active human participant in the retrieval process are now being developed. Another distinction between recognition and retrieval is evident in less-specialized domains, such as web search. These applications, among the most challenging for CBIR, are inherently concerned with ranking (i.e., reordering database images according to their measured similarity to a query example even if there is no image similar to the example) rather than classification (i.e., a binary partitioning process deciding whether an observed object matches a model), as the result of *similarity-based retrieval*.

Image retrieval by similarity is the true distinguishing feature of a CBIR system, of which recognition-based systems should be regarded as a special case (see Table 2.1). Specifically, *(1)* the true qualifying feature of CBIR systems is the manner in which human cooperation is exploited in performing the retrieval task; *(2)* from the viewpoint of expected performance, CBIR systems typically

Table 2.1. Typical Features of Recognition and Similarity Retrieval Systems (see text)

	Recognition	Similarity Retrieval
Target performance	High precision	High recall, any precision
System output	Database partition	Database reordering/ranking
Interactivity	Low	High
User modeling	Not important	Important
Built-in intelligence	High	Low
Application domain	Narrow	Wide
Semantic level	High	Application-dependent
Annotation	Manual	Automatic
Semantic range	Narrow	Wide
View invariance	Yes	Application-dependent

require that all relevant images be retrieved, regardless of the presence of false positives (high recall, any precision); conversely, the main scope of image-recognition systems is to exclude false positives, namely, to attain a high precision in the classification; *(3)* recognition systems are typically required to be invariant with respect to a number of image-appearance transformations (e.g., scale, illumination, etc.). In CBIR systems, it is normally up to the user to decide whether two images that differ (e.g., with respect to color) should be considered identical for the retrieval task at hand; *(4)* as opposed to recognition, in which uncertainties and imprecision are commonly managed automatically during the process, in similarity retrieval, it is the user who, being in the retrieval loop, analyzes system responses, refines the query, and determines relevance. This implies that the need for intelligence and reasoning capabilities inside the system is reduced. Image-recognition capabilities, allowing the retrieval of objects in images much in the same way as words, are found in a dictionary, are highly appealing to capture high-level semantics, and can be used for the purpose of visual retrieval. However, it is evident from our discussion that CBIR typically requires versatility and adaptation to the user, rather than the embedded intelligence desirable in recognition tasks. Therefore, design efforts in CBIR are currently being devoted to combine light weight, low semantics image representations with human-adaptive paradigms, and powerful system–user interaction strategies.

2.2.2 Visible Image Retrieval Applications

VisIR can be defined as a branch of CBIR that deals with images produced with visible spectrum technology.

Because visible images are obtained through a large variety of mechanisms, including photographic devices, video cameras, imaging scanners, computer graphics software, and so on, they are neither expected to adhere to any particular technical standard of quality or resolution nor to any strict content characterization. In this chapter, we focus on general-purpose systems for retrieval of photographic imagery.

Every CBIR application is characterized by a typical set of possible queries reflecting a specific semantic content. This section classifies several important VisIR applications based on their semantic requirements; these are partitioned into three main levels.

Low Level. In this level, the user's interest is concentrated on the basic perceptual features of visual content (dominant colors, color distributions, texture patterns, relevant edges and 2D shapes, and uniform image regions) and on their spatial arrangement. Nearly all CBIR systems should support these kind of queries [3,4]. Typical application domains for low-level queries are retrieval of trademarks and fashion design. Trademark image retrieval is useful to designers for the purpose of visual brainstorming or to governmental organizations that need to check if a similar trademark already exists. Given the enormous number of registered trademarks (on the order of millions), this application must be designed to work fully automatically (actually, to date, in many European patent organizations, trademark similarity search is still carried out in a manual way, through visual browsing). Trademark images are typically in black and white but can also feature a limited number of unmixed and saturated colors and may contain portions of text (usually recorded separately). Trademark symbols usually have a graphic nature, are only seldom figurative, and often feature an ambiguous foreground or background separation. This is why it is preferable to characterize trademarks using descriptors such as color statistics and edge orientation [5–7].

Another application characterized by a low semantic level is fashion design: to develop new ideas, designers may want to inspect patterns from a large collection of images that look similar to a reference color and/or texture pattern. Low-level queries can support the retrieval of art images also. For example, a user may want to retrieve all paintings sharing a common set of dominant colors or color arrangements, to look for commonalities and/or influences between artists with respect to the use of colors, spatial arrangement of forms, and representation of subjects, and so forth. Indeed, art images, as well as many other real application domains, encompass a range of semantic levels that go well beyond those provided by low-level queries alone.

Intermediate Level. This level is characterized by a deeper involvement of users with the visual content. This involvement is peculiarly emotional and is difficult to express in rational and textual terms. Examples of visual content with a strong emotional component can be derived from the visual arts (painting, photography). From the viewpoint of intermediate-level content, visual art domains are characterized by the presence of either figurative elements such as people, manufactured objects, and so on or harmonic or disharmonic color contrast. Specifically, the shape of single objects dominates over color both in artistic photography (in which, much more than color, concepts are conveyed through unusual views and details, and special effects such as motion blur) and in figurative art (of which

Magritte is a noticeable example, because he combines painting techniques with photographic aesthetic criteria). Colors and color contrast between different image regions dominate shape in both medieval art and in abstract modern art (in both cases, emotions and symbols are predominant over verisimilitude). Art historians may be interested in finding images based on intermediate-level semantics. For example, they can consider the meaningful sensations that a painting provokes, according to the theory that different arrangements of colors on a canvas produces different psychological effects in the observer.

High Level. These are the queries that reflect data classification according to some rational criterion. For instance, journalism or historical image databases could be organized so as to be interrogated by genre (e.g., images of prime ministers, photos of environmental pollution, etc.). Other relevant application fields range from advertising to home entertainment (e.g., management of family photo albums). Another example is encoding high-level semantics in the representation of art images, to be used by art historians, for example, for the purpose of studying visual iconography (see Section. 2.4). State-of-the-art systems incorporating high-level semantics still require a huge amount of manual (and specifically textual) annotation, typically increasing with database size or task difficulty.

Web-Search. Searching the web for images is one of the most difficult CBIR tasks. The web is not a structured database — its content is widely heterogeneous and changes continuously.

Research in this area, although still in its infancy, is growing rapidly with the goals of achieving high quality of service and effective search. An interesting methodology for exploiting automatic color-based retrieval to prevent access to pornographic images is reported in Ref. [8]. Preliminary image-search experiments with a noncommercial system were reported in Ref. [9]. Two commercial systems, offering a limited number of search facilities, were launched in the past few years [10,11]. Open research topics include use of hierarchical organization of concepts and categories associated with visual content; use of simple but highly discriminant visual features, such as color, so as to reduce the computational requirements of indexing; use of summary information for browsing and querying; use of analysis or retrieval methods in the compressed domain; and the use of visualization at different levels of resolution.

Despite the current limitations of CBIR technologies, several VisIR systems are available either as commercial packages or as free software on the web. Most of these systems are of general purpose, even if they can be tailored to a specific application or thematic image collection, such as technical drawings, art images, and so on. Some of the best-known VisIR systems are included in Table. 2.2. The table reports both standard and advanced features for each system. Advanced features (to be discussed further in the following sections) are aimed at complementing standard facilities to provide enhanced data representations, interaction with users, or domain-specific extensions. Unfortunately, most of the techniques implemented to date are still in their infancy.

Table 2.2. Current Retrieval Systems

Name	Low-Level Queries	Advanced Features	References
Chabot	C	Semantic queries	[12]
IRIS	C,T,S	Semantic queries	[13]
MARS	C,T	User modeling, interactivity	[14]
NeTra	C,R,T,S	Indexing, large databases	[15]
Photobook	S,T	User modeling, learning, interactivity	[16]
PICASSO	C,R,S	Semantic queries, visualization	[4]
PicToSeek	C,R	Invariance, WWW connectivity	[17]
QBIC	C,R,T,S,SR	Indexing, semantic queries	[18]
QuickLook	C,R,T,S	Semantic queries, interactivity	[19]
Surfimage	C,R,T	User modeling, interactivity	[20]
Virage	C,T,SR	Semantic queries	[11]
Visual Retrievalware	C,T	Semantic queries, WWW connectivity	[10]
VisualSEEk	R,S,SR	Semantic query, interactivity	[21]
WebSEEk	C,R	Interactivity, WWW connectivity	[9]

C = global color, R = color region, T = texture, S = shape, SR = spatial relationships. "Semantic queries" stands for queries either at intermediate-level or at high-level semantics (see text).

2.3 ADVANCED DESIGN ISSUES

This section addresses some advanced issues in VisIR. As mentioned earlier, VisIR requires a new processing model in which incompletely specified queries are interactively refined, incorporating the user's knowledge and feedback to obtain a satisfactory set of results. Because the user is in the processing loop, the true challenge is to develop support for effective human–computer dialogue. This shifts the problem from putting intelligence in the system, as in traditional recognition systems, to interface design, effective indexing, and modeling of users' similarity perception and cognition. Indexing on the WWW poses additional problems concerned with the development of metadata for efficient retrieval and filtering.

Similarity Modeling. Similarity modeling, also known as user modeling, requires internal image representations that closely reflect the ways in which users interpret, understand, and encode visual data. Finding suitable image representations based on low-level, perceptual features, such as color, texture, shape, image structure, and spatial relationships, is an important step toward the development of effective similarity models and has been an intensively studied CBIR research topic in the last few years. Yet, using image analysis and pattern-recognition algorithms to extract numeric descriptors that give a quantitative measure of perceptual features is only part of the job; many of the difficulties still remain to be addressed. In several retrieval contexts, higher-level semantic primitives such as objects or even emotions induced by visual material should also be extracted from images and represented in the retrieval system, because it is these higher-level features, which, as semioticians and psychologists suggest, actually convey meaning to the observer (colors, for example, may induce particular sensations according to their chromatic properties and spatial arrangement). In fact, when direct manual annotation of image content is not possible, embedding higher-level semantics into the retrieval system must follow from reasoning about perceptual features themselves.

A process of semantic construction driven by low-level features and suitable for both advertising and artistic visual domains was recently proposed in Ref. [22] (see also Section. 2.4). The approach characterizes visual meaning through a hierarchy, in which each level is connected to its ancestor by a set of rules obtained through a semiotic analysis of the visual domains studied.

It is important to note that completely different representations can be built starting from the same basic perceptual features: it all depends on the intepretation of the features themselves. For instance, color-based representations can be more or less effective in terms of human similarity judgment, depending on the color space used.

Also of crucial importance in user modeling is the design of similarity metrics used to compare current query and database feature vectors. In fact, human similarity perception is based on the measurement of an appropriate distance in a *metric psychological space*, whose form is doubtlessly quite different from the metric spaces (such as the Euclidean) typically used for vector comparison. Hence, to be truly effective, feature representation and feature-matching models should somehow replicate the way in which humans assess similarity between different objects. This approach is complicated by the fact that there is no single model of human similarity. In Ref. [23], various definitions of similarity measures for feature spaces are presented and analyzed with the purpose of finding characteristics of the distance measures, which are relatively independent of the choice of the feature space.

System adaptation to individual users is another hot research topic. In the traditional approach of querying by visual example, the user explicitly indicates which features are important, selects a representation model, and specifies the range of model parameters and the appropriate similarity measure. Some researchers have pointed out that this approach is not suitable for general databases of arbitrary content or for average users [16]. It is instead suitable to domain-specific retrieval applications, in which images belong to a homogeneous set and users are experts. In fact, it requires that the user be aware of the effects of the representation and similarity processing on retrieval. A further drawback to this approach is its failure to model user's subjectivity in similarity evaluation. Combining multiple representation models can partially resolve this problem. If the retrieval system allows multiple similarity functions, the user should be able to select those that most closely model his or her perception.

Learning is another important way to address similarity and subjectivity modeling. The system presented in Ref. [24] is probably the best-known example of subjectivity modeling through learning. Users can define their subjective similarity measure through selections of examples and by interactively grouping similar examples. Similarity measures are obtained not by computing metric distances but as a compound grouping of precomputed hierarchy nodes. The system also allows manual and automatic image annotation through learning, by allowing the user to attach labels to image regions. This permits semantic groupings and the usage of textual keys for querying and retrieving database images.

Interactivity. Interfaces for content-based interactivity provide access to visual data by allowing the user to switch back and forth between navigation, browsing, and querying. While querying is used to precisely locate certain information, navigation and browsing support exploration of visual information spaces. Flexible interfaces for querying and data visualization are needed to improve the overall performance of a CBIR system. Any improvement in interactivity, while pushing toward a more efficient exploitation of human resources during the retrieval process, also proves particularly appealing for commercial applications supporting nonexpert (hence more impatient and less adaptive) users. Often a good interface can let the user express queries that go beyond the normal system representation power, giving the user the impression of working at a higher semantic level than the actual one. As an example, sky images can be effectively retrieved by a blue color sketch in the top part of the canvas; similarly, "all leopards" in an image collection can be retrieved by querying for texture (possibly invariant to scale), using a leopard's coat as an example.

There is a need for query technology that will support more effective ways to express composite queries, thus combining high-level textual queries with queries by visual example (icon, sketch, painting, and whole image). In retrieving visual information, high-level concepts, such as the type of an object, or its role if available, are often used together with perceptual features in a query; yet, most current retrieval systems require the use of separate interfaces for text and visual information. Research in data visualization can be exploited to define new ways of representing the content of visual archives and the paths followed during a retrieval session. For example, new effective visualization tools have recently been proposed, which enable the display of whole visual information spaces instead of simply displaying a limited number of images [25].

Figure 2.1 shows the main interface window of a prototype system, allowing querying by multiple features [26]. In the figure, retrieval by shape, area, and color similarity of a crosslike sketch is supported with a very intuitive mechanism, based on the concept of "star." Explicitly, an n-point star is used to perform an n-feature query, the length of each star point being proportional to the relative relevance of the feature with which it is associated. The relative weights of the three query features are indicated by the three-point star shown at query composition time (Fig. 2.2): an equal importance is assigned to shape and

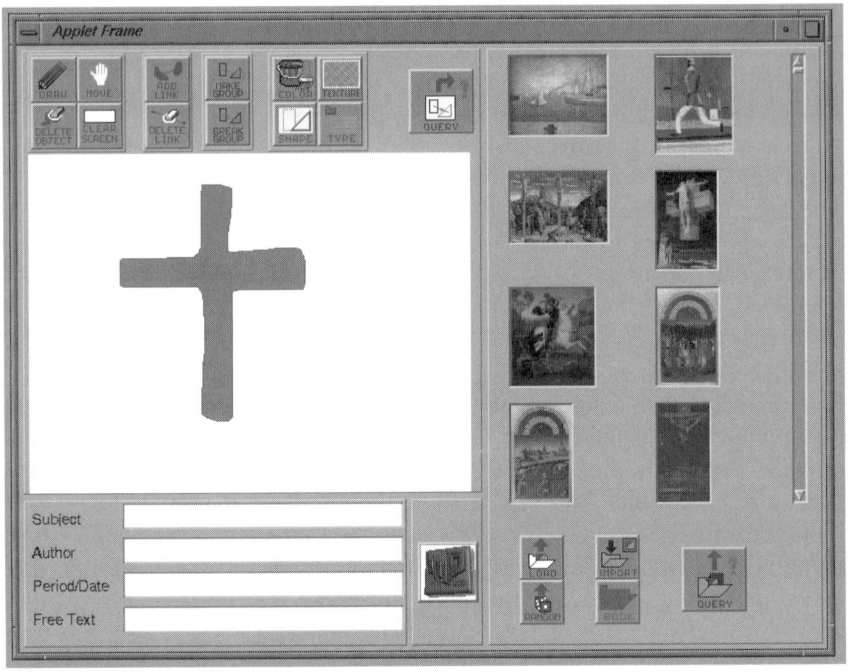

Figure 2.1. Image retrieval with conventional interaction tools: query space and retrieval results (thumbnail form). A color version of this figure can be downloaded from *ftp://wiley.com/public/sci_tech_med/image_databases*.

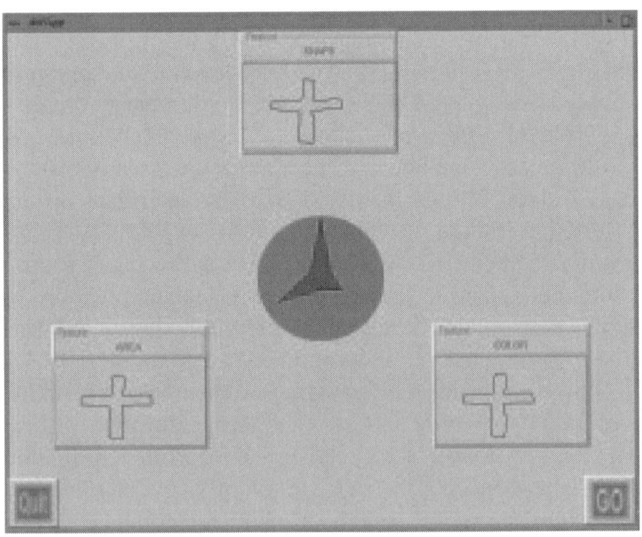

Figure 2.2. Image retrieval with advanced interaction tools: query composition in "star" form (see text). A color version of this figure can be downloaded from *ftp://wiley.com/public/sci_tech_med/image_databases*.

area, while a lesser importance is assigned to color. Displaying the most relevant images in thumbnail format is the most common method to present retrieval results (Fig. 2.1). Display of thumbnails is usually accompanied by display of the query, so that the user can visually compare retrieval results with the original request and provide relevant feedback accordingly [27]. However, thumbnail display has several drawbacks: *(1)* thumbnails must be displayed on a number of successive pages (each page containing a maximum of about 20 thumbnails); *(2)* for multiple-feature queries, the criteria for ranking the thumbnail images is not obvious; *(3)* comparative evaluation of relevance is difficult and is usually limited to thumbnails in the first one or two pages.

A more effective visualization of retrieval results is therefore suggested. Figure 2.3 shows a new visualization space that displays retrieval results in star form rather than in thumbnail form. This representation is very useful for compactly describing the individual similarity of each image with respect to the query and about how images sharing similar features are distributed inside the database. In the example provided, which refers to the query of Figures 2.1–2.2, stars located closer to the center of the visualization space have a higher similarity with respect to the query (the first four of them are reported at the sides of the visualization space). Images at the bottom center of the visualization space are characterized by a good similarity with respect to the query in terms of area and color, but their shape is quite different from that of the query. This method of visualizing results permits an enhanced user–system synergy for the progressive

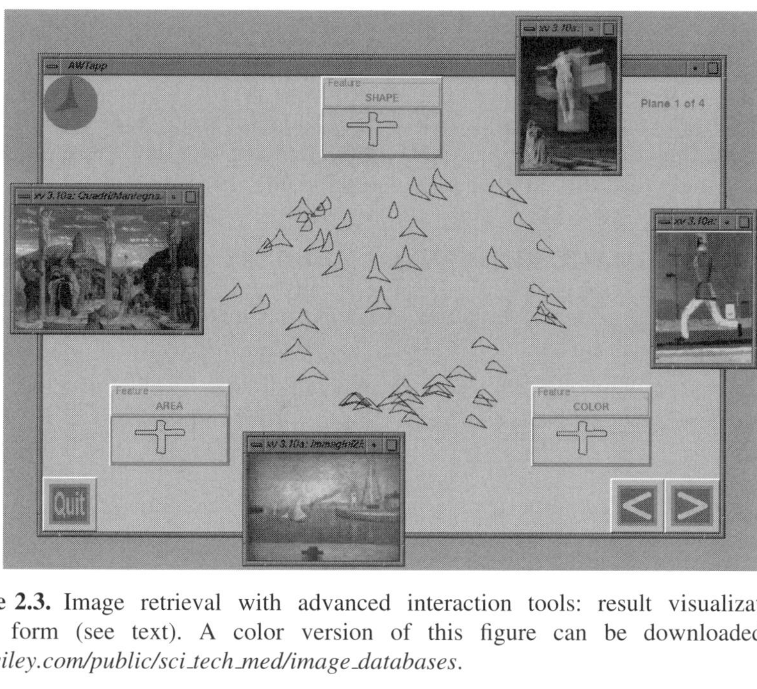

Figure 2.3. Image retrieval with advanced interaction tools: result visualization in "star" form (see text). A color version of this figure can be downloaded from *ftp://wiley.com/public/sci_tech_med/image_databases*.

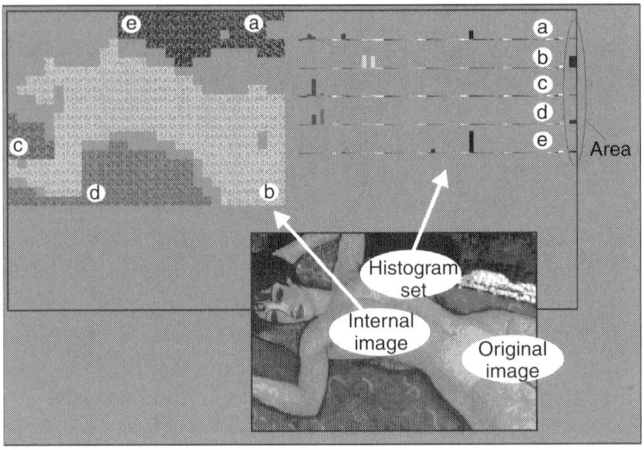

Figure 2.4. Visualization of internal query representation. A color version of this figure can be downloaded from *ftp://wiley.com/public/sci_tech_med/image_databases*.

refinement of queries and allows for a degree of uncertainty in both the user's request and the content description. In fact, the user is able to refine his query by a simple change in the shape of the query star, based on the shape of the most relevant results obtained in the previous iteration.

Another useful method for narrowing the semantic gap between the system and the user is to provide the user with a visual interpretation of the internal image representation that allows them to refine or modify the query [28]. Figure 2.4 shows how the original external query image is transformed into its internal counterpart through a multiple-region content representation based on color histograms. The user is able to refine the original query by directly reshaping the single histograms extracted from each region and examining how this affects the visual appearance of the internal query; the latter, and not the external query, is the one actually used for similarity matching inside the database.

2.4 VISIBLE IMAGE RETRIEVAL EXAMPLES

This section shows several examples of image retrieval using packages developed at the Visual Information Laboratory of the University of Florence [4]. These packages include a number of advanced retrieval features. Some of these features have been outlined earlier and are also present in several other available VisIR packages. The examples are provided in increasing order of representation complexity (semantic demand), ranging from trademark through art images and iconography. For the purpose of efficient system design, image representation was designed to support the most common query types, which in general are strictly related to how images are used in the targeted application domain.

Retrieval of Trademarks by Low-Level Content. Because of domain characteristics of trademark images, the representation used in this case is based on

Figure 2.5. Retrieval of trademarks by shape only. A color version of this figure can be downloaded from *ftp://wiley.com/public/sci_tech_med/image_databases*.

very simple perceptual features, namely, edge orientation histograms and their moments to represent shape and color histograms. Image search can be based on color and shape taken in any proportion. Shape moments can be excluded from the representation to enable invariance with respect to image size.

Figures 2.5 to 2.7 show three different retrieval tasks from an experimental database of 1,000 entries (in all cases, the example is in the upper left window of the interface). Figure 2.5 shows the result in the case of retrieval by shape only: notice that, besides being totally invariant to scale (see the third ranked image), the chosen representation is also partially invariant to partial writing changes. Retrieval by color only is shown in Figure 2.6; all the trademarks retrieved contain at least one of the two dominant colors of the example. The third task, shown in Figure 2.7, is to perform retrieval based on both color and shape, shape being dominant to color. All trademarks with the white lion were correctly retrieved, regardless of the background color.

Retrieval of Paintings by Low- and Intermediate-Level Content. The second example demonstrates retrieval from an experimental database featuring hundreds of modern art paintings. Both low- and intermediate-level queries are supported. From our discussion, it is apparent that color and shape are the most important image characteristics for feature-based retrieval of paintings. Image regions are extracted automatically by means of a multiresolution color segmentation technique, based on an energy-minimization process. Chromatic qualities are represented in the $L^*u^*v^*$ space, to gain a good approximation of human color

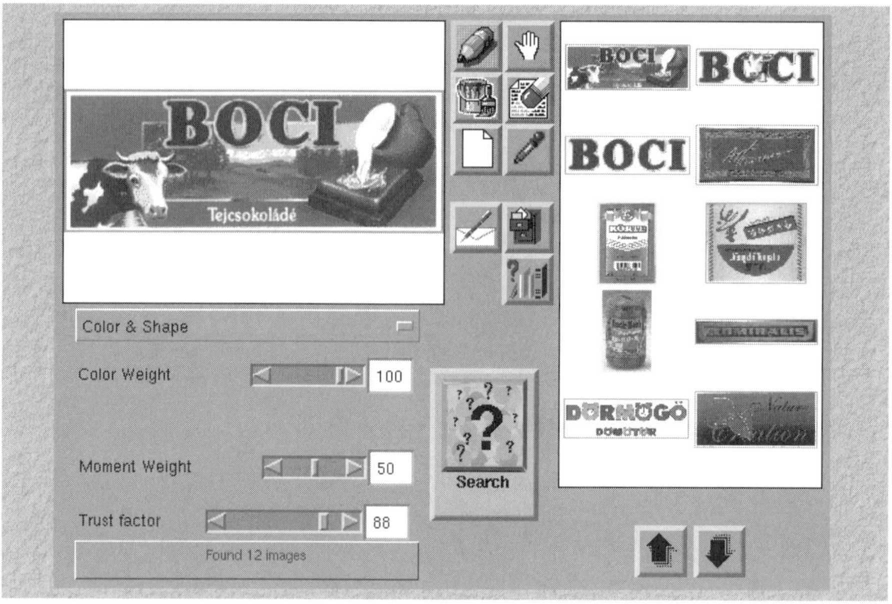

Figure 2.6. Retrieval of trademarks by color only. A color version of this figure can be downloaded from *ftp://wiley.com/public/sci_tech_med/image_databases*.

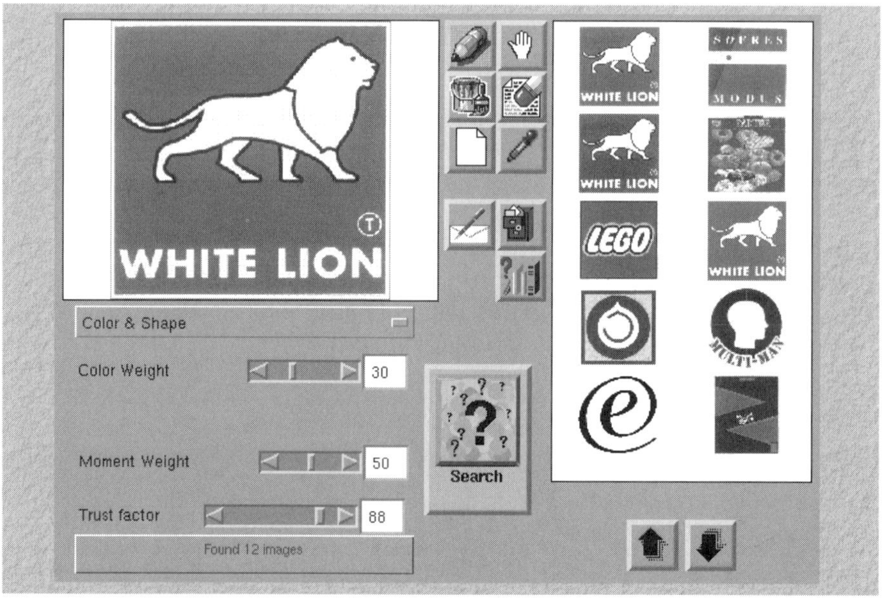

Figure 2.7. Retrieval of trademarks by combined shape and color. A color version of this figure can be downloaded from *ftp://wiley.com/public/sci_tech_med/image_databases*.

perception, and similarity of color regions is evaluated considering both chromatic and spatial attributes (region area, location, elongation and orientation) [29]. A more sophisticated color representation than that for trademarks is required because of much more complex color content of art images. The multiresolution strategy that has been adopted allows the system to take into account color regions scattered throughout an image. Figure 2.8 shows color similarity retrieval results using a painting by Cezanne as the query image. Notice how many of the retrieved images are actually paintings by the same painter; this is sensible, as it reflects the preference of each artist for specific color combinations.

Objects are annotated manually (but not textually) in each image by drawing their contour. For the purpose of shape-based retrieval, queries are submitted by sketch; query and database shapes are compared using an energy-minimization procedure, in which the sketch is elastically deformed to best fit the target shape [32]. Querying by sketch typically gives the user the (false, but pleasant) impression that the system is more "intelligent" than it really is; in fact, the system would be unable to extract an object shape from an example query image without the manual drawing made by the user. Results of retrieval by shape are shown in Figure 2.9, in response to a horse query. Many of the retrieved images actually include horses or horse-like figures.

Figure 2.8. Retrieval of art paintings by color similarity. A color version of this figure can be downloaded from *ftp://wiley.com/public/sci_tech_med/image_databases*.

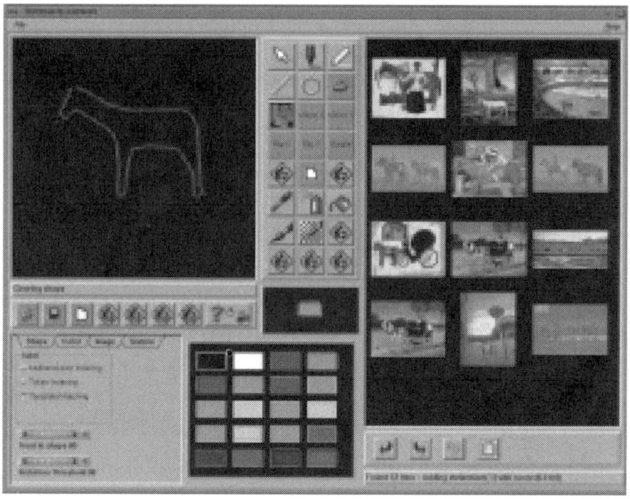

Figure 2.9. Retrieval of art paintings by shape similarity. A color version of this figure can be downloaded from *ftp://wiley.com/public/sci_tech_med/image_databases*.

Retrieval of Paintings by Semiotic Content. As a second example of the way intermediate-level content can be represented and used, this section reviews the approach that has been recently proposed in Ref. [22] for enhancing the semantic representation level for art images according to semiotic principles. In this approach, a content representation is built through a process of syntactic construction, called "compositional semantics," featuring the composition of higher semantic levels according to syntactic rules operating at a perceptual feature level. The rules are directly translated from the aesthetic and psychological theory of Itten [31] on the use of color in art and the semantics that it induces. Itten observed that color combinations induce effects such as harmony, disharmony, calmness and excitement, which are consciously exploited by artists in the composition of their paintings. Most of these effects are related to high-level chromatic patterns rather than to physical properties of single points of color. The theory characterizes colors according to the categories of *hue*, *luminance*, and *saturation*. Twelve hues are identified as fundamental colors, and each fundamental color is varied through five levels of luminance and three levels of saturation. These colors are arranged into a chromatic sphere, such that perceptually contrasting colors have opposite coordinates with respect to the center of the sphere (Fig. 2.10). Analyzing the polar reference system, four different types of contrasts can be identified: contrast of *pure colors, light-dark, warm-cold, quality (saturated-unsaturated)*. Psychological studies have suggested that, in western culture, red-orange environments induce a sense of warmth (yellow through red-purple are *warm* colors). Conversely, green blue conveys a sensation of cold (yellow-green through purple are *cold* colors). Cold sensations can be emphasized by the contrast with a warm color or damped by its coupling with a highly cold tint. The term *harmonic accordance* refers to combinations

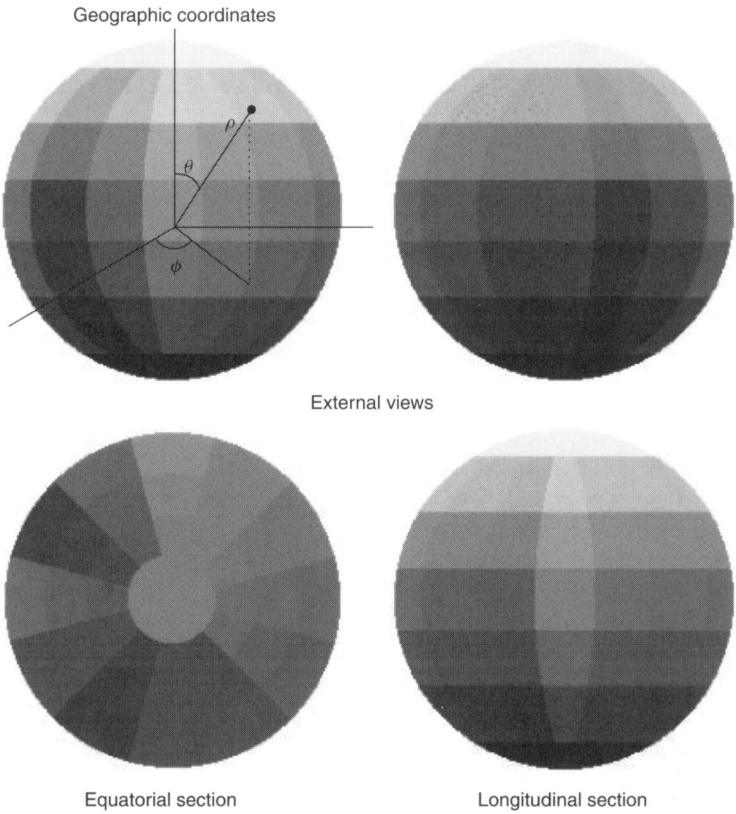

Figure 2.10. The itten sphere. A color version of this figure can be downloaded from *ftp://wiley.com/public/sci_tech_med/image_databases*.

of hue and tone that are pleasing to the human eye. Harmony is achieved by the creation of color combinations that are selected by connecting locations through regular polygons inscribed within the chromatic sphere.

Figure 2.11 shows the eight best-ranked images retrieved by the system in response to four reference queries, addressing contrasts of luminance, warmth, saturation, and harmony, respectively. Tests show good agreement between human opinions (from interviews) and the system in the assignment of similarity rankings [22]. Figure 2.12 shows an example of retrieval of images characterized by two large regions with contrasting luminance, from a database of several hundred fifteenth to twentieth century paintings. Two dialog boxes are used to define properties (hue and dimension) of the two sketched regions of Figure 2.12. Retrieved paintings are shown in the right part of Figure 2.12. The 12 best matched images display a relevant luminance contrast, featuring a black region over a white background. Images ranked in the second, third, and fifth to seventh positions are all examples of how the contrast of luminance between large regions can be used to convey the perception of different planes of depth.

Figure 2.11. Best-ranked images according to queries for contrast of luminance (top row), contrast of saturation (second row), contrast of warmth (third row) and harmonic accordance (bottom row). A color version of this figure can be downloaded from *ftp://wiley.com/public/sci_tech_med/image_databases*.

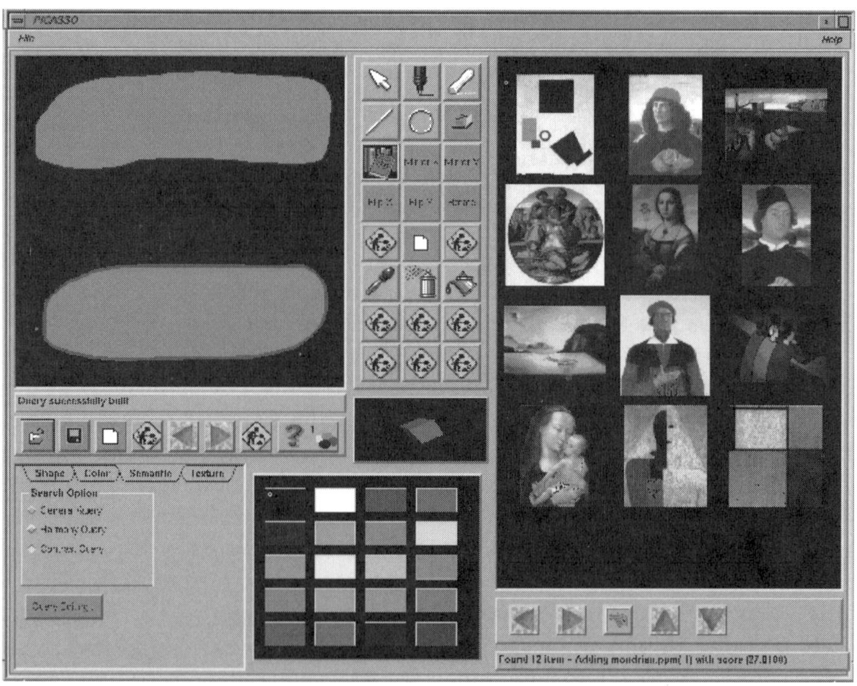

Figure 2.12. Results of a query for images with two large regions with contrasting luminance. A color version of this figure can be downloaded from *ftp://wiley.com/public/sci_tech_med/image_databases*.

Retrieval of Renaissance Paintings by Low- and High-Level Content. Iconographic study of Renaissance paintings provides an interesting example of simultaneous exploitation of low- and high-level descriptors [32]. In this retrieval example, spatial relationships and other features such as color or texture are combined with textual annotations of visual entities. Modeling of spatial relationships is obtained through an original modeling technique that is able to account for the overall distribution of relationships among the individual pixels belonging to the two regions. Textual labels are associated with each manually marked object (in the case of Fig. 2.13, these are "Madonna" and "angel"). The spatial relationship between an observing and an observed

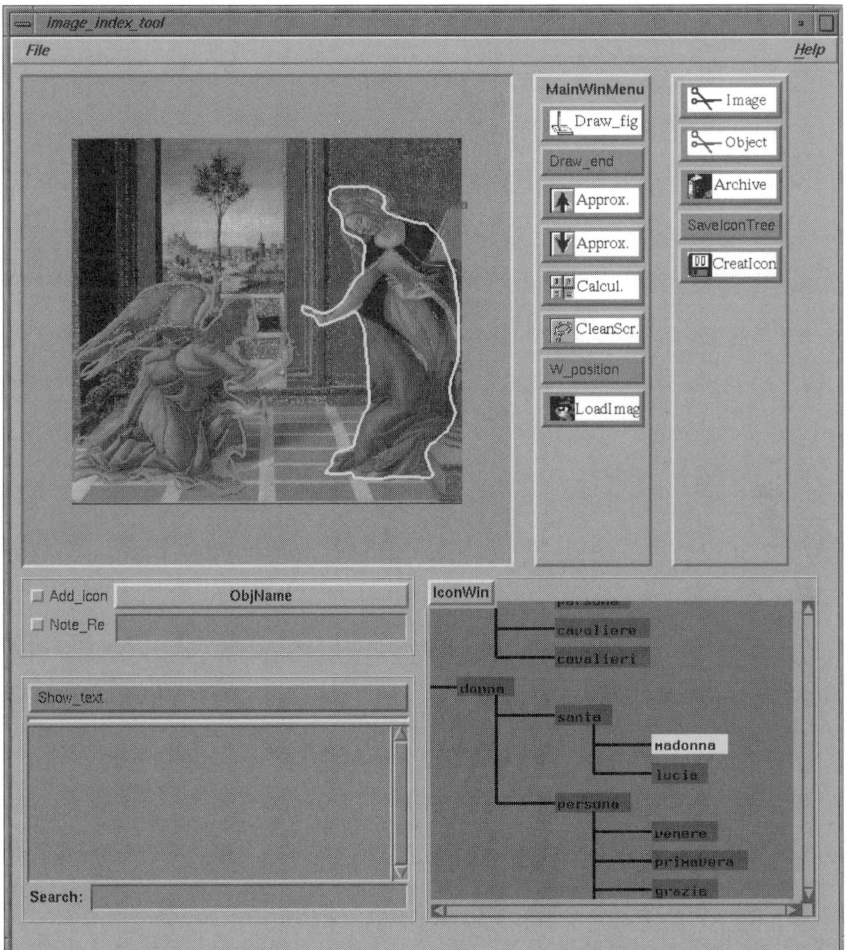

Figure 2.13. Manual annotation of image content through graphics and text. A color version of this figure can be downloaded from *ftp://wiley.com/public/sci_tech_med/image_databases*.

object is represented by a finite set of equivalence classes (the *symbolic walk-throughs*) on the sets of possible paths leading from any pixel in the observing object to any pixel in the observed object. Each equivalence class is associated with a weight, which provides an integral measure of the set of pixel pairs that are connected by a path belonging to the class, thus accounting for the degree to which the individual class represents the actual relationship between the two regions. The resulting representation is referred to as a *weighted walk-through* model. Art historians can, for example, perform iconographic search by finding, for example, all paintings featuring the Madonna and another figure in a desired spatial arrangement (in the query of Figure 2.14, *left*, the configuration is that of a famous annunciation). Retrieval results are shown in Figure 2.14. Note that all the top-ranked images depict annunciation scenes in which the Madonna is on the right side of the image. Because of the strong similarity in the spatial arrangement of figures — spatial arrangement has a more relevant weight than figure identity in this example — nonannunciation paintings, including the Madonna and a saint, are also retrieved.

Figure 2.14. Iconographic search: query submission and retrieval results. A color version of this figure can be downloaded from *ftp://wiley.com/public/sci_tech_med/image_databases*.

2.5 CONCLUSION

In this chapter, a discussion about current and future issues in content-based VisIR design was presented with an eye to applications. The ultimate goal of a new-generation visual retrieval system is to achieve complete automatic annotation of content and reduce the semantic gap by skillfully exploiting user's intelligence and objectives. This can be obtained by stressing the aspects of human similarity modeling and user–system interactivity. The discussion and the concrete retrieval examples illustrate that, despite the huge efforts made in the last few years, research on visual retrieval is still in its infancy. This is particularly true for applications intended not for professional or specialist use, but for the mass market, namely, for naive users. Designing effective retrieval systems for general use is a big challenge that will not only require extra research efforts to make systems friendly and usable but also open new markets and perspectives in the field.

ACKNOWLEDGMENTS

The authors would like to thank the editors, L. Bergman and V. Castelli, for their kindness and support. G. Baldi, S. Berretti, P. Pala, and E. Vicario from the Visual Information Laboratory of the University of Florence provided the example images shown in Section 2.4. Thanks to all.

REFERENCES

1. R. Chellappa, C.L. Wilson, and S. Sirohey, Human and machine recognition of faces: a survey, *Proc. IEEE* **83**(5), 705–740 (1995).
2. C.R. Shyu et al., ASSERT: a physician-in-the-loop content-based retrieval system for HRCT image databases, *Comput. Vis. Image Understand.* **75**(1/2), 175–195 (1999).
3. E. Binaghi, I. Gagliardi, and R. Schettini, Image retrieval using fuzzy evaluation of color similarity, *Int. J. Pattern Recog. Artif. Intell.* **8**(4), 945–968 (1994).
4. A. Del Bimbo, *Visual Information Retrieval*, Morgan Kaufmann, San Francisco, Calif, 1999.
5. J.K. Wu et al., Content-based retrieval for trademark registration, *Multimedia Tools Appl.* **3**(3), 245–267 (1996).
6. J.P. Eakins, J.M. Boardman, and M.E. Graham, Similarity retrieval of trade mark images, *IEEE Multimedia* **5**(2), 53–63 (1998).
7. A.K. Jain and A. Vailaya, Shape-based retrieval: a case study with trademark image database, *Pattern Recog.* **31**(9), 1369–1390 (1998).
8. D. Forsyth, M. Fleck, and C. Bregler, Finding naked people, *Proceedings of the European Conference on Computer Vision*, Springer-Verlag, 1996.
9. S.-F. Chang, J.R. Smith, M. Beigi, and A. Benitez, Visual Information retrieval from large distributed online repositories, *Commun. ACM* **40**(12), 63–71 (1997).

10. J. Feder, Towards image content-based retrieval for the world-wide web, *Adv.Imaging* **11**(1), 26–29 (1996).
11. J.R. Bach et al., The virage image search engine: an open framework for image management, *Proceedings of the SPIE International Conference on Storage and Retrieval for Still Image and Video Databases*, 1996.
12. V.E. Ogle and M. Stonebraker, Chabot: retrieval from a relational database of images, *IEEE Comput.* **28**(9), 40–48 (1995).
13. P. Alshuth et al., IRIS image retrieval for images and video, *Proceedings of the First International Workshop on Image Database and Multimedia Search*, 1996.
14. T. Huang et al., Multimedia analysis and retrieval system (MARS) project, in P.B. Heidorn and B. Sandore, eds., *Digital Image Access and Retrieval*, 1997.
15. W.-Y. Ma and B.S. Manjunath, NeTra: a toolbox for navigating large image databases, *Multimedia Syst.* **7**, 184–198 (1999).
16. R. Picard, T.P. Minka, and M. Szummer, Modeling user subjectivity in image libraries, *Proceedings of the IEEE International Conference on Image Processing ICIP'96*, 1996.
17. T. Gevers and A.W.M. Smeulders, The PicToSeek WWW image search system, *Proceedings of the International Conference on Multimedia Computing and Systems, IEEE ICMCS'99*, Florence, Italy, 1999.
18. M. Flickner, et al., Query by image and video content: the QBIC system, *IEEE Comput.* **28**(9), 310–315 (1995).
19. G. Ciocca, and R. Schettini, A relevance feedback mechanism for content-based image retrieval, *Inf. Process. Manage.* **35**, 605–632 (1999).
20. C. Nastar et al., Surfimage: a flexible content-based image retrieval system, *ACM Multimedia*, 1998.
21. J.R. Smith and S.-F. Chang, Querying by color regions using the visualSEEk content-based visual query system, in M.T. Maybury, ed., *Intelligent Multimedia Information Retrieval*, 1997.
22. C. Colombo, A. Del Bimbo, and P. Pala, Semantics in visual information retrieval, *IEEE Multimedia* **6**(3), 38–53 (1999).
23. S. Santini and R. Jain, Similarity measures, *IEEE Trans. Pattern Anal. Machine Intell.* **21**(9), 871–883 (1999).
24. T. Minka and R. Picard, Interactive learning with a society of models, *Pattern Recog.* **30**(4), 565–582 (1997).
25. A. Gupta, S. Santini, and R. Jain, In search of information in visual media, *Commun. ACM* **40**(12), 35–42 (1997).
26. A. Del Bimbo and P. Pala, Image retrieval by multiple features combination, Technical Note, Department of Systems and Informatics, University of Florence, Italy, 1999.
27. Y. Rui, T.S. Huang, M. Ortega, and S. Mehotra, Relevance feedback: a powerful tool for interactive content-based image retrieval, *IEEE Trans. Circuits Systems Video Technol.* **8**(5), 644–655 (1998).
28. C. Colombo and A. Del Bimbo, Color-induced image representation and retrieval, *Pattern Recog.* **32**, 1685–1695 (1999).
29. J. Itten, *Kunst der Farbe*, Otto Maier Verlag, Ravensburg, Germany, 1961 (in German).

30. E. Vicario and He Wengxe, Weighted walkthroughs in retrieval by content of pictorial data, *Proceedings of the IAPR-IC International Conference on Image Analysis and Processing*, 1997.

31. A. Del Bimbo, M. Mugnaini, P. Pala, and F. Turco, Visual querying by color perceptive regions, *Pattern Recog.* **31**(9), 1241–1253 (1998).

32. A. Del Bimbo and P. Pala, Retrieval by elastic matching of user sketches, *IEEE Trans. Pattern Anal. Machine Intell.* **19**(2), 121–132 (1997).

3 Satellite Imagery in Earth Science Applications

H.K. RAMAPRIYAN
NASA, Goddard Space Flight Center, Greenbelt, Maryland

3.1 INTRODUCTION

Remote sensing is the science of measuring characteristics of interest from a distance. Our focus in this chapter is the remote sensing of Earth from instruments flown on aircraft or spacecraft. Imaging from remote sensors has had a long history, starting early in the twentieth century with photographs from balloons and aircraft. In recent years, there has been a proliferation of aerial and space-borne sensors that image the Earth at various resolutions. There is considerable international interest in remote sensing, both in the public and in the private sectors. The data from remote sensors come in many forms, such as images, profiles, and so on. However, images tend to dominate the archives of remotely sensed data both in volume and in variety. The applications of remote sensing are numerous in both civilian and military arenas. Examples of civilian applications include daily weather forecasting, long-term climate studies, monitoring atmospheric ozone, forecasting crops, and helping farmers with precision agriculture.

A variety of data collection systems exist today to obtain image and nonimage data using remote sensing. Instruments that obtain image data are in general referred to as *imagers*. Measurements such as surface height obtained by altimeters and reflected radiance from the Earth at various wavelengths, obtained by radiometers, spectrometers, or spectroradiometers, are represented as images. The number of wavelength ranges (spectral bands) used by imaging instruments can vary from one (panchromatic) to hundreds (hyperspectral). A variety of mechanisms are used in sensing, including across-track and along-track scanning (Section 3.4.2), resulting in the need for algorithms modeling the sensing geometry to ensure that the images are properly mapped (registered) to a ground coordinate system. Usually, several detectors are used to obtain images from a given instrument, resulting in the need for proper cross-calibration, to ensure that the numbers obtained from the different detectors have the same physical meaning. Images are obtained at various resolutions (or pixel sizes), ranging from one meter to a few kilometers.

Image Databases: Search and Retrieval of Digital Imagery, Edited by Vittorio Castelli and Lawrence D. Bergman.
ISBN 0-471-32116-8 Published 2002 John Wiley & Sons, Inc.

Generally, low-resolution images are used for frequent and global coverage of the Earth, whereas high-resolution images are used for occasional and detailed coverage of selected areas.

Remotely sensed images must be radiometrically and geometrically corrected to ensure that they provide accurate information. The corresponding processing usually includes corrections and derivation of "higher levels" of information (beyond gray levels and colors of pixels) such as chlorophyll concentration, sea surface temperature, cloud heights, ice motion, and land cover classes. In designing a database for remotely sensed image data, it is important to understand the variety of data collection systems, the types of processing performed on the data, and the various ways in which the data and the derived information are accessed. The goal of this chapter is to discuss the issues associated with managing remotely sensed image data, with a particular focus on the problems unique to such data, and to provide a few examples of how some existing systems handle those problems.

Section 3.2 gives a brief history of remote sensing. Section 3.3 provides a discussion of applications with two examples of assessing human impact on the Earth's environment. Section 3.4 covers data collection systems briefly with emphasis on defining terminology relevant to obtaining and managing image data. Section 3.5 is a discussion of the types of errors and artifacts in remotely sensed images and the corrections required before proceeding with higher levels of information extraction. Section 3.6 outlines processing steps to derive useful information from remotely sensed images. Section 3.7 addresses the implications of the variety of collection systems, processing, and usage patterns on the storage and access of remotely sensed image data. Section 3.8 gives a few examples of systems managing such data and how they address the issues identified in Section 3.7. Section 3.9 concludes the chapter with a summary of the key points.

3.2 HISTORICAL BACKGROUND AND REMOTE SENSING MISSIONS

A brief history of remote sensing, with a focus on land remote sensing, can be found in Ref. [1]. An extensive survey of airborne and space-borne missions and sensors for observing the Earth is given in Ref. [2]. The latter reference describes more than 125 space-borne missions, several of which are series of multiple satellites, and more than 190 airborne sensors. Some of the interesting facts from these references are summarized in the following text to illustrate the variety of applications and the breadth of international interest in remote sensing.

Remote sensing of Earth is said to have started with the first photograph from a balloon over Paris taken by Gaspard Felix Tournachon in 1895 (see *http://observe.ivv.nasa.gov/nasa/exhibits/history/*). By 1909, aerial photographs of the Earth were being taken for various applications. The first military Earth-observing satellite, called *Discoverer*, was launched in August 1960. The data were initially meant to support biomedical research and Earth observations. However, a few months after launch, the data were classified secret and became unavailable for civilian purposes. The first satellite for civilian applications was launched by the National Aeronautics and Space Administration (NASA) and the Department of Defense (DOD) in August 1960. It was the first experimental weather satellite and was called the *Television Infrared Observation Satellite* (TIROS-1). This led to a series of satellites that became operational in 1966 as TIROS Operational Satellites (TOS), to be renamed the *National Oceanic and Atmospheric Administration* (NOAA) *Polar Orbiting Environmental Satellites* (POES) in 1970. This was followed in 1978 with a series of NOAA weather satellites carrying the Advanced Very High-Resolution Radiometer (AVHRR) that have been used for both meteorologic applications and studies of vegetation and land use. NASA launched the first of the series of satellites dedicated to land remote sensing in July 1972. This was initially called the *Earth Resources Technology Satellite* (ERTS-1) and was later renamed *Landsat-1*. Since then, there have been several Landsat satellites. The latest in the series, Landsat-7 was launched in April 1999. While Landsat provides relatively high-resolution data (30 m), AVHRR provides coarser resolution (1.1 km) data, but more frequent observations of a given location on Earth. The series of NOAA Geostationary Operational Environmental Satellites (GOES) provide continuous observations of the Earth at an even coarser resolution. These are principally used for continuous monitoring of atmospheric phenomena and for supporting weather forecasts. The satellite series called *SPOT*, designed by the Centre National d'Etudes Spatiales (CNES) in France, has been providing remotely sensed land images since 1986. The latest in the series, SPOT 4, was launched in March 1998. In September 1999, Space Imaging, Inc., a private company in the United States launched IKONOS, a satellite for high-resolution (1-m panchromatic and 4-m multispectral) imaging. Since the launch of IRS-1A, in March 1988, India has had a series of remote sensing satellites, called *IRS*. There have been other satellites such as the Nimbus series (Nimbus-1, launched in August 1964, to Nimbus-7, launched in October 1978), SeaSat (launched in June 1978) and Sea star (with the SeaWiFS instrument launched in August 1997) that have been used mainly for ocean, coastal zone, and fishery applications.

NASA initiated a program called the *Mission to Planet Earth* (MTPE) in the 1980s. This is a part of the broader U.S. Global Change Research Program (USGCRP). The MTPE is now renamed the *Earth Science Enterprise*. There are several partners from other agencies (e.g., NOAA, U.S. Geological Survey, Department of Energy) and countries (e.g., Australia, Brazil, Canada, Finland, France, Japan, Netherlands) in this program. The purpose of this comprehensive program is to study the Earth as an integrated and coupled system, consisting of the atmosphere, oceans, and landmasses interacting with each other over a range of spatial and temporal scales [3–6]. Phase 1 of this program consisted of many spacecraft, several of which are still operational, including NASA missions: Earth Radiation Budget Satellite (ERBS), Upper Atmospheric Research Satellite (UARS), Topography Experiment for Ocean Circulation (TOPEX/Poseidon — joint with France), Tropical Rainfall Measuring Mission (TRMM — joint with Japan). Several non-NASA missions that are considered part of the Phase 1 of MTPE include NOAA-12 and NOAA-14, European Remote Sensing Satellites (ERS-1 and–2), Japanese Earth Resources Satellite (JERS-1), and Radarsat (Canada). Phase 2 of this program consists of the Earth Observing System (EOS). EOS was considered the centerpiece of the MTPE and continues to be the biggest part of NASA's Earth Science Program. EOS consists of a series of satellites and a variety of instruments that will monitor the Earth from space. The primary purpose of EOS is to establish a long-term basis for determining the extent, causes, and consequences of global climate change. The first two EOS instruments were launched on TRMM in November 1997. The first major EOS satellite, Terra (formerly known as EOS-AM), was launched in December 1999. This is to be followed by Aqua (formerly known as EOS-PM) in 2001 and Aura (formerly known as EOS CHEM) in 2003. Complete details of all satellites and instruments constituting the EOS Program can be found in the *Earth Science Enterprise/EOS Reference Handbook* [6].

3.3 APPLICATIONS OF REMOTE SENSING

Remotely sensed data have many different civilian and military applications in diverse disciplines. A few examples of civilian applications are as follows: characterizing and studying variations in atmospheric ozone, quantifying and identifying causes and effects of pollution, forecasting weather, monitoring volcanic eruptions, forest fires, floods and other natural hazards, tracking sea-ice motion, mapping and studying temporal changes in global biomass productivity, studying deforestation and desertification, topographical mapping, forecasting crops, supporting precision agriculture, monitoring urban change, land use planning, and studying long-term climate change. These applications range from providing detailed information covering small areas to individuals and small organizations for commercial purposes to generating global-scale information that is relevant in formulating international policies. Examples of international policies in which remotely sensed information has played a significant role include the 1987 Montreal protocol for eliminating chlorofluorocarbons (CFCs) [7] and the emission-reducing accords from the Kyoto Climate Change Conference in December 1997 [8]. Although accuracy requirements may vary from application to application, a common theme is that decisions with individual, regional, national, or international impact are made using information derived from remote sensing data. Especially in cases in which the information is used in making a public policy that affects the lives of millions of people, it is extremely important that the quality of the data and the scientific basis of the algorithms that are used to derive conclusions from the data are well understood, documented, and preserved for posterity. Preserving all the data and related information and making them conveniently accessible to users are as important as collecting the data using remote sensing systems.

Many interesting applications, images, and animations can be found at the URLs listed at the end of this chapter. We will consider two examples of applications of remote sensing. The first provides an illustration of a time series of data from NASA's Total Ozone Measuring System (TOMS) instruments used to observe the progression of the Antarctic ozone concentration over the past several years. The second provides an example of observing deforestation over time using Landsat data.

3.3.1 Antarctic Ozone

Ozone (O_3) in the Earth's atmosphere is critical to the life on the surface of the Earth [9]. Although it is a lethal pollutant at lower altitudes, it screens the ultraviolet (UV) radiation that destroys cells in plants, animals, and humans at high altitudes. Extreme exposure to UV radiation causes skin cancer. Ground-based instruments and those flown aboard balloons, aircraft, and spacecraft have been used extensively for measuring ozone concentration. The ozone concentration is measured in parts per million (the number of O_3 molecules per million molecules of air) and is typically only a few parts per million. Measurements show that about 90 percent of the ozone in the atmosphere is in the stratosphere (altitudes between 10 and 50 km). Therefore, the ozone layer is generally referred to as the *stratospheric ozone layer*. The "thickness" of the ozone layer is measured in "Dobson Units (DU)." To define DU, imagine that, all the ozone contained in a vertical column of atmosphere above a given ground location is brought to sea level and at room temperature. The average thickness of such a layer of ozone over the globe is 3 mm (about the thickness of two stacked pennies). This is designated as 300 DU. Despite its very low concentration, ozone is critical to the survival of life on Earth.

In the 1920s, CFCs, a family of chemicals, were developed as a safe substitute for flammable substances such as ammonia for use in refrigerators and spray cans. Over subsequent decades, there was an enormous growth in the use of CFCs. Although the amount of chlorine occurring naturally in the atmosphere is very low, CFCs introduced a significant amount of chlorine into the ozone layer. Under certain conditions, chlorine has the potential for destroying large amounts of ozone. This effect of reducing ozone concentration has, in fact, been observed, especially over Antarctica.

In 1985, Farman and coworkers [10] showed that ozone was disappearing over Antarctica and that the measured amounts were much less than the natural low values. This led to an intensive measurement campaign and analyses that have yielded a nearly complete characterization of the physical and chemical processes controlling Antarctic ozone. Concerns over the health of the ozone layer led, in 1987, to the international agreement, called the *Montreal Protocol* that restricted and ultimately phased out the production of CFCs [45]. There is a time lag of years, however, between the stopping of the production of CFCs and the reduction of their concentration in the stratosphere. As the CFCs begin to decrease, it is expected that the Antarctic ozone amounts should begin to recover.

Several types of measurements have been made on a global scale to monitor the ozone layer. Remotely sensed images from a variety of sources, including space-borne instruments, aircraft, and ground-based stations, were needed for the thorough analysis of cause and effect relationships required to support a decision about CFCs. Remotely sensed images from the TOMS instruments are being

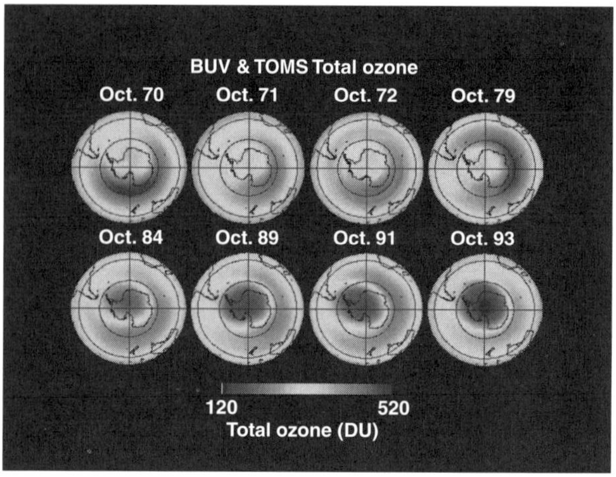

Figure 3.1. The progression of the hole in the ozone layer between 1970 and 1993, imaged by the Total Ozone Measuring System (TOMS) instruments. A color version of this figure can be downloaded from *ftp://wiley.com/public/sci_tech_med/image_databases*.

used for ongoing monitoring of the ozone concentration. The TOMS instruments have been flown on several spacecraft, starting with Nimubs-7 in 1978. The series of images shown in Figure 3.1 illustrates the progression of the ozone hole during the period 1970 through 1993. [Before 1978 images were obtained from the backscatter ultraviolet (BUV) instrument on Nimbus 4]. Each image shows a color representation of the thickness of the total ozone column measured in DUs. The images represent the monthly means of thickness for October of each year displayed. As shown in the color scale, the thickness is the smallest in the blue areas. Generation of these images involves several steps, starting with obtaining instrument-observed radiance values, deriving ozone concentration values, and mapping them to a standard polar projection for display. Access to image data from TOMS can be obtained through *http://toms.gsfc.nasa.gov and http://daac.gsfc.nasa.gov*.

3.3.2 Deforestation

Reduction of forest areas around the world due to natural causes, such as forest fires, and human activities, such as logging and converting of forested regions into agricultural or urban regions, is referred to as *deforestation*. Deforestation has significant impact on the global carbon cycle and biodiversity. The removal of large trees and the burning of debris to clear the land increase the carbon dioxide content of the atmosphere, which may have an impact on climate. Tropical rain forests occupy about 7 percent of the land area of the Earth. However, they are home to more than half of the living plant and animal species. Thus, deforestation can lead to massive extinction of plant and animal species. The largest tropical rain forest in the world is the Amazon Rain Forest. It covers parts of Bolivia, Brazil, Colombia, Ecuador, and Peru. An example of deforestation over time is shown in Figure 3.2. This shows two Landsat images of Rondonia, Brazil. The

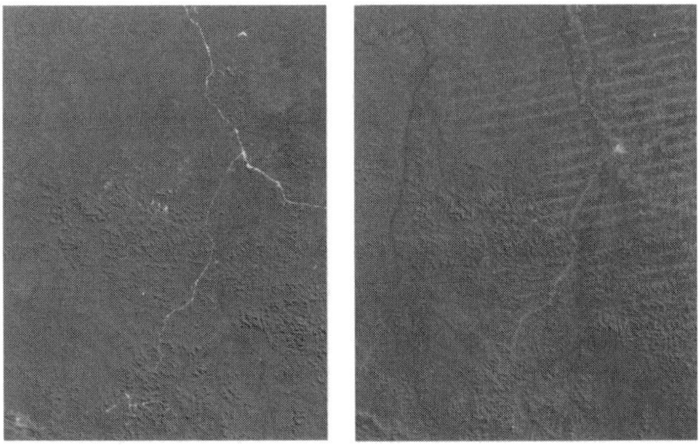

Figure 3.2. Example of deforestation in Rondonia, Brazil, as it appears in Landsat TM images. A color version of this figure can be downloaded from *ftp://wiley.com/public/sci_tech_med/image_databases*.

left image was obtained in 1975 and the right image in 1986. Significant increase in human population occurred between 1975 and 1986, resulting in colonization of the region adjacent to the main highway and conversion of forestland to agricultural use. It is easy to see these areas in the 1986 image — they appear as a fish bone pattern. By accurately coregistering images such as these (i.e., overlaying them), comparing them, and using classification techniques discussed in Section 3.6, it is possible to obtain accurate estimates of the extent of deforestation. By analyzing a large number of Landsat images such as these (it takes about 210 Landsat images to cover the Brazilian Amazon Basin), it has been shown that between 1975 and 1988, about 5.6 percent of the Brazilian Amazon Basin became deforested. The impact on biodiversity is even greater than that indicated by this estimate of deforestation, because the natural plants and animals in the forest are adversely affected by isolation of previously contiguous habitats. Contiguous areas of less than 100 km^2 are considered isolated. Greater exposure to winds and predators at the boundary between forested and deforested areas also affects the natural plants and animals. The habitat within 1 km of the forest boundary is considered to be affected in this manner. With these considerations, it is estimated that about 14.4 percent of the habitat for natural plant and animal life in Brazil was impacted [11]. Acquiring remotely sensed images on a global scale periodically and over a long period of time, and archiving them along with ancillary data (i.e., data other than the remotely sensed image data needed for analysis), metadata, and the results of analyses, will help monitor deforestation, assist in policy making, and aid in studying the impacts of changes in policy.

Because of the importance of this issue, there are several global and regional scale initiatives to monitor the forests of the world over time. Examples of global initiatives are as follows:

- The international Global Observations of Forest Cover (GOFC) Project.
- NASA Landsat Pathfinder Humid Tropical Forest Inventory Project (HTFIP).

- Commission of the European Communities Topical Ecosystem Environment Observation by Satellite (TREES) Project.
- High-Resolution Data Exchange Project of the Committee on Earth Observation Satellites (an international affiliation of space agencies) and the International Geosphere Biosphere Program.
- The multinational Global Forest Mapping Program (GFMP) led by the Earth Observation Research Center (EORC) of the National Space Development Agency of Japan (NASDA).

Regional initiatives include the following:

- North American Landscape Characterization (NALC) Project
- Regional Multiresolution Land Characteristics (MRLC) covering the conterminous United States;
- U.S. Forest Inventory and Analysis (FIA) and the Canadian National Forestry Database Program (NFDP).

More details about these and other programs can be found in Ref. [12].

3.4 DATA COLLECTION SYSTEMS

There are a large variety of systems for collecting remotely sensed data. These can be categorized in several ways according to the

- type of instrument (imager, sounder, altimeter, radiometer, spectrometer, etc.),
- mechanics of the instrument (push broom, whisk broom, serial cross-track, parallel cross-track, conical scan, step-staring, etc.),
- sensing mechanism — passive or active,
- viewing characteristics — pointable or fixed, nadir- or off-nadir-looking, single- or multiangle (mono or stereo),
- spectral characteristics measured (panchromatic, multispectral, hyperspectral),
- spatial resolution (high, moderate, low),
- observed wavelength range (UV, visible, near infrared, thermal, microwave, etc.),
- platform — aircraft, spacecraft, and
- altitude (in case of airborne sensors) or orbits (in the case of spaceborne sensors) — sun-synchronous, geosynchronous, geostationary, low inclination.

Some of the foregoing terms, especially the ones contributing to data management issues, are defined in the following text. Because the focus of this chapter is on image data, the discussion will be limited to the terms relating to imaging instruments. For a more complete discussion of terminology see Refs. [2,13].

3.4.1. Instrument Types

Instruments used in remote sensing belong to one of the following categories:

- *Imager.* (Imaging Instrument) An instrument that has one or more sensors (also called detectors) that measure characteristics of the remote object (e.g., the Earth) and that produces measurements that can be represented as an image. Most of the imagers used in remote sensing acquire images electronically by measuring the radiance incident at the sensor(s), convert the data into digital format, and transmit the results to a receiving system on the ground.
- *Altimeter.* An instrument whose purpose is to measure altitudes. Altitudes are measured over a "reference ellipsoid" — a standard for the zero altitude surface of the Earth. The altitudes can be represented as a gray scale or color-coded two-dimensional image or as a three-dimensional surface.
- *Radiometer.* An instrument that measures radiance values (either reflected or emitted) from the Earth's surface in a given set of wavelength bands of the electromagnetic spectrum.
- *Spectrometer.* An instrument that measures the spectral content of radiation incident at its sensor(s).
- *Spectroradiometer.* An instrument that measures both the radiance values and their spectral distribution.

3.4.2 Mechanics

Generally, unlike conventional cameras, an imaging instrument does not obtain an image as a "snap shot" at a single point in time. It uses a relatively small number of sensors and relies on some form of scanning mechanism and on the motion of the aircraft (or spacecraft) to measure radiance from different parts of the scene being imaged. Consider the general imaging geometry shown in Figure 3.3. Here, a detector D measures the radiance reflected from point P on Earth. S is the source of illumination, which is generally the Sun. The detector actually measures radiance from a finite region surrounding P, called

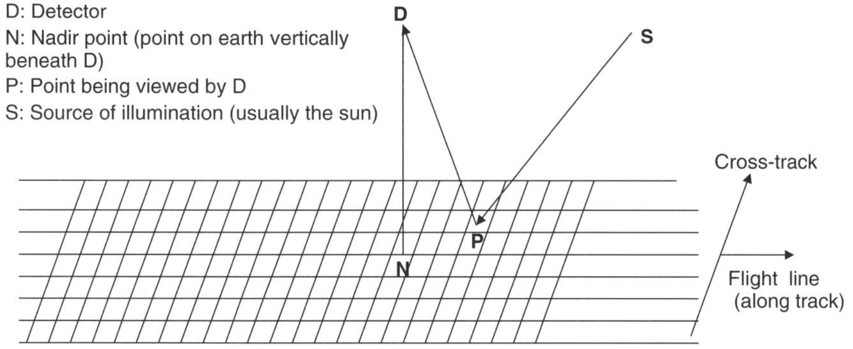

Figure 3.3. General imaging geometry.

the *instantaneous field of view* (IFOV). (Note that the size of an IFOV is loosely referred to as resolution. Each IFOV results in a pixel in the sensed image). As the platform (spacecraft or aircraft) moves along its path, the IFOV traces a small strip on the ground. By using an array of detectors in an instrument, the radiance values from an array of IFOVs can be measured simultaneously. Wide ground swaths are imaged using various combinations of scanning mechanisms, arrays of detectors, and platform motion. Two of the commonly used combinations and the synthetic-aperture radar instrument are discussed in the following list:

- *Across-Track (Whisk Broom) Scanner.* Using an oscillating (or rotating) mirror, an across-track scanner traces a scan line along which the detector measures radiance values of an array of IFOVs. The continuous signal measured by the detector is sampled and converted to digital counts through an analog-to-digital conversion process. Thus, a scan line results in a row of pixels in the image. As the platform (spacecraft or aircraft) moves, successive scan lines are traced. The instrument can have several detectors, so that, as the mirror oscillates, n scan lines can be traced simultaneously. The platform velocity and scanning period are matched to avoid overlaps or gaps between successive sets of n scan lines. If $n = 1$, then the instrument is called a *serial cross-track scanner.* If $n > 1$, then it is called a *parallel cross-track scanner.*
- *Along-Track (Push Broom) Scanner.* An along-track scanner uses a linear array of detectors arranged perpendicular to the direction of platform motion. There is no scanning mirror. Each detector measures the radiance values along a track parallel to the platform motion, thus generating a column of pixels in the resulting image. The set of detectors in the linear array generates a row of pixels at a time.
- *Synthetic Aperture.* Radar instruments (see active sensing described in the following section) measure reflected signals from the ground as the platform moves and mathematically reconstruct high-resolution images, creating images as if obtained with a very large antenna. These are called *synthetic-aperture radar instruments* (SAR).

3.4.3 Sensing Mechanism

Sensing mechanisms can be either passive or active.

- *Passive.* A passive sensor measures emitted and/or reflected radiance values from the Earth without an active source of radiation in the sensor. The source of illumination with passive sensors is usually the sun.
- *Active.* An active sensor provides its own source of radiation, usually in a narrow spectral band (e.g., radar or laser) and measures the reflected (echo) radiance.

3.4.4 Viewing Characteristics

Depending on the acquisition direction, instruments can be categorized as follows:

Nadir-Looking. *Nadir* is the point (point N in Figure 3.3) on Earth that is vertically below the sensor. The set of all points vertically below a platform as it moves is referred to as the *nadir track*. A nadir-looking instrument images a swath (narrow or broad) on either side of the nadir track. An off-nadir- or side-looking instrument images a swath on one side or the other of the nadir track. To describe the imaging more precisely, one needs to specify the maximum and minimum "look angles" viewed by the instrument in the cross-track direction. There are also instruments that view in the off-nadir directions along track.

- *Pointable.* Some instruments are fixed on the platform, and the direction they point to does not change, except for scanning and minor variations in the platform attitude (its relative orientation with respect to the Earth). There are other instruments whose pointing direction can be controlled so that areas of interest are imaged using commands from the ground.
- *Multiangle.* Some instruments have multiple sets of detectors that can image a given ground location from different angles within a short span of time. This permits a "stereo" capability useful for developing digital elevation maps. Multiangle views of Earth are also useful to study the effects of varying lengths of atmospheric column and "bidirectional" reflectance properties (i.e., differences in the reflectance of objects when viewed from two different directions).

3.4.5 Spectral Characteristics Measured

An instrument may measure reflected or emitted radiance values in broad or narrow spectral bands and in a small or large set of spectral bands. The spectral resolution of a sensor is defined as the narrowest spectral bandwidth that it can measure. Depending on the spectral resolution and number of bands measured, the instruments are categorized as follows:

- *Panchromatic.* A panchromatic instrument measures radiance values over a wide spectral range (usually covering the entire visible spectrum and part of the ultraviolet spectrum).
- *Multispectral.* A multispectral imager measures radiance values in several spectral bands. It may have several detectors sensitive to each spectral band, and, if there are n spectral bands, they generate n radiance values for each pixel observed.
- *Hyperspectral.* A hyperspectral imager is a particular case of multispectral imager, in which the number n of spectral bands is large (usually greater than 200) and the width of each spectral band is small. The spectral bands are narrow enough and sufficiently closely spaced to allow each n-dimensional vector of measured radiance values to approximate the continuous spectrum corresponding to the observed pixel.

3.4.6 Spatial Resolution

The *spatial resolution* is defined as the minimum distance between two points on the ground that the sensor is able to distinguish. It depends on the sensor

Table 3.1. Examples of Imaging Instruments

Platform	Instrument	Type	Mechanics	Sensing Mechanism	Viewing Characteristics	Spectral Characteristics	Special Resolution	Maximum Data Rate (Megabits per second)
EOS Terra	ASTER-VNIR	Radiometer	Push broom	Passive	Pointable (cross-track); same arbit stereo with second, aft-pointing push broom array	Multispectral (3 bands)	15 m	62
EOS Terra	ASTER-SWIR	Radiometer	Push broom	Passive	Pointable (cross-track)	Multispectral (6 bands)	30 m	23
EOS Terra	ASTER-TIR	Radiometer	Cross-track scanning	Passive	Pointable (cross-track)	Multispectral (5 bands)	90 m	4.2
EOS Terra	MISR	Spectro-radiometer Push broom	Passive	Multiangle (9 different along track angles)	Multispectral (4 bands)	Commandable (275 m, 550 m or 1.1 km)	9	
EOS Terra and Aqua	MODIS	Spectro-radiometer	Cross-track scanning	Passive	Nadir-looking, broad swath	Multispectral (36 bands)	250 m, 500 m, 1 km at nadir, depending on the spectral band	10.6
EOS Aura	OMI	Spectrometer	Push broom	Passive	Nadir-looking, broad swath	Hyperspectral (740 bands)	13 km	0.8(avg)
Landsat-7	ETM+	Radiometer	Cross-track scanning	Passive	Nadir-looking	Multispectral (7 band) and Panchromatic	Multispectral 30 m: panchromatic 15 m	150
Aircraft	AVIRIS	Spectrometer	Cross-track scanning	Passive	Nadir-looking	Hyperspectral (224 bands)	20 m (with flight altitude = 20 km)	20.4
SPOT-4	HRVIR	Radiometer	Push broom	Passive	Pointable (cross-track)	Multispectral (3 band) and Panchromatic	Multispectral 20 m: panchromatic 10 m	50
Radarsat	SAR	Radar	Synthetic aperture	Active	Side-looking	Single band	Variable depending on mode, standard is 25 m by 28 m	105
Space shuttle	SIR-C	Radar	Synthetic aperture	Active	Side-looking: variable look-angle	Two bands	25 m	180

itself and on the distance between the sensor and the ground. Sometimes the resolution is specified in angular units (microradians). Most often, however, the spatial resolution is specified in meters (or kilometers) representing one side of a square area on the ground constituting a pixel. High resolution in remote sensing usually refers to pixel sizes less than or equal to 100 m. Moderate resolution ranges from 100 to 500 m. Low resolution refers to pixel sizes above 500 m.

Table 3.1 shows a few examples of imaging instruments categorized according to the above characteristics. This table also shows the peak data rates from each of these instruments. The amount of data collected and transmitted by the instruments depends on the data rates and the "duty cycle" (percentage of time that they collect data).

3.5 ERRORS, ARTIFACTS, AND REQUIRED CORRECTIONS

In general, the goal of a remote sensing system is to measure certain parameters of interest that pertain to a given area of the Earth. Many distortions cause the measurements to differ from their ideal values or to be assigned to the wrong pixel locations. This is illustrated by two highly simplified examples in Figure 3.4.

Figure 3.2a shows how radiation from locations other than that desired enters a detector. The desired location here is a small neighborhood around point P. The Earth is illuminated by the Sun S, and the radiation from the desired location is reflected to the detector D. In addition, radiation scattered by point A in the atmosphere reaches the detector. Also, radiation reflected from the point P′ is scattered by point B in the atmosphere and reaches the detector.

Figure 3.4b shows how a pixel can be "misplaced" or shifted if information about elevation is ignored. Geographic coordinates are assigned to each pixel, depending on the angular displacement of the observed point relative to a reference direction (for e.g., the vertical). Suppose a feature (for e.g., a mountain or a tall building) with elevation h is present at point P on Earth. Then, the radiation from that feature will be observed along the line DQ (rather than DP). Thus, if the elevation information is ignored, the observation is assigned to a pixel number corresponding to the angle NDQ (rather than NDP). In effect, the resulting image will appear as if the radiation at Q were arising from the point P' on Earth.

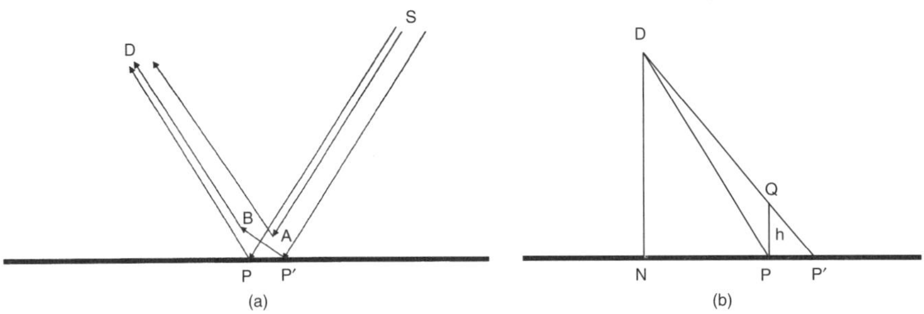

Figure 3.4. **(a)** Atmospheric effects. **(b)** Elevation effect.

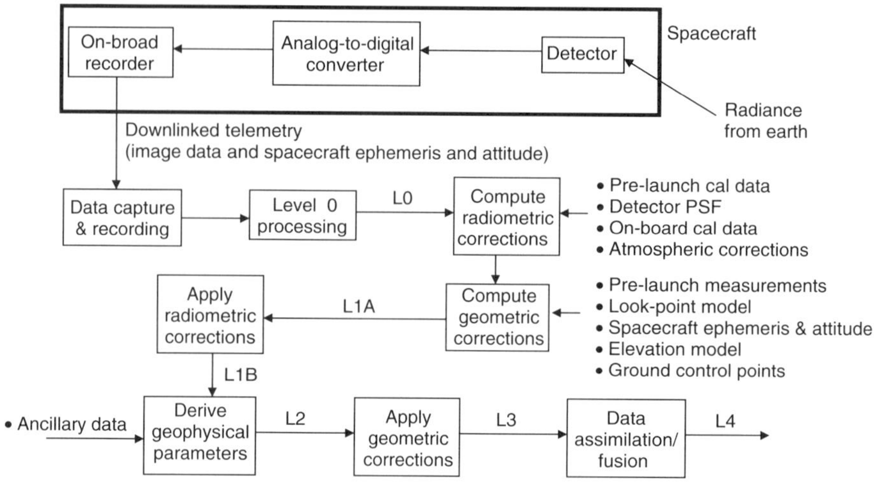

Figure 3.5. "Generic" data flow.

Figure 3.5 shows a "generic" data flow diagram to illustrate the various steps in the acquisition, correction of errors and artifacts, and generation of useful information from image data. In the following sections, we will address the correction of telemetry errors and artifacts, radiometric errors, and geometric errors.

3.5.1 Telemetry Errors and Artifacts

Telemetry errors are likely to occur when the data are received from the satellite at a ground station. Because of the errors in various parts of the sensing, recording, and communications systems, data bits may be "flipped." The bit flips are minimized using error-detecting and error-correcting codes (e.g., Reed-Solomon codes). Typical specifications for satellite telemetry data are that bit errors before correction be fewer than 1 in 10^5. Generally, the post correction rates are required to be fewer than 1 in 10^6 to 1 in 10^7. Observed post correction error rates tend to be significantly lower (e.g., 1 in 10^{12}).

In the case of satellites with multiple sensors on board, data from different sensors may be interleaved in the transmission to the ground stations. Some data may be downlinked directly and others may be played back from onboard recorders. The data may be out of time sequence, that is, some of the data observed earlier may be downlinked later. In fact, data may be received at multiple ground stations and may need to be assembled into a properly time-ordered data stream. All these effects are referred to as *telemetry artifacts*. Removal of such artifacts involves separating data from various instruments into individual data sets, arranging them in proper time order, and subdividing them into files covering some meaningful (usually fixed) time period. Such files are called *production data sets* (PDSs). The time period covered by PDSs may range from 2 hours to 24 hours and usually depends on the instrument, its data rate and application, so that the sizes of data sets are reasonable, and the data are available for higher levels of processing and analysis at a reasonable time after observation. Typically, for EOS instruments, the files range in size from 200 MB to 6 GB.

3.5.2 Radiometric Errors

For purposes of illustration, consider a multispectral sensor imaging the Earth's surface with a cross-track scanning mechanism, such as the Landsat Thematic Mapper (TM). The sensor can have multiple spectral bands and multiple detectors in each of the spectral bands. Under given solar illumination conditions, each detector measures the reflected light in a given spectral band. The reflectance in multiple spectral bands characterizes the area being viewed on Earth. Ideally, the numbers recorded by each of the detectors in a given spectral band should be the same when they view the same target. However, there are several sources of detector-to-detector variation. The atmosphere affects the amount of reflected light reaching the detectors. The atmospheric effect depends on the viewing angle of the detectors: the farther from nadir a given location on Earth is, the longer the atmospheric column that the reflected light passes through, and the greater the attenuation. The effect of the atmosphere also depends on the spectral band in which a detector is measuring because the atmospheric absorption is wavelength-dependent. Detectors also may have nonlinear responses to incident radiation. Ideally, a detector should record a point on Earth as a point in the image. However, real detectors generate a "spread" or "smear" in the image corresponding to a given point on Earth. This is a measurable characteristic of a detector and is called its *point-spread function* (PSF). Because point-spread functions of the detectors differ from the ideal, the values measured for a given location on Earth are affected by the values from its neighboring locations.

Knowledge of all these effects is required to retrieve the detector's ideal response, that is, to radiometrically calibrate the detector's response. The calibration of the detector responses requires prelaunch measurements of a known "standard" source of radiation. Also, each detector, while in orbit, makes frequent measurements of an onboard calibration source. Some instruments, for purposes of calibration, may use occasional views of "constant" sources of radiance, such as deep space, the Sun, and/or the Moon. Such calibration data are generally stored as a part of the instrument data stream.

3.5.3 Geometric Errors

Acquired images are subject to geometric distortions. Ideally, we would like to know the exact location on Earth that a detector views at any given instant, and associate the value recorded by the detector with that location. The geometric model that determines (estimates) the location to which a detector points is sometimes referred to as the *look-point* model. Some of the geometric effects to be considered in constructing the look-point model are detector-to-detector displacements; location (ephemeris) of the spacecraft relative to the Earth; orientation (attitude) of the spacecraft; scanning and detector sampling frequency; variation of pixel size (area viewed by a detector) due to viewing angle; pixel displacements due to atmospheric refraction; pixel displacements due to elevation effects, and desired map projection.

Geometric calibration consists of applying knowledge of these effects to determine the pixel placements. Geometric calibration performed by modeling the known distortions indicated earlier is called *systematic correction*. Because of errors in the knowledge of parameters that define the look-point model, there generally are residual errors. These can be corrected using ground control points (GCPs). GCPs are identifiable objects in images for which corresponding ground coordinates can be accurately determined from a map (or another image that has been geometrically corrected). Prelaunch measurements of the detector configuration, validation of the scanning geometry model, and validation of the geometric correction process using targets with known geometry are essential. For each image that is observed, the geometric correction parameters need to be computed and stored along with the image data.

The specific types of prelaunch measurements, calibration procedures, onboard calibration mechanisms, and the radiometric and geometric calibration parameters to be stored with the data vary from instrument to instrument. However, in all cases, it is essential to maintain the calibration parameters in order to interpret the remotely sensed data meaningfully and obtain accurate information from them.

3.6 PROCESSING

3.6.1 Processing Levels

As remotely sensed data are received, corrected, and processed to derive useful information, various intermediate products are generated. It is convenient to refer to such products by their "levels of processing." NASA's EOS Program uses the following definitions consistent with those provided by the Committee on Data Management, Archiving and Computing (CODMAC) [6]. In Figure 3.5, these levels are shown as L0, L1A, and so on. In general, Level 0 data cannot be represented as images, whereas Level 1A and above can (even though exceptions do exist).

Level 0. Reconstructed, unprocessed instrument or payload data at full resolution; any and all communication artifacts (e.g., synchronization frames, communication headers, and duplicate data) removed. The PDSs defined in Section 3.5.1 are Level 0 data products.

Level 1A. Reconstructed, unprocessed instrument data at full resolution, time-referenced, and annotated with ancillary information, including radiometric and geometric calibration coefficients, and georeferencing parameters (e.g., platform ephemeris) computed and appended but not applied to the level 0 data.

Level 1B. Level 1A data that have been processed to sensor units (by applying the radiometric corrections).

Level 2. Derived geophysical variables at the same resolution and location as the Level 1 source data. Several examples of geophysical variables are given in the following text. For example, sea surface temperature and land surface moisture are geophysical variables derived from the measured radiance values constituting a Level 1B product.

Level 3. Derived geophysical variables mapped on uniform space–time grid scales, usually with some completeness and consistency.

Level 4. Model output or results from analyses of lower levels of data (e.g., variables derived from multiple measurements).

Not all instruments have products at all these levels. For convenience, some of the instrument teams have defined other intermediate levels also. For example, the science team responsible for the moderate resolution imaging spectroradiometer (MODIS) instrument on EOS defines a Level 2G product as an intermediate step in geometric corrections to map a Level 2 product onto a standard grid to produce a Level 3 product [14].

Several examples of geophysical variables referred to in the foregoing definitions of Level 2 and Level 3 products are grouped as characteristics of the atmosphere, land, and oceans as follows:

Atmosphere. atmospheric temperature profile, atmospheric humidity profile, aerosol vertical structure, cloud height, cloud-top temperature, aerosol optical depth, top of the atmosphere fluxes, lightening events, cirrus ice content, cloud-top altitude, concentrations of various gases such as chlorofluorocarbon (CFC), methane, ozone, carbon monoxide, and nitrous oxide.

Land. land topography, vegetation topography, surface reflectance, surface emissivity, surface kinetic temperature, surface temperature, ice sheet elevation, ice sheet roughness, land surface moisture, snow water equivalent, day–night temperature difference, and snow cover.

Oceans. sea surface temperature, ocean surface wind speed, sea ice concentration, sea surface topography, chlorophyll-A pigment concentration, chlorophyll fluorescence, and water-leaving radiance.

In addition, Level 4 products are produced from models that combine (by data assimilation or fusion) several of the lower-level products, to characterize certain phenomena such as weather, global circulation, primary productivity, carbon cycle, and so on.

Either individual geophysical variables or groups of several of them constitute *data products*. The term *standard products* is used in the EOS Program to refer to “data products that are generated as a part of a research investigation using EOS data that are of wide research utility, are routinely generated, and in general are produced for spatially and/or temporally extensive subsets of the data.”

The term *special data products* is used in the EOS Program to refer to “data products that are generated as part of a research investigation using EOS data and that are produced for a limited region or time period, or products that are not accepted as standard by the EOS Investigators’ Working Group (IWG) and

NASA Headquarters ... Special products may be reclassified later as standard products."

In addition to the standard and special products discussed earlier, many other value-added products can be derived for applications to specific regions of Earth or to specific disciplines. Several such products are being produced by the Working Prototype Earth Science Information Partners (WP-ESIPs) participating in NASA's Federation Experiment [6]. Most of the products generated by the EOS Program are global in scale, owing to the goals of the program to study the Earth as a system. However, there are many remote sensing systems (and some of the instruments on EOS) that acquire and process data at a high resolution over small regions of the Earth. The following discussion provides a sampling of methods used in deriving information from such multispectral (or hyperspectral) sensors. There are several textbooks on image processing and multispectral image analysis that cover these topics in much greater detail [13,15–18]. The discussion here is qualitative and avoids much of the mathematical detail needed for a more thorough treatment of this topic. The products containing the derived information in these cases are usually categorized as Level 3 and above, because they are typically mapped to standard ground coordinates (rather than sensor coordinates) on a grid.

From the point of view of accessing and manipulating data, the operations on multispectral images can be categorized as single-band (or single-image) operations, multiband (or multiimage) operations, and data-merging (multitemporal, multisensor, image and ancillary data).

3.6.2 Single-Band Operations

In single-band or single-image operations, each of the spectral bands in a multispectral image is handled separately. These operations are used for enhancing the images for visual analysis and interpretation, for removing artifacts of the sensing system, for radiometric and geometric corrections (see Section 3.5), or for spatial feature extraction. Some of the most common single-band operations are described here.

3.6.2.1 Contrast Stretch. Sensor data in a single image generally fall within a narrower range than that of display devices. Color display devices with 8 bits per color permit 256 levels (0 through 255), but the values from a sensor might span a different range. The input pixel values of the image are modified to output values using a linear or nonlinear function that maps the smallest number to 0 and the largest to 255. This improves the contrast in the image and assists an analyst during manual interpretation.

3.6.2.2 Histogram Equalization. A disadvantage of a linear stretch is that the output gray levels are assigned equally to input values regardless of whether they occur rarely or frequently. Frequently occurring gray levels represent a larger part of the image. Therefore, to increase the contrast in a large percentage of the image area, variable stretching of the input ranges is performed on the basis of the frequency of occurrence of input values. The larger the frequency, the wider the range of output values assigned. The result is that the histogram of the output image approximates a uniform distribution.

3.6.2.3 Selective Saturation. A user may be interested in a specific area of the image and may not care about the rest. In such a case, the image values in the area of interest may be stretched to the maximum output range (0 to 255) and the values in the other parts of the image be allowed to "saturate." That is, the contrast stretching function may map some pixel values outside the area of interest to numbers below 0 or above 255. Output values below 0 are set to 0 and those above 255 are set to 255.

3.6.2.4 Sensor Noise Removal. Occasional dropouts (or flipped bits) in sensor values may appear in images as individual pixels, whose values are very different from those of their neighboring pixels. Such values are adjusted using median filtering. A given pixel's value is replaced by the median value of a set of pixels in a 3×3 or 5×5 neighborhood centered on the given pixel. This processing step facilitates visual interpretation. However, for accurate analyses, it may be more useful simply to mark such pixels as "wrong" values.

3.6.2.5 Destriping. With multiple detectors in a given spectral band (as in parallel cross-track and along-track scanners), the images may appear striped, because the different sensors have slightly different responses, and therefore generate slightly different output values even while viewing the same target. For example, a uniform source of reflectance such as a desert or a lake may appear in the image as having a set of horizontal stripes. Although such images must be rigorously calibrated radiometrically for accurate analytical work (see previous section on Radiometric errors), it is possible to use simple algorithms to remove the striping in the image for visual analysis. An example of such an algorithm is based on computing the histograms of the subsets of the image obtained by individual detectors. Thus, if there are n detectors in the instrument, n histograms are obtained. The mean and standard deviation of each histogram are compared to, say, those of the first histogram. For each histogram, except the first, two adjustment factors are constructed: a gain, computed as the ratio of the variance of the first histogram to its variance; and a bias, computed as the difference of the mean of the first histogram and its mean. Each of the subimages corresponding to the individual detectors is then corrected by adding the bias factor to it and multiplying the result by the gain factor.

3.6.2.6 Correcting Line Dropouts. Occasionally, because of telemetry errors, images may have line dropouts—0 values for all or part of a scan line. Such dropouts appear as black lines in an image. For visual purposes, they can be corrected by assigning the average of the pixel values from the lines above and below to each affected pixel.

3.6.2.7 Spatial Filtering. Spatial filters emphasize or block image data at various spatial frequencies. Slow variations in brightness (e.g., over deserts and bodies of water) have low spatial frequency, whereas rapid variations (e.g., at edges between fields and roads, lines of crops in agricultural fields — in high-resolution images) have high spatial frequency. Low-pass (or low-emphasis) filters are designed to reduce the high-frequency components of the image and thus suppress local detail. High-pass (or high-emphasis) filters emphasize the local detail and suppress the overall variations in the image. Spatial filtering uses the input pixel values in a neighborhood of each pixel to determine the values of the output pixel. A simple low-pass filter is an averaging filter that replaces each pixel value by the average of the pixel values in a 3×3 or 5×5 neighborhood centered at the given pixel. A simple high-pass filter replaces each pixel value by the difference between the input value and the value of the output of an averaging filter at that pixel.

Both types of filters are particular cases of "convolution filters." Convolution filters are implemented using an $n \times n$ matrix of "weights," where n is usually an odd number. The matrix is used as a "moving window" that is positioned over each possible location in the input image. The weights and the corresponding input pixel values are multiplied, and the resulting products are all added to form the output pixel value. The 3×3 averaging filter uses all weights equal to 1/9. A simple 3×3 high-pass filter uses all weights equal to $-1/9$ except at the center, where the weight is 8/9. The effect of convolution filtering on an image depends on the set of weights and the size of the convolution matrix. For example, the larger the value of n for an averaging filter, the greater the low-frequency enhancement (and the more smeared the appearance of the output image). The high-pass filter discussed earlier removes all low-frequency variations in the image. However, by varying the center weight of the convolution matrix, it is possible to retain different degrees of low-frequency input data and hence vary the amount of edge enhancement obtained.

3.6.2.8 Fourier Analysis. The filters discussed earlier manipulate the image in the spatial domain [i.e., the (x, y) coordinate system in which the image is obtained]. It is possible to manipulate them in a "transform domain." In the Fourier transform domain, an image is expressed as a sum of a two-dimensional set of sinusoidal functions with different frequencies, amplitudes, and phases. The frequencies (u, v) form the coordinate system for the Fourier transform domain. The amplitudes and phases are recorded for each point (u, v) in the Fourier domain. There are standard algorithms for fast computation of Fourier transforms. The Fourier transform is invertible: the original image values can be recovered from the transform. It can be shown that convolution in the spatial domain is equivalent to multiplication of corresponding values in the Fourier transform domain. Thus, to perform a convolution, one can obtain the Fourier transforms of the input image and the convolution weight matrix, multiply the two Fourier transforms point by point, and obtain the inverse Fourier transform of the result. This method is significantly faster than computing the convolution in the spatial domain unless the filter matrix is very small. In addition, it is sometimes convenient to design filters in the frequency domain. This is done by observing the image displayed in the Fourier domain to highlight some of the frequency anomalies in the original image. Those frequencies are then suppressed directly in the Fourier domain (i.e., they are set to zero). A "clean" image is then derived by obtaining the inverse [13].

3.6.3 Multiband Operations

Multiband (or multiimage) operations combine the data from two or more spectral bands (or images) to facilitate visual interpretation or automated information extraction. Usually, the purpose of interpretation or information extraction is to distinguish objects on the ground or land cover types. The most common multiband operations are now described briefly.

3.6.3.1 Spectral Ratios. Ratios of corresponding pixel values in a pair of spectral bands are used to compensate for varying illumination effects, such as those caused by surface slopes. In those cases, the measured reflectance values for a given object type may be significantly different in different parts of the image. However, the ratios between the values in two spectral bands remain approximately the same. The ratios are different for different object types. Therefore, it is often possible to discriminate between different types of objects using spectral ratios. However, it is also possible that the spectral ratios hide some of the differences between object types that are not due to variations in illumination. If the absolute reflectance of two objects is different but the slopes of their spectra are the same in a given spectral region, they may yield the same spectral ratio. Because pairs of spectral bands are used to generate ratios, many ratio images can be generated from a multispectral input image. For example, for a Landsat thematic mapper image with six nonthermal spectral bands, there are 30 possible ratio images. The ratio images can be displayed in combinations of three (or with two ratio images and one of the input spectral bands) to generate color composites. Thus, a very large number of combinations are possible. A criterion for selecting which ratios to display relies on the amount of variance in a given ratio image and the correlation between ratio images: it is desirable to use images with the highest variance and minimum correlation. An optimum index factor (OIF) is defined on the basis of these criteria to select ratios to display [19].

3.6.3.2 Principal Components. Significant correlation may exist between spectral bands of a multispectral image. That is, two or more spectral bands in the image may convey essentially the same information. A scatter plot of the values in two spectral bands that are highly correlated shows most of the values close to a straight line. Thus, by using a linear combination of the two bands, the data values can be projected along the line that captures most of the variance in the data. Generalizing this to n dimensions, one can reduce the effective dimensionality of the data by "packing" the information into fewer dimensions that capture most of the variance in the image. This is done by computing the covariance matrix of the spectral bands. The covariance matrix is then diagonalized using eigenvector analysis [20].

The eigenvectors are used to produce linear combinations of spectral bands, called principal components, which are uncorrelated and whose variances are equal to the eigenvalues. The principal components that correspond to the largest eigenvalues capture most of the intensity variations across the image.

3.6.3.3 ***Canonical Components.*** As discussed earlier, principal components treat a multispectral image as a whole in determining the correlation between spectral bands. Canonical components are a variation of this concept, wherein the linear combinations of the original spectral bands are computed in order to maximize the visual dissimilarity between objects belonging to different user-selected classes [13].

3.6.3.4 ***Decorrelation Stretch.*** The principal components of a multispectral image can be used to perform a "decorrelation stretch" to enhance color display of a highly correlated data. The three most significant components are first obtained using principal components analysis. Each of the components is then independently stretched in contrast to take advantage of the full dynamic range of the display. The stretched data are then transformed back into the original spectral coordinates. This process increases the color saturation in the display better than a simple contrast stretch of the original spectral bands.

3.6.3.5 ***Vegetation Components.*** Certain combinations of spectral bands are found to emphasize differences between vegetation and other types of land cover as well as the differences among various types of vegetation. For example, in the NOAA AVHRR sensor, combinations of Channel 1 (visible band) and Channel 2 (near infrared band) are found to be indicative of green vegetation. Such combinations are therefore called *vegetation indices*. A simple vegetation index (VI) is given by the pixel-by-pixel difference ($C_2 - C_1$), where C_2 and C_1 are the image values in the two channels. The Normalized Difference Vegetation Index (NDVI) is defined as follows:

$$\mathrm{NDVI} = (C_2 - C_1)/(C_2 + C_1)$$

Both VI and NDVI have large values for healthy vegetation because of its high reflectivity in the infrared band. The NDVI is the preferred index for global vegetation monitoring because it is a ratio and, as discussed earlier (see paragraph on Spectral Ratios), compensates for differences in illumination conditions, surface slopes, aspect, and so on. The NDVI has been used to produce extensive and frequent maps of global vegetation using AVHRR data [21–23]. (see *http://edcdaac.usgs.gov/dataproducts.html*). In Ref. [24], an empirically determined linear transformation called the '*Tasseled Cap*' transformation is defined for Landsat multispectral scanner (MSS) data that maps most of the data into two components — brightness and greenness. The latter component is strongly correlated with the amount of vegetation. This concept has been extended by Crist and Cicone [25] to map six bands of Landsat TM data (other than the thermal

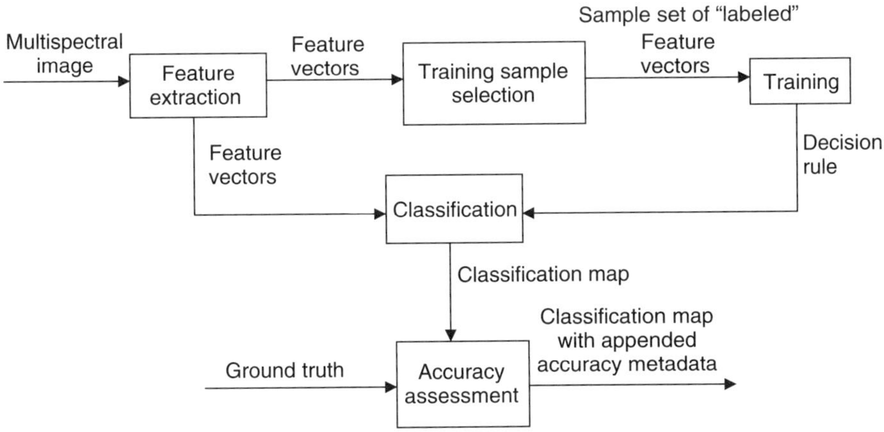

Figure 3.6. Steps in image classification.

band) into three components that emphasize soils, vegetation, and wetness. For examples of other work related to vegetation mapping see Refs. [26–31].

3.6.4 Image Classification

Classification is the process of assigning a label representing a meaningful category (or class) to each pixel in an image, on the basis of multispectral values of the pixel (and possibly its neighbors). For example, Labels 1, 2, 3, and 4 could be assigned respectively to pixels determined to be forest, agriculture, urban, and water. The label image could then be displayed by assigning a unique and distinctive color to each label to highlight the different classes. Although classification is a multiband operation, owing to the variety of techniques and its importance it is discussed here as a separate section. Typically, classification involves decision rules with parameters that must be estimated. Generally, classification algorithms have the following phases: feature extraction, training (or learning), labeling, and accuracy assessment (or validation). Figure 3.6 shows these steps and the inputs and outputs involved.

3.6.4.1 Feature Extraction. Features are numerical characteristics based on which classification decisions are made. That is, they help discriminate between the different classes. They should have values as close as possible for pixels or regions of the same class and as dissimilar as possible for those of different classes. Generally, several features are used together (constituting a "feature vector") for a given pixel (or a region) to which the class label is to be assigned. A feature vector can simply be the one-dimensional array of multispectral measurements at a given pixel. One can apply a principal components or canonical components transformation (discussed earlier) and assemble a multichannel image consisting of the components accounting for a predetermined amount (i.e., at least 95 percent) of the image variance. The feature vector for a given pixel then is the one-dimensional array of values in that multichannel image. Alternatively, one can combine textural (i.e., local variations in the neighborhood of a pixel) and spectral values into feature vectors.

3.6.4.2 ***Training (or Learning).*** The training or learning step in a classification algorithm is where the parameters of a "decision rule" are estimated. A decision rule is essentially a set of mathematical functions (also called *discriminant functions*) that are evaluated to decide the label to be assigned to each feature vector. The corresponding curves (in two dimensions) or hypersurfaces (in higher dimensional spaces) are referred to as *decision surfaces*. Two examples of decision surfaces are shown in Figure 3.7. Here, the feature vectors are two-dimensional. In general, feature vectors from multispectral images have much higher dimensionality. The scatter plots show three distinct classes, denoted by o, +, and −, respectively. Figure 3.7a shows ellipses and Figure 3.7b shows straight lines separating these classes. In the higher dimensional case, these become hyperellipsoids and hyperplanes, respectively. First, suppose that there is a known, complete, and valid physical model of the process that determines the observed feature vector given a particular class. Also, suppose that it is possible to invert the model. Then, given an observed feature vector, it is possible to use the inverse model and assign a class label to it. However, physical models are not always known. Even if physical models are known to characterize the observing process, deviations of the pixels from the ideal classes modeled cause the observations to be different from the predicted values. Examples of distorting phenomena that make it difficult to model the observations physically are mixed pixels, slope and aspect variations, and so forth. Even as the state of the art in measurements and physical modeling improves, it is necessary to account for the residuals through a statistical model. The decision rules can thus be based on a combination of physical and statistical models.

Examples of decision rules are as follows:

- *Minimum Distance.* Each class is represented by the mean of the feature vectors of a set of samples from that class. An observed feature vector is assigned to the class that has the closest mean.

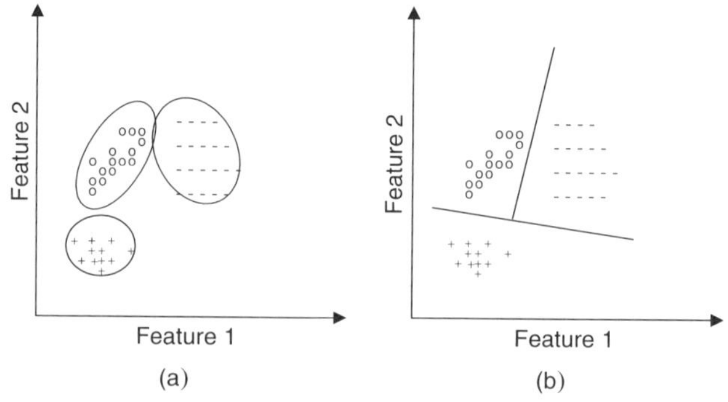

Figure 3.7. Decision rules.

- *Linear Discriminant Functions.* The multidimensional space of feature vectors is separated into different regions by hyperplanes. An observation is assigned to a class depending on the region to which it belongs.
- *Parallelepiped.* Each class is represented by a parallelepiped (a box with sides parallel to the axes of the feature space). An observation is assigned to a class, depending on the parallelepiped to which it belongs.
- *Gaussian Maximum Likelihood.* Each class is modeled using a Gaussian distribution using a mean vector and a covariance matrix — it is assumed that the observations from a given class are normally distributed. On the basis of these distributions, an observed feature vector is used to compute the probability (likelihood) of belonging to each of the different classes. The observed feature vector is assigned to the class for which the likelihood is maximal.

These and other rules are discussed with more mathematical detail in several references [13,15]. The parameters in the decision rules can be estimated using an identified set of "training samples" for which a user assigns labels. The user may have ancillary information about the image, such as a corresponding map, or may use visual interpretation of small segments of the image to identify training samples. This process is called supervised learning. Estimation of the accuracy of the resulting classification is part of the supervised learning process. This may be done by identifying a set of "test samples" that are distinct from the training samples. The class labels of the test samples are known. The accuracy (or goodness) of the discriminant functions can be estimated by using the discriminant functions to label the test samples and comparing the computed labels with the known labels.

One could also present the randomly sampled subset of an image to an algorithm that groups it into smaller subsets called *clusters* by some criterion of similarity between samples belonging to a given cluster. The clusters are then used to estimate the parameters of the decision rules. Such a process is called *unsupervised learning* and by itself does not produce semantically meaningful labels. However, clusters can be visually analyzed by an expert, who assigns a class label to each of them. An image is then classified by assigning each feature vector the semantic label of the cluster to which it belongs.

3.6.4.3 Labeling. After the parameters of the decision rules (discriminant functions) are estimated, each pixel in the image is assigned a label according to the decision rule. Note that spectral classes or class labels that are assigned only on the basis of feature vector values are not necessarily "information classes." For example, there may be several spectral classes corresponding to forest, several corresponding to agricultural regions, and so on. A reassignment of the spectral class labels to information class labels may be needed to obtain a classification map with physically meaningful labels. It may also be necessary to perform some "smoothing" of the labels to avoid "salt and pepper" appearance of classification maps that do not reflect reality.

3.6.4.4 Accuracy Assessment (Validation). The results of classification need to be validated by comparison with ground truth such as maps or in situ observations of a set of sample areas. This could be a more extensive process than the use of "test samples" discussed in the previous section on training. Photointerpretation and consistency checks may be used. The most accurate and valid comparisons are obtained if in situ observations of ground truth are made simultaneously with the acquisition of remotely sensed data. There are many variations of the general approach discussed earlier. A combined of spectral, spatial, and textural features can be considered. For example, one could perform segmentation of the image into relatively homogeneous sets of contiguous pixels and then assign single labels to each such class on the basis of statistical models or other criteria Ref. [32,33].

3.6.5 Hyperspectral Analyses

Hyperspectral sensors are characterized by a very large number of narrow and contiguous spectral bands. Such sensors are also called *imaging spectrometers* [34]. For each pixel, a spectrum of the energy arriving at the sensor is recorded. The spectral bands are narrow enough to provide a good approximation to the continuous spectrum. Typical hyperspectral sensors use 200 or more spectral bands. For example, the airborne visible-infrared imaging spectrometer (AVIRIS) collects data in 224 bands, in the range of 400 to 2500 nm with a resolution of 10 nm. With hyperspectral sensors, the potential exists for matching the observations at a given pixel with spectra of known materials and identifying the materials at the pixel location. Generally, the spectra of numerous materials are available in databases of laboratory measurements. The various radiometric and geometric errors, such as those discussed in Section 3.5, need to be corrected first. Rather than comparing the observed spectra with a large number of spectra in a database, it is useful to identify a small number of potential candidates that may be present at the given location to narrow down the search. This could be done using some a priori knowledge, if available. Expert system approaches have been explored for matching the AVIRIS spectrum for each pixel with laboratory spectra for various minerals [35]. In addition, pixels contain mixtures of different materials. Therefore, the observed spectra may not match any of the laboratory spectra in the database. However, they can be used to estimate proportions of the constituent materials that best match the given observation.

3.6.6 Data Fusion

Although remotely sensed images from a given sensor are quite rich in information, it is through combination of such images with other sources of data that one derives more complete information and applies it to real-world problems. The process of using multiple data sets together is referred to as *data fusion*, *data merging*, or *interuse*. Images observed by a sensor could be merged with

- images from other sensors (multisensor);
- images obtained by the same sensor at other times (multitemporal);

- images obtained by different detectors from the same sensors at different resolutions (multiresolution — e.g., ETM+ on Landsat-7 has a panchromatic band at 15-m resolution, 6 nonthermal bands at 30-m resolution, and 1 thermal band at 60-m resolution);
- several layers of ancillary data in a geographic information system (GIS)

In all these cases, it is important to have the images properly coregistered (relative to each other) or georegistered (relative to a ground coordinate system). The geometric corrections discussed in Section 3.5.3 assist in such registration. Sometimes, it is necessary to project the images onto a geographic coordinate system (e.g., universal transverse mercator — UTM grid with 10-m pixel sizes). When such corrections are required, the image value to be assigned to a given pixel P are computed using the image values in a small neighborhood of a "pixel" P′ in the input image. The geometric transformation from the desired output coordinate system to the input image coordinate system maps the pixel P to P′. The coordinates of P′ will generally be fractional. This process of computing the image values to be assigned to P is called *resampling*, because the image is being sampled in a different coordinate system to estimate what the sensor would have seen if it were sampling along that coordinate system. Because resampling introduces errors, it is important to minimize the number of times an image is resampled, that is, all the necessary geometric corrections and transformations must be accumulated and applied together to the original image (rather than applying them sequentially and generating intermediate resampled images).

The utility of image merging can be seen in many different applications. Examples of uses of merged multitemporal observations are improved land cover classification, change detection, display of daily variations (as in cloud maps in TV weather reports), and study of seasonal and interannual variations (e.g., time-sequenced images of the Antarctic ozone maps). Many interesting visualizations have been recently produced from temporal sequences of derived global data products, such as sea surface topography (*http://podaac.jpl.nasa.gov/tpssa/images/tpssa.mov?251,155*), ozone concentration (*http://daac.gsfc.nasa.gov/CAMPAIGN_DOCS/ATM_CHEM/graphics/October_1991_Ozone.mov and http://toms.gsfc.nasa.gov/multi/multi.html*), biosphere and a variety of other parameters (*http://seawifs.gsfc.nasa.gov/SEAWIFS/IMAGES/MOVIES.html*). Overlays of remotely sensed data (e.g., Landsat TM, Shuttle Imaging Radar) on digital elevation maps (DEM) have been used to generate synthetic stereoscopic images and perspective-view images. Also, it is possible to generate DEMs using stereo-pairs of satellite images and overlay spectral information from the instruments on such DEMs (for example, see *http://asterweb.jpl.nasa.gov/gallery/gallery.htm?name=Fuji*). Merging topographical data and remotely sensed data is useful in classification because the knowledge of elevation and slope can be used in addition to spectral data in identifying land cover types.

In generating the products discussed in the beginning of Section 3.6, the various instrument teams in the EOS Program use data from other instruments on EOS and ancillary data from NOAA and USGS. Examples of ancillary data are global vegetation index, snow/ice cover, stratospheric ozone profiles, medium-range weather forecast, ship/buoy observations, and digital elevation maps.

3.7 IMPLICATIONS FOR STORAGE AND ACCESS

From the discussion of data sources, processing, and applications, several characteristics of remotely sensed images that impose requirements on their storage and retrieval can be derived.

It is important to maintain information (metadata) about the images to keep track of them and search for them when needed. The data are very diverse in volume, characteristics, processing level, and format. Remotely sensed data are used by diverse communities of users. This implies that several different access patterns need to be supported. There are many providers of remote sensing data, and users often need data from multiple sources. Remote sensing data are usually large in volume because of a combination of their global nature, spatial resolution, and temporal frequency. Considerable expense is involved in satellite systems and instruments for acquiring the data, which, obviously, cannot be reacquired for a time period that has passed. Therefore, all data deemed of sufficient value need to be permanently preserved. A brief discussion of the implications of each of these issues is provided in the following sections.

3.7.1 Metadata

To track the millions of images that are typical in large remote sensing data systems, it is necessary to maintain information about the images that can be regarded as "tags" or "indexes." These "metadata" may be stored along with the image data and/or in a separate database with pointers to help locate the images from tertiary storage devices. Some of the metadata may be used for searching and accessing images, whereas other metadata may be information of interest in using the data. Generally, metadata consists of several attributes. Some of the attributes are associated with a large set (collection) of images, whereas other attributes need to be specified for each granule (a *granule* is the smallest entity tracked by a database — it can be a single image or a set of a few images). Examples of collection level attributes are as follows:

- *General Description.* Product name, discipline, topic, term, variable, collection version, and so on.
- *Data Origin.* Campaign, platform, instrument, sensor, and so on.
- *Spatial Coverage.* One of the several ways of specifying the geographic area covered by the images in the collection (e.g., latitude and longitude of the corners of a bounding rectangle).
- *Temporal Coverage.* One of several ways of specifying the time range over which the images in the collection were obtained (e.g., starting date and time and ending date and time; a single date and time; starting date and time and the periodicity).
- *Contact.* Name, address, telephone number, e-mail address, and so on.

Examples of granule level attributes are as follows:

- *General Description.* Name, size estimate, date of production, process input, ancillary data, associated browse image(s), software version used to produce the granule, pointers to software documentation, and quality measures.
- *Data Origin.* Campaign, platform, instrument, sensor, model, and so on.
- *Spatial Coverage.* One of the several ways of specifying the geographic area covered by the images in the granule (e.g., latitude and longitude of the corners of a bounding rectangle).
- *Temporal Coverage.* One of the several ways of specifying the time range over which the images in the granule were obtained. (e.g., starting date and time and ending date and time; a single date and time; starting date and time and the periodicity).

The federal geographic data committee (FGDC) has established standards for metadata content with which all geographic data managed by U.S. federal government agencies must comply [36].

3.7.2 Diversity of Data

As shown in Section 3.4 of this chapter, remotely sensed data are obtained from a variety of satellites and instruments and pertain to many science disciplines. It is important that organizations that maintain and support such data have a good understanding of the data and their usage. Some broad expertise in the disciplines covered by the data sets is necessary to support users of such data. This makes it difficult to have common database solutions that apply to all types of data. From an organizational point of view, it is necessary to distribute the responsibility of data management among multiple organizations, each focused on a subset of disciplines and managing the data sets appropriate to those disciplines. From a technical point of view, it is necessary to define a large variety of data types and store the data as multiple collections of related data. To enable merging and interuse of the variety of data sets, it is necessary either to establish a small number of common standard formats or to provide format translation tools and software tools for resampling to common grids. It is necessary to manage the information about the data availability across multiple sites and provide search and order tools. Examples of standards used for image data are common data format (CDF), network common data form (NetCDF), and hierarchical data format (HDF). Each of these formats is really a flexible environment for representing the data with a suite of software tools. More information on standard formats will be provided in the discussion of examples of systems supporting remotely sensed image data presented in Section 3.8.

3.7.3 Diversity of Users

Except in the case of image databases with a rather narrow focus and a well-established applications area, it is difficult to predict the demand and usage patterns for the data. Remote sensing is an area in which new applications are discovered frequently and new communities of users tend to grow. The statistics in the charts at *http://ivanova.gsfc.nasa.gov/charts* illustrate the number and diversity of users of NASA's Distributed Active Archive Centers. The organizational implications of this include recognizing that personnel-assisting users should have a broad understanding of users' needs and that support must be available for new data providers focused on serving different user communities. One technical consequence of this diversity is the difficulty in predicting the load on the database systems. It is necessary to gather usage statistics, assess them, and be prepared to augment system capacity and capabilities as needed. Clear on-line documentation, multiple layers of indexes to data, aliases to accommodate differences in terminology, and easy-to-use search and order facilities are needed. Just as distributed implementation helps in supporting diverse sets of data, it also helps in serving a diverse user community by focusing attention on the needs of smaller subcommunities.

3.7.4 Access Patterns

Given the variety of users, applications, and types of processing, image data and metadata are accessed from the data archives in many different ways. First, users may access just the metadata to find out about the characteristics of an image collection, how the images were obtained, algorithms used for processing, and so on. Users may use metadata for locating the images that cover specific spatial regions and intervals of time. Before ordering, accessing, or acquiring the images, users may want to view (or "browse") versions of images at a reduced resolution, to obtain an idea of data quality, cloud cover, and so on. The users may then order specific granules from the archives. Depending on the size of the granules, the data can be downloaded through the Internet or shipped on media, such as CD-ROMs or tapes. Some users may be interested in obtaining entire collections of image data pertaining to specific geographic regions or application disciplines, to provide value-added services to other users. A common user requirement, especially on image data collections wherein the granules are large in size (e.g., >1 GB each) is to obtain subsets of images that meet their specifications. Some examples of methods for defining subimages are to specify

- the top-left and bottom-right corners of a rectangular area of interest in terms of line and pixel numbers or latitude and longitude;
- one or more polygonal areas of interest, by providing the coordinates of a sequence of vertices (as line and pixel numbers or latitude and longitude);
- subsampling (e.g., discarding every other line and pixel in the image);
- content-based rules depending on the content of the image of interest (e.g., in an image representing elevations, provide all pixels with elevation values greater than 500 m);
- content-based rules depending on the content of ancillary data (e.g., in a Landsat image, provide all the multispectral pixel values for locations with

soil moisture greater than a certain value, where soil moisture is the ancillary data that is registered with, i.e., overlaid on, the Landsat image of interest)

Subsetting is just one example of the methods for reducing the amount of data to be shipped (or transmitted) to meet the user's needs more closely than sending entire granules or collections of image data. Clearly, the image data archive performs some computations while extracting subsets. The computations may involve just the metadata or the image granules themselves. This idea can be extended to allow more general computations at the image data archive. For example, users may be permitted to submit data mining algorithms to the archive and obtain the resulting information (rather than the image data).

3.7.5 Diversity of Data Providers

It is expected that the number and variety of providers of remote sensing data will continue to grow. Providers will be from different scientific disciplines and may have varying levels and types of responsibility. They range from government organizations with responsibility to serve "all comers" and nonprofit organizations with focused discipline responsibilities to "value-added" data providers and commercial outfits that work for profit. Interface standards, different levels and types of interoperability, and corresponding protocols are therefore required for data, metadata, messages, and so on, to facilitate exchanges among groups of providers or providers and users. It is important to devise mechanisms to identify which providers own the data sets needed by the users. Examples of providing interoperability and of the standards adopted for some of the systems managing access to remotely sensed data are discussed in Section 3.8.

3.7.6 Large Volumes

Remote sensing imagers, in general, and multispectral or hyperspectral sensors, in particular, produce very large volumes of data. The volumes of the U.S. federal government's (NASA, NOAA, and USGS) remotely sensed data holdings are currently growing at about 1 petabyte (PB) per year and are expected to grow at about 2 PB per year after 2005, resulting in about 18 PB by 2010. Economical storage and access to these data involve

- Data compression;
- A balance between on-line (possibly RAID) and near-line storage (with robotic access) to ensure fast response on database searches and downloading of small files, while maintaining the bulk of the image data on more economical media;
- Providing the appropriate file sizes to balance the trade-off between size of individual granules (small granules can be efficiently downloaded over computer networks) and the number of granules to be managed (maintaining and indexing a large number of granules is a computationally expensive task);

- Providing the ability for users to browse reduced-resolution data before ordering or accessing the data;
- Providing subsets of granules upon request;
- Providing users with the ability to search for data of interest and to narrow down the searches (e.g., by specifying spatial, temporal and/or parametric criteria, and coincidences with other data sets of interest) to minimize extraneous data transfers.

3.7.7 Permanent Storage

Data acquired for a specific, fleeting operational purpose does not have to be archived permanently. However, most satellite-acquired image data do not fall into this category. Remotely sensed data are expensive to obtain. Additionally, it is important to maintain a continuous and consistent record for applications such as long-term climate studies. Any data from the past that are lost can never be reacquired.

These considerations dictate several storage requirements. At a minimum, raw data and all ancillary data, documentation, and software required to generate higher levels of products must be permanently stored. “Ancillary” data include calibration parameters, prelaunch and onboard calibration data, any in situ measurements used for validation of satellite-derived products, and so on. Any data products that require special expertise and quality control to generate should be considered for permanent storage. Just as important is the preservation of the metadata and search tools, to ensure that the data of interest can still be located several years in the future. The media must ensure long-term survival of data or, alternatively, data should be migrated sufficiently frequently to newer media. Quality checks should be performed to ensure data integrity. Technology upgrades should ensure that the data continue to be readable.

3.8 EXAMPLES OF SYSTEMS THAT STORE OR PROVIDE ACCESS TO REMOTELY SENSED DATA

There are several organizations and systems that store or provide access to remotely sensed data. It is beyond the scope of this chapter to perform an exhaustive survey of such systems. This section will discuss a few of them that are supported by the U.S. government and universities with reference to the issues discussed in Section 3.7. The various systems address different needs of the user and provider communities: no single system currently provides all the functionalities needed by all of these communities. The following discussion covers the salient features of each of the systems but is not to be construed as a comparative evaluation. All the systems rely on the World Wide Web (WWW) to provide user-access to data and information. All of these systems are currently operational, in that they actually serve specific user communities, and at the same time are under development, in that they are providing evolutionary enhancements to their capabilities.

NASA's Global Change Master Directory offers a mechanism for data providers to advertise their holdings and for users to discover data sets of interest [37,38]. The U.S. Global Change Research Program gives a listing of and access to many government providers of remotely sensed data at *http://www.gcdis.usgcrp.gov/*. NASA's Earth Science Enterprise Program has developed a distributed system, called *the EOS Data and Information System* (EOSDIS), with a broad set of responsibilities to manage NASA's Earth science data. This system addresses many of the issues associated with diversity, large volumes, and permanency discussed in Section 3.7. In addition, NASA's Earth Science Enterprise is conducting a "Federation Experiment." This experiment supports a set of "Working Prototype Earth Science Information Partners" (WP-ESIPs), to increase flexibility in addressing the diversity issues and to help in defining directions for the Earth Science Enterprise's data systems and services for the future. The Alexandria Digital Library (ADL) being developed at the University of California, Santa Barbara (UCSB), is a distributed library for geographically referenced information [39]. The Distributed Oceanographic Data System (DODS) is a system developed by the University of Rhode Island and the Massachusetts Institute of Technology for facilitating user access to distributed oceanographic data [40]. Both ADL and DODS address the issue of minimizing the "cost of entry" of diverse providers of remotely sensed data.

3.8.1 Global Change Master Directory (GCMD)

The GCMD is supported by NASA's Earth Science Enterprise with the participation of several national and international organizations. It is a comprehensive directory providing descriptions of data sets relevant to research in global change. The directory has been "mirrored" at many sites through the Committee on Earth Observation Satellites' (CEOS) International Directory Network (IDN). The GCMD database includes more than 8500 descriptions of data sets in various disciplines — climate change, agriculture, the atmosphere, biosphere, hydrosphere and oceans, geology, geography, and human dimensions of global change. These descriptions are provided in a standard format, called the *directory interchange format* (DIF). The DIF contains a predefined, specific set of metadata — covering 30 key aspects of data — to be placed in the database to facilitate search for data set information. These attributes include geographic coordinates for bounding areas and alphanumeric fields containing a list of locations. The providers of data sets supply uniform resource locators (URLs) or descriptions of their data sets to the GCMD using a web-based registration form. To encourage participation by providers with a minimum amount of effort, the GCMD also accommodates a shorter version of the DIF called '*Skinny DIF*.' A variety of interfaces are provided for searching the database. The results of a search are metadata records that provide information on the location and nature of the data (e.g., parameters measured, geographic location, and time range). A recent addition to GCMD is a search interface to Earth science–related software tools and services. The organization at NASA Goddard Space Flight Center that manages the GCMD participates in several national and international groups promoting metadata standards. These include the Federal Geographic Data Committee (FGDC) for Content Standard for Digital Geospatial Metadata, the Canadian Earth Observation Network (CEONet), the Government Information Locator Service (GILS), the Z39.50 Search and Retrieval Protocol, the Catalog Interoperability Protocol (CIP), the National Biological Information Infrastructure (NBII), the Dublin Core Metadata Initiative, and the Australia New Zealand Land Information Council (ANZLIC).

The GCMD uses extensible stylesheet language (XSL) for translation among several metadata formats, and allows flexibility in dealing with the issue of diverse providers and users requiring different levels of metadata detail. The GCMD has established a hierarchical structure for the parameter key words (valid names for parameters). Various other groups, including the FGDC Clearinghouse, NOAA, CEOS IDN, and EOSDIS, have used this structure. The staff supporting the GCMD acts as the maintenance body for the parameter key words and the DIF standard to ensure interoperability.

The latest version of GCMD is designed as a distributed system that is not limited to a specific database architecture. This design is intended to allow automated exchange of metadata content among Earth science collaborators. A local database agent for each partner captures database updates and broadcasts them to the other cooperating nodes. Thus, the exchange of metadata and the validation of content are distributed over several nodes. The management of the controlled vocabulary, however, is performed by one administrative node.

3.8.2 EOS Data and Information System (EOSDIS)

NASA's Earth Science Enterprise Program has developed a distributed system called the Earth Observing System (EOS) Data and Information System (EOSDIS) with a broad set of responsibilities to manage NASA's Earth science data. The development of this system was started in 1990 at the time the EOS program of satellites and science research was initiated to address the study of long-term global climate change. Since then, EOSDIS has evolved in architecture and capabilities, with interim working versions supporting earth science data from NASA's past and current missions.

3.8.2.1 EOSDIS Requirements. The key functional requirements of EOSDIS are as follows:

- Planning, scheduling, command, and control of EOS spacecraft and instruments;
- Data capture and telemetry processing;
- Product generation;
- Data archival, management, and distribution;
- Information management;
- User support.

The major components of EOSDIS are discussed as follows:

3.8.2.2 EOSDIS Components. The components of EOSDIS are EOS Data and Operations System (EDOS), the EOSDIS Core System (ECS), the Distributed Active Archive Centers (DAACs), and Science Investigator-led Processing Systems (SIPSs) and networks that connect these together. The EDOS receives the raw data stream from the satellites, separates the data by instrument, and performs the initial processing and backup archiving. NASA's operational networks are used for mission-critical data transfers. Data transfers among non-mission-critical components of EOSDIS and with users are handled by partnering with existing and evolving national network infrastructure. The ECS has two major segments. The first, called the *Flight Operations Segment* (also known as the EOS Mission Operations System-EMOS) provides the capabilities for satellite and instrument command and control. The second, called the Science Data Processing Segment (SDPS) provides the capabilities for data product generation using science software provided by the instrument teams, ingest of data from various sources, archival, and distribution. The DAACs process the raw data into useful products, handle user product searches, requests, and orders, and distribute data to the user community, through the Internet or media. The DAACs also archive the data and information for future use. Each DAAC focuses on the data needs of a specific segment of the user community based on scientific disciplines. A list of the DAACs and their scientific disciplines is given in Table 3.2. The DAACs accomplish their work using a combination of ECS and other systems. Most of the EOS product generation at the DAACs is carried out using science software provided by the instrument teams. In many cases, instrument teams produce all their standard data products operationally and deliver them to the DAACs. The instrument teams' systems for such product generation are referred to as *SIPSs*. Thus, the part of EOSDIS that handles data beyond capture and initial processing is a distributed system with several independent and interacting components. The ECS is a large system with a homogeneous design but is geographically distributed at the DAACs. There are SIPSs and DAAC-unique components that have interfaces with ECS. There are also SIPSs and DAAC-unique components that do not interface with ECS but provide processing, archiving, and distribution services as a part of the overall EOSDIS.

3.8.2.3 EOSDIS "Version 0"—Distributed Implementation and Interoperability. The initial version of EOSDIS, called *Version 0*, was developed during 1990 to 1994 as a collaborative effort between the DAACs and the Earth Science Data and Information System (ESDIS) Project at the NASA Goddard Space Flight Center. The goal of this development was to make the "heritage" Earth science data more broadly available to the community. The approach was to improve interoperability among the heterogeneous data systems that existed at the organizations hosting the DAACs while also establishing the DAACs as operational entities. Interoperability was chosen to be at the inventory level to support users in searching and ordering data sets through a single interface, called

Table 3.2. NASA's EOSDIS Distributed Active Archive Centers (DAACs)

DAAC	Location	Discipline(s)	URL
Alaska SAR Facility (University of Alaska)	Fairbanks, AK	Sea Ice and Polar Processes Imagery	http://www.asf.alaska.edu
EROS Data Center (U.S. Geological Survey)	Sioux Falls, SD	Land Features and Processes Imagery	http://edcwww.cr.usgs.gov/landdaac/
Goddard Space Flight Center (NASA)	Greenbelt, MD	Upper Atmosphere, Atmospheric Dynamics and Global Biosphere	http://daac.gsfc.nasa.gov/
Jet Propulsion Laboratory (NASA)	Pasadena, CA	Ocean Circulation and Air-Sea Interaction	http://podaac.jpl.nasa.gov
Langley Research Center (NASA)	Hampton, VA	Radiation Budget, Clouds, Aerosols and Tropospheric Chemistry	http://eosweb.larc.nasa.gov
Marshall Space Flight Center (NASA)	Huntsville, AL	Hydrology	http://www-nsidc.colorado.edu/
National Snow and Ice Data Center (University of Colorado)	Boulder, CO	Polar Processes, Cryosphere and Climate	http://www-nsidc.colorado.edu/
Oak Ridge National Laboratory (Department of Energy)	Oak Ridge, TN	Biogeochemical Dynamics	http://www-eosdis.ornl.gov
Socio-Economic Data and Applications Center (Consortium for International Earth Science Information Network - CIESIN)	Palisades, NY	Human Interactions in Global Change	http://sedac.ciesin.org/

the *Version 0 Information Management System* (V0 IMS). The V0 IMS provided a web-based client to handle user queries for data based on spatial and temporal bounds and other criteria such as sensor, platform, and geophysical parameters. Optionally, the users could also specify a set of DAACs as a search parameter if they knew which DAACs contained the data of interest to them. A data dictionary with valid names for all the parameters was established. The client transmitted the user requests to the DAACs' local systems using a standard protocol. Each of the DAACs had a local interoperability layer that translated the user requests into queries understandable to the local database management systems. The inventories would be searched against the criteria, and the search results would be transmitted to the client for assembling and presenting to the users. Figure 3.8 illustrates this process. The DAACs needed to ensure that the data sets were made visible through the V0 IMS interface for them to be searchable through the common client. The DAACs also developed individual user interfaces supporting search and order as well as additional specialized services appropriate to their disciplines.

The Hierarchical Data Format (HDF), developed by the National Center for Supercomputing Applications (NCSA) at the University of Illinois, was selected as a standard format for distribution for data sets of general interest. Native formats of the data sets were also supported. Improvements to metadata content and documentation were made to the heritage data held at the DAACs. The DAACs continue to serve a growing community of tens of thousands of users with more than 900 image and nonimage data sets. See catalog of data sets and the science data plan at *http://spsosun.gsfc.nasa.gov/spso/sdp/sdphomepage.html* for details on the data sets. The interoperability approach with the V0 IMS has been extended to several data centers outside the United States to constitute a truly international network of interoperable data providers.

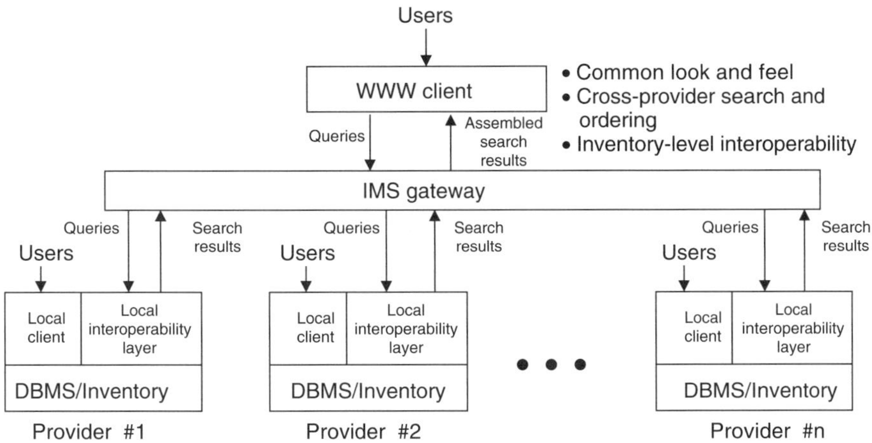

Figure 3.8. Version 0 IMS architecture.

3.8.2.4 EOSDIS with ECS—"Homogeneous Core" with Interfaces to Distributed Components. The latest version of EOSDIS has been supporting Landsat-7 since April 1999 and Terra since December 1999 with the ECS, while continuing to provide the capabilities of Version 0. The ECS development has taken an approach different from that of Version 0 EOSDIS, enforcing greater homogeneity in the system design across the geographically distributed components. This is the case in all areas—data ingest, production planning, processing, archiving, data management, and user access. A high-level description of the other aspects of the architecture can be found in Ref. [3]. The V0 IMS has evolved into a new client called the *EOS Data Gateway* (EDG), taking advantage of more recent technology and the richer metadata provided for EOS data sets. EDG is used for searching and ordering data in the ECS and non-ECS data servers at the DAACs and other international data centers. Access to EDG can be obtained at *http://eos.nasa.gov/imswelcome*. The ECS has standard interfaces for exchange of data with the SIPSs. Also, the ECS interfaces with capabilities developed at the DAACs to provide specialized services. Examples of such capabilities are billing and accounting at the EROS Data Center (EDC) DAAC and a database system at the Langley Research Center (LaRC) DAAC to support quality assessment of data products from the multiangle imaging spectroradiometer (MISR) instrument.

An important aspect of the ECS architecture is its data model. Conceptually, the data model can be represented as a pyramid, as shown in Figure 3.9 [41]. The upper levels of the pyramid may be considered indexes to data (traditionally called *metadata*) and the lower layers are the different levels of data products

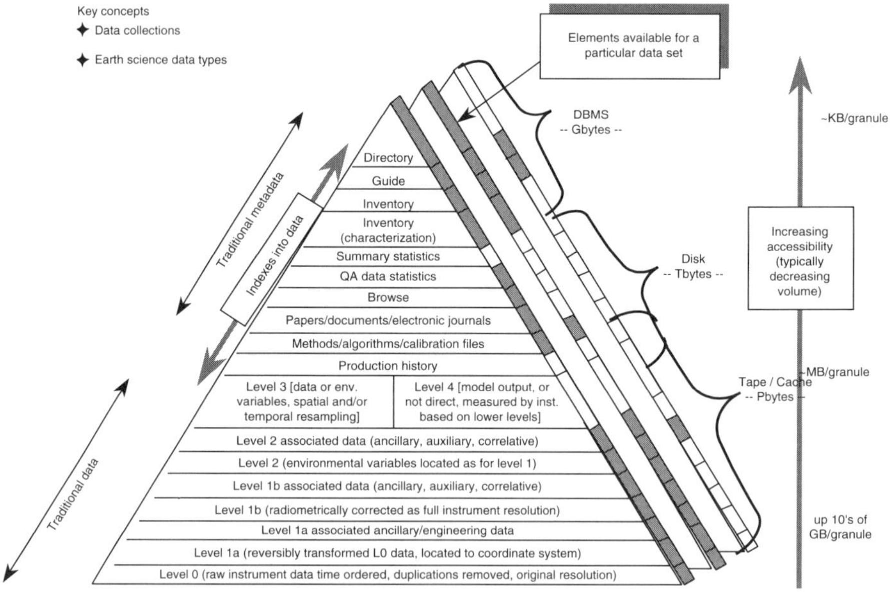

Figure 3.9. ECS data pyramid.

discussed in Section 3.6.1. Indexes in the higher levels of the pyramid point to the data sets in the lower levels to assist in locating them. All the data holdings are conceptually grouped into collections of granules. Each such collection is called an *Earth science data type* (ESDT). The granule sizes can vary from collection to collection. Not all collections need to have the same structure of data within the pyramid. Applicable services can be defined for each ESDT. The collections involve various types of data — swaths (time sequences of scan lines, profiles, or other array data), images, time-series data, gridded data, point data, delivered algorithm packages, and so forth.

All data products generated from EOS instruments are required to have metadata conforming to the ECS metadata model. This facilitates keeping track of the many millions of granules, archiving them for the years to come, and locating them upon user request. A more detailed discussion of the ECS metadata model can be found in Ref. [42]. The metadata model is consistent with the Federal Geographic Data Committee standards for metadata content. The model provides for up to 287 metadata attributes to describe the ESDTs. However, for a given ESDT, only a fraction of them would be required. The metadata are provided at both the collection level (attributes and values shared by all granules in the collection) and at the granule level (attributes and values specific to a given granule). Examples of these attributes are given in Section 3.7.1.

In addition, there are attributes associated with browse granules (subsampled images to aid users in deciding whether to order a full-resolution image), delivered algorithm packages (software, documentation, etc.), documents, production history, and quality assessment.

Most of the data products generated from the EOS instrument data are in a standard format called *HDF-EOS*. This format is based on the standard HDF discussed earlier, with additional conventions, data types, and metadata. At a minimum, HDF-EOS products are HDF products that include ECS core metadata (i.e., the minimal set of metadata that are essential for supporting ECS search services). HDF-EOS also uniquely accommodates specific data types, metadata, and conventions tailored to EOS data. Three specific data types defined on HDF-EOS are called *point, grid, and swath*. These permit spatial and temporal queries on the file contents. Any tool that processes standard HDF files can read an HDF-EOS file. Although HDF-EOS geolocation or temporal information is accessible using standard HDF calls, the particular association between that information and the data themselves will not be apparent. Software tool kits are provided for writing and reading HDF-EOS data sets. Some support for HDF-EOS using commercial tools is available. It is expected that, with the significant quantity of data and number of data sets available in HDF-EOS, there will be more commercial development of tools, including translation tools into other popular formats. (See *http://hdfeos.gsfc.nasa.gov/hdfeos/workshop.html* for examples of activities in support of HDF-EOS standard format). As mentioned earlier, most of the EOS data products are generated in HDF-EOS. However, exceptions do exist and are made when there is strong justification based on scientific, technical, and economic reasons.

3.8.2.5 EOSDIS Federation Experiment—Increase in Distributed Implementation. EOSDIS, with its present implementation including ECS, the DAACs, and the SIPSs addresses many of the issues of diversity, large volumes, and permanency discussed in Section 3.7. However, its primary orientation is toward disciplined, schedule-driven, and operational generation of standard products. In response to a 1995 recommendation by the National Research Council [43] and to increase the flexibility in incorporating evolving technologies and address the diversity issues, NASA started a "Federation Experiment" in 1998. This experiment supports a set of "Working Prototype Earth Science Information Partners (WP-ESIPs)." There are three types of ESIPs defined. Type-1 ESIPs, currently the DAACs, are responsible for standard data and information products requiring disciplined adherence to schedules. Type-2 ESIPs are responsible for data and information products in support of Earth system science that are developmental or research-oriented in nature, and emphasize innovation and flexibility. Type-3 ESIPs provide data and information products, through joint endeavor agreements with NASA, to a broader set of users than the global change research community. The three types of ESIPs together constitute a "Working Prototype Federation (WPF)." A succinct description of the WPF and a list of the Type-2 and Type-3 WP-ESIPs that were competitively selected in 1998 are given in Ref. [6]. Details about the federation can be found at *http://www.esipfed.org*. Given the autonomous and highly distributed nature of the ESIPs, one of the key activities is to form "clusters" with voluntary participation to address common scientific or technical problems. One of these clusters addresses interoperability issues and standards. Another cluster is focused on content-based search and data mining. More details about the clusters can be found at *http://www.esipfed.org/clusters*. As of this writing, the Federation experiment is still in progress and is expected to help define directions for the Earth Science Enterprise's data systems and services for the future.

3.8.3 The Alexandria Digital Library (ADL)

The Alexandria Digital Library is a distributed library for geographically referenced information being developed at the University of California, Santa Barbara [39]. The library manages remotely sensed and other data—digital and analog. Its main goals are to make the jobs as easy as possible for both the providers and the users of such information. The library facilitates the addition of new collections by accepting a very wide selection of existing metadata schemata. The effort on the part of the providers of new collections is minimized. The library facilitates the users' access to the collections by supporting the execution of a single query against multiple heterogeneous collections. Thus, the goal is to enable heterogeneous providers while attempting to provide a homogeneous view to users. To handle these somewhat conflicting goals, ADL uses a concept called *search buckets*. Search buckets are a set of generic parameters intended primarily for querying and are high-level containers for metadata from multiple sources. All holdings accessible through ADL can be queried using the attributes in the search buckets. The search bucket scheme currently has the following attributes:

- *Geographic Location.* "Footprint" (point, bounding box, polygon, etc.) in geographic coordinates. Each object in an ADL collection must be associated with at least one footprint. It is possible for an object to be associated with more than one, possibly joint footprints. The geographic location bucket has the coordinates of the vertices of the geographic polygons bounding the footprints of the object. Query operations "contains" and "overlaps" are defined for this search bucket.
- *Type.* Form (e.g., map, aerial photograph, etc.) or content (e.g., hydrographic feature, airport, etc.). ADL has a controlled hierarchical vocabulary of valid terms to be used to describe the types. The query operation on this bucket is to obtain an exact match on the term at some node (or leaf) in the hierarchy.
- *Format.* Format(s) in which the holding can be delivered, both on-line and off-line. Format names need to be provided for both digital and nondigital data. Where possible, the controlled vocabulary conforms to commonly understood standard terminology. It is possible to assign multiple formats to a single digital object.
- *Topical Text.* Text gleaned from detailed metadata associated with the object that describes any topics or themes. This is the most loosely specified search bucket. Queries on this bucket and the following four buckets are of the form "any word," "all words," and "exact phrase" ("Any word" queries return "true" if any of the specified words exist in the text being searched. "All words" queries require that all the words exist, but their order in the text is not important. "Exact phrase" queries require that the words be found in the exact sequence in the text being searched.)
- *Assigned Term.* Subject headings, index terms, key words, and others that are considered significant by the original catalogers of the object. This is a proper subset of the topical text.
- *Originator.* Author, agency, publisher, and others responsible for the creation or dissemination of the object. This could include funding agencies, curators, and so on.
- *Date Range.* Beginning and ending dates of coverage, publication, and so on. These are specified as pairs of beginning and ending dates, and can be viewed as "time footprints."
- *Identifier.* These are unique identifiers provided or maintained by the originators of the objects for their own purposes. These do not have to conform to the ADL's controlled vocabulary but generally provide a simple and convenient mechanism for users familiar with the conventions to locate the objects. It is possible, however, for a user to receive "false hits" because of two different providers using the same identifier with different meanings.

Type and format are the only search buckets for which a set of valid terms is mandated by ADL. Providers are free to choose their own vocabulary for the other search buckets. Each ADL collection provides mappings between the search bucket attributes and its own individual metadata fields. One of the reasons for keeping the number of search buckets small is to simplify the mappings. The semantics of the search buckets are fairly precise to permit expressive queries, although query operators are loosely defined. For example, the operators "overlaps" and "contains" defined for the geographic location search bucket do not indicate whether the objects are defined over a spherical or planar surface. There is no obligation beyond best efforts on the part of the collection servers to provide support for the query operators.

The ADL architecture consists of a middleware server that provides multiple clients a homogeneous view of multiple heterogeneous servers providing collections of data in the distributed library. The clients formulate queries in terms of the search buckets. The middleware translates the queries and forwards them to the collection servers, that interpret these queries in ways meaningful to them, and provide responses.

Each collection server is registered with the middleware with collection-level metadata structured in XML according to an ADL-defined standard. Not all collection servers need to support all the search buckets. The metadata indicate which buckets a collection server supports.

3.8.4 DODS — Distributed Oceanographic Data System

The Distributed Oceanographic Data System (DODS) is being developed by a number of institutions led by the University of Rhode Island and the Massachusetts Institute of Technology (*http://unidata.ucar.edu/packages/dods*). This is an example of a system that addresses the issues of diversity of providers and users. The basic premises of DODS are that data producers should also be data providers and that users should be free to use applications software of their choice to access and manipulate the data. DODS is a software package that provides access to data on any network-accessible DODS server. The users can obtain and use data regardless of the format in which they are archived. DODS does not put constraints on the content or format of the semantic metadata associated with the data and therefore simplifies the data provider's task. However, the services available to the users depend on the presence of appropriate metadata.

Like the other systems discussed earlier, DODS is also a client-server system. There is no central authority that funds or controls the clients and servers. Therefore, the system is in a state of flux, with the clients and servers joining and leaving it at will. This could be looked upon as analogous to informal sharing of data tapes among scientists and researchers in the pre-Web era. A "central registry" is planned for DODS with voluntary participation by servers to indicate the type and location of data provided. The data are not located in any centralized archive but each of the large number of servers make relatively small amounts of data available to users. In concept, this is analogous to making documents available on the WWW. In fact, DODS servers are standard http servers equipped with a set of DODS common gateway interface (CGI) programs.

The data model of DODS is based on common data types of programming languages such as C. In addition, it supports URLs, lists, sequences, and grids. Sequences are used to store relational data, such as those in a relational database. Grids are used to store arrays that have mapping vectors associated with their indices. The goal in DODS is to provide the ability to handle data in various formats supplied by servers through the use of format-specific APIs. As of September 2000, DODS APIs supported the following formats [40]:

- *NetCDF.* Developed by UCAR. Supports gridded data such as satellite data, interpolated ship data, or current meter data.
- *JGOFS.* Relational data such as sequences created by the Joint Global Ocean Flux Study (JGOFS) project for use with oceanographic station data.
- *HDF.* Developed by NCSA. Supports gridded data.
- *HDF-EOS.* Adaptation of HDF to EOS products. DODS server developed by NASA Jet Propulsion Laboratory. Supports gridded and point data.
- *DSP.* Developed at the University of Miami/RSMAS. Oceanographic and geophysical satellite data. Provides support for image processing. Primarily used for AVHRR and CZCS data. GRIB — World Meteorological Organization (WMO) format for the storage of weather information and the exchange of weather product messages. Support for gridded binary data. The GRIB server makes use of grid analysis and display system (GrADS, *http://grads.iges.org/grads*) to read GRIB data. GrADS then serves a DODS data stream.
- *FreeForm.* On-the-fly conversion of arbitrarily formatted data, including relational data and gridded data. May be used for sequence data, satellite data, model data, or any other data format that can be described in the flexible FreeForm format definition language.
- *Native DODS.* The DODS class library may be used directly by a client program. It supports relational data, array data, gridded data, and a flexible assortment of data types.
- *FITS.* Used by the astronomy and solar physics communities.
- *CDF.* Developed by the National Space Science Data Center (NSSDC) at the NASA Goddard Space Flight Center.

Users or clients request data with URLs, and the query expressions are a part of the URL. The query expressions consist of two parts — projection and selection. The projection part identifies which variables from a data set are to be returned and the selection part applies criteria on the values of those variables. Both projection and selection parts can include functions. Every DODS server supports a base set of functions and may have additional unique sets of functions.

DODS provides for two types of interoperability among servers. Given the diversity of providers, some providers may wish to supply data with the minimum of metadata that may still be of use to many users. Some other providers, such as data centers, adhere to rigorous metadata standards and provide data with a rich set of metadata. Accommodating the former set of providers is referred to as *broad interoperability*. This maximizes the number of participants in the DODS environment. In general, however, it is also true that the utility of data increases with the increase in metadata content. For cases in which metadata are available, it should be possible to take advantage of them. This aspect of interoperability is referred to as *depth of interoperability*. The depth of interoperability is not uniform across the DODS servers, but this is not considered a disadvantage. DODS provides for increasing the depth of interoperability by allowing metadata to be included when available and to be updated as more metadata become available.

3.9 SUMMARY AND CONCLUSION

In this chapter, we have provided a broad treatment of issues related to managing and handling databases of remotely sensed images. We started with a brief historical background on remote sensing, dating from the early twentieth century to the present. There is considerable international interest in remote sensing as evidenced by the large number of airborne and space-borne instruments collecting image data globally and locally at various spatial resolutions, spectral bands, and temporal frequencies. Remotely sensed images are used in a variety of applications. A few examples of civilian applications are daily weather forecasting, long-term climate studies, monitoring atmospheric ozone, monitoring global forest cover to assess the extent of deforestation over time, forecasting crops, and helping farmers with precision agriculture. Although both image and nonimage data are acquired from remote sensing instruments, image data dominate the archives in both volume and variety. Especially for applications that affect public policy, it is essential that remotely sensed data be preserved along with information about how they were acquired and processed.

Depending on the data collection systems, imaging mechanisms, sensor spectral characteristics, and so on, it is necessary to apply various corrections to the image data to best approximate the remote sensing image that would have been acquired under "ideal" conditions. Corrections include removal of telemetry artifacts, radiometric calibration, and geometric correction. Many types of higher level information can be derived from image data. These include geophysical parameters, such as chlorophyll concentration, sea surface temperature, cloud heights, surface winds, ozone concentration, ice motion, snow cover, and vegetation index. There are several data management issues associated with supporting processing to higher levels and providing access to both the raw image data and the derived products. To track millions of images typical in remote sensing data systems, it is necessary to maintain a rich collection of metadata that provides indexes to the data. Given the diversity of image data, it is necessary to establish a small set of standard formats or provide translation tools and to provide software tools to assist in reading and manipulating the data. Given the diversity of users, it is difficult to predict usage and access patterns. Accesses to data may include content-based searches, various types of subsetting, and data mining. This implies that image database systems should monitor usage and be prepared to augment capacity and capabilities as required. Also, clear on-line documentation should be provided and aliases should be allowed for terminology used in searching and ordering data. Given the diversity of providers, it is important to establish interface standards that permit interoperability. The "cost of entry" for a provider should be kept low, and the users' access to data should be made easy. Large volumes and the need for permanent storage pose additional challenges.

Four systems have been discussed as examples of how some of the issues and challenges discussed in the foregoing paragraph are addressed. These systems differ significantly from each other in the requirements they address and their size and complexity. The GCMD is a comprehensive directory providing descriptions of data sets relevant to research in global change. The EOSDIS is a distributed system with a broad set of responsibilities to manage NASA's Earth science data. The ADL is a distributed library for geographically referenced information that includes both digital and analog data. The DODS is a software package that provides access to data on any network-accessible server and that makes it easy for users to obtain and use data essentially independent of the native format. There are many more systems that manage remotely sensed image data and the reader is encouraged to explore the references for details about them.

3.10 ACKNOWLEDGMENTS

The author gratefully acknowledges the assistance of Rich McPeters and Darrel Williams of the NASA GSFC in the development of the Antarctic Ozone and Deforestation subsections of Section 3.3.2. Lola Olsen of NASA GSFC, James Frew of University of California, Santa Barbara, and Peter Cornillon of the University of Rhode Island provided pointers to assist the author in the development of subsections of Section 3.8 on GCMD, ADL and DODS, respectively. Michael Moore of NASA GSFC provided Figure 3.9, the ECS Data Pyramid, and Richard Ullman of NASA GSFC helped with the material on HDF-EOS data format standard. The author is grateful to Kenneth McDonald, Dorothy Perkins and Carl "Skip" Reber of NASA GSFC, and the editors (Lawrence Bergman and Vittorio Castelli of IBM Thomas J. Watson Research Center) for their thorough review and comments on the drafts of this chapter. Special thanks are due to Dorothy Perkins for her encouragement and support in the author's efforts to develop this chapter.

REFERENCES

1. S.A. Morain, A brief history of remote sensing applications, in D. Silverman et al., eds., *People and Pixels—Linking Remote Sensing and Social Science, National Research Council*, National Academy Press, Washington, D.C., 1998.
2. H.J. Kramer, Observation of the Earth and its environment, *Survey of Missions and Sensors*, 3rd ed., Springer-Verlag, Berlin, 1996.

3. G. Asrar and H.K. Ramapriyan, Data and information system for Mission to Planet Earth, *Remote Sensing Rev.* **13**, 1–25 (1995).
5. J. Dozier and H.K. Ramapriyan, Planning for the EOS Data and Information System (EOSDIS), *The Science of Global Environmental Change*, NATO ASI, 1991.
6. NASA, M. King and R. Greenstone, eds., *1999 EOS Reference Handbook: A Guide to NASA's Earth Science Enterprise and the Earth-Observing System*, NASA Goddard Space Flight Center, pp. 34–48 1999; (*http://eos.nasa.gov/*)
7. I.H. Rowlands, The fourth meeting of the parties to the Montreal Protocol: Report and reflection, *Environment*, **35**(6), 25–34 (1993).
8. S.R., Fletcher, 98-2: Global Climate Change Treaty: The Kyoto Protocol, *Congressional Research Service Report for Congress*, The National Council for Science and the Environment, Washington, D.C., 1998; (*http://www.cnie.org/nle/clim-3.html*)
9. R.M. Todaro, ed., Stratospheric Ozone, *An Electronic Textbook*, NASA Goddard Space Flight Center; *http://see.gsfc.nasa.gov/edu/SEES/strat/class/S_class.htm*, 2000.
10. J.C. Farman, B.G. Gardiner, and J.D. Shanklin, Large losses of total ozone in Antarctica reveal seasonal ClO_x/NO_x interaction, *Nature* **15**, 207–210 (1985).
11. D.L. Skole, and C.J. Tucker, Evidence for tropical deforestation, fragmented habitat, and adversely affected habitat in the Brazilian Amazon 1978–1988, *Science* **260**, 1905–1910 (1993).
12. D.L. Skole, W.A. Salas, and V. Taylor eds., *Global Observations of Forest Cover: Fine Resolution Data and Product Design Strategy*, Report of a Workshop, CNES Headquarters, Paris, France, 23–25 September 1998.
13. T.M. Lillesand and R.W. Kiefer, *Remote Sensing and Image Interpretation*, 4th ed., Wiley and Sons, New York, 2000.
14. R.E. Wolfe, D.P. Roy, and E. Vermote, MODIS land data storage, gridding and compositing methodology: level 2 Grid, *IEEE Trans. Geosci. Remote Sensing*, **35**, 1324–1338 (1998).
15. J.A. Richards, *Remote Sensing Digital Image Analysis, An Introduction*, Springer-Verlag, Berlin, 1993.
16. K.R. Castellman, *Digital Image Processing*, Prentice Hall, New York, 1996.
17. J.R. Jensen, *Introductory Digital Image Processing: A remote Sensing Perspective*, Prentice Hall, Englewood Cliffs, N.J., 1996.
18. P.J. Gibson, and C.H. Power, *Introductory Remote Sensing: Digital Image Processing and Applications*, Routledge, London, New York, 2000.
19. P.S., Chavez, Jr. et al., Statistical method for selecting Landsat MSS ratios, *J. App. Photo. Eng.*, **8**,23–30, (1982).
20. M.M. Nicholson *Fundamentals and Techniques of Mathematics for Scientists*, Wiley and Sons, New York, 1961, pp. 460–464.
21. J.T. Townshend, eds., Improved Global Data for Land Applications, IGBP Global Change Report No. 20, The International Geosphere Biosphere Programme: A Study of Global Change of the Council of Scientific Unions, Stockholm, 1992.
22. M.E. James, and S. Kalluri, The Pathfinder AVHRR land data set: An improved coarse resolution data set for terrestrial monitoring, *Int. J. Remote Sensing* **15**, 3347–3364 (1994).
23. J.R.G. Townshend et al., The 1-km AVHRR global data set: needs of the International Geosphere Biosphere Program, *Int. J. Remote Sensing* **15**, 3319–3332 (1994).

24. R.J. Kauth, and G.S. Thomas, The tasseled cap — a graphic description of spectral-temporal development of agricultural crops as seen by Landsat, *Proceedings of the 2nd International Symposium on Machine Processing of Remotely Sensed Data*, Purdue University, West Lafayette, Ind. 1976 pp. 4B 41–51.
25. E.P. Crist, and R.C. Cicone, Application of the tasseled cap concept to simulated Thematic Mapper data, *Photo. Eng. Remote Sensing* **50**(3), 343–352 (1984).
26. A.R. Huete, A soil-adjusted vegetation index (SAVI), *Remote Sensing Environ.* **25**, 295–309, (1988).
27. F.G. Hall, K.F. Huemmrich, and S.N. Goward, Use of narrow-band spectra to Estimate the fraction of absorbed photosynthetically active radiation, *Remote Sensing of Environment* **33**, 47–54 (1990).
28. Y.J. Kaufman, and D. Tanre, Atmospherically resistant vegetation index (ARVI) for EOS-MODIS, *IEEE Trans. Geosci Remote Sensing* **30**(2), 261–270 (1992).
29. S.W. Running et al, Terrestrial remote sensing science and algorithms planned for the moderate resolution imaging spectrometer (MODIS) of the Earth Observing System (EOS), *The In. J. Remote Sensing*, **15**, 3587–3620 (1994).
30. J. Chen, New land cover and leaf area index mapping for Canada, *Presentation at the EOS IWG Meeting*, Tucson, Ariz., April 2000.
31. A.R. Huete, Advanced vegetation indices from MODIS, *Presentation at the EOS IWG Meeting*, Tucson, Ariz., April 2000.
32. J.C. Tilton, Image segmentation by region growing and spectral clustering with a natural convergence criterion, *Proceedings of the IGARSS 1998 Conference*, Seattle, Wash. pp. 1776–1778, July 6–10, 1998.
33. Tilton, J.C. and W.T. Lawrence, Interactive analysis of hierarchical image segmentation, *Proceedings of the IGARSS 2000 Conference*, Honolulu, Hawaii, July 24–28, 2000.
34. A. H. Goetz, et al., Imaging spectrometry for Earth remote sensing, *Science* **228**(4704), 1147–1153 (1985).
35. F.A. Kruse, and A.B. Lefkoff, Hyperspectral imaging of the Earth's surface — an expert system-based analysis approach, *Proceedings of the International Symposium on Spectral Sensing Research*, Maui, Hawaii, November 1992.
36. FGDC, *Content Standard for Digital Geospatial Metadata*, Federal Geographic Data Committee, 1998, Reston, Va., (see *http://fgdc.gov/metadata/contstan.html*)
37. L.M. Olsen, Discovering and using global databases, in R. Tateishi and D. Hastings, *Global Environmental Databases: Present Situation; Future Directions*, International Society for Photogrammetry and Remote Sensing (ISPRS), Geocarto International Centre, Hong Kong, 2000.
38. S.G Smith and R.T. Northcutt, Improving multiple site services: The GCMD proxy server system implementation, *EOGEO 2000: Earth Observation (EO) & Geo-Spatial (GEO) Web and Internet Workshop 2000*, April 17–19, 2000. *http://gcmd.nasa.gov/conferences/EOGEO2000/Smith_Northcutt.html*
39. J. Frew, et al., Generic query metadata for geospatial digital libraries, *Proceedings of the 3rd IEEE META-DATA Conference*, Bethesda, Md., April 1999; *http://www.computer.org/proceedings/meta/1999/papers/55/jfrew.htm*
40. P.C. Cornillon, Personal Communication, December 2000.

41. R. Williamson, Treatment of Metadata within the EOSDIS Core System Architecture, Technical Paper (221-TP-005-001), Hughes Information Technology Systems Technical Paper prepared under contract NAS5-60000, 1996; *http://edhs1.gsfc.nasa.gov/waisdata/sdp/pdf/tp2250501.pdf.*
42. T. Dopplick, (ed.), The role of metadata in EOSDIS, 160-TP-013-001, Hughes Information Technology Systems Technical Paper prepared under contract NAS5-60000, Upper Marlboro, Md. 1997; *http://edhs1.gsfc.nasa.gov/waisdata/sdp/pdf/tp1601301.pdf*)
43. NRC, *A Review of the U. S. Global Change Research Program and NASA's Mission to Planet Earth/Earth Observing System*, National Academy Press, Washington, D.C., 1995.
44. NASA Catalog of Data Sets and Services Available from the EOS Distributed Active Archive Centers (DAACs), 1999; *http://spsosun.gsfc.nasa.gov/spso/sdp/sdphomepage .html*
45. UNEP, The 1987 Montreal Protocol on Substances that Deplete the Ozone Layer; *http://www.unep.org/ozone/mont_t.htm*

ADDITIONAL READING

http://Earthobservatory.nasa.gov/

http://edc.usgs.gov/

http://eospso.gsfc.nasa.gov/eos_homepage/dp/

http://ltpwww.gsfc.nasa.gov/MODIS/MODIS.html

http://modis-atmos.gsfc.nasa.gov/

http://modis-atmos.gsfc.nasa.gov/products.html

http://modis-atmos.gsfc.nasa.gov/IMAGES/index.html

http://modis-ocean.gsfc.nasa.gov/

http://modis-ocean.gsfc.nasa.gov/refs.html

http://modis-land.gsfc.nasa.gov/

http://visibleEarth.nasa.gov/

http://www.ncdc.noaa.gov/

4 Medical Imagery

STEPHEN WONG and KENT SOO HOO, JR.
University of California at San Francisco, San Francisco, California

4.1 INTRODUCTION

Medical imaging has its roots in the accidental discovery of a new class of electromagnetic radiation, X rays, by Wilhelm Conrad Roentgen in 1895. The first X-ray radiograph ever taken was of his wife's hand, revealing a picture of the living skeleton [1]. In the subsequent decades, physicians refined the art of X-ray radiography to image the structural and physiological state of internal organs such as the stomach, intestines, lungs, heart, and brain.

Unlike the gradual evolution of X-ray radiography, the convergence of imaging physics and computers has spawned a revolution in medical imaging practice over the past two decades. This revolution has produced a multitude of new digital imaging modalities: film scanners, diagnostic ultrasound, computed tomography (CT), magnetic resonance imaging (MRI), digital subtraction angiography (DSA), single-photon-emission computed tomography (SPECT), positron-emission tomography (PET), and magnetic source imaging (MSI) to name just a few [2,3]. Most of these modalities are routinely being used in clinical applications, and they allow in vivo evaluation of physiology and anatomy in ways that conventional X-ray radiography could never achieve. Digital imaging has revolutionized the means to acquire patient images, provides flexible means to view anatomic cross sections and physiological states, and frequently reduces patient radiation dose and examination trauma. The other 70 percent of radiological examinations are done using conventional X rays and digital luminescent radiography. These analog images can be converted into digital format for processing by using film digitizers, such as laser scanners, solid-state cameras, drum scanners, and video cameras.

Medical images are digitally represented in a multitude of formats depending on the modality, anatomy, and scanning technique. The most outstanding feature of medical images is that they are almost always displayed in gray scale rather than color, with the exception of Doppler ultrasound and pseudocolor nuclear medicine images. A two-dimensional (2D) medical image has a size of

Image Databases: Search and Retrieval of Digital Imagery, Edited by Vittorio Castelli and Lawrence D. Bergman.
ISBN 0-471-32116-8

Table 4.1. Dimensions and sizes of biomedical images

Modality	Image Dimension	Gray Level (Bits)	Average Size/Exam.
Nuclear medicine	128×128	8 or 16	2 MB
MRI	256×256	12	8–20 MB
Ultrasound	512×512	8	5–8 MB
Doppler ultrasound	512×512	24	15–24 MB
DSA	512×512	8	4–10 MB
CT	512×512	12	20 MB
Spiral or helical CT	512×512	12	40–150 MB
Digital electronic microscopy (DEM)	512×512	8	varies
Digital color microscopy (DCM)	512×512	24	varies
Cardiac catheterization	512×512 or 1024×1024	8	500–1000 MB
Digitized X-ray films	2048×2048	12	8 MB
Computed radiography	2048×2048	12	8–32 MB
Digitized mammogram	4096×4096	12	64 MB (a pair)

$M \times N \times k$ bits, where M is the height in pixels and N is the width, and where there are 2^k gray levels. Table 4.1 lists the average number of megabytes (MB) per examination generated by medical imaging technologies, where a 12-bit image is represented by 2 bytes in memory. The size of an image and the number of images taken in one patient examination varies with the modality. As shown in Table 4.1, except for digital electronic microscopy (DEM) and digital color microscopy (DCM), which are pathological and histological images of microscopic tissues, all the modalities are classified as radiological images (that broadly include images for use in other medical disciplines such as cardiology and neurology) and used for diagnosis, treatment, and surgery-planning purposes. Each radiological examination follows a well-defined procedure. One examination (about 40 image slices) of X-ray CT with uniform image slice size of $512 \times 512 \times 12$ bits is around 20 MB, whereas one digital mammography image usually generates 32 MB of data.

Digital imaging modalities produce huge amounts of image data that require the creation of new systems for visualization, manipulation, archiving, and transmission. The traditional method of handling images using paper and films cannot possibly satisfy the needs of the modern, digitally enabled radiological practice. Picture archiving and communication systems (PACS) have been developed in the past decade to handle the large volume of digital image data generated in radiology departments, and proponents envision an all-digital, filmless radiology department in the near future. Today's managed care environment further demands the reduction of medical costs, and computer systems can help to streamline the process of handling all patient data, including images. Telemedicine enables physicians to consult with regional expert centers using wide area networks and telephones, improving the quality of care and also eliminating the cost of maintaining such expertise on-site at smaller clinics or rural hospitals. In addition, there is great interest in integrating all the health care information systems into one computerized patient record (CPR) in order to reduce costs and to provide full access to longitudinal patient data and history for care providers.

4.2 APPLICATIONS

The most prevalent clinical application of medical image database systems (MIDS) is acquiring, storing, and displaying digital images so that radiologists can perform primary diagnosis. These systems are responsible for managing images from the acquisition modalities to the display workstations. Advanced communication systems are enabling doctors to exchange voice, image, and textual data in real time, over long distances in the application known as *teleconsultation*. Finally, researchers are utilizing MIDS in constructing brain atlases for discovering how the brain is organized and how it functions.

4.2.1 Display Workstations

Clinicians interact with MIDS through display workstations. Clinicians interpret images and relevant data using these workstations, and the results of their analysis become the diagnostic report, which is permanently archived in hospital and radiology information systems (HIS and RIS). Generally, the clinician enters the patient name or hospital identification into the display station's query field to survey which image studies are available. The clinician selects only those images that need to be transferred from the central storage archive to the display workstation for the task at hand.

The six basic types of display workstations support six separate clinical applications: diagnosis, review, analysis, digitization and printing, interactive teaching, and desktop applications. Radiologists make primary diagnoses using *diagnostic workstations*. These workstations are constructed using the best hardware available and may include multiple high-resolution monitors (having a significantly higher dynamic range than typical displays and a matrix of 2,000 × 2,000 or 2,500 × 2,000 pixels) for displaying projection radiographs. Redundant arrays of inexpensive disks (RAID) are used for local storage to enable rapid retrieval of images with response time on the order of 1 to 2 seconds. In addition to the primary diagnosis, radiologists and referring physicians often review cases in the hospital wards using a *review workstation*. Review workstations may not require high-resolution monitors, because the clinician is not generating a primary diagnosis and the referring physicians will not be looking for every minute detail. *Analysis workstations* differ from diagnostic and review workstations in that they are used to extract useful parameters from images. An example of a useful parameter might be the volume of a brain tumor: a clinician would then perform a region of interest (ROI) analysis by outlining the tumor on the images, and the workstation would calculate its volume. Clinicians obtain hard copies (printouts) of digital medical images at *digitizing and printing workstations*, which consist of a paper printer for pictorial report generation. When a patient is examined at other hospitals, the workstation's laser film scanner allows the radiology department technician to digitize hard copy films from outside the department and store the digitized copy into the local image archival system. An *interactive teaching workstation* is used to train radiologists in the art of interpreting medical images; a software program leads the student through a series of images and multiple-choice questions that are intended to teach him/her how to recognize various pathologies. Finally, physicians or researchers need to generate lecture slides for teaching and research materials from images and related data in the MIDS. The *desktop workstation* uses everyday computer equipment to satisfy requirements that are outside the scope of daily clinical operations.

As examples, a pair of multimedia physician workstation prototypes developed at University of California, San Francisco (UCSF) is described using an object-oriented multimedia graphical user interface (GUI) builder. Age assessment of pediatric bone images and Presurgical planning in epilepsy are the two supported applications.

In the first application, a pediatrician assesses bone age and compares it with the chronological age of the patient based on a radiological examination of the skeletal development of a left-hand wrist. A discrepancy indicates abnormalities in skeletal development. Query of the database for pediatric hand bone images can be by image content, for example, by radius bone age or ratio of epiphyseal and metaphyseal diameters; by patient attributes, for example, by name, age, and exam_date; or by a combination of these features. Programs for extracting features of hand bone images were discussed in Refs. [4,5]. The sliders in the "Query-by-Image Attributes" window can be used to specify the range of the image attributes for data retrieval. The Image Database System (IDBS) returns with a list of five patients and representative thumbnail images satisfying the combined image- and patient-attribute constraints. The user can click on any thumbnail image to retrieve, visualize, and analyze the original digitized hand radiographs (Fig. 4.1).

The second application, assisting the presurgical evaluation of complex partial seizure is illustrated in Figure 4.2. Here, the user specifies the structural, functional, and textual attributes of the MRI studies of interest. The IDBS returns a list of patients satisfying the query constraints and a set of representative images in thumbnail form. The user then clicks on one of the thumbnail images to zoom to full size or to retrieve the complete three-dimensional (3D) MRI data set for further study. After studying the retrieved images, the user can update the database with new pictures of interest, regions of interest, image attributes, or textual reports.

4.2.2 An Application Scenario: Teleconsultation

Consolidation of health care resources and streamlining of services has motivated the development of communication technologies to support the remote diagnosis,

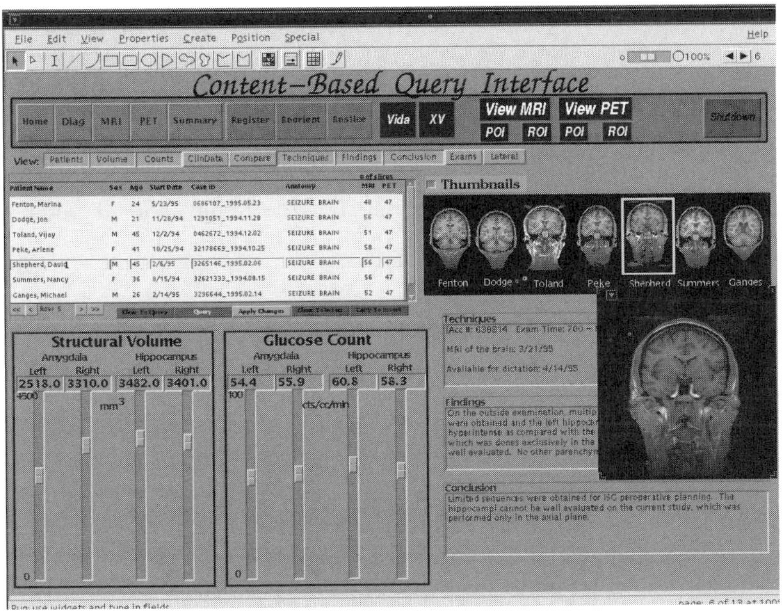

Figure 4.1. Content-based retrieval of MRI images based on ranges, structural volume, and functional glucose count of the amygdala and hippocampus. A color version of this figure can be downloaded from *ftp://wiley.com/public/sci_tech_med/image_databases*.

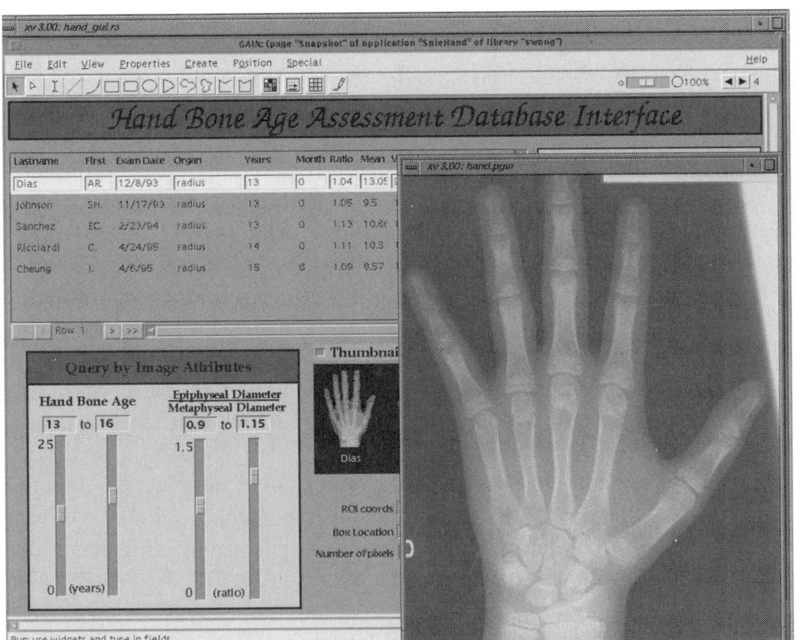

Figure 4.2. Content-based retrieval for hand-bone imaging based on hand-bone age and epiphyseal and metaphyseal diameter ratio. A color version of this figure can be downloaded from *ftp://wiley.com/public/sci_tech_med/image_databases*.

consultation, and management of patient cases. For the referring physician to access the specialist located in an expert medical center, the specialist must have access to the relevant patient data and images. Telemedicine is simply the delivery of health care using telecommunications and computer technologies. Teleradiology adds radiological images to the information exchange. In the past, textual and image information was exchanged on computer networks and the consultation between doctors was carried out over conventional phone lines. Teleconsultation enables the real time interaction between two physicians and improves the mutual understanding of the case. Both physicians see the exact image on their computer monitors, and each of them can see the mouse pointer of the other. When one physician outlines an area of interest or changes a window or level setting, the other physician's computer monitor is automatically updated with the new settings.

A neuroradiological teleconsultation system has been implemented between the UCSF main hospital and Mt. Zion hospital for emergency consultations and cooperative readouts [6]. Images are transferred from the referring site (Mt. Zion) to the expert center at UCSF over local area network using digital imaging and communications in medicine (DICOM) protocols and transmission control protocol/Internet protocol (TCP/IP). During the consultation, information is exchanged over both TCP (stream) and UDP (datagram) channels for remote control and display synchronization. Conversation is over regular telephone lines.

4.2.3 Image Archives for the Research Community: Brain Atlases

In addition to being used for diagnostic purposes, imagery finds an important application as reference for clinical, research, and instructional purposes. Brain atlases provide a useful case in point. In this section, the construction of brain atlases [7] and their use is described briefly.

Historically, brain maps have relied almost exclusively on a single analysis technique, such as analysis at the cellular level [8], 3D tomography [9], anatomic analysis [10], PET [11], functional MRI [12], and electrophysiology [13]. Although each of these brain maps is individually useful for studying limited aspects of brain structure and function, they provide far more information when they are combined into a common reference model such as a brain atlas.

The problem of combining data from different sources (both from different patients and from different modalities) into a single representation is a common one throughout medical imagery and is central to the problem of brain atlas construction. Brain atlases typically employ a common reference system, called *stereotaxic space*, onto which individual brains are mapped. The deformable atlas approach assumes that there exists a prototypical template of human brain anatomy and that individual patient brains can be mapped onto this template by continuous deformation transformations. Such mappings include piecewise affine transformations [14], elastic deformations [15], and fluid-based warping transforms [16,17]. In addition to geometric information, the atlas can also contain anatomic models to ensure the biological validity of the results of the mapping process [18].

As an alternative to a single deformable model, the probabilistic approach employs a statistical confidence limit, retaining quantitative information on intersubject variations in brain architecture [19]. Since no "ideal" brain faithfully represents all brains [19,20], probabilistic models can be used to capture variations in shape, size, age, gender, and disease state. A number of different techniques for creating probabilistic atlases have been investigated [21–24].

Brain atlases have been used in a number of applications including automatic segmentation of anatomy to measure and study specific regions or structures [25], [26,27]; statistical investigation of the structural differences between the atlas and a subject brain to detect abnormal pathologies [28]; and automatic labeling of neuroanatomic structures [28].

4.3 CHALLENGES

An MIDS stores medical image data and associated textual information for the purpose of supporting decision making in a health care environment. The image data is multimodal, heterogeneous, and changing over time. Patients may have different parts of the body imaged by using any number of the available imaging modalities, and disease progression is tracked by repeating the imaging exams at regular timely intervals. A well-designed imaging database can outperform the capabilities of traditional film library storage and compensate for limitations in human memory. A powerful query language coupled with an easy-to-use graphic user interface can open up new vistas to improve patient care, biomedical research, and education.

Textual medical databases have attained a high degree of technical sophistication and real-world usage owing to the considerable effort expended in applying traditional relational database technology in the health field. However, the inclusion of medical images with other patient data in a multimodal, heterogeneous imaging database raises many new challenges, owing to fundamental differences between the information acquired and represented in images and that in text. The following have been identified as key issues [29,30]:

1. *Large Data Sets.* The sheer size of individual data sets differentiates imaging records from textual records, posing new problems in information management. Images acquired in one examination can range from one or two megabytes in nuclear medicine modalities to around 32 megabytes each in mammograms and digital radiographs. A major hospital typically generates around one terabyte of digital imaging data per year [31]. Because of the large volumes, traditional methods employed in textual databases are inadequate for managing digital imagery. Advanced algorithms are required to process and manage multimodal images and their associated textual information.
2. *Multimodality.* Medical imaging modalities are differentiated by the type of biomedical information, for example, anatomic, biochemical, physiological, geometric, and spatial, that they can reveal of the body organ under

study in vivo, for example, brain, heart, chest, and liver. Modalities are selected for diagnosis depending on the type of disease, and it is the job of the radiologist to synthesize the resulting image information to make a decision. Features and information contained in multimodal images are diverse and interrelated in complex ways that make interpretation and correlation difficult. For example, Figure 4.3 shows both a CT scan and an MRI scan of the torso, and despite imaging the same part of the body, the two images look very different. CT is especially sensitive to hard tissue such as bone, but it presents soft tissue with less contrast. On the other hand, MRI renders soft tissue with very high contrast but does not image bone as well as CT. Scans of PET and CT look entirely different from one another and are also distinct from other modalities, such as computed radiography (CR) and ultrasound. PET acquires images of different body parts from those of mammographic images (Fig. 4.4). Even within the same modality and for the same anatomy, two sets of medical images can vary greatly in slice thickness, data set orientation, scanning range, and data representation. Geometric considerations, such as location and volume, are as important as organ functionality in the image interpretation and diagnosis.

3. *Data Heterogeneity.* Medical image data are heterogeneous in how they are collected, formatted, distributed, and displayed. Images are acquired

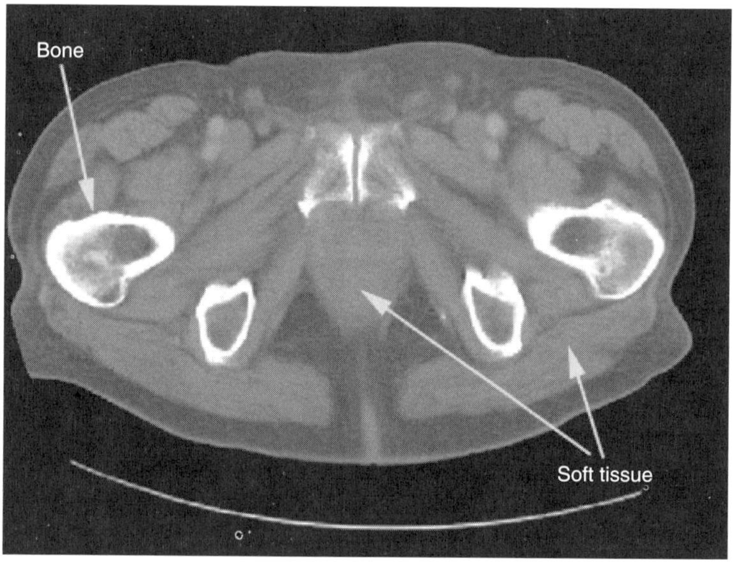

(a)

Figure 4.3. **(a)** Single image slice from a CT scan of the body. Note that bone appears as areas of high signal intensity (white). The soft tissue does not have very good contrast. **(b)** Single image slice from a MRI scan of the body. Unlike CT, bone does not show up as areas of high intensity; instead, MRI is especially suited to imaging soft tissue. (Courtesy of A. Lou).

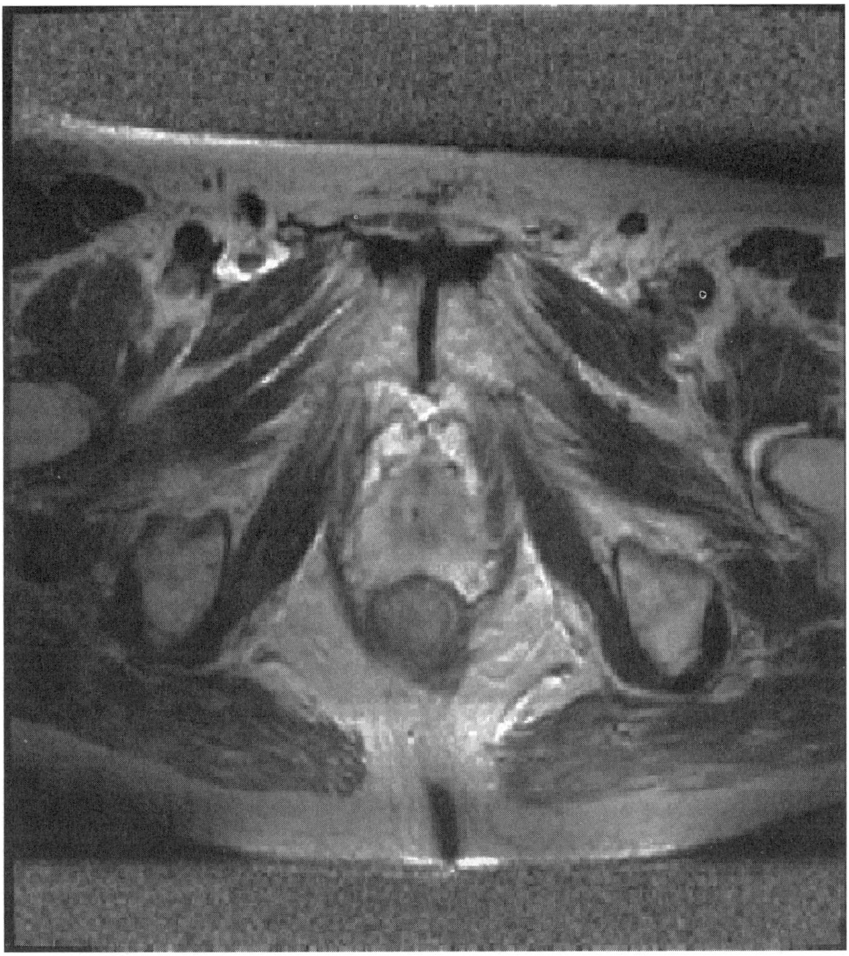

(b)

Figure 4.3. (*Continued*)

from the scanners of different modalities and in different positions, represented in internal data formats that vary with modality and manufacturer, and differ in appearance, orientation, size, spatial resolution, and in the number of bits per pixel. For example, the CT image of Figure 4.3 is 512×512 pixels in size, whereas the MRI image contains 256×256 pixels. It is worth noting that, with the exception of Doppler ultrasound, diagnostic images are acquired and displayed in gray scale. Hence issues pertaining to color, such as the choice of color space, do not arise for medical images. Color images are edited only for illustration purposes, for example, in pseudocolor nuclear medicine; physicians rarely use color images in diagnosis and therapy workups.

4. *Structural and Functional Contexts.* Structural information in a medical image contributes essential knowledge of the disease state as it affects the morphology of the body. For example, the location of a tumor, with respect to its adjacent anatomic structures (spatial context), has profound implications in therapeutic planning, whereas monitoring of growth or shrinkage of that tumor (geometric context) is an important indicator of the patient's progress in therapy. However, what distinguishes medical images from most other types of digital images is the representation of functional information (e.g., biochemistry and physiology) about body parts, in addition to their anatomic contents and structures. As an example, fluorodeoxyglucose PET scans show the relative oxygen consumption of brain tissue — areas of low oxygen consumption (i.e., dark areas in the PET image) correspond to tissue that is hypometabolic and may be dead or dying. The PET findings can then be compared with MRI findings in expectation that areas of hypometabolism in PET correspond to areas of tissue atrophy in the MRI. The preceding example demonstrates the power of utilizing more than one imaging modality to bolster the clinical decision-making process.
5. *Imprecision.* Because of limited spatial resolution and contrast and the presence of noise, medical images can only provide the physician with an approximate and often imprecise representation of anatomic structures and physiological functionalities. This phenomenon applies to the entire

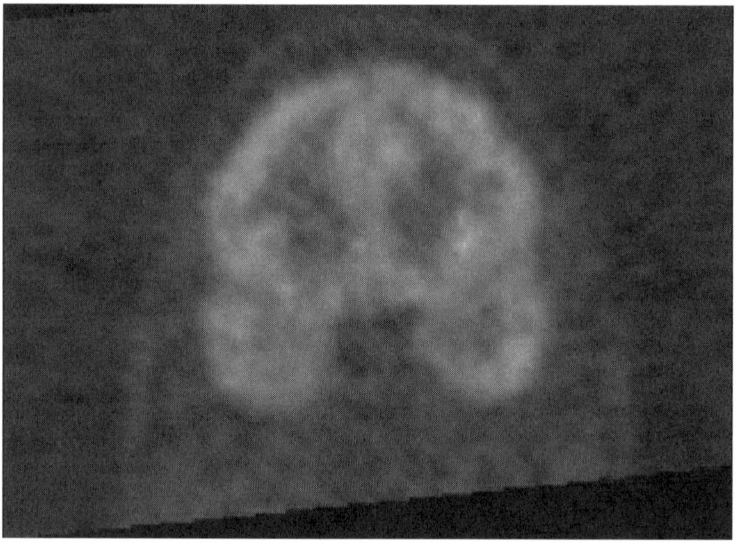

(a)

Figure 4.4. **(a)** FDG-PET image of the brain, coronal plane, 128 × 128 × 8 bits, **(b)** Mammography image, 4096 × 4096 × 12 bits.

(b)

Figure 4.4. *(Continued)*

data sets and to features within individual images. The boundary of a tumor, for example, may be fuzzy owing to inadequate resolution of the imaging modality. Yet, the accurate delineation of a tumor is an essential first step for curative therapy. The imprecision of image resolution is often compounded by the vague description of features extracted from the images or ambiguous coding of disease classification in diagnostic reports. For instance, the diagnosis "acute myocardial infarction, anterior wall" imparts a sense of certainty and specificity and can be linked to ICD-9 (International Classification of Diseases, ninth revision) code 410.10. On the other hand, an agreeable definition has yet to be reached within the medical community for the diagnosis "left ventricular aneurysm." New, more expressive data or knowledge models that can cope with such imprecision are required.

6. *Temporal Dimension.* Tracking the disease state and monitoring patient progress over time are fundamental to diagnostic and therapeutic decisions and to outcome assessment in long-term follow-up. The ability to define and track temporal relations in the image sets of a patient taken at different periods, together with the medical history of that patient, is an essential component of medical image databases. As the database expands to incorporate a large mass of similar patient data, tools developed for intrasubject temporal monitoring can also be extended to intersubject temporal comparison to improve prognostic and diagnostic outcomes.
7. *Infrastructure Support.* Technological and administrative barriers make gathering a complete body of textual and image information for analysis a major challenge. Most databases and information systems are stand-alone entities under the control of individual medical sections and departments. These administrative entities are reluctant to build bridges to other information systems for fear of losing control of their data. Interfacing disparate information systems is a nontrivial technological problem because of differing hardware platforms, communication protocols, and data formats. What is needed is an integrated communication infrastructure that interfaces with diverse sources of images, patient data, and medical reference materials in a way that is transparent to the clinical user.
8. *Security.* Along with multimedia data integration comes a new issue: "How do we ensure integrity and privacy for medical images and records that exist only in easily altered and disseminated digital forms?" This issue is especially relevant when an image database framework is connected to national and international medical database networks. An insecure information system is not likely to be acceptable to the conservative medical community because of legal or medical issues. The effort of applying cryptographic techniques to medical images, without noticeable effect on system performance, is in its infancy [32,33].
9. *Registration.* Medical image registration is often required to geometrically align two or more 3D image data sets so that voxels representing the same underlying anatomic structure may be superimposed or directly compared. For instance, registration of functional images obtained using nuclear medicine modalities, such as PET or SPECT, with anatomic MRI images is of particular importance in neurological diagnosis, because it allows the intrinsically better spatial resolution of the MR image to be used in interpreting the functional activities of the brain.

4.4 ENABLING TECHNOLOGIES

4.4.1 Large Image Management

The requirements of long-term data storage, rapid image transmission to display workstations, and maintaining cost control require the stratification of storage subsystems with regards to speed, cost, and capacity. This stratification is formally known as hierarchical storage management (HSM), a solution based on the idea of managing a hierarchy of storage media [34]. Each level of the hierarchy has a different level of performance, capacity, and associated cost. The key algorithms that make HSM functionally viable are based on the notion of file migration. Files are migrated between levels based on usage patterns and memory costs.

The most expensive and best performing level of HSM involves the local hard disk storage of the display workstations themselves. Images residing on these local disks can be displayed in a matter of seconds, but the cost of maintaining large amounts of magnetic disk storage has to be balanced with performance. Local magnetic disks typically hold the radiological examinations for several days. The next level of storage is the PACS controller's own large-capacity magnetic disks or RAID storage as a short-term data cache. Holding from 10 to 60 gigabytes of medical images, the PACS controller stores about two weeks' worth of images in the average hospital (600 beds). In this way, images belonging to a given patient during a hospital stay will remain on the PACS controller's magnetic disks until the patient is discharged or transferred.

Finally, HSM utilizes a relational database management system to efficiently store and update textual data and indexes of images on optical disks. First, images are migrated from the PACS controller's magnetic disks to erasable magneto-optical disks. After an appropriate period of time, all the imaging studies of a particular patient are grouped together and burned to the next lowest level of storage, that is, write once read many (WORM) disks in an optical jukebox, for permanent data storage. Optical disks are durable and can be transported without fear of data loss. Long data life is essential to maintain the integrity of medical records that must be kept for a number of years in the United States.

Clinicians demand short response times when retrieving medical images. In the past, the only way to truly satisfy such demands was to buy large, expensive magnetic disk storage systems for each display workstation. Images stored at the PACS controller required an order of magnitude longer response time because of the bottleneck in the Ethernet communication network. Recent advances in high-speed networking technology (e.g., Fast-Ethernet and ATM) have greatly reduced the communication time and enabled the design of PACS without large magnetic disks at the display workstations. This reduces costs of storage and maintenance and provides better quality assurance from the central PACS controller.

4.4.2 Feature Extraction and Indexing

To take advantage of the rich information content of medical images, clinicians analyze images using analysis workstations to obtain clinically useful features that

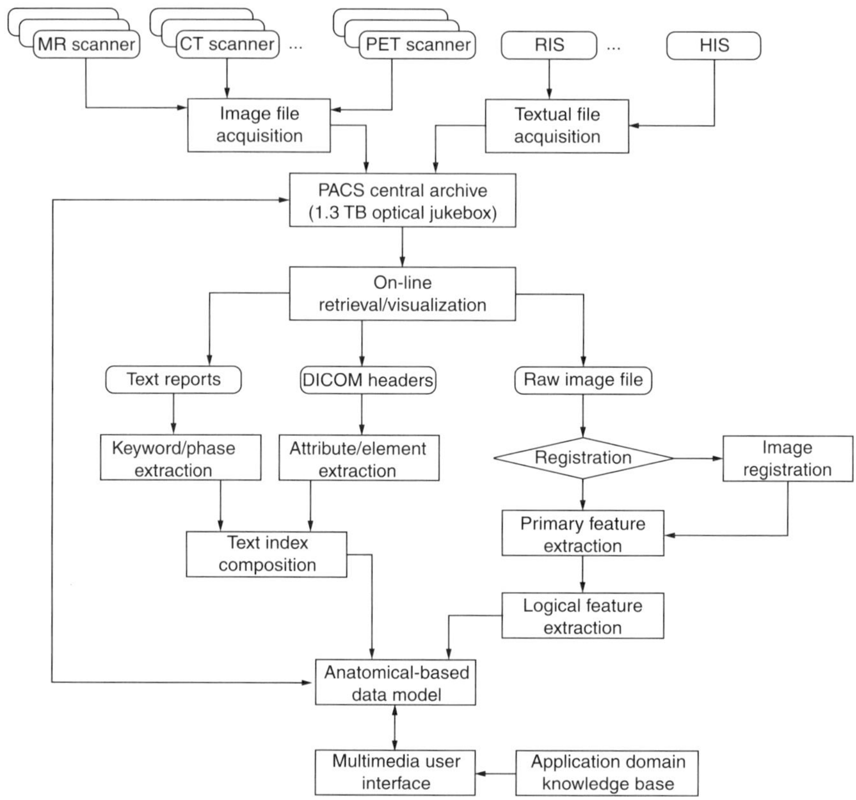

Figure 4.5. The operational flow of extracting image and text features into an anatomic based data model for subsequent content-based image indexing in IDBS. Specific knowledge or heuristics is triggered to aid the query and navigation of the medical image database.

describe the images. Figure 4.5 illustrates the operational steps that are taken to extract image and textual features from on-line image data. The feature extraction is based on the a priori approach, rather than the dynamic and automatic feature extraction during user query employed in many nonmedical image database applications [35,36]. The a priori approach requires that the features be extracted from every image data set before storage in the database. These features form an index to the images against which queries may be dispatched. In *dynamic* feature extraction, the user first composes a query and then the database system automatically analyzes the images during query execution. The a priori approach is advantageous in that the queries are executed quickly because the image features are already contained in the index. The disadvantage is that the types of queries that will be submitted to the database must be determined prior to building the image feature indices.

Image features are divided into primitive and logical. *Primitive features* are directly obtained from the medical images and include volume, shape, and texture of organs in CT images as well as metabolic activities of brain tissue in PET scans. To extract primitive features, regions of interest are manually or semiautomatically outlined in images (for example, MRI slices). *Logical features* are abstract representations of images at various levels of detail and represent deeper domain semantics. For example, the extracted volume of an anatomic structure is characterized as normal if it is consistent with established reference data. These logical features are synthesized from primitive ones and additional domain knowledge. The type and number of extracted features depend on the specific application. For example, in epilepsy presurgical planning, the following image features are used for indexing: MRI anatomic volume, PET glucose uptake count, magnetic resonance spectroscopy (MRS) spectra, and magnetoencephalography (MEG) dipole polarization for the amygdala and hippocampus regions of the brain.

Textual features are also essential in medical database indexing. The extraction and composition of textual data from the diagnostic reports and medical images can be automatic. For example, key words or phrases are often automatically extracted from the physician's textual reports for indexing purposes. Medical images commonly have an image header containing textual information about the image, such as patient name, institution, date, time, scanning technique, patient position, and so on. As an example, all the UCSF PACS image files have DICOM headers (described in Section 5.2), which contain patient and imaging exam information. The DICOM header is organized into sequential data element tags, each consisting of a group number and element number. For example, the value of patient's name is located in group 0010, element 0010 (Table 4.2). This value is automatically extracted and entered into the column for patient name.

4.4.3 Image Registration

Image registration permits the combination of different types of functional (such as PET and SPECT images) and structural information (such as MRI images), setting the stage for feature extraction. At UCSF, neurologists use the Ratio Image Uniformity algorithms developed by Woods for registration of neuro-images including PET, MRI, MRS, and MEG [37]. The correlated image data sets are encoded into a targeted data model to enable definitive indexing in image query. For example, registering the functional images of PET with the MRI images of the same patient allows the intrinsically better spatial resolution of MR

Table 4.2. Data Element Tags from the DICOM header

Group	Element	Name
0010	0010	Patient's Name
0010	0020	Patient ID
0018	0015	Body Part Examined

images to be used in quantitatively analyzing functional information (metabolic count of glucose consumption) of captured PET scans. There are more than 30 published techniques to carry out the goals of medical image registration. The image registration is an essential technique in extracting image features to store in the underlying image database for subsequent database retrieval.

4.5 STANDARDS

Different platforms, protocols, modalities, and manufacturers have always made the transfer of image and text data between health care information systems difficult. In order to increase the interoperability of imaging systems and devices, industry standards have been developed that address both data format and communication protocols. Some major health care industry standards are Health Level 7 (HL7) for textual data and DICOM for image data. The HL7 standard makes it possible to share medical textual information between the hospital information systems (HIS), radiology information systems (RIS), and PACS. The DICOM standard addresses the issues of converting medical images into a standardized data format and the communication between systems and devices.

4.5.1 PACS

The first generation of MIDS is the PACS. The intent of PACS is to provide management and fast review of the vast volumes of image and text files in a digital radiology department. PACS is a system integration of many components, including image acquisition devices, computers, communication networks, image display workstations, and database management systems. PACS has been the most common means during the last decade for acquisition, storage, communication, and display of digital images related to radiology, and its success has recently extended to include other imaging specialities, such as cardiology, pathology, and dentistry [38].

The operational flow of an image dataset through a PACS commences when an acquisition computer captures the image data set from the imaging scanner and immediately routes the data set to the brains of the PACS, the PACS controller. The PACS controller sends the data set to the database management system for long-term storage in the archive and may route the data set to appropriate remote medical display stations for radiological interpretation. The radiologist generates a diagnostic report for the data set, and the report is appended to the image data set in the central archive.

Depending on the application, a PACS can be a simple or a complex system. For example, a PACS for an intensive care unit can be a simple system consisting of a video camera for digitization of radiographs, a broadband video system to transmit the images, and a video monitor to receive and display images. On the other hand, a departmental PACS is comprehensive and requires careful planning and large capital investment. During the past decade, several large-scale PACS have been developed and are in clinical trial and use [38].

In spite of these technological advances, medical imaging records are still typically archived and transmitted using hand-carried film jackets. Fundamental system integration and operational issues have not yet been completely resolved. PACS standardizes the architectural components of medical image management systems and provides an infrastructure for developing medical imaging records using standard data exchange and protocols for different image devices. However, medical imaging records today still suffer from notable issues such as the lack of explicit and automatic work flow process management and of cost-effective means for high-performance networking and storage.

4.5.1.1 PACS Acquisition. PACS acquisition computers are responsible for transferring images from the local storage of the digital imaging system into the PACS network. This transfer is accomplished using interface methods specified by the manufacturer of the acquisition hardware. The interfaces range from proprietary hardware interfaces to open systems communication. For example, many commercial film laser digitizers use the small computer systems interface (SCSI). The Imatron Cine CT scanner (Imatron Company, Oyster Point, CA) employs a direct memory access (DMA) approach, whereby the acquisition computer is connected to the medical imaging scanner through a dual port RAM. Many MR manufacturers take advantage of the network file system (NFS) protocol so that the acquisition computer can remotely mount the imaging system's local hard drive through a local area network. Lately, open systems communication has emerged as the most promising approach to attach imaging systems to the PACS network. In this open systems communication approach, the acquisition computer and the host computer of the imaging system are connected by a computer network and communicate through standard communication protocols such as DICOM 3.0.

4.5.1.2 Preprocessing. Once PACS has acquired a set of images, they are processed before being sent to the database management subsystem for archival storage. The acquisition computer, the PACS controller, or both machines may execute these preprocessing tasks. The first of the three types of image preprocessing is converting the image data from the manufacturer's format to the DICOM representation. The second type involves compressing images to save storage space. Compression schemes are mostly lossless owing to legal or medical issues, although lossy compression has been used for ancillary reading of images or for browsing of PACS images. The compressed images are decoded for display by either the PACS controller or by the display workstation. The last type of image preprocessing prepares the image for optimal viewing at the display workstation. The factors for presenting the best image on the screen are correct formatted size, good brightness and contrast adjustment, correct orientation, and no distracting background. The third stage image-processing algorithms are modality-specific because those factors that work well for one modality may not work well for another.

4.5.1.3 PACS Controller. The PACS controller is the brain of the PACS, controlling the two main functions of the system, namely, archiving and communication. The PACS controller contains a storage system that can handle the enormous storage demands of multimedia medical applications and the high transfer-rate requirements of multimedia data types, such as images of various dimensions (2D, 3D, and 4D) and modalities, free text, structured data, and voice dictation reports. Acting as an image traffic cop, the PACS controller manages the flow of images within the entire PACS from the acquisition computers to various end points, such as display workstations or film printers. The PACS controller is a multitasking, multiprocessor computer with SCSI databases and interface capabilities to various networks, namely, Ethernet, fiber distributed data interface (FDDI), frame relay, and asynchronous transfer mode (ATM).

Many researchers in the field have criticized the inadequacy of PACS for database management. Yet, they have failed to observe the significant role of a new generation of PAC systems in creating imaging databases. The vast storehouse of multimodal images and textual data consolidated in a HI-PACS (hospital-integrated PACS) overcomes many of the administrative and technological barriers in gathering scattered and fragmented medical images and textual data. HI-PAC systems represent the most advanced communication and networking environment found in hospitals today and can thus serve as a ready-made infrastructure to support imaging database experiments that are difficult to simulate or evaluate in isolation.

4.5.2 DICOM

The DICOM Standard specifies a nonproprietary digital image format, file structure, and data interchange protocol for biomedical images and image-related information. The standard has its roots in two generations of previous standards defined by the American College of Radiology (ACR) and the National Electrical Manufacturers Association (NEMA), and these were known as ACR/NEMA 1.0 (released in 1985) and 2.0 (released in 1988). The DICOM Standard is now maintained by the multispeciality DICOM Standards Committee. ACR/NEMA 1.0 and 2.0 are based on the layered ISO-OSI (open systems interconnect) model, with physical, transport or network, session, and presentation and application layers. The presentation and application layers consist of a highly structured message format — a series of data elements, each of which contains a piece of information. The data elements are addressed by means of an "element name," which consists of a pair of 16-bit unsigned integers ("group number," "data element number").

DICOM is a complete specification of the elements required to achieve a practical level of automatic interoperability between biomedical imaging computer systems — from application layer to bit-stream coding. Vendors following the DICOM interface specifications can expect their equipment to communicate reliably over the network with other vendor's DICOM-compliant equipment. The Standard describes how to format and exchange medical images and associated information. DICOM's message protocol provides the communications framework for DICOM services and is compatible with TCP/IP.

The DICOM services are divided into two groups: (*1*) composite services that are optimized for image interchange and (*2*) normalized services for broader information management functionality. The DICOM semantic data model represents real-world entities (e.g., images, protocols, or diagnostic reports) by templates of attributes. DICOM information object descriptions (IODs) document the specifications of these templates, and the DICOM composite or normalized services operate upon members of an IOD. An IOD and its corresponding set of DIMSE (DICOM message service element) services combine to form a service-object pair (SOP), and an individual SOP exists to serve a specific purpose. DICOM message transactions between two application programs commence with association establishment. The application programs use the DIMSE protocol to generate and receive DICOM messages, and during the association establishment process, the two programs negotiate data structures and services to be used. DICOM service classes support five general application areas: imaging procedure management, network image management, image interpretation management, network print management, and off-line storage media management.

4.5.3 Health Level 7 (HL7) Standard

The Health Level 7 (HL7) standard governs electronic data exchange in a health care environment, particularly for hospital applications. The main goal is to simplify the interface implementation between computer applications from multiple vendors. This standard emphasizes data formats and protocols for exchanging certain key textual data among health care information systems, such as RIS and HIS. HL7 is based on the highest level of the open system interconnection (OSI) model of the International Standards Organization (ISO). Because of the trend toward electronic patient record and medical imaging records, the DICOM and HL7 community are working together in fulfilling the data exchange needs among health care information systems and medical imaging systems [39].

4.6 SYSTEMS INTEGRATION

Recent development of HI-PACS aims to remedy the shortcomings of first-generation PAC systems [40]. Figure 4.6 provides a schematic diagram of the HI-PACS installed in the UCSF. The implementation of this HI-PACS emphasizes recognized and implemented standards, open systems connectivity, HSM, database integration, and security. The PACS fiber-optic backbone, ATM OC-12c, 622 Megabits per second (Mbps), has been installed interconnecting four major facilities at UCSF (Moffitt and Long Hospitals, the ambulatory care clinic, and the campus library) to provide a fully connected data bank that links various clinical databases, imaging devices, and medical reference sources. The next generation of image information management systems, currently under research and development by major vendors and research centers, would provide further close coupling between PACS and more administratively oriented RIS and HIS by

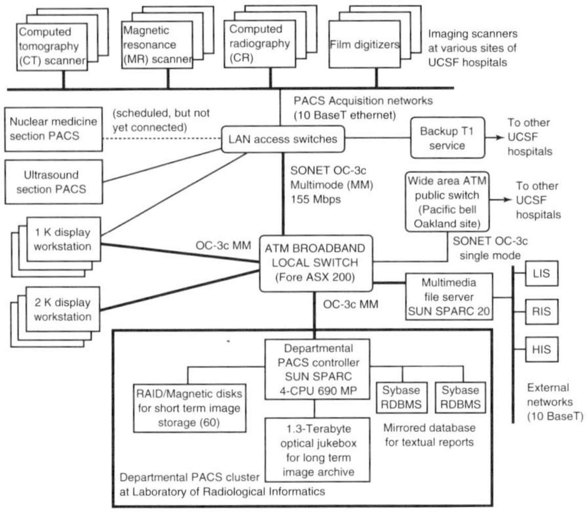

Figure 4.6. Schematic diagram of the hospital integrated PACS at UCSF.

merging and automating PACS and RIS work flows, integrating the merged image work flow with textual oriented HIS, and sharing one logical image database across the digital hospital enterprise. It is worth noting that, in this new architecture, the distinction between PACS and RIS will cease to exist. Wide area connections between the HI-PACS and affiliated hospitals utilize T1 or asynchronous transmission mode networks.

The original intent of PACS is to provide management and distribution of image files in a digital radiology department. Recent efforts have focused on gathering images of different modalities and coupling them with the information carried in the patient reports for better correlation of diagnosis findings [40]. The file system management handles only query by artificial keys, such as a patient's name or a hospital ID, and lacks the means to organize, synthesize, and present medical images and associated text to the users in a structured way for database applications.

4.7 CONCLUSION

The advent of new digital medical imaging modalities is opening new frontiers for investigating the structure and function of the human body and at the same time presents challenges in the form of data heterogeneity, multimodality, differing structural or functional contexts, and imprecision. PACS has answered the need for a digital medical image management system to support radiological diagnosis and also serves as a foundation for developing more sophisticated medical image management systems that support content-based image retrieval, image processing, and teleconsultation. The DICOM Standard has facilitated the interfacing of medical imaging components over computer networks to support data interchange for biomedical images and image-related information. Research in the area of brain atlasing will enable the collective analysis of multimodal neuroimages of large populations to further the understanding of how the brain is organized and how it functions. Content-based image indexing expands the functionality of the PACS by enabling clinicians and researchers to search through image databases using knowledge of what the desired image will look like instead of artificial key descriptions. The ultimate goals are the improvement of patient care, education, and basic understanding of human biology.

APPENDIX

A number of specialized terms apply to medical image modalities and management systems. This appendix contains a small glossary of the corresponding acronyms used in the chapter.

CPR	Computerized patient record
CT	Computed tomography
DCM	Digital color microscopy
DEM	Digital electronic microscopy
DICOM	Digital imaging and communications in Medicine
DIMSE	DICOM message service element
DSA	Digital subtraction angiography
HI-PACS	Hospital-integrated picture archiving and communication systems
HIS	Hospital information systems
HL7	Health Level 7
IDBS	Image database system
ICD	International classification of diseases
MEG	Magnetoencephalography
MIDS	Medical image database systems
MRI	Magnetic resonance imaging
MRS	Magnetic resonance spectroscopy
MSI	Magnetic source imaging
PACS	Picture archiving and communication systems
PET	Positron-emission tomography
RIS	Radiological information systems
ROI	Region Of interest
SPECT	Single-photon-emission computed tomography

REFERENCES

1. E. Trevert, *Something About X rays for Everybody*, Bubier Publishing, Lynn, Mass., 1986.
2. *Digital Image Processing in Radiology*, Williams & Wilkins, Baltimore, Md., 1985.

3. J.D. Newell and C.A. Kelsey, *Digital Imaging in Diagnostic Radiology*, Churchill Livingstone, New York, 1990.
4. E. Pietka et al., Computer-assisted phalangeal analysis and skeletal age assessment, *IEEE Trans. Med. Imaging* **10**(4), 616–620 (1991).
5. E. Pietka et al., Feature extraction in carpal-bone analysis, *IEEE Trans. Med. Imaging* **12**(1), 44–49 (1993).
6. J.N. Stahl et al., *Experiences in real time teleconsultation in neuroradiology*, SPIE Medical Imaging, San Diego, Calif., 1999.
7. A. Toga and P. Thompason, *Measuring, mapping, and modeling brain structure and function, SPIE Medical Imaging Symposium*, SPIE Lecture Notes, Newport Beach, Calif., 1997.
8. D.V. Essen and J. Maunsell, Hierarchical organization and functional streams in the visual cortex, *Trans Neurol. Sci.* **6**, 370–375 (1983).
9. H. Damasio, *Human Brain Anatomy in Computerized Images*, Oxford University Press, New York, 1995.
10. J. Talairach and G. Szikla, *Atlas d'Anatomie stereotaxique du telencephale: etudes anatomo-radiologiques*, Masson & Cie, Paris, France, 1967.
11. S. Minoshima et al., Stereotactic PET atlas of the human brain: aid for visual interpretation of functional brain images, *J. Nucl. Med.* **35**, 949–954 (1994).
12. D.L. Bihan, Functional MRI of the brain: principles, applications and limitations, *Neuroradiology* **23**(1), 1–5 (1996).
13. M. Avoli et al., Electrophysiological analysis of human neocortex in vitro: experimental techniques and methodological approaches, *Can. J. Neurol. Sci.* **18**, 636–639 (1991).
14. J. Talairach and P. Tournoux, *Co-Planar Stereotaxic Atlas of the Human Brain*, Thieme, New York, 1988.
15. R. Bajcsy and S. Kovacic, Multiresolution elastic matching, *Comput Vis., Graphics, Image Process.* **46**, 1–21 (1989).
16. G. Christensen et al., A deformable neuroanatomy textbook based on viscous fluid mechanics, *27th Annual Conference on Information Sciences and Systems* 1993.
17. G. Christensen et al., Deformable templates using large deformation kinematics, *IEEE Trans. Image Process.* **5**(10), 1435–1447 (1996).
18. P. Thompson et al., High-resolution random mesh algorithms for creating a probabilistic 3D surface atlas of the human brain, *NeuroImage* **3**, 19–34 (1996).
19. J. Mazziota et al., A probabilistic atlas of the human brain: theory and rationale for its development, *NeuroImage* **2**, 89–101 (1995).
20. P. Roland and K. Zilles, Brain atlases — a new research tool, *Trends Neurosci.* **17**(11), 458–467 (1994).
21. A. Evans et al., An MRI-based stereotactic brain atlas from 300 young normal subjects, Proceedings of 22nd Symposium of the Society for Neuroscience, Anaheim, Calif., 1992.
22. N. Andreasen et al., Thalamic abnormalities in schizophrenia visualized through magnetic resonance image averaging, *Science* **266**, 294–298 (1994).
23. T. Paus et al., Human cingulate and paracingulate sulci: pattern, variability, asymmetry, and probabilistic map, *Cerebral Cortex* **6**, 207–214 (1996).

24. P. Thompson and A. Toga, Detection, visualization, and animation of abnormal anatomic structure with a deformable probabilistic brain atlas based on random vector field transformations, *Med. Image Anal.* **1**(4), 271–294 (1997).
25. J. Haller et al., Three-dimensional hippocampal MR morphometry with high-dimensional transformation of a neuroanatomic alas, *Radiology* **202**(2), 504–510 (1997).
26. D. Iosifescu et al., An automated registration algorithm for measuring MRI subcortical brain structures, *NeuroImage* **6**(1), 13–25 (1997).
27. S. Warfield et al., Automatic identification of gray matter structures from MRI to improve the segmentation of white matter lesions, *Med. Robotics Comp. Assist. Surg. (MRCAS)* (1995).
28. D. Collins, C.J. Holmes, T.M. Peters and A.C. Evans, Automatic 3D model-based neuroanatomical segmentation, *Human Brain Mapping* **3**, 190–208 (1995).
29. S. Zink and C. Jaffe, Medical image databases, *Invest. Radiol.* **28**(4), 366–372 (1993).
30. S.T.C. Wong et al., Issues and applications of networked medical imaging library, *Int. J. Digital Libr.* **1**(3), 209–218 (1997).
31. Y. Kim et al., Requirements for PACS workstation, *Proceedings of the Second International Conference on Image Management and Communication in Patient Care*, IEEE Computer Society Press, Kyoto, Japan, 1991.
32. S.T.C. Wong and H. Huang, Authenticity techniques for PACS images and records, *SPIE 2435: Medical Imaging Proceedings — PACS Design and Evaluation*, SPIE, San Diego, Calif., 1995.
33. M. Epstein et al., Security for the digital information age of medicine: Issues, applications, and implementation, *J. Digital Imaging* **11**(1), 33–44 (1998).
34. S.T.C. Wong et al., Architecture of next-generation information management systems for digital radiology enterprises, *SPIE Medical Imaging Conference*, San Diego, Calif., 2000.
35. V. Guidivada and V. Raghavan, Content-based image retrieval systems, *IEEE Computer*, 18–22 (1995).
36. M. Flickner et al., Query by image and video content: The QBIC system, *IEEE Computer* **28**(9), 23–32 (1995).
37. S.T.C. Wong et al., Use of multidimensional, multimodal imaging and PACS to support neurological diagnosis, *SPIE 2433, Medical Imaging — Function and Physiology of Multidimensional Medical Images*, SPIE, Newport Beach, Calif., 1995.
38. H. Huang et al., Picture archiving and communication system (PACS), *J. Digital Imaging* **5**(1), 22–25 (1992).
39. W.D. Bidgood et al., Medical data standards: Controlled terminology for clinically-relevant indexing and selective retrieval of biomedical images, *Int. J. Digital Libr.* **1**(3), 278–287 (1997).
40. M. Osteaux, *A Second Generation PACS Concept*, Springer-Verlag, New York, 1992.
41. J. Gee et al., Bayesian approach to the brain image matching problem, Institute for research in cognition science, Technical Report 8 1995.
42. E. Hoffman, VIDA (volumetric image display and analysis) operational manual, Department of Radiology, University of Iowa College of Medicine, Iowa City, Iowa, 1994.

5 Images in the Exploration for Oil and Gas

PETER TILKE
Schlumberger–Doll Research Center, Ridgefield, Connecticut

5.1 INTRODUCTION

Images are central to the task of exploring for and producing oil and gas (hydrocarbons) from the Earth's subsurface. To understand their utility, one must look at both how hydrocarbons are formed and how we explore for them.

Oil and gas (hydrocarbons) are generally found in the pores of sedimentary rocks, such as sandstone or limestone. These rocks are formed by the burial of sediment over millions of years and its subsequent chemical alteration (*diagenesis*). In addition to the sediment, organic material is also buried and subjected to the same high pressures and temperatures that turn the sediment into rock. This organic material eventually becomes oil and gas.

Over time, the oil and gas migrates upward through porous and permeable rock or fractures because it is less dense than the surrounding groundwater. Most of these hydrocarbons reach the surface and either evaporate or dissipate. However, a small fraction of these migrating hydrocarbons become trapped in the subsurface.

A hydrocarbon trap forms when an impermeable rock, such as shale, lies above a porous rock, such as sandstone or limestone. Traps are often associated with faults or folds in the rock layers. The exploration for hydrocarbons generally begins with the search for these traps.

Oil exploration may begin with the acquisition of *two-dimensional (2D) seismic* data in an area of interest. These data may be thought of as two-dimensional images vertically slicing through the Earth, each slice being tens of kilometers long and several kilometers deep. If a candidate area is located on these images, then a *three-dimensional (3D) seismic survey* may be acquired over the region. This survey yields a 3D image of the subsurface.

Image Databases: Search and Retrieval of Digital Imagery, Edited by Vittorio Castelli and Lawrence D. Bergman.
ISBN 0-471-32116-8

The 3D seismic images are then carefully analyzed and interpreted. If a trap is identified, and enough supporting evidence suggests that economical deposits of hydrocarbons are present, then the decision to drill a well might be made.

After the well is drilled, wireline logs are acquired to image the rock strata penetrated by the well. If these wireline images and other supporting data suggest that hydrocarbons are present in the trap, then a core might be acquired over the small interval of interest for detailed analysis of the rock.

The depicted scenario is just one possible use of imagery in the hunt for hydrocarbons. There are, however, many other steps involved in exploration and production, some of which are discussed later in this chapter.

To interpret and manage these data, the petroleum industry relies on large software systems and databases. Through the 1980s, oil companies developed much of this software in-house for interpreting and managing oil fields. Most oil companies have traditionally had a heterogeneous mix of software tools that include vendor-supplied products and homegrown applications. Communication between these products typically involved exporting the data as ASCII text files and importing the data into another application.

Just as they have long outsourced the acquisition of data, during the 1990s the oil companies increasingly outsourced the development of software. Numerous vendors now produce specialized applications that manage specific aspects of oil field development. To address the resulting interoperability nightmare, the major oil companies invested substantial effort to standardize data storage and exchange formats. In particular, the Petrotechnical Open Software Corporation (POSC) was created as a nonprofit organization whose purpose is to produce open specifications (called *Energy eStandards*) for leveraging and integrating information technologies.

The late 1990s also saw the explosion of the Internet and the associated evolution of tools and standards for business-to-business e-commerce. POSC and the rest of the oil industry are embracing these new opportunities to build even more open data exchange standards.

This chapter introduces some of the types of image data acquired during the hydrocarbon exploration and production task. This is followed first by a discussion of how these data are processed and integrated with each other and an analysis of data management issues. Finally, an overview of some of the most well-known interpretation and analysis systems is presented.

5.2 DATA CHARACTERISTICS

A wide variety of image data is acquired from the subsurface during the hydrocarbon exploration task. Some of the principal technologies involved in image acquisition are discussed in this section.

5.2.1 Wireline Logs

Wireline logging is the most common means for analyzing the rocks intersected by a well (Section 5.2.2). A well is "logged" after an interval has been drilled (for e.g., 3,000 feet). In logging the well, several different types of equipment are involved:

- The "tool" assembly, which contains the instruments that measure the rock and fluid properties in the well.
- The data acquisition system, located at the surface, which stores and analyzes the data.
- The cable or "wireline," which serves as the mechanical and data communication link between the downhole tool and the surface data acquisition system.
- The hoisting equipment used to raise and lower the tool in the well.

The drill and drill pipe are first removed from the well, leaving the newly drilled well full of a high-density fluid (the drilling mud). The tool assembly is then lowered to the bottom of the well and slowly pulled to the surface, making various measurements (electrical, acoustic, and nuclear) of the surrounding rock and fluids as it passes up through the different geologic strata. These measurements generate a continuous stream of data up the "wireline" to the data acquisition system on the surface. These data are displayed on a "log" that presents the measurements about the rocks and fluids as a function of depth. The data are also recorded digitally for further processing and analysis.

The tool assembly is composed of numerous instruments, each of which measures a different physical property of the rock and the fluid contained in the pore spaces. Depending on the complexity of the rock and fluid being analyzed, and the clients' budget, 10 or more types of measurements may be required to obtain the desired information.

Some measurements examine the natural nuclear radiation emitted by the rocks; others measure the formation's response to bombardment by gamma rays or neutrons. There are yet other measurements that observe how induced vibrational (acoustic) waves are transmitted through the rock. Electrical measurements observe the conductivity of the surrounding rocks and fluids: salt water is conductive, whereas oil and gas are nonconductive.

The typical wireline logging tool resembles a long thin pipe. The Schlumberger combined magnetic resonance (CMR) tool is typical. The tool is 14 ft long with a diameter of 5.3 in. It can operate in holes with a diameter as small as 5.875 in. On the CMR tool, the sensor is a 6-in-long pad, which presses against the rock wall. The remaining 13.5 ft of the tool contain the power supply, computer hardware, and telemetry equipment needed to support the sensor.

As hostile environmental conditions exist in the well, all components of the logging tool are engineered to operate under extreme conditions. Temperatures can exceed 400 °F and pressures can exceed 20,000 psi. Pulling the tools through the well can subject them to high shock and vibration. Chemicals in the well are often extremely corrosive.

The FMS (Formation MicroScanner) and FMI (Formation MicroImager) tools are used to image the circumference of the borehole. Both these tools have very closely spaced electrodes. As such, they produce and measure electrical current that flows near the well bore surface, rather than deep in the rock strata. Therefore, they measure localized electrical properties of the rock formations and yield high-resolution images.

Figure 5.1 illustrates an FMS tool. The FMS consists of four orthogonal imaging pads, each containing 16 microelectrodes or *buttons* (Fig. 5.2), which

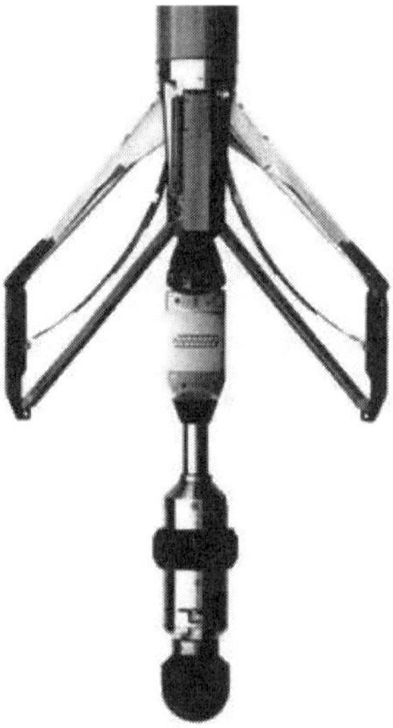

Figure 5.1. Formation MicroScanner (FMS) sonde (*http://www.ldeo.columbia.edu/BRG/ODP/LOGGING/MANUAL/MENU/contents.html, ODP Logging Manual*).

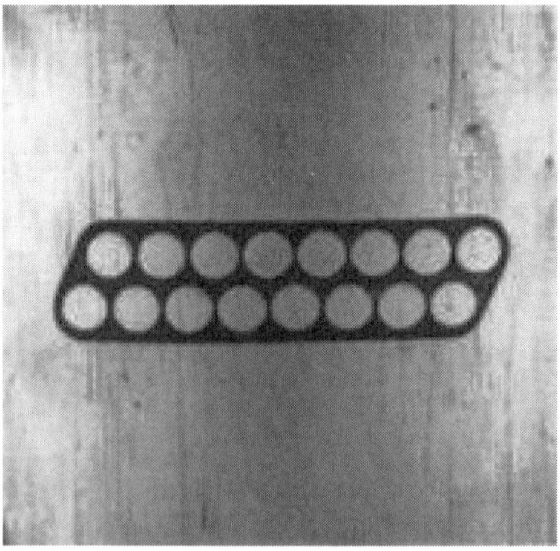

Figure 5.2. Detailed view of the 16 electrodes on one of the four FMS pads (*http://www.ldeo.columbia.edu/BRG/ODP/LOGGING/MANUAL/MENU/contents.html, ODP Logging Manual*).

are in direct contact with the borehole wall during the recording. After a portion of the well has been drilled, the FMS sonde is lowered into the deepest part of the interval of interest. The sonde is then slowly pulled up the well with the button current intensity being sampled every 2.5 mm. The tool works by emitting a focused current from the four pads into the formation. The current intensity variations are measured by the array of buttons on each of the pads. The FMI tool is very similar to the FMS tool. It has eight pads instead of four, and produces a more continuous image around the circumference of the borehole. An example of an FMI image is illustrated in Figure 5.3.

Despite the power of 2D imaging tools such as FMI and FMS, the majority of logging tools are single channel, that is, for a given depth only one measurement is made for a particular physical property. Thus, as the tool is being pulled up the hole, it is taking "snapshots" of the surrounding rock at regular intervals. The

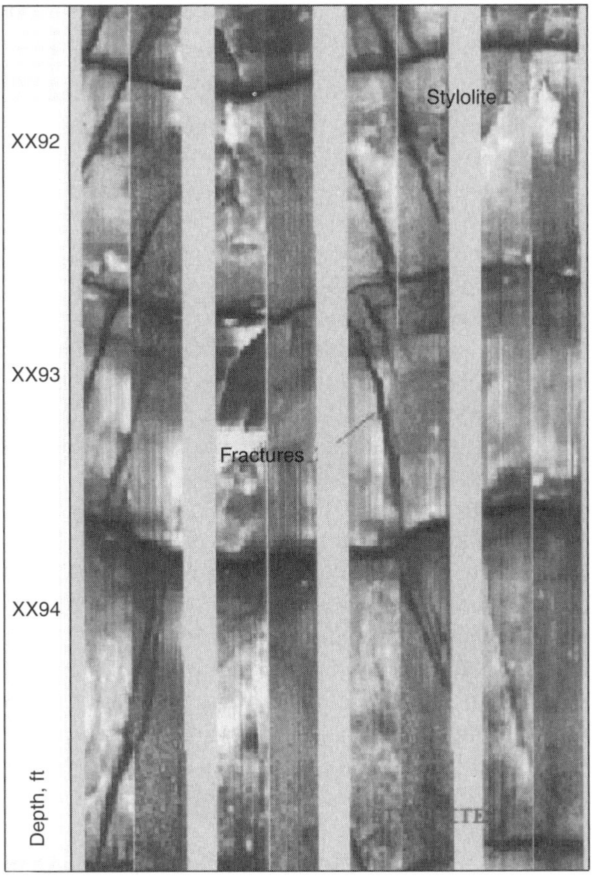

Figure 5.3. Sub-horizontal stylolites(wide dark bands) and inclined fractures (narrow dark lines) in a Middle East carbonate formation [Akbar et al., Classic interpretation problems: evaluating carbonates, *Oilfield Rev.*, Winter, 38–57 (1995)]. A color version of this figure can be downloaded from *ftp://wiley.com/public/sci_tech_med/image_databases*.

typical depth-interval spacing for the single-channel logging tools is 6 inches. The measurements taken at a specific depth are termed frames. Other tools, such as the CMR, acquire multiple measurements at each frame. For example, the CMR tool measures the magnetic resonance relaxation time at each frame, which has varying signal intensity as a function of time.

A relatively standard presentation for wireline logging data has evolved over the years. In this presentation, the vertical axis of the cartesian plot is the independent (depth) variable, whereas the horizontal axis is the dependent (measurement) variable. Some measurements are scaled linearly, while others are scaled logarithmically, resulting in parallel plots. Imagery from FMI and FMS tools is typically displayed in an unwrapped format in which the vertical axis is depth and the horizontal axis is the azimuth around the borehole. This format presents the entire circumference of the borehole, although certain visual distortions result (Fig. 5.3).

5.2.2 Logging While Drilling

The vast majority of vertical or deviated oil and gas wells are "logged" with wireline technology. "Horizontal wells" that are steered to follow the geologic strata at depth instead use a specialized technology called *logging while drilling* or LWD.

LWD is the measurement of the petrophysical properties of the rock penetrated by a well during the drilling of the hole. LWD is very similar to wireline logging in that physical measurements are made on the rock but differs greatly in that the measurements are made during the drilling of wells rather than after. With LWD, the logging tools are integrated into the *bottom hole assembly* (BHA) of the drill string. Although expensive, and sometimes risky, LWD has the advantage of measuring properties of the rock before the drilling fluids invade deeply. Further, many well bores prove to be difficult or even impossible to measure with conventional wireline logging tools, especially highly deviated wells. In these situations, the LWD measurement ensures that some measurement of the subsurface is captured in the event that wireline operations are not possible.

The BHA is located at the end of a continuous section of coiled tubing. Drilling mud is pumped down the center of the coiled tubing so that the hydraulic force of the mud drives the mud motor, which in turn drives the drill bit at the end of the BHA. The logging tools are located within the BHA but behind the drill bit.

The resistivity at the bit (RAB) tool makes resistivity measurements around the circumference of the borehole. The RAB tool also contains a gamma ray detector, which supplies a total gamma ray measurement. An azimuthal positioning system allows the gamma ray measurement and certain resistivity measurements to be acquired around the borehole, thereby generating a borehole image. The RAB tool may be connected directly behind the bit or further back in the BHA.

In LWD, the acquired logging data is delivered to the surface through mud pulse telemetry: positive and negative pressure waves are sent up through the mud column. The bandwidth of this telemetry system (less than 10 bits per second) is

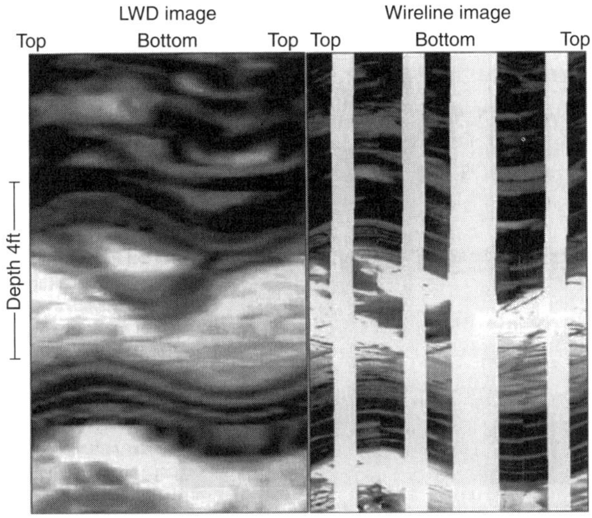

Figure 5.4. Comparison of LWD (RAB) image with an FMI image in a deviated well. Note the characteristic sinusoidal pattern caused by the intersection of the rock strata with the cylindrical borehole (*http://www.ldeo.columbia.edu/BRG/ODP/LOGGING/MANUAL/MENU/contents.html, ODP Logging Manual*). A color version of this figure can be downloaded from *ftp://wiley.com/public/sci_tech_med/image_databases.*

much lower than that supported by the conventional wireline telemetry. Because drilling speeds are typically very low (less than 100 feet per hour), a lot of data can be delivered to the surface even with the low bandwidth. Thus, many of the same measurements that can be made with wireline logging can be made with LWD

Figure 5.4 illustrates a comparison of LWD RAB tool and wireline electrical imaging FMI tool measurements of dense fracturing in consolidated sediments. Both images of the interior of the borehole wall are oriented to the top and bottom of the deviated (nonvertical) well. Note that the RAB tool has inferior bed resolution (by a factor of 30) than the FMI, although it provides complete circumferential coverage.

As noted earlier, LWD is generally used in highly deviated or horizontal wells where it is not possible to lower a wireline tool into the hole. Highly deviated and horizontal wells are generally geosteered, that is, the driller can control in real time the direction of the drill. Geosteering requires an understanding of where the drill bit is relative to the surrounding rock. LWD is well suited to this purpose. Because the well is being "logged" as it is passing through the rock formations, the driller knows when the drill has entered or left the zone of interest, thereby allowing the geosteering activity to be controlled in near real time.

5.2.3 Core Images

A core is a cylindrical sample of rock collected from a well. Conventionally, when a well is drilled, the diamond drill bit pulverizes the rock. To retrieve a consolidated section of core, a coring tool is required. A coring tool is essentially a hollow pipe that cuts out a cylinder of the rock without pulverizing it. The rock is then preserved inside the pipe and brought to the surface.

The first coring tool appeared in 1908 in Holland. The first one used in the United States appeared some years later (1915) and was a piece of modified drill pipe with a saw-toothed edge for cutting — much like a milling shoe [3].

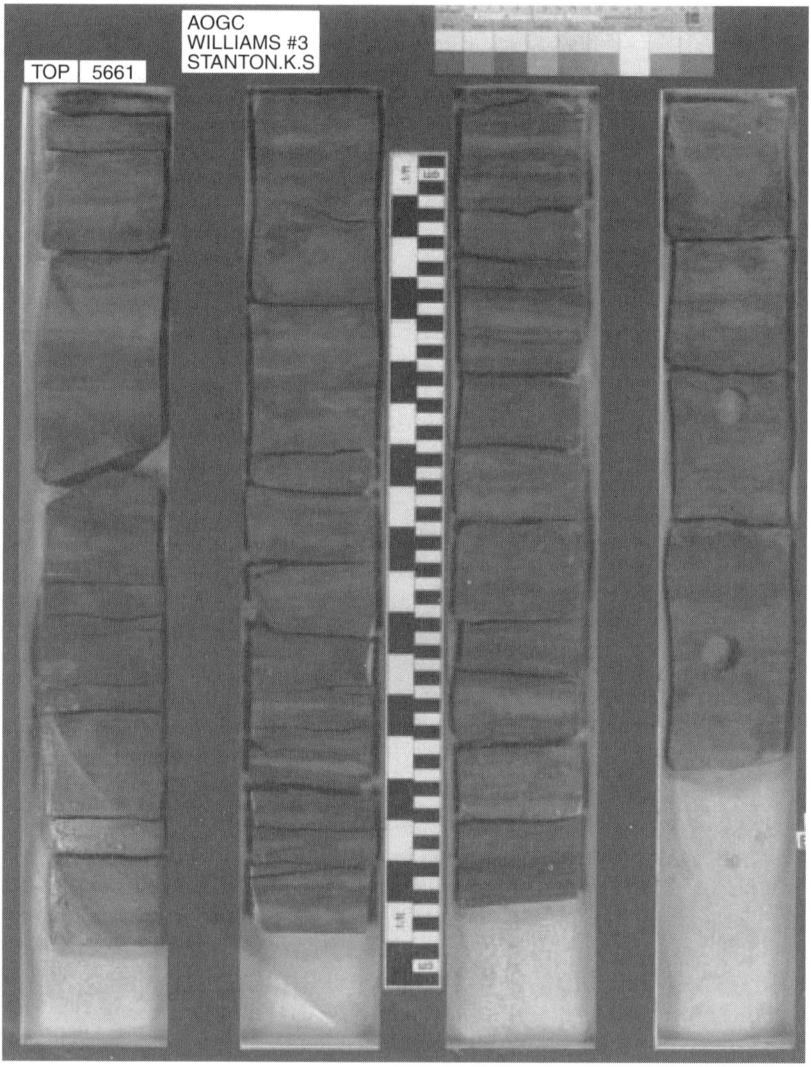

Figure 5.5. Slabbed core in boxes. Note the holes in the core where rock samples have been removed for further analysis (*http://crude2.kgs.ukans.edu/DPA/BigBow/CoreDesc, Kansa Geological Survey, Big Bow Field*). A color version of this figure can be downloaded from *ftp://wiley.com/public/sci_tech_med/image_databases*.

Once collected, the cores are placed in core boxes. The boxes are labeled with the well identification information and marked with the measured depths of each piece. In many cases the core is sliced down the axis of the cylinder ("slabbed") so that a flat surface of the rock is exposed for visual inspection (Fig. 5.5). The core is then typically stored in large core "warehouses." Traditionally, geologists and technicians would then visually inspect the core and have samples extracted for further analysis. Increasingly, these "slabbed" (and "unslabbed") cores are digitally photographed.

After the core has been boxed and possibly slabbed, small samples are taken for higher-resolution analysis (Figs 5.5 and 5.6). The data obtained from the core include photographic images, measurements of physical properties, such as porosity and permeability, and microphotographs of thin sections. Quite often, even higher-resolution imaging is required to fully understand the properties of the rock. In these cases, scanning electron microscopy (SEM) may be necessary.

There are no standards for core photographs. Only recently have laboratories begun capturing the images digitally. Those cores that were photographed are now being "scanned" at varying resolutions.

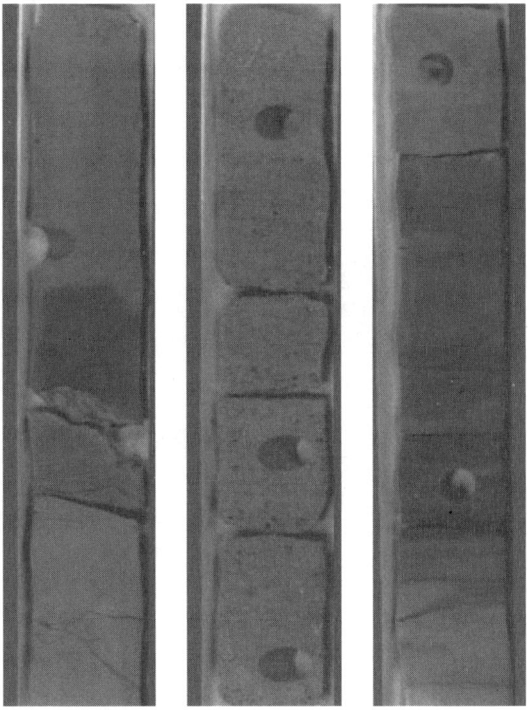

Figure 5.6. Slabbed core from a single well, illustrating variability in rock color, layering, and texture. Note the holes in the core where rock samples have been removed for further analysis (*http://crude2.kgs.ukans.edu/DPA/BigBow/CoreDesc, Kansa Geological Survey, Big Bow Field*). A color version of this figure can be downloaded from *ftp://wiley.com/public/sci_tech_med/image_databases*.

A common technique when photographing core is to take two photographs: one in white light, the other in ultraviolet light. Ultraviolet light is useful because oil becomes luminescent, and the oil-saturated rock then becomes easily distinguishable from the oil-free rock.

5.2.4 Seismic Data

Seismic imaging is the process through which acoustic waves reflected from rock layers and structures are observed and integrated to form one-, two-, and three-dimensional images (1D, 2D, and 3D) of the Earth's subsurface. The resulting images allow us to interpret the geometric and material properties of the subsurface.

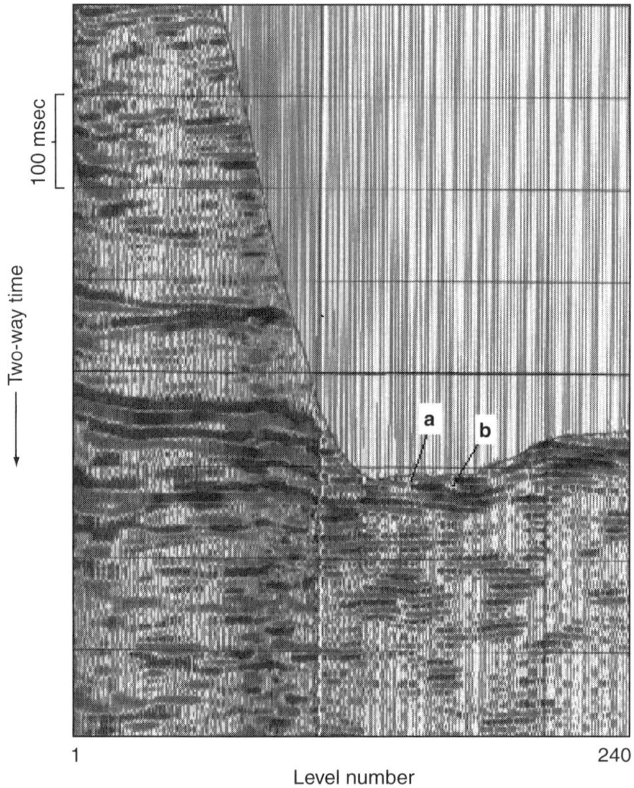

Figure 5.7. VSP data in a horizontal well (red trace). The data show three important features; two faults marked A and B, which appear as anticipated in the reflected image, together with evidence of dipping. The apparent formation dips seem to be parallel to the borehole until very near total depth. This turned out to be entirely consistent with the Formation MicroScanner (FMS)–computed dips [Christie et al., Borehole seismic data sharpen the reservoir image, *Oilfield Rev.*, Winter, 18–31 (1995)]. A color version of this figure can be downloaded from *ftp://wiley.com/public/sci_tech_med/image_databases*.

At the scale of reflection seismic imaging, the Earth is, to a first-order approximation, a vertically stratified medium. These stratifications have resulted from the slow, constant deposition of sediments, sands, ash and so forth. As a result of compaction, erosion, change of sea level, and many other factors, the geologic, and hence the seismic character of these layers varies with the depth and age of the rock.

Seismic data acquisition uses low-frequency sound waves generated by explosives or mechanical means on the Earth or ocean surface. As these waves travel downward, they cross rock layers; some of their energy is reflected back to the surface and detected by sensors called *geophones* (on land) or *hydrophones* (in the ocean).

Modern digital recording systems allow the recording of data from more than 10,000 geophones simultaneously. Sophisticated seismic-processing software then integrates these data using the physics of wave propagation to yield 3D images of the subsurface.

It should be noted that not all seismic data is acquired with both the reflection source and the receivers being on the surface of the Earth. Often, the receivers are located within the borehole, a practice commonly known as vertical seismic profiling (VSP). This approach can often yield very high-resolution images at the depth of the reservoir (Fig. 5.7).

Seismic data from modern 3D surveys is typically represented as 3D arrays of 1-, 2-, or 4-byte floats. Seismic interpretation applications present the user with a wide spectrum of tools to visualize the data in 3D voxelated volumes or as 2D slices through the volumes. In addition to storing the volumes as different resolution float arrays, each volume may be stored three times — once for every dimension. This permits the data to be rapidly accessed in each of the primary dimensions of the volume.

5.3 SELECTED APPLICATION SCENARIOS

This section provides an overview of a number of typical applications of imagery in the exploration and production of oil and gas.

5.3.1 Seismic Exploration

Seismic images are the modern mainstay of oil exploration. Today a single 3D seismic survey may cover hundreds of square kilometers and be comprised of tens of gigabytes of data. Explorationists (the oil company professionals who search for hydrocarbons in the subsurface) use seismic images for a wide variety of tasks in their work, including structural interpretation, stratigraphic interpretation, and horizon and formation attribute analysis.

Structural interpretation involves the analysis and modeling of the geometry of the geologic strata, which may be deformed by folding and disrupted by faulting (Fig. 5.8).

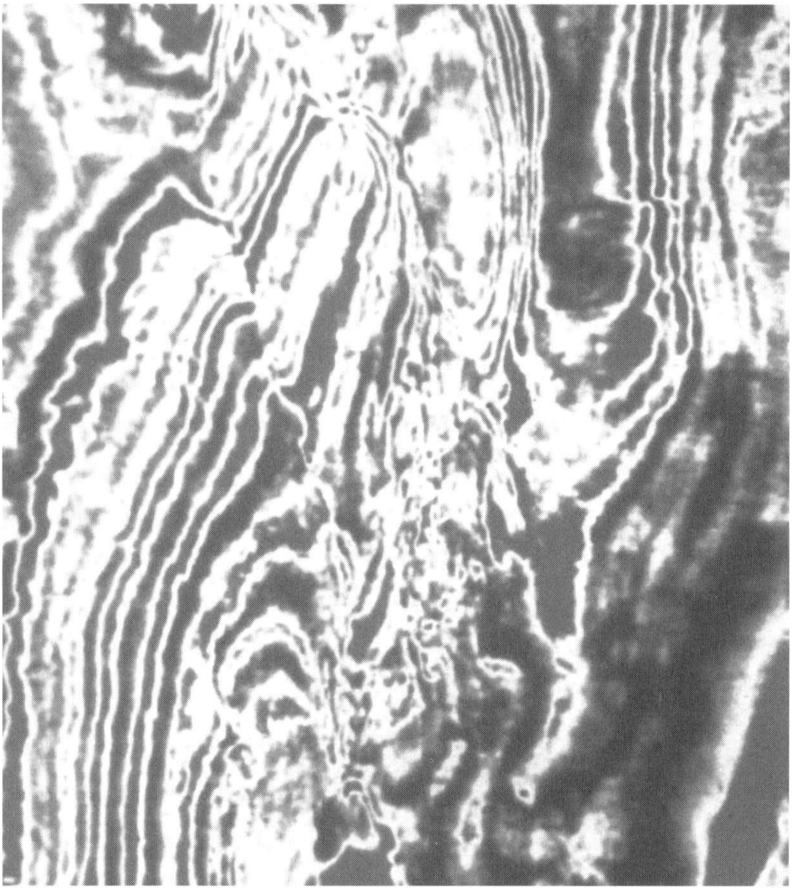

Figure 5.8. Horizontal section through a 3D seismic volume illustrating folded (curved) rock layers being terminated by faults (A.R. Brown, *Interpretation of three-dimensional seismic data*, 5th ed., AAPG and SEG, 1999, p. 514). A color version of this figure can be downloaded from *ftp://wiley.com/public/sci_tech_med/image_databases*.

Stratigraphic interpretation involves the analysis of how the rock varies spatially as a function of different depositional environments. For example, seismic data may be used to identify a meandering river (Fig. 5.9).

By calibrating seismic attributes with other data, such as well log–derived information, maps of horizon (layer boundary) or formation (layer volume) material properties may be made (Fig. 5.10).

5.3.1.1 Identification of "Bright Spots." The term *bright spot* is used in the industry when it is believed that pools of gas or oil have been directly observed by seismic imagery. Bright spots are very high-amplitude signals that often result from large changes in acoustic impedance, for example, when a gas-saturated

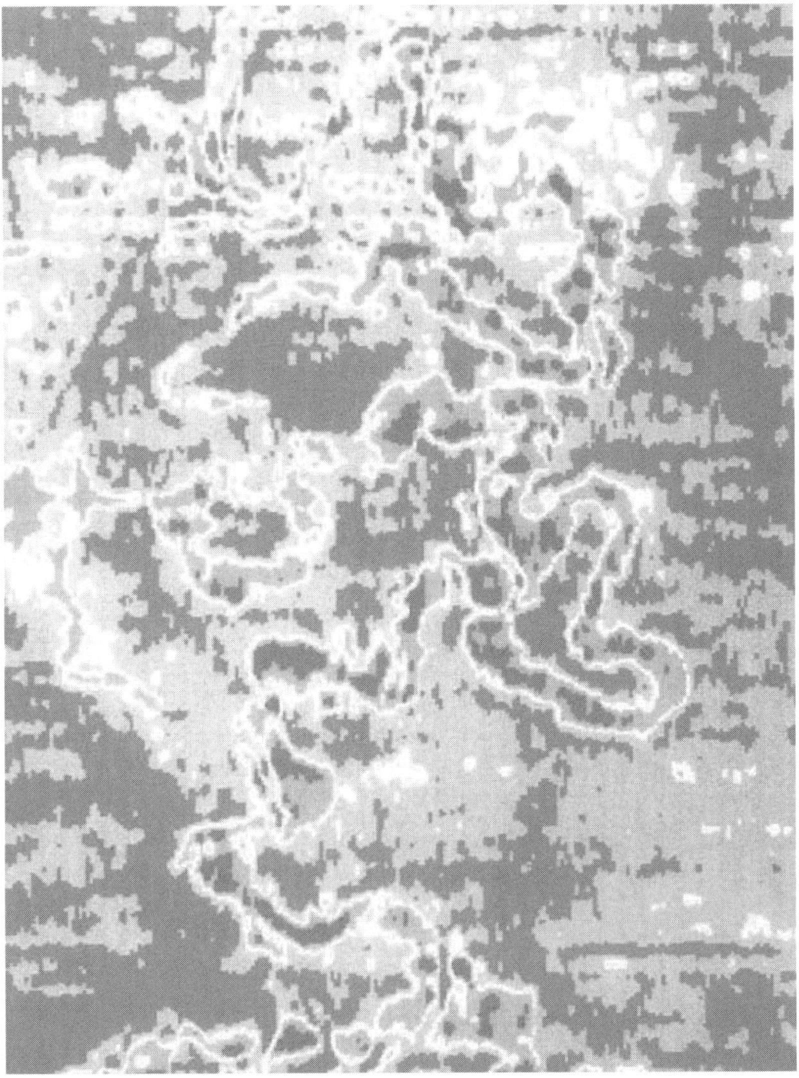

Figure 5.9. Horizontal slice through a 3D seismic volume illustrating a meandering river (A.R. Brown, *Interpretation of three-dimensional seismic data*, 5th ed., AAPG and SEG, 1999, p. 514). A color version of this figure can be downloaded from *ftp://wiley.com/public/sci_tech_med/image_databases*.

sand underlies a shale layer, but can also be caused by phenomena other than the presence of hydrocarbons, such as a change in rock type.

Figure 5.11 is a vertical section through a 3D seismic volume that illustrates a bright spot caused by two gas filled sand layers. The layers are dipping down to the right. Note the "flat spot" at the lower right termination of the bright spots. A flat spot is caused by the horizontal (due to gravity) boundary between

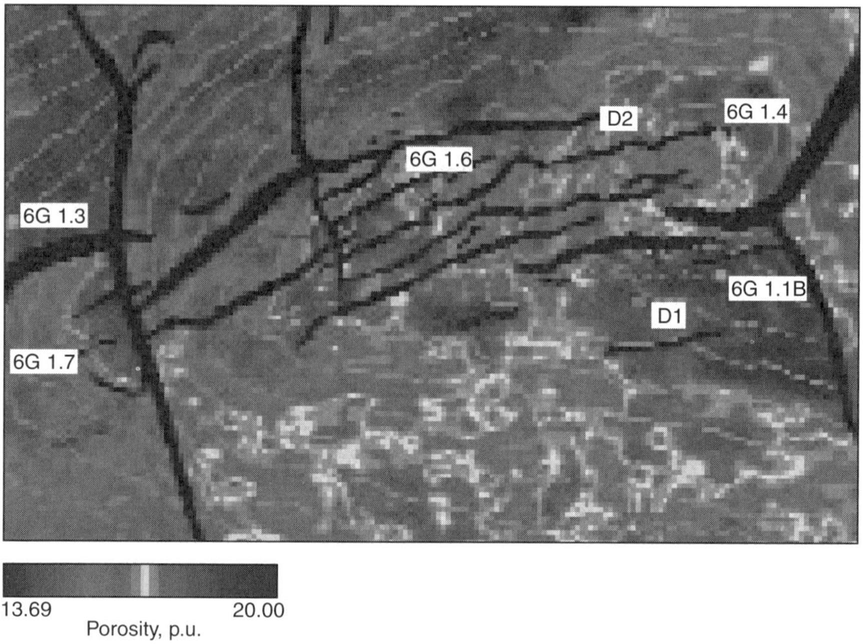

Figure 5.10. Porosity map of geologic horizon based on seismic attributes calibrated against well data [Ariffin et al., Seismic tools for reservoir management, *Oilfield Rev.*, Winter, 4–17 (1995)]. A color version of this figure can be downloaded from *ftp://wiley.com/public/sci_tech_med/image_databases*.

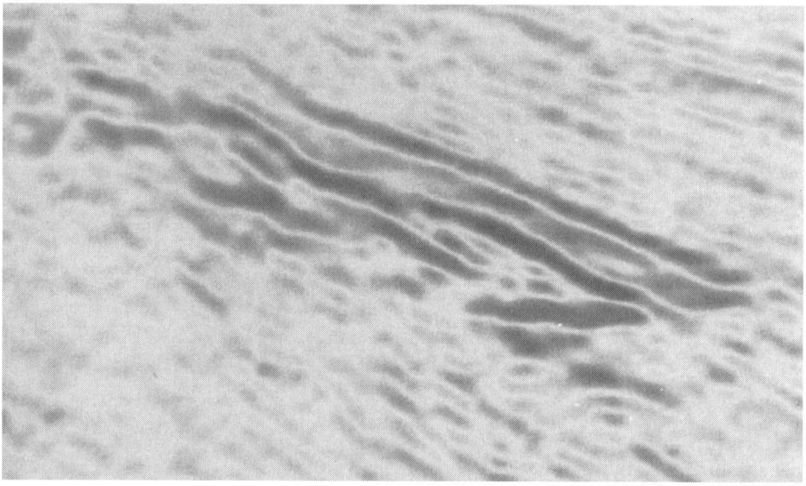

Figure 5.11. Bright spots caused by two dipping and layers filled with gas. Horizontal flat spots caused by the gas (above) giving way to water (below) (A.R. Brown, *Interpretation of three-dimensional seismic data*, 5th ed., AAPG and SEG, 1999, p. 514). A color version of this figure can be downloaded from *ftp://wiley.com/public/sci_tech_med/image_databases*.

the gas-filled sandstone above and the water-filled sandstone below. As noted earlier, bright spots can be caused by changes in rock type, but the presence of a horizontal flat spot strongly supports the premise that the bright spot is caused by a fluid boundary.

5.3.1.2 Identification of Stratigraphic Features. Generally, large volumes of rock are very similar in their composition and internal geometry. This is because uniform depositional environments often have large spatial extents. For example, the sediments blanketing the outer continental shelves are often relatively uniform layers of shale. Other environments, such as near-shore deltas or coral reefs, vary rapidly in a spatial sense. Seismic imagery provides a very powerful tool for interpreting and identifying these features.

Figure 5.9 is a horizontal section through a three-dimensional seismic volume illustrating a meandering river system. This image is analogous to the view from an airplane of the modern Mississippi river. From an understanding of the physics of river behavior, the exploration geologist can then make inferences about which parts of the river system have sand deposits and therefore potential hydrocarbon accumulations.

5.3.2 Formation Evaluation with Wireline Images

Wireline logging is the basis of an entire science called *petrophysics* or *rock physics*. Professional organizations exist for this science, such as the Society of Professional Well Log Analysts (*http://www.spwla.org/*).

Although the single-channel or one-dimensional logging tools are typically focused at measuring the petrophysical properties of the rocks, applications of the imaging tools (FMS and FMI) are more varied and include

- Mapping of the internal geometry of the rock: the orientation of the strata, the frequency of the layering, and the orientation and frequency of fractures.
- Detailed correlation of coring and logging depths. Depths measured by wireline length (because of cable stretch) differ from the measured depth of core, which is derived from drill pipe length. FMI, FMS, and core images are of comparable resolution and may therefore be used to correlate with each other.
- Precise positioning of core sections in which core recovery is less than 100 percent.
- Analysis of depositional environments. The internal geometry of the rock layers may be indicative of the ancient environment in which they were deposited.

5.3.2.1 Bedding Geometry. A great deal of information about the rock penetrated by a well can be inferred from conventional well logs. These measurements, combined with an understanding of the geologic environment will generally yield information about the rock types and their fluid content. Of comparable importance to understanding the rock's constituents is the understanding of the rock's geometry. Wireline imagery can yield a great deal of information in this regard.

Gross geometric features including the dip of the strata with respect to the borehole can be deciphered. As sediments are generally deposited in horizontal layers, if the strata are no longer horizontal then inferences about the post depositional folding and faulting of the sediments may be made. Geologists are normally very careful in making these interpretations and typically use extensive supporting evidence, such as seismic interpretation. Figures 5.3 and 5.4 illustrate FMI and LWD images of dipping rock layers intersecting the well. The sinusoidal pattern is due to the image being a planar projection of the cylindrical wall of the well bore.

In addition to the gross geometry of the geologic strata, the internal geometry of the rock layers can also be deciphered with wireline imagery. For example, sand dunes often display a characteristic crisscross pattern of rapidly changing sediment orientation.

Some rock types are characterized by thick (>1 m) featureless intervals, whereas others might be characterized by thin (<10 cm) laminar layering. This type of information can also be revealed by wireline imagery. Figure 5.4 illustrates alternating thin and thick layers.

5.3.2.2 ***Fracture Identification and Interpretation.*** One of the great challenges to developing an oil field is understanding the role of fractures in the behavior of fluids within the rock. Although a precise understanding of the porosity and permeability of the rock can be obtained by a variety of means (described later), a single fracture could dominate the flow of fluids through the reservoir. Fractures can also influence borehole stability: the rock may slip along one of these fractures and destroy the borehole. Wireline imagery is a very powerful tool for determining not only the intensity of fracturing in the rock but also the orientation and size of the fractures.

An example of fractures revealed with wireline imagery is illustrated in Figure 5.3. Here, subhorizontal stylolites (zones where rock material has dissolved) are cut by vertical fractures in a middle eastern limestone formation.

5.3.3 Formation Evaluation with Core Photos

The geologist uses core data for detailed lithologic examination and determination of rock age. Direct measures of porosity and permeability can also be made on the core samples. Wireline logging measurements, which might provide indirect measures of the porosity and permeability, can then be calibrated with the core data.

The analysis of core images can give the geologist detailed information on the stratigraphy and structure of the portion of the subsurface sampled by the core. Information not revealed by remote sensing techniques (logging and seismic) is often apparent at this scale and resolution.

The most significant visual property of the rock in a core photo is the color (Fig. 5.6). Color, however, can be deceiving. Although pure sandstone might possess a "sandy" color, even small amounts of mineral impurities in the sand can yield a significantly different color. The process of *diagenesis*, in which the sand becomes rock as cement forms between the grains, can further alter the color. Alternatively, if dark brown or black hydrocarbons fill the pores of the sandstone, then the entire rock may assume the color of the hydrocarbons.

5.3.3.1 Rock Texture Analysis. The finely laminated nature of some rock can only be revealed at the scale of a core: these thin beds are commonly invisible even to the highest-resolution remote sensing tools. Another phenomenon that is often only visible in core is fine fractures. Even tiny fractures can significantly increase the porosity of the rock and its consequent capacity to transmit fluids.

Grain size (the size of the grains comprising the rock), pore size (the size of the fluid filled space between the grains), and pore connectivity (which determines how well fluids will flow through the rock) are all crucial parameters in understanding how the oil field will behave when attempts are made to extract fluids from the surrounding reservoir rock. Core photos are a powerful tool that give the geologist an opportunity to visually inspect the rock and make inferences about the rock properties to supplement observations made with the wireline logging and imaging tools (Fig. 5.6).

5.3.3.2 Trace Fossil and Paleoenvironment Analysis. As noted earlier, there are vast areas of the oil field that are not sampled directly by an oil well. Therefore, one of the great challenges associated with interpreting well data is predicting the types of rock that occur between the wells. To aid this, geologists use core images to build an understanding of the ancient (paleo) environment in which the sediments were originally deposited. For example, if the sediments observed in a well were deposited in a river, then inferences about rock types between wells will be quite different than if the rocks were deposited in a beach environment.

By examining core photos for trace fossils, such as ancient burrows (Fig. 5.12), paleontologists can infer what types of animals lived in the sediment and therefore infer the environment in which the sediments were deposited.

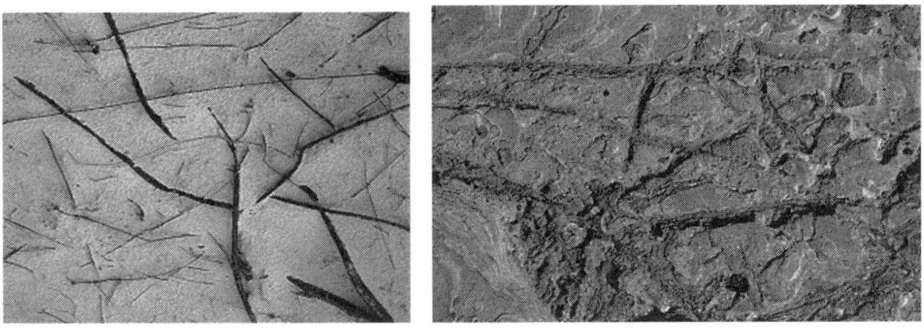

Figure 5.12. Photos comparing modern roots in soil with ancient fossilized roots in rock. These types of trace fossils are often visible in Core (*http://www.emory.edu/COLLEGE/ENVS/research/ichnology/images.htm, Trace Fossil Image Database*). A color version of this figure can be downloaded from *ftp://wiley.com/public/sci_tech_med/image_databases*.

5.3.4 Porosity Analysis with Microscopic Imagery

Diagenesis (the chemical and physical alteration of sediment during its burial and conversion to rock) will typically result in minerals being deposited between grains, thereby "cementing" these grains together to form rock. Alternatively, portions of the grains may be dissolved, with the dissolved material being precipitated elsewhere to form"cement." In either scenario, the space between the grains (porosity) and their interconnectivity (permeability) is reduced.

Photomicrographs (images from light microscopy) are powerful tools in developing an understanding of the style of diagenesis and mineral alteration that has affected the rock. Figure 5.13 illustrates an example of limestone with intergranular porosity.

Often, the rock may have had a complex history during its burial. For example, initial diagenesis might result in the formation of cement by the precipitation of

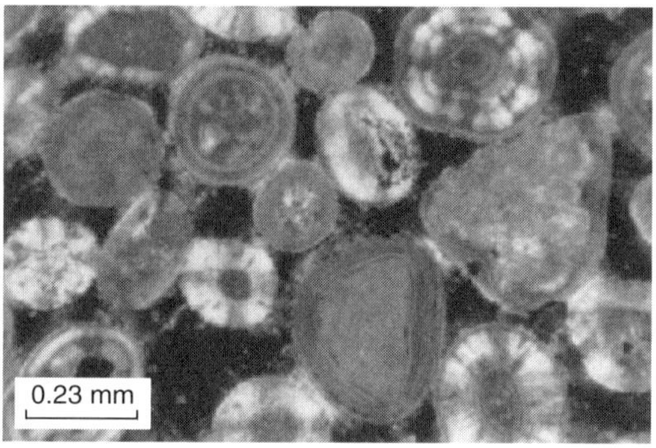

Figure 5.13. Unfilled interparticle porosity (black) in an oolitic limestone [Akbar et al., Classic interpretation problems: evaluating carbonates, *Oilfield Rev.*, Winter, 38–57 (1995)]. A color version of this figure can be downloaded from *ftp://wiley.com/public/sci_tech_med/image_databases*.

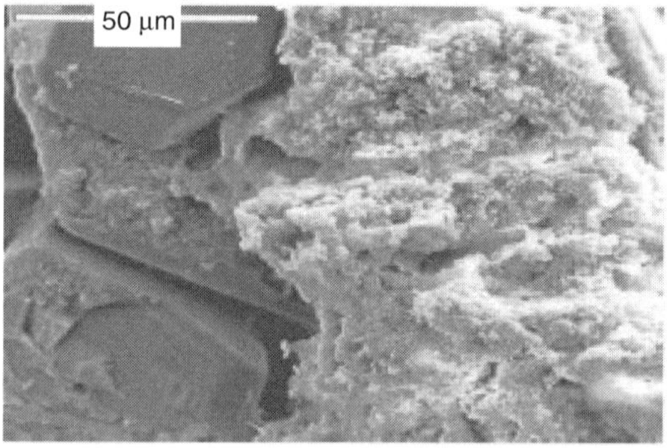

Figure 5.14. SEM Image of quartz grains in a sandstone. The minerals on the left are relatively unaltered with intragranular primary porosity. The minerals on the right have been altered and have developed secondary porosity.

minerals between adjacent grains with an associated reduction in permeability. A subsequent geologic event may then cause dissolution of this cement and the original grains, resulting in enhanced porosity. This phenomenon is sometimes termed *secondary porosity*. Although many techniques are available to measure the porosity and permeability of the rock, it is often crucial to understand the timing of these events. For example, if secondary porosity developed before oil migrated to the rock, then the likelihood of finding oil in this type of rock is enhanced. However, if the secondary porosity developed after the migration of the oil, then the probability of the oil being able to flow through the rock is reduced.

Light microscopy alone may not be sufficiently powerful to distinguish multiple episodes of diagenesis. SEM imaging on the other hand can very often yield definitive results. Figure 5.14 illustrates both primary and secondary porosity.

5.4 ENABLING TECHNOLOGIES

5.4.1 Processing

Most oil field measurements that appear as images do so after sophisticated digital signal processing. In fact, the oil-exploration industry is one of the principal consumers of supercomputers for this very reason. A short review of some of this processing follows.

5.4.1.1 Scale Issues. One of the greatest challenges to integrating the data required to explore for hydrocarbons is to understand the range in scale of these data.

The acquisition of modern 3D seismic data has revolutionized the exploration and production of hydrocarbons. However, the major problem with seismic data is its relatively low resolution. This resolution is limited by the acoustic properties of rock and how these properties attenuate the reflected signals. For targets at 2- to 3-km depth, the upper acoustic frequency is normally less than 50 Hz, which, if the rock has a velocity of 3,000 ms^{-1}, implies a maximum resolution of about 60 m. Figure 5.15 illustrates such a 50-Hz wavelength in relation to a reservoir. A modern seismic survey can span tens of kilometers on the surface of the Earth and penetrate up to 10 kilometers into the Earth.

At the other end of the scale, when a well is drilled, the surrounding rock is imaged at the scale of centimeters. Occasionally, the rock is actually sampled for more careful analysis. For example, to understand the subtle variations in permeability that will determine whether a well is going to be economical, it may be necessary to examine the intergranular structures at the micron level (Fig. 5.14).

5.4.1.2 Data Type Specific Processing

Wireline Logging and Logging While Drilling. As discussed earlier, the FMI, FMS and RAB tools measure the electrical conductivity of the surrounding rock.

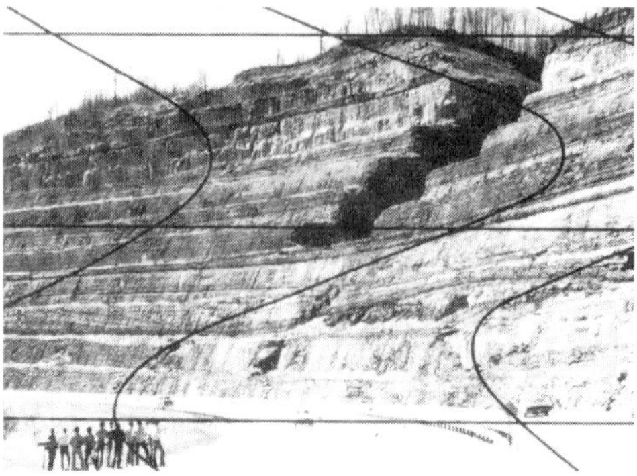

Figure 5.15. 50-Hz seismic waves compared to an outcrop of rock [A. Ziolkowski, Multi-well imaging of reservoir fluids, *Leading Edge*, **18**(12), (1999).] The horizontal lines are spaced at half the wavelength of the waves. The illustration suggests the large volume of rock contained in a single wavelet.

However, there are numerous environmental variables that must be taken into account before these measurements can be meaningfully interpreted. For example, the high-density drilling fluid that fills the well during logging may have left a "cake" on the borehole surface that prevents the tools from making direct contact with the rock. This will alter the measured conductivity and must be taken into account. The drilling fluid also has electrical properties that influence the signal; this must also be accounted for.

Once these "environmental" effects have been accounted for, further processing transforms the current intensity measurements, which now reflect the microresistivity variations of the formation, into high-resolution color images of variable intensity. Typically, there is a one-to-one correspondence between a resistivity measurement and a pixel in this conversion to an image. Thus, each pad of the 4-pad FMS tool has 16 sensors yielding 4 16 pixel wide images, whereas the 8 pads FMI tool has 24 sensors on each pad, yielding 8 24 pixel wide images. Conventionally, a white-to-dark-brown 32-bit color scale is used to represent FMS, FMI, and RAB images (Fig. 5.4).

Seismic Imagery. Seismic waves traveling through the Earth often have very complex paths; they will be refracted, reflected, and diffracted. In order to image the Earth through the complicated distorting heterogeneous subsurface, we need to be able to undo all the resulting wave-propagation effects. This is the goal of seismic imaging: to transform a suite of seismic waves recorded at the surface of the Earth into a spatial image of some property of the Earth (usually reflection strength or amplitude).

There are two types of spatial variations of the Earth's properties:

- Smooth variations associated with processes such as compaction. These gradual changes cause ray paths to be gently turned or refracted.
- Sharp changes, mostly in the vertical direction, which are associated with changes in rock type and, to a lesser extent, faulting and fracturing. It is

these short wavelength features that give rise to the reflections that we see on seismic sections.

Reflection seismology is primarily sensitive to the latter. As noted earlier, the integration of these data and physical phenomena related to acoustic wave propagation in layered media has resulted in the oil industry being one of the principal consumers of supercomputers.

5.4.1.3 Data Fusion. The oil industry is presented with a wide spectrum of imagery at a variety of scales. In the interpretation of an oil field, it is necessary to integrate as much data as possible to arrive at a complete analysis. Just a few examples of combining these data and the associated challenges are discussed in the following sections.

Time-to-Depth Conversion. In a seismic survey, the vertical dimension of the measurement represents the time required for the sound wave to travel from the surface of the Earth to the horizon, reflect, and return to the surface; this is commonly referred to as *two-way travel time* (TWT). Naturally, this time is a function of the vertically and laterally varying velocity of sound waves in the rock. Sophisticated data analysis and interpretation is required to derive this complex velocity function for a given area. Only when this is achieved can the time-based seismic data be transformed into a depth-based image. This task is referred to as *time-to-depth* conversion. Once the seismic has been "depth converted," it is possible to integrate these data with other measurements that are depth based.

Figure 5.10 illustrates a map of the rock porosity in a geologic formation. This map is based on the attributes in the seismic image. It is possible to infer actual porosity values from the seismic image because the depth-converted seismic data has been calibrated with wells in which the porosity was directly measured.

Calibration of Core and Wireline Logging Data. One interesting challenge in oil exploration is getting an accurate estimate of the depth of a given measurement. As with the challenge of reconciling the depth of an observation in a well with the time-based seismic observation (see the previous section), there is a challenge in reconciling core data with wireline (e.g., microresistivity) data. Wireline data is acquired by lowering the measuring instrument into the well on a sophisticated cable. The logging tool is then pulled up the well as it is acquiring data from the surrounding rock. The tool does not slide smoothly but typically gets stuck by the friction of the surrounding rock until the tension in the cable is high enough for the tool to break free. This, combined with the weight of the tool, the cable, and the stress of the surrounding high-density fluid that fills the borehole causes the cable to stretch by varying amounts. Although the tension in the cable is measured at the surface, there is significant uncertainty in the actual depth of the tool at any given time. On the other hand, as discussed earlier, core data is acquired by lowering a core barrel into the well. Instead of being at the end of a cable, the core barrel is at the end of a drill pipe. The drill pipe is built by connecting individual pipe segments together (each segment is typically 30 ft in length). The depth of a core is therefore determined precisely by counting the number of drill pipe segments.

A common way of reconciling the driller's (core) depth with logger's (wireline) depth is to make a gamma ray log directly from the core data. This core-based gamma ray log is then pattern matched with the wireline — derived gamma ray.

Once this depth matching has been achieved, the core data presents a very high-resolution image of the rock interval measured with the wireline tools. Note that the different depth domains are not an issue for RAB and other LWD data, which are measured in driller's depth.

Use of Scanning Electron Microscopy (SEM) Imagery to Validate Hypotheses. SEM is often used in conjunction with other lower-resolution imaging techniques. For example, certain wireline measurements combined with analysis of petrographic images (Fig. 5.13) might yield precise estimates of porosity for example, 31 percent. However, a detailed analysis of the SEM images might be necessary to understand the history of the porosity development. Thus, by combining the SEM observations (e.g., Fig. 5.14), it might be possible to say that of the 31 percent porosity, 25 percent is primary and the remaining 6 percent is secondary.

5.4.2 Data Management

The vast majority of image data used by the petroleum industry is in the private domain. Oil and gas companies and oil field service companies spend billions of dollars annually in acquiring data for exploring and producing hydrocarbons. Furthermore, much of these data have been collected over many decades and still have value today. However, the volume of acquired data (particularly seismic) is growing exponentially as companies have moved from acquiring 2D seismic data to 3D, and now to four-dimensional seismic data (4D)(3D over time). Also, the spatial extent of these surveys is also increasing.

The data storage, retrieval, and loading processes in current use are inefficient, labor-intensive and wasteful. Data are typically stored off-line or off-site on tape of various vintages, making retrieval very time consuming and requiring trained technicians to locate data, retrieve tapes, reformat, and load data into a computer-aided exploration application.

The problem with current practice is that seismic and well data is often dispersed, and there is no complete index or location map to facilitate access; this critical data resource is scattered throughout the corporate enterprise and beyond in application data stores, the corporate archive, warehouses, and with data brokers. The user of these data can never be sure that the data package for a project area is complete; there may be additional relevant data at an obscure location that were overlooked. The industry consensus has it that users of these data spend on average 60 percent of their time gathering and loading (rather than evaluating) data.

5.4.2.1 Storage. There is a rapidly growing business within the oil industry devoted to the management of a corporation's data. Service companies such as GeoQuest (*http://www.geoquest.com*) are now offering software and consulting services to organize a company's data into an easily accessible format. The promise of these services is that a company's users will have near-instantaneous access to the organized data in a format that is useful for their particular applications.

These data-archiving systems store the data in digital (e.g., Sony DMS), automatic tape libraries for high-performance, near-line mass storage. The latest generation of this technology supports scalable tape libraries with data capacities up to 11 petabytes. The latest digital tape format (DTF) cassettes can store up to 200 GB of uncompressed data with search speeds of 1.4 gigabytes per second.

5.4.2.2 Formats and Standards

Core. Core images are typically stored in TIFF (Appendix A) to preserve the resolution of the original digital image, although the images are increasingly being stored in JPEG format (see Appendix) because of the popularity of web tools and delivery.

Wireline Logging and Logging While Drilling Data. Microresistivity images are typically stored in DLIS files (see Appendix) along with other log data. Interpretation applications load DLIS data into their own proprietary formats.

Seismic

PROPRIETARY FORMATS. For active interpretations, oil companies typically store their seismic image data in one of the following proprietary formats:

- SeisWorks™ — This is the native format for Landmark Graphics Corporation (*http://www.lgc.com*) seismic interpretation system.
- Charisma™ — This is the native format for GeoQuest's (*http://www.geoquest.com*) Charisma seismic interpretation system.
- IES-X™ — This is the native format for GeoQuest's (*http://www.geoquest.com*) IES-X seismic interpretation system.

SEG-Y FORMAT. The SEG-Y format is one of several tape standards developed by the Society of Exploration Geophysicists (*http://www.seg.com*). It is the most common format used for seismic data in the exploration and production industry. However, it was created in 1973 and many different "modernized" flavors exist.

SEG-Y was designed for storing a single line of seismic data on IBM 9-track tapes attached to IBM mainframe computers. Some of the features of SEG-Y that are outdated today include the use of an EBCDIC descriptive header (rather than the now-standard ASCII), use of IBM floating-point data (rather than the now-standard IEEE), and single-line storage (rather than the now-common 3D surveys). Most of the variations in modern SEG-Y varieties result from trying to overcome these limitations.

5.4.2.3 ***Interoperability.*** All the major seismic interpretation vendors support import and export to the SEG-Y format so that the data can be used by the seismic interpretation application of choice.

In addition, some vendors have expended great efforts to have real-time interoperability between their seismic and well interpretation products (e.g., GeoQuest and Landmark Graphics).

The current problem is that much of this real-time interoperability only takes place between single-vendor applications. Since many oil companies would prefer not to be tied to a single vendor, considerable effort has been devoted to defining interoperability standards. The most notable recent effort in this direction is the OpenSpirit initiative (*http://www.openspirit.com*). OpenSpirit is a vendor-neutral, platform-independent application framework. OpenSpirit will allow oil companies to select and integrate best-in-class applications, independently of their chosen data management solution. OpenSpirit will also allow independent software vendors to develop applications that work with all the popular data management solutions, including GeoQuest's and Landmark's systems.

The idea behind OpenSpirit is that all the participating OpenSpirit applications exchange data through an OpenSpirit server using the OpenSpirit data model. The OpenSpirit data server then has back end connections to the proprietary databases. The vendors themselves would typically implement these back end connectors.

5.4.2.4 ***Retrieval.*** The major oil industry application vendors use relational databases to store their data. The bulk data, well logs and seismic, are stored in proprietary binary file formats. These binary files are referenced from within the relational databases, which also contain the metadata, such as image dimensions and spatial information.

5.4.2.5 ***Optimized Retrieval.*** An interesting example of optimized data retrieval is the extraction of 2D seismic images (planes) from 3D volumes. Although most seismic interpretation applications allow any arbitrarily oriented 2D surface to be extracted from a seismic volume, some applications (e.g., Charisma Section 6.1.1.1) organize the 3D data into three duplicate volumes, each optimized to extract planes, which are normal to the principal axes of the volume. These principal axes are the vertical (acoustic travel-time) direction, the horizontal (in-line) direction parallel to the direction in which the geophones and hydrophones were arranged, and the mutually orthogonal cross-line direction.

An alternative approach to storing multiple copies of the 3D seismic volumes is to "brick" the volumes. The IESX seismic interpretation system (Section 6.1.1.2) takes this approach. This technique simply dissects the main volume into smaller bricks. Only those bricks that contain the data being actively interpreted are delivered to the client application.

During interpretation of seismic data, decisions are also made with regard to how precise the data needs to be. Generally, seismic data is losslessly compressed, with reduction in resolution only at the time of delivery to an end user. For example, seismic data is typically stored as arrays of 4-byte floats, but might be converted to single bytes for human interpretation.

Interestingly, lossy image storage solutions such as JPEG are becoming increasingly popular because of the Internet. Core photos or wireline images can now be delivered to a web browser as JPEG images.

5.4.2.6 ***Model Based Retrieval.*** A routine part of geologic interpretation is identifying the rock layers or intervals that comprise the subsurface. All the data model schemes that support the oil exploration and production task (e.g., Epicenter, Section 6.3) support this type of interpretation.

Wireline and Core imagery data are typically stored as image files outside the relational database, which stores the nonimagery data. The imagery is indexed in the database by well identify, top depth, bottom depth, and other parameters (e.g., white light versus ultraviolet light image).

Using an interpretation application that supports a valid data model, the geologist will interpret a well and define horizons (layer boundaries) and intervals (volumes of rock intersected by the well). These interpretations are based on a variety of data, including the wireline and core imagery.

When an application displays imagery, data is always retrieved using the acquisition parameters (well, top, and bottom depths), along with the relevant interpretation parameters (horizons and intervals). A similar tight coupling between the relational metadata and the bulk image data exists for all seismic interpretation applications.

It should be noted that not all data models are implemented as relational databases. Increasingly, proprietary "geometry engines" are being used to manage the complex geometries of the subsurface. However, the image data is still stored separately from the geometry.

5.4.2.7 ***Content-Based Retrieval.*** Efficient content-based retrieval has long been an objective of vendors of interpretation software for the oil and gas industry. Recently, a number of very sophisticated applications aimed at achieving this objective have become available.

SeisClass (Section 6.1.1.3) is an application focused at automatically interpreting seismic imagery based on spectral and textural characteristics. Areas and volumes of the seismic images are classified. The resulting classes may be calibrated to wells, so that the classes may be assigned semantic attributes. For example, a certain classification may correspond to an interval identified in a well as "cross-bedded sandstone."

BorTex (Section 6.1.1.4) analyzes borehole imagery data in conjunction with conventional wireline logs to automatically classify different portions of the well. It also identifies "spots" and "patches" from images for quantification of vugs (empty spaces) and volume connectivity.

5.5 CHALLENGES AND OPEN PROBLEMS

The petroleum industry is faced with numerous challenges in efficiently acquiring, managing and utilizing its image data. A few of these challenges include the following:

- *Data Volume.* Particularly in terms of three-dimensional seismic data. Seismic surveys are becoming ever larger, with corporate databases now having terabyte inventories. Routine acquisition of four-dimensional (time-lapse) seismic will also strain a company's ability to process, manage, and interpret the data.
- *Database Standardization.* Although great effort has been made over the last 10 years to develop industry-wide database standards, such as POSC and OpenSpirit, most oil companies are forced to make single-vendor decisions. It is currently very difficult to allow applications from different vendors to seamlessly work together. It is possible that the rapidly emerging open standards-based Internet technologies may serendipitously lead to truly integrated systems in the oil industry.
- *Legacy Software.* Software development and advancement moves very slowly in the oil industry. There are several reasons for this. First, the data are very heterogeneous and their interrelationships very complex. Once these databases have evolved, they are very difficult to change. Second, the market for this software is relatively small and the unit cost is consequently very high. Software vendors are challenged to develop new tools while maintaining their existing systems.
- *Bandwidth.* Although the explosion of the Internet has brought many exciting opportunities to the oil and gas industry, it has also brought numerous challenges. One of the greatest challenges in managing image data is dealing with limited bandwidth. The networked world of the Internet implies distributed users, data, and applications. No matter how clever the software solutions are, this inevitably implies the necessity to rapidly deliver large volumes of data.

APPENDIX

A.1 Overview of Current Systems

A.1.1 GeoFrame™. Released by GeoQuest in 1993, GeoFrame™ is a project database and a suite of reservoir characterization applications that enables the interactive sharing of data and interpretations within broad exploration and production (E& P) domains such as geology, geophysics, petrophysics, reservoir modeling, and reservoir engineering.

Below are some example applications from the GeoFrame™ suite that specifically address automated image analysis and interpretation.

A.1.1.1 Charisma™. The Charisma™ seismic interpretation system is part of the GeoFrame POSC-compliant integrated reservoir characterization system.

Beyond basic seismic interpretation, Charisma has full support for several advanced interpretation features:

- 3D seismic attribute extraction. A seismic amplitude volume can be processed to represent numerous other attributes.
- Geologic horizons can be extracted automatically from the amplitude data.
- Processing utilities are available to the interpreter to apply a variety of transformations including phase rotation, time shift, deconvolution, and filtering
- Automatic discontinuity detection highlights subtle faults, and fractures

A.1.1.2 IESX™. IESX™ is another seismic interpretation system that is part of GeoQuest's GeoFrame™ reservoir characterization system. IESX™ has many of the same basic and advanced features of Charisma™, but a different user interface and customer base. A powerful feature of IESX™ is its ability to easily combine data from multiple seismic surveys. 3D visualization and interpretation is another powerful feature.

A.1.1.3 SeisClass™. The SeisClass™ multiattribute classification tool kit is designed to automate the seismic attribute analysis and interpretation task. The technology supporting SeisClass™ is fully integrated with GeoFrame and uses the reservoir's seismic attributes to generate class and probability maps. Once a given fluid or rock type is captured by a set of attributes and calibrated by one or more wells, similar potential reservoirs can be identified in neighboring undrilled structures or basins.

All the data in the GeoFrame™ database, including interpreted surfaces, attributes and geologic markers are a direct input to the classification process. SeisClass™ can be used with pre- and poststack seismic data. With the advent of multicomponent and time-lapse seismic data, SeisClass™ can be used to determine fluid type and monitor fluid migration for complete reservoir characterization.

SeisClass™ has multiple classification algorithms that use any combination of seismic attribute grids as the input. Integrated with GeoFrame™, the software accesses a large number of new, instantaneous volume attributes that completely represent and capture the seismic signal — going beyond seismic waveshape.

A.1.1.4 BorTex™. The BorTex™ texture classification software automatically obtains rock texture from dip meter and image logs. BorTex™ derives new attributes from logs and automatically classifies the texture in both elastic and carbonate environments. It also identifies "spots" and "patches" from images for quantification of vugs (empty spaces) and volume connectivity in carbonates.

***A.1.2 OpenWorks*™.** Landmark Graphics (*http://www.lgc.com*) delivered its first system for interpreting 3D seismic data in 1984. As the oil industry embraced 3D seismic data and the technology evolved over the last 20 years, so has Landmarks' influence. It remains one of the leading vendors of integrated oil field interpretation software.

In addition to its suite of geologic interpretation and mapping software, Landmark sports several seismic interpretation and analysis systems:

SeisWorks™. SeisWorks™ is one of the industry's best-known 3D seismic interpretation and analysis systems. SeisWorks™ supports seismic interpretation in either time or depth. SeisWorks™ includes full multisurvey merge capabilities allowing a user to easily combine 2D with 3D projects, and to merge multiple 3D projects without data reformatting or reloading. The seismic balance functions allow for the correction of differences in amplitude, phase and frequency across multiple surveys and within 2D projects. Faults can be interpreted and edited on vertical seismic sections and time slices. SeisWorks™ uses Landmarks OpenWorks™ database, which allows data and interpretations to be between all of Landmarks interpretation and modeling applications.

EarthCube™. EarthCube™ provides a 3D, seismic interpretation and visualization system. Key features that allow the user to manipulate data include opacity display using volume rendering, zooming and rotation, chair displays and animation planes. The seismic slice plane animation allows the interpreter to create arbitrary seismic slice planes in any orientation - vertical, horizontal, arbitrary or at oblique angles - then drive the slice planes throughout the seismic volume for interpretation.

PAL™. (post stack attribute library) enables the interpreter to extract attributes from SeisWorks™ data. PAL™ allows the interactive computation of statistical and complex attributes, which can be accessed by numerous applications throughout the interpretation process.

A.2 Managing Images

The following three tables (Tables 5.1–5.3) summarize the information on storage and compression formats that are relevant to the chapter.

Table 5.1. Format Portability

Widely Supported	Mostly Microsoft Windows	Mostly UNIX	Others
JPEG [2] GIF PostScript	BMP (Windows BitMaP)	PBM, PGM, PPM	TIFF[a] SGI[b] CGM[c] PDS[d]

[a] Because of the complexity of the format, different implementations of TIFF might be incompatible.
[b] Available on silicon graphics machines. Some applications, such as XV, understand the format.
[c] Computer graphics metafile (CGM) is poorly supported by DTP packages.
[d] Picture description standard (PDS) developed by Schlumberger, is a graphic metafile format to efficiently describe, store and transport log graphics.

Table 5.2. Compression Types, Algorithms, and Color Support

File Format	Compression Type	Compression Algorithm	Color Support
GIF	Lossless (8-bit) Lossy (24-bit)	Color-quantization and LZW [10]	256 colors. 24-bit color is quantized to 8 bits.
JPEG	Lossless Lossy	Predictive Coding and Huffman [11]or AC [12]. Block-DCT and quantization and run-length coding. User-selectable parameter controls the loss.	Both lossless and lossy support 8-bit gray scale images and 24-bit color images. Color images are encoded by compressing separately the red, green, and blue bands.
BMP	Lossless	Optional run-length coding.	1-, 4-, 8-, and 24-bit color. 1-, 4-, and 8-bit color use table-lookup.
TIFF	Lossless	LZW or PackBits	Up to 24-bit color.
PBM (PGM, PPM)	None	None	PBM: up to 24-bit color images, PGM/PPM are gray scale versions.
PostScript	Level 2: lossless/lossy	Various (including JPEG)	1-, 2-, 4-, or 8-bit color. Also 24-bit support.
CGM	Lossless	Optional run-length coding.	24-bit color support
PDS	Lossless	Optional run-length coding.	24-bit color support

Table 5.3. Image Quality, Design Goals, and Suitability

File Format	Lossy Image Quality [3]	Design Target	Suitability for Oil Industry Data
JPEG	User-selected.	Natural images	Web-based applications
BMP	NA	Bitmaps for Windows	PC-based log and seismic applications
TIFF	Supports numerous schemes	General imagery. Versions for scientific data (e.g., GeoTIFF)	Nonlossy storage of all image data
CGM	NA	Vector and bitmap graphics	Poorly supported by DTP packages
PDS	NA	Log graphics	Log graphics

Note: The assessment of the image quality refers to lossy compression. If a format supports both lossless and lossy compression, the column refers only to the lossy mode.

A.3 Data Models and Schemas

A system for managing the complex spectrum of images discussed in the preceding text, requires much more than efficient file formats. Rich data models, which describe the complex entities and their interrelationships, are necessary to manage the context of the images. The data models for representing this richness have evolved significantly over the past several decades.

Name	Description
LAS	LAS is the standard published by the Canadian Well Logging Society for ASCII data. These files are limited in size and are suitable for timely exchange and quick exploration of basic well log data.
LIS	Schlumberger introduced the LIS data format in the late 1970s. It was the de facto industry standard until it was superseded by DLIS in the late 1980s. Legacy applications, which use LIS instead of DLIS, still exist.
DLIS	DLIS is an industry-standard file format for well logs as defined by American Petroleum Institute Recommended Practice 66. The complex and diverse data sets acquired at a modern well site are typically stored and exchanged in DLIS format.
WellLogML	The explosion of the World Wide Web in the late 1990s has seen an interest by the petroleum industry in leveraging this technology. One outgrowth of this interest is WellLogML [14],the XML (Extensible Markup Language) DTD (Document Type Definition) to represent Well Log in a form that can easily be exchanged across the World Wide Web.
SEG-Y	SEG-Y is the standard file format for storing seismic data.
Epicentre	As noted earlier, POSC [15] developed is the 1990s a rich data model named *Epicentre*. The current version of Epicentre is composed of more than 750 real-world technical and business objects concerned with petroleum exploration and production. In POSC's data-modeling terminology, these objects are called *entities*.
OpenSpirit	Open*Spirit* is a vendor-neutral, platform-independent application framework. Open*Spirit* allows E&P companies to select and integrate best-in-class applications, independent of their chosen data management solution. Open*Spirit* allows software vendors to develop applications that work with all the popular data management solutions, including GeoQuest's GeoFrame and Landmark's OpenWorks.

REFERENCES

1. *http://www.ldeo.columbia.edu/BRG/ODP/LOGGING/MANUAL/MENU/contents.html*, ODP Logging Manual.
2. Akbar et al., Classic Interpretation Problems: Evaluating Carbonates, *Oil Field Rev.* (Winter) 38–57 (1995).
3. G. Anderson, *Coring and core analysis handbook,* PennWell Books 1975.
4. *http://crude2.kgs.ukans.edu/DPA/BigBow/CoreDesc*, Kansas Geological Survey, Big Bow Field.
5. Christie et al., Borehole seismic data sharpen the reservoir image, *Oil field Rev.* (Winter) 18–31 (1995).
6. A.R. Brown, *Interpretation of Three-Dimensional Seismic Data*, 5th Ed., AAPG and SEG (1999) p. 514
7. Ariffin et al., Seismic Tools for Reservoir Management, *OilField Rev.* (Winter) 4–17 (1995).
8. *http://www.emory.edu/COLLEGE/ENVS/research/ichnology/images.htm*, Trace Fossil Image Database.
9. A. Ziolkowski, Multiwell imaging of reservoir fluids, *Leading Edge* **18**(12), (1999).
10. T.A. Welch, A technique for high-performance data compression, *IEEE Comput. Mag.* **17**,9–19 (1984).
11. T.J. Cover, and J.A. Thomas, *Elements of Information Theory*, Wiley & Sons, 1991.
12. I.H. Witten, R.M. Neal, and J.G. Cleary, Arithmetic coding for data compression, *Commun. ACM* **30**(6), 520–540 (1987).
13. W. Pennebaker and J.L. Mitchell, *JPEG still image data compression standard,* Van Nostrand Reinhold, New York, 1993.
14. *http://www.posc.org/ebiz/WellLogML/*, WellLogML DTD.
15. *http://www.posc.org.*

6 Storage Architectures for Digital Imagery

HARRICK M. VIN
University of Texas at Austin, Austin, Texas

PRASHANT SHENOY
University of Massachusetts, Amherst, Massachusetts

Rapid advances in computing and communication technologies coupled with the dramatic growth of the Internet have led to the emergence of a wide variety of multimedia applications, such as distance education, on-line virtual worlds, immersive telepresence, and scientific visualization. These applications differ from conventional distributed applications in at least two ways. First, they involve storage, transmission, and processing of heterogeneous data types — such as text, imagery, audio, and video — that differ significantly in their characteristics (e.g., size, data rate, real-time requirements, and so on). Second, unlike conventional best-effort applications, these applications impose diverse performance requirements — for instance, with respect to timeliness — on the networks and operating systems. Unfortunately, existing networks and operating systems do not differentiate between data types, offering a single class of best-effort service to all applications. Hence, to support emerging multimedia applications, existing networks and operating systems need to be extended along several dimensions.

In this chapter, issues involved in designing storage servers that can support such a diversity of applications and data types are discussed. First, the specific issues that arise in designing a storage server for digital imagery are described, and then the architectural choices for designing storage servers that efficiently manage the storage and retrieval of multiple data types are discussed. Note that as it is difficult, if not impossible, to foresee requirements imposed by future applications and data types, a storage server that supports multiple data types and applications will need to facilitate easy integration of new application classes and data types. This dictates that the storage server architecture be extensible, allowing it to be easily tailored to meet new requirements.

Image Databases: Search and Retrieval of Digital Imagery, Edited by Vittorio Castelli and Lawrence D. Bergman.
ISBN 0-471-32116-8

The rest of the chapter is organized as follows. We begin by examining techniques for placement of digital imagery on a single disk, a disk array, and a hierarchical storage architecture. We then examine fault-tolerance techniques employed by servers to guarantee high availability of image data. Next, we discuss retrieval techniques employed by storage servers to efficiently access images and image sequences. We then discuss caching and batching issues employed by such servers to maximize the number of clients supported. Finally, we examine architectural issues in incorporating all of these techniques into a general-purpose file system.

6.1 STORAGE MANAGEMENT

6.1.1 Single Disk Placement

A storage server divides images into *blocks* while storing them on disks. In order to explore the viability of various placement models for storing these blocks on magnetic disks, some of the fundamental characteristics of these disks are briefly reviewed. Generally, magnetic disks consist of a collection of platters, each of which is composed of a number of circular recording tracks (Fig. 6.1). Platters spin at a constant rate. Moreover, the amount of data recorded on tracks may increase from the innermost track to the outermost track (e.g., in the case of zoned disks). The storage space of each track is divided into several disk blocks, each consisting of a sequence of physically contiguous sectors. Each platter is associated with a read or write head that is attached to a common actuator. A cylinder is a stack of tracks at one actuator position.

In such an environment the access time of a disk block consists of three components: *seek time*, *rotational latency*, and *data-transfer time*. Seek time is the time required to position the disk head on the track, containing the desired data and is a function of the initial start-up cost to accelerate the disk head and the number of tracks that are traversed. Rotational latency, on the other hand, is the time for the desired data to rotate under the head before it can be read or

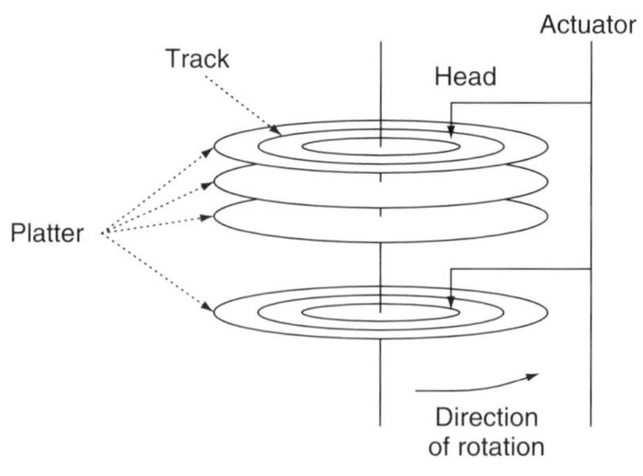

Figure 6.1. Architectural model of a conventional magnetic disk.

written and is a function of the angular distance between the current position of the disk head and the location of the desired data, as well as the rate at which platters spin. Once the disk head is positioned at the desired disk block, the time to retrieve its contents is referred to as the *data-transfer time*; it is a function of the disk block size and data-transfer rate of the disk.

The placement of data blocks on disks is generally governed by contiguous, random, or constrained placement policy. Contiguous placement policy requires that all blocks belonging to an image be placed together on the disk. This ensures that once the disk head is positioned at the beginning of an image, all its blocks can be retrieved without incurring any seek or rotational latency. Unfortunately, the contiguous placement policy results in disk fragmentation in environments with frequent image creations and deletions. Hence, contiguous placement is well suited for read-only systems (such as compact discs, CLVs, and so on.), but is less desirable for a dynamic, read-write storage systems.

Storage servers for read-write systems have traditionally employed random placement of blocks belonging to an image on disk [1,2]. This placement scheme does not impose any restrictions on the relative placement on the disks of blocks belonging to a single image. This approach eliminates disk fragmentation, albeit at the expense of incurring high seek time and rotational latency overhead while accessing an image.

Clearly, the contiguous and random placement models represent two ends of a spectrum; whereas the former does not permit any separation between successive blocks of an image on disk, the latter does not impose any constraints at all. The constrained or the clustered placement policy is a generalization of these extremes; it requires the blocks to be clustered together such that the maximum seek time and rotational latency incurred while accessing the image does not exceed a predefined threshold.

For the random and the constrained placement policies, the overall disk throughput depends on the total seek time and rotational latency incurred per byte accessed. Hence, to maximize the disk throughput, image servers use as large a block size as possible.

6.1.2 Multidisk Placement

Because of the large sizes of images and image sequences (i.e., video streams), most image and video storage servers utilize disk arrays. Disk arrays achieve high performance by servicing multiple input-output requests concurrently and by using several disks to service a single request in parallel. The performance of a disk array, however, is critically dependent on the distribution of the workload (i.e., the number of blocks to be retrieved from the array) among the disks. The higher the imbalance in the workload distribution, the lower is the throughput of the disk array.

To effectively utilize a disk array, a storage server interleaves the storage of each image or image sequence among the disks in the array. The unit of data interleaving, referred to as a *stripe unit*, denotes the maximum amount of logically contiguous data that is stored on a single disk [82,3]. Successive stripe units of an object are placed on disks, using a round-robin or random allocation algorithm.

Conventional file systems select stripe unit sizes that minimize the *average* response time while maximizing throughput. In contrast, to decrease the frequency of playback discontinuities, image and video servers select a stripe unit size that minimizes the *variance* in response time while maximizing throughput. Although small stripe units result in a uniform load distribution among disks in the array (and thereby decrease the variance in response times), they also increase the overhead of disk seeks and rotational latencies (and thereby decrease throughput). Large stripe units, on the other hand, increase the array throughput at the expense of increased load imbalance and variance in response times. To maximize the number of clients that can be serviced simultaneously, the server should select a stripe unit size that balances these trade-offs. Table 6.1 illustrates typical block or stripe unit sizes employed to store different types of data.

The degree of striping — the number of disks over which an image or an image sequence is striped — is dependent on the number of disks in the array. In relatively small disk arrays, striping image sequences across all disks in the array (i.e., wide-striping) yields a balanced load and maximizes throughput. For large disk arrays, however, to maximize the throughput, the server may need to stripe image sequences across subsets of disks in the array and replicate their storage to achieve load balancing. The amount of replication for each image sequence depends on the popularity of the image sequence and the total storage-space constraints.

6.1.2.1 From Images to Multiresolution Imagery. The placement technique becomes more challenging if the imagery is encoded using a multiresolution encoding algorithm. In general, multiresolution imagery consists of multiple layers. Although all layers need be retrieved to display the imagery at the highest resolution, only a subset of the layers need to be retrieved for lower resolution displays. To efficiently support the retrieval of such images at different resolutions, the placement algorithm needs to ensure that the server access only as much data as needed and no more. To ensure this property, the placement algorithm should store multiresolution images such that: (*1*) each layer is independently

Table 6.1. Typical Block or Stripe Unit Size for Different Data Types

Data Type	Storage Requirement	Block or Stripe Unit Size
Text	2–4 KB	0.5–4 KB
Gif Image	64 KB	4–8 KB
Satellite Image	60 MB	16 KB
MPEG Video	1 GB	64–256 KB

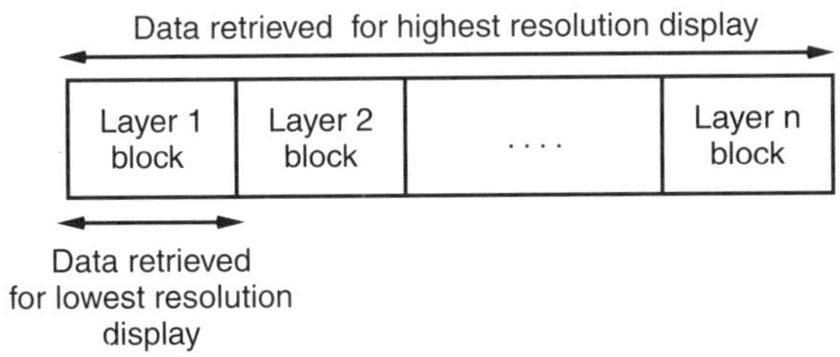

Figure 6.2. Contiguous placement of different layers of a multiresolution image. Storing data from different resolutions in separate disk blocks enables the server to retrieve each resolution independently of others; storing these blocks contiguously enables the server to reduce disk seek overheads while accessing multiple layers simultaneously.

accessible, and (2) the seek and rotational latency while accessing any subset of the layers is minimized. Although the former requirement can be met by storing layers in separate disk blocks, the latter requirement can be met by storing these disk blocks adjacent on disk. Observe that this placement policy is general and can be used to interleave any multiresolution image or video stream on the array. Figure 6.2 illustrates this placement policy.

6.1.2.2 From Images to Video Streams. Consider a disk array–based video server. If the video streams are compressed using a variable bit rate (VBR) compression algorithm, then the sizes of frames (or images) will vary. Hence, if the server stores these video streams on disks using fixed-size stripe units, each stripe unit will contain a variable number of frames. On the other hand, if each stripe unit contains a fixed number of frames (and hence data for a fixed playback duration), then the stripe units will have variable sizes. Thus, depending on the striping policy, retrieving a fixed number of frames will require the server to access a fixed number of variable-size blocks or a variable number of fixed-size blocks [4,5,6].

Because of the periodic nature of video playback, most video servers service clients by proceeding in terms of periodic rounds. During each round, the server retrieves a fixed number of video frames (or images) for each client. To ensure continuous playback, the number of frames accessed for each client during a round must be sufficient to meet its playback requirements. In such an architecture, a server that employs variable-size stripe units (or fixed-time stripe units) accesses a fixed number of stripe units during each round. This uniformity of access, when coupled with the sequential and periodic nature of video retrieval, enables the server to balance load across the disks in the array. This efficiency, however, comes at the expense of increased complexity of storage-space management.

The placement policy that utilizes fixed-size stripe units, on the other hand, simplifies storage-space management but results in higher load imbalance across the disks. In such servers, load across disks within a server may become unbalanced, at least transiently, because of the arrival pattern of requests. To smoothen out this load imbalance, servers employ dynamic load-balancing techniques. If multiple replicas of the requested video stream are stored on the array, then the server can attempt to balance load across disks by servicing the request from the least-loaded disk containing a replica. Further, the server can exploit the sequentiality of video retrieval to prefetch data for the streams to smoothen out variation in the load imposed by individual video stream.

6.1.3 Utilizing Storage Hierarchies

The preceding discussion has focused on fixed disks as the storage medium for image and video servers. This is primarily because disks provide high throughput and low latency relative to other storage media such as tape libraries, optical juke boxes, and so on. The start-up latency for devices such as tape libraries is substantial as it requires mechanical loading of the appropriate tape into a reader station. The advantage, however, is that they offer very high storage capacities (Table 6.2).

In order to construct a cost-effective image and video storage system that provides adequate throughput, it is logical to use a hierarchy of storage devices [7,8,9,10]. There are several possible strategies for managing this storage hierarchy, with different techniques for placement, replacement, and so on. In one scenario, a relatively small set of frequently requested images and videos are placed on disks and the large set of less frequently requested data objects are stored in optical juke boxes or tape libraries. In this storage hierarchy there are several alternatives for managing the disk system. The most common architecture is the one in which disks are used as a staging area (cache) for the secondary storage devices and the entire image and video files are moved from the tertiary storage to the disk. It is then possible to apply traditional cache-management techniques to manage the content of the disk array.

For very large-scale servers, it is also possible to use an array of juke boxes or tape readers [10]. In such a system, images and video objects may need to be striped across these tertiary storage devices [11]. Although striping can improve I/O throughput by reading from multiple tape drives in parallel, it can also increase contention for drives (because each request accesses all drives). Studies have shown that such systems must carefully balance these trade-offs by choosing an appropriate degree of striping for a given workload [11,12].

Table 6.2. Tertiary Storage Devices

	Disks		Tapes	
	Magnetic	Optical	Low-End	High-End
Capacity	40 GB	200 GB	500 GB	10 TB
Mount Time	0 sec	20 sec	60 sec	90 sec
Transfer Rate	10 MB/s	300 KB/s	100 KB/s	1,000 KB/s

6.2 FAULT TOLERANCE

Most image and video servers are based on large disk arrays, and hence the ability to tolerate disk failures is central to the design of such servers. The design of fault-tolerant storage systems has been a topic of much research and development over the past decade [13,14]. In most of these systems, fault-tolerance is achieved either by *disk mirroring* [15] or *parity encoding* [16,17]. Disk arrays that employ these techniques are referred to as *redundant array of independent disks* (RAID). RAID arrays that employ disk mirroring achieve fault-tolerance by duplicating data on separate disks (and thereby incur a 100 percent storage-space overhead). Parity encoding, on the other hand, reduces the overhead considerably by employing error-correcting codes. For instance, in a RAID level five disk array, consisting of D disks, parity computed over data stored across $(D - 1)$ disks is stored on another disk (e.g., the left-symmetric parity assignment shown in Figure 6.3a) [18,19,17]. In such architectures, if one of the disks fails, the data on the failed disk is recovered using the data and parity blocks stored on the surviving disks That is, each user access to a block on the failed disk causes one request to be sent to each of the surviving disks. Thus, if the system is load-balanced prior to disk failure, the surviving disks would observe at least twice as many requests in the presence of a failure [20].

The *declustered parity* disk array organization [21,22,23] addresses this problem by trading some of the array's capacity for improved performance in the presence of disk failures. Specifically, it requires that each parity block protect some smaller number of data blocks [for e.g., $(G - 1)$]. By appropriately distributing the parity information across all the D disks in the array, such a policy ensures that each surviving disk would see an on-the-fly reconstruction load increase of $(G - 1)/(D - 1)$ instead of $(D - 1)/(D - 1) = 100\%$ [Fig. 6.3b].

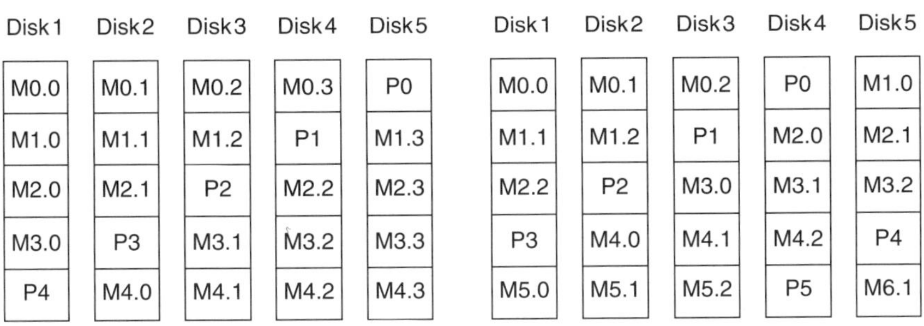

(a) Left-symmetric data organization in RAID level 5 disk array with G = D = 5

(b) Declustered parity organization with G = 4 and D = 5

Figure 6.3. Different techniques for storing parity blocks in a RAID-5 architecture. (**a**) depicts the left-symmetric parity organization, in which the parity group size is same as the number of disks in the array; (**b**) depicts the declustered parity organization in which the parity group size is smaller than the number of disks. $M_{i.j}$ and P_i denote data and parity blocks, respectively, and $P_i = M_{i.0} \oplus M_{i.1} \cdots \oplus M_{i.(G-2)}$.

In general, with such parity-based recovery techniques, increase in the load on the surviving disks in the event of a disk failure results in deadline violations in the playback of video streams. To prevent such a scenario with conventional fault-tolerance techniques, servers must operate at low levels of disk utilization during the fault-free state. Image and video servers can reduce this overhead by exploiting the characteristics of imagery. There are two general techniques that such servers may use.

- A video server can exploit the sequentiality of video access to reduce the overhead of on-line recovery in a disk array. Specifically, by computing parity information over a sequence of blocks belonging to the same video stream, the server can ensure that video data retrieved for recovering a block stored on the failed disk would be requested by the client in the near future. By buffering such blocks and then servicing the requests for their access from the buffer, this method minimizes the overhead of the on-line failure recovery process.
- Because human perception is tolerant to minor distortions in images, a server can exploit the inherent redundancies in images to *approximately* reconstruct lost image data using error-correcting codes instead of perfectly recovering image data stored on the failed disk. In such a server, each image is partitioned into subimages and if the subimages are stored on different disks, then a single disk failure will result in the loss of fractions of several images. In the simplest case, if the subimages are created in the pixel domain (i.e., prior to compression) such that none of the immediate neighbors of a pixel in the image belong to the same subimage, then even in the presence of a single disk failure, all the neighbors of the lost pixels will be available. In this case, the high degree of correlation between neighboring pixels will make it possible to reconstruct a reasonable approximation of the original image. Moreover, no additional information will have to be retrieved from any of the surviving disks for recovery.

Although conceptually elegant, such *precompression image partitioning* techniques significantly reduce the correlation between the pixels assigned to the same subimage and hence adversely affect image-compression efficiency [24,25]. The resultant increase in the bit rate requirement may impose higher load on each disk in the array even during the fault-free state, thereby reducing the number of video streams that can be simultaneously retrieved from the server. A number of postcompression partitioning algorithms that address this limitation have been proposed [26,27]. The concepts in postcompression partitioning is illustrated by describing one such algorithm, namely, the loss-resilient joint photographic expert group (JPEG) (LRJ).

6.2.1 Loss-Resilient JPEG (LRJ) Algorithm

As human perception is less sensitive to high-frequency components of the spectral energy in an image, most compression algorithms transform images into the frequency domain so as to separate low- and high-frequency components. For instance, the JPEG compression standard fragments image data into a sequence of 8×8 pixel blocks and transforms them into the frequency domain using discrete cosine transform (DCT). DCT uncorrelates each pixel block into an 8×8 array of coefficients such that most of the spectral energy is packed in the fewest number of low-frequency coefficients. Although the lowest frequency coefficient (referred to as the *DC coefficient*) captures the average brightness of the spatial block, the remaining set of 63 coefficients (referred to as the *AC coefficients*) capture the details within the 8×8 pixel block. The DC coefficients of successive blocks are difference-encoded independent of the AC coefficients. Within each block, the AC coefficients are quantized to remove high-frequency components, scanned in a zigzag manner to obtain an approximate ordering from lowest to highest frequency and finally run-length and entropy-encoded. Figure 6.4 depicts the main steps involved in the JPEG compression algorithm [28].

The loss-resilient JPEG (LRJ) algorithm is an enhancement of the JPEG compression algorithm and is motivated by the following two observations:

- Because the DC coefficients capture the average brightness of each 8×8 pixel block and because the average brightness of pixels gradually changes across most images, the DC coefficients of neighboring 8×8 pixel blocks are correlated. Consequently, the value of DC coefficient of a block can be reasonably approximated by extrapolating from the DC coefficients of the neighboring blocks.

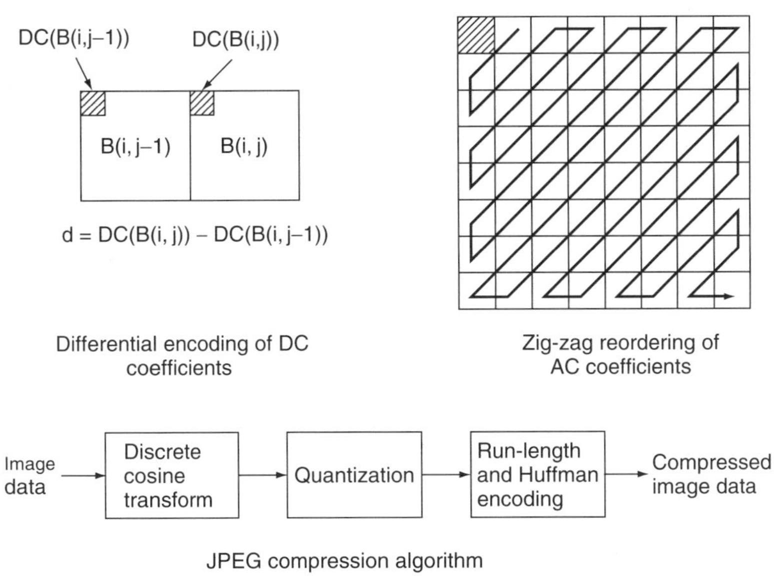

Figure 6.4. JPEG compression algorithm.

- Owing to the very nature of DCT, the set of AC coefficients generated for each 8×8 block are uncorrelated. Moreover, because DCT packs the most amount of spectral energy into a few low-frequency coefficients, quantizing the set of AC coefficients (by using a user-defined normalization array) yields many zeroes, especially at higher frequencies. Consequently, recovering a block by simply substituting a zero for each of the lost AC coefficient is generally sufficient to obtain a reasonable approximation of the original image (at least as long as the number of lost coefficients are small and are scattered throughout the block).

Thus, even when parts of a compressed image have been lost, a reasonable recovery is possible if: (*1*) the image in the frequency domain is partitioned into a set of N subimages such that none of the DC coefficients in the eight-neighborhood of a block belong to the same subimage, and (*2*) the AC coefficients of a block are scattered among multiple subimages. To ensure that none of the blocks contained in a subimage are in the eight-neighborhood of each other, N should be at least 4 [27]. To scatter the AC coefficients of a block among multiple subimages, the LRJ compression algorithm employs a scrambling technique, which when given a set of N blocks of AC coefficients, creates a new set of N blocks such that the AC coefficients from each of the input blocks are equally distributed among all of the output blocks (Fig. 6.5). Once all the blocks within the image have been processed, each of the N subimages can be independently encoded.

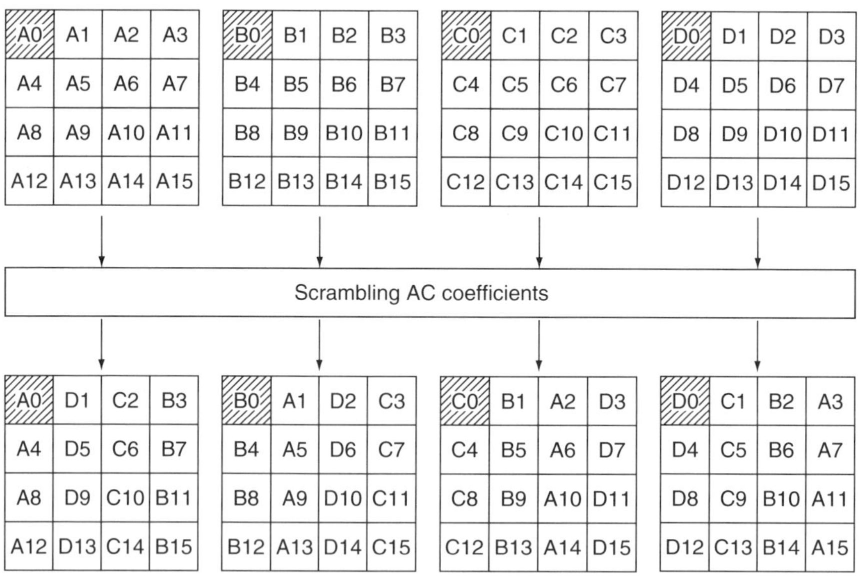

Figure 6.5. Scrambling AC coefficients. Here A_0, B_0, C_0, and D_0 denote DC coefficients, and $\forall i \in [29, 30] : A_i, B_i, C_i$, and D_i represent AC coefficients.

At the time of decompression, once each subimage has been run-length- and Huffman-decoded, the LRJ algorithm employs an unscrambler to recover blocks of the original image from the corresponding blocks of the subimages. In the event that the information contained in a subimage is not available, the unscrambling module also performs a predictive reconstruction of the lost DC coefficients from the DC coefficients of the neighboring 8×8 blocks. Lost AC coefficients, on the other hand, are replaced by zeroes. Because the scrambler module employed by the encoder ensures that each block within a subimage contains coefficients from several blocks of the original image, the artifacts yielded by such a recovery mechanism are dispersed over the entire reconstructed image, thereby significantly improving the visual quality of the image.

There are several salient features of a fault-tolerance architecture based on LRJ.

- The failure recovery process does not impose any additional load on the disk array, because each image in the video stream is reconstructed by extrapolating information retrieved from the surviving disks.
- The reconstruction process is carried out at client sites, because the recovery of lost image data is integrated with the decompression algorithm. This is an important departure from the conventional RAID technology — distributing the functionality of failure recovery to client sites will significantly enhance the scalability of multi-disk multimedia servers.
- Client sites will be able to reconstruct a video stream even in the presence of multiple disk failures, as the recovery process only exploits the inherent redundancy in imagery. The quality of the reconstructed image, albeit, will degrade with increase in the number of simultaneously failed disks.
- The unscrambling algorithms in LRJ can be adapted to mask packet losses due to network congestion as well, as the cause of the data loss is irrelevant to the recovery algorithm.

Observe also that although the quality of the recovered image in the presence of a single disk failure is acceptable for most applications, to prevent any accumulation of errors across multiple disk failures, the server must also maintain parity information to perfectly recover the contents of the failed disk onto a spare disk. In such a scenario, on-line reconstruction onto a spare disk can proceed simply by issuing low-priority read requests to access media blocks from each of the surviving disks [20]. By assigning low priority to each read request issued by the on-line reconstruction process, the server can ensure that the performance guarantees provided to all the clients are met even in the presence of disk failures.

6.3 RETRIEVAL TECHNIQUES

Traditionally, storage servers have employed two fundamentally different architectures for the storage and retrieval of images and image sequences. Storage

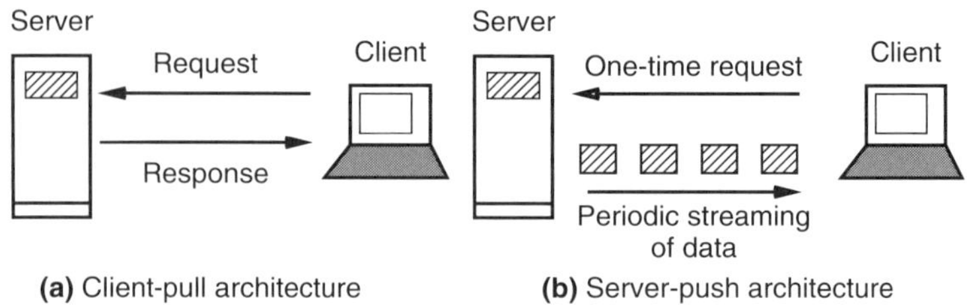

Figure 6.6. Client-pull and server-push architectures for retrieving data.

servers that employ the *client-pull* architecture retrieve data from disks only in response to an explicit client request. Servers that employ the *server-push* or *streaming* architecture, on the other hand, periodically retrieve and transmit data to clients without explicit client requests. Figure 6.6 illustrates these two architectures. From the perspective of retrieving images and image sequences, both architectures have their advantages and disadvantages.

Because its request-response nature, the client-pull architecture is inherently suitable for one-time requests for an image or a portion of an image (e.g., the low-resolution component of a multiresolution image). Adapting the client-pull architecture for retrieving image sequences, however, is difficult. This is because maintaining continuity of playback for an image sequence requires that retrieval requests be issued sufficiently in advance of the playback instant. To do so, applications must estimate the response time of the server and issue requests appropriately. As the response time varies dynamically depending on the server and the network load, client-pull-based applications that access image sequences are nontrivial to develop, [31]. Alternatively, rather than estimating the response time before each request, a client can issue requests based on the worst-case response time; however, such a strategy can significantly increase the client's buffer space requirements. The server-push architecture does not suffer from these disadvantages and therefore is better suited for retrieving image sequences. In such an architecture, the server exploits the sequential nature of data playback by servicing clients in periodic *rounds*. In each round the server determines the amount of data that needs to be retrieved for each client and issues read requests for these clients. Data retrieved in a round is buffered and transmitted to clients in the next round. Because of the round-based nature of data retrieval, clients need not send periodic requests for data retrieval; hence, this architecture is suitable for efficiently retrieving image sequences. The server-push architecture is, however, inappropriate for aperiodic or one-time requests for image data.

Although conventional applications are best efforts in nature, certain image applications need performance guarantees from the storage server. For instance, to maintain continuity of playback for image sequences, a storage server must guarantee that it will retrieve and transmit images at a certain rate. Retrieval of images for applications such as virtual reality impose bounds on the server response time. To provide performance guarantees to such applications, a storage server must employ resource reservation techniques (also referred to as *admission control* algorithms). Typically, such techniques: (*1*) determine the resource requirements for each new client, (*2*) admit the client only if the resource available at the server sufficient to meet its resource requirements. Admission control algorithms can provide either deterministic or statistical guarantees, depending on whether they reserve resources based on the worst-case load or a probability distribution of the load [32,33]. Regardless of the nature of guarantees provided by admission control algorithms, designing such algorithms for the server-push architecture is simple — the sequential and periodic nature of data retrieval enables the server to accurately predict the data rate requirements of each client and reserve resources appropriately. Designing admission control algorithms for client-pull architectures, on the other hand, is challenging (because the aperiodic nature of client requests makes it difficult to determine and characterize the resource requirements of a client).

A fundamental advantage of the client-pull architecture is that it is inherently suitable for supporting adaptive applications with dynamically changing resource availability. This is because with changes in resource availability, the client can alter its request rate to keep pace with the server. For instance, if the load on a central processing unit (CPU) increases or the response time estimates indicate that the network is congested, an adaptive application can reduce its bandwidth requirements by requesting only a subset of data, or by requesting the delivery of a lower-resolution version of the same object. The server-push architecture, on the other hand, does not assume any feedback from the clients. In fact, admission of a client for service constitutes a "contract" between the server and the client: the server guarantees that it will access and transmit sufficient information during each round so as to meet the data rate requirements of the client, and the client guarantees that it will keep pace with the server by consuming all the data transmitted by a server during a round within a round duration. Any change in resource availability or client requirements necessitates a renegotiation of this contract, making the design of the server and adaptive applications more complex.

Finally, regardless of the architecture, all storage servers employ disk scheduling algorithms to improve I/O performance through intelligent scheduling of disk requests. Typically, disk requests issued by video servers have deadlines. Conventional disk scheduling algorithms, such as SCAN and shortest access time first (SATF) [34,35,36], schedule requests based on their physical location on disk (so as to reduce disk seek and rotational latency overheads) and ignore other requirements such as deadlines. To service requests with deadlines, several disk scheduling algorithms have been proposed. The simplest of these scheduling algorithms is earliest deadline first (EDF). EDF schedules requests on the order of their deadlines but ignores the relative positions of requested data on disk. Hence, it can incur significant seek time and rotational latency overhead. This limitation has been addressed by several disk scheduling algorithms, including priority SCAN (PSCAN), earliest deadline SCAN, SCAN-EDF, feasible deadline SCAN (FD-SCAN), and shortest seek earliest deadline by order/value (SSEDO, SSEDV) [29,37,38,39]. These algorithms start from an EDF schedule and reorder requests without violating their deadlines such that the seek time and rotational latency overhead is reduced. In homogeneous environments, depending on the application requirements, a storage server can employ a scheduling algorithm from one of these two classes. Neither class of algorithms is appropriate for heterogeneous computing environments consisting of a mix of best-effort and real-time applications. For such environments, sophisticated disk schedulers that (*1*) support multiple application classes simultaneously, (*2*) allocate disk bandwidth among classes in a predictable manner, and (*3*) align the service provided within each class with application needs are more appropriate[40].

6.4 CACHING AND BATCHING ISSUES

In addition to managing data on disks, a storage server employs an in-memory buffer cache to improve performance. Typically, such a buffer cache is used to store frequently accessed images or image sequences; requests for these objects are then serviced from the cache rather than from disk. Doing so not only improves user response time but also reduces the load on the disk subsystem and increases the number of clients that can be supported by the server. Managing such a cache requires the server to employs a cache replacement policy to decide which objects to replace from the cache and when. Typically, a storage server employs a cache replacement policy such as the *least recently used* (LRU) or the *least frequently used* (LFU) to manage cached image objects. These policies improve cache hit ratios by replacing the least recently accessed object or the object with the least access frequency, respectively. Although such cache replacement policies work well for workloads that exhibit locality, they perform poorly for video workloads, because such objects are predominantly accessed in a sequential manner. Policies such as *interval caching* that are optimized for sequential access workloads are more suitable for such objects [41]. Interval caching requires a server to cache the interval between two users accessing the same multimedia file; the server then services the trailing user using the cached data (thereby saving disk bandwidth for that request). Observe that, in this case, the cache is employed to store subsequences of an object rather than that of entire objects.

Batching is another technique that is frequently employed by storage servers to maximize the number of clients supported. Batching delays a new user request, for a duration referred to as the *batching interval*, with the expectation that more requests for the same multimedia object may arrive within that duration. If multiple requests are indeed received for the same stream within the batching interval then the server can service all the requests by retrieving a single stream from the disks. The longer the batching interval, the larger is the probability of receiving multiple requests for the same stream within the interval and hence larger is the gain due to batching [42]. However, the larger the batching interval, the larger is the start-up latency for requests. Batching policies attempt to find a balance between this trade-off. One approach for reducing the start-up latency is called *piggybacking* (or *catching*). In this technique, requests are serviced immediately on their arrival. However, if the server began servicing a request for the same stream sometime in the recent past, then the server attempts to service the two requests in a manner such that the servicing of the new request catches up with that of the previous request. If this is successful, the server then services both these requests as a single stream from the disks.

Both caching and batching achieve similar goals — that of improving the number of clients supported — but they employ different trade-offs to do so. The former technique trades memory buffers, whereas the latter technique trades user latency to improve the number of clients supported. In certain scenarios, caching can be employed to replace batching — rather than batch multiple requests for the same object, a server may choose to cache an object on its first access and service subsequent requests from the cache. Hybrid schemes that employ a combination of caching and batching can also be employed to further improve server performance.

6.5 ARCHITECTURAL ISSUES

Sections 6.1, 6.2, and 6.3 examined placement, failure recovery, and retrieval techniques that are suitable for image and video servers. In this section, the method of incorporation of these techniques into a general-purpose file system and the implications of doing on the file system architecture is examined.

There are two methodologies for designing file systems that simultaneously support heterogeneous data types and applications: (*1*) a *partitioned* architecture that consists of multiple component file servers, each optimized for a particular data type (and glued together by an integration layer that provides a uniform interface to access these files); and (*2*) an *integrated* architecture that consists of a single file server that stores all data types. Figure 6.7 illustrates these architectures.

Because techniques for building file servers optimized for a single data type are well known [1,43], partitioned file systems are easy to design and implement. In such file systems, resources (disks, buffers) are statically partitioned among component file servers. This causes requests that access, different component servers to access mutually exclusive set of resources, thereby preventing interference between user requests (e.g., servicing best-effort requests does not violate deadlines of real-time requests). The partitioned architecture, however, has the following limitations:

- Static partitioning of resources in such servers is typically governed by the expected workload on each component server. If the observed workload deviates significantly from the expected, then repartitioning of resources may be necessary. Repartitioning of resources such as disks and buffers is tedious and may require the system to be taken off-line [44]. An alternative to repartitioning is to add new resources (e.g., disks) to the server, which causes resources in underutilized partitions to be wasted.

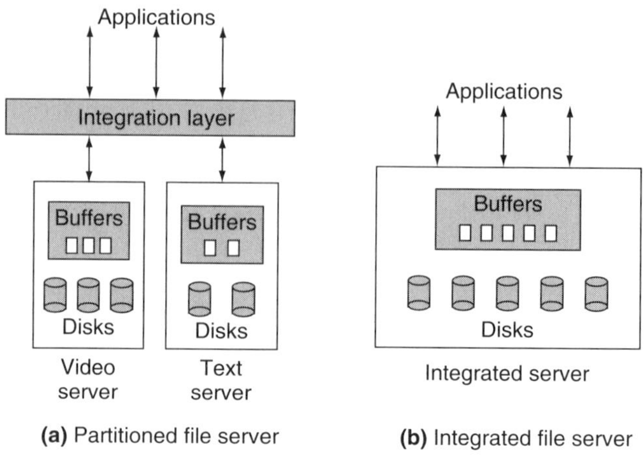

Figure 6.7. Partitioned and integrated file servers supporting text or images and video applications. The partitioned architecture divides the server resources among multiple component file systems and employs an integration layer that provides a uniform mechanism to access files. The integrated architecture employs a single server that multiplexes all the resources among multiple application classes.

- The storage-space requirements of files stored on a component file server can be significantly different from their bandwidth requirements. In such a scenario, allocation of disks to a component server will be governed by the maximum of the two values. This can lead to under-utilization of either storage space or disk bandwidth on the server.

The main feature of the integrated file system architecture is dynamic resource allocation: storage space, disk bandwidth, and buffer space are allocated to data types on demand; static partitioning of these resources is not required. This feature has several benefits. First, by co-locating a set of files with large storage space but small bandwidth requirements with another set of files with small storage space but large bandwidth requirements, this architecture yields better resource utilization. Second, because resources are allocated on demand, this architecture can easily accommodate dynamic changes in access patterns. Finally, because all the resources are shared by all applications, more resources are available to service each request, which in turn improves the performance.

Such improvements in the resource utilization, however, come at the expense of increased complexity in the design of the file system. This is because wide disparity in the applications or data requirements dictate that a single storage management technique or policy is often inadequate to meet the requirements of all applications and data types. For instance, the best-effort service model, although adequate for many applications, is clearly unsuitable for applications and data types that impose timeliness constraints. Consequently, a key principle in designing integrated file systems is that they should enable the coexistence of multiple data type–specific and application-specific policies. For instance, to align the service it provides to the needs of individual data types, an integrated file system should enable the coexistence of data type–specific policies for common file system tasks such as placement, metadata management, caching, and failure recovery. Similarly, it should support multiple retrieval policies, such as client-pull and server-push, as well as multiple application classes with different performance requirements, such as best-effort, soft real time, and throughput-intensive (interactive applications need low average response times, real-time applications need bounds on their response times, whereas throughput-intensive applications need high aggregate throughput). Enabling the co-existence of such diverse techniques requires the development of mechanisms that achieve high resource utilization through sharing, at the same time isolating the service exported to the different application classes [45].

Figure 6.8 depicts a two-layer architecture for implementing such an integrated file system. This architecture separates data type–independant and application independent mechanisms from specific policies and implements these mechanisms and policies in separate layers. The lower layer implements core file system mechanisms for placement, retrieval, caching, and metadata management that are required for all applications and data types. The upper layer then employs these mechanisms to instantiate specific polices each tailored for a particular data type or an application class; multiple policies can coexist because the mechanisms in the lower layer are designed to multiplex resources among various classes. To illustrate, in case of placement, the lower layer may consist of a storage manager that can allocate a disk block of any size, whereas the upper layer uses the storage manager to instantiate different placement policies for different data types. A placement policy for video, for instance, might stripe all files and use a stripe unit size of 64 KB to do so, whereas that for text might choose a block size of 4 KB and store all blocks of a file on a single disk. In case of retrieval, the disk scheduling mechanisms exported by the lower layer should allow the upper layer to implement different retrieval policies — the server-push retrieval policy for video files and the client-pull policy for textual and image files. Similarly, the mechanisms exported by the buffer manager in the lower layer should enable different cache replacement policies to be instantiated in the upper layer (e.g., the

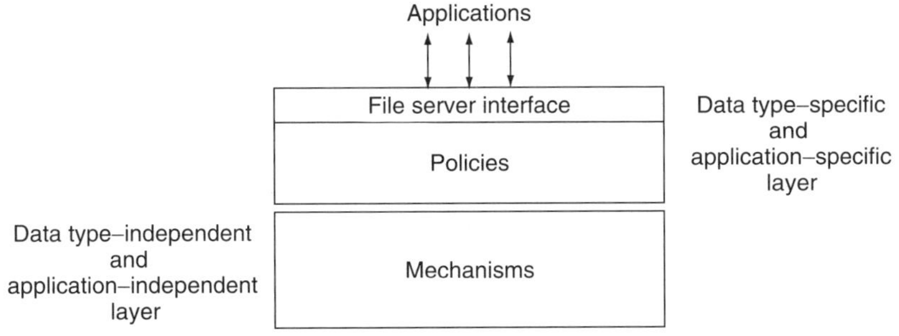

Figure 6.8. A two-layer file system architecture that separates mechanisms from policies.

LRU policy for text and image files, interval caching for video files). Observe that such a two layer architecture is inherently extensible — implementing a powerful set of mechanisms in the lower layer enables new application and data types to be supported by adding appropriate policies to the upper layer.

Although the storage servers employing the partitioned architecture were common in the early 1990s (due to the concurrent and independent development of conventional file systems and video-on-demand servers), integrated file systems have received significant attention recently. Several research projects, such as Symphony [45], Fellini [46] and Nemesis [47], as well as commercial efforts, such as IBM's Tiger Shark [30] and SGI's XFS [44], have resulted in storage servers employing an integrated architecture.

6.6 CONCLUSION

Emerging multimedia applications differ from conventional distributed applications in the type of data they store, transmit, and process, and also in the requirements they impose on the networks and operating systems. In this chapter, the focus was on the problem of designing storage servers that can meet the requirements of these emerging applications. The techniques for designing a storage server for digital imagery and video streams were described and then the architectural issues in incorporating these techniques into a general-purpose file system was examined.

We conclude by noting that a quality-of-service (QoS) aware file system is just one piece of the end-to-end infrastructure required to support emerging distributed applications; to provide applications with the services they require, such file systems will need to be integrated with appropriate networks and operating systems.

REFERENCES

1. M.K. McKusick et al., A fast file system for UNIX, *ACM Trans. Comput. Syst.* **2**(3), 181–197 (1984).
2. F.A. Tobagi et al., Streaming RAID — a disk array management system for video files, *Proceedings of ACM Multimedia'93*, Anaheim, Calif., 1993, pp. 393–400.
3. H. Garcia-Molina and K. Salem, Disk striping, *International Conference on Data Engineering* (ICDE), Los Angeles, Calif., February 1986, pp. 336–342.
4. E. Chang and A. Zakhor, Scalable video placement on parallel disk arrays, *Proceedings of IS & T/SPIE International Symposium on Electronic Imaging: Science and Technology*, San Jose, Calif., February 1994.
5. S. Paek, P. Bocheck, and S.F. Chang, Scalable MPEG2 video servers with heterogeneous QoS on parallel disk arrays, *Proceedings of the 5th International Workshop on Network and Operating System Support for Digital Audio and Video*, Durham, NH, April 1995, pp. 363–374.

6. H.M. Vin, S.S. Rao, and P. Goyal, Optimizing the placement of multimedia objects on disk arrays. *Proceedings of the 2nd IEEE International Conference on Multimedia Computing and Systems*, Washington, D.C., May 1995, pp. 158–165.
7. Robert M. Geist and Kishor S. Trivedi, *Optimal Design of Multilevel Storage Hierarchies*, **C-31**, 249–260, (1982).
8. B.K. Hillyer and A. Silberschatz, On the modeling and performance characteristics of a serpentine tape drive, *Proceedings of ACM Sigmetrics Conference*, Philadelphia, Pa. May 1996, pp. 170–179.
9. J. Menon and K. Treiber, *Daisy: Virtual Disk Hierarchical Storage Manager*, **25**(3), 37–44 (1997).
10. S. Ranade, ed,. *Jukebox and Robotic Tape Libraries for Mass Storage*, Meckler Publishing, London, U.K., 1992.
11. A. Drapeau, Striped Tertiary Storage Systems: *Performance and reliability*, PhD thesis, University of California, Berkeley, Calif. 1993.
12. A.L. Drapeau and R.H. Katz, Striping in large tape libraries, *Proceedings of Supercomputing '93*, Portland, Ore., November 1993, pp. 378–387.
13. P. Cao et al., The TickerTAIP parallel RAID architecture, *Proceedings of the 20th International Symposium on Computer Architecture* (ISCA), San Diego, Calif., May 1993, pp. 52–63.
14. J. Menon and J. Cortney, The Architecture of a fault-tolerant cached RAID controller, *Proceedings of the 20th International Symposium on Computer Architecture* (ISCA), San Diego, Calif., May 1993. pp. 76–86.
15. D. Bitton and J. Gray, Disk shadowing, *Proceedings of the 14th Conference on Very Large Databases*, Los Angeles, Calif., 1988, pp. 331–338.
16. G. Gibson and D. Patterson, Designing disk arrays for high data reliability, *J. Parallel Distrib. Comput.*, **17**(1–2), 4–27 (1993).
17. D. Patterson, G. Gibson, and R. Katz, A case for redundant array of inexpensive disks (RAID), *Proceedings of ACM SIGMOD '88*, Chicago, Ill., June 1988, pp. 109–116.
18. J. Gray, B. Horst, and M. Walker, Parity striping of disc arrays: low-cost reliable storage with acceptable throughput, *Proceedings of the 16th Very Large Data Bases Conference*, Brisbane, Australia, 1990, pp. 148–160.
19. E.K. Lee and R. Katz, Performance Consequences of Parity Placement in Disk Arrays, *Proceedings of the International Conference on Architectural Support for Programming Languages and Operating Systems* (ASPLOS-IV), Santa Clara, Calif., 1991, pp. 190–199.
20. M. Holland, G. Gibson, and D. Siewiorek, Fast, on-line recovery in redundant disk arrays, *Proceedings of the 23rd International Symposium on Fault Tolerant Computing* (FTCS), Toulouse, France, 1993, pp. 422–431.
21. M. Holland and G. Gibson, Parity declustering for continuous operation in redundant disk arrays, *Proceedings of the 5th International Conference on Architectural Support for Programming Languages and Operating Systems (ASPLOS-V)*, Boston, Mass., October pp. 23–35. 1992.
22. A. Merchant and P.S. Yu, Design and Modeling of Clustered RAID, *Proceedings of the International Symposium on Fault Tolerant Computing*, Boston, Mass., 1992, pp. 140–149.

23. R.R. Muntz and J.C.S. Lui, Performance analysis of disk arrays under failure, *Proceedings of the 16th Very Large Data Bases Conference*, Brisbane, Australia, 1990, pp. 162–173.
24. E.J. Posnak, et al., Techniques for resilient transmission of JPEG video streams, *Proceedings of Multimedia Computing and Networking*, San Jose, Calif., February 1995, pp. 243–252.
25. C.J. Turner and L.L. Peterson, Image transfer: an end-to-end design, *Proceedings of ACM SIGCOMM'92*, Baltimore, August 1992, pp. 258–268.
26. J.M. Danskin, G.M. Davies, and X. Song, Fast lossy internet image transmission, *Proceedings of the 3rd ACM Conference on Multimedia*, San Francisco, Calif., November 1995, pp. 321–332.
27. H.M. Vin, et al., P.J. Shenoy, and S. Rao, Efficient failure recovery in multidisk multimedia servers. *Proceedings of the 25th International Symposium on fault tolerant computing systems*, Pasadena, Calif., June1995, pp. 12–21.
28. W.B. Pennebaker and J.L. Mitchell, *JPEG Still Image Data Compression Standard*, Van Nostrand Reinhold, New York, 1993.
29. R.K. Abbott and H. Garcia-Molina, Scheduling I/O requests with deadlines: a performance evaluation, *Proceedings of IEEE Real-time Systems Symposium (RTSS)*, Lake Buena Vista, Fla., December 1990, pp. 113–124.
30. R. Haskin, Tiger shark-a scalable file system for multimedia, *IBM J. Res. Dev.*, **42**(2), 185–197, (1998).
31. S.S. Rao, H.M. Vin, and A. Tarafdar, Comparative evaluation of server-push and client-pull architectures for multimedia servers, *Proceedings of NOSSDAV '96*, Zushi, Japan, April 1996, pp. 45–48.
32. H.M. Vin et al., A statistical admission control algorithm for multimedia servers, *Proceedings of the ACM Multimedia'94*, San Francisco, Calif., October 1994, pp. 33–40.
33. H.M. Vin, A. Goyal, and P. Goyal, Algorithms for designing large-scale multimedia servers, *Comput. Commun.*, **18**(3), 192–203, (1995).
34. T. Teorey and T.B. Pinkerton, *A comparative analysis of disk scheduling policies, Commun. ACM* **15**(3), 177–184 (1972).
35. D.M. Jacobson and J. Wilkes, Disk scheduling algorithms based on rotational position, Technical report, Hewlett Packard Labs, HPL-CSP-91-7, 1991.
36. M. Seltzer, P. Chen, and J. Ousterhout, Disk scheduling revisited, *Proceedings of the 1990 Winter USENIX Conference*, Washington, D.C., January 1990, pp. 313–323.
37. S. Chen et al., Performance evaluation of two new disk scheduling algorithms for real-time systems, *J. Real-Time Syst.*, **3**, 307–336 (1991).
38. A.L. Narasimha Reddy and J. Wyllie, Disk scheduling in multimedia I/O system, *Proceedings of ACM Multimedia'93*, Anaheim, Calif., August 1993, pp. 225–234.
39. P. Yu, M.S. Chen, and D.D. Kandlur, Design and analysis of a grouped sweeping scheme for multimedia storage management, *Proceedings of 3rd International Workshop on Network and Operating System Support for Digital Audio and Video*, San Diego, November 1992, pp. 38–49.
40. P Shenoy and H M. Vin, Cello: a disk scheduling framework for next generation operating systems, *Proceedings of ACM SIGMETRICS Conference*, Madison, Wis, June1998, pp. 44–55.

41. A. Dan and D. Sitaram, A generalized interval caching policy for mixed interactive and long video workloads, *Proceedings of Multimedia Computing and Networking (MMCN) Conference*, San Jose, Calif., 1996, pp. 344–351.

42. A. Dan, D. Sitaram, and P. Shahabuddin, Scheduling policies for an on-demand video server with batching, *Proceedings of the 2nd ACM International Conference on Multimedia*, San Fransisco, Calif., October 1994, pp. 15–23.

43. M. Vernick, C. Venkatramini, and T. Chiueh, Adventures in building the stony brook video server, *Proceedings of ACM Multimedia '96*, Boston, Mass., 1996.

44. M. Holton and R. Das, XFS: a next generation journalled 64-bit file system with guaranteed rate I/O, Technical report, Silicon Graphics 1996; http://oss.sgi.com/projects/xfs/publications.html

45. P.J. Shenoy et al., Symphony: an integrated multimedia file system, *Proceedings of the SPIE/ACM Conference on Multimedia Computing and Networking (MMCN'98)*, San Jose, Calif, January 1998, pp. 124–138.

46. C. Martin et al., The Fellini multimedia storage server in. *Multimedia Information Storage and Management*, S.M. Chung, ed., Kluwer Academic Publishers, Norwell, Mass. 1996.

47. Timothy Roscoe, *The Structure of a Multi-service Operating System.* PhD thesis, University of Cambridge Computer Laboratory, Cambridge, U.K., 1995; Available as Technical Report No. 376.

7 Database Support for Multimedia Applications

MICHAEL ORTEGA-BINDERBERGER, KAUSHIK CHAKRABARTI
University of Illinois at Urbana–Champaign, Illinois

SHARAD MEHROTRA
University of California, Irvine California

7.1 INTRODUCTION

Advances in high-performance computing, communication, and storage technologies, as well as emerging large-scale multimedia applications, have made the design and development of multimedia information systems one of the most challenging and important directions of research and development within computer science. The payoffs of a multimedia infrastructure are tremendous — it enables many multibillion dollar-a-year application areas. Examples are medical information systems, electronic commerce, digital libraries (such as multimedia data repositories for training, education, broadcast, and entertainment), special-purpose databases, (such as face or fingerprint databases for security), and geographic information systems storing satellite images, maps, and so forth.

An integral component of the multimedia infrastructure is a *multimedia database management system*. Such a system supports mechanisms to extract and represent the content of multimedia objects, provides efficient storage of the content in the database, supports content-based queries over multimedia objects, and provides a seamless integration of the multimedia objects with the traditional information stored in existing databases. A multimedia database system consists of multiple components, which provide the following functionalities:

- *Multimedia Object Representation.* Techniques or models to succinctly represent both structure and content of multimedia objects in databases.
- *Content Extraction.* Mechanisms to automatically or semiautomatically extract meaningful features that capture the content of multimedia objects and that can be indexed to support retrieval.

Image Databases: Search and Retrieval of Digital Imagery, Edited by Vittorio Castelli and Lawrence D. Bergman.
ISBN 0-471-32116-8

- *Multimedia Information Retrieval.* Techniques to match and retrieve multimedia objects on the basis of the similarity of their representation (i.e., similarity-based retrieval).
- *Multimedia Database Management.* Extensions to data management technologies of indexing and query processing to effectively support efficient content-based retrieval in database management systems.

Many of these issues have been extensively addressed in other chapters of this book. Our focus in this chapter is on how content-based retrieval of multimedia objects can be integrated into database management systems as a primary access mechanism. In this context, we first explore the support provided by existing object-oriented and object-relational systems for building multimedia applications. We then identify limitations of existing systems in supporting content-based retrieval and summarize approaches proposed to address these limitations. We believe that this research will culminate in improved data management products that support multimedia objects as "first-class" objects, capable of being efficiently stored and retrieved on the basis of their internal content.

The rest of the chapter is organized as follows. In Section 7.2, we describe a simple model for content-based retrieval of multimedia objects, which is widely implemented and commonly supported by commercial vendors. We use this model throughout the chapter to explain the issues that arise in integrating content-based retrieval into database management systems (DBMSs). In Section 7.3, we explore how the evolution of relational databases into object-oriented and object-relational systems, which support complex data types and user-defined functions, facilitates the building of multimedia applications [1]. We apply the analysis framework of Section 7.3 to the Oracle, the Informix, and the IBM DB2 database systems in Section 7.4. The chapter then identifies limitations of existing state-of-the-art data management systems from the perspective of supporting multimedia applications. Finally, Section 7.5 outlines a set of research issues and approaches that are crucial for the development of next-generation database technology that will provide seamless support for complex multimedia information.

7.2 A MODEL FOR CONTENT-BASED RETRIEVAL

Traditionally, content-based retrieval from multimedia databases was supported by describing multimedia objects with textual annotations [2–5]. Textual information retrieval techniques [6–9] were then used to search for multimedia information indirectly using the annotations. Such a *text-based approach* suffers from numerous limitations, including the impossibility of scaling it to large data sets (because of the high degree of manual effort required to produce the annotations), the difficulty of expressing visual content (e.g., texture or patterns or shape in an image) using textual annotations, and the subjectivity of manually generated annotations.

To overcome several of these limitations, a *visual feature–based approach* has emerged as a promising alternative, as is evidenced by several prototype [10–12] and commercial systems [13–17]. In a visual feature–based approach, a multimedia object is represented using visual properties; for example, a digital photograph may be represented using color, texture, shape, and textual features. Typically, a user formulates a query by providing examples and the system returns the "most similar" objects in the database. The retrieval consists of ranking the similarity between the feature-space representations of the query and of the images in the database. The query process can therefore be described by defining the models for objects, queries, and retrieval.

7.2.1 Object Model

A multimedia object is represented as a collection of extracted features. Each feature may have multiple representations, capturing it from different perspectives. For instance, the color histogram [18] descriptor represents the color distribution in an image using value counts, whereas the color moments [19] descriptor represents the color distribution in an image using statistical parameters (e.g., mean, variance, and skewness). Associated with each representation is a similarity function that determines the similarity between two descriptor values. Different representations capture the same feature from different perspectives. The simultaneous use of different representations often improves retrieval effectiveness [11], but it also increases the dimensionality of the search space, which reduces retrieval efficiency, and has the potential for introducing redundancy, which can negatively affect effectiveness.

Each feature space (e.g., a color histogram space) can be viewed as a multidimensional space, in which a feature vector representing an object corresponds to a point. A metric on the feature space can be used to define the dissimilarity between the corresponding feature vectors. Distance values are then converted to similarity values. Two popular conversion formulae are $s = 1 - d$[1] and $s = \exp(-d^2/2)$, where s and d denote similarity and distance, respectively. With the first formula, if d is measured using the *Euclidean distance function*, s becomes the *cosine similarity* between the vectors, whereas if d is measured using the *Manhattan distance function*, s becomes the *histogram intersection similarity* between them. Although cosine similarity is widely used in key word–based document retrieval, histogram-intersection similarity is common for color histograms. A number of image features and feature-matching functions are further described in Chapters 8 to 19.

7.2.2 Query Model

The query model specifies how a query is constructed and structured. Much like multimedia objects, a query is represented as a collection of features. One

[1] The conversion formula assumes that the space is normalized to guarantee that the maximum distance between points is equal to 1.

difference is that a user may simultaneously use multiple example objects, in which case the query can be represented in either of the following two ways [20]:

- *Feature-Based Representation.* The query is represented as a collection of features. Each feature contains a collection of feature representations with multiple values. Each value corresponds to a specific feature descriptor of a particular object.
- *Object-Based Representation.* A query is represented as a collection of objects and each object consists of a collection of feature descriptors.

In either case, each component of a query is associated with a weight indicating its relative importance.

Figure 7.1 shows a structure of a query tree in an object-based model. In the figure, the query structure consists of multiple objects O_i, and each object is represented as a collection of multiple-feature values R_{ij}.

7.2.3 Retrieval Model

The retrieval model determines the similarity between a query tree and the objects in the database. The leaf level of the tree corresponds to feature representations. A similarity function specific to a given representation is used to evaluate the similarity between a leaf node (R_{ij}) and the corresponding feature representation of the objects in the database. Assume, for example, that the leaf nodes of a query tree correspond to two different color representations—color histogram and color moments. Although histogram intersection [18] may be used to evaluate the similarity between the color histogram of an object and that of the query, the weighted Euclidean distance metric may be used to compute the similarity between the color moments descriptor of an object and that of the query. The matching (or retrieval) process at the feature representation level produces one ranked list of results for each leaf of the query tree. These ranked lists are combined using a combining function to generate a ranked list describing the match results at the parent node. Different functions may be used to merge ranked lists at different nodes of the query tree, resulting in different retrieval

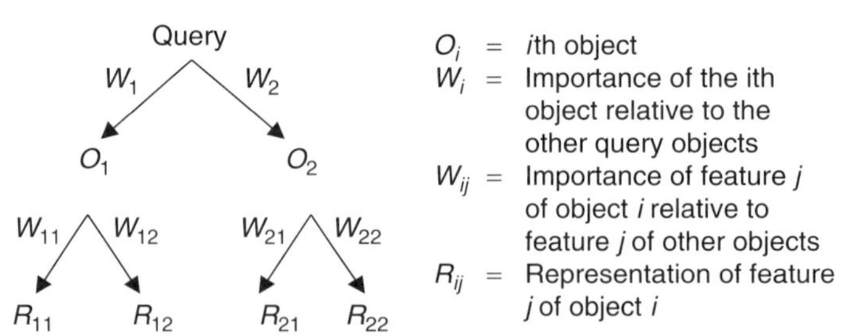

Figure 7.1. Query model.

models. A common technique used is the *weighted summation model*. Let a node N_i in the query tree have children N_{i1} to N_{in}. The similarity of an object O in the database with node N_i (represented as $similarity_i$) is computed as:

$$similarity_i = \sum_{j=1}^{n} w_{ij}\ similarity_{ij}$$

$$\text{where } \sum_{j=1}^{n} w_{ij} = 1 \tag{7.1}$$

and $similarity_{ij}$ is the measure of similarity of the object with the jth child of node N_i.

Many other retrieval models to generate overall similarity between an object and a query have been explored. For example, in Ref. [21], a Boolean model suitably extended with fuzzy and probabilistic interpretations is used to combine ranked lists. A Boolean operator — AND ($\wedge$), OR ($\vee$), NOT ($\neg$) — is associated with each node of the query tree, and the similarity is interpreted as a fuzzy value or a probability and combined with suitable merge functions. Desirable properties of such merge functions are studied by Fagin and Wimmers in Ref. [22].

7.2.4 Extensions

In the previous section, we have described a simple model for content-based retrieval that will serve as the base reference in the remainder of the chapter. Many extensions are possible and have been proposed. For example, we have implicitly assumed that the user provides appropriate weights for nodes at each level of the query tree (reflecting the importance of a given feature or node to the user's information need [6]). In practice, however, it is difficult for a user to specify the precise weights. An approach followed in some research prototypes (e.g., MARS [11], MindReader [23]) is to learn these weights automatically using the process of *relevance feedback* [20,24,25]. Relevance feedback is used to modify the query representation by altering the weights and structure of the query tree to better reflect the user's subjective information need.

Another limitation of our reference model is that it focuses on representation and content-based retrieval of images — it has limited ability to represent structural, spatial, or temporal properties of general multimedia objects, (e.g., multiple synchronized audio and video streams) and to model retrieval based on these properties. Even in the context of image retrieval, the model described needs to be appropriately extended to support a more structured retrieval based on local or region-based properties. Retrieval based on local region-specific properties and the spatial relationships between the regions has been studied in many prototypes including Refs. [26–30].

7.3 OVERVIEW OF CURRENT DATABASE TECHNOLOGY

In this section, we explore how multimedia applications requiring content-based retrieval can be built using existing commercial data management systems. Traditionally, relational database technology has been geared toward business applications, in which data is mostly represented in tabular form with simple atomic attributes. Relational systems usually support only a handful of data types — a numeric type with its usual variations in precision[2], a text type with some variations in the assumptions about the storage space available[3], some temporal data types, such as date and time with some variations[4]. Providing support for multimedia objects in relational database systems poses many challenges. First, in contrast to the limited storage requirements of traditional data types, multimedia data, such as images, video, and audio are quite voluminous — a single record may span several pages. One alternative is to store the multimedia data in files outside the DBMS control with only *pointers* or references to the multimedia object stored in the DBMS. This approach has numerous limitations because it makes the task of optimizing access to data difficult, and, furthermore, prevents DBMS access control over multimedia types. An alternative solution is to store the multimedia data in databases as *binary large objects* (BLOBs), which are supported by almost all commercial systems. BLOB is a data type used for data that does not fit into one of the standard categories, because of its large size or its widely variable length, or because the only needed operation is storage, rather than interpretation, analysis, or manipulation.

Although modern databases provide effective mechanisms to store very large multimedia objects in a BLOB, BLOBs are uninterpreted sequences of bytes, which cannot represent the rich internal structure of multimedia data. Such a structure can be represented in a DBMS using the support for user-defined abstract data types (ADTs) offered by modern object-oriented and object-relational databases. Such systems also provide support for user-defined functions (UDFs) or methods, which can be used to implement similarity retrieval for multimedia types. Similarity models, implemented as UDFs, can be called from within structured query language (SQL), allowing content-based retrieval to be seamlessly integrated into the database query language. In the remaining section we discuss the support for ADTs, UDFs, and BLOBs in modern databases that provides the core technology for building multimedia database applications.

---

[2] Typically, numeric data can be of integral type, fractional data, such as floating point in various precisions, and specialized money types, such as packed decimal, that retained high precision for detailed money transactions.

[3] Notably, the *char* data type specifies a maximum length of a character string and this space is always reserved. *Varchar* data in contrast occupies only the needed space for the stored character string and also has a maximum length.

[4] Variations of temporal data types include *time*, *date*, *datetime* sometimes with a precision specification, such as year down to hours, *timestamp* used to mark a specific time for an event, and *interval* to indicate the length of time.

7.3.1 User-Defined Abstract Data Types

The basic relational model requires tables to be in the first normal form [31], where every attribute is atomic. This poses serious limitations in supporting applications that deal with objects or data types with rich internal structure. The only recourse is to translate between the complex structure of the applications and the relational model every time an object is read or written. This results in extensive overhead, which makes the relational approach unsuitable for advanced applications that require support for complex data types.

These limitations of relational systems have resulted in much research and commercial development to extend the database functionality with rich user-defined data types in order to accommodate the needs of advanced applications. Research in extending the relational database technology has proceeded along two parallel directions.

The first approach, referred to as the *object-oriented database* (OODBMS) approach, attempts to enrich object-oriented languages, such as C++ and Smalltalk, with the desirable features of databases, such as concurrency control, recovery, and security, while retaining support for the rich data types and semantics of object-oriented languages. Examples of systems that have followed this approach include research prototypes such as in Ref. [32] and a number of commercial products [33,34].

The object-relational database (ORDBMS) systems, on the other hand, approach the problem of adding additional data types by extending the existing relational model with the full-blown type hierarchy of object-oriented languages. The key observation was that the concept of domain of an attribute need not be restricted to simple data types. Given its foundation in the relational model, the ORDBMS approach can be considered a less radical evolution than the OODBMS approach. The ORDBMS approach produced such research prototypes as Postgres [35] and Starburst [36] and commercial products such as Illustra [1]. The ORDBMS technology has now been embraced by all major vendors including Informix [37], IBM DB2 [38], Oracle [39], Sybase [40], and UniSQL [41] among others. The ORDBMS model has been incorporated in the SQL-3 standards.

Although OODBMSs provide the full power of an object-oriented language, they have lost ground to ORDBMSs. Interested readers are referred to Ref. [1] for insight into reasons for this development from both a technical and commercial perspective. In the following section of this chapter, we will concentrate on the ORDBMS approach.

The object-relational model retains relational model concepts of tables and columns in tables. Besides the basic types, it provides for additional user-defined ADTs and for collections of basic and user-defined types. The functions that operate on these ADTs, known as UDFs are written by the user and are equivalent to methods in the object-oriented context. In the object-relational model, the fields of a table may correspond to basic DBMS data types, to other ADTs, or can even just contain storage space whose interpretation is entirely left to the user-defined methods for the type [37]. The following example illustrates how a user may create an ADT and include it in a table definition:

```
create type ImageInfoType ( date varchar(12) ,
                            location_latitude real ,
                            location_longitude real )

create table SurveyPhotos ( photo_id integer
                            primary key not null,
                            photographer varchar(50)
                            not null,
                            photo blob not null,
                            photo_location
                            ImageInfoType not null)
```

The type *ImageInfoType* defines a structure for storing the location at which a photograph was taken, together with the date stored as a string. This can be useful for nature survey applications wherein a biologist may wish to attach a geographic location and a date to a photograph. This abstract data type is then used to create a table with an id for the photograph, the photographer's name, the photograph itself (stored as a BLOB), and the location and date when it was taken.

ORDBMSs extend the basic SQL language to allow UDFs (once they are compiled and registered with the DBMS) to be called directly from within SQL queries, thereby providing a natural mechanism for developing domain-specific extensions to databases. The following example shows a sample query that calls a UDF on the type declared earlier:

```
select photographer, convert_to_grayscale(photo)
       from SurveyPhotos
       where within_distance(photo_location,
                             '1', '30.45, -127.0')
```

This query returns the photographer and a gray scale version of the image stored in the table. The *within_distance* UDF is a predicate that returns "true" if the place where the image was shot is within 1 mile of the given location. This UDF ignores the date on which the picture was taken, demonstrating how predicates are free to implement any semantically significant properties of an application. Note that the UDF *convert_to_grayscale*, which converts the image to gray scale, is not a predicate because it is applied to an attribute in the *select* clause and returns a gray scale image.

ADTs also provide for type inheritance and, as a consequence, polymorphism. This introduces some problems in the storage of ADTs, as existing storage mangers assume that all rows in a table share the same structure. Several strategies have been developed to cope with this problem [42], including dynamic interpretation, and using distinct physical tables for each possible type of a larger, logical table. Section 7.5.1 contains more details on this topic.

7.3.2 Binary Large Objects

As mentioned previously, BLOBs are used for data that does not fit into any of the conventional data types supported by a DBMS. BLOBs are used as a data type for objects that are either large, have wildly varying size, cannot be represented by a traditional data type, or whose data might be corrupted by character table translation[5]. Two main characteristics set BLOBs apart from other data types: they are stored separately from the record [43] and their data type is just a string of bytes.

BLOBs are stored separately owing to their size: if placed in-line with the record, they could span multiple pages and hence introduce loss of clustering in the table storage. Furthermore, applications frequently choose only to access other attributes and not BLOBs — or to access BLOBs selectively on the basis of other attributes. Indeed, BLOBs have a different access pattern than other attributes. As observed in Ref. [44], it is unreasonable to assume that applications will read and/or update all the bytes belonging to a BLOB at once. It is more reasonable to assume that only portions or substrings (byte or bit) will be read or updated during individual operations. To cope with such an access pattern, many DBMSs distinguish between two types of BLOBs:

- *Regular BLOBs*, in which the application receives the whole data in a host variable all at once, and
- *Smart BLOBs*, in which the application receives a handle and uses it to read from the BLOB using the well-known file system interfaces *open*, *close*, *read*, *write*, and *seek*. This allows fine-grained access to the BLOB.

Besides these two mechanisms to deliver BLOBs from the database to applications (i.e., either through whole chunks or through a file interface), a third option of a streaming interface is also possible. Such an interface is important for guaranteing timely delivery of continuous media objects, such as audio or video. Currently, to the best of our knowledge, no DBMS offers a streaming interface to BLOBs. Continuous media objects are stored outside the DBMSs in specialized storage servers [45] and accessed from applications directly and not through a database interface. This may, however, change with the increasing importance of continuous media data in enterprise computing.

BLOBs present an additional challenge. Unless a BLOB is part of a query predicate, it is best to avoid the inclusion of the corresponding column during query processing, to save an extra file access and, more importantly, to prevent

[5] Most DBMSs support data types that could be used to store objects of miscellaneous types. For example, a small image icon can be represented using a *varchar* type. The icon would be stored in-line with the record instead of separately (as would be the case if the image icon is stored as a BLOB). Even though there may be performance benefits from storing the icon in-line (say it is very frequently accessed), it may still not be desirable to store it as a *varchar* since the icon may get corrupted in transmission and interpretation across different hardware (because of the differences in character set representation across different machines). Such data types, sensitive to character translation, should be stored as BLOBs.

thrashing of the database buffers resulting from the large size of BLOBs. For this reason, BLOB handles are often used, and when the user requests the BLOB content, separate database buffers are used to complete this transfer.

For access control purposes, BLOBs are treated as a single atomic field in a record. Large BLOBs could, in principle, be shared by multiple users, but the most fine-grained locking unit in current databases is a tuple (or row) lock, which simultaneously locks all the fields inside the tuple, including the BLOBs. Some of the SQL extensions needed to support parallel operations from applications into database systems are discussed in Ref. [46].

7.3.3 Support for Extensible Indexing

Although user-defined ADTs and UDFs provide adequate modeling power to implement advanced applications with complex data types, the existing access methods that support the traditional relational model (i.e., B-tree and hashing) may not provide for efficient retrieval of these data types. Consider, for example, a data type corresponding to the geographic location of an object. A spatial data structure such as an R-tree [47] or a grid file [48] might provide much more efficient retrieval of objects based on spatial location than a collection of B-trees, each indexing separate spatial dimensions. Access methods that exploit the semantics of the data type may reduce the cost of retrieval. As discussed in Chapters 14 and 15, this is certainly true for multimedia types such as images, in which features (e.g., color, texture, and shape) used to model image content correspond to high-dimensional feature spaces. Retrieval of multimedia objects based on similarity in these feature spaces cannot be adequately supported using B-trees or, for that matter, common multidimensional data structures such as R-trees and region quad-trees that are currently supported by certain commercial DBMSs. Specialized access methods (Chapters 14 and 15) need to be incorporated into the DBMS to support efficient content-based retrieval of multimedia objects.

Commercial ORDBMS vendors support extensible access methods [49,50] because it is not feasible to provide native support for all possible type-specific indexing mechanisms. These type-specific access methods can then be used by the query processor to access data (i.e. implement type-specific UDFs) efficiently. Although these systems support extensibility at the level of access methods, the interface exported for this purpose is at a fairly low level and requires that access method implementors write their own code to pack records into pages, maintain links between pages, handle physical consistency as well as concurrency control for the access method and so on. This makes access method integration a daunting task. Other (cleaner) approaches to adding new type-specific access methods are currently a topic of active research [51] and will be discussed in Section 7.5.2.3.

7.3.4 Integrating External Data Sources

Many data sources are external to database systems, therefore it is important to extend querying capabilities to such data. This can be accomplished by providing a relational interface to external data — making it look like tables, or by storing external data in the database while maintaining an external interface for traditional applications to access the data. These two approaches are discussed next in more detail.

External data can be made to appear as an internal database table by registering UDFs that access resources external to the database server, even including remote services such as search engines, remote servers, and so forth. For example, Informix has extended its Universal Server to offer the capability of "Virtual Tables" (VTI), in which the user defines a set of functions designed to access an external entity and make it appear to be a normal relational table that is suitable for searching and updating. Similarly, DB2 uses table functions and special SQL *TABLE* operators to simulate the existence of an internal table. The primary aim of the table functions is to access external search engines to assist DB2 in computing the answers for a query. A detailed discussion of their support is found in Ref. [52].

Another approach to integrate external data is based on the realization that much unstructured data (up to 90 percent) resides outside of DBMSs. This led several vendors to develop a way to extend their database offerings to incorporate such external data into the database while maintaining its current functional characteristics intact. IBM developed an extension to their DB2 database called *Datalinks*, in which a DBMS table can contain a column that is an "external file." This file is accessible by the table it logically resides in and through the traditional file system interface. Users have the illusion of interacting with a file system with traditional file system commands while the data is stored under DBMS control. In this way, traditional applications can still access their data files without restrictions and enjoy the recovery and protection benefits of the DBMS. This functionality implies protection against data corruption.

Similarly, the Oracle Internet File System [53,54] addresses the same problem by modifying the file system to store files in database tables as BLOBs. The Oracle Internet File System is of interest here because it allows normal users, including web servers, to access images through file system interfaces, while retaining all DBMS advantages.

These advantages translate into small changes to existing delivery infrastructure such as web servers and text-processing programs, while retaining advanced functionality including searching, storage management, and scalability.

7.3.5 Commercial Extensions to DBMSs

We have discussed the evolution of the traditional relational model to modern extensible database technology that supports user-defined ADTs and functions and the ability to call such functions from SQL. These extensions provide a powerful mechanism for third-party vendors to develop domain-specific extensions to the basic database management system. Such extensions are called *Datablades* in Informix, *Data Cartridges* in Oracle, and *Extenders* in DB2. Many datablades are commercially available for the Informix Universal Server — some of which are shipped as standard packages whereas others can be purchased separately. Examples of datablades include the *Geodetic datablade* that supports all the important data types and functions for geospatial applications and includes an R-tree implementation for indexing spatio-temporal data types. Other available datablades include the Time series Datablade for time-varying numeric data such as stocks, the Web Datablade that provides a tight coupling between the database server and a web server and a Video Foundation Datablade to handle video files. Similar cartridges and extenders are also available for Oracle and DB2, respectively.

Besides commercially available datablades, cartridges, or extenders, users can develop their own domain-specific extensions. For this purpose, each DBMS supports an API that a programmer must conform to in developing the extensions. Details of the API offered by Informix can be found in Ref. [55]. The API supported by Oracle (referred to as the Oracle Data Cartridge Interface (ODCI)) is discussed in Ref. [56].

Although each of the different systems (i.e., Informix, Oracle, and DB2) support the notion of extensibility, they differ somewhat in the degree of control and protection offered. Informix supports extensibility at a low level with very fine-grained access to the database server. There are a considerable number of hooks into the server to customize many aspects of query processing. For example, for predicates involving UDFs over user-defined types[6], the predicate functions have access to the conditions in the where clause itself. This level of access allows for very flexible functionality and speed, at a certain cost to safety — Informix relies on the developers of datablades to follow their protocol closely and not do any damage. Another feature offered by the Informix Datablade API is allowing UDFs to acquire and maintain memory across multiple invocations. Memory is released by the server on the basis of the duration specified by the data type (i.e., transaction duration, query duration, etc.). Such a feature simplifies the task of implementing certain UDFs (e.g., user-level aggregation and grouping operators).

Although Informix offers a potentially more powerful model for extensibility, IBM DB2 is the only system that isolates the server from faults in UDFs by allowing the execution of UDFs in their own separate address space [38] in addition to the server address space. With this fine-grained fault containment, errors in UDFs will not bring the database server off-line.

7.4 IMAGE RETRIEVAL EXTENSIONS TO COMMERCIAL DBMSs

In this section, we discuss the image retrieval extensions available in commercial systems. We specifically explore the image retrieval technologies supported by Informix Universal Server, Oracle, and IBM DB2 products. These products offer a wide variety of desirable features designed to provide integrated image retrieval

[6] These are special UDFs declared as operators.

in databases. We illustrate some of the functionalities offered by discussing how applications requiring image retrieval can be built in these systems. Although other vendors support a subset of the desired technologies, none integrate them to the same degree; therefore, the effort required to create multimedia applications with these other systems is generally quite large.

To demonstrate how image retrieval applications can be built using database extensions for commercial DBMSs, we will use a very simple example of a digital catalog of color pictures. In this application, a collection of pictures is stored in a table. For each picture, the photographer and date are stored in a table. The basic table schema is as follows:

- *Photo_id.* an integer number to identify the item in the catalog
- *Photographer.* a character string with the photographer's name
- *Date.* the date the picture was taken; for simplicity we will use a character string instead of a date data type
- *Photo.* the photo image and its necessary features for retrieval

The implementation of the *photo* attribute differs between products and is described in the following subsections. In addition to these attributes, any additional attributes, tables, and steps necessary to store such a catalog in the database, and to execute content-based retrieval queries, will be illustrated for each of the three systems.

7.4.1 Informix Image Retrieval Datablade

The Informix system includes a complete media asset management suite (called *Informix Media360* (TM) [57]) to manage digital content in a central repository. The product is designed to handle any media type, including images, maps, blueprints, audio, and video, and is extensible to support additional media types. It manages the entire life cycle of media objects, from production to delivery and archiving, including access control and rights management. The product is integrated with image, video, and audio catalogers and image, video key-frame, and audio content-based search functionality. This suite includes asset management software and a number of content-specific datablades to tackle data type–specific needs. The Excalibur Visual Retrievalware Datablade [17] is one such type-specific datablade that manages the storage, transcoding, and content-based search of images. The image datablade is also used for video key-frame search. Image retrieval based on color, texture, shape, brightness layout, color structure, and image aspect ratio is supported. Color refers to the global color content of the image (i.e., regardless of its location). Texture seeks to distinguish such properties as smoothness or graininess of a surface. Shape seeks to express the shape of objects: for example, a balloon is a circular shape. Brightness layout captures the relative energy as a function of location in the image and, similarly, color structure seeks to localize the color properties to regions of the image.

A similarity score is computed for each image in the database, to determine the degree to which it satisfies a query. All feature-to-feature matches are weighted with user-supplied weights and combined into a final score. Only those images with a score above a given similarity threshold are returned to the user and the remaining images are deemed not relevant to the query. The datablade supports data types to store images and their image feature vectors. Feature vectors combine all the feature representations supported into a single attribute for the whole image. Therefore, no subimage or region searching is possible.

In order to build an image retrieval application using the image datablade in Informix, the following tasks must be performed:

1. Install Informix with the Universal Data Option and the Excalibur Visual Retrievalware Datablade product. Then configure the necessary table and index storage space in the server.
2. Create a database to store all tables and auxiliary data required for our example. We will call this the *Gallery* database.

   ```
   CREATE DATABASE Gallery;
   ```

3. Create a table with the desired fields, two of which are for image retrieval. Following our example, this statement creates such a table:

   ```
   CREATE TABLE photo_collection ( photo_id integer
                primary key not null,
                photographer varchar(50) not null,
                date varchar(12) not null,
                photo IfdImgDesc not null,
                fv IfdFeatVect)
   ```

   The *photo* field stores the image descriptor and the *fv* field stores the feature vector for the image, which will be used for content-based search.
4. Insert data into the table with all the values except for the *fv* field that will be filled elsewhere:

   ```
   INSERT INTO photo_collection (photo_id,
               photographer, date, photo) VALUES
               (3, 'Ansel Adams', '03/06/1995',
               IfdImgDescFromFile('/tmp/03.jpg'))
   ```

   Notice that the feature vector attribute was not specified and thus retains a value of NULL. More photo collection entries can be added using this method.
5. At a later time, the features are extracted to populate the *fv* attribute in the table:

```
UPDATE photo_collection
       SET fv = GetFeatureVector(photo)
       WHERE fv IS NULL
```

This command sets the feature vector attribute for tuples in which the features have not yet been extracted, that is, where the *fv* attribute is NULL. The features are extracted from each *photo* with the *GetFeatureVector* UDF that is part of the datablade. Manually extracting the feature information and updating it in the table is desirable if many images are loaded quickly and feature extraction can be performed at a later time. An alternative to manual feature extraction is to automatically extract the features when each tuple is inserted or updated. To accomplish this, a database trigger can be created that will automatically execute the foregoing statement whenever there is an update to the tuple.

Once the Images are loaded and the features extracted, the *Resembles* function is used to retrieve those images similar to a given image. The *Resembles* function accepts a number of parameters:

- The database image and query feature vectors to be compared.
- A real number between 0 and 1 that is a cutoff threshold in the similarity score. Only images that match with a score higher than the threshold are returned. We refer to such a cutoff as the *alpha cut* value.
- A weighting value for each of the features used. The weights do not have to add up to any particular value, but their sum cannot exceed 100. Weights are relative, so the weights (1,1,1,1,2,1) and (5,5,5,5,10,5) are equivalent.
- An output variable that contains the returned match score value.

6. Query the *photo_collection* table with an example image.

The user provides an image feature vector as a query template. This feature vector can either be stored in the table or correspond to an external image. Using a feature vector for an image already in the table requires a self join to identify the query feature vector. A feature vector for an external image requires calling the *GetFeatureVector* UDF.

The first example uses an image already in the table (the one with image id 3) as the query image:

```
SELECT g.photo_id, score
       FROM photo_collection g, photo_collection s
       WHERE
           s.photo_id = 3
         AND
           Resembles(g.fv,s.fv,0.0,1,1,1,0,0,0,
                     score #REAL)
       ORDER BY score
```

The *Resembles* function takes two extracted feature vectors (here *g.fv* and *s.fv*), computes a similarity score, and compares it to the indicated threshold. In this example, the threshold is 0.0, which means all images will be returned to the user. Following the threshold, six values in the argument list identify the weights for each of the features. Here, only the first three features (color, shape, and texture) are used, whereas the remaining three are unused (their weights are set to 0). The last parameter is an output variable named *score* of type REAL, which contains the similarity score for the image match between the query feature vector *s.fv* and the images stored in the table. The score is then used to sort the result tuples to provide a ranked output.

The next example uses an external image as the query image with all features used for matching and a nonzero threshold specified:

```
SELECT photo_id, score
       FROM photo_collection
       WHERE Resembles(fv, GetFeatureVector
             (IfdImgDescFromFile('/tmp/03.jpg')),
             0.80, 10, 30, 40, 10, 5, 5, score #REAL)
       ORDER BY score
```

Note how the features are extracted in situ by the *GetFeatureVector* function and passed to the *Resembles* function to compute the score between each image and the query image. In this query, only those images with a match score greater than 0.8 will be returned.

7.4.2 DB2 UDB Image Extender

IBM offers a full content management suite that, like the Media Asset Management Suite of Informix, provides a range of content administration, delivery, privilege management, protection, and other services. The IBM Content Manager product has evolved over a number of years, incorporating technology from several sources including OnDemand, DB2 Digital Library, ImagePlus, and VideoCharger. The early focus of these products was to provide integrated storage for and access to data of diverse types (e.g., scanned handwritten notes, images, etc.). These products, however, only provided search based on metadata. For example, searching was supported on manually entered attributes associated with each digitized image but not on the image itself. This, however, changed with the conversion of the IBM QBIC[7] prototype image retrieval system into a

[7] QBIC [13], standing for *Query By Image Content*, was the first commercial content-based Image Retrieval system and was initially developed as an IBM research prototype. Its system framework and techniques had profound effects on later Image Retrieval systems. QBIC supports queries based on example-images, user-constructed sketches and drawings, and selected color and texture patterns. The color features used in QBIC are the average (R,G,B), (Y,i,q), (L,a,b), and MTM (Mathematical

DB2 Extender. DB2 now offers integrated image search from within the database through the DB2 UDB Image Extender, which supports several color and texture feature representations.

In order to build the image retrieval application using the Image Extender, the following tasks need to be performed:

1. Install DB2 and the Image Extender and configure the necessary storage space for the server. This installs a number of extender-supplied user-defined distinct types and functions.
2. Create a database to store all tables and auxiliary data required for our example. We will call this the *Gallery* database.

   ```
   CREATE DATABASE Gallery;
   ```

3. Enable the *Gallery* database for Image searches. From the command line (not the SQL interpreter), use the Extender manager and execute:

   ```
   db2ext ENABLE DATABASE Gallery FOR DB2IMAGE
   ```

   This example uses the DB2 UDB version for UNIX and Microsoft Windows operating systems.
4. Create a table with the desired fields:

   ```
   CREATE TABLE photo_collection (
                photo_id integer PRIMARY KEY
                NOT NULL, photographer varchar(50)
                NOT NULL, date varchar(12) NOT NULL,
                photo DB2IMAGE)
   ```

5. Enable the table *photo_collection* for content-based image retrieval. This step again uses the external Extender manager, and is composed of several substeps.
   - Set up the main table and create auxiliary tables and indexes.

     ```
     db2ext ENABLE TABLE photo_collection FOR DB2IMAGE
     USING TSP1,,LTSP1
     ```

     This creates some auxiliary support tables used by the Extender to support image retrieval for the *photo_collection* table. These tables are stored in the database table-space named "*TSP1*" whereas the supporting large objects (BLOBs) are stored in the "*LTSP1*" table-space. The necessary indexes on auxiliary tables are also created in this step.

Transform to Munsell) coordinates, and a k element Color Histogram. Its texture feature is an improved version of the Tamura texture representation [58], namely, combinations of coarseness, contrast, and directionality. Its shape feature consists of shape area, circularity, eccentricity, major axis orientation, and a set of algebraic moments invariants.

- Enable the *photo* column for content-based image retrieval. This step again uses the external Extender manager.

  ```
  db2ext ENABLE COLUMN photo_collection photo
  FOR DB2IMAGE
  ```

  This makes the *photo* column active for use with the Image Extender and creates triggers that will update the auxiliary administrative tables in response to any change (insertion, deletion, and update) to the data in table *photo_collection*.
- Create a catalog for querying the column by image content. This is done with the Extender manager.

  ```
  db2ext CREATE QBIC CATALOG photo_collection
  photo ON
  ```

  This creates all the support tables necessary to execute a content-based image query. The key word *ON* indicates that the cataloging process (i.e., the feature extraction) will be performed automatically; otherwise, periodic manual recataloging is necessary.
- Open a catalog for adding features, for which feature extraction is to take place; only those features present in the catalog will be available for querying. Using the Extender manager, we issue the following command:

  ```
  db2ext OPEN QBIC CATALOG photo_collection photo
  ```

- Add to the catalog the features to be extracted from the images. Here we will add all four supported features.

  ```
  db2ext ADD QBIC FEATURE QbColorFeatureClass
  db2ext ADD QBIC FEATURE
         QbColorHistogramFeatureClass
  db2ext ADD QBIC FEATURE QbDrawFeatureClass
  db2ext ADD QBIC FEATURE QbTextureFeatureClass
  ```

  These correspond to *Average Color*, *Histogram Color*, *Positional Color*, and *Texture*. Not all features need to be present; including unnecessary features will only decrease performance.
- Close the catalog.

  ```
  db2ext CLOSE QBIC CATALOG
  ```

6. Insert into the *photo_collection* table. The examples presented here use *embedded* SQL to access a DB2 database server.

```
EXEC SQL BEGIN DECLARE SECTION;
  long int_Stor;
  long the_id;
EXEC SQL END DECLARE SECTION;

  the_id = 1; /* the image id */
  int_Stor = MMDB_STORAGE_TYPE_INTERNAL;

EXEC SQL INSERT INTO photo_collection VALUES(
                :the_id, /* id */
                'Ansel Adams', /* name */
                '6/9/2000', /* date */
                DB2IMAGE( /* Image Extender UDF*/
                  CURRENT SERVER,
                  /* database server name */
                  '/images/pic.jpg'
                  /* image source file*/
                  'ASIS', /* keep image format*/
                  :int_Stor,
                  /* store in DB as BLOB*/
                  'BW Picture') /* comment*/
                );
```

This insert populates the image data in the auxiliary tables and stores an image handle into the *photo_collection* table. The DB2IMAGE UDF uses the current server, reads the image located in */images/pic.jpg*, and stores it in the server as specified by the *int_Stor* variable. The image is stored without a format change, and the discovery of the image format is left to the Image Extender as specified by the *ASIS* option. Features are extracted and stored for the image. The comment “BW picture” is attached to the image in the auxiliary tables. The DB2IMAGE UDF offers several different parameter lists (i.e., it is an overloaded function), to support different sources to import images.

7. Query the *photo_collection* table with an example-image.

```
SELECT T.photo_id, T.photographer, S.SCORE
       FROM photo_collection T,
            TABLE (QbScoreTBFromStr(
                  'QbColorFeatureClass
                  color=<255,0,0> 2.0 and
                  QbColorHistogramFeatureClass
                      file=<server,
                      "/img/pic1.gif"> 3.0 and
                  QbDrawFeatureClass
                      file=<server,
```

```
                        "/img/pic1.gif"> 1.0 and
                    QbTextureFeatureClass
                        file=<server,
                        "/img/pic1.gif"> 0.5',
                   photo_collection,
                   photo,
                   100)
             ) AS S
    WHERE CAST(S.IMAGE_ID as varchar(250))
      = CAST(T.photo as varchar(250))
```

This query uses the image stored in */img/pic1.gif* as a query image and uses all four features. The *QbScoreTBFromStr* UDF takes a query string, an enabled table (*photo_collection*), a column (*photo*) name, and a maximum number of images to return. This UDF returns a table with two columns. The first column is named *IMAGE_ID* and contains the image handle used by the Image Extender in the original table (i.e., table *photo_collection*). The second column is named *SCORE* and is a numeric value, which denotes the query to image similarity score interpreted as a distance. A score of 0 denotes a perfect match and higher values indicate progressively worse matches.

The query string is structured as an *and* separated chain of *feature name*, *feature value*, and *feature weight* triplets. The *feature name* indicates which feature to match. The *feature value* is a specification of the value for the desired feature and can be specified in several ways: (*1*) literally specifying the values, which is cumbersome as it requires that the user know the internal representation of each feature, (*2*) an image handle returned by the Image Extender itself so an already stored image can be used as the query, and (*3*) an external file, for which the features are extracted and used. The example mentioned here uses the first approach for the average color feature, specifying an average color of red. The remaining three features use the third approach and use an external image, from which features are extracted for the query. The *feature weight* indicates the weight for this feature and is relative to the other features — if a weight is omitted, then a default value of 1.0 is assumed.

The table returned by the *QbScoreTBFromStr* UDF is joined on the image handle with the *photo_collection* table to retrieve the *photo_id* and *photographer* attributes and keep the score of the image match with the query.

7.4.3 Oracle Visual Image Retrieval Cartridge

Like Informix and IBM, Oracle supports a comprehensive media management framework named *Oracle Intermedia* that incorporates a number of technologies. Oracle Intermedia is designed with the objective of managing diverse media by providing many services from long-term archival to content-based search of text and images and, video storage and delivery. The Oracle Intermedia media management suite [59] contains a number of products designed to manage rich multimedia content particularly in the context of the web. Specifically, it includes components to handle audio, image, and video data types. A sample application for this product would be an on-line music store that wishes to offer music samples, photos of the CD cover and performers, and a sample video of the performers. Intermedia is a tool box that includes a number of object-relational data types, indices, and so on that provide storage and retrieval facilities to web servers, and other delivery channels including streaming video and audio servers. The actual media data can be stored in the server for full control or externally, without full transactional support in a file system, web server, streaming server, or other user-defined source. Functions implemented by this suite include among others dynamic image transcoding to provide both thumbnails and full-resolution images to the client upon request. As part of the Intermedia suite, the Oracle Visual Image Retrieval (VIR) product supplied by Virage [16,60,61][8] provides image-search capabilities.

VIR supports matching on global color, local color, texture, and structure. Global color captures the image's global color content, whereas local color takes into account the location of the color in the image. Texture distinguishes different patterns and nuances in images such as smoothness or graininess. Structure seeks to capture the overall layout of a scene such as the horizon in a photo or the tall vertical boxes of skyscrapers. The product supports arbitrary combinations of the supported feature representations as a query. Users can adjust the weights associated with the features in the query according to the aspects they wish to emphasize. A score that incorporates the matching of all features is computed for each image through a weighted summation of the individual feature matches. The score is akin to the distance between two images where lower (positive) values indicate higher similarity and larger values indicate lower similarity. Only those images with a score below a given threshold are returned, and the remaining images are deemed not relevant to the query. Oracle VIR uses a proprietary index to speed up the matching, referred to as an index of type *ORDVIRIDX*.

We now specify the steps needed to build an image retrieval application. The example code presented here uses Oracles PL/SQL language extensions. PL/SQL is a procedural extension to SQL. To support image retrieval, the following steps are required:

1. Install Oracle8i Enterprise Edition and the VIR products and suitably configure storage table-spaces.
2. Create a Database to store all tables and auxiliary data required for our example. We will call this the *Gallery* database.

```
CREATE DATABASE Gallery;
```

[8] Virage also provides a version of its image retrieval system to Informix and is supported as a datablade.

3. Create a table with the desired attributes and the image data type.

```
CREATE TABLE photo_collection (
             photo_id number PRIMARY KEY NOT NULL,
             photographer VARCHAR(50) NOT NULL,
             date VARCHAR(50) NOT NULL,
             photo ORDSYS.ORDVir);
```

4. Insert images into the newly created table. In Oracle, this will be done through the PL/SQL language, as there are multiple steps to insert an image.

```
DECLARE
    image ORDSYS.ORDVIR;
    the_id NUMBER;
BEGIN
    the_id :=1; -- use a serial number
    INSERT INTO photo_collection VALUES (
           the_id, 'Ansel Adams', '03/06/1995',
   ORDSYS.ORDVIR(ORDSYS.ORDImage(ORDSYS.ordsource
     (empty_BLOB(), 'FILE', 'ORDVIRDIR',
     'the_image.jpg', sysdate, 0),
     NULL, NULL, NULL, NULL, NULL, NULL, NULL),
     NULL));
    SELECT photo INTO image
           FROM photo_collection
           WHERE photo_id = the_id
           FOR UPDATE;
    image.SetProperties;
    image.import(NULL);
    image.Analyze;
    UPDATE photo_collection
           SET photo = image
           WHERE id = the_id;
END
```

The insert command only stores an image descriptor, not the image itself. To get the image, first its properties have to be determined using the `SetProperties` command. Then the image itself is loaded in with the `import(NULL)` command and its features extracted with the `Analyze` command. Lastly the table is updated with the image and its extracted features.

5. Create an index on the features to speed up the similarity queries.

```
CREATE INDEX imgindex
       ON catalog_photos(photo.signature)
```

```
INDEXTYPE IS ordsys.ordviridx
PARAMETERS ('ORDVIR_DATA_TABLESPACE = tbs_1,
ORDVIR_INDEX_TABLESPACE = tbs_2');
```

Here *tbs_1* and *tbs_2* are suitable table-spaces that provide storage.

6. Query the *catalog_photos* table.

   The following example selects images that are similar to an image already in the table with id equal to 3.

```
SELECT T.photo_id,T.photo,ORDSYS.VIRScore(50)SCORE
       FROM catalog_photos T, catalog_photos S
       WHERE
           S.photo_id = 3
         AND
           ORDSYS.VIRSimilar(T.photo.signature,
            S.photo.signature, 'globalcolor="0.2"
            localcolor="0.3" texture="0.1"
            structure="0.4" ', 20.0, 50)=1;
```

   This statement returns three columns: the first one is the *id* of the returned image, the second column is the image itself, and the third column is the score of the similarity between the query image and the result image (the parameter to the *VIRScore* function is discussed in the following text). The query does a self join to fetch the value *S.photo.signature* for the image with an id of 3, which is the signature of the query image. The image similarity computation is performed by the *VIRSimilar* function in the query condition. This function has five arguments:

   - T.photo.signature, the compared images features.
   - S.photo.signature, the query image features.
   - A string value that describes the features and weights to be used in matching. This example has the string

     ```
     'globalcolor="0.2" localcolor="0.3" texture="0.1"
     structure="0.4" '
     ```

     The value 0.0 for a weight indicates that the feature is unimportant, and the value 1.0 indicates the highest importance for that feature. Only those features listed are used for matching. If, for example, global color is not required, then it may be removed from the list. In this example, all features are used and their weights are 0.2 for global color, 0.3 for local color, 0.1 for texture, and 0.4 for structure.
   - The fourth parameter is a threshold for deciding which images are similar enough to the query signature to be returned as results. The Image

Retrieval Cartridge uses a distance interpretation of similarity. A score of 0 indicates that the signatures are identical, whereas scores higher than 0 indicate progressively worse matches. In this example, the threshold value is 20.0, that is, those images with a score larger than 20.0 will not be returned in response to the query.

- The last value is optional and is used to recover the computed similarity score. The alert reader may have noticed that the *VIRSimilar* function is in a *where* clause, a Boolean condition, and therefore must return true or false, as opposed to the computed similarity score. The function returns true if the computed score is below the threshold, and false otherwise. If the query wishes to list the similarity score of each returned image, as is the case here, a different mechanism is required to retrieve the score elsewhere in the query. This parameter value is thus used to uniquely identify the similarity score (computed by the *VIRSimilar* function) within the query to make it available elsewhere in the query through the use of the *VIRScore* function. *VIRScore* retrieves the similarity score by providing the same number as in the *VIRSimilar* function. This key-based identification mechanism enables multiple calls to scoring functions within the same query.

  The final step in the query is to sort the result in increasing order of SCORE such that the most similar image will be the first one returned.

  This example uses an image already in the table as the query image, but an external image may also be used. To do this, extra steps are required, similar to the *insert* command where an external image is read in and its features are extracted and used in the *VIRSimilar* function. This scenario does not require a self join as the query feature vector is directly accessible.

Additional functionality is provided by a third-party software package from Visual Technology. This component supports special-purpose operators for searching for human faces among images stored in the database. Besides image search, the VIR package offers a number of additional operational options such as image format conversion and on-demand image transcoding of query results.

7.4.4 Discussion

We have discussed the extensions supported for incorporating images and multimedia into databases by three of the major DBMS vendors. All the vendors discussed offer media asset management suites to archive and manage digital media. Their offerings differ in the details of their composition, scope, and source, (i.e., third party versus home grown) and their maturity. The image retrieval capabilities of all vendors are approximately comparable. Despite minor administrative differences in table and column setup, once the tables and permissions are set properly, the insertion and querying processes are comparable. Each of the image retrieval products discussed earlier essentially supports the base content-based image retrieval model discussed in Section 7.2. There is, however, one difference.

In Section 7.2, the model permits several query example-images, but so far in this section we only considered single example-image queries. Multiple example-image query support is beyond the current query model implemented by these vendors but is not impossible to implement. Indeed, the model can be incorporated in a query, although in an exposed fashion — exposed because now the user writing the query is exposed to the retrieval model and is responsible for formulating a query properly. To see how such a query can be specified, we will use Informix as an example:

```
SELECT photo_id, (score2 * 0.6 + score2 * 0.4)
       as score
       FROM photo_collection
       WHERE  Resembles(fv,
                GetFeatureVector(IfdImgDescFromFile(
                '/img/query1.jpg')), 0.60, 10,
                30, 40, 10, 5, 5, score1 #REAL)
         AND  Resembles(fv, GetFeatureVector(
               IfdImgDescFromFile('/img/query2.jpg')),
                0.60, 20, 20, 20, 5, 5, 5,
                score2 #REAL)
        ORDER BY score
```

This query uses two external images, *query1.jpg* and *query2.jpg* and computes the score between each individual image in the table and the *query1.jpg* and *query2.jpg* image feature vectors *fv* resulting in one score for each of the two example-images. Then it combines both scores with a weighted summation with 60 percent of weight for *query1.jpg* and 40 percent of the weight to *query2.jpg*. Notice that both *Resembles* function calls specify a threshold of 0.60 and that they use different weights for different features.

Figure 7.2 shows the query tree that corresponds to this example. In this figure, the leaf nodes correspond to actual values v_{ij} for the query image i and the feature j.

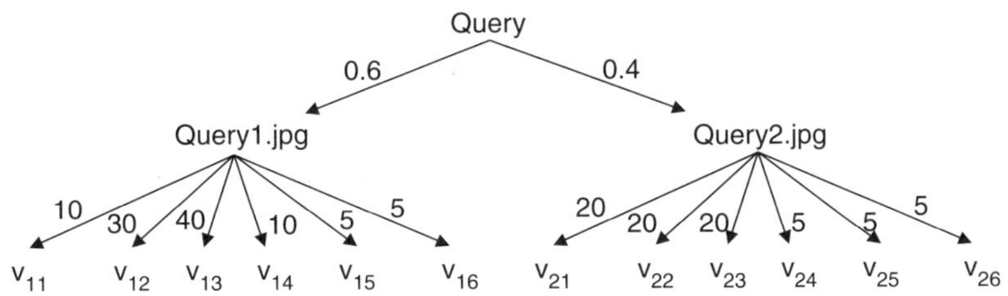

Figure 7.2. Query example.

It is not clear if the feature-based model described in Section 7.2 can be supported by existing systems. Furthermore, we note that none of the products currently available is powerful enough to support region-based image retrieval, relevance feedback mechanisms, or "merge" functions other than weighted summation at different levels of the query tree. Extending image retrieval with these functionalities is a significant research challenge, which the research community has yet to address.

Finally, we note that the foregoing description of the image extensions to commercial DBMSs is certainly not complete. Besides content-based image retrieval, products include many functions that are designed to handle operational considerations, such as image format conversions and image processing. Interested readers are referred to the product manuals.

7.5 CURRENT RESEARCH

The advent of object-relational technology has greatly facilitated the development of content-based image retrieval applications on top of commercial database systems. Using ADTs, UDFs, and BLOBs, applications can extract the visual features of images, store the features in relational tables (along with the raw images themselves), and use these features to compute query matches. Although this represents significant progress, several proposals to improve the earlier mentioned approach have appeared in the research literature. One of them is an efficient technique to implement ADT on top of relational storage managers. Another issue is that of allowing users to easily integrate multidimensional indexing structures into the DBMS and use them as access methods. This will allow applications to build indexes on the image features and use them to efficiently answer content-based queries. To realize the full potential of the feature indexes, the processing of content-based queries (i.e., top-k and threshold-based queries) must be pushed inside the database engine. Commercial systems, such as those described in Section 7.4, retrieve all the matching objects from the database with their computed scores and then perform most of the processing (i.e., sorting and pruning) as an independent step. This misses out on opportunities for optimization and efficient evaluation of content-based queries. Pushing the processing into the engine would open up such optimization opportunities, leading to tremendous performance gains. Another proposal is that of efficient support for similarity joins to facilitate the finding of similar pairs of images.

7.5.1 Implementing ADTs Using Relational Storage Managers

Although ADTs have appeared in mainstream commercial databases [37–40], they present several challenges in terms of storage management. ADTs support varied functionalities, such as inheritance, polymorphism, substitutability, encapsulation, structures, and collections among others. We discuss the storage management problems that arise when an ADT is defined as an aggregation of base data types and/or already defined ADTs (like the way `structs` are defined in C). In our discussion, we do not consider "opaque" types in which the system treats the type as an (uninterpreted) chunk of memory, which is interpreted by the UDFs [37]. We also do not consider the functions defined for the ADT here but will cover them in more detail in Section 7.5.3.1.

Consider an ADT for a few geometric shapes in two dimensions[9]:

```
Type 2dShape ( )
Type Point inherits from 2dShape ( x,y :integer)
Type Circle inherits from 2dShape
     ( x,y, radius :integer)
Type Rectangle inherits from 2dShape
     ( x1,y1, x2,y2 :integer)
Type Triangle inherits from 2dShape
     ( x1,y1, x2,y2, x3,y3 :integer)
```

Suppose we want to associate one or more regions with each image in our *Gallery* database from Section 7.4. The idea is to create image maps for the users to click on. Assuming that each region is one of the two-dimensional (2d) shapes[10] mentioned above, we now create a table to store the regions.

```
create table photo_regions(region_id integer, photo_id
integer, region 2dShape)
```

This table would allow a region to be a point, a circle, a rectangle or a triangle by virtue of type substitutability. Now, we add the following data to our table[11]:

```
insert into photo_regions values (1, 1, Point
            (100,100))
insert into photo_regions values (2, 1, Circle
            (10,10, 5))
insert into photo_regions values (3, 1, Rectangle
            (50,60, 80,90))
insert into photo_regions values (4, 1, Triangle
            (0,0, 5,5, 5,0))
```

Here, we insert a point located at the coordinates (100, 100), a circle of radius 5 centered at the point (10, 10), a rectangle with opposing corner points (50, 60)

[9] Here we have used generic SQL pseudo-code. For specific vendor implementations and syntax, the appropriate manual should be consulted.

[10] More flexible shapes, such as polygons are necessary for such an application. Here we restrict ourselves to the above shapes, as our goal is to show the problems faced in storage management of ADTs and not to provide a complete image mapping solution.

[11] We assume that the appropriate object constructors have been defined (i.e., "Point(x, y)" has been defined as a constructor for the Point type).

and (80, 90) and a triangle with the three corners (0, 0), (5, 5), and (5, 0). Each of these tuple stores one integer for the *region_id*, one integer for the *photo_id*, and an internal fixed-size tuple header whose size depends on the DBMS used. The format of the rest of the information in all four tuples differs from each other: the first tuple needs to store two more integers (in addition to header, region_id and photo_id), the second needs three more, the third needs four more, and the fourth needs to store six more integers. The question is how to organize these tuples on disk in order to handle the diversity among them without sacrificing query efficiency. The following options are available:

1. *One table for each possible data type.* Within this scheme, although there is only one logical table *photo_regions*, the system creates five physical tables, one each of 2dShape, Point, Circle, Rectangle, and Triangle[12]. Each table has a uniform and fixed schema, and it is up to the query processor to look in all the physical tables for a query on the logical table. The advantages of this approach are that regular relational storage managers can be used, the tuples have fixed length and are therefore more amenable to optimizations, and, because the schema for each physical table is known in advance, no dynamic interpretation of object types is required. The disadvantages are that the query processor must decide which tables to search for a query and, on some occasions, it might be necessary to search all the physical tables. More importantly, there could be an explosion in the number of physical tables if the inheritance hierarchy is deep. The Postgres and Illustra systems used an approach similar to this one [35,1].
2. *Co-locate tuples of different types in one table.* In this approach, a single physical table is used to store all the five different types of tuples. Like approach 1, no dynamic decoding of the object type is required, as the layout and column information of each tuple type is fully precomputed. Another advantage is that all the tuples are stored in the same table, avoiding the need for multiple-table lookups. The disadvantage is that there could be an explosion of the number of tuple types in the table. This approach is used in the MARS file system.
3. *Flatten ADT and map to regular relation.* In this approach, all the tuples are stored in a single table, which is managed by a regular relational storage manager (i.e., the storage manager need not support multiple tuple types per relation). All the types are expanded into their components and stored in individual columns of the table. The columns that are not used are filled with NULL values. In this approach, the *photo_regions* table would have 17 columns (region_id, photo_id, two columns for Point, three for Circle, four for Rectangle and six for Triangle)[13], and most of them will contain NULL

[12] There should be no table for 2dShape itself assuming it is a pure abstract data type whose only purpose is to serve as the common superclass, that is there can be no instantiations of this type. However, here we have included 2dShape as a normal ADT.

[13] In practice, one more column is required to keep track of which object is stored in the table.

values as only those columns that correspond to the actual object stored will be non-NULL (e.g., only 4 columns for a Point object would be non-NULL and the remaining 13 would be NULL). The advantage of this approach is that it can be readily implemented in regular relational storage managers. The disadvantages are that space is wasted and additional work is required in the query processor to dynamically interpret the correct columns for a tuple. Note that, as in the earlier approaches, there could be an explosion in storage requirements because here the number of columns required may increase rapidly.

4. *Serialize object in-line and dynamically interpret content to determine type.* In this approach, the table schema is exactly as desired with three attributes, one each for region_id, photo_id, and 2dShape. The last attribute is now stored as a variable length column, either in-line in the tuple, or out of line in a BLOB if its size is too large. This approach has several advantages. It is the most flexible because it can most easily handle changes in the type hierarchy (the other three approaches must make significant changes in the schema of the table(s) when the type hierarchy changes.) It also avoids the combinatorial explosion and space overhead problems of the previous approaches. The only disadvantage is the overhead of dynamically interpreting the contents of each tuple to determine its type. IBM DB2 follows a similar approach to store ADTs [42]. Sybase also follows a similar approach for Java objects [62].

A study on the implementation of ADTs comparing several variations of approaches 3 and 4 can be found in Ref. [42]. Storage management of rich data types has also been addressed by object-oriented databases [33, 34].

Another important problem in ORDBMSs that is relevant to image retrieval is the management of collection-type attributes. An example of such an attribute is the polygonal contour-shape descriptor (represented by the corner points, the number of which can vary from shape to shape). Such attributes are usually handled by co-location or by using side tables. In the co-location approach, the items in the collection attribute of a tuple are stored along with the rest of the tuple with an optional pointer to an overflow area. Figure 7.3a shows how the items $\{val1, val2, val3\}$ in the collection attribute A of a tuple t would be stored. The advantage of this approach is efficiency, as all the items in the collection will be co-located with the tuple most of the time, (i.e., no overflow pointer required). The disadvantages are that updates to a tuple may cause the use of the overflow areas, thus increasing fragmentation and degrading performance. In addition, the storage manager must be able to support coexistence of tuples from different schemes in the same file. In the side-table approach, there is a base table and there is a separate side table for each column with a collection attribute. Each tuple t in the base table stores a system generated handle h for each collection attribute A. The handle h is a key into a side table where a tuple $\langle h, item\rangle$ is stored for each item *item* in the collection attribute A of tuple t. Figure 7.3b shows how the same table t with items

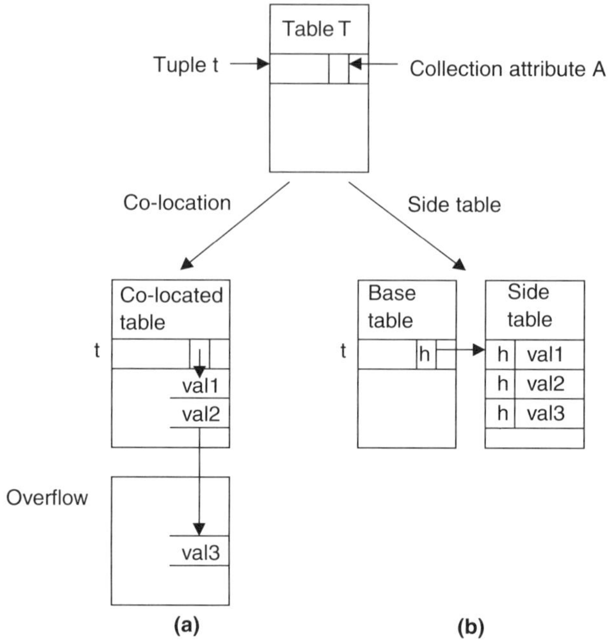

Figure 7.3. Two ways of implementing collections inside attributes, **(a)** The co-location approach, **(b)** The side-table approach.

$\{val1, val2, val3\}$ in the collection attribute A is stored using this approach. An advantage of this approach is that it does not require any special support from storage managers, as all tuples in a relation are the same. Fragmentation in the side table can also be avoided by having the file clustered on the handle. A clear disadvantage is that potentially expensive joins or table lookups are required.

7.5.2 Multidimensional Access Methods

As discussed in Section 7.2, image retrieval systems represent the content of the images using visual features such as color, texture and shape. Processing content-based queries on large image collections can be speeded up significantly by building indices on the individual features (known as the feature indices or simply F-indices) and using them to answer content-based queries. Because the feature spaces are high-dimensional in nature (e.g., 32-dimensional color histogram space), novel indexing techniques must be developed and incorporated into the DBMS (Chapters 14 and 15). The purpose of a feature index is to efficiently retrieve the best matches with respect to that feature by executing a range search or a k-nearest neighbor (k-NN) search on the multidimensional index structure. How these individual feature matches returned by the feature indices can be used to obtain the overall best matches will be discussed in Section 7.5.3.1.

In this section, we discuss research issues that arise in designing index structures that can execute range and k-NN searches efficiently over image feature spaces, in supporting new types of queries for image retrieval applications and in integrating multidimensional index structures as access methods into the DBMS at the end.

*7.5.2.1 **Designing Index Structures for Image Feature Spaces.*** The main problem that arises in indexing image feature spaces is high dimensionality. For example, the color histograms used in the MARS system are usually 32-dimensional or 64-dimensional [63]. Many multidimensional index structures do not scale to such high dimensionalities [64]. Designing scalable index structures has been an active area of research and is discussed in detail in Chapters 14 and 15.

*7.5.2.2 **Supporting Multimedia Queries on Top of Multidimensional Index Structures.*** Traditionally, multidimensional index structures support only point, range, and k-NN queries (with a single query point) and only the Euclidean distance function. In multimedia retrieval, the retrieval model defines what a match between two images means with respect to each individual feature. The measure of match (rather, mismatch) is defined in terms of a distance function. The retrieval model uses arbitrary distance functions (typically an L_p metric) and arbitrary weights along the dimensions of the feature space to capture the visual perception of the user. This implies that the index structure must support arbitrary distance functions and arbitrary weights along the dimensions that are specified by the user at query time. Such techniques have been developed in Refs. [65–67]. Another requirement of the index structure is to support multiexample queries, because the user might submit multiple images as part of the query (Section 7.2). Such queries are particularly important for retrieval models that represent the query using multiple query points [24,68]. A multipoint query Q_F for a feature F is formally defined as $Q_F = \langle n_F, P_F, W_F, D_F \rangle$, where n_F is the number of points in the query, $P_F = \{P_F^{(1)}, \ldots, P_F^{(n_F)}\}$ is the set of n_F points in the feature space, $W_F = \{w_F^{(1)}, \ldots, w_F^{(n_F)}\}$ are the corresponding weights, and D_F is a distance function, which, given two points in the feature space, returns the distance between them (usually a weighted L_p metric). The distance between the multipoint query Q_F and an object point O_F with respect to feature F is defined as the aggregate of the distances between O_F and the individual points $P_F^{(i)} \in P_F$ in Q_F. The weighted sum

$$D_F(Q_F, O_F) = \sum_{i=1}^{n_F} w_F^{(i)} D_F(P_F^{(i)}, O_F) \tag{7.2}$$

may be used as an aggregation function. The individual point-to-point distance $D_F(P_F^{(i)}, O_F)$ is given by a weighted L_p metric

$$D_F(P_F^{(i)}, O_F) = \left[\sum_{j=1}^{d_F} \mu_F^{(j)} (|P_F^{(i)}[j] - O_F[j]|)^p \right]^{1/p} \tag{7.3}$$

where d_F is the dimensionality of the feature space and $\mu_F^{(j)}$ denotes the *intra-feature weight* associated with the jth dimension. This is the aggregation function used in the MARS system. The problem is to find the k-NN of Q_F using the F-index.

One way to implement a multipoint query is the multiple expansion approach proposed by Porkaew and coworkers [20] and Wu and coworkers [68]. The approach explores the nearest neighbors of each individual point $P_F^{(i)}$ using the traditional single-point k-NN algorithm and combines them. An alternate way, proposed in Ref. [24,67], is to develop a new k-NN algorithm that can handle multipoint queries. The latter technique involves *(1)* redefining the MINDIST function, which is used to compute the distance of an index node from the query and *(2)* using the distance function described earlier to compute the distance of an indexed object from the multipoint query. Experiments show that the latter technique can process a multipoint query much more efficiently than the multiple expansion approach [67].

7.5.2.3 Integration of Multidimensional Index Structures as Access Methods in a DBMS. Although there exist several research challenges in designing scalable index structures and developing algorithms for efficient content-based search using them, one of the most important practical challenges is that of integration of such indexing mechanisms as access methods (AMs) in a DBMS. Building a database server with native support for all possible kinds of complex multimedia features and feature-specific indexing mechanisms, along with support for feature-specific queries or operations is not feasible. The solution is to build an extensible database server that allows the application developer to define data types and related operations as well as indexing mechanisms on the stored data, which the database query optimizer can exploit to access the data efficiently. As discussed in Section 7.3.3, commercial ORDBMSs have started providing extensibility options for users to incorporate their own index structures. As pointed out earlier, the interfaces exposed by current commercial systems are too low level and place the burden of writing structural maintenance code (i.e., concurrency control) on the access method implementor. The *Generalized Search Tree* (GiST) [51] provides a more elegant solution to the earlier-mentioned problem.

Generalized Search Tree (GiST). A GiST is a balanced tree where the root has a fanout between 2 and M and the other nodes have variable fanout between kM and M. The constant k must satisfy the inequalities $\frac{2}{M} \leq k \leq \frac{1}{2}$, and is termed the *minimum fill factor of the tree*. Leaf nodes in a GiST contain (p, ptr) pairs, where p is a predicate that is used as a search key and ptr is the identifier of some tuple in the database. Nonleaf nodes contain (p, ptr) pairs, where p is a predicate used as a search key (referred to as bounding predicate (BP) [69]) and

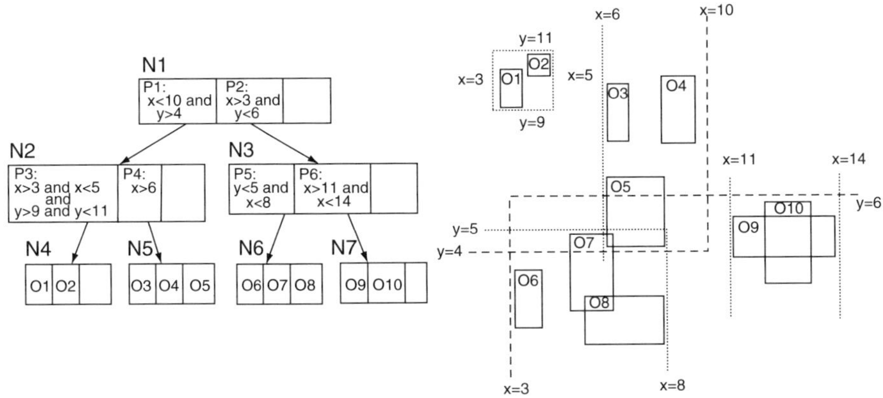

Figure 7.4. A GiST for a key set comprised of rectangles in two-dimensional space. Note that the bounding predicates are arbitrary (i.e., not necessarily bounding rectangles as in R-trees).

ptr points to another tree node. The predicates can be arbitrary as long as they satisfy the following condition: the predicate p in a leaf node entry (p, ptr) must hold for the tuple identified by ptr, and the bounding predicate p in a nonleaf node entry (p, ptr) must hold for any tuple reachable from ptr. A GiST for a key set composed of 2d rectangles is shown in Figure 7.4.

Generalizing the notion of a search key to an arbitrary predicate makes GiST extensible, both in the data types it can index and the queries it can support. GiST is like a "template"—the application developer can implement a new AM using GiST by simply registering a few (domain-specific) extension methods with the DBMS. Examples of the extension methods are *Consistent*(E, q), which, given an entry $E = (p, ptr)$ and a query predicate q, returns false if $p \wedge q$ can be guaranteed to be unsatisfiable and true otherwise, and *Penalty*(E_1, E_2), which, given two entries $E_1 = (p_1, ptr_1)$, $E_2 = (p_2, ptr_2)$, returns a domain-specific penalty for inserting E_2 into the subtree rooted at E_1. GiST uses the extension methods provided by the AM developer to implement the standard index operations: search, insertion, and deletion. For example, the search operation uses *Consistent*(E, q) to determine which nodes to traverse to answer the query, whereas the insert operation uses *Penalty*(E_1, E_2) to determine the leaf node to place the inserted item in. The AM developer thus controls the organization of keys within the tree and the behavior of the search operation, thereby specializing GiST to the desired AM. The original GiST paper deals only with range queries [51]. Several extensions to support more general queries (i.e., ranked or nearest neighbor queries) on top of GiST are proposed in [70].

Concurrency Control in GiST. Although GiST reduces the effort of integrating new AMs in DBMSs considerably, it does not automatically provide concurrency control. It is essential to develop efficient techniques to manage concurrent access to data through the GiST, before it can be supported by "commercial strength"

DBMSs. Concurrent access to data through an index structure introduces two independent concurrency control problems:

- Preserving consistency of the data structure in the presence of concurrent insertions, deletions, and updates.
- Protecting search regions from phantoms.

Techniques for concurrency control (CC) in multidimensional data structures and, in particular, GiST have been proposed recently [69,71,72]. Developing CC techniques for GiST is particularly beneficial because the CC code can be implemented once by the database developer — the AM developer does not need to implement individual algorithms for each AM.

Preserving Consistency of GiST. We first discuss the consistency problem and its solution. Consider a GiST (configured as, e.g., an R-tree) with a root node R and two children nodes A and B. Consider two operations executing concurrently on the R-tree: an insertion of a new key $k1$ into B and a deletion of a key $k2$ from B. Suppose the deletion operation examines R and discovers that $k2$, if present, must be in B. Before it can examine B, the insertion operation causes B to split into B and B', as a result of which $k2$ moves to B' (and subsequently updates R). The delete operation now examines B and incorrectly concludes that $k2$ does not exist. To avoid the above problem, Kornaker and coworkers propose a link-based technique that was originally used in B-trees [71]. By adding a right link between a node and its split-off right sibling and a node sequence number to every node, the operations (i.e., the deletion operation in the mentioned example here) can detect whether the node has split since the parent was examined and, if so, whether it can compensate for the missed splits by following the right links.

Phantom Protection in GiST. We now move on to the problem of phantom protection. Consider a transaction T1 reading a set of data items from a GiST that satisfy some search predicate Q. Transaction T2 then inserts a data item that satisfies Q and commits. If T1 now repeats its scan with the same search predicate Q, it gets a set of data items (known as "phantoms") different from the first read. Phantoms must be prevented to guarantee serializable execution. Note that object-level locking [73] does not prevent phantoms because even if all objects currently in the database that satisfy the search predicate are locked, concurrent insertions[14] into the search range cannot be prevented. There are two general strategies to solve the phantom problem, namely, *predicate locking* and its engineering approximation *granular locking*. In predicate locking, transactions acquire locks on predicates rather than on individual objects. Although predicate locking is a complete solution to the phantom problem, it is usually too costly [73]. In contrast, in granular locking, the predicate space is divided into a set

[14] These insertions may be a result of insertion of new objects, updates to existing objects, or rolling-back deletions made by other concurrent transactions.

of lockable resource granules. Transactions acquire locks on granules instead of on predicates. The locking protocol guarantees that if two transactions request conflicting-mode locks on predicates p and p' such that $p \wedge p'$ is satisfiable, then the two transactions will request conflicting locks on at least one granule in common. Granular locks can be set and released as efficiently as object locks. An example of the granular locking approach is the *multigranularity locking protocol* (MGL) [74]. Application of MGL to the key space associated with a B-tree is referred to as *key range locking* (KRL) [74,75].

In Ref. [71], Kornaker and coworkers develop a solution for phantom protection in GiSTs based on predicate locking. In the proposed protocol, a searcher attaches its search predicate Q to all the index nodes whose BPs are consistent with Q. Subsequently, the searcher acquires shared mode locks on all objects "consistent" with Q. An inserter checks the object to be inserted against all the search predicates attached to the node in which the insertion takes place. If it conflicts with any of them, the inserter attaches its predicate to the node (to prevent starvation) and waits for the conflicting transactions to commit. If the insertion causes a BP of a node N to grow, the predicate attachments of the parent of N are checked with the new BP of N and are replicated at N if necessary. The process is carried out top-down over the entire path where node BP adjustments take place. Similar predicate checking and replication is done between sibling nodes during split propagation. The details of the protocol can be found in Ref. [71].

In Ref. [69], Chakrabarti and Mehrotra propose an alternative approach based on granular locking. Note that the granular locking technique for B-trees, called key range locking (KRL), cannot be applied for phantom protection in multidimensional data structures because it relies on a total order of key values, which does not exist for multidimensional data. Imposing an artificial total order (say a Z-order [76]) over multidimensional data to adapt KRL is not a viable technique either. The first step is to define lockable resource granules over the multidimensional key space. One way to define the granules is to statically partition the key space (e.g., as a grid) and treat each partition (i.e., each grid cell) as a granule. The problem with such a partitioning is that it does not adapt to the key distribution: some granules may contain many more keys than others, causing them to become "hot spots." In Ref. [69], the authors use the predicate space partitioning generated by the GiST to define the granules. There is a lockable granule $TG(N)$ associated with each index node N of a GiST whose coverage is defined by the *granule predicate* $GP(N)$ associated with the node. $GP(N)$ is defined as follows. Let P denote the parent node of N (P is NULL if N is the root node) and $BP(N)$ denote the bounding predicate of N. The granule predicate $GP(N)$ of node N is equal to $BP(N)$ if N is the root and $BP(N) \wedge GP(P)$ otherwise. For example, the granule predicate associated with the nonleaf node $N2$ in Figure 7.4 is $P1 = (x < 10) \wedge (y > 4)$, whereas that associated with leaf node $N5$ is $P1 \wedge P4 = (6 < x < 10) \wedge (y > 4)$. The granules associated with leaf nodes are called *leaf granules*, whereas those associated with nonleaf nodes are called *nonleaf granules*. Note that the above partitioning scheme does not suffer from the "hot spot" problem of static partitioning because the granules dynamically adapt to the key distribution as keys are inserted into and deleted from the GiST.

Once the granules are defined, the authors develop lock protocols for the various operations on the GiST. As mentioned earlier, for correctness, if two operations conflict, they must request conflicting locks on at least one granule in common. The protocol exploits, in addition to shared mode (S) and exclusive mode (X) locks, *intention* mode locks that represent the intention to set locks at finer granularity. The compatibility matrix for the various lock modes used by the protocol can be found in Ref. [69]. The lock protocol of the search operation is simple. A searcher acquires commit-duration S-mode locks on all granules (both leaf and nonleaf) "consistent" with its search predicate. Note that in this technique, unlike the approach of Ref. [71], the searcher does not acquire object-level locks. The lock protocol of the insertion operation is slightly more involved. Let O be the object being inserted and g be the granule corresponding to the leaf node in which O is being inserted. The protocol has the following two cases. If the insertion does not cause g to grow, the inserter acquires *(1)* a commit-duration IX-mode lock on g where the IX-mode is an intention mode (intention to set shared or exclusive mode locks at finer granularity) and *(2)* a commit-duration X-mode lock on O. Otherwise, the insertion acquires *(1)* a commit-duration IX-mode lock on g *(2)* a commit-duration X-mode lock on O and *(3)* a *short*-duration IX-mode lock on TG(LU-node) where the LU-node (lowest unchanged node) denotes the lowest node in the insertion path whose GP does not change because of the insertion. The protocol mentioned here guarantees that a transaction cannot insert an object into the search region of another concurrently running transaction, that is, it will request a conflicting lock on at least one common granule and hence will block till the search transaction is over. The correctness proofs and the lock protocols of the other operations can be found [69].

7.5.3 Supporting Top-*k* Queries in Databases

In content-based image retrieval, almost all images match the query image to some degree or another. Users are typically not interested in all matching images (i.e., all images with degree of match >0) as that might retrieve the entire database. Instead, they are interested in only the top few matching images. There are two ways of retrieving the top few images. *Top-k* queries return the k best matches, irrespective of their scores. For example, in Section 7.4.2, we requested the top 100 images matching */image/pic1.gif*. *Range queries* or *alpha-cut* queries return all the images whose matching score exceeds a user-specified threshold, irrespective of their number. For example, in Section 7.4.1, we requested all images whose degree of match to the image */tmp/03.jpg* exceeds the alpha-cut of 0.8[15]. Database query optimizers and query processors

[15] For both types of queries, the user typically expects the answers to be ranked the basis of on their degree of match (the best matches before the less good ones). For top-k queries, a "get more" feature is desirable so that the user can ask for additional matches if she wants.

do not support queries with user-specified limits on result cardinality; the limiting of the result cardinalities in the examples (in Section 7.4) is achieved at the application level (by Excalibur Visual Retrievalware in Informix, QBIC in DB2 and Virage in Oracle). The database engine returns all the tuples that satisfy the non-image selection predicates, if any, or all tuples otherwise; the application then evaluates the image match for each returned tuple and retains only those that satisfy the user-specified limit. This causes large amounts of wasted work by the database engine (as it accesses and retrieves tuples, most of which are eventually discarded), leading to long response times. Significant performance improvements can be obtained by pushing the top-k and range query processing inside the database engine. In this section, we discuss query-optimization and query-processing issues that arise in that context.

7.5.3.1 Query Optimization. Relational query languages, particularly SQL, are declarative in nature: they specify what the answers should be and not how they are to be computed. When a DBMS receives an SQL query, it first validates the query and then determines a strategy for evaluating it. Such a strategy is called the *query-evaluation plan* or simply *plan* and is represented using an operator tree [77]. For a given query, there are usually several different plans that will produce the same result; they differ only in the amount of resources needed to compute the result. The resources include time and memory space in both disk and main memory. The query optimizer first generates a variety of plans by choosing different orders among the operators in the operator tree and different algorithms to implement these operators, and then chooses the best plan on the basis of available resources [77]. The two common strategies to compute optimized plans are *(1) rule-based* optimization [36] and *(2) cost-based* optimization [78]. In the rule-based approach, a number of heuristics are encoded in the form of production rules that can be used to transform the query tree into an equivalent tree that is more efficient to execute. For example, a rule might specify that selections are to be pushed below joins because this reduces the sizes of the input relations and hence the cost of the join operation. In the cost-based approach, the optimizer first generates several plans that would correctly compute the answers to a query and computes a cost estimate for each plan. The system maintains some running statistics for each relation (i.e., number of tuples, number of disk pages occupied by the relation, etc.) and for each index (i.e., number of distinct keys, number of pages, etc.), which are used to obtain the cost estimates. Subsequently, the optimizer chooses the plan with the lowest estimated cost [78].

Access Path Selection for Top-k Queries. Pushing top-k query processing inside the database engine opens up several query optimization issues. One of them is access path selection. The access path represents how the top-k query accesses the tuples of a relation to compute the result. To illustrate the access path-selection problem, let us consider an example image database in which the images are represented using two features, color and texture. Assuming that all the extracted feature values are stored in the same tuple along with other image information (i.e., the photo_id, photographer and date in the example in Section 7.4), one option is to sequentially scan through the entire table, compute the similarity score for each tuple by first computing the individual feature scores and then combining them using the merge function, and then retain the k tuples with the highest similarity scores. This option may be too slow, especially if the relation is very large. Another option that avoids this problem is to index each feature using a multidimensional index structure. With the indexes in place, the optimizer has several choices of access paths:

- Filter the images on the color feature (using k-NN search on the color index), access the full records of the returned images, which contain the texture feature values, and compute the overall score.
- Filter the images on the texture feature, analyze the full records of the returned images, which contain the color feature values, and compute the overall score.
- Use both the color and texture indexes to find the best matches with respect to each feature individually and merge the individual results[16].

Note the number of execution alternatives increases exponentially with the number of features. The presence of other selection predicates (i.e., the "date ≥'01/01/2000' " predicate in the preceding example) also increases the size of the execution space. It is up to the query optimizer to determine the access path to be used for a given query. Database systems use a cost-based technique for access path selection as proposed by Selinger and coworkers [78]. To apply this technique, several issues need to be considered. In image databases, the features are indexed using multidimensional index structures, which serve as access paths to the relation. New kinds of statistics need to be maintained for such index structures and new cost formulae need to be developed for accurate estimation of their access costs. In addition, the cost models for top-k queries are likely to be significantly different from traditional database queries that return all tuples satisfying the user-specified predicates. The cost model would also depend on the retrieval model used, that is, on the similarity functions used for each individual feature and the ones used to combine the individual matches (Section 7.2.3). Such cost models need to be designed.

In Ref. [79], Chaudhari and Gravano propose a cost model to evaluate the costs of the various execution alternatives[17] and develop an algorithm to determine the cheapest alternative. The cost model relies on techniques for estimating selectivity of queries in individual feature spaces, estimating the costs of k-NN searches using individual feature indices, and probing a relation for a tuple to evaluate

[16] Yet another option would be to create a combined index on color and texture features so that the earlier-mentioned query can be answered using a single index. We do not consider this option in this discussion.

[17] The authors do not consider all the execution alternatives but only a small subset of them (called *search-minimal executions*) [79]. Also, the authors only consider Boolean queries and do not handle more complex retrieval models (i.e., weighted sum model, probabilistic model).

one or more selection predicates. Most selectivity estimation techniques proposed so far for multidimensional feature spaces work well only for low-dimensional spaces but are not accurate in the high-dimensional spaces commonly used to represent images features [80–82]. More suitable techniques (based, for instance, on fractals) are beginning to appear in the literature [83,84]. Work on cost models for range and k-NN searches on multidimensional index structures includes earlier proposals for low-dimensional index structures (i.e., R-tree) in Ref. [85,86] and more recent work for higher-dimensional spaces in Ref. [87,88].

Optimization of Expensive User-Defined Functions. The system may need to evaluate multiple selection predicates on each tuple accessed through the chosen access path. Relational query optimizers typically place no importance on the order in which the selection predicates are evaluated on the tuples. The same is true for projections. Selections and projections are assumed to be zero-time operations. This assumption is not true in content-based image retrieval applications in which selection predicates may involve evaluating expensive UDFs. Let us consider the following query on the `photo_collection` table in Section 7.4.1:

```
/* Retrieve all photographs taken since the year 2000 */
/* that match the query image more than 80%. */
SELECT photo_id, score
       FROM photo_collection
       WHERE Resembles(fv, GetFeatureVector(
              IfdImgDescFromFile('/tmp/03.jpg')),
              0.80, 10, 30, 40, 10,
              5, 5, score #REAL)
       AND
              date >= '01/01/2000'
       ORDER BY score
```

The query has two selection predicates: the Resembles predicate and the predicate involving the date. The first one is a complex predicate that may take hundreds or even thousands of instructions to compute, whereas the second one is a simple predicate that can be computed in a few instructions. If the chosen access path is a sequential scan over the table, the query will run faster if the second selection is applied before the first because doing so minimizes the number of calls to Resembles. The query optimizer must, therefore, take into account the computational cost of evaluating the UDF to determine the best query plan. Cost-based optimizers use only the selectivity of the predicates to order them in the query plan but do not consider their computational complexities. In Ref. [89,90], Hellerstein and coworkers use both the selectivity and the cost of selection predicates to optimize queries with expensive UDFs. In Ref. [91], Chaudhari and Shim propose dynamic programming-based algorithms to optimize queries with expensive predicates.

The techniques discussed in the preceding text deal with UDF optimization when the functions appear in the *where* clause of an SQL query. Expensive UDFs can also appear in the projection clause as operations on ADTs. Let us consider the following example taken from Ref. [92]. A table stores images in a column and offers functions to crop an image and apply filters to it (e.g., a sharpening filter). Consider the following query (using the syntax of [95]):

```
select image.sharpen().crop(0.0, 0.0, 0.1, 0.1)
from image_table
```

The user requests that all images be filtered using *sharpen* and then *cropped* in order to extract the portion of the image inside the rectangular region with diagonal end points (0.0, 0.0) and (0.1, 0.1). Sharpening an image first and then cropping is wasteful as the entire image would be sharpened and 99 percent of it would be discarded later (assuming the width and height of the images are 1.0). Inverting the execution order to *image.crop(0.1,0.1).sharpen()* reduces the total central processing units (CPU) cost. It may not be always possible for the user to enter the operations in the best order (i.e., *crop* function before the *sharpen* function), specially in the presence of relational views defined over the underlying tables [92]. In such cases, the optimizer should reorder these functions to optimize the CPU cost of the query. The Predator project [93] proposes to use Enhanced-ADTs or E-ADTs to address the above problem. The E-ADTs provide information regarding the execution cost of various operations, their properties (i.e., commutativity between *sharpen* and *crop* operations in the preceding example), and so on, which the optimizer can use to reorder the operations and reduce the execution cost of the query. In some cases, it might be possible to remove function calls. For example, if X is an image, *rotate()* is a function that rotates an image and *count_different_colors()* is a function that counts the number of different colors in an image, the operation *X.rotate().count_different_colors()* can be replaced by *X.count_different_colors()*, thus saving the cost of rotation. Reference [92] documents performance improvements of up to several orders of magnitude using these techniques.

7.5.3.2 Query Processing. In the earlier section, we discussed how pushing the top-k query support into the database engine can lead to choice of better query-evaluation plans. In this section, we discuss algorithms that the query processor can use to execute top-k queries for some of the query-evaluation plans discussed in the previous section.

Evaluating Top-k Queries. Let us again consider an image database with two features, color and texture, each of which is indexed using a multidimensional index structure. Let F_{color} and F_{texture} denote the similarity functions for the color and texture features individually. Examples of individual feature similarity functions (or equivalent distance functions) are the various L_p metrics. Let F_{agg} denote the function that combines (or aggregates) the individual similarities (with respect to color and texture features) of an image to the query image to obtain its overall similarity to the query image. Examples of aggregation functions are weighted summation, probabilistic and fuzzy conjunctive and disjunctive models and so on [21]. The functions F_{color}, $F_{texture}$, and F_{agg}, and their associated weights together constitute the retrieval model (Section 7.2.3). In order to support top-k queries inside the database engine, the engine must allow users to plug in their desired retrieval models for the queries and tune the weights and the functions in the model at query time. The query optimization and evaluation must be based on the retrieval model specified for the query. We next discuss some query-evaluation algorithms that have been proposed for the various retrieval models.

One of the evaluation plans for this example database, discussed in Section 7.5.3.1, is to use the individual feature indexes to find the best matches with respect to each feature individually and then merge the individual results. Fagin [94] proposed an algorithm to evaluate a top-k query efficiently according to this plan. The input to this algorithm is a set of ranked lists X_i generated by the individual feature indices (by the k-NN algorithm). The algorithm accesses each X_i in sorted order on the basis of its score and maintains a set $L = \cap_i X_i$ that contains the intersection of the objects retrieved from the input ranked lists. Once L contains k objects, the full tuples of all the items in $\cup_i X_i$ are probed (by accessing the relation), their overall scores are computed and the tuples with the k best overall scores are returned. This algorithm works as long as F_{agg} is monotonic, that is, $F_{agg}(x_1, \ldots, x_m) \leq F_{agg}(x'_1, \ldots, x'_m)$ for $x_i \leq x'_i$ for every i. Most of the interesting aggregation functions such as the weighted sum model and the fuzzy and probabilistic conjunctive and disjunctive models satisfy the monotonicity property. Fagin also proposes optimizations to his algorithm for specific types of scoring functions [94].

Although Fagin proposes a general algorithm for all monotonic aggregation functions, Ortega and coworkers [21,95] propose evaluation algorithms that are tailored to specific aggregation functions (i.e., separate algorithms for weighted sum, fuzzy conjunctive, and disjunctive models and probabilistic conjunctive and disjunctive models). This approach allows incorporating function-specific optimizations in the evaluation algorithms and is used by the MARS [10] system. One of the main advantages of these algorithms is that they do not need to probe the relation for the full tuples. This can lead to significant performance improvements because, according to the cost model proposed in Ref. [94], the total database access cost due to probing can be much higher than the total cost due to sorted access (i.e., accesses using the individual feature indices). Another advantage comes from the *demand-driven data flow* followed in Ref. [21]. While Fagin's approach retrieves objects from the individual streams and buffers them until it reaches the termination condition ($|L| \geq k$) and then returns all the k objects to the user, the algorithms in Ref. [21] retrieve only the necessary number of objects from each stream in order to return the next best match. This demand-driven approach reduces the wait time of intermediate answers in temporary files or buffers between the operators in a query tree. On the other hand, in Ref. [94], the items returned by the individual feature indexes must wait in a temporary file or buffer until the completion of the probing and sorting process. Note that both approaches are incremental in nature and can support the "get more" feature efficiently. Several other optimizations of these algorithms have been proposed recently [96,97].

An alternative approach to evaluating top-k queries has been proposed by Chaudhuri and Gravano [79,98]. It uses the results in Ref. [94] to convert top-k queries to *alpha-cut* queries and processes them as filter conditions. Under certain conditions (uniquely graded repository), this approach is expected to access no more objects than the strategy in Ref. [94]. Much like the former approach, this approach also requires temporary storage and sorting of intermediate answers before returning the results. Unlike the former approaches, this approach cannot support the "get more" feature without re-executing the query from scratch. Another way to convert top-k queries to threshold queries is presented in Ref. [99]. This work mainly deals with traditional data types. It uses selectivity information from the DBMS to probabilistically estimate the value of the threshold that would retrieve the desired number of items and then uses this threshold to execute a normal range query. Carey and Kossman propose techniques to limit the answers in an ORDER BY query to a user-specified number by placing stop operators in the query tree [100,101].

Similarity Joins. Certain queries in image retrieval applications may require join operations. An example is finding all pairs of images that are most similar to each other. Such joins are called *similarity joins.* A join between two relations returns every pair of tuples from the two relations that satisfy a certain selection predicate[18]. In a traditional relation join, the selection predicate is precise (i.e., equality between two numbers); hence, a pair of tuples either does or does not satisfy the predicate. This is not true for general similarity joins in which the selection predicate is imprecise (i.e., similarity between two images): each pair of tuples satisfies the predicate to a certain degree but some pairs satisfy the predicate more than other pairs. Thus just using similarity as the join predicate would return almost all pairs of images including pairs with very low similarity scores.

Because the user is typically interested in the top few best matching pairs, we must restrict the result to only those pairs with good matching scores. This notion of restricted similarity joins have been studied in the context of geographic proximity distance [102–104] and in the similarity context [105–110]. The problem of a restricted similarity join between two data sets A and B containing d-dimensional points is defined as follows [106,110]. Given points $X = (x_1, x_2, \ldots, x_d) \in A$ and $Y = (y_1, y_2, \ldots, y_d) \in B$ and a threshold distance ε, the result of the join contains all pairs (X, Y) whose distance $D_d^\varepsilon(X, Y)$ is less than ε. The distance function $D_d^\varepsilon(X, Y)$ is typically an L_p metric (Chapter 14), but other distance measures are also possible.

A number of nonindexed and indexed methods have been proposed for similarity joins. Among the nonindexed ones, the nested loop join is the simplest but has the highest execution cost. If $|A|$ and $|B|$ denote the cardinality of the data

[18] Note that the two input relation to a join can be the same relation (known as a self join).

sets A and B, respectively, then the nested loop join has a time complexity of $|A| \times |B|$, which degenerates to a quadratic cost if the data sets are similarity sized. Among the indexed methods, one of the earliest proposed ones is the R-Tree-based method that is presented in Ref. [105]. This R-Tree method traverses the structure of two R-Trees synchronously matching corresponding branches in the two trees. It expands each bounding rectangle by $\varepsilon/2$ on each side along each dimension and recursively searches each pair of overlapping bounding rectangles. Most other index-based techniques for similarity joins employ variations of this technique [106]. The generalization of the multidimensional similarity join technique described above (which can be applied to obtain similar pairs with respect to individual features) to obtain overall similar pairs of images remains a research challenge.

7.6 CONCLUSION

The evolution of traditional relational databases into powerful extensible object-relational systems has facilitated the development of applications that require storage of multimedia objects and retrieval based on their content. In order to support content-based retrieval, the representation of the multimedia object (object model) must capture its visual properties. Users formulate content-based queries by providing examples of objects similar to the ones they wish to retrieve. Such queries are internally mapped to a feature-based representation (query model). Retrieval is performed by computing similarity between the multimedia object and the query on the basis of feature values, and the results are ranked by the computed similarity values. The key technologies provided by modern databases that facilitate the implementation of applications requiring content-based retrieval are the support for user-defined data types, including UDFs and ways to call these functions from within SQL. Content-based retrieval models can be incorporated within databases using these extensibility options: the internal structure and content of multimedia objects can be represented in DBMSs as abstract data types, and similarity models can be implemented as UDFs. Most major DBMSs now support multimedia extensions (either developed in house or by third-party developers) that consist of predefined multimedia data types and commonly used functions on those types including functions that support similarity retrieval. Examples of such extensions include the Image Datablade supported by the Informix Universal Server and the QBIC extender of DB2.

Although the existing commercial object-relational databases have come a long way in providing support for multimedia applications, there are still many technical challenges that need to be addressed in incorporating multimedia objects into DBMSs. Among the primary challenges are those of extensible query processing and query optimization. Multimedia similarity queries differ significantly from traditional database queries — they deal with high-dimensional data sets, for which existing indexing mechanisms are not sufficient. Furthermore, a user is typically interested in retrieving the top-k matching answers (possibly progressively) to the query. Many novel indexing methods that provide efficient retrieval over high-dimensional multimedia feature spaces have been proposed. Furthermore, efficient query-processing algorithms for evaluating top-k queries have been developed. These indexing mechanisms and query-processing algorithms need to be incorporated into database systems. To this end, database systems have begun to support extensibility options for users to add type-specific access methods. However, current mechanisms are limited in scope and quite cumbersome to use. For example, to incorporate a new access method, a user has to address the daunting task of concurrency control and recovery for the access method. Query optimizers are still not sufficiently extensible to support optimal access path selection based on UDFs and access methods. Research on these issues is ongoing and we believe that solutions will be incorporated into future DBMSs, resulting in systems that efficiently support content-based queries on multimedia types.

ACKNOWLEDGMENTS

This work was supported by NSF CAREER award IIS-9734300 and in part by the Army Research Laboratory under Cooperative Agreement No. DAAL01-96-2-0003.

REFERENCES

1. M. Stonebreaker and D. Moore, *Object-Relational DBMSs, The Next Great Wave.* Morgan Kaufman, San Francisco, Calif., (1996).
2. F. Rabitti and P. Stanchev, GRIM DBMS: A GRaphical IMage Database Management System, *Vis. Database Syst., IFIP TC2/WG2.6 Working Conf. Vis. Database Syst.,* **1**, 415–430 (1989).
3. T.G. Aguierre Smith, Parsing movies in context. *Summer Usenix Conference*, Nashville, Tennessee, June 1991, pp. 157–167.
4. S. Flank, P. Martin, A. Balogh, and J. Rothey, PhotoFile: A Digital Library for Image Retrieval, *Proc. 2nd Int. Conf. Multimedia Comput. Syst.*, Washington, D.C., 1995, pp. 292–295.
5. H. Jiang, D. Montesi, and A. Elmagarmid, Videotext database system, *IEEE Proc. Int. Conf. Multimedia Comput. Syst.*, Ottawa, Ontario, Canada, 1997, pp. 344–351.
6. G. Salton and M.J. McGill, *Introduction to Modern Information Retrieval*, McGraw-Hill Book Company, New York (1983).
7. R.R. Korfhage, *Information Storage and Retrieval*, Wiley Computer Publishing, New York 1997.
8. G. Kowalski, *Information Retrieval Systems: Theory and Implementation*, Kluwer Academic Publishers, Norwell, Mass. 1997.
9. C. Faloutsos and D. Oard, A survey of information retrieval and filtering methods. Technical Report CS-TR-3514, Department of Computer Science, University of Maryland, College Park, Md., 1995.
10. A. Pentland, R.W. Picard, and S.Sclaroff, Photobook: Content-based manipulation of image databases, *Int. J. Comput. Vis.* **18**(3), 233–254 (1996).

11. T.S. Huang, S. Mehrotra, and K. Ramchandran, Multimedia analysis and retrieval system (MARS) project, Proc of 33rd Annual Clinic on Library Application of Data Processing — Digital Image Access and Retrieval, (1996).

12. J.R. Smith and S.-F. Chang, Visually Searching the Web for Content, *IEEE Multimedia* **4**(3), 12–20 (1997).

13. M. Flickner, H. Sawhney, W. Niblack, and J. Ashley, Query by Image and Video Content: The QBIC System, *IEEE Computer* **28**(9), 23–32 (1995).

14. C. Faloutsos et al., Efficient and effective querying by image content, Technical Report RJ 9453 (83074), IBM Research Report, San Jose, Calif., August 1993.

15. W. Niblack et al., The QBIC project: Querying images by content using color, texture and shape, *IBM Research Report*, San Jose, Calif., August 1993.

16. J.R. Bach et al., The virage image search engine: An open framework for image management, *Proc. SPIE, Storage and Retrieval for Still Image Video Databases* **2670**, 76–87 (1996).

17. Informix, *Excalibur Image DataBlade Module User's Guide, Version 1.2*, Informix, 1999.

18. M.J. Swain, Interactive indexing into image databases, *Storage and Retrieval for Image and Video Databases*, **1908**, 95–103, (1993).

19. M.K̃. Hu, *Visual Pattern Recognition by Moment Invariants,* in *Computer Methods in Image Analysis*, IEEE Computer Society, Los Angeles, Calif. (1977).

20. K. Porkaew, S. Mehrotra, M. Ortega, and K. Chakrabarti, Similarity search using multiple examples in MARS, *Proc. Int. Conf. Vis. Inf. Syst.* 68–75 (1999).

21. M. Ortega et al., *IEEE Trans. Knowledge Data Eng.* **10**(6), 905–925 (1998).

22. R. Fagin and E.L. Wimmers, Incorporating user preferences in multimedia queries, *Proc. Int. Conf. Database Theory (ICDT '97)* **1186**, 247–261, (1997).

23. Y. Ishikawa, R. Subramanya, and C. Faloutsos, Mindreader: Querying databases through multiple examples, *Proc. 24th Int. Conf. Very Large Data Bases VLDB '98* **24**, 218–227, (1998).

24. K. Porkaew, K. Chakrabarti, and S. Mehrotra, Query refinement for content-based multimedia retrieval in MARS, *Proc. 7th. ACM Int. Conf. Multimedia*, 235–238 (1999).

25. Y. Rui, T.S. Huang, M. Ortega, and S. Mehrotra, Relevance feedback: A power tool for interactive content-based image retrieval, *IEEE Trans. Circuits Syst. Video Technol.* **8**(5), 644–655 (1998).

26. A. Natsev, R. Rastogi, and K. Shim, Walrus: A similarity retrieval algorithm for image databases, *Proc. 1999 ACM SIGMOD Int. Conf. Manage. Data* **28**, 395–406, (1999).

27. C. Carson et al., Blobworld: A system for region-based image indexing and retrieval, *Proc. 3rd Int. Conf. Vis. Inf. Syst.* **1614**, 509–516 (June 1999).

28. M. Ortega-Binderberger, S. Mehrotra, K. Chakrabarti, and K. Porkaew, WebMARS: A Multimedia Search Engine for Full Document Retrieval and Cross Media Browsing, *6th Int. Workshop Multimedia Inf. Syst. (MIS'00)* 72–81 (2000).

29. J.R. Smith and S.-F. Chang, Integrated spatial and feature image query, *Multimedia Syst. J.* **7**(2), 129–140 (1997).

30. C.-S. Li et al., Framework for efficient processing of content-based fuzzy cartesian queries, *Proc. SPIE, Storage and Retrieval for Media Databases 2000* **3972**, 64–75 (2000).
31. E.F. Codd, A relational model of data for large shared data banks, *Commun. ACM.* **13**(6), 377–387 (1970).
32. M.J. Carey et al., The Architecture of the EXODUS extensible DBMS, *Proc. 1986 Int. Workshop Object-Oriented database syst.* 52–65 (September 1986).
33. F. Bancilhon, C. Delobel, and P. Kanellakis, *Building an Object-Oriented Database System: The Story of O2*, The Morgan Kaufmann Series in Data Management Systems, Los Altos, Calif., 1992.
34. C. Lamb, G. Landis, J. Orenstein, and D. Weinreb, The objectstore database system, *Commun. ACM*, **34**(63), 50–63 (1991).
35. M. Stonebraker and G. Kemnitz, The postgres next-generation database management system, *Commun. ACM* **34**(10), 78–92 (1991).
36. L.M. Haas, J.C. Freytag, G.M. Lohman, and H. Pirahesh, Extensible query processing in starburst, *Proc. 1989 ACM SIGMOD Int. Conf. Manage. Data* **18**, 377–388 (1989).
37. Informix, *Getting Started with Informix Universal Server, Version 9.1*, Informix, March 1997.
38. D.D. Chamberlin, *A Complete Guide to DB2 Universal Database*. Morgan Kaufmann, Los Altos, Calif., 1998.
39. ORACLE, *Oracle 8i Concepts, Release 8.1.6*, Oracle, (1999).
40. Sybase, *Sybase Adaptive Server Enterprise, Version 12.0*, Sybase, (1999).
41. W. Kim, Unisql/x unified relational and object-oriented database system. *Proc. 1994 ACM SIGMOD Int. Conf. Manage. Data* 481 (1994).
42. You-Chin (Gene) Fuh et al., Implementation of SQL3 Structured Type with Inheritance and Value Substitutability, *Proceedings of the 25th International Conference on Very Large Data Bases VLDB '99*, Edinburgh, Scotland, 1999.
43. D.D. Chamberlin et al., SEQUEL 2:A Unified Approach to Data Definition, Manipulation, and Control, *IBM J. Res. Dev.*, **20**(6), 560–575 (1976).
44. S. Khoshafian and A.B. Baker, *Multimedia and Imaging Databases*, Morgan Kaufmann Publishers, San Francisco, Calif. 1996.
45. J.L. Bruno et al., Disk scheduling with quality of service guarantees, *IEEE Int. Conf. Multimedia Comput. Syst.*, Florence, Italy, June 1999, pp. 400–405.
46. V. Gottemukkala, A. Jhingran, and S. Padmanabhan, Interfacing parallel applications and parallel databases, in A. Gray and P.- Å Larson, eds., *Proc. 13th Int. Conf. on Data Engineering*, IEEE Computer Society Birmingham, U.K, 1997.
47. A. Guttman, R-tree: a dynamic index structure for spatial searching, *Proc. 1984 ACM SIGMOD Int. Conf. Manage. Data* **14**, 47–57 (June 1984).
48. J. Neivergelt et al., *ACM Trans. Database Systems (TODS)* **9**(1), 38–71 (1984).
49. R. Bliuhute, S. Saltenis, G. Slivinskas, and C. Jensen, Developing a datablade for a new index, *Proc. 15th Int. Conf. Data Eng.* 314–323, (March 1999).
50. J. Srinivasan et al., Extensible indexing: A framework for integrating domain-specific indexing schemes into oracle8i, *Proc. 16th Int. Conf. Data Eng.* 91–100 (February 2000).

51. J. Hellerstein, J. Naughton, and A. Pfeffer, Generalized search trees in database systems, *Proc. 21st Int. Conf. Very Large Data Bases VLDB'95* 562–573 (September 1995).
52. S. Dessloch and N. Mattos, Integrating SQL databases with content—specific search engines. *Proceedings of the International Conference on Very Large Data Bases VLDB '97*, IBM Database Technology Institute, Santa Teresa Lab. Athens, Greece 1997, pp. 528–537.
53. ORACLE, *Oracle Internet File System, User's Guide, Release 1.0*, Oracle, (2000).
54. ORACLE, *Oracle Internet File System, Developers's Guide, Release 1.0*, Oracle, (2000).
55. Informix, *Informix Universal Server–Datablade Programmer's Manual Version 9.1*, Informix, March 1997.
56. ORACLE, *Oracle Data Cartridge, Developers's Guide, Release 8.1.5*, Oracle, (1999).
57. Informix, *Media360, Any kind of content. Everywhere you need it*, Informix, 2000.
58. H. Tamura et al., Texture features corresponding to visual perception, *IEEE Trans. Systems, Man and Cybernetics*, SMC-**8**(6), 460–473 (1978).
59. ORACLE, *Oracle 8i inter Media Audio, Image and Video, User's Guide and Reference*, Oracle, (1999).
60. A. Gupta and R. Jain, Visual Information Retrieval, *Commun. ACM* **40**(5), 70–79 (1997).
61. ORACLE, *Oracle 8i Visual Information Retrieval, Users Guide and Reference*, Oracle, (1999).
62. Sybase, *Java in Adaptive Server Enterprise, Version 12*, Sybase, October (1999).
63. K. Chakrabarti and S. Mehrotra, The Hybrid Tree: An Index Structure for High Dimensional Feature Spaces, *Proc. 15th Int. Conf. Data Eng.* 440–447 (March 1999).
64. K. Beyer, J. Goldstein, R. Ramakrishnan, and U. Shaft, When is "nearest neighbor" meaningful? *Proceedings of the International Conference on Database Theory (ICDT '99)*, Jerusalem, Israel, 1999.
65. F. Korn, et al., Fast nearest neighbor search in medical image databases, *Proc. 22nd Int. Conf. Very Large Data Bases VLDB '96* 215–226 (September 1996).
66. T. Seidl and H.P. Kriegel, Optimal multistep k-nearest neighbor search, *Proc. 1998 ACM SIGMOD Int. Conf. Manage. Data* **27**, 154–165 (June 1998).
67. K. Chakrabarti, K. Porkaew M. Ortega, and S. Mehrotra, Evaluating Refined Queries in Top-*k* Retrieval Systems, Technical Report TR-MARS-00-04, University of California, Irvine; online at *http://www-db.ics.uci.edu/pages/publications/*, 2000.
68. L. Wu, C. Faloutsos, K. Sycara, and T. Payne, Falcon: Feedback adaptive loop for content-based retrieval, *Proc. 26th Int. Conf. Very Large Data Bases VLDB 2000* 297–306 (2000).
69. K. Chakrabarti and S. Mehrotra, Efficient concurrency control in multidimensional access methods, *Proc. 1999 ACM SIGMOD Int. Conf. Manage. Data* 25–36 (June 1999).
70. P. Aoki, Generalizing "search" in generalized search trees, *Proc. 14th Int. Conf. Data Eng.* 380–389 (1998).
71. M. Kornacker, C. Mohan, and J. Hellerstein, Concurrency and recovery in generalized search trees, *Proc. 1997 ACM SIGMOD Int. Conf. Manage. Data* 62–72 (1997).
72. K. Chakrabarti and S. Mehrotra, Dynamic granular locking approach to phantom protection in R-trees, *Proc. 14th Int. Conf. Data Eng.* 446–454 (February 1998).

73. J. Gray and A. Reuter, *Transaction Processing: Concepts and Techniques*, Morgan Kaufmann, San Mateo, Calif., 1993.
74. D.B. Lomet, Key range locking strategies for improved concurrency, *Proc. 19th Int. Conf. Very Large Data Bases VLDB '93*, 655–664 (August 1993).
75. C. Mohan, ARIES/KVL: A key value locking method for concurrency control of multiaction transactions operating on B-tree indexes, *Proc. 16th Int. Conf. Very Large Data Bases VLDB '92* 392–405, (August 1990).
76. J. Orenstein and T. Merett., A class of data structures for associative searching, *Proc. 3rd ACM SIGACT-SIGMOD Symp. Principles Database Syst.* 181–190, (1984).
77. H.G. Molina, J.D. Ullman, and J. Widom, *Database System Implementation*, Prentice Hall, New York 1999.
78. P.G. Selinger, et al., Access path selection in a relational database management system, In P.A. Bernstein, ed., *Proceedings of the 1979 ACM SIGMOD International Conference on Management of Data ACM*, Boston, Mass., pp. 23–34 (1979).
79. S. Chaudhuri and L. Gravano, Optimizing queries over multimedia repositories, *Proc. 1996 ACM SIGMOD Int. Conf. Manage. Data* 91–102 (June 1996).
80. V. Poosala and Y. Ioannidis, Selectivity estimation without the attribute value independence assumption, *Proc. 23rd Int. Conf. Very Large Data Bases VLDB '97* 486–495 (August 1997).
81. Y. Matias, J.S. Vitter, and M. Wang, Wavelet-based histograms for selectivity estimation. *Proc. 1998 ACM SIGMOD Int. Conf. Manage. Data* 448–459 (June 1998).
82. S. Acharya, V. Poosala, and S. Ramaswamy, Selectivity estimation in spatial databases, *Proc. 1999 ACM SIGMOD Int. Conf. Manage. Data* 13–24 (June 1999).
83. A. Belussi and C. Faloutsos, Estimating the selectivity of spatial queries using the 'correlation' fractal dimension, *Proc. 21st Int. Conf. on Very Large Data Bases VLDB '95* 299–310 (September 1995).
84. C. Faloutsos, B. Seeger, A. Traina, and C. Traina, Jr., Spatial join selectivity using power laws, *Proc. 2000 ACM SIGMOD Int. Conf. Manage. Data* 177–188, June 2000.
85. C. Faloutsos and I. Kamel, Beyond Uniformity and Independence: Analysis of R-trees Using the Concept of Fractal Dimension, *Proc. 13th ACM Symp. Principles of Database Systems, PODS '94* **13**, 4–13 (May 1994).
86. Y. Theodoridis and T. Sellis, A Model for the Prediction of R-tree Performance, *Proc. 15th ACM Symp. Principles Database Syst. PODS'96* **15**, 161–171 (June 1996).
87. S. Berchtold, C. Bohm, D. Keim, and H. P. Kriegel, A cost model for nearest neighbor search in high dimensional data spaces, *Proc. 16th ACM Symp. Principles of Database Systems*, Tucson, Ariz, May 1997.
88. B.U. Pagel, F. Korn, and C. Faloutsos, Deflating the dimensionality curse using multiple fractal dimensions, *Proc. 16th Int. Conf. Data Eng.* 589–598 (March 2000).
89. J.M. Hellerstein and M. Stonebraker, Predicate migration: Optimizing queries with expensive predicates, *Proc. 1993 ACM SIGMOD Int. Conf. Manage. Data* **22**, 267–276 (May 1993).
90. J.M. Hellerstein, Practical predicate placement, *Proc. 1994 ACM SIGMOD Int. Conf. Manage. Data* **23**, 325–335 (June 1994).

91. S. Chaudhuri and K.Shim, Optimization of queries with user-defined predicates, *Proc. 22nd Int. Conf. Very Large Data Bases VLDB '96* 87–98 (September 1996).
92. P. Seshadri, E-ADTs and Relational Query Optimization, Technical report, Cornell University Technical Report, June (1998).
93. P. Seshadri, Enhanced abstract data types in object-relational databases, *VLDB J.* **7**(3), 130–140 (August 1998).
94. R. Fagin, Combining fuzzy information from multiple systems, *Proc. 15th ACM Symp. Principles Database Systems, PODS '96* **115**, 216–226 (June 1996).
95. M. Ortega, et al., Supporting Similarity Queries in MARS, *Proc. of ACM Multimedia 1997* 403–413, (1997).
96. S. Nepal and M.V. Ramakrishna, Query processing issues in image (multimedia) databases, *Proc. 15th Int. Conf. Data Eng.* 22–29 (March 1999).
97. U. Guntzer, W. Balke, and W. Kiebling, Optimizing Multi-Feature Queries for Image Databases, *Proc. 26th Int. Conf. on Very Large Data Bases VLDB 2000* 419–428 (September 2000).
98. S. Chaudhuri and L. Gravano, Evaluating top-k selection queries, *Proceedings of the 25th International Conference on Very Large Data Bases VLDB'99*, Edinburgh, Scotland, September 1999.
99. D. Donjerkovic and R. Ramakrishnan, Probabilistic optimization of top-n queries, *Proceedings of the International Conference on Very Large Data Bases VLDB '99*, Edinburgh, Scotland, September 1999.
100. M.J. Carey and D. Kossmann, On Saying "Enough Already!" in SQL, *Proc. 1997 ACM SIGMOD Int. Conf. Manage. Data* 219–230 (May 1997).
101. M.J. Carey and D. Kossmann, Reducing the Braking Distance of an SQL Query Engine, *Proc. 24th Int. Conf. Very Large Data Bases VLDB '98* 158–169 (1998).
102. W.G. Aref and H. Samet, Cascaded spatial join algorithms with spatially sorted output, *Proc. 4th ACM Workshop Adv. Geogr. Inf. Syst.* 17–24, (1997).
103. G. Hjaltason and H. Samet, Incremental distance join algorithms for spatial databases, *Proceedings of 1998 ACM SIGMOD International Conference on Management of Data*, Seattle, Wash., USA, June 1998.
104. W.G. Aref and H. Samet, Optimization for spatial query processing, G.M. Lohman, A. Sernadas, and R. Camps, eds., *Proc. 17th Int. Conf. on Very Large Data Bases VLDB '92*, Morgan Kaufmann Barcelona, Catalonia, Spain, 1991 pp. 81–90.
105. T. Brinkhoff, H.-P. Kriegel, and B. Seeger, Efficient processing of spatial joins using R-Trees, in P. Buneman and S. Jajodia, eds., *Proceedings of the 1993 ACM SIGMOD International Conference on Management of Data* ACM Press Washington, D.C. 1993, pp. 26–28.
106. J.C. Shafer and R. Agrawal, Parallel algorithms for high-dimensional proximity joins for data mining applications, *Proc. 23rd Int. Conf. Very Large Data Bases VLDB '97* 176–185 (August 1997).
107. K. Alsabti, S. Ranka, and V. Singh, An efficient parallel algorithm for high dimensional similarity join. *Proceedings of the International Parallel and Distributed Processing Symposium*, Orlando, Florida, March 1998.
108. K. Shim, R. Srikant, and R. Agrawal, High-dimensional similarity joins, *Proc. 13th Int. Conf. on Data Eng.* 301–311 (April 1997).

109. A.N. Papadopoulos and Y. Manolopoulos, Similarity query processing using disk arrays, *Proc. 1998 ACM SIGMOD Int. Conf. Manage. Data* 225–236 (1998).
110. N. Koudas and K.C. Sevcik, High dimensional similarity joins: Algorithms and performance evaluation, *Proc. 14th Int. Conf. Data Eng.* 466–475 (February 1998).

8 Image Compression — A Review

SHEILA S. HEMAMI
Cornell University, Ithaca, New York

8.1 INTRODUCTION

Compression reduces the number of bits required to represent a signal. The appropriate compression strategy is a function of the type of signal to be compressed. Here, we focus on images, which can be single component (e.g., gray scale) or multiple component (e.g., three-component color or higher-component remote sensing data). Each component can be considered to be an "image" — a two-dimensional (2D) array of pixels, and this chapter reviews the fundamentals of image compression as a 2D signal with specific statistical characteristics. Application to multicomponent imagery is achieved by separately compressing each component. Compression of the higher-dimensional multicomponent data is possible, it is very uncommon, so we concentrate on 2D image compression.

Compression can be thought of as redundancy reduction; its goal is to eliminate the redundancy in the data to provide an efficient representation that preserves only the essential information. Compression can be performed in one of the two regimes: lossless compression and lossy compression. Lossless compression permits an exact recovery of the original signal and permits compression ratios for images of not more than approximately 4 : 1. In lossy compression, the original signal cannot be recovered from the compressed representation. Lossy compression can provide images that are visually equivalent to the original at compression ratios that range from 8 : 1 to 20 : 1, depending on the image content. Incorporation of human visual system characteristics can be important in providing high-quality lossy compression. Higher compression ratios are possible, but they produce a visual difference between the original and the compressed images.

A block diagram of a typical generic image-compression system is shown in Figure 8.1 and consists of three components: pixel-level redundancy

Image Databases: Search and Retrieval of Digital Imagery, Edited by Vittorio Castelli and Lawrence D. Bergman.
ISBN 0-471-32116-8

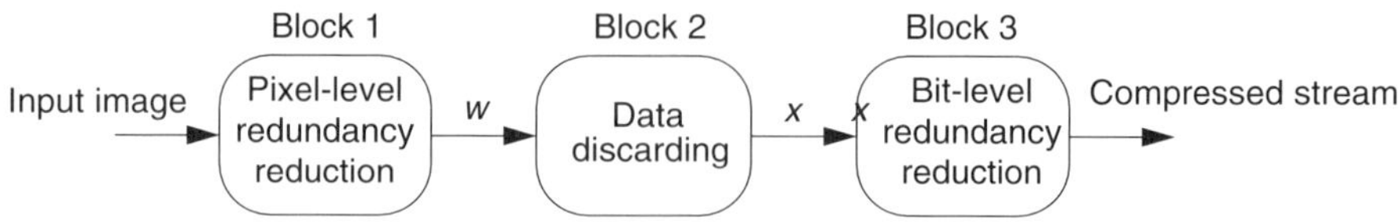

Figure 8.1. Three components of an image-compression system.

reduction, data discarding, and bit-level redundancy reduction. A lossless image-compression system omits the data-discarding step, and as such, lossless compression results from redundancy reduction alone. A lossy algorithm uses all three blocks, although extremely efficient techniques can produce excellent results even without the third block. Although both compression types can be achieved using simpler block diagrams (e.g., omitting the first block), these three steps are required to produce state-of-the-art lossy image compression. Each of these blocks is described briefly.

Pixel-level redundancy reduction performs an invertible mapping of the input image into a different domain in which the output data w is less correlated than the original pixels. The most efficient and widely used mapping is a frequency transformation (also called a *transform code*), which maps the spatial information contained in the pixels into a frequency space, in which the image data is more efficiently represented numerically and is well matched to the human visual system frequency response. Data discarding provides the "loss" in lossy compression and is performed by quantization of w to form x. Both statistical properties of images and human visual system characteristics are used to determine how the data w should be quantized while minimally impacting the fidelity of the images. Fidelity can be easily measured numerically but such metrics do not necessarily match subjective judgments, making visually pleasing quantization of image data an inexact science. Finally, bit-level redundancy reduction removes or reduces dependencies in the data x and is itself lossless.

Instead of studying the blocks sequentially, this chapter begins by describing basic concepts in both lossless and lossy coding: entropy and rate-distortion theory (RD theory). Entropy provides a computable bound on bit-level redundancy reduction and hence lossless compression ratios for specific sources, whereas RD theory provides a theory of lossy compression bounds. Useful for understanding limits of compression, neither the concept of entropy nor RD theory tell us how these bounds may be achieved and whether the computed or theorized bounds are absolute bounds themselves. However, they suggest that the desired lossless or lossy compression is indeed possible. Next, a brief description of the human visual system is provided, giving an understanding of the relative visual impact of image information. This provides guidance in matching pixel-level redundancy reduction techniques and data-discarding techniques to human perception. Pixel-level redundancy reduction is then described, followed by quantization and bit-level redundancy reduction. Finally, several standard and nonstandard state-of-the-art image compression techniques are described.

8.2 ENTROPY — A BOUND ON LOSSLESS COMPRESSION

Entropy provides a computable bound by which a source with a known probability mass function can be losslessly compressed. For example, the "source" could be the data entering Block 3 in Figure 8.1; as such, entropy does not suggest how this source has been generated from the original data. Redundancy reduction prior to entropy computation can reduce the entropy of the processed data below that of the original data.

The concept of entropy is required for *variable-rate* coding, in which a code can adjust its own bit rate to better match the local behavior of a source. For example, if English text is to be encoded with a fixed-length binary code, each code word requires $\lceil \log_2 27 \rceil = 5$ bits/symbol (assuming only the alphabet and a space symbol). However, letters such as "s" and "e" appear far more frequently than do letters such as "x" and "j." A more efficient code would assign shorter code words to more frequently occurring symbols and longer code words to less frequently occurring symbols, resulting in a lower average number of bits/symbol to encode the source. In fact, the entropy of English has been estimated at 1.34 bits/letter [1], indicating that substantial savings are possible over using a fixed-length code.

8.2.1 Entropy Definition

For a discrete source X with a finite alphabet of N symbols $(x_0, \ldots, x_{N-1})$ and a probability mass function of $p(x)$, the entropy of the source in bits/symbol is given by

$$H(X) = -\sum_{n=0}^{N-1} p(x_n) \log_2 p(x_n) \tag{8.1}$$

and measures the average number of bits/symbol required to describe the source. Such a discrete source is encountered in image compression, in which the acquired digital image pixels can take on only a finite number of values as determined by the number of bits used to represent each pixel.

It is easy to show (using the method of Lagrange multipliers) that the uniform distribution achieves maximum entropy, given by $H(X) = \log_2 N$. A uniformly distributed source can be considered to have maximum randomness when compared with sources having other distributions — each alphabet value is no more likely than any other. Combining this with the intuitive English text example mentioned previously, it is apparent that entropy provides a measure of the compressibility of a source. High entropy indicates more randomness; hence the source requires more bits on average to describe a symbol.

8.2.2 Calculating Entropy — An Example

An example illustrates the computation of entropy the difficulty in determining the entropy of a fixed-length signal. Consider the four-point signal [3/4 1/4 0 0]. There are three distinct values (or symbols) in this signal, with probabilities 1/4,

1/4, and 1/2 for the symbols 3/4, 1/4, and 0, respectively. The entropy of the signal is then computed as

$$H = -\tfrac{1}{4}\log_2\tfrac{1}{4} - \tfrac{1}{4}\log_2\tfrac{1}{4} - \tfrac{1}{2}\log_2\tfrac{1}{2} = 1.5 \text{ bits/symbol}. \tag{8.2}$$

This indicates that a variable length code requires 1.5 bits/symbol on average to represent this source. In fact, a variable-length code that achieves this entropy is [10 11 0] for the symbols [3/4 1/4 0].

Now consider taking the Walsh-Hadamard transform of this signal (block-based transforms are described in more detail in Section 8.5.2). This is an invertible transform, so the original data can be uniquely recovered from the transformed data. The forward transform is given by

$$\frac{1}{2}\begin{bmatrix} 1 & 1 & 1 & 1 \\ 1 & 1 & -1 & -1 \\ 1 & -1 & -1 & 1 \\ 1 & -1 & 1 & -1 \end{bmatrix}\begin{bmatrix} 3/4 \\ 1/4 \\ 0 \\ 0 \end{bmatrix} = \begin{bmatrix} 1/2 \\ 1/2 \\ 1/4 \\ 1/4 \end{bmatrix} \tag{8.3}$$

with a resulting entropy easily calculated as 1 bit/symbol. With a simple forward transform before computing the entropy and an inverse transform to get the original signal back from the coded signal, the entropy has been reduced by 0.5 bit/symbol. The entropy reduction achieved by a different signal representation suggests that measuring entropy is not as straightforward as plugging into the mathematical definition; with an appropriate invertible signal representation, the entropy can be reduced and the original signal still represented.

Although the entropy example calculations given earlier are simple to compute, the results and the broader definition of entropy as the "minimum number of bits required to describe a source" suggests that defining the entropy of an image is not as trivial as it may seem. An appropriate pixel-level redundancy reduction such as a transform can reduce entropy. Such redundancy reduction techniques for images are discussed later in the chapter; however, it should be mentioned that pixel transformation into the "right" domain can reduce the required bit rate to describe the image.

8.2.3 Entropy Coding Techniques

Entropy coding techniques, also known as *noiseless coding*, *lossless coding*, or *data compaction* coding, are variable-rate coding techniques that provide compression at rates close to the source entropy. Although the source entropy provides a lower bound, several of these techniques can approach this bound arbitrarily closely. Three specific techniques are described.

Huffman coding achieves variable-length coding by assigning code words of differing lengths to different source symbols. The code word length is directly proportional to $-\log(f(x))$, where $f(x)$ is the frequency of occurrence of the symbol x, and a simple algorithm exists to design a Huffman code when the source symbol probabilities are known [2]. If the probabilities are all powers of (1/2), then the entropy bound can be achieved exactly by a binary Huffman code. Because a code word is assigned explicitly to each alphabet symbol, the minimum number of bits required to code a single source symbol is 1. The example variable-length code given in the previous section is a Huffman code.

In *arithmetic coding*, a variable number of input symbols are required to produce each code symbol. A sequence of source symbols is represented by a subinterval of real numbers within the unit interval [0,1]. Smaller intervals require more bits to specify them; larger intervals require fewer. Longer sequences of source symbols require smaller intervals to uniquely specify them and hence require more bits than shorter sequences. Successive symbols in the input data reduce the size of the current interval proportionally to their probabilities; more probable symbols reduce an interval by a smaller amount than less probable symbols and hence add fewer bits to the message. Arithmetic coding is more complex than Huffman coding; typically, it provides a gain of approximately 10 percent more compression than Huffman coding in imaging applications.

Lempel-Ziv-Welch (LZW) coding is very different from both Huffman and arithmetic coding in that it does not require the probability distribution of the input. Instead, LZW coding is dictionary-based: the code "builds itself" from the input data, recursively parsing an input sequence into nonoverlapping blocks of variable size and constructing a dictionary of blocks seen thus far. The dictionary is initialized with the symbols 0 and 1. In general, LZW works best on large inputs, in which the overhead involved in building the dictionary decreases as the number of source symbols increases. Because of its complexity and the possibility to expand small data sets, LZW coding is not frequently used in image-compression schemes (it is, however, the basis for the Unix utilities *compress* and *gzip*).

8.3 RATE-DISTORTION THEORY—PERFORMANCE BOUNDS FOR LOSSY COMPRESSION

Lossy compression performance bounds are provided by rate-distortion theory (RD theory) and are more difficult to quantify and compute than the lossless compression performance bound. RD theory approaches the problem of maximizing fidelity (or minimizing distortion) for a class of sources for a given bit rate. This description immediately suggests the difficulties in applying such theory to image compression. First, fidelity must be defined. Numerical metrics are easy to calculate but an accepted numerical metric that corresponds to perceived visual quality has yet to be defined. Secondly, an appropriate statistical description for images is required. Images are clearly complex and even sophisticated statistical models for small subsets of image types fail to adequately describe the source for RD theory purposes. Nevertheless, the basic tenets of RD theory can be applied operationally to provide improved compression performance in a system. The aim of this section is to introduce readers to the concepts of RD theory and their applications in operational rate distortion.

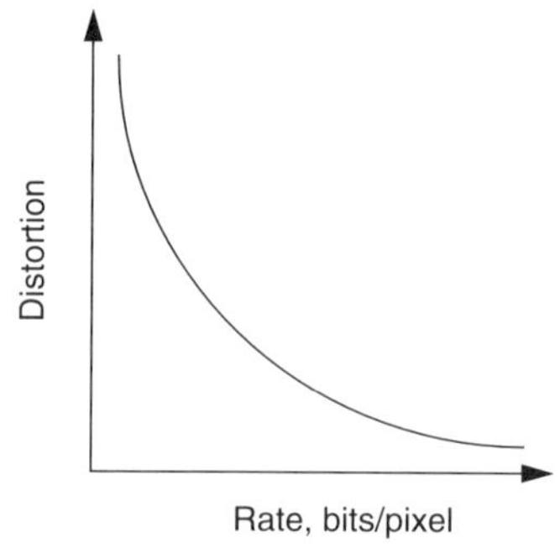

Figure 8.2. A sample rate-distortion curve.

A representative RD curve is shown in Figure 8.2 — as the rate increases, distortion decreases, and vice versa. RD theory provides two classes of performance bounds. Shannon theory, introduced by Claude Shannon seminal works [3,4], provides performance bounds as the data samples to be coded are grouped into infinitely long blocks. Alternatively, high-rate low-distortion theory provides bounds for fixed block size as the rate approaches infinity. Although the second class of bounds is more realistic for use in image compression (an image has a finite number of pixels), both classes only provide existence proofs; they are not constructive. As such, performance bounds can be derived, no instruction is provided on designing a system that can achieve them. Hence how can RD theory be applied to practical image compression?

First, consider a simple example. Suppose that an image-compression algorithm can select among one of several data samples to add to the compressed stream. Data sample 1 requires three bits to code and reduces the mean-squared error (MSE) of the reconstructed image by 100; data sample 2 requires 7 bits to code and reduces the MSE by 225. Which sample should be added to the data stream? A purely rate-based approach would select the first sample — it requires fewer bits to describe. Conversely, a purely distortion-based approach would select the second sample, as it reduces the MSE by over twice the first sample. An RD-based approach compares the trade-off between the two: the first sample produces an average decrease in MSE per bit of $100/3 = 33.3$ and the second produces an average decrease in MSE per bit of $225/7 = 321/7$. The RD-based approach selects data sample 1 as maximizing the decrease in MSE per bit. In other words, the coefficient that yields a steeper slope for the RD curve is selected.

The previous example demonstrates how RD theory is applied in practice; this is generally referred to as determining *operational* (rather than theoretical) RD curves. When dealing with existing compression techniques (e.g., a particular transform coder followed by a particular quantization strategy, such as JPEG or a zerotree-based wavelet coder), RD theory is reduced to operational rate distortion — for a given system (the compression algorithm) and source model (a statistical description of the image), which system parameters produce the best RD performance? Furthermore, human visual system (HVS) characteristics must be taken into account even when determining operational RD curves. Blind application of minimizing the MSE subject to a rate constraint for image data following a redundancy-reducing transform code suggests that the average error introduced into each quantized coefficient be equal, and that such a quantization strategy will indeed minimize the MSE over all other step size selections at the same rate. However, the human visual system is not equally sensitive to errors at different frequencies, and HVS properties suggest that more quantization error can be tolerated at higher frequencies to produce the same visual quality. Indeed, images compressed with HVS-motivated quantization step sizes are of visually higher quality than those compressed to minimize the MSE.

The operational RD curve consists of points that can be achieved using a given compression system, whereas RD theory provides existence proofs only. The system defines the parameters that must be selected (e.g., quantizer step sizes), and a constrained minimization then solves for the parameters that will provide the best RD trade-offs. Suppose there are N sources to be represent using a total of R bits/symbol; these N sources could represent the 64 discrete cosine transform (DCT) coefficients in a joint photographic experts group (JPEG) compression system or the 10 subband coefficients in a three-level hierarchically subband-transformed image (both the DCT and subband transforms are described in Section 8.5). For each source, there is, an individual RD curve, which may itself be operationally determined or generated from a model, that indicates that source i will incur a distortion of D_{ij} when coded at a rate of R_{ij}at operating point j. Then the operational RD curve is obtained by solving the following constrained minimization:

For each source i, find the operating point $y(i)$ that minimizes the distortion

$$D = f(D_{1y(1)}, D_{2y(2)}, \ldots, D_{Ny(N)}) \quad \text{such that} \quad \sum_{\mathrm{i}=1}^{N} R_{iy(i)} \leq R \qquad (8.4)$$

Most commonly, the distortion is additive and $D = \Sigma_{\mathrm{i}=1}^{N} D_{iy(i)}$. This constrained minimization can be solved using the method of Lagrange multipliers. When solved, the result is that to minimize the total distortion D, each source should operate at a point on its RD curve such that the tangents to the curves are equal; that is, the operating points have equal slopes. The minimization finds that slope.

Both RD theory and operational RD curves provide a guiding tenet for lossy image compression: maximize the quality for a given bit rate. Although some image-compression algorithms actually use RD theory to find operating parameters, more commonly, the general tenet is used without explicitly invoking the theory. This yields theoretically suboptimal compression, but as Section 8.8 will show, the performance of many compression algorithms is still an excellent event without explicit RD optimization.

8.4 HUMAN VISUAL SYSTEM CHARACTERISTICS

Lossy image compression must discard information in the image that is not or is only minimally visible, producing the smallest possible perceptible change to the image. To determine what information can be discarded, an elementary understanding of the HVS is required. Understanding the HVS has been a topic of research for over a century, but here we review the points salient to providing high-quality lossy image compression.

8.4.1 Vision and Luminance-Chrominance Representations

Light enters the eye through the pupil and strikes the retina at the back of the eye. The retina contains two types of light receptors: cones and rods. Approximately eight million cones located in the central portion of the retina and sensitive to red, blue, or green light provide color vision under high-illumination conditions, such as in a well-lighted room. Each cone is connected to its own nerve end, providing high resolution in *photopic* (color) vision. Approximately 120 million rods are distributed over the entire retina and provide vision at low-illumination levels, such as a moonlit night (*scotopic* vision). A single nerve end is connected to multiple rods; as such, resolution is lower and rods provide a general picture of the field of view without color information. With midrange illumination, both rods and cones are active to provide *mesopic* vision. Because most digital images are viewed on well-lit displays, the characteristics of photopic vision are most applicable to digital imaging and compression.

The HVS processes color information by converting the red, green, and blue data from the cones into a luminance-chrominance space, with the luminance channel having approximately five times the bandwidth of the chrominance channel. Consequently, much more error in color (or chrominance) than in luminance information can be tolerated in compressed images. Color digital images are often represented in a luminance-chrominance color space (one luminance component, and two chrominance components). The chrominance components are often reduced in size by a factor of 2 in each dimension through low-pass filtering followed by downsampling; these lower-resolution chrominance components are then compressed along with the full-size luminance component. In decompression, the chrominance components are upsampled and interpolated to full size for display. No noticeable effects are seen when this is applied to natural images, and it reduces the amount of chrominance information by a factor of 4 even before the compression operation.

Because understanding and representation of color is itself a well-developed science, the remainder of this section will focus on the HVS characteristics for monochrome (gray scale) images on which most lossy image-compression algorithms rely. The resulting characteristics are typically also applied to chrominance data without modification.

8.4.2 The Human Contrast Sensitivity Function and Visibility Thresholds

Studies on perception of visual stimuli indicate that many factors influence the visibility of noise in a degraded image when compared with the original. These factors are functions of the image itself and include the average luminance of the image, the spatial frequencies present in the image, and the image content.

Because images can have widely varying average luminances and content, the first and third factors are more difficult to include in an image-compression algorithm for general use. However, all images can be decomposed into their frequency content and the HVS sensitivities to different frequencies can be incorporated into an algorithm.

The human *contrast sensitivity function* (CSF) is a well-accepted, experimentally obtained description of spatial frequency perception and plots contrast sensitivity versus spatial frequency. A common contrast measure is the Michelson contrast, given in terms of minimum and maximum luminances in the stimulus $l_{\min}$ and $l_{\max}$ as $C = (l_{\max} - l_{\min})/(l_{\max} + l_{\min})$. The visibility threshold (VT) is defined as the contrast at which the stimulus can be perceived, and the contrast sensitivity is defined as 1/VT. The units of spatial frequency are cycles/degree, where a cycle refers to a full period of a sinusoid, and degrees are a measure of visual range, where the visual field is described by 180°. Spatial frequency is a function of viewing distance, so the same sinusoid represents a higher spatial frequency at a larger viewing distance. The CSF has been determined experimentally with stimuli of sinusoidal gratings at differing frequencies. Figure 8.3 plots a representative CSF. This function peaks around 5–10 cycles/degree and exhibits exponential falloff—humans are exponentially less sensitive to higher frequencies.

The CSF represents measured sensitivities to a simple stimuli that is single frequency. Although images can be decomposed into individual frequencies, they in general consist of many such frequencies. Factors influencing the VTs for a complex stimuli include luminance masking, in which VTs are affected by background luminance and contrast masking, in which VTs are affected for one image component in the presence of another. Contrast masking is sometimes informally referred to as *texture masking* and includes the interactions of different frequencies. The combination of luminance and contrast masking is referred to as *spatial masking*. When spatial masking is exploited, more compression artifacts can be hidden in appropriate parts of the an image. For example, an observer is less likely to see compression artifacts in a dark, textured region, when compared

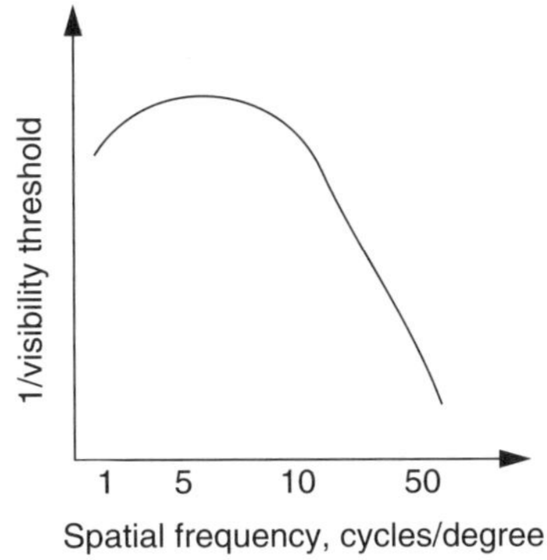

Figure 8.3. The human contrast sensitivity function.

with artifacts in a midgray flat region. However, fully exploiting spatial masking in compression is difficult because it is fairly image-dependent.

The CSF is nonorientation-specific. A HVS model that incorporates orientation frequency is the *multichannel model* [5], which asserts that the visual cortex contains sets of neurons (called *channels*) tuned to different spatial frequencies at different orientations. Although the multichannel model is itself not typically applied directly to obtaining VTs, it is used as an argument for using wavelet transforms (described in Section 8.5).

8.4.3 Application to Image Compression

Although the CSF can be mapped directly to a compression algorithm (see [6–8] for details), it is more common to experimentally measure the VTs for basis functions of the transform used in an image-compression algorithm. These VTs are then translated to quantizer step sizes such that quantization-induced distortion in image components will be below the measured VTs. Such an application assumes that results from individual experimental stimuli such as a single basis function or band-pass noise add independently, so that the measured VTs are equally valid when all transform coefficients in an image are simultaneously quantized. This approach is argued to be valid when all individual distortions are *subthreshold* that is, they are all below the experimentally measured VTs. Such an application is image-independent — only measured VTs are used in determining a quantization strategy. Quantization can be made image-dependent by modifying the VTs by incorporating various spatial masking models [9].

Roughly speaking, then, a good image-compression algorithm will discard more higher frequencies than lower frequencies, putting more compression artifacts in the frequencies to which the eye is less sensitive. Note that if the data-discarding step is uniform quantization, this result is in conflict with that from RD theory, which indicates that all frequencies should be quantized with the same step size. As such, a perceptually weighted distortion measure is required to obtain the best-looking images when using an RD technique.

8.5 PIXEL-BASED REDUNDANCY REDUCTION

In this section, techniques for redundancy reduction in images are examined. These include predictive coding and transform coding. The high redundancy present in image pixels can be quantified by the relatively high correlation coefficients and can be intuitively understood by considering predicting a single pixel. High correlation intuitively means that given a group of spatially close pixels and an unknown pixel in that group, the unknown pixel can be predicted with very little error from the known pixels. As such, most of the information required to determine the unknown pixel is contained in the surrounding pixels and the unknown pixel itself contains relatively little information that is not represented in the surrounding pixels. Predictive coding exploits this redundancy by attempting to predict the current data sample from surrounding data and can be applied both in the pixel domain and selectively on transform coded image data. If the prediction is done well, the resulting coded data contains much less redundancy (i.e., has lower correlation) than the original data.

Transformation from the pixel domain to a domain in which each data point represents independent information can also eliminate this redundancy. It is not coincidental that state-of-the-art compression algorithms employ frequency transformations as a method of pixel-based redundancy reduction. A transform can be considered to be a spectral decomposition, providing a twofold insight into the operation of transform coding. First of all, image data is separated into spatial frequencies, which can be coded according to human perception. Secondly, the spectral information (or *coefficient* data) is significantly less correlated than the corresponding pixel information and hence is easier to represent efficiently.

This section describes two types of frequency transformations: block-based transforms and wavelet transforms. Block-based transform coding has been very widely used in compression techniques for images, due in great part to the use of the DCT for the still-image coding standard JPEG [10] and in the video coding standard *motion pictures experts group* (MPEG) [11]. Wavelet transform coding is an alternative to block-based transform coding and is the transform used in JPEG-2000 [12]. Wavelet decompositions naturally lend themselves to progressive transmission, in which more bits result in improvement either in a spatially scalable manner (in which the size of the decoded image increases) or in a quality-scalable manner (in which the quality of the full-size decoded image increases). It has been argued that representing images using their wavelet transforms is well suited to the HVS because wavelets provide a decomposition that varies with both scale and orientation, which matches the HVS multichannel model.

Many excellent texts exist on both transform coding techniques, and the interested reader is directed to those listed in the bibliography Ref. [13].

8.5.1 Predictive Coding

In predictive coding, rather than directly coding the data itself, the coded data consists of a difference signal formed by subtracting a prediction of the data from the data itself. The prediction for the current sample is usually formed using past data. A predictive encoder and decoder are shown in Figure 8.4, with the difference signal given by d. If the internal loop states are initialized to the same values at the beginning of the signal, then $y = x$. If the predictor is ideal at removing redundancy, then the difference signal contains only the "new" information at each time instant that is unrelated to previous data. This "new" information is sometimes referred to as the *innovation*, and d is called the *innovations process*. If predictive coding is used, an appropriate predictor must be determined.

Predictors can be nonlinear or linear. A nonlinear predictor can in general outperform a linear predictor at removing redundancy because it is not restricted in form, but can be difficult or impossible to implement. The predictor that minimizes the MSE between the current sample and its prediction is nonlinear and is given by the conditional expectation operator: the MMSE predictor of x given z is $E(x|z)$. However, this predictor is impossible to implement in practice.

An N-step linear predictor is given as

$$\text{Pred}\{x(n)\} = \sum_{i=1}^{N} \alpha_i x(n-i) \tag{8.5}$$

The prediction coefficients α_i that minimize the MSE $E\{x(n) - \text{Pred}\{x(n)\})^2\}$ can be easily found to be given by

$$\begin{bmatrix} \alpha_l \\ \alpha_N \end{bmatrix} = \begin{bmatrix} 1 & \rho_1 & \rho_{N-1} \\ \rho_1 & & \\ \rho_{N-1} & \rho_1 & 1 \end{bmatrix}^{-1} \begin{bmatrix} \rho_1 \\ \rho_N \end{bmatrix} \tag{8.6}$$

where ρ_i is the i-th-step correlation coefficient of x. Linear predictors are easy to implement as FIR filters. A special case of linear prediction is one-step prediction. From Eq. (8.6), the optimal one-step prediction coefficient is given by $\alpha_1 = \rho_1$. However, a more common predictor is to take $\alpha_1 = 1$, in which case the predictor is simply the previous data sample and can be easily implemented with a delay element. This is known as *differential pulse code modulation* or DPCM.

When predictive coding is combined with a data-discarding step (namely, quantization), care must be taken to ensure that the resulting error does not accumulate in the decoded samples. If a quantizer is placed between the encoding and decoding operations shown in Figure 8.4, each decoded sample $y(n)$ will contain not only the quantization error associated with quantizing $d(n)$ but also the quantization error associated with quantizing all previous samples $d(n-1), d(n-2), \ldots$ To avoid such error accumulation, the encoder must include the quantized data in the predictor, as shown in Figure 8.5. The decoder is the same as in Figure.

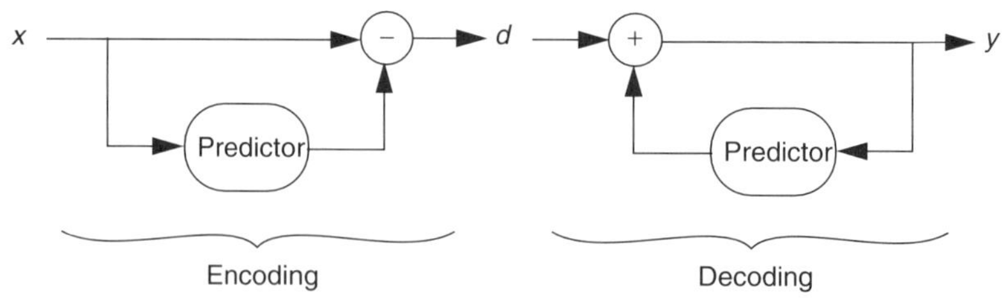

Figure 8.4. Predictive encoding and decoding.

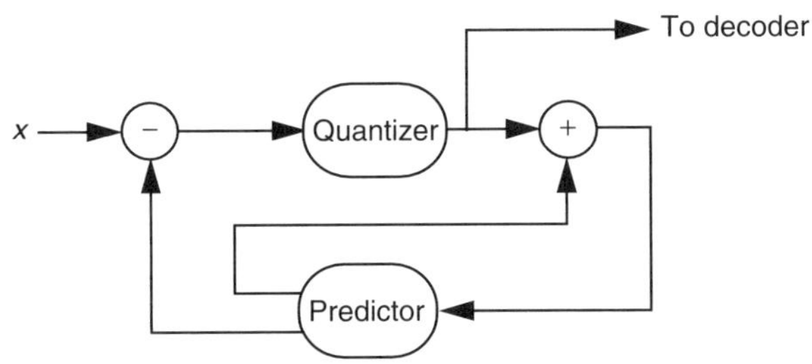

Figure 8.5. Predictive encoding with quantization in the prediction loop to avoid error accumulation.

8.5.2 Block-Based Transforms

The block-based transform coding procedure consists of segmenting an image into typically square blocks and applying an orthonormal transform to each block. The following sections first describe generic block-based transform coding and then describe a specific transform, the DCT.

In one-dimensional transform coding, an input signal $x(n)$ is first segmented into blocks of length N, where N is the size of the transform. Each block, represented as a column vector p, is then multiplied by an orthonormal transform matrix T of size $N \times N$ (T may be unitary, but most transforms used in image compression are real). The columns of T are the basis vectors of the particular transform, and the transform is applied by forming $c = T'p$. The vector c consists of the *transform coefficients*, each of which is the result of an inner product of a basis vector and the block p. Because T is orthonormal, the data vector is recovered from the transform coefficients by simply writing it as an expansion of the corresponding basis vectors: $p = Tc$. If no lossy coding of the coefficients has taken place, t the transform provides exact invertibility, since $Tc = TT'p = p$.

Block-based transform coding easily extends to two dimensions by applying the transform independently in each dimension. In the case of images, this corresponds to a horizontal and vertical application. Hence, the data segment is now a 2D matrix P of size $N \times N$ that is referred to as a *pixel block*. The corresponding transform coefficients represent the inner product of the 2D pixel block with the 2D basis functions, which are the outer products of the one-dimensional basis vectors with each other. The coefficients are obtained by first applying the transform to the columns of P by forming $\tilde{C} = T'P$ and then by applying the transform to the resulting rows of $\tilde{C}$ by forming $C = \tilde{C}T = T'CT$. The pixel block is recovered from the coefficient block by pre- and postmultiplying the coefficient block by T and T', respectively: $P = TCT'$. Again, the 2D transform obviously provides exact invertibility.

In the context of lossy data compression, a transform that minimizes the error between the original and decompressed signals and still provides high compression is desirable. Under certain assumptions, the Karhunen-Loeve transform (KLT) approximately accomplishes this goal [13]. The KLT diagonalizes the data autocovariance matrix by performing an eigen-decomposition: the transform matrix is the eigenvector matrix, and the transform coefficients are the eigenvalues. As such, the KLT coefficients are completely uncorrelated.

An example of a widely-used block-based transform is the DCT. The DCT basis functions are cosines. Several versions of the DCT exist, but the version used in JPEG is considered here. The transform matrix T is given by

$$T_{m,k} = \alpha_k \cos\left(\frac{(2m+1)k\pi}{2N}\right)$$

$$\alpha_0 = \sqrt{\frac{1}{N}}, \quad \alpha_k = \sqrt{\frac{2}{N}} \quad k \neq 0 \tag{8.7}$$

For small block sizes, the pixels in the block are highly correlated, and this DCT is asymptotically equivalent to the KLT for fixed N as the one-step correlation coefficient ρ approaches 1. Thus the DCT coefficients within a block are considered approximately uncorrelated.

The basis vectors for the 2D DCT are the outer products of horizontal and vertical cosine functions of frequencies ranging from DC to $(N-1)/2$. The coefficient $c_{0,0}$ is called the *DC coefficient*, and the remaining coefficients $c_{k,l}$ are called *AC coefficients*. As the coefficient indices k and l in the coefficient block increase, the corresponding vertical and horizontal spatial frequencies increase. The basis functions for an 8×8 DCT are illustrated in Figure 8.6.

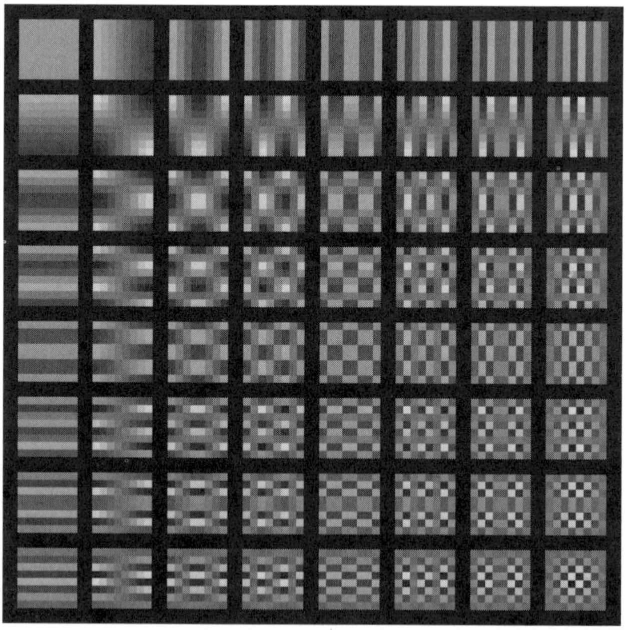

Figure 8.6. DCT basis functions for an 8×8 transform.

8.5.3 Subband and Wavelet Transforms

Instead of decomposing individual blocks into their frequency components, subband and wavelet transforms operate on the entire image, decomposing it into, in the common case of separable filters, high- and low-pass filtered and decimated images, or *bands*, in the horizontal and vertical directions. Each band can be individually coded to match its distribution and to incorporate human perception of its features.

The ideal two-band subband transform separates the input signal into orthogonal bands, as depicted in Figure 8.7. The orthogonal bands provide a decomposition in frequency while completely representing the original signal. In practice, however, orthogonal bands are neither implementable nor necessary, and the success of transform rests on the filters possessing certain implementable symmetry properties. A one-dimensional two-band subband transform system is shown in Figure 8.8. The input signal $x(n)$ is both low-pass and high-pass filtered and then subsampled in the *analysis* procedure. The resulting subsampled signals, called *subband coefficients*, can then be coded and transmitted. To recover the original signal from the subband coefficients, the low and high-frequency subband coefficients are upsampled and again low-pass and high-pass filtered and then summed in the *synthesis* procedure.

The low- and high-frequency subband coefficients shown in Figure 8.8 can be used as inputs to another analysis bank. In this way, the signal can be recursively decomposed and the frequency bands can be made narrower.

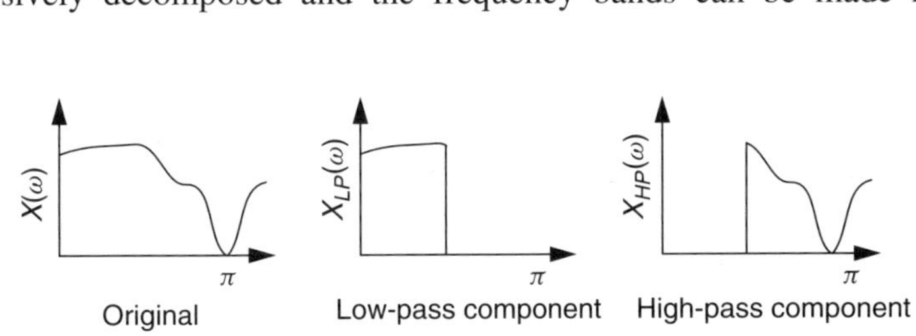

Figure 8.7. An ideal two-band decomposition (before subsampling).

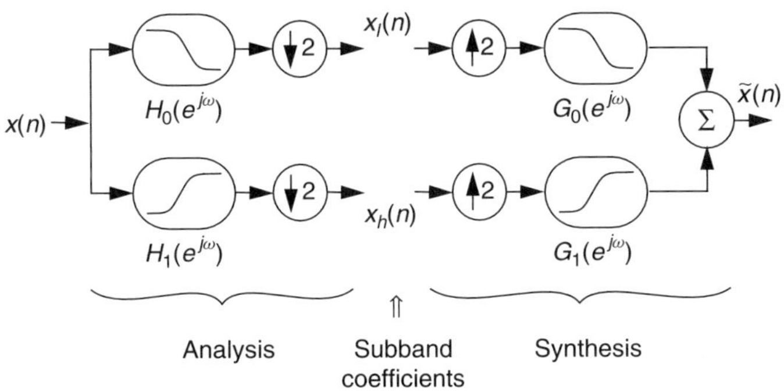

Figure 8.8. A one-dimensional subband analysis-synthesis system.

Recursive decomposition takes the form of *full-band decomposition*, in which each subband signal is input to an analysis bank, or *hierarchical decomposition* (also called *octave decomposition*), in which only the low-frequency signal is recursively decomposed. Each level of analysis is termed a *decomposition level* or *scale*. Thus if k represents the number of decomposition levels, in a full-band decomposition the total number of bands is 2^k, and in a hierarchical decomposition the total number of bands is $k + 1$. The output of the low-pass filter of the last analysis level is the *low-frequency band* and the remaining are *high-frequency bands*. Of the high-frequency bands, that with the lowest-frequency information is at the output of the high-pass filter of the last analysis level, whereas the output of the high-pass filter in the first analysis level contains the highest-frequency information. When certain filters are used with a hierarchical decomposition, the resulting transform is called a *wavelet transform* and the coefficients are called *wavelet coefficients*. The basis functions representing the image in this case are scaled and translated versions of a discrete time function given by the high-frequency synthesis filter impulse response.

Subband and wavelet transforms are easily extended to two dimensions by analyzing the input signal independently in the horizontal and vertical directions, as shown in Figure 8.9. Again, a recursive decomposition is obtained by analyzing the output subbands in either a full-band or a hierarchical fashion. Full-band decompositions contain 4^k bands, whereas hierarchical decompositions contain $4 + 3(k - 1)$ bands, for k levels of decomposition. Hierarchical decompositions are often represented as shown in Figure 8.10, with the lowest-frequency band in the upper left-hand corner and bands from a single level of analysis arranged in 2×2 fashion into a square.

One obvious benefit of representing images with subband or wavelet transforms is that they naturally provide *spatial scalability* — images of varying sizes can be easily generated from the decomposition by stopping the synthesis procedure at an appropriate point. Such scalability is attractive when the end users

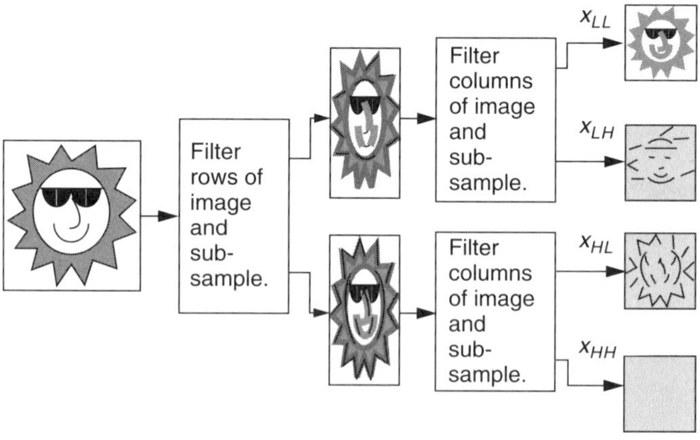

Figure 8.9. Two-dimensional subband analysis.

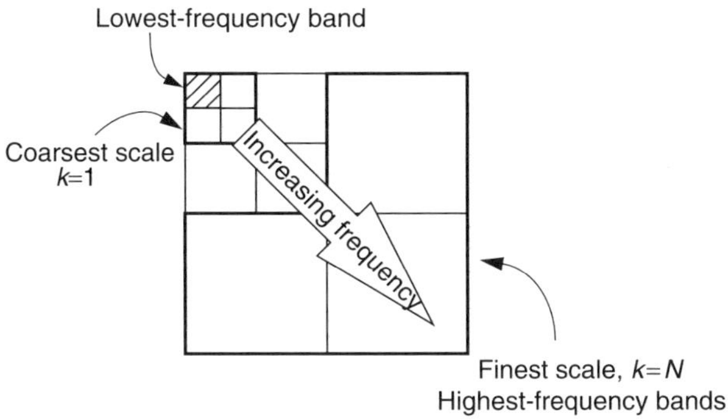

Figure 8.10. Nomenclature in the representation of a hierarchical subband/wavelet decomposition of an image.

of the image may have different viewing environments or communication bandwidths.

8.6 QUANTIZATION

A frequency transformation alone provides no compression (although the example in Section 8.2.2 demonstrates that the transformed data can have lower entropy than the original data). A transform is simply a mapping of the image from one space into another, where the number of samples are conserved. However, consideration of the nonuniform frequency sensitivity of the HVS suggests that the high-frequency information can be discarded or at least not reproduced perfectly and that the visual fidelity of the resulting image will not be significantly compromised. Discarding of information is a special case of *quantization*, and it is quantization in general that provides the lossy part of lossy image compression.

Quantization is a mapping of a possibly infinite number of input levels to a finite number of outputs, thereby providing an inexact but more efficient representation of data. One of the simplest examples of quantization is the assignment of letter grades at the end of a course — for each student, the total number of points earned is represented by one of five letter grades. Obviously, quantization is a noninvertible procedure — once an input has been quantized, it cannot be recovered exactly.

8.6.1 Uniform Quantization

A typical uniform quantizer input-output curve is shown in Figure 8.11. The real line on the horizontal axis is segmented into seven regions, or "bins," and all input data in each bin is quantized to one of the seven reconstruction levels. This quantizer is a uniform, midtread quantizer. Uniform refers to the identical size of

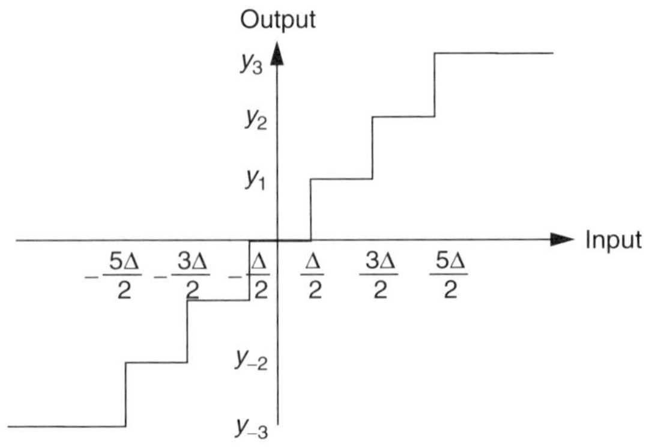

Figure 8.11. A uniform, midtread quantizer input–output functional; $y_i = i\Delta$.

the bins (except the two infinite-length bins at either end of the curve), whereas midtread refers to the fact that a "tread" of the staircase sits on the horizontal axis centered at zero and that zero is a reconstruction level. (A midriser quantizer does not have zero as an output level. Midtread quantizers are preferable for image compression because they set small values to zero rather than possibly increasing them, which could be seen as amplifying low-level noise.) The reconstruction levels are the midpoints of the bins; this provides low (although not generally optimal) distortion ease of design. Note that the quantizer error is finite and the middle in five bins, with maximum value $\Delta/2$; this region is called the *granular* region of the quantizer. However, the error can be infinite in the outer two bins; these are collectively called the *overload* region of the quantizer. A well-designed quantizer will minimize the probability of operation in the overload region for its input source distribution.

If N bits are available to represent a quantized source x, then 2^N input bins and output levels can be specified. A midtread uniform quantizer that is symmetric about $x = 0$ has an odd number of output levels that can be taken as $2^N - 1$. For N being large, we take $2^N - 1 \approx 2^N$. A common technique for bin-size selection is to take

$$\Delta = \frac{2\sigma\gamma}{2^N} \tag{8.8}$$

where σ is the standard deviation of the source, the denominator represents the number of output levels and γ is a constant known as the *loading factor*. Typical values of γ are 2–4, and the loading factor can be adjusted to minimize or set to zero the probability of quantizer overload. Assuming that N is large and that the error induced by quantization $e = Q(x) - x$ is uniformly distributed within each of the bins yields a distortion incurred by uniform quantization with the step size given in Eq. (8.8)

$$D = \tfrac{1}{3}\gamma^2\sigma^2 2^{-2N} \tag{8.9}$$

This equation provides a modeled RD curve for uniform quantization with N being large, which can be used in the RD minimization Eq. (8.4).

8.6.2 Nonuniform Quantization

Nonuniform quantizers allow more flexibility than uniform quantizers, but they do not have equally sized bins and are more complicated to both design and implement than uniform quantizers. A methodical technique for both design and analysis of nonuniform quantizers is known as *companding*, in which a nonuniform quantizer is modelled as an invertible point process, followed by uniform quantization and then the inverse of the point process [19]. Quantizers designed in such a way are very commonly used in speech applications. For images, a more common technique of designing nonuniform quantizers is known as the LBG algorithm (for Linde, Buzo, and Gray) [20], which is an iterative technique for designing a nonuniform quantizer that minimizes the MSE of the quantized data with a known source distribution or training set. Nonuniform quantizers are not commonly used in image-compression applications because their performance can be generally matched by uniform quantization followed by entropy coding, although the LBG algorithm can be applied in multiple dimensions to achieve vector quantization, which has been applied to image compression [20].

8.6.3 Selection of Quantizer Parameters for Image Compression

For a uniform quantizer, the only specification required is the number of bins and the overload boundaries. The number of bins can be determined by the number of bits available. If an operational RD minimization is performed using Eq. (8.9) to specify the distortion of each source in Eq. (8.4), the resulting bit allocations produce equal quantizer step sizes for each source. This approach allows a range of compression ratios and produces compressed images with theoretically minimum distortion for a given bit rate, but is not visually optimized. A second approach is to incorporate HVS characteristics directly in determining the quantizer step sizes. Such strategies are often based on experimentation or well-accepted HVS properties. The two approaches can be combined by weighting the distortions in Eq. (8.4) for the different sources as a function of the frequencies that each source represents.

However, even simpler approaches are used. The JPEG-recommended quantization matrices were determined on the basis of experimentation using DCT basis functions, so for DCT-based coding, the JPEG matrix is typically scaled to obtain the desired bit rate (this procedure requires that the image is iteratively compressed until the desired bit rate is achieved). These quantization matrices are given in Figure 8.12. Note that the quantizer step sizes generally increase with increasing frequency and that the chrominance step sizes are much larger than the luminance step sizes, corresponding to the CSF behavior and the lower sensitivity to chrominance information. A similar approach can be applied to

$$\begin{bmatrix} 16 & 11 & 10 & 16 & 24 & 40 & 51 & 61 \\ 12 & 12 & 14 & 19 & 26 & 58 & 60 & 55 \\ 14 & 13 & 16 & 24 & 40 & 57 & 69 & 56 \\ 14 & 17 & 22 & 29 & 51 & 87 & 80 & 62 \\ 18 & 22 & 37 & 56 & 68 & 109 & 103 & 77 \\ 24 & 35 & 55 & 64 & 81 & 104 & 113 & 92 \\ 49 & 64 & 78 & 87 & 103 & 121 & 120 & 101 \\ 72 & 92 & 95 & 98 & 112 & 100 & 103 & 99 \end{bmatrix} \begin{bmatrix} 17 & 18 & 24 & 47 & 99 & 99 & 99 & 99 \\ 18 & 21 & 26 & 66 & 99 & 99 & 99 & 99 \\ 24 & 26 & 56 & 99 & 99 & 99 & 99 & 99 \\ 47 & 66 & 99 & 99 & 99 & 99 & 99 & 99 \\ 99 & 99 & 99 & 99 & 99 & 99 & 99 & 99 \\ 99 & 99 & 99 & 99 & 99 & 99 & 99 & 99 \\ 99 & 99 & 99 & 99 & 99 & 99 & 99 & 99 \\ 99 & 99 & 99 & 99 & 99 & 99 & 99 & 99 \end{bmatrix}$$

Figure 8.12. The JPEG-recommended luminance and chrominance quantization matrices.

subband or wavelet coding in which quantizer step sizes are selected on the basis of CSF [21].

A second approach to selecting quantizer step sizes for subband or wavelet-based coding involves applying weights to the distortion model of individual bands that decrease with increasing frequency to approximately model the CSF. These weights are not well accepted and many different techniques for selecting them have been proposed [22]. Then the optimal bit allocation problem is solved.

In newer image-compression algorithms, compression is provided implicitly rather than explicitly. Coefficients are coded in order of decreasing magnitude, where the threshold for coding decreases by a factor of 2 with each coding pass. As such, in each pass, coefficients are effectively quantized to reconstruction levels, the number of which double with each pass and whose reconstruction levels are modified with each pass. This implicit quantization can be modified to include visual characteristics by weighting the coefficients before coding, with weights selected according to HVS properties [23]. In these algorithms, the bit allocation is automatic; no explicit allocation is performed.

8.7 LOSSLESS IMAGE COMPRESSION SYSTEMS

The simplest technique for providing lossless image compression is to simply entropy-code the pixel values. However, as demonstrated in the entropy examples of Section 8.2, further gains can be obtained by first reducing the redundancy in the pixel data. Any combination of redundancy reduction and entropy coding can be applied to images. As long as no data is discarded through quantization, the compression technique is lossless and the original pixels can be recovered. Here, both GIF and lossless JPEG are briefly discussed. No images are shown because the compression is lossless; therefore, the decompressed images are identical to the originals. Compression ratios of 2 : 1 to 4 : 1 are typical for lossless image compression techniques operating on natural images, yielding image representations of 4–2 bits/pixel for gray scale images.

8.7.1 (Graphics Interchange Format (GIF)) Compression

GIF is a compression algorithm for general graphics-style inputs, of which images are one. A color table is first created, with one entry for each color in the image.

The image is then raster-scanned and an index of table entries is generated to represent the image. These indices are then coded using a variation on LZW coding called *variable-length-code LZW compression*. Because a color table is used in the encoding procedure, the GIF compression procedure is identical, regardless of whether a color or gray scale image is being compressed.

8.7.2 Lossless JPEG

JPEG's lossless mode uses 2D prediction on pixels. The prediction is formed from three neighboring pixels: the pixel above, to the left, and diagonally above and to the left of the pixel being coded. Eight options for the prediction function are available. Entropy coding follows the predictive coding and can be either Huffman or arithmetic coding. Because of patent restrictions, Huffman coding is most commonly used. If multicomponent (i.e., color) images are to be compressed, each color plane is predicted and entropy-coded separately.

8.8 LOSSY IMAGE COMPRESSION SYSTEMS

This section describes several lossy image compression systems, including baseline JPEG and two wavelet-based techniques. Many image compression techniques have been proposed; the techniques described here were selected on the basis of their performance, popularity, and relevance to JPEG-2000.

8.8.1 Baseline JPEG

JPEG is the only current standard in existence for still gray scale and color-image coding. This section describes its key features. Further details can be found in Ref. [10]. Lossy JPEG compression can be baseline, as described below, or extended. All JPEG decoders must be able to decode baseline JPEG.

The transform code block size in JPEG is 8×8 pixels and the transform used is the DCT as given in Eq. (8.7). Individual pixel blocks are transformed to form coefficient blocks and the coefficients are all scalar quantized, using either the default JPEG quantization matrix or a scaled version (where the scaling factor is user-specified). The quantized DC coefficient is subtracted from the quantized DC coefficient of the previous block, forming the difference that is then coded using a variable-length code, which is not a Huffman code but provides compression near the entropy bound. The quantized AC coefficients are traversed in a zig-zag scan on the entries in the 2D coefficient matrix, starting in the upper left-hand corner, as illustrated in Figure 8.13. This reorders the quantized AC coefficients into a one-dimensional vector arranged approximately in order of increasing frequency. Groups of sequential zeroes in the vector are then *run-length coded*; that is, they are replaced with a single number indicating the length of the zero-run. Finally, symbols are formed from the quantized AC coefficients and the zero-run lengths as pairs indicating number of zeroes preceding a nonzero coefficient, quantized

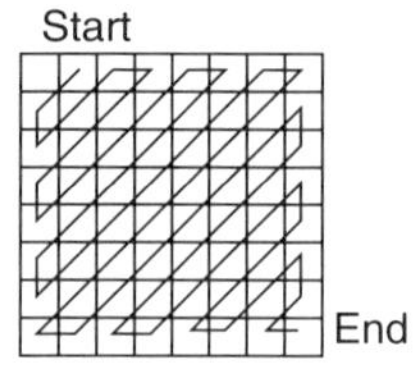

Figure 8.13. AC coefficient scanning order to produce the zig-zig scan.

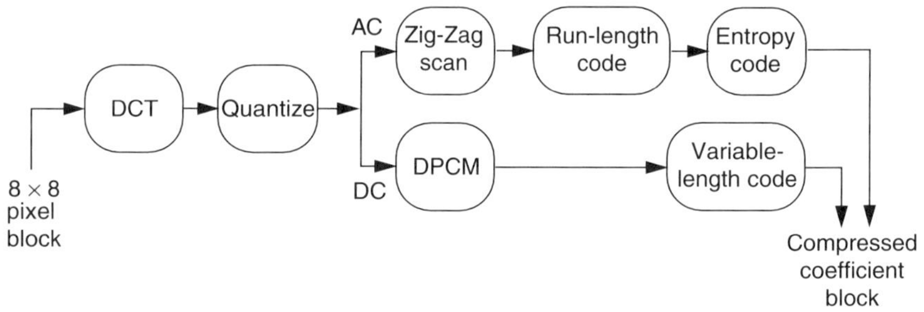

Figure 8.14. The JPEG encoding procedure.

AC coefficient, and these symbols are entropy coded using either Huffman or arithmetic coding (the first value in the pair is zero for a coefficient preceded by a nonzero coefficient). The encoding procedure is illustrated in Figure 8.14. At the decoder, the procedure is simply reversed. Arithmetic coding can be used for both the DC and AC data, but is not commonly used because of patent restrictions.

JPEG does not specify quantization tables, although the recommended tables are often used. The compression ratios that are achievable by using JPEG can be varied by scaling the recommended tables or by defining new tables with appropriate step sizes.

8.8.2 Zerotree-Based Embedded Wavelet Coders

Zerotree-based embedded wavelet coders operate on the basis of two observations. First, in a wavelet transform of an image, small coefficients at low frequencies often imply that coefficients at higher frequencies corresponding to the same spatial location are also small. And secondly, representing large coefficients early in the bit stream produces a large distortion reduction, which thereby provides a high slope for the RD curve. These coders produce a single embedded bit stream from which the best-reconstructed images in the MSE sense can be extracted at any bit rate. The first zerotree-based wavelet coder was EZW [24], followed by CREW [25], and SPIHT [26]. The SPIHT coder builds on the concepts introduced in EZW to outperform the original method even without EZW's requirement of an arithmetic coder. This section describes the SPIHT coder as representative of zerotree-based embedded wavelet coders.

Generally, zerotree-based embedded wavelet coders scan coefficients in a predefined order. In each scan, coefficients are compared to a threshold to determine whether the coefficient is to be encoded (above threshold) or not (below threshold). The encoding is performed bit plane by bit plane and is known as successive refinement or successive approximation quantization. No explicit consideration of rate is performed; only distortion reduction is considered.

The SPIHT algorithm scanning reduces the number of magnitude comparisons by partitioning the coefficients into subsets. The set partitioning is a spatial orientation tree rooted in the lowest frequency band (the number of levels is a user option), grouped in 2×2 adjacent coefficients with each node having either no descendents or four offsprings, as shown in Figure 8.15. The coding of coefficients involves a sequence of sorting and refinement passes applied with decreasing magnitude thresholds. In the sorting pass, coefficients are labeled as significant or insignificant with respect to the current magnitude threshold, and a bit indicating this label, is included in the bit stream (an extra sign bit is immediately sent when a coefficient is first labeled significant). A significant coefficient has magnitude above the current threshold, whereas an insignificant coefficient has magnitude below the current threshold. After the significance information is determined for all coefficients in the scanning order, the refinement pass adds resolution to those coefficients already labeled significant at some threshold. Because of the first observation given earlier, this partitioning ensures that insignificant subsets contain a large number of elements.

The efficiency in zerotree-based embedded wavelet coders comes not from efficient representation of nonzero coefficients but in the extreme efficiency of representing large numbers of coefficients that are zero by a single symbol.

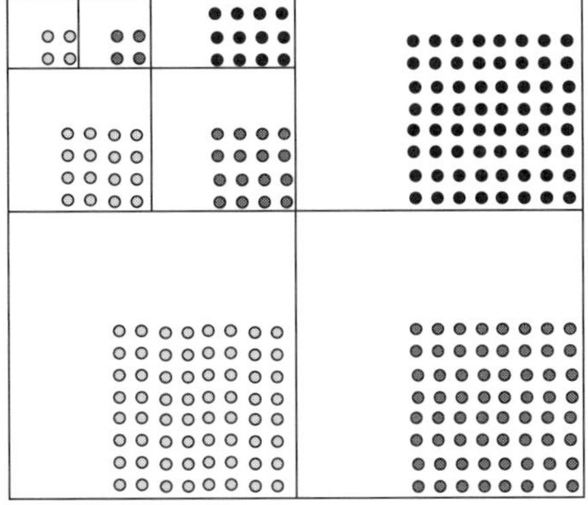

Figure 8.15. Spatial orientation trees used in SPIHT. Of ever four coefficients in the lowest frequency band, one is not a tree root and the other three are roots to three different trees. Dots of the same color are in the same area.

8.8.3 Rate-Distortion-Based Embedded Wavelet Coders

Although the zerotree-based embedded wavelet coders described in the previous section perform better than JPEG, they operate only to minimize distortion — no consideration of rate takes place during encoding. A type of embedded coder that explicitly incorporates rate and distortion is the rate-distortion-based embedded (RDE) wavelet coder. In these coders, coefficients are encoded bit plane by bit plane in an embedded manner. However, instead of scanning all coefficients in a predefined order, these coders try to optimize the coding order so as to code coefficients with larger RD slope earlier in the bit stream.

In an RDE coder, each bit plane coding involves the calculation of the RD slope for all the coefficients and coding of the one with the largest slope. This procedure repeats until the desired bit rate is reached. For this type of coder, it is essential to efficiently calculate the RD slope for each coefficient at the encoder and convey the ordering information to the decoder. If the actual operating RD slope is calculated, the coding order has to be transmitted explicitly because the decoder does not have a priori knowledge to replicate the calculation. In this case, the overhead of the position information can be too high to take advantage of the RD-optimized ordering [27]. As an alternative, an RD-optimization technique proposed in Ref. [28] calculates the expected RD slope on the basis of available information at each coding pass so that the decoder can follow the same procedure. This coder outperforms SPIHT but at an high computational cost. Coding results also demonstrate better embedding performance with higher gains at lower bit rates.

8.8.4 Performance Comparisons

Figure 8.16 plots PSNR versus bit rate for *lena*, a 512×512 image from the well-known USC database. These results are representative for the

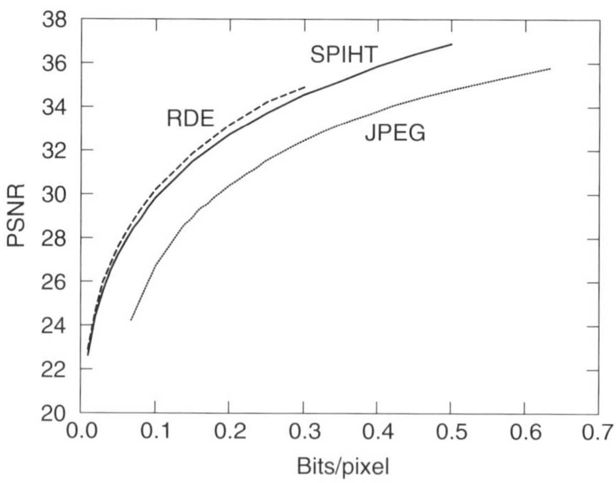

Figure 8.16. PSNR versus rate for *lena*.

general performance of JPEG, SPIHT, and RDE [28]. The JPEG results are approximately 2 dB below the SPIHT results, which are in turn 0.5–1 dB below the RDE results. Although the actual differences vary from image to image, the general trends are the same.

Figure 8.17 shows the original image and compressed versions at 0.1 bits/pixel, using all three algorithms. This is a very low bit rate, and compression artifacts can be seen in each image. However, the nature of the artifacts varies, depending on whether the transform is block-based (as in JPEG) or wavelet-based (as in SPIHT and RDE). The JPEG image was obtained by scaling the default quantization matrix by an integer value such that the resulting quantized image achieved the target bit rate. The resulting quantizer step sizes are large enough

Figure 8.17. A comparison of compression techniques at 0.1 bits/pixel: **(a)** original *lena*, **(b)** JPEG, PSNR = 26.7 db, **(c)** SPIHT, PSNR = 29.4 dB, **(d)** RDE, PSNR = 30.2 db. Coarse quantization of DC coefficients in the JPEG image produces extreme blockiness, whereas coarse implicit quantization of high-frequency coefficients in the SPIHT and RDE images produces severe ringing artifacts.

(a) (b)

Figure 8.18. A comparison of compression techniques at 0.3 bits/pixel: **(a)** JPEG, PSNR = 32.5 dB, **(b)** SPIHT, PSNR = 34.1. Both blocking artifacts and ringing are still apparent in the JPEG and SPIHT images, respectively, although not nearly as noticeable as at the lower bit rate.

such that most AC coefficients are quantized to zero and the DC coefficients are extremely coarsely quantized. As a result the image is represented by its coarsely quantized average values within each 8×8 block, producing the lack of detail and severe blocking artifacts in the image. In contrast, the wavelet-based coders do not exhibit blocking but do have severe ringing around strong edges. Both SPIHT and RDE provide implicit quantization via the bit plane coding. At this rate, the implicit quantization step size is still quite large, providing coarse quantization. As a result, many of the higher-frequency coefficients are zero, yielding the loss of texture in the hat and the ringing.

Figure 8.18 shows the same image at 0.3 bits/pixel for both JPEG and SPIHT (the RDE image is visually identical to the SPIHT image). At this higher rate, the JPEG image exhibits faint blocking artifacts, whereas the SPIHT image exhibits faint ringing. Psychovisual experimentation has shown that ringing artifacts are preferred to blocking artifacts in approximately 75 percent of comparisons [29].

Computationally, both JPEG and SPIHT are fairly fast algorithms, requiring at most only a few seconds on any reasonable machine. In contrast, the RDE algorithm requires nearly three orders of magnitude more time, which translates to several hours. A suboptimal, faster variation of the algorithm significantly reduces this time, but given the small PSNR differences and negligible visual differences.

8.9 SOME COMMENTS ON JPEG-2000

JPEG-2000 is the next-generation image-compression standard, expected to be in Draft international standard form by late 2000. A single mode of operation will allow compression, ranging from lossy to lossless and providing many features not currently easily achieved with the current JPEG standard. This section briefly describes basic operation of the JPEG-2000 compression algorithm and resulting features.

JPEG-2000 is based on a wavelet transform, and suggests a hierarchical wavelet transform and default integer wavelet filters for both lossy and lossless encoding but allows user-defined arbitrary-size filters and arbitrary wavelet-decomposition trees. Three quantization options are available: trellis-coded quantization [30], explicit scalar quantization, and implicit scalar quantization achieved using bit plane encoding. Visual weighting can be incorporated to take advantage of HVS properties in one of two ways, using either fixed weights (selected on the basis of viewing conditions and achieved by scaling the quantization step size in a given subband) or weights that change during the encoding–decoding process (selected on the basis of current bit rate and implemented using an arbitrary reordering of the coefficient bit planes). In JPEG-2000, the bit-level redundancy reduction technique is arithmetic coding. The data can be ordered and indexed in the bit stream so as to allow both spatial and quality scalability. Additionally, region-of-interest coding is included and allows a spatially variable quality. The new standard is expected to provide compression ratios up to 30 percent higher than the present standard, depending on the image size and bit rate.

8.10 CONCLUSION

This chapter has reviewed the fundamental concepts in image compression: pixel-level redundancy reduction, data-discarding, and bit-level redundancy reduction. Design of a practical compression algorithm that provides high quality at a variety of bit rates requires an understanding of and successful integration of all three concepts. The ultimate algorithm selected for any application should provide the required quality and features with an execution time suited to the application. With a comprehension of the basics presented here, the reader will be well suited to make informed algorithmic selections.

REFERENCES

1. T. Cover and J. Thomas, *Information Theory*, Wiley & Sons, New York, 1991.
2. D. Huffman, A method for the construction of minimum-redundancy codes, *Proc. IRE* **40**, 1098–1101 (1952).
3. C.E. Shannon, A mathematical theory of communication, *Bell System Technical J.* **27**, 279–423 (1948).
4. C.E. Shannon, Coding theorems for a discrete source with a fidelity criterion, in *IRE National Convention Record*, Part 4, pp. 142–63, 1959.
5. R. Sekuler and R. Blake, *Perception*, 3rd ed., McGraw-Hill, New York, 1994.

6. P.W. Jones et al., Comparative study of wavelet and DCT decompositions with equivalent quantization and encoding strategies for medical images, *Proceedings of SPIE Medical Imaging*, San Diego, Calif., March 1995, pp. 571–582.
7. S. Daly, Application of a noise-adaptive contrast sensitivity function to image data compression, *Opt. Eng.* **29**(8), 977–987 (1990).
8. C.-H. Chou and Y.-C. Li, A perceptually tuned subband image coder based on the measure of just-noticeable distortion profile, *IEEE Trans. Circuits Syst. Video Technol.* **5**(6), 467–476, (1995).
9. J.A. Solomon, A.B. Watson, and A.J. Ahumada, Jr., Visibility of DCT basis functions: effects of contrast masking, *Proceedings of Data Compression Conference*, Snowbird, Utah, March 1994 pp. 361–370.
10. W.B. Pennebaker and J. Mitchell, *JPEG Still Image Data Compression Standard*, Van Nostrand Reinhold, New York, 1992.
11. B.G. Haskell, A. Puri, and A. Netravali, *Digital Video: An Introduction to MPEG-2*, Chapman & Hall, New York, 1997.
12. M. Rabbani, JPEG-2000: Background, Scope, and Technical Description, Cornell University School of Electrical Engineering Colloquium Talk, December 1998.
13. K.R. Rao and P. Yip, *Discrete Cosine Transform*, Academic Press, San Diego, Calif., 1990.
14. R.J. Clarke, *Transform Coding of Images*, Academic Press, San Diego, Calif., 1985.
15. J.W. Woods, *Subband Image Coding*, Kluwer Academic Publishers, Boston, Mass., 1991.
16. B. Haskell and A. Netravali, *Digital Pictures*, Plenum Press, New York, 1988.
17. M. Rabbani and P.W. Jones, *Digital Image Compression Techniques*, SPIE Optical Engineering Press, Bellingham, Washington, 1991.
18. N. Jayant and P. Noll, *Digital Coding of Waveforms*, Prentice Hall, Englewood Cliffs, N.J., 1984.
19. A. Gersho, Principles of Quantization, *IEEE Commun. Soc. Mag.* **15**(5), 16–29 (1977).
20. A. Gersho and R.M. Gray, *Vector Quantization and Signal Compression*, Kluwer Academic Publishers, Boston, Mass., 1992.
21. R.J. Safranek and J.D. Johnston, A perceptually tuned subband image coder with image dependent quantization and postquantization data compression, *Proceedings of IEEE ICASSP'89*, New York, May 1989, pp. 1945–1948.
22. M.G. Ramos and S.S. Hemami, Perceptually-based scalable image coding for packet networks, *Journal of Electronic Imaging* **7**(7), 453–463 (1998).
23. I. Hontsch, L.J. Karam, and R.J. Safranak, A perceptually tuned embedded zerotree image coding, *Proceedings of IEEE International Conference on Image Processing*, Santa Barbara, Calif., October 1997, pp. 41–44.
24. J.M. Shapiro, Embedded image coding using zerotrees of wavelet coefficients, *IEEE Trans. Signal Processing* **41**(12), 3445–3462 (1993).
25. A. Zandi et al., CREW: compression with reversible embedded wavelets, *Proceedings of Data Compression Conference*, Snowbird, Utah, March 1995, pp. 212–22.
26. A. Said and W.A. Pearlman, A new, fast, and efficient image codec based on set partitioning in hierarchical trees, *IEEE Trans. Circuits Syst. Video Technol.* **6**(3), 243–250 (1996).

27. W.K. Carey, L.A. Von Pischke, and S.S. Hemami, Rate-distortion based scalable progressive image coding, *SPIE Conference on Mathematics of Data and Image Coding, Compression, and Encryption*, San Diego, Calif., July 1998.
28. J. Li and S. Lei, An embedded still image coder with rate-distortion optimization, *Proc. SPIE Visual Commun. and Image Process.* **3309**, 36–48, (1998).
29. M.G. Ramos and S.S. Hemami, Perceptually scalable image compression for packet-based networks, *J. Electronic Imaging*, special issue on *Image/Video Compression and Processing for Visual Commun.* July (1998).
30. M.W. Marcellin and T.R. Fischer, Trellis coded quantization of memoryless and Gauss-markov sources, *IEEE Trans. Commun.* **38**(1), 82–93 (1990).
31. O. Rioul and M. Vetterli, Wavelets and signal processing, *IEEE Signal Process. Mag.* **8**(4), 14–38 (1991).

9 Transmission of Digital Imagery

JEFFREY W. PERCIVAL
University of Wisconsin, Madison, Wisconsin

VITTORIO CASTELLI
IBM T.J. Watson Research Center, Yorktown Heights, New York

9.1 INTRODUCTION

The transmission of digital imagery can impose significant demands on the resources of clients, servers, and the networks that connect them. With the explosive growth of the internet, the need for mechanisms that support rapid browsing of on-line imagery has become critical.

This is particularly evident in scientific imagery. The increase in availability of publicly accessible scientific data archives on the Internet has changed the typical scientist's expectations about access to data. In the past, scientific procedures produced proprietary (PI-owned) data sets that, if exchanged at all, were usually exchanged through magnetic tape. Now, the approach is to generate large online data archives using standardized data formats and allow direct access by researchers. For example, NASA's Planetary Data System is a network of archive sites serving data from a number of solar system missions. The Earth-Observing System will use eight Distributed Active Archive Centers to provide access to the very large volume of data to be acquired.

Although transmission bandwidth has been increasing with faster modems for personal networking, upgrades to the Internet, and the introduction of new networks such as Internet 2 and the Next Generation Internet, there are still a number of reasons because of which bandwidth for image-transmission will continue to be a limited resource into the foreseeable future.

Perhaps the most striking of these factors is the rapid increase in the resolution of digital imagery and hence the size of images to be transmitted. A case in point is the rapid increase in both pixel count and intensity resolution provided by the solid-state detectors in modern astronomical systems. For example, upgrading from a 640×480 8-bit detector to a $2{,}048 \times 2{,}048$ 16-bit detector represents a data growth of about a factor of 30. Now, even $2{,}048^2$ detectors seem small; new astronomical

Image Databases: Search and Retrieval of Digital Imagery, Edited by Vittorio Castelli and Lawrence D. Bergman.
ISBN 0-471-32116-8

detectors are using $2{,}048 \times 4{,}096$ detectors in mosaics to build units as large as $8{,}192^2$ pixels. This is a factor of 400 larger than the previously mentioned 8-bit image. The Sloan Digital Sky Survey will use thirty $2{,}048^2$ detectors simultaneously and will produce a 40 terabyte data set during its lifetime.

This phenomenon is not limited to astronomy. For example, medical imaging detectors are reaching the spatial and intensity resolution of photographic film and are replacing it. Similarly, Earth-observing satellites with high-resolution sensors managed by private companies produce images having $12{,}000^2$ pixels, which are commercialized for civilian use.

In addition to image volume (both image size and number of images), other factors are competing for transmission bandwidth, including the continued growth in demand for access and the competition for bandwidth from other application such as telephony and videoconferencing. Therefore, it does not seem unreasonable to expect that the transmission of digital imagery will continue to be a challenge requiring careful thought and a deft allocation of resources.

The transmission of digital imagery is usually handled through the exchange of raw, uncompressed files, losslessly compressed files, or files compressed with some degree of lossiness chosen in advance at the server. The files are first transmitted and then some visualization program is invoked on the received file. Another type of transmission, growing in popularity with archives of large digital images, is called *progressive transmission*. When an image is progressively transmitted from server to client, it can be displayed by the client as the data arrive, instead of having to wait until the transmission is complete. This allows browsing in an archive even over connections for which the transmission time of a single image may be prohibitive. In this chapter each of these transmission schemes and their effect on the allocation of resources between server, network, and client are discussed.

9.2 BULK TRANSMISSION OF RAW DATA

This is the simplest case to consider. Error-free transmission of raw digital images is easily done using the file transfer protocol (FTP) on any Internet-style (TCP/IP) connection. Image compression can be used to mitigate the transmission time by decreasing the total number of bytes to be transmitted.

When used to decrease the volume of transmitted data, the compression usually needs to be lossless, as further data analysis is often performed on the received data sets. A lossless compression is exactly reversible, in that the exact value of each pixel can be recovered by reversing the compression. Many compression algorithms are lossy, that is, the original pixel values cannot be exactly recovered from the compressed data. Joint photographic experts group (JPEG)[1] and graphics interchange format (GIF) (see Chapter 8) are examples of such algorithms. Lossy compression is universally used for photographic images transmitted across the World Wide Web. Interestingly, it is becoming increasingly important in transmitting scientific data, especially in applications in which the images are manually interpreted, rather than processed, and where the bandwidth between server and client is limited.

Compression exploits redundancy in an image, which can be large for certain kinds of graphics such as line drawings, vector graphics, and computer-generated images. Lossless compression of raw digital imagery is far less efficient because digital images from solid-state detectors contain electronic noise, temperature-dependent dark counts, fixed-pattern noise, and other artifacts. These effects reduce the redundancy, for example, by disrupting long runs of pixels that would otherwise have the same value in the absence of noise. A rule of thumb is that lossless compression can reduce the size of a digital image by a factor of 2 or 3.

The cost of transmitting compressed images has three components: the cost of compression, the cost of decompression, and the cost of transmission. The latter decreases with the effectiveness of the compressed algorithm: the bigger the achieved compression ratio, the smaller the transmission cost. However, the first two costs increase with the achieved compression ratio: when comparing two image-compression algorithms, one usually finds that the one that compresses better complex is more[1]. Additionally, the computational costs of compressing and decompressing are quite often similar (although asymmetric schemes exist where compression is much more expensive than decompression). In an image database, compression is usually performed once (when the image is ingested into the database) and therefore its cost is divided over all the transmissions of the image. Hence, the actual trade-off is between bandwidth and decompression cost, which depends on the client characteristics. Therefore, the compression algorithm should be selected with client capabilities in mind.

A number of high-performance, lossless image-compression algorithms exist. Most use wavelet transforms of one kind or another, although simply using a wavelet basis is no guarantee that an algorithm is exactly reversible. A well-tested, fast, exactly reversible, wavelet-based compression program is HCOMPRESS[2]. Source code is available at *www.stsci.edu*.

Finally, it is easily forgotten in this highly networked world that sometimes more primitive methods of bulk transmission of large data sets still hold some sway. For example, the effective bandwidth of a shoebox full of Exabyte tapes sent by overnight express easily exceeds 100 megabits per second for 24 hours.

9.3 PROGRESSIVE TRANSMISSION

Progressive transmission is a scheme in which the image is transmitted from server to client in such a way that the client can display the image as it arrives, instead of waiting until all the data have been received.

Progressive transmission fills an important niche between the extremes of transmitting either raw images in their entirety or irreversibly reduced graphic products.

[1] This assertion needs to be carefully qualified: to compress well in practice, an algorithm must be tailored to the characteristics of actual images. For example, a simple algorithm that treats each pixel as an independent random variable does not perform as well on actual images as a complex method that accounts for dependencies between neighboring pixels.

Progressive transmission allows users to browse an archive of large digital images, perhaps searching for some particular features. It has also numerous applications in scientific fields. Meteorologists often scan large image archives looking for certain types or percentages of cloud cover. The ability to receive, examine, and reject an image while receiving only the first 1 percent of its data is very attractive. Astronomers are experimenting with progressive techniques for remote observing. They want to check an image for target position, filter selection, and telescope focus before beginning a long exposure, but the end-to-end network bandwidth between remote mountain tops and an urban department of astronomy can be very low. Doing a quality check on a $2{,}048^2$ pixel, 16-bit image over a dial-up transmission control protocol (TCP) connection seems daunting, but it is easily done with progressive image-transmission techniques.

Some progressive transmission situations are forced on a system. The Galileo probe to Jupiter was originally equipped with a 134,400 bit-per-second transmission system, which would allow an image to be transmitted in about a minute. The high-gain antenna failed to deploy; however, it resulted in a Jupiter-to-Earth bandwidth of only about 10 bits per second. Ten days per image was too much! Ground system engineers devised a makeshift image browsing system using spatially subsampled images (called *jail bars*, typically one or two image rows spaced every 20 rows) to select images for future transmission. Sending only every twentieth row improves the transmission time, but the obvious risk of missing smaller-scale structure in the images is severe. Figure 9.1 shows the discovery image of Dactyl, the small moon orbiting the asteroid Ida. Had Dactyl been a little smaller, this form of image browsing might have prevented its discovery.

Ideally, progressive transmission should have the following properties.

- It should present a rough approximation of the original image very quickly. It should improve the approximation rapidly at first and eventually reconstruct the original image.

Figure 9.1. Discovery image of Dactyl, a small moon orbiting the asteroid Ida. Had the moon been a little smaller, it could have been missing in the transmitted data.

- It should capture features at all spatial and intensity scales early in the transmission, that is, broad, faint features should be captured in the early stages of transmission as easily as bright, localized features.
- It should support interactive transmission, in which the client can use the first approximations to select "regions of interest," which are then scheduled for transmission at a priority higher than that of the original image. By "bootstrapping" into a particular region of an image based on an early view, the client is effectively boosting bandwidth by discarding unneeded bits.
- No bits should be sent twice. As resolution improves from coarse to fine, even with multiple overlapping regions of interest having been requested, the server must not squander bandwidth by sending the client information that it already has.
- It should allow interruption or cancellation by the client, likely to occur while browsing images.
- It should be well behaved numerically, approximately preserving the image statistics (e.g., the pixel-intensity histogram) throughout the transmission. This allows numerical analysis of a partially transmitted image.

Progressive image transmission is not really about compression. Rather, it is better viewed as a scheduling problem, in which one wants to know which bits to send first and which bits can wait until later. Progressive transmission uses the same algorithms as compression, simply because if a compression algorithm can tell a compressor which bits to throw away, it can also be used to sense which bits are important.

9.3.1 Theoretical Considerations

In this section, we show that progressive transmission need not require much more bandwidth than nonprogressive schemes.

To precisely formulate the problem, we compare a simple nonprogressive scheme to a simple progressive scheme using Figure 9.2. Let the nonprogressive scheme be ideal, in the sense that in order to send an image with distortion (e.g., mean-square error, MSE, or Hamming distance) no larger than D_N, it needs to send R_N bits per pixel and that the point (R_N, D_N) lies on the rate-distortion curve[3] defined in Chapter 8, Section 8.3. No other scheme can send fewer bits and produce an image of the same quality.

The progressive scheme has two stages. In the first, it produces an image having distortion no larger than D_1 by sending R_1 bits per pixel and in the second it improves the quality of the image to $D_2 = D_N$ by sending further R_2 bits per pixel. Therefore, both schemes produce an image having the same quality.

Our wish list for the progressive scheme contains two items: first we would like to produce the best possible image during the initial transmission, namely, we wish the point (R_1, D_1) to lie on the rate-distortion curve, namely $R_1 = R(D_1)$ (constraint nr 1), second, we wish overall to transmit the same number of bits

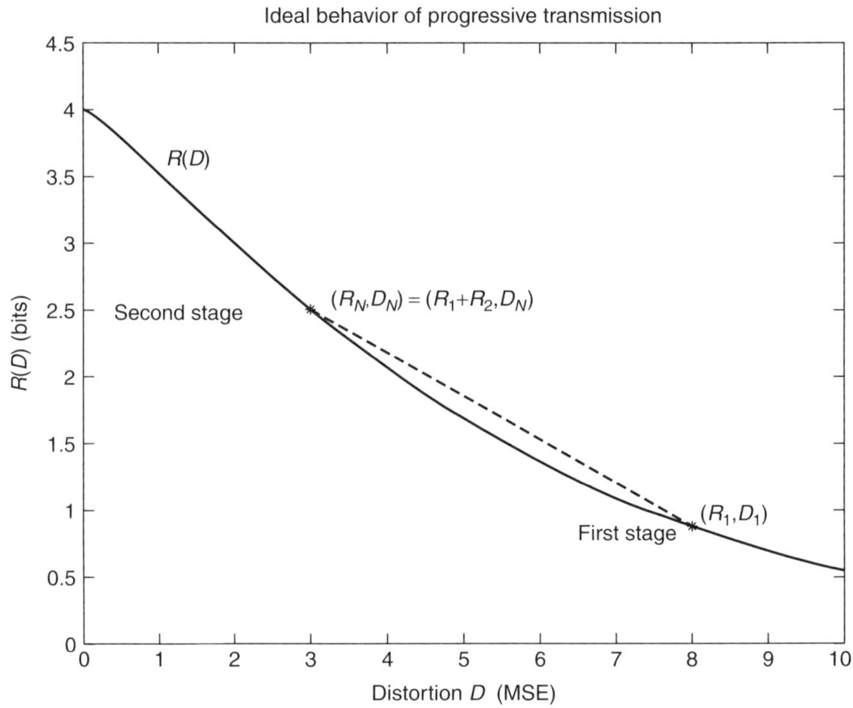

Figure 9.2. Ideal behavior of a successive refinement system: the points describing the first and second stage lie on the rate-distortion curve $R(D)$.

R_N as the nonprogressive scheme, that is, we wish $R_1 + R_2 = R_N = R(D_N) = R(D_2)$ (constraint nr 2).

In this section it is shown that it is not always possible to satisfy both constraints and that recent results show that constraints 1 and 2 can be relaxed to $R_1 < R(D_1) + 1/2$ and $R_1 + R_2 \leq R(D_2) + 1/2$, respectively.

The first results are due to Equitz and Cover [4], who showed that the answer depends on the source (namely, on the statistical characteristics of the image), and that although, in general, the two-stage scheme requires a higher rate than the one-stage approach, there exist necessary and sufficient conditions under which $R_1 = R(D_1)$ and $R_1 + R_2 = R(D_2)$ (the sources for which the two equalities hold for every D_1 and D_2 are called *successively refinable*[2]). An interesting question is whether there are indeed sources that do not satisfy Equitz and Cover's

[2] More specifically, a sufficient condition for a source to be successively refinable is that the original data I, the better approximation I_2, and the coarse approximation I_1 form a Markov chain in this order, that is, if I_1 is conditionally independent of I given I_2. In simpler terms, the conditional independence condition means that if we are given the finer approximation of the original image, our uncertainty about the coarser approximation is the same regardless of whether we are given the original image.

conditions. Unfortunately, sources that are not successively refinable do exist: an example of such a source over a discrete alphabet is described in Ref. [3], whereas Ref. [5] contains an example of a continuous source that is not successively refinable. This result is somewhat problematic: it seems to indicate that the rate-distortion curve can be used to measure the performance of a progressive transmission scheme only for certain types of sources.

The question of which rates are achievable was addressed by Rimoldi [6], who refined the result of Equitz and Cover: by relaxing the condition that $R_1 = R(D_1)$ and $(R_1 + R_2) = R(D_2)$, the author provided conditions under which pairs of rates R_1 and R_2 can be achieved, given fixed distortions D_1 and D_2. Interestingly, in Ref. [6], D_1 and D_2 need not be obtained with the same distortion measure. This is practically relevant: progressive transmission methods in which the early stages produce high-quality approximations of small portions of the image and poor-quality renditions of the rest are discussed later (e.g., in telemedicine, a radiographic image could be transmitted with a method that quickly provides a high-quality image of the area of interest and a blurry version of the rest of the image [7], which can be improved in later stages. Here, the first distortion measure could concentrate on the region of interest, whereas subsequent measures could take into account the image as a whole.)

Although Rimoldi's regions can be used to evaluate the performance of a progressive transmission scheme, a more recent result [8] provides a simpler answer. For any source producing independent and identically distributed samples[3] under squared error distortion for an m-step progressive transmission scheme, any fixed set of m distortion values $D_1 > D_2 \ldots > D_m$, Lastras and Berger showed that there exists an m-step code that operates within $1/2$ bit of the rate-distortion curve at all of its steps (Fig. 9.3). This is a powerful result, which essentially states that the rate-distortion curve can indeed be used to evaluate a progressive transmission scheme: an algorithm that at some step achieves a rate that is not within $1/2$ bit of the rate-distortion curve is by no means optimal and can be improved upon.

The theory of successive refinements plays the same role for progressive transmission as the rate-distortion theory for lossy compression.

In particular, it confirms that it is possible, in principle, to construct progressive transmission schemes that achieve transmission rates comparable to those of nonprogressive methods.

This theory also provides fundamental limits to what is achievable and guidelines to evaluate how well a specific algorithm performs under given assumptions. Such guidelines are sometimes very general and hence difficult to specialize to actual algorithms. However, the field is relatively young and very active; some of the more recent results can be applied to specific categories of progressive transmission schemes, such as the bounds provided in Ref. [9] for multiresolution coding.

---

[3] Lastras's thesis also provides directions on how to extend the result to stationary ergodic sources.

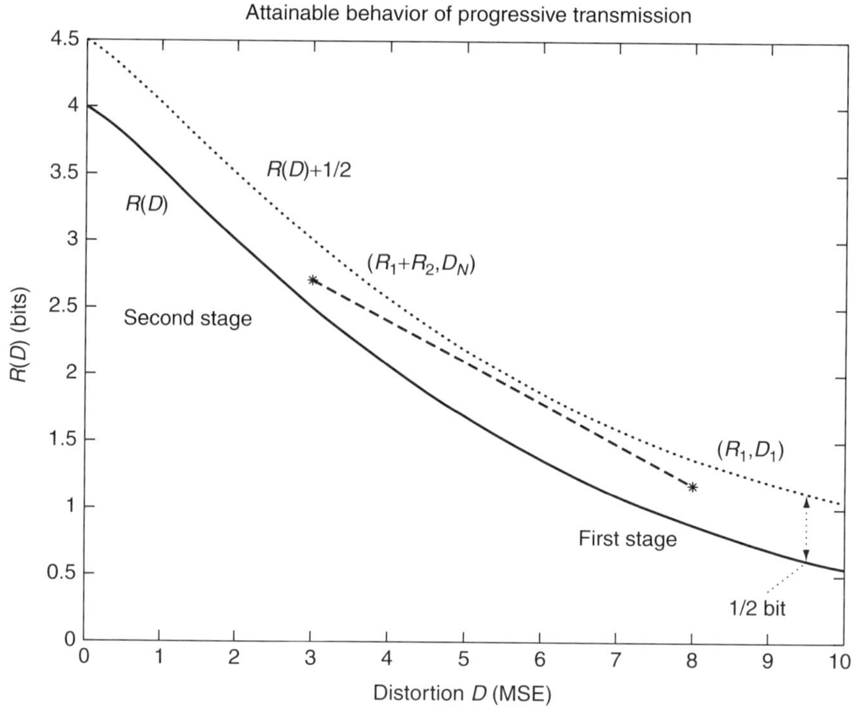

Figure 9.3. Attainable behavior of a progressive transmission scheme: each stage is described by a point that lies within $1/2$ bits of the rate-distortion curve.

Note, finally, that there is a limitation to the applicability of the theory of successive refinements to image transmission: a good distortion measure that is well-matched to the human visual system is not known. The implications are discussed in Section 9.3.3.

9.3.2 Taxonomies of Progressive Transmission Algorithms

Over the years, a large number of progressive transmission schemes have appeared in the literature. Numerous progressive transmission methods have been developed starting from a compression scheme, selecting parts of the compressed data for transmission at each stage, and devising algorithms to reconstruct images from the information available at the receiver after each transmission stage. The following taxonomy, proposed by Tsou [10] and widely used in the field, is well suited to characterize this class of algorithm because it focuses on the characteristics of the compression scheme. Tsou's taxonomy divides progressive transmission approaches into three classes:

Spatial-Domain Techniques. Algorithms belonging to this class compress images without transforming them. A simple example consists of dividing the image into bit planes, compressing the bit planes separately, and scheduling the transmission to send the compressed bit planes in order of significance. Dividing an 8-bit image I into bit planes consists of creating eight images with pixel values equal to 0 or 1 — the first image contains the most significant bit of the pixels of I, the last image contains the least significant bit, and the intermediate images contain the intermediate bits.

A more interesting example is progressive vector quantization (VQ): the image I is first vector-quantized (Chapter 8, Section 8.6.2) at low rate, namely, with a small codebook, which produces an approximation I_1. The difference $I - I_1$ between the original image and the first coarse approximation is further quantized, possibly with a different codebook, to produce I_2, and the process is repeated. The encoded images $I_1, I_2, \ldots$ are transmitted in order and progressively reconstructed at the receiver.

Transform-Domain Techniques. Algorithms belonging to this category transform the image to a specific space (such as the frequency domain), and compress the transform. Examples of this category include progressive JPEG and are discussed in Section 9.4.1.

Pyramid-Structured Techniques. This category contains methods that rely on a multiresolution pyramid, which is a sequence of approximations of the original image I at progressively coarser resolution and larger scale (i.e., having smaller size). The coarsest approximation is losslessly compressed and transmitted; subsequent steps consist of transmitting only the information necessary to reconstruct the next finer approximation from the received data. Schemes derived from compression algorithms that rely on subband coding or on the wavelet transform (Chapter 8, Sections 8.5.3 and 8.8.2) belong to this category, and in this sense, the current category overlaps the transform-domain techniques.

Numerous progressive transmission algorithms developed in recent years are not well categorized by Tsou's taxonomy.

Chee [11] recently proposed a different classification system, which uses Tsou's taxonomy as a secondary categorization. Chee's taxonomy specifically addresses the transmission mechanism, rather than the compression characteristics, and contains four classes:

Multistage Residual Methods. This class contains algorithms that progressively reduce the distortion of the reconstructed image. Chee assigns to this class only methods that operate on the full-resolution image at each stage: multiresolution-based algorithms are assigned to the next category. This category includes multistage VQ [12] and the transform-coding method proposed in Ref. [13].

Our discussion of successive refinements in Section 9.3.1. is directly relevant to this class of methods.

Hierarchical Methods. These algorithms analyze the images at different scales to process them in a hierarchical fashion. Chee divides this class into nonresidual coder, residual multiscale coders, and filter-bank coders.

- *Nonresidual coders* perform a multiscale decomposition of the image and include quadtree-coders [14,15], binary-tree coders [16], spatial pyramid coders [17,18], and subsampling pyramids [19].
- *Residual coders* differ from nonresidual coders in that they compute and encode the residual image at each level of the decomposition (the difference between the original image and what is received at that stage). The well-known Laplacian pyramid can be used to construct a hierarchical residual coder [20]. A theoretical analysis of this category of coders can be found in Ref. [21].
- *Filter-bank coders* include wavelet-based coders and subband coders. Wavelet-based coders send the lowest resolution version of the image first and successively transmit the subbands required to produce the approximation at the immediately higher resolution. A similar approach is used in subband coders [22]. The theoretical analysis of Ref. [9] is directly relevant to this group of methods.

Successive Approximation Methods. This class contains methods that progressively refine the precision (e.g., the number of bits) of the reconstructed approximations. Methods that transmit bit planes belong to this category: at each stage the precision of the reconstructed image increases by 1 bit. Chee assigns to this category bit planes methods, tree-structured vector quantizers, full-search quantizers with intermediate codebooks [23], the embedded zerotree wavelet coder (Chapter 8, Section 8.8.2), and the successive approximation mode of the JPEG standard (Section 9.4.1.1).

Note that these methods, and in particular, transform-domain methods, are not guaranteed to monotonically improve the fidelity of the reconstructed image at each stage, if the fidelity is measured with a single-letter distortion measure (i.e., a measure that averages the distortions of individual pixels) [1].

Methods Based on Transmission Sequences. In this category, Chee groups methods that use a classifier to divide the data into portions, prioritize the order in which different portions are transmitted, and include a protocol for specifying transmission order to the receiver. The prioritization process can aim at different goals, such as reducing the MSE or improving the visual appearance of the reconstructed image at each step.

In Ref. [11] the author assigns to this class the spectral selection method of the JPEG standard (Section 9.4.1.1), Efstratiadi's Filter Bank Coder [24], and several block-based spatial domain coders [25,26].

9.3.3 Comparing Progressive Transmission Schemes

Although it is possible to compare different progressive transmission schemes [11], no general guidelines exist. However, the following broad statements can be made:.

- The application field and the characteristics of the data might directly determine the most appropriate transmission approach. In some cases, starting from a thumbnail (which progressively increases in size) is preferable to receiving, for example, the low-contrast full-size image produced by a bit plane successive approximation algorithm (which becomes progressively sharper) or the blocky full-size image produced by a multistage vector quantizer. In other cases, the thumbnail is the least useful of the three representations. There is no mathematical way of characterizing which of the three images is more suitable for a specific application domain.
- The theory of successive refinements provides a reference point to assess and compare bandwidth requirements. It can be very useful for comparing similar approaches but might not be effective for comparing heterogeneous methods, such as a multiresolution scheme and a successive approximation algorithm. Additionally, different compression methods produce different types of artifacts in intermediate images; the lack of a distortion measure matched to the human visual system means that an intermediate image with certain artifacts can be substantially preferable to another with different artifacts, even though their measured distortion is the same.
- The specific application often imposes constraints on the characteristics of the associated compression algorithm and consequently reduces the set of possible candidate transmission schemes. For instance, some applications might require lossless compression, whereas others can tolerate loss; moreover, different lossy compression algorithms introduce different artifacts, whose severity depends on the intended use of the data.

9.4 SOME EXAMPLES

9.4.1 Transform Coding

Because raw digital images are typically difficult to compress, one often resorts to representing the image in another mathematical space (see Chapter 8). The Fourier transform (FT, Chapter 16), the discrete cosine transform (DCT, Chapters 8 and 16), and the wavelet transform (WT, Chapters 8 and 16) are examples of transformations that map images into mathematical spaces having properties that facilitate compression and transmission. They represent images as linear combinations of appropriately selected functions called *basis functions*.

The DCT and WT in particular are at the heart of numerous progressive transmission schemes. The next two sections analyze them in detail.

9.4.1.1 Discrete Cosine Transform Coding. The DCT uses cosines of varying spatial frequencies as basis functions. Lossy JPEG uses a particular type of DCT called *block-DCT*: the image is first divided into nonoverlapping square blocks of size 8×8 pixels, and each tile is independently transformed with DCT. In JPEG, the reversible DCT step is followed by irreversible quantization of the DCT coefficients. The table used for quantization is not specified by the standard and, in principle, could be selected to match the requirements of specific applications. In practice, there is no algorithm to accomplish this task and even the quantization tables recommended in the standard for use with photographic images were constructed by hand, using essentially a trial-and-error approach.

DCT coding supports progressive transmission easily, if not optimally. Progressive JPEG is now supported in many Web browsers. There are two main progressive JPEG modes.

The first progressive transmission mode uses a successive approximation scheme. During the first pass a low-precision approximation of all the DCT coefficients is transmitted to the client. Using this information the client can reconstruct a full-sized initial image, but one that will tend to have numerous artifacts. Subsequent transmissions successively reduce errors in the approximation of the coefficients and the artifacts in the image. The rationale for this approach is that the largest coefficients capture a great deal of the image content even when transmitted at reduced precision.

The second method is a spectral selection approach which belongs to the transmission-sequence category. First the server sends the DC pixels (corresponding to spatial frequency equal to zero) of each image block to the client. The client can then reconstruct and display a scaled-down version of the original image, containing one pixel per each 8^2 block. Each pixel contains the average value of the 8^2 block. In each subsequent transmission stage the server sends the AC coefficients required to double the size of the received image, until all the data is received by the client. This scheme is an effective way of generating thumbnail images without redundant transmission of bits. The thumbnail can be used to select, say, the desired image, and at the beginning of the transmission the client can use the thumbnail to populate the DC pixel locations of an otherwise empty DCT buffer. The server begins the full transmission not by repeating the DC values, which the client already has, but starts right in with the first scan of low-frequency pixels. The main problem with using DCTs in a tiled image for progressive transmission is that the tile size imposes a minimum resolution on the image as a whole. That is, every 8^2 tile contributes to the first scan regardless of its similarity to its neighbors. Bandwidth is used to express the DC level of each tile, even when that tile's DC level may be shared by many of its neighbors: the basis functions of the DCT do not exploit coherence on scales larger than 8^2.

9.4.1.2 Integer Wavelet Transform Coding. Using wavelet transforms for image processing and compression is a subject that is both vast and deep. We will not delve deeply into the mathematics or algorithms of wavelet transformations but refer the reader to Chapter 8 for an introduction and for references.

In this section, we restrict ourselves to fast, exactly reversible, integer-based transforms. It turns out that a number of different wavelet bases meet these criteria. Therefore, we will discuss in generic terms what such transforms look like, what properties they lend to progressive transmission, and how they optimize the use of transmission bandwidth.

In a generic integer wavelet transform, the first pass scans through the image and forms nearest-neighbor sums and differences of pixels. On a second pass, it scans through what is essentially a 2×2 block average of the original image, one whose overall dimensions have been reduced by a factor of 2. After forming the nearest-neighbor sums and differences, the third pass then operates on a 4×4 block averaged version of the original. This hierarchical decomposition of the image lends the wavelet transform its special powers. As the data are transmitted by bit plane, all wavelet coefficients that capture details too small or faint to be of interest at a certain stage are equal to zero.

A characteristic appearance of an image that has been wavelet-inverted using only partially received coefficients is the variation in pixel size: pixels are big where the image is not changing very much and they are small near edges and small-scale features where the image is changing rapidly. This is a truly dynamic bandwidth management. Bandwidth is used just where it is needed (expressing small pixels) and is conserved where not needed (the large, fixed areas in an image). It is also automatic, in that it falls naturally out of the transform. No special image processing, such as edge detection or content determination, is required.

There are an endless variety of integer-based wavelet transforms. They vary according to small differences in how they calculate their nearest-neighbor sums and differences. It turns out that there is not a large difference in performance between them. Figure 9.4 shows the performance of different transform coders, measured as mean-square error as a function of transmitted data volume. For our purposes, the horizontal axis is proportional to elapsed transmission time for a constant bandwidth.

We notice several facts. First, the DCT coder is obviously worse during the early stages of the transmission. Second, the family of integer-based wavelet coders perform pretty much alike. The differences between them are always much smaller than the difference between their envelope and the performance of the DCT coder. Note that the DCT coder used for Figure 9.4 is a bit plane coder, not the pixel-ordering coders that are officially sanctioned by the JPEG standard.

9.4.2 Color Images

Color images provide an extra point of attack on bandwidth usage: we can exploit the correlation in content between the separate red, green, and blue color components. Any good file compressor, like JPEG, exploits this correlation between colors as well, but it has particular relevance in progressive transmission.

Color images are typically expressed using three component images, one each in the colors of red, green, and blue (RGB). Often, there is a strong correlation in image content between each of the color bands. A classic method of dealing with this correlation, used for decades in color TV broadcasting, is to switch the scene into a different color space using the transformation

$$Y = 0.299R + 0.587G + 0.114B$$

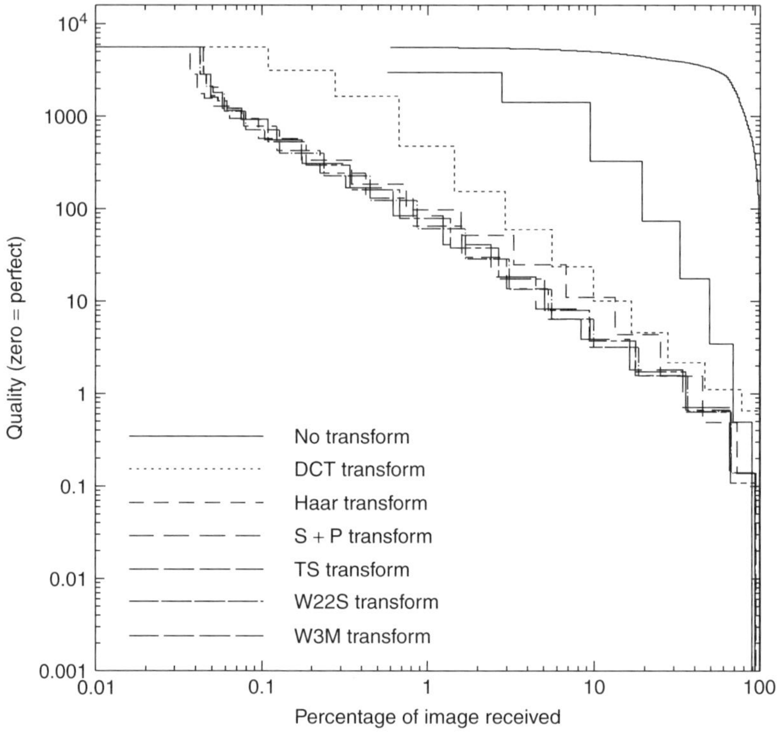

Figure 9.4. Mean-squared error as a function of fraction of image received.

$$Cb = 128 - (0.167734R) - (0.331264G) + (05B)$$
$$Cr = 128 + (0.5R) - (0.418688G) - (0.081312B)$$

and reverse the transformation when displaying the image (There are many variants on this transformation; we use this one to illustrate the idea.) The Y-component is called the *luminance* and can be used as a gray scale representation of the original image. This signal is used by black and white TV sets when receiving a color signal. The other two components represent color differences and are much less correlated in image content. These "chroma" channels are often very compressible.

A good progressive image-transmission system should exploit such correlations between the components of multiband imaging. Such correlation is not restricted to RGB systems, for example, multiband spectral imaging detectors in Earth-observing systems often produce highly correlated image components. There may be multiple groups of correlated components, with the number of correlated spectral bands in each group being much larger than three. A transformation similar to that mentioned earlier can be designed for multiband imagery with any number of components.

9.4.3 Extraction, Coding, and Transmission of Data

We will now step through an actual progressive transmission and discuss the details of the process. Our intent is to outline the steps and considerations any good progressive image-transmission system should have, instead of exhaustively documenting any specific process or step.

The server first ingests the image. The image can be transformed either on-the-fly or in advance. The choice depends on whether the server has been supplied with preprocessed, previously transformed images. Preprocessing is used to avoid the CPU processing required to perform the transformation in real time.

Wavelet transforms produce negative numbers for some pixels, and even if the absolute value of the coefficient is small, sign extension in 32-bit or 64-bit integers can generate many unneeded 1-bits that can foil the entropy coders (Chapter 8). Signs must be handled separately, usually by separating them from their associated values and dealing with a completely nonnegative transform. Signs must be carefully reunited with their associated coefficients at the client in time for them to express the desired effect before the client inverts the transform.

The server then extracts bit planes, or blocks of pixels, and performs entropy coding on them to reduce their size. Entropy coding may be done in advance as well, although this complicates the serving of regions of interest. If the progressive transmission is interactive, the server may need to reverse the entropy coding and rebuild the image in order to extract the requested region of interest.

Bit clipping is an important part of the interactive mode of progressive transmission. The client may request overlapping regions of interest and the degree of overlap may be quite high. For example, the client may be cropping an image and the crop may be slightly wrong; recropping with just a small change in size or position can result in a great deal of overlap. Because the goal of serving regions of interest is to represent the requested region exactly (losslessly), there can be a large transmission penalty in mismanaging such regions. A well-behaved interactive server will keep track of the bit plane sections and pixel blocks already sent and will clip (zero) out duplicate bits before sending.

In an interactive session, it is important to quantize the transmitted data messages into reasonably timed units. That is, when sending a bit plane that may take, for example, a minute to complete, the client may be blocked from requesting and receiving regions of interest before that time. The transactions must be quantized such that the server can respond to interactive requests and interpolate the transmission of the newly requested areas before falling back to the originally scheduled bits.

9.4.4 Examples

A progressive image-transmission system that meets each of the ideal capabilities of Section 9.1 has been implemented at the University of Wisconsin. Here we show some examples using this system.

Figure 9.5 shows a true-color (24-bit) image progressively transmitted to a byte count that is only 0.1 percent of the original. This represents a compression ratio of nearly 1,000. Note the effect of the dynamic spatial resolution: the pixels are small and dense around the edge and face of the child but are large and sparse in the background, where the file cabinets present a visually uninteresting background. Although a detailed inspection indicates that there is much to be improved, holding the picture at arm's length nevertheless shows that this point in the progression serves nicely as a thumbnail image.

Figure 9.6 shows the same image as in Figure 9.5, but captured at a factor of 300 in lossiness. Considerable improvement is seen in fingers, forehead, and hair.

In Figure 9.7 we jump all the way to a factor of 80 in lossiness. Remember that this is still only about 1 percent of the total image volume. We use examples at such aggressive levels of lossiness because of the high performance of the algorithm; at the 10 percent point, the image is visually indistinguishable from the original and no further improvement is apparent.

Finally, in Figure 9.8 we show the effects of selecting regions of interest. In this case, the approximation of Figure 9.5 was used to outline a box using the mouse in our graphical user interface. Upon selection, the region of interest was immediately extracted from the wavelet transform, previously sent bits were clipped (zeroed out) to avoid retransmission, and the region was progressively sent to the client.

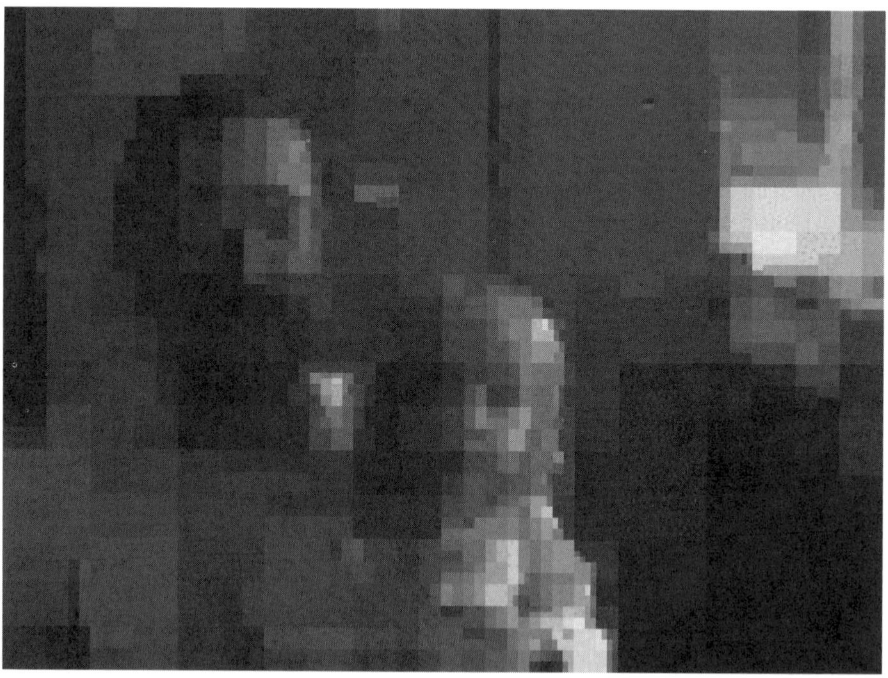

Figure 9.5. Result of sending 0.1 percent of the coefficients. A color version of this figure can be downloaded from *ftp://wiley.com/public/sci_tech_med/image_databases*.

Figure 9.6. Result of sending 0.3 percent of the coefficients. A color version of this figure can be downloaded from *ftp://wiley.com/public/sci_tech_med/image_databases*.

Figure 9.7. Result of sending 1 percent of the coefficients. A color version of this figure can be downloaded from *ftp://wiley.com/public/sci_tech_med/image_databases*.

Figure 9.8. Selecting a region of interest in an image: the region of interest is extracted from the wavelet transform, previously sent bits are clipped to avoid retransmission, and the region is progressively sent to the client. A color version of this figure can be downloaded from *ftp://wiley.com/public/sci_tech_med/image_databases*.

9.5 SUMMARY

Progressive transmission of large digital images offers the powerful new capability of interactively browsing large image archives over relatively slow network connections. Browsers can enjoy an effective bandwidth that appears as much as one hundred times greater than the actual bandwidth delivered by the network infrastructure.

Interactivity allows users to examine an image very quickly and then either reject it as a candidate for complete transmission or outline regions of interest that quickly follow at a higher priority.

Progressive transmission is a form of image compression in which lossiness is played out as a function of elapsed time rather than file size as in normal compression. No degree of lossiness need be chosen in advance, and different clients can customize the quality of the received image simply by letting more time pass during its receipt.

Even when fully transmitting a lossless image, progressive transmission is still more efficient than transmitting the raw image, because the transform and entropy coding at its core are the same as the ones used in normal file compression.

REFERENCES

1. W. Pennebaker and J.L. Mitchell, *JPEG Still Image Data Compression Standard*, Van Nostrand Reinhold, New York, 1993.

2. R. White, High performance compression of astronomical images, Technical Report, Space Telescope Science Institute, 1992.
3. T. Berger, *Rate Distortion Theory: a Mathematical Basis for Data Compression*, Prentice Hall, Englewood Cliffs, N.J., 1971.
4. W. Equitz and T. Cover, Successive refinements of information, *IEEE Trans. Information Theory* **37**, 269–275 (1991).
5. J. Chowan and T. Berger, Failure of Successive Refinement for Symmetric Gaussian Mixtures, *IEEE Trans. Information Theory* **43**, 350–352, (1991).
6. B. Rimoldi, Successive refinements of information: Characterization of the Achievable Rates, *IEEE Trans. Information Theory* **40**, 253–259 (1994).
7. J. Chow, Interactive selective decompression of medical images, *Proc. IEEE Nucl. Sci. Symp.* **3**, 1855–1858 (1996).
8. L. Lastras and T. Berger, All sources are nearly successively refinable, *IEEE Trans. Inf. Theory* (2001), in press.
9. M. Effros, Distortion-rate bounds forfixed- and variable-rate multiresolution source codes, *IEEE Trans. Inf. Theory* **45**, 1887–1910 (1999).
10. K.-H. Tsou, Progressive image transmission: a review and comparison of techniques, *Opt. Eng.* **26**(7), 581–589 (1987).
11. Y.-K. Chee, A survey of progressive image transmission methods, *Int. J. Imaging Systems Techno.* (2000).
12. B.-H. Juang and A. Gray, Multiple stage vector quantization for speech coding, *Proc. IEEE ICASSP 82* **1**, 597–600 (1982).
13. L. Wang and M. Goldberg, Progressive image transmission by transform coefficient residual error quantization, *IEEE Trans. Commun.* **36**, 75–87 (1988).
14. R. Blanford, Progressive refinement using local variance estimators, *IEEE Trans. Commun.* **41**(5), 749–759 (1993).
15. G. Sullivan and R. Baker, Efficient quadtree coding of images and video, *IEEE Trans. Image Process.* **3**, 327–331 (1994).
16. K. Knowlton, Progressive transmission of grey-scale and binary pictures by simple, efficient, and lossless encoding schemes, *Proc. IEEE* **68**(7), 885–896 1980.
17. S. Tanimoto, Image transmission with gross information first, Technical Report 77-10-06, Department of computer science, University of Washington, Seattle, 1977.
18. M. Goldberg and L. Wang, Comparative performance of pyramid data structures for progressive image transmission, *IEEE Trans. Commun.* **39**(4), 540–547 (1991).
19. M. Viergever and P. Roos, Hierarchical interpolation, *IEEE Eng. Med. Bio.* **12**, 48–55 (1993).
20. P. Burt and A.E.H., The Laplacian pyramid as a compact image coder, *IEEE Trans. Commun.* **31**(4), 532–540, (1983).
21. S. Park and S. Lee, The coding gains of pyramid structures in progressive image transmission, *Proc. SPIE Vis. Commun. Image Process.'90* **1360**, 1702–1710 (1990).
22. P. Westerink, J. Biemond, and D. Boekee, Progressive transmission of images using image coding, *Proc. IEEE ICASSP 89* 1811–1814 (1989).
23. E. Riskin, R. Ladner, R.-Y. Wang, and L. Atlas, Index assignment for progressive transmission of full-search vector quantization, *IEEE Trans. Image Process.*, **3**(3), 307–311 (1994).

24. S. Efstratiadis, B. Rouchouze, and M. Kunt, Image compression using subband/wavelet transform and adaptive multiple-distribution entropy coding, *Proc. SPIE Vis. Commun. Image Process. '92* **1818**, 753–764 (1992).
25. N. Subramanian, A. Kalhan, and V. Udpikar, Sketch and texture coding approach to monochrome image coding, *Int. Conf. Image Process. Appl.*, 29–32 FIND (1992).
26. S. Caron and J.-F. Rivest, Progressive image transmission by segmentation- based coding, *J. Vis. Commun. Image Represent.* **7**(3), 296–303 (1996).

10 Introduction to Content-Based Image Retrieval — Overview of Key Techniques

YING LI and C.-C. JAY KUO
University of Southern California, Los Angeles, California
X. WAN
U.S. Research Lab, San Jose, California

10.1 INTRODUCTION

Advances in modern computer and telecommunication technologies have led to huge archives of multimedia data in diverse application areas such as medicine, remote sensing, entertainment, education, and on-line information services. This is similar to the rapid increase in the amount of alphanumeric data during the early days of computing, which led to the development of database management systems (DBMS). Traditional DBMSs were designed to organize alphanumeric data into interrelated collections so that information retrieval and storage could be done conveniently and efficiently. However, this technology is not well suited to the management of multimedia information. The diversity of data types and formats, the large size of media objects, and the difficulties in automatically extracting semantic meanings from data are entirely foreign to traditional database management techniques. To use this widely available multimedia information effectively, efficient methods for storage, browsing, indexing, and retrieval [1,2] must be developed. Different multimedia data types may require specific indexing and retrieval tools and methodologies. In this chapter, we present an overview of indexing and retrieval methods for image data.

Since the 1970s, image retrieval has been a very active research area within two major research communities — database management and computer vision. These research communities study image retrieval from two different angles. The first is primarily text-based, whereas the second relies on visual properties of the data [3].

Image Databases: Search and Retrieval of Digital Imagery, Edited by Vittorio Castelli and Lawrence D. Bergman.
ISBN 0-471-32116-8

Text-based image retrieval can be traced back to the late 1970s. At that time, images were annotated by key words and stored as retrieval keys in traditional databases. Some relevant research in this field can be found in Refs. [4,5]. Two problems render manual annotation ineffective when the size of image databases becomes very large. The first is the prohibitive amount of labor involved in image annotation. The other, probably more essential, results from the difficulty of capturing the rich content of images using a small number of key words, a difficulty which is compounded by the subjectivity of human perception.

In the early 1990s, because of the emergence of large-scale image collections, content-based image retrieval (CBIR) was proposed as a way to overcome these difficulties. In CBIR, images are automatically indexed by summarizing their visual contents through automatically extracted quantities or features such as color, texture, or shape. Thus, low-level numerical features, extracted by a computer, are substituted for higher-level, text-based manual annotations or key words. Since the inception of CBIR, many techniques have been developed along this direction, and many retrieval systems, both research and commercial, have been built [3].

Note that ideally CBIR systems should automatically extract (and index) the semantic content of images to meet the requirements of specific application areas. Although it seems effortless for a human being to pick out photos of horses from a collection of pictures, automatic object recognition and classification are still among the most difficult problems in image understanding and computer vision. This is the main reason why low-level features such as colors [6–8], textures [9–11], and shapes of objects [12,13] are widely used for content-based image retrieval. However, in specific applications, such as medical or petroleum imaging, low-level features play a substantial role in defining the content of the data.

A typical content-based image retrieval system is depicted in Figure 10.1 [3]. The image collection database contains raw images for the purpose of visual display. The visual feature repository stores visual features extracted from images needed to support content-based image retrieval. The text annotation repository contains key words and free-text descriptions of images. Multidimensional indexing is used to achieve fast retrieval and to make the system scalable to large image collections.

The retrieval engine includes a query interface and a query-processing unit. The query interface, typically employing graphical displays and direct manipulation techniques, collects information from users and displays retrieval results. The query-processing unit is used to translate user queries into an internal form, which is then submitted to the DBMS. Moreover, in order to gap the bridge between low-level visual features and high-level semantic meanings, users are usually allowed to communicate with the search engine in an interactive way.

We will address each part of this structure in more detail in later sections.

This chapter is organized as follows. In Section 10.2, the extraction and integration of some commonly used features, such as color, texture, shape,

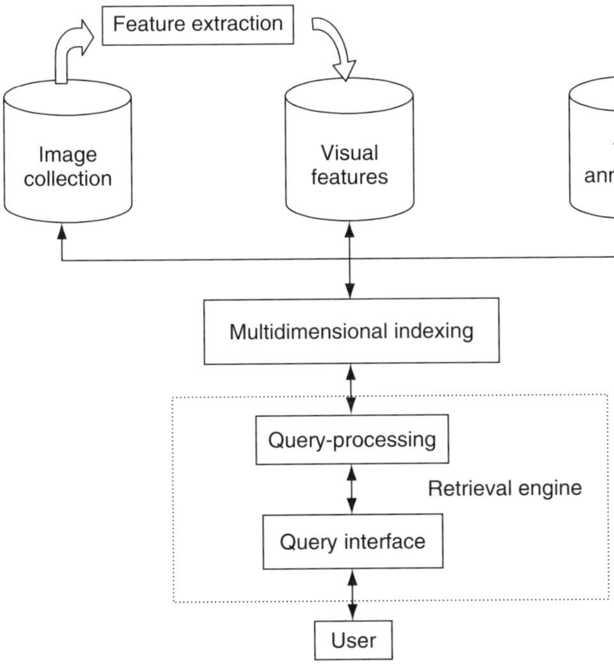

Figure 10.1. An image retrieval system architecture.

object spatial relationship, and so on are briefly discussed. Some feature indexing techniques are reviewed in Section 10.4. Section 10.5 provides key concepts of interactive content-based image retrieval, and several main components of a CBIR system are also discussed briefly. Section 10.6 introduces a new work item of the ISO/MPEG family, which is called the "Multimedia Content Description Interface" or MPEG-7 in short, which defines a standard to describe and define multimedia content features and descriptors. Finally, concluding remarks are drawn in Section 10.7.

10.2 FEATURE EXTRACTION AND INTEGRATION

Feature extraction is the basis of CBIR. Features can be categorized as general or domain-specific. General features typically include color, texture, shape, sketch, spatial relationships, and deformation, whereas domain-specific features are applicable in specialized domains such as human face recognition or fingerprint recognition.

Each feature may have several representations. For example, color histogram and color moments are both representations of the image color feature. Moreover, numerous variations of the color histogram itself have been proposed, each of which differs in the selected color-quantization scheme.

10.2.1 Feature Extraction

10.2.1.1 Color. Color is one of the most recognizable elements of image content [14] and is widely used in image retrieval because of its invariance with respect to image scaling, translation, and rotation. The key issues in color feature extraction include the color space, color quantization, and the choice of similarity function.

Color Spaces. The commonly used color spaces include RGB, YCbCr, HSV, CIELAB, CIEL*u*v*, and Munsell spaces. The CIELAB and CIEL*u*v* color spaces usually give a better performance because of their improved perceptual uniformity with respect to RGB [15]. MPEG-7 XM V2 supports RGB, YCbCr, HSV color spaces, and some linear transformation matrices with reference to RGB [16].

Color Quantization. Color quantization is used to reduce the color resolution of an image. Using a quantized color map can considerably decrease the computational complexity during image retrieval. The commonly used color-quantization schemes include uniform quantization, vector quantization, tree-structured vector quantization, and product quantization [17–19]. In MPEG-7 XM V2 [16], three quantization types are supported: linear, nonlinear, and lookup table.

10.3 SIMILARITY FUNCTIONS

A similarity function is a mapping between pairs of feature vectors and a positive real-valued number, which is chosen to be representative of the visual similarity between two images. Let us take the color histogram as an example. There are two main approaches to histogram formation. The first one is based on the global color distribution across the entire image, whereas the second one consists of computing the local color distribution for a certain partition of the image. These two techniques are suitable for different types of queries. If users are concerned only with the overall colors and their amounts, regardless of their spatial arrangement in the image, then indexing using the global color distribution is useful. However, if users also want to take into consideration the positional arrangement of colors, the local color histogram will be a better choice.

A global color histogram represents an image I by an N-dimensional vector, $\mathbf{H}(I) = [\mathbf{H}(I, j), j = 1, 2, \ldots, N]$, where N is the number of quantization colors and $\mathbf{H}(I, j)$ is the number of pixels having color j. The similarity of two images can be easily computed on the basis of this representation. The four common types of similarity measurements are the L1 norm [20], the L2 norm [21], the color histogram intersection [7], and the weighted distance metric [22]. The L1 norm has the lowest computational complexity. However, it was shown in Ref. [23] that it could produce false negatives (not all similar images are retrieved). The L2 norm (i.e., the Euclidean distance) is probably the most widely used metric.

However, it can result in false positives (dissimilar images are retrieved). The color histogram intersection proposed by Swain and Ballard [7] has been adopted by many researchers because of its simplicity and effectiveness. The weighted distance metric proposed by Hafner and coworkers [22] takes into account the perceptual similarity between two colors, thus making retrieval results consistent with human's visual perception. Other weighted matrices for similarity measure can be found in Ref. [24]. See Chapter 14 for a more detailed description of these metrics.

Local color histograms are used to retrieve images on the basis of their color similarity in local spatial regions. One natural approach is to partition the whole image into several regions and then extract color features from each of them [25,26]. In this case, the similarity of two images will be determined by the similarity of the corresponding regions. Of course, the two images should have same number of partitions with the same size. If they happen to have different aspect ratios, then normalization will be required.

10.3.1 Some Color Descriptors

A compact color descriptor, called a *binary representation of the image histogram*, was proposed in Ref. [27]. With this approach, each region is represented by a binary signature, which is a binary sequence generated by a two-level quantization of wavelet coefficients obtained by applying the two-dimensional (2D) Haar transform to the 2D color histogram. In Ref. [28], a scalable blob histogram was proposed, where the term *blob* denotes a group of pixels with homogeneous color. One advantage of this descriptor is that images containing objects with different sizes and shapes can be easily distinguished without color segmentation. A region-based image retrieval approach was presented in Ref. [29]. The main idea of this work is to adaptively segment the whole image into sets of regions according to the local color distribution [30] and then compute the similarity on the basis of each region's dominant colors, which are extracted by applying color quantization.

Some other commonly used color feature representations in image retrieval include color moments and color sets. For example, in Ref. [31], Stricker and Dimai extracted the first three color moments from five partially overlapped fuzzy regions. In Ref. [32], Stricker and Orengo proposed to use color moments to overcome undesirable quantization effects. To speed up the retrieval process in a very large image database, Smith and Chang approximated the color histogram with a selection of colors (color sets) from a prequantized color space [33,34].

10.3.2 Texture

Texture refers to visual patterns with properties of homogeneity that do not result from the presence of only a single color or intensity [35]. Tree barks, clouds, water, bricks, and fabrics are examples of texture. Typical textural features include contrast, uniformity, coarseness, roughness, frequency, density, and directionality. Texture features usually contain important information about the structural arrangement of surfaces and their relationship to the surrounding environment [36]. To date, a large amount of research in texture analysis has been done as a result of the usefulness and effectiveness of this feature in application areas such as pattern recognition, computer vision, and image retrieval.

There are two basic classes of texture descriptors: statistical model-based and transform-based. The first approach explores the gray-level spatial dependence of textures and then extracts meaningful statistics as texture representation. In Ref. [36], Haralick and coworkers proposed the co-occurrence matrix representation of texture features, in which they explored the gray-level spatial dependence of texture. They also studied the line-angle-ratio statistics by analyzing the spatial relationships of lines and the properties of their surroundings. Interestingly, Tamura and coworkers addressed this topic from a totally different viewpoint [37]. They showed, on the basis of psychological measurements, that six basic textural features were coarseness, contrast, directionality, line-likeness, regularity, and roughness. This approach selects numerical features that correspond to characteristics of the human visual system, rather than on statistical measures of the data and, therefore, seems well suited to the retrieval of natural images. Two well-known CBIR systems (the QBIC system [38] and the MARS system [39,40]) adopted Tamura's texture representation and made some further improvements. Liu and Picard [10] and Niblack and coworkers [11,41] used a subset of the above mentioned 6 features, namely contrast, coarseness, and directionality models to achieve texture classification and recognition.

A human texture perception study, conducted by Rao and Lohse [42], indicated that the three most important orthogonal dimensions are "repetitiveness," "directionality," and "granularity and complexity."

Some commonly used transforms for transform-based texture extractions are the discrete cosine transform (DCT transform), the Fourier-Mellin transform, Polar Fourier transform, and the Gabor and the wavelet transform. Alata and coworkers [43] proposed classifying rotated and scaled textures by using the combination of a Fourier-Mellin transform and a parametric 2D spectrum estimation method called *harmonic mean horizontal vertical* (HMHV). Wan and Kuo [44] extracted the texture features in the joint photographic experts group (JPEG) compressed domain by analyzing AC coefficients of the DCT transform. The Gabor filters proposed by Manjunath and Ma [45] offer texture descriptors with a set of "optimum joint bandwidth." A tree-structured wavelet transform presented by Chang and Kuo [46] provides a natural and effective way to describe textures that have dominant middle- or high-frequency subbands. In Ref. [47], Nevel developed a texture feature–extraction method by matching the first and the second-order statistics of wavelet subbands.

10.3.3 Shape

Two major steps are involved in shape feature extraction. They are object segmentation and shape representation.

10.3.3.1 Object Segmentation. Image retrieval based on object shape is considered to be one of the most difficult aspects of content-based image retrieval because of difficulties in low-level image segmentation and the variety of ways a given three-dimensional (3D) object can be projected into 2D shapes. Several segmentation techniques have been proposed so far and include the global threshold-based technique [21], the region-growing technique [48], the split-and-merge technique [49], the edge-detection-based technique [41,50], the texture-based technique [51], the color-based technique [52], and the model-based technique [53]. Generally speaking, it is difficult to do a precise segmentation owing to the complexity of the individual object shape, the existence of shadows, noise, and so on.

10.3.3.2 Shape Representation. Once objects are segmented, their shape features can be represented and indexed. In general, shape representations can be classified into three categories [54]:

- *Boundary-Based Representations (Based on the Outer Boundary of the Shape).* The commonly used descriptors of this class include the chain code [55], the Fourier descriptor [55], and the UNL descriptor [56].
- *Region-Based Representations (Based on the Entire Shape Region).* Descriptors of this class include moment invariants [57], Zernike moments [55], the morphological descriptor [58], and pseudo-Zernike moments [56].
- *Combined Representations.* We may consider the integration of several basic representations such as moment invariants with the Fourier descriptor or moment invariants with the UNL descriptor.

The Fourier descriptor is extracted by applying the Fourier transform to the parameterized 1 D boundary. Because digitization noise can significantly affect this technique, robust approaches have been developed such as the one described in Ref. [54], which is also invariant to geometric transformations. Region-based moments are invariant with respect to affine transformations of images. Details can be found in Ref. [57,59,60]. Recent work in shape representation includes the finite element method (FEM) [61], the turning function developed by Arkin and coworkers [62], and the wavelet descriptor developed by Chuang and Kuo [63].

Chamfer matching is the most popular shape-matching technique. It was first proposed by Barrow and coworkers [64] for comparing two collections of shape fragments and was then further improved by Borgefors in Ref. [65].

Besides the aforementioned work in 2D shape representation, some research has focused on 3D shape representations. For example, Borgefors and coworkers [66] used binary pyramids in 3D space to improve the shape and the topology preservation in lower-resolution representations. Wallace and Mitchell [67] presented a hybrid structural or statistical local shape analysis algorithm for 3D shape representation.

10.3.4 Spatial Relationships

There are two classes of spatial relationships. The first class, containing topological relationships, captures the relations between element boundaries. The second class containing orientation or directional relationships captures the relative positions of elements with respect to each other. Examples of topological relationships are "near to," "within," or "adjacent to." Examples of directional relationships are "in front of," "on the left of," and "on top of." A well-known method to describe spatial relationship is the attributed-relational graph (ARG) [68] in which objects are represented by nodes, and an arc between two nodes represents a relationship between them.

So far, spatial-based modeling has been widely addressed, mostly in the literature on spatial reasoning, for application areas such as geographic information systems [69,70]. We can distinguish two main categories that are called *qualitative* and *quantitative spatial modeling*, respectively.

A typical application of the qualitative spatial model to image databases, based on symbolic projection theory, was proposed by Chang [7]; it allows a bidimensional arrangement of a set of objects to be encoded into a sequential structure called a *2D string*. Because the 2D string structure reduces the matching complexity from a quadratic function to a linear one, the approach has been adopted in several other works [72,73].

Compared to qualitative modeling, quantitative spatial modeling can provide a more continuous relationship between perceived spatial arrangements and their representations by using numeric quantities as classification thresholds [74,75].

Lee and Hsu [74] proposed a quantitative modeling technique that enables the comparison of the mutual position of a pair of extended regions. In this approach, the spatial relationship between an observer and an observed object is represented by a finite set of equivalence classes based on the dense sets of possible paths leading from any pixel of one object to that of the other.

10.3.5 Features of Nonphotographic Images

The discussion in the previous section focused on features for indexing and retrieving natural images. Nonphotographic images such as medical and satellite images can be retrieved more effectively using special-purpose features, owing to their special content and their complex and variable characteristics.

10.3.5.1 Medical Images. Medical images include diagnostic X-ray images, ultrasound images, computer-aided tomographical images, magnetic resonance images, and nuclear medicine images. Typical medical images contain many complex, irregular objects. These exhibit a great deal of variability, due to difference in modality, equipment, procedure, and the patient [76]. This variability poses a big challenge to efficient image indexing and retrieval.

Features suitable for medical images can be categorized into two basic classes: text-based and content-based.

Text-Based Features. Because of the uniqueness of each medical image (for example, the unique relationship between a patient and an X-ray image of his or her lungs at a particular time), text-based features are widely used in some medical image retrieval systems. This information usually includes the institution name, the institution patient identifier, patient's name and birth date, patient study identifiers, modality, date, and time [76].

Usually, these features are incorporated into labels, which are digitally or physically affixed to the images and then used as the primary indexing key in medical imaging libraries.

Content-Based Features. Two commonly used content-based features are shape and object spatial relationship, which are very useful in helping physicians locate images containing the objects of their interest. In Ref. [76], Cabral and coworkers proposed a new feature called *anatomic labels.* This descriptor is associated with the anatomy and pathology present in the image and provides a means for assigning (unified medical language system) (UMLS) labels to images or specific locations within images.

10.3.5.2 Satellite Images. Recent advances in sensor and communication technologies have made it practical to launch an increasing number of space platforms for a variety of Earth science studies. The large volume of data generated by the instruments on the platforms has posed significant challenges for data transmission, storage, retrieval and dissemination. Efficient image storage, indexing, and retrieval systems are required to make this vast quantity of data useful.

The research community has devoted a significant amount of effort to this area [77–80]. In CBIR systems for satellite imagery, different image features are extracted, depending on the type of satellite images and research purposes. For example, in a system used for analyzing aurora image data [79], the authors extract two types of features. Global features include the aurora area, the magnetic flux, the total intensity and the variation of intensity, and radial features along a radial line from geomagnetic north such as the average width and the variation of width. In Ref. [77], shape and spatial relationship features are extracted from a National Oceanographic and Atmospheric Adminstration (NOAA) satellite image database. In a database system for the Earth observing satellite image [80], Li and Chen proposed an algorithm to progressively extract and compare different texture features, such as the fractal dimension, coarseness, entropy, circular Moran autocorrelation functions, and spatial gray-level difference (SGLD) statistics, between an image and a target template. In Ref. [78], Barros and coworkers explored techniques for the exploitation of spectral distribution information in a satellite image database.

10.3.6 Some Additional Features

Some additional features that have been used in the image retrieval process are discussed in the following section.

10.3.6.1 Angular Spectrum. Visual properties of an image are mainly related to the largest objects it contains. In describing an object, shape, texture, and orientation play a major role. In many cases, because shape can also be defined in terms of presence and distribution of oriented subcomponents, the orientation of objects within an image becomes a key attribute in the definition of similarity to other images. On the basis of this assumption, Lecce and Celentano [81] defined a metric for image classification in the 2D space that is quantified by signatures composed of angular spectra of image components. In Ref. [8.2], an image's Fourier transform was analyzed to find the directional distribution of lines.

10.3.6.2 Edge Directionality. Edge directionality is another commonly used feature. In Ref. [82], Lecce and Celentano detected edges within an image by using the Canny algorithm [83] and then applied the Hough transform [84], which transforms a line in Cartesian coordinate space to a point in polar coordinate space, to each edge point. The results were then analyzed in order to detect main directions of edges in each image.

10.3.7 Feature Integration

Experience shows that the use of a single class of descriptors to index an image database does not generally produce results that are adequate for real applications and that retrieval results are often unsatisfactory even for a research prototype. A strategy to potentially improve image retrieval, both in terms of speed and quality of results, is to combine multiple heterogeneous features.

We can categorize feature integration as either sequential or parallel. Sequential feature integration, also called *feature filtering*, is a multistage process in which different features are sequentially used to prune a candidate image set. In the parallel feature-integration approach, several features are used concurrently in the retrieval process. In the latter case, different weights need to be assigned appropriately to different features, because different features have different discriminating powers, depending on the application and specific task. The feature-integration approach appears to be superior to using individual features and, as a consequence, is implemented in most current CBIR systems. The original Query by Image Content (QBIC) system [85] allowed the user to select the relative importance of color, texture, and shape. Smith and Chang [86] proposed a spatial and feature (SaFe) system to integrate content-based features with spatial query methods, thus allowing users to specify a query in terms of a set of regions with desired characteristics and simple spatial relations.

Srihari [20] developed a system for identifying human faces in newspaper photographs by integrating visual features extracted from images with texts obtained from the associated descriptive captions. A similar system based on textual and image content information was also described in Ref. [87]. Extensive experiments show that the use of only one kind of information cannot produce satisfactory results. In the newest version of the QBIC system [85], text-based key word search is integrated with content-based similarity search, which leads to an improvement of the overall system performance. The virage system [88] allows queries to be built by combining color, composition (color layout), texture, and structure (object boundary information).

The main limitation of feature integration in most existing CBIR systems is the heavy involvement of the user, who must not only select the features to be used for each individual query, but must also specify their relative weights. A successful system that is built upon feature integration requires a good understanding of how the matching of each feature is performed and how the query engine uses weights to produce final results. Sometimes, even sophisticated users find it difficult to construct queries that return satisfactory results. An interactive CBIR system can be designed to simplify this problem and is discussed in Section 10.5.

10.4 FEATURE INDEXING

Normally, image descriptors are represented by multidimensional vectors, which are often used to measure the similarity of two images by calculating a descriptor distance in the feature space. When the number of images in the database is small, a sequential linear search can provide a reasonable performance. However, with large-scale image databases, indexing support for similarity-based queries becomes necessary. In regular database systems, data are indexed by key entities, which are selected to support the most common types of searches. Similarly, the indexing of an image database should support an efficient search based on image contents or extracted features. In traditional relational database management systems (RDBMS), the most popular class of indexing techniques is the B-tree family, most commonly the B^+-tree [89]. B-trees allow extremely efficient searches when the key is a scalar. However, they are not suitable to index the content of images represented by high-dimensional features. The R-tree [90] and its variations are probably the best-known multidimensional indexing techniques.

10.4.1 Dimension Reduction

Experiments indicate that R-Trees [90] and R*-Trees [91] work well for similarity retrieval only when the dimension of the indexing key is less than 20. For a higher dimensional space, the performance of these tree-structured indices degrades rapidly. Although the dimension of a feature vector obtained by concatenating multiple descriptors is often in the order of 10^2, the number of nonredundant dimensions is typically much lower. Thus, dimension reduction should be performed before indexing the feature vectors with a multidimensional indexing technique. There are two widely used approaches to dimension reduction: the Karhunen-Loeve transform (KLT) [92] and the column-wise clustering [93].

KLT and its variations have been used in dimension reduction in many areas such as features for facial recognition, eigen-images, and principal component analysis. Because KLT is a computationally intensive algorithm, recent work has been devoted to efficient computation of approximations suitable for similarity indexing, which include the fast approximation to KLT [94], the low-rank singular value decomposition (SVD) update algorithm [95], and others.

Clustering is another useful tool to achieve dimension reduction. The key idea of clustering is to group a set of objects with similar feature or features into one class. Clustering has been developed in the context of lossy data compression (where it is known as vector quantization) and in pattern recognition (where it is the subject of research on unsupervised learning). It has also been used to group similar objects (patterns and documents) together for information retrieval applications. It can also be used to reduce the dimensionality of a feature space as discussed in Ref. [93].

10.4.2 Indexing Techniques

The universe of multidimensional indexing techniques is extremely vast and rich. Here, we limit ourselves to citing the bucketing algorithm, the k-d tree [96], the priority k-d tree [97], the quad-tree [98], the K-D-B tree [99], the hB-tree [96], the R-tree [90,100] and its variants R^+-tree [101] and the R^*-tree [91]. Among them, the R-tree and its variants are the most popular. An R-tree is a B-tree-like indexing structure where each internal node represents a k-dimensional hyper-rectangle rather than a scalar. Thus, it is suitable for high-dimensional indexing and, in particular, for range queries. The main disadvantage of the R-tree is that rectangles can overlap so that more than one subtree under a node may have to be visited during a search. This results in a degraded performance.

In 1990, Beckman and Kridgel [91] proposed the best dynamic R-tree variant called the R^**-tree*, which minimized the overlap among nodes, thus yielding an improved performance.

Recent research work includes the development of new techniques, such as the VAM k-d tree, the VAMSplit R-tree, and the 2D h-tree, as well as comparisons of the performance of various existing indexing techniques in image retrieval [92,97].

10.5 INTERACTIVE CONTENT-BASED IMAGE RETRIEVAL

In early stages of the development of CBIR, research was primarily focused on exploring various feature representations, hoping to find a "best" representation for each feature. In these systems, users first select some visual features of interest and then specify the weight for each representation. This burdens the user by requiring a comprehensive knowledge of low-level feature representations in the retrieval system. There are two more important reasons why these systems are limited: the difficulty of representing semantics by means of low-level features and the subjectivity of the human visual system.

- *The Gap Between High-Level Semantics and Low-Level Features.* The query process in these systems consists of finding the best matches in the repository to low-level features computed from the input query examples. However, users typically wish to query the database based on semantics, such as "show me a sunset image," but not on low-level image features, such as "show me a predominantly red and orange image." Unfortunately, the latter query will result in retrieval of many nonsunset images having dominant red and orange colors. Obviously, low-level features are not good representations of image content (especially of photographic images) because they do not carry semantic meaning. Furthermore, low-level features cannot adequately represent highly complicated and widely varied image content.
- *The Subjectivity of Human Perception.* Different persons, or the same person under different circumstances, may perceive the same visual content differently. For example, one user may be interested in the color appearance of an image, whereas another may prefer the facial appearance of people. More importantly, when a user feels that two images are similar, it often means that they have similar semantic meanings, rather than being visually similar.

To conclude, the "best" representations and fixed weights of early CBIR systems cannot effectively model high-level concepts and user's subjective perception. Recent research in CBIR has shifted to an interactive process that involves the human as a part of the retrieval process. Examples include interactive region segmentation [102], interactive image annotation [103], the use of supervised learning before retrieval [104], automatic similarity matching toolkit selection [105], and interactive integration of key words and high-level concepts [106]. Figure 10.2 shows the overview of a general interactive CBIR system [107].

There are four main parts in this system: the image database, the feature database, the similarity metric selection part, and the feature relevance computation part. At the start of processing a query, the system has no a priori knowledge about the query; thus all features are considered equally important and are used to compute the similarity measure. The top N similar images will be returned to the user as retrieval results, and the user can further refine it by sending relevance feedback to the system until he or she is satisfied. The learning-based feature relevance computation part is used to recompute the weights of each feature on the basis of user's feedback, and the metric selection part is used to choose the best similarity metric for the input feature weight vector on the basis of reinforcement learning.

By considering user's feedback, the system can automatically adjust the query and provide a better approximation to the user's expectation. Moreover, by adopting relevance feedback, burdens of concept mapping and specification of weights are removed. Now, the user only needs to mark images that are relevant to the query — the weight of each feature used for relevance computation

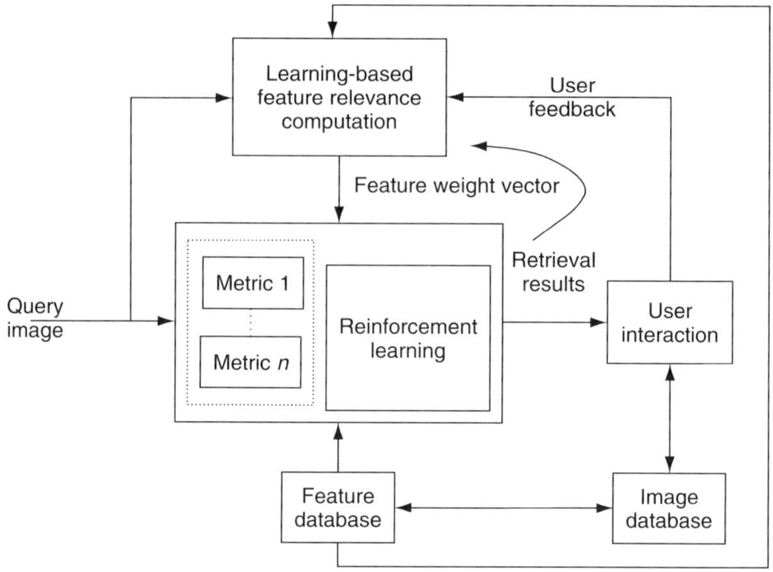

Figure 10.2. Overview of an interactive retrieval system.

is dynamically updated to model high-level concepts and subjective perception. Examples of interactive CBIR systems include MARS [108], Photobook and its recent version, FourEyes [103,109], IRIS [110], WebSEEK [106], QBIC [85], PicHunter [111], and so on. We will briefly discuss main components of an interactive retrieval system in the next section.

10.5.1 Interactive Retrieval Interface

An interactive retrieval interface allows the user to formulate queries. There are typically two phases to formulating a query. The first is the initial specification and the second is the refinement. Both processes are briefly described in the following sections.

10.5.1.1 Initial Query Formulation. Query-by-example interfaces are designed to help the user of a CBIR system in formulating queries. In most cases, users do not have an exact idea of what they want, so they may wish to describe their targets as "something like this image, but with more blue color or with more people," or "I will know it when I see it." To help users quickly form a query, three types of tools are generally used: browsing, sketching, and feature editing.

There are two basic types of browsing tools: those that support sequential browsing and those that support browsing by features. In sequential browsing, images are presented to users sequentially on the basis of their physical storage location in the database. However, if the users have some rough idea of what they want, for example, a flower image or a beach image, they can browse the database according to a specific feature, which can speed up the search process.

Sketching tools are useful if the user has particular requirements for the spatial locations of objects within an image (e.g., an image with blue sky, brown fields with sun rising in the upper left). By providing a rough sketch of the desired layout, the user can retrieve images with very specific spatial characteristics.

Feature-editing tools allow experienced users to edit or modify features of a query image. For example, users can directly edit a color histogram and make a query to find images whose color histogram is similar to the edited one. All three types of tools described here can also be combined to provide users a more flexible way to form their queries.

10.5.2 Relevance Feedback Processing

Once a query has been formulated, the system returns an initial set of results. As discussed in the preceding section, all features used in the similarity metric are considered equally important because the user's preference is not specified. This is also known as the equal importance criterion. Using the initial result set, the user can give some positive or negative feedback to the system. For example, labels such as "highly relevant," "relevant," "no opinion," "irrelevant," and "highly irrelevant" can be attached to the images. The query, augmented by labeled images, is then resubmitted and processed by the search engine. This is an iterative process — the feedback provided during multiple iterations can be accumulated until the user resets the system to submit a completely new query. This feedback-retrieval cycle can be repeated until the user is satisfied with the results. This iterative cycle is known as *relevance feedback.*

Initial retrieval in a relevance feedback system assumes equal weighting for all features. However, when there is a significant discrepancy between the system's definition of similarity and the user's definition, the retrieved results will tend to be unsatisfactory.

Different features should be weighted differently during the search, reflecting the importance attached to them by the user. For example, the dissimilarity between the query image and target images can be measured by a weighted Euclidean distance, wherein the more important features have larger weights. If the query consists of a collection of examples, the weights can be computed from the examples. Typically, one computes the empirical standard deviation of each feature from the example set and uses its inverse as weight. In the example of Figure 10.3, a threshold value is also computed from the examples. If the distance of a feature vector from the centroid of the positive example exceeds the threshold, the feature vector is declared irrelevant and not returned by the query. From the data, it appears that the value of feature Y is more important in distinguishing between relevant and irrelevant images than the value of feature X; hence, a larger weight is assigned to Y. The weighted distance and the threshold define a separating surface (an ellipse): feature vectors within the separating surface are considered relevant, whereas those outside are considered

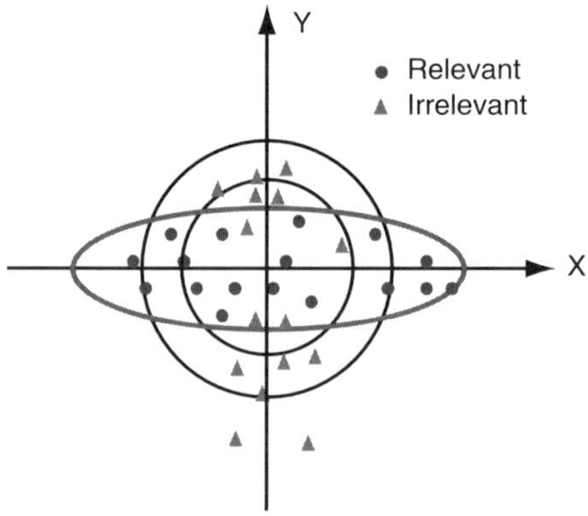

Figure 10.3. Comparison of the separating surfaces defined by weighted and unweighted distances in the feature space.

irrelevant. If an unweighted distance were used, the separating surface would simply be a (hyper)sphere.

In the interactive retrieval of images system (IRIS) developed by University of Southern California (USC) [110], two weight-updating rules were proposed. The first one is that the smaller the variance of a feature in the relevant set, the more important it is, and the larger is the assigned weight. In other words, if the variance of one certain feature is large, then it cannot be a critical feature. The second rule is that if the variance of a certain feature in the relevant set is similar to that in the irrelevant set, this feature cannot be important because it is not an effective separator for different image sets.

Some similar concepts are also explored by other CBIR systems, such as MARS [108], which uses a standard deviation-based weight-updating approach.

10.6 THE MPEG-7 STANDARD

In 1998, the International Standard Organization (ISO) or Moving Picture Expert Group (MPEG) began developing a standard to describe multimedia data contents and to support content-based multimedia management. This new member of the MPEG family, called "multimedia content description interface," or MPEG-7 for short, will enable semantic descriptions of multimedia data, including still pictures, graphics, 3D models, audio, speech, and video. Standard representations of image features, extracted objects, and object relationships will allow a variety of applications, including multimedia search and editing, to use a wide range of data sources.

Figure 10.4 shows a highly abstract block diagram of a possible MPEG-7 processing chain [112]. This chain includes feature extraction (analysis), standard descriptions, and the search engine (application). MPEG-7 will not specify detailed algorithms for feature extraction or application implementations but will only standardize the description, which provides a common interface between

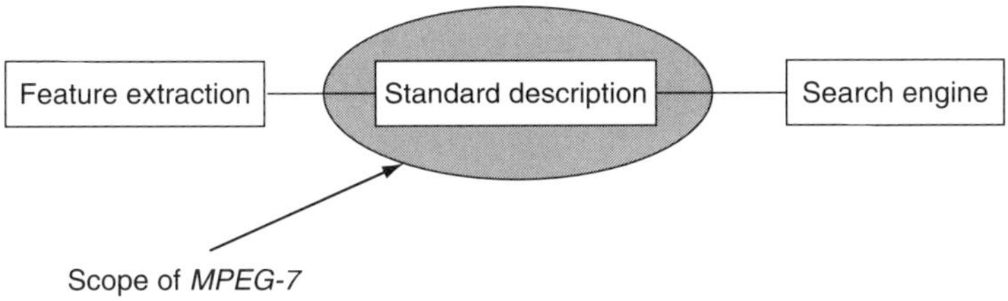

Figure 10.4. Scope of MPEG-7.

the other two parts. Some potential MPEG-7 applications include education, journalism, tourism information, entertainment, investigation services, geographic information systems, and so on [113].

The MPEG-7 framework consists of four major components [112]:

A set of descriptors (Ds). A descriptor is a representation of a feature and it defines the syntax and semantics of the feature representation. Multiple descriptors can be assigned to a single feature. For example, the average color [114], the dominant color [114], and the color histogram [7] can all be descriptors of the color feature.

A set of description schemes (DS). A description scheme (DS) specifies the structure and semantics of the relationship between various components, which may be both descriptors and description schemes. Usually, description schemes refer to subsystems that solve image classification and organization problems or describe image contents with specific indexing structures. Some examples include a classification DS that contains the description tools to allow material classification or a segment DS that represents a section of a multimedia content item [115].

A language to specify description schemes (DDL). A description definition language (DDL) allows the creation of new description schemes and descriptors. It also allows the extension and modification of existing description schemes. Now, the MPEG-7 DDL group has decided to adopt XML (eXtensible markup language) schema language with MPEG-7-specific extensions as the description definition language.

One or more ways to encode the description. Figure 10.5 illustrates a hypothetical MPEG-7 chain [112]. The square boxes depict tools for specific tasks, such as encoding or decoding, whereas the circular boxes represent static elements, such as a description. The shaded boxes in the figure highlight the elements standardized by MPEG-7.

In summary, MPEG-7 will specify a standard set of descriptors that can be used to describe various types of multimedia information. It will also standardize ways to define other descriptors and structures for descriptors and their relationships. This description (a combination of descriptors and description schemes) will be associated with the content itself, thus allowing fast and efficient search for material of interest.

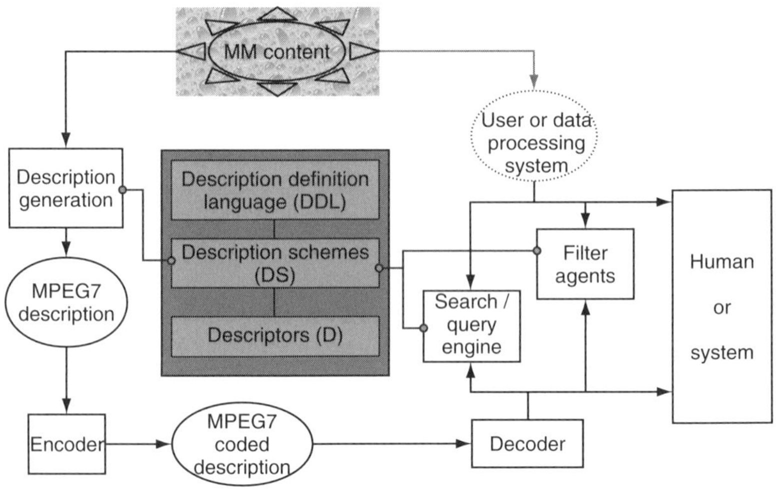

Figure 10.5. An MPEG-7 processing pipeline.

10.7 CONCLUSION

In this chapter, past and current technical achievements in visual feature extraction and integration, multidimensional indexing, and CBIR system design are reviewed. A new family member of ISO/MPEG, known as MPEG-7, which aims to create a standard for describing the content of multimedia data is also briefly introduced. Although much progress in CBIR technology has been realized in recent years, there are still many open research issues. One of the critical issues is how to move beyond simple human-in-loop scheme to further bridge the semantic gap between high-level concepts and low-level visual features in current CBIR system. Some researchers choose to approach this problem by first classifying all images into several meaningful classes and then perform query only within semantically related class. How to achieve effective high-dimensional indexing to support search of large image collections is another important issue. Furthermore, as the World Wide Web continues to expand, web-based image search engines become increasingly desirable. Although there are a number of very successful text-based search engines, such as Yahoo, Alta Vista, Infoseek, and so forth, web-based image search engines are still in their infancy. More technical breakthroughs are required to make image search engines as successful as their text-based counterparts.

Currently, MPEG-7 is under rapid development and has captured the attention of many potential user communities. As discussed in Section 10.6, only the description itself will be standardized by MPEG-7; the other two parts, namely, feature extraction and the design of multimedia search engines, are completely left open for industry competition. Thus, more advanced research results are expected to emerge in the years to come.

REFERENCES

1. R. Jain, Workshop report: NSF workshop on visual information management systems, *Proceedings of SPIE: Storage and Retrieval for Image and Video Databases*, San Jose, Calif., February 1993.
2. R. Jain, A. Pentland, and D. Petkovic, NSF-ARPA workshop report, *NSF-ARPA Workshop on Visual Information Management Systems*, Boston, Mass., June 1995.
3. Y. Rui, T.S. Hang, and S.-Fu Chang, Image retrieval: Current technique, promising directions, and open issues, *J. Vis. Commun. Image Represent.* **10**, 39–62 (1999).
4. N.S. Chang and K.S. Fu, A relational database system for images, Technical Report TR-EE 79–28, Purdue University, Purdue, IN, 1979.
5. S.K. Chang, C.W. Yan, D.C. Dimitroff, and T. Arndt, An intelligent image database system, *IEEE Trans. Software Eng.* **14**(5), 681–688 (1988).
6. M. Stricker and A. Dimai, Color indexing with weak spatial constraints, *Proc. SPIE: Storage and Retrieval for Still Image and Video Databases IV* **2670**, 29–41 (1996).
7. M. Swain and D. Ballard, Color indexing, *Int. J. Comput. Vis.* **7**(1), 11–32 (1991).
8. H. Zhang, C.L.Y. Gong, and S. Smolia, Image retrieval based on color features: An evaluation study, *Proc. SPIE: Digital Image Storage and Archiving Systems* **2606**, 212–220 (1995).
9. L.M. Kaplan and C.-C.J. Kuo, Terrain texture synthesis with an extended self-similar model, *Proceedings of SPIE: Visual data exploration and analysis II*, San Jose, Calif., February 1995.
10. F. Liu and R. Picard, Periodicity, directionality and randomness: Wold features for image modeling and retrieval, Technical Report No. 320, MIT Media Laboratory and Modeling Group, Boston, Mass., 1994.
11. W. Niblack et al., Updates to the QBIC system, *Proc. SPIE: Storage and Retrieval for Image and Video Database VI* **3312**, 150–161 (1997).
12. Z. Lei, T. Tasdizen, and D.B. Cooper, Object signature curve and invariant shape patches for geometric indexing into pictorial databases, *Proceedings of SPIE: Multimedia Storage and Archiving Systems*, Dallas, Tex. November 1997.
13. R. Mehrotra and J. Gary, Similar-shape retrieval in shape data management, *IEEE Comput.* **28**, 57–62 (1995).
14. G. Wyszecki and W. Stiles, Color Science: Concepts and Methods, Wiley & Sons, New York, 1982.
15. M.J. Swain, Interactive indexing into image database, *Proc. SPIE: Storage Retrieval Image Video Databases* **1908**, 95–103 (1993).
16. MPEG Requirements Group, MPEG-7 Visual part of experimentation Model Version 2.0, *Doc. ISO/MPEG N2822, MPEG Vancouver Meeting*, Vancouver, Canada, July 1999.
17. P. Heckbert, Color image quantization for Frame Buffer Display, *Comput. Graphics* **16**(3), 297–304 (1982).
18. C. Jacobs, A. Finkelstein, and D. Salesin, Fast multiresolution image querying, Technical Report 95-01-06, University of Washington, Washington, 1995.
19. X. Wan and C.-C.J. Kuo, Color distribution analysis and quantization for image retrieval, *Proc. SPIE Storage Retrieval Still Image Video Databases IV* **2670** 8–16 (1996).

20. R.K. Srihari, Automatic indexing and content-based retrieval of captioned images, *IEEE Comput. Mag.* **28**(9), 49–56 (1995).
21. D.C. Tseng, Y.F. Li, and C.T. Tung, Circular histogram thresholding for color image segmentation, *Proc. 3rd Int. Conf. Doc. Anal. Recog.* **2**, 673–676 (1995).
22. J. Hafner et al., Efficient color histogram indexing for Quadratic Form Distance Functions, *IEEE Trans. Pattern Recog. Machine Intell.* **17**, 729–736 (1995).
23. M. Stricker, Bounds for the discrimination power of color indexing techniques, *Proc. SPIE: Storage Retrieval Image Video Databases II* **2185**, 15–24 (1994).
24. IBM Almaden Research Center, Technical summary of color descriptors for MPEG-7, *MPEG-7 proposal P*165, *MPEG-7 Seoul Meeting*, Seoul, Korea, March 1999.
25. C. Faloutsos, et al., Efficient and effective querying by image content, Technical Report, IBM Research Report, No. 9453, 1993.
26. T.S. Chua, K.-L. Tan, and B.C. Ooi, Fast signature-based color-spatial image retrieval, *Proc. IEEE Conf. Multimedia Comput. and Syst.* 480–484 (1997).
27. Philips Research, Binary Representation of Image Histograms, *MPEG-7 proposal P652*, *MPEG-7 Seoul Meeting*, Seoul, Korea, March 1999.
28. Sharp Laboratories of American, Scalable blob histogram descriptor, *MPEG-7 proposal P430, MPEG-7 Seoul Meeting*, Seoul, Korea, March 1999.
29. Y. Deng and B.S. Manjunath, A color descriptor for MPEG-7: Variable-bin histogram, *MPEG-7 proposal P76, MPEG-7 Seoul Meeting*, Seoul, Korea, March 1999.
30. Y. Deng and B.S. Manjunath, A technique for fully automated color image segmentation, *MPEG-7 proposal P427, MPEG-7 Seoul Meeting*, Seoul, Korea, March 1999.
31. M. Stricker and A. Dimai, Color indexing with weak spatial constraints, *Proc. SPIE: Storage and Retrieval for Still Image and Video Databases IV* **2670**, 29–40 (1996).
32. M. Stricker and M. Orengo, Similarity of color image, *Proc. SPIE Storage and Retrieval for Image and Video Databases III* **2420**, 381–392 (1995).
33. J.R. Smith and S.F. Chang, Single color extraction and image query, *Proc. IEEE Int. Conf. Image Proc.* **3**, 528–533 (1995).
34. J.R. Smith and S.F. Chang, Tools and techniques for color image retrieval, *Proc. SPIE: Storage and Retrieval for Sill Image and Video Databases IV* **2670**, 426–437 (1996).
35. J.R. Smith and S.-F. Chang, Automated binary texture feature sets for image retrieval, *Proc. ICASSP-96*, Atlanta, GA, **4**, 2241–2246 (1996).
36. R.M. Haralick, K. Shanmugam, and I. Dinstein, Texture features for image classification, *IEEE Trans. Sys. Man. Cyb.* **SMC-3**(6), 1345–1350 (1973).
37. H. Tamura, S. Mori, and T. Yamawaki, Texture features corresponding to visual perception, *IEEE Trans. Sys. Man. Cyb.* **SMC-8**(6),780–786 (1978).
38. W. Niblack et al., The QBIC project: Querying images by content using color, texture and shape, *Proceedings of the SPIE: Storage and Retrieval for Image and Video Databases*, San Jose, Calif., February 1993.
39. T.S. Huang, S. Mehrotra, and K. Ramachandran, Multimedia analysis and retrieval system (MARS) project, *Proceedings of 33rd Annual Clinic on Library Application of Data Processing-Digital Image Access and Retrieval*, Urbana-Champaign, IL, March 1996.

40. M. Ortega et al., Supporting similarity queries in MARS, *Proc. ACM Conf. Multimedia*, 403–413 (1997).
41. W. Niblack, et al., The QBIC project: querying images by content using color, texture and shape, *Proceedings SPIE: Storage and Retrieval for Image and Video Database* **1908**, 173–181 (1993).
42. A.R. Rao and G.L. Lohse, Towards a texture naming system: identifying relevant dimensions of texture, *IEEE Conf. Vis.* 220–227 (1993).
43. O. Alata, C. Cariou, C. Ramannanjarasoa, and M. Najim, Classification of rotated and scaled textures using HMHV spectrum estimation and the Fourier-Mellin Transform, *Proceedings of the IEEE International Conference on Image Processing*, Chicago, October 1998.
44. X. Wan and C.-C. Jay Kuo, Image retrieval based on JPEG compressed data, *Proc. SPIE: Multimedia Storage and Archiving Systems* **2916**, 104–115 (1996).
45. B.S. Manjunath and W. Ma, Texture features for browsing and retrieval of image data, *IEEE Trans. Pattern Anal. Machine Intell.* **18**(8), 837–842 (1996).
46. T. Chang and C.-C. J. Kuo, Texture analysis and classification with tree-structured wavelet transform, *IEEE Trans. Image Process.* **2**(4), 429–441 (1993).
47. A.V. Nevel, Texture synthesis via matching first and second order statistics of a wavelet frame decomposition, *IEEE Int. Conf. Image Process.* 72–76 (1998).
48. N. Ikonomatakis, K.N. Plataniotis, M. Zervakis, and A.N. Venetsanopoulos, Region growing and region merging image segmentation, *Proc. Digital Signal Process. Proc., DSP 97., 1997 13th Int. Conf.* **1**, 299–302 (1997).
49. M.D.G. Montoya, C. Gil, and I. Garcia, Load balancing for a class of irregular and dynamic problems: region growing image segmentation algorithms, *Parallel and Distributed Processing, PDP'99. Proc. Seventh Euromicro Workshop*, 163–169 (1999).
50. W. Ma and B. Manjunath, Edge Flow: A Framework of Boundary Detection and Image Segmentation, *Proceedings of the IEEE: Computer Society Conference on Computer Vision and Pattern Recognition*, Puerto Rico, June 1997.
51. O. Schwartz and A. Quinn, Fast and accurate texture-based image segmentation, *Image Process., Proc. Int. Conf.* **3**, 121–124 (1996).
52. R. Battiti, Low level image segmentation with high level 'emergent properties': color based segmentation, *Ind. Appl. Machine Intell. Vis.*, Int. Workshop 128–132 (1989).
53. A. Hoogs and R. Bajcsy, Model-based learning of segmentations, *Pattern Recog. Proc. 13th Int. Conf.* **4**, 494–499 (1996).
54. Y. Rui, A. C. She, and T.S. Huang, Modified Fourier descriptors for shape representation — a practical approach, *Proceedings of First International Workshop on Image Databases and Multimedia Search*, Amsterdam, Netherlands, August 1996.
55. A.K. Jain, *Fundamentals of Digital Image Processing*, Prentice Hall, New York, 1986, pp. 342–430.
56. B.M. Mehtre, M. Kankanhalli, and W.F. Lee, Shape measures for content-based image retrieval: A comparison, *Inf. Process. Manage.* **33**(3), 40–48 (1997).
57. M.K. Hu, Visual pattern recognition by moment invariants, computer methods in image analysis, *IEE Trans. Inf. Theory* **IT-8**, 179–187 (1962).
58. L. Prasad, Morphological analysis of shapes, *CNLS Research Highlights*, Los Alamos National Laboratory, Los Alamos, NM, July 1997.

59. D. Kapur, Y.N. Lakshman, and T. Saxena, Computing invariants using elimination methods, *Proc. IEEE Int. Conf. Image Proc.* **3**, 335–341 (1995).
60. L. Yang and F. Albregtsen, Fast computation of invariant geometric moments: A new method giving correct results, *Proc. IEEE Int. Conf. Image Proc.* 201–204 (1994).
61. A. Pentland, R.W. Picard, W. Rosalind, and S. Sclaroff, Photobook: Tools for content-based manipulation of image databases, *Proc. SPIE 23rd AIPR Workshop: Image and Information Systems: Applications and Opportunities* **2368**, 37–50 (1995).
62. E.M. Arkin et al., An efficiently computable metric for comparing polygonal shapes, *IEEE Transactions on Pattern Analysis and Machine Intelligence* **13**(3), 209–216 (1991).
63. G.C.-H. Chuang and C.-C.J. Kuo, Wavelet descriptor of planar curves: Theory and Applications, *IEEE Trans. Image Proc.* **5**(1), 56–70 (1996).
64. H.G. Barrow, Parametric correspondence and chamfer matching: Two new techniques for image matching, *Proc. 5th Int. Joint Conf. Artificial Intell.* 130–140 (1977).
65. G. Borgefors, Hierarchical chamfer matching: A parametric edge matching algorithm, *IEEE Trans. Pattern Anal. Machine Intell.* **10**(6), 849–865 (1988).
66. G. Borgefors et al., On the Multiscale Representation of 2D and 3D Shapes, *Graphical Models Image Proc.* **61**(1), 44–62 (1999).
67. T. Wallace and O. Mitchell, Three-dimensional shape analysis using local shape descriptors, *IEEE Trans. Pattern Anal. Machine Intell.* **PAMI-3**(3), 310–323 (1981).
68. S. Gold and A. Rangarajan, Graph matching by graduated assignment, *Proc. IEEE Comput. Soc. Conf. Comput. Vis. Pattern Recog.* 239–244 (1996).
69. M.J. Egenhofer and R. Franzosa, Point-set topological spatial relations, *Int. J. Geogr. Inf. Sys.* **5**(2), 161–174 (1991).
70. A.U. Frank, Qualitative spatial reasoning about distances and directions in geographical space, *J. Vis. Lang. Comput.* **3**(3), 343–371 (1992).
71. S.K. Chang and E. Jungert, Pictorial data management based upon the theory of symbolic projections, *J. Visual Lang. Comput.* **2**(2), 195–215 (1991).
72. E. Jungert, Qualitative spatial reasoning for determination of object relations using symbolic interval projections, *IEEE Int. Workshop on Vis. Lang. VL'93*, 83–87 (1993).
73. S.Y. Lee and F. Hsu, Spatial reasoning and similarity retrieval of images using 2D C-string knowledge representation, *Pattern Recog.* **25**(3), 305–318, (1992).
74. A. Del Bimbo and E. Vicario, *Using weighted spatial relationships in retrieval by visual contents*, *CBAVIL*, 35–39 (1998).
75. V.N. Gudivada and V.V. Raghavan, Design and evaluation of algorithms for image retrieval by spatial similarity, *ACM Trans. Inf. Syst.* **13**(2), 115–144 (1995).
76. J.E. Cabral, Jr., C. Lau, A. Pumrin, and A.J. Sun, Medical image description scheme —P391, *MPEG Seoul Meeting*, Seoul, Korea, March 1999.
77. A. Kitamoto, C.M. Zhou, and M. Takagi, Similarity retrieval of NOAA satellite imagery by graph matching, *Proc. SPIE: Storage and Retrieval for Image and Video Databases* **1908**, 60–73, (1993).

78. J. Barros, J. French, and W. Martin, System for indexing multi-spectral satellite images for efficient content-based retrieval, *Proc. SPIE: Storage and Retrieval for Image and Video Databases III* **2420**, 228–237 (1995).

79. R. Samadani, C. Han, and L.K. Katragadda, Content-based event selection from satellite images of the aurora, *Proc. SPIE: Storage and Retrieval for Image and Video Databases* **1908**, 50–59 (1993).

80. C.S. Li and M.S. Chen, Progressive texture matching for Earth observing satellite image databases, *Proc. SPIE: Multimedia Storage and Archiving Systems* **2916**, 150–161 (1996).

81. V. Di Lecce and A. Celentano, A FFT based technique for image signature generation, *Proc. SPIE: Storage and Retrieval for Image and Video Database V*,**3022**, 457–466 (1997).

82. V. Di Lecce and Andrea Guerriero, An evaluation of the effectiveness of image features for image retrieval, *J. Vis. Commun. Image Represent.* **10**, 1–12 (1999).

83. J. Canny, A computational approach to edge detection, *IEEE Trans. Pattern Anal. Machine Intell.* **8**(6), 679–698 (1986).

84. P.V.C. Hough, Method and means for recognizing complex patterns, U.S. Patent 3, 069, 654, December **18**, (1962).

85. M. Flickner et al., Query by image and video content: the QBIC system, *IEEE Comput.* **28**, 23–32 (1995).

86. J.R. Smith and S.-F. Chang, SaFe: A general framework for integrated spatial and feature image search, *IEEE 1st Multimedia Signal Processing Workshop*, June 1997.

87. V.E. Ogle and M. Stonebraker, Chabot: Retrieval from a relational database of images, *IEEE Comput. Mag.* **28**(9) (1995).

88. J.R. Bach et al., The virage image search engine: An open framework for image management, *Proc. SPIE: Storage and Retrieval for Still Image and Video Databases IV* **2670**, 76–87 (1996).

89. R. Elmasri and S. Navathe, *Fundamentals of Database Systems*, Benjamin Cummings, Addison Wesley, Boston, MA, 1994 pp. 116–128.

90. T. Brinkhoff, H. Kriegel, and B. Seeger, Efficient processing of spatial joins using R-Trees, *Proc. ACM SIGMOD* 237–246 (1993).

91. N. Beckmann, H.-P. Kriegel, R. Schneider, and B. Seeger, The R*-tree: An efficient and robust access method for points and rectangles, *Proc. ACM SIGMOD* 322–331 (1990).

92. R. Ng and A. Sedighian, Evaluating multidimensional indexing structures for images transformed by principal component analysis, *Proc. SPIE: Storage and Retrieval for Still Image and Video Databases IV* **2670**, 50–61 (1996).

93. G. Salton and M.J. McGill, *Introduction to Modern Information Retrieval*, McGraw-Hill, New York, 1983.

94. C. Faloutsos and K.-I. David Lin, Fastmap: A fast algorithm for indexing, data-mining and visualization of traditional and multimedia datasets, *Proc. ACM SIGMOD* 163–174 (1995).

95. S. Chandrasekaran et al., An eigenspace update algorithm for image analysis, *CVGIP: Graphic. Models Image Process. J.* 551–556 (1997).

96. D.B. Lomet and B. Salzberg, A robust multimedia-attribute search structure, *Proc. Fifth Int. Conf. Data Eng.* 296–304 (1989).

97. D. White and R. Jain, Similarity indexing: Algorithms and performance, *Proc. SPIE: Storage and Retrieval for Still Image and Video Databases IV* **2670**, 62–73 (1996).
98. S.-F. Chang, Compressed-domain techniques for image/video indexing and manipulation, *Proc. ICIP95, Special Session on Digital Library and Video on Demand* **1**, 314–316 (1995).
99. V. Ng and T. Kameda, Concurrent access to point data, *Proc. 25th Annu. Int. Conf. Comput. Software Appl. Conf. COMPSAC'97* 368–373 (1997).
100. A. Guttman, R-tree: A dynamic index structure for spatial searching, *Proc. ACM SIGMOD* 47–57 (1984).
101. T. Sellis, N. Roussopoulos, and C. Faloutsos, The R^+-tree: A dynamic index for multidimensional objects, *Proc. 12th VLDB*, 507–518 (1987).
102. D. Daneels et al., Interactive outlining: An improved approach using active contours, *Proc. SPIE: Storage and Retrieval for Image and Video Databases.* **1908**, 226–233 (1993).
103. T.P. Minka and R.W. Picard, Interactive learning using a society of models, *Proc. IEEE CVPR* 447–452 (1996).
104. W.Y. Ma and B.S. Manjunath, Texture features and learning similarity, *Proc. IEEE Conf. Comput. Vis. Pattern Recog.* 425–430 (1996).
105. Y. Rui, T.S. Huang, S. Mehrotra, and M. Ortega, Automatic matching tool selection using relevance feedback in MARS, *Proc. Int. Conf. Vis. Inf. Retrieval*, 45–50 (1998).
106. J.R. Smith and S.-F. Chang, An image and video search engine for the World-Wide Web, *IS&T/SPIE Symposium on Electronic Imaging: Science and Technology (ET '97)—Storage and Retrieval for Image and Video Database V*, San Jose, Calif., February 1997.
107. B. Bhanu, J. Peng, and S. Qing, Learning feature relevance and similarity metrics in image databases, *CBAVIL* 14–18 (1998).
108. Y. Rui, T.-S. Huang, and S. Mehrotra, Content-based image retrieval with relevance feedback in MARs, *Proc. IEEE Int. Conf. Image Proc.* **2**, 815–816 (1997).
109. A. Pentland et al., Photobook: Tools for content-based manipulation of image databases, *Proc. SPIE: Storage and Retrieval for Image and Video Databases II* **2185**, 34–47 (1994).
110. Z. Yang, X. Wan, and C.-C. J. Kuo, Interactive Image Retrieval: Concept, procedure and tools, *Proceedings of the IEEE 32nd Asilomar Conference*, Montery, Calif., November 1998.
111. M.L. Miller, S.M. Omohundro, and P.N. Yianilos, Target testing and the PicHunter bayesian multimedia retrieval system, *Proc. Third Forum on Research and Technology Advances in Digital Library*, 66–57 (1996).
112. MPEG Requirements Group, MPEG-7 context, objectives and technical roadmap, Doc. *ISO/MPEG N2729, MPEG Seoul Meeting*, Seoul, Korea, March 1999.
113. MPEG Requirements Group, MPEG-7 applications document v.8, *Doc. ISO/MPEG N2728, MPEG Seoul Meeting*, Seoul, Korea, March 1999.
114. X. Wan and C.-C.J. Kuo, Pruned octree feature for interactive retrieval, *Proc. SPIE Multimedia Storage and Archiving Systems II* Dallas, Tex., October 1997.
115. MPEG Multimedia Description Scheme Group, MPEG-7 multimedia description schemes WD (version 2.0), *Doc. ISO/MPEG N3247, MPEG Noordwijkerhout Meeting*, The Netherlands, March 2000.

11 Color for Image Retrieval

JOHN R. SMITH
IBM T.J. Watson Research Center, Hawthorne, New York

11.1 INTRODUCTION

Recent progress in multimedia database systems has resulted in solutions for integrating and managing a variety of multimedia formats that include images, video, audio, and text [1]. Advances in automatic feature extraction and image-content analysis have enabled the development of new functionalities for searching, filtering, and accessing images based on perceptual features such as color [2,3], texture [4,5], shape [6], and spatial composition [7]. The content-based query paradigm, which allows similarity searching based on visual features, addresses the obstacles to access color image databases that result from the insufficiency of *key word* or text-based annotations to completely, consistently, and objectively describe the content of images. Although perceptual features such as color distributions and color layout often provide a poor characterization of the actual semantic content of the images, content-based query appears to be effective for indexing and rapidly accessing images based on the similarity of visual features.

11.1.1 Content-Based Query Systems

The seminal work on content-based query of image databases was carried out in the IBM query by image content (QBIC) project [2,8]. The QBIC project explored methods for searching for images based on the similarity of global image features of color, texture, and shape. The QBIC project developed a novel method of prefiltering of queries that greatly reduces the number of target images searched in similarity queries [9]. The MIT Photobook project extended some of the early methods of content-based query by developing descriptors that provide effective matching as well as the ability to reconstruct the images and their features from the descriptors [5]. Smith and Chang developed a fully automated content-based query system called *VisualSEEk*, which further extended content-based querying of image databases by extracting regions and allowing searching based on their spatial layout [10]. Other content-based image database systems

Image Databases: Search and Retrieval of Digital Imagery, Edited by Vittorio Castelli and Lawrence D. Bergman.
ISBN 0-471-32116-8

such as WebSEEk [11] and ImageRover [12] have focused on indexing and searching of images on the World Wide Web. More recently, the MPEG-7 "Multimedia Content Description Interface" standard provides standardized descriptors for color, texture, shape, motion, and other features of audiovisual data to enable fast and effective content-based searching [13].

11.1.2 Content-Based Query-by-Color

The objective of content-based query-by-color is to return images, color features of which are most similar to the color features of a query image. Swain and Ballard investigated the use of color histogram descriptors for searching of color objects contained within the target images [3]. Stricker and Orengo developed color moment descriptors for fast similarity searching of large image databases [14]. Later, Stricker and Dimai developed a system for indexing of color images based on the color moments of different regions [15]. In the spatial and feature (SaFe) project, Smith and Chang designed a 166-bin color descriptor in HSV color space and developed methods for graphically constructing content-based queries that depict spatial layout of color regions [7]. Each of these approaches for content-based query-by-color involves the design of color descriptors, including the selection of the color feature space and a distance metric for measuring the similarity of the color features.

11.1.3 Outline

This chapter investigates methods for content-based query of image databases based on color features of images. In particular, the chapter focuses on the design and extraction of color descriptors and the methods for matching. The chapter is organized as follows. Section 11.2 analyzes the three main aspects of color feature extraction, namely, the choice of a color space, the selection of a quantizer, and the computation of color descriptors. Section 11.3 defines and discusses several similarity measures and Section 11.4 evaluates their usefulness in content-based image-query tasks. Concluding remarks and comments for future directions are given in Section 11.5.

11.2 COLOR DESCRIPTOR EXTRACTION

Color is an important dimension of human visual perception that allows discrimination and recognition of visual information. Correspondingly, color features have been found to be effective for indexing and searching of color images in image databases. Generally, color descriptors are relatively easily extracted and matched and are therefore well-suited for content-based query. Typically, the specification of a color descriptor[1] requires fixing a color space and determining its partitioning.

[1] In this chapter we use the term "feature" to mean a perceptual characteristic of images that signifies something to human observers, whereas "descriptor" means a numeric quantity that describes a feature.

Images can be indexed by mapping their pixels into the quantized color space and computing a color descriptor. Color descriptors such as color histograms can be extracted from images in different ways. For example, in some cases, it is important to capture the global color distribution of an image. In other cases, it is important to capture the spatially localized apportionment of the colors to different regions. In either case, because the descriptors are ultimately represented as points in a multidimensional space, it is necessary to carefully define the metrics for determining descriptor similarity.

The design space for color descriptors, which involves specification of the color space, its partitioning, and the similarity metric, is therefore quite large. There are a few evaluation points that can be used to guide the design. The determination of the color space and partitioning can be done using color experiments that perceptually gauge intra and interpartition distribution of colors. The determination of the color descriptors can be made using retrieval-effectiveness experiments in which the content-based query-by-color results are compared to known ground truth results for benchmark queries. The image database system can be designed to allow the user to select from different descriptors based on the query at hand. Alternatively, the image database system can use relevance feedback to automatically weight the descriptors or select metrics based on user feedback [16].

11.2.1 Color Space

A color space is the multidimensional space in which the different dimensions represent the different components of color. Color or colored light, denoted by function $F(\lambda)$, is perceived as electromagnetic radiation in the range of visible light ($\lambda \in \{380\text{ nm} \ldots 780\text{ nm}\}$). It has been verified experimentally that color is perceived through three independent color receptors that have peak response at approximately red (r), green (g), and blue (b) wavelengths: $\lambda_r = 700$ nm, $\lambda_g = 546.1$ nm, $\lambda_b = 435.8$ nm, respectively. By assigning to each primary color receptor a response function $c_k(\lambda)$, where $k \in \{r, b, g\}$, the linear superposition of the $c_k(\lambda)$'s represents visible light $F(\lambda)$ of any color or wavelength λ [17]. By normalizing $c_k(\lambda)$'s to reference white light $W(\lambda)$ such that

$$W(\lambda) = \bar{c}_r(\lambda) + \bar{c}_g(\lambda) + \bar{c}_b(\lambda), \tag{11.1}$$

the colored light $F(\lambda)$ produces the tristimulus responses (R, G, B) such that

$$F(\lambda) = R\,\bar{c}_r(\lambda) + G\,\bar{c}_g(\lambda) + B\,\bar{c}_b(\lambda). \tag{11.2}$$

As such, any color can be represented by a linear combination of the three primary colors (R, G, B). The space spanned by the R, G, and B values completely describe visible colors, which are represented as vectors in the 3D RGB color space. As a result, the RGB color space provides a useful starting point for representing color features of images. However, the RGB color space is not perceptually uniform. More specifically, equal distances in different areas and along different dimensions of the 3D RGB color space do not correspond to equal perception of color dissimilarity. The lack of perceptual uniformity results in the need to develop more complex vector quantization to satisfactorily partition the RGB color space to form the color descriptors. Alternative color spaces can be generated by transforming the RGB color space. However, as yet, no consensus has been reached regarding the optimality of different color spaces for content-based query-by-color. The problem originates from the lack of any known single perceptually uniform color space [18]. As a result, a large number of color spaces have been used in practice for content-based query-by-color.

In general, the RGB colors, represented by vectors $\mathbf{v}_c$, can be mapped to different color spaces by means of a color transformation T_c. The notation $\mathbf{w}_c$ indicates the transformed colors. The simplest color transformations are linear. For example, linear transformations of the RGB color spaces produce a number of important color spaces that include YIQ (NTSC composite color TV standard), YUV (PAL and SECAM color television standards), $YCrCb$ (JPEG digital image coding standard and MPEG digital video coding standard), and opponent color space OPP [19]. Equation (11.3) gives the matrices that transform an RGB vector into each of these color spaces. The YIQ, YUV, and $YCrCb$ linear color transforms have been adopted in color picture coding systems. These linear transforms, each of which generates one luminance channel and two chrominance channels, were designed specifically to accommodate targeted display devices: YIQ—NTSC color television, YUV—PAL and SECAM color television, and $YCrCb$—color computer display. Because none of the color spaces is uniform, color distance does not correspond well to perceptual color dissimilarity.

The opponent color space (OPP) was developed based on evidence that human color vision uses an opponent-color model by which the responses of the R, G, and B cones are combined into two opponent color pathways [20]. One benefit of the OPP color space is that it is obtained easily by linear transform. The disadvantages are that it is neither uniform nor natural. The color distance in OPP color space does not provide a robust measure of color dissimilarity. One component of OPP, the luminance channel, indicates brightness. The two chrominance channels correspond to blue versus yellow and red versus green.

$$T_c^{YIQ} = \begin{bmatrix} 0.299 & 0.587 & 0.114 \\ 0.596 & -0.274 & -0.322 \\ 0.211 & -0.523 & 0.312 \end{bmatrix}$$

$$T_c^{YUV} = \begin{bmatrix} 0.299 & 0.587 & 0.114 \\ -0.147 & -0.289 & 0.436 \\ 0.615 & -0.515 & -0.100 \end{bmatrix}$$

$$T_c^{YCrCb} = \begin{bmatrix} 0.2990 & 0.5870 & 0.1140 \\ 0.5000 & -0.4187 & -0.0813 \\ -0.1687 & -0.3313 & 0.5000 \end{bmatrix}$$

$$T_c^{OPP} = \begin{bmatrix} 0.333 & 0.333 & 0.333 \\ -0.500 & -0.500 & 1.000 \\ 0.500 & -1.000 & 0.500 \end{bmatrix} \tag{11.3}$$

Although these linear color transforms are the simplest, they do not generate natural or uniform color spaces. The Munsell color order system was desined to be natural, compact, and complete. The Munsell color order rotational system organizes the colors according to natural attributes [21]. Munsell's *Book of Color* [22] contains 1,200 samples of color chips, each with a value of hue, saturation, and chroma. The chips are spatially arranged (in three dimensions) so that steps between neighboring chips are perceptually equal.

The advantage of the Munsell color order system results from its ordering of a finite set of colors by perceptual similarities over an intuitive three-dimensional space. The disadvantage is that the color order system does not indicate how to transform or partition the RGB color space to produce the set of color chips. Although one transformation, named the mathematical transform to Munsell (MTM), from RGB to Munsell HVC was investigated for image data by Miyahara [23], there does not exist a simple mapping from color points in RGB color space to Munsell color chips. Although the Munsell space was designed to be compact and complete, it does not satisfy the property of uniformity. The color order system does not provide for the assessment of the similarity of color chips that are not neighbors.

Other color spaces such as HSV, CIE 1976 ($L^*a^*b^*$), and CIE 1976 ($L^*u^*v^*$) are generated by nonlinear transformation of the RGB space. With the goal of deriving uniform color spaces, the CIE[2] in 1976 defined the CIE 1976 ($L^*u^*v^*$) and CIE 1976 ($L^*a^*b^*$) color spaces [24]. These are generated by a linear transformation from the RGB to the XYZ color space, followed by a different nonlinear transformation. The CIE color spaces represent, with equal emphasis, the three characteristics that best characterize color perceptually: *hue*, *lightness*, and *saturation*. However, the CIE color spaces are inconvenient because of the necessary nonlinearity of the transformations to and from the RGB color space.

Although the determination of the optimum color space is an open problem, certain color spaces have been found to be well-suited for content-based query-by-color. In Ref. [25], Smith investigated one form of the *hue*, *lightness*, and *saturation* transform from RGB to HSV, given in Ref. [26], for content-based query-by-color. The transform to HSV is nonlinear, but it is easily invertible. The HSV color space is natural and approximately perceptually uniform. Therefore, the quantization of HSV can produce a collection of colors that is also compact and complete. Recognizing the effectiveness of the HSV color space for content-based query-by-color, the MPEG-7 has adopted HSV as one of the color spaces for defining color descriptors [27].

[2] Commission Internationale de l'Eclairage

11.2.2 Color Quantization

By far, the most common category of color descriptors are color histograms. Color histograms capture the distribution of colors within an image or an image region. When dealing with observations from distributions that are continuous or that can take a large number of possible values, a histogram is constructed by associating each bin to a set of observation values. Each bin of the histogram contains the number of observations (i.e., the number of image pixels) that belong to the associated set. Color belongs to this category of random variables: for example, the color space of 24-bit images contains 2^{24} distinct colors. Therefore, the partitioning of the color space is an important step in constructing color histogram descriptors.

As color spaces are multidimensional, they can be partitioned by multidimensional scalar quantization (i.e., by quantizing each dimension separately) or by vector quantization methods. By definition, a vector quantizer Q_c of dimension k and size M is a mapping from a vector in k-dimensional space into a finite set $\mathcal{C}$ that contains M outputs [28]. Thus, a vector quantizer is defined as the mapping $Q_c : \Re^k \rightarrow \mathcal{C}$, where $\mathcal{C} = (\mathbf{y}_0, \mathbf{y}_1, \ldots, \mathbf{y}_{M-1})$ and each $\mathbf{y}_m$ is a vector in the k-dimensional Euclidean space $\Re^k$. The set $\mathcal{C}$ is customarily called a *codebook*, and its elements are called *code words*. In the case of vector quantization of the color space, $k = 3$ and each code word $\mathbf{y}_m$ is an actual color point. Therefore, the codebook $\mathcal{C}$ represents a gamut or collection of colors.

The quantizer partitions the color space $\Re^k$ into M disjoint sets R_m, one per code word that completely covers it:

$$\bigcup_{m=0}^{M-1} R_m = \Re^k \qquad \text{and} \qquad R_m \bigcap R_n \qquad \forall \quad m \neq n. \tag{11.4}$$

All the transformed color points $\mathbf{w}_c$ belonging to the same partition R_m are quantized to (i.e., represented by) the same code word $\mathbf{y}_m$:

$$R_m = \{\mathbf{w}_c \in \Re^k : Q_c(\mathbf{w}_c) = \mathbf{y}_m\}. \tag{11.5}$$

A good color space quantizer defines partitions that contain perceptually similar colors and code words that well approximate the colors in their partition. The quantization Q_c^{166} of the HSV color space developed by Smith in Ref. [25] partitions the HSV color space into 166 colors. As shown in Figure 11.1, the HSV color space is cylindrical. The cylinder axis represents the *value*, which ranges from blackness to whiteness. The distance from the axis represents the *saturation*, which indicates the amount of presence of a color. The angle around the axis is the *hue*, indicating tint or tone. As the hue represents the most perceptually significant characteristic of color, it requires the finest quantization. As shown in Figure 11.1, the primaries, red, green, and blue, are separated by 120 degrees in the hue circle. A circular quantization at 20-degree steps separates the hues so that the three primaries and yellow, magenta, and cyan are each represented with three subdivisions. The other color dimensions are quantized more coarsely

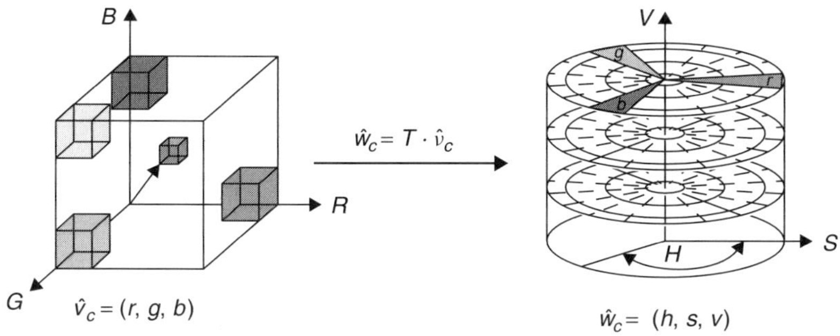

Figure 11.1. The transformation T_c^{HSV} from RGB to HSV and quantization Q_c^{166} gives 166 HSVcolors = 18 *hues* × 3 *saturations* × 3 *values* + 4 *grays*. A color version of this figure can be downloaded from *ftp://wiley.com/public/sci_tech_med/image_databases.*

because the human visual system responds to them with less discrimination; we use three levels each for value and saturation. This quantization, Q_c^{166}, provides $M = 166$ distinct colors in HSV color space, derived from 18 hues (H) × 3 saturations (S) × 3 values (V) + 4 grays [29].

11.2.3 Color Descriptors

A color descriptor is a numeric quantity that describes a color feature of an image. As with texture and shape, it is possible to extract color descriptors from the image as a whole, producing a global characterization; or separately from different regions, producing a local characterization. Global descriptors capture the color content of the entire image but carry no information on the spatial layout, whereas local descriptors can be used in conjunction with the position and size of the corresponding regions to describe the spatial structure of the image color.

11.2.3.1 Color Histograms. The vast majority of color descriptors are color histograms or derived quantities. As previously mentioned, mapping the image to an appropriate color space, quantizing the mapped image, and counting how many times each quantized color occurs produce a color histogram. Formally, if $\mathbf{I}$ denotes an image of size $W \times H$, $\mathbf{I}^q(i, j)$ is the color of the quantized pixel at position i, j, and $\mathbf{y}_m$ is the mth code word of the vector quantizer, the color histogram h_c has entries defined by

$$h_c[m] = \sum_{i=0}^{W-1} \sum_{j=0}^{H-1} \delta(I^q(i, j), \mathbf{y}_m), (m = 1, \ldots, M), \tag{11.6}$$

where the Kronecker delta function, $\delta(\cdot, \cdot)$, is equal to 1 if its two arguments are equal, and zero otherwise.

The histogram computed using Eq. 11.6 does not define a distribution because the sum of the entries is not equal to 1 but is the total number of pixels of the image. This definition is not conducive to comparing color histograms of images having different size. To allow matching, the following class of normalizations can be used:

$$\mathbf{h}^r = \frac{\mathbf{h}}{\left(\sum_{m=0}^{M-1} |h[m]|^r\right)^{1/r}}, \quad (r = 1, 2). \tag{11.7}$$

Histograms normalized with $r = 1$ are empirical distributions, and they can be compared with different metrics and dissimilarity indices. Histograms normalized with $r = 2$ are unit vectors in the M-dimensional Euclidean space, namely, they lie on the surface of the unit sphere. The similarity between two such histograms can be represented, for example, by the angle between the corresponding vectors, captured by their inner product.

11.2.3.2 Region Color. One of the drawbacks of extracting color histograms globally is that it does not take into account the spatial distribution of color across different areas of the image. A number of methods have been developed for integrating color and spatial information for content-based query. Sticker and Dimai developed a method for partitioning each image into five nonoverlapping spatial regions [15]. By extracting color descriptors from each of the regions, the matching can optionally emphasize some regions or can accommodate matching of rotated or flipped images. Similarly, Whsu and coworkers developed a method for extracting color descriptors from local regions by imposing a spatial grid on images [30]. Jacobs and coworkers developed a method for extracting color descriptors from wavelet-transformed images, which allows fast matching of the images based on location of color [31]. Figure 11.2 illustrates an example of extracting localized color descriptors in ways similar to that explored in [15] and [30], respectively. The basic approach involves the partitioning of the image into multiple regions and extracting a color descriptor for each region. Corresponding region-based color descriptors are compared in order to assess the similarity of two images.

Figure 11.2a shows a partitioning of the image into five regions: r_0–r_4, in which a single center region, r_0, captures the color features of any center object. Figure 11.2b shows a partitioning of the image into sixteen uniformly spaced regions: g_0–g_{15}. The dissimilarity of images based on the color spatial descriptors can be measured by computing the weighted sum of individual region dissimilarities as follows:

$$d_{q,t} = \sum_{m=0}^{M-1} w_m d_{q,t}(r_m^q, r_m^t), \tag{11.8}$$

where r_m^q is the color descriptor of region m of the query image, r_m^t is the color descriptor of region m of the target image, and w_m is the weight of the m-th distance and satisfies $\sum w_m = 1$.

Alternately, Smith and Chang developed a method by matching images based on extraction of prominent single regions, as shown in Figure 11.3 [32]. The

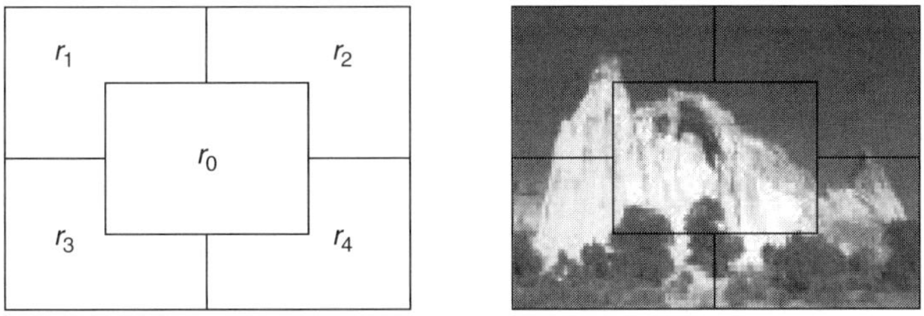

(a)

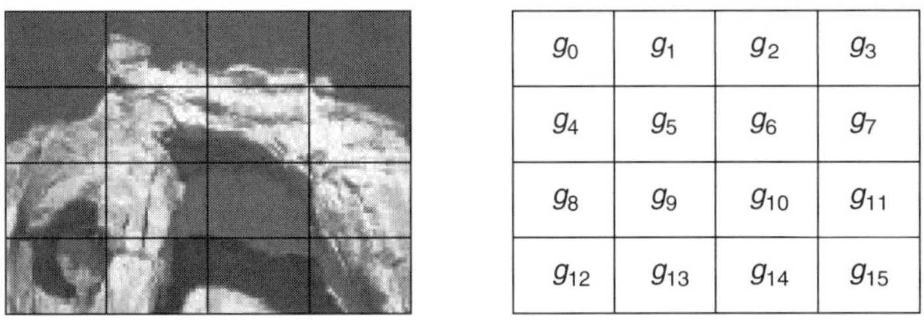

(b)

Figure 11.2. Representation of spatially localized color using region-based color descriptors. A color version of this figure can be downloaded from *ftp://wiley.com/public/sci_tech_med/image_databases*.

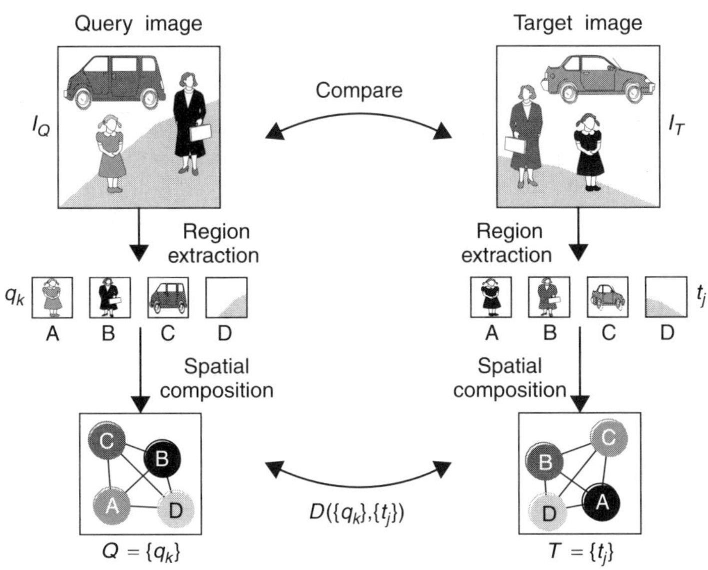

Figure 11.3. The integrated spatial and color feature query approach matches the images by comparing the spatial arrangements of regions.

VisualSEEk content-based query system allows the images to be matched by matching the color regions based on color, size, and absolute and relative spatial location [10]. In [7], it was reported that for some queries the integrated spatial and color feature query approach improves retrieval effectiveness substantially over content-based query-by-color using global color histograms.

11.3 COLOR DESCRIPTOR METRICS

A color descriptor metric indicates the similarity, or equivalently, the dissimilarity of the color features of images by measuring the distance between color descriptors in the multidimensional feature space. Color histogram metrics can be evaluated according to their retrieval effectiveness and their computational complexity. Retrieval effectiveness indicates how well the color histogram metric captures the subjective, perceptual image dissimilarity by measuring the effectiveness in retrieving images that are perceptually similar to query images. Table 11.1 summarizes eight different metrics for measuring the dissimilarity of color histogram descriptors.

11.3.1 Minkowski-Form Metrics

The first category of metrics for color histogram descriptors is based on the Minkowski-form metric. Let $\mathbf{h}_q$ and $\mathbf{h}_t$ be the query and target color histograms, respectively. Then

$$d_{q,t}^r = \left[\sum_{m=0}^{M-1} |h_q(m) - h_t(m)|^r \right]. \tag{11.9}$$

As illustrated in Figure 11.4, the computation of Minkowski distances between color histograms accounts only for differences between corresponding color bins. A Minkowski metric compares the proportion of a specific color within image q to the proportion of the same color within image t, but not to the proportions of

Table 11.1. Summary of the Eight Color Histogram Descriptor Metrics ($\mathcal{D}1$–$\mathcal{D}8$)

Metric	Description	Category
$\mathcal{D}1$	Histogram L_1 distance	Minkowski-form ($r = 1$)
$\mathcal{D}2$	Histogram L_2 distance	Minkowski-form ($r = 2$)
$\mathcal{D}3$	Binary set Hamming distance	Binary Minkowski-form ($r = 1$)
$\mathcal{D}4$	Histogram quadratic distance	Quadratic-form
$\mathcal{D}5$	Binary set quadratic distance	Binary quadratic-form
$\mathcal{D}6$	Histogram Mahalanobis distance	Binary quadratic-form
$\mathcal{D}7$	Histogram mean distance	First moment
$\mathcal{D}8$	Histogram moment distance	Higher moments

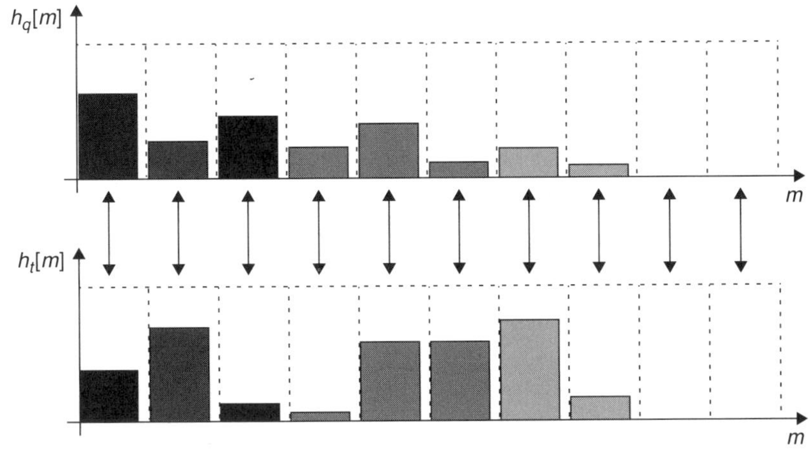

Figure 11.4. The Minkowski-form metrics compare only the corresponding-color bins between the color histograms. As a result, they are prone to false dismissals when images have colors that are similar but not identical.

other similar colors. Thus, a Minkowski distance between a dark red image and a lighter red image is measured to be the same as the distance between the same dark red image and a perceptually more different blue image.

11.3.1.1 Histogram Intersection ($\mathcal{D}1$). Histogram intersection was investigated for color image retrieval by Swain and Ballard in [3]. Their objective was to find known objects within images using color histograms. When the object (q) size is less than the image (t) size and the color histograms are not normalized, $|\mathbf{h}_\mathrm{q}|$ is less than or equal to $|\mathbf{h}_\mathrm{t}|$ (where $|\mathbf{h}|$ denotes the sum of the histogram-cell values, $\sum_{m=0}^{M-1} h(m)$). The intersection of color histograms $\mathbf{h}_\mathrm{q}$ and $\mathbf{h}_\mathrm{t}$ is measured by

$$d_{q,t} = 1 - \frac{\sum_{m=0}^{M-1} \min[h_q(m), h_t(m)]}{|\mathbf{h}_\mathrm{q}|}, \tag{11.10}$$

As defined, Eq (11.10) is not a distance metric because it is not symmetric: $d_{q,t} \neq d_{t,q}$. However, Eq (11.10) can be modified to produce a metric by making it symmetric in $\mathbf{h}_\mathrm{q}$ and $\mathbf{h}_\mathrm{t}$ as follows:

$$d'_{q,t} = 1 - \frac{\sum_{m=0}^{M-1} \min[h_q(m), h_t(m)]}{\min(|\mathbf{h}_\mathrm{q}|, |\mathbf{h}_\mathrm{t}|)}. \tag{11.11}$$

Alternatively, when the color histograms are normalized, so that $|\mathbf{h}_{\mathrm{q}}| = |\mathbf{h}_{\mathrm{t}}|$, both Eq (11.10) and Eq (11.11) are metrics. It is shown in [33] that, when $|\mathbf{h}_{\mathrm{q}}| = |\mathbf{h}_{\mathrm{t}}|$, the color histogram intersection is given by

$$\mathcal{D}1(q,t) = \sum_{m=0}^{M-1} |h_q(m) - h_t(m)|, \tag{11.12}$$

where $\mathcal{D}1(q,t) = d_{q,t} = d'_{q,t}$. The metric $\mathcal{D}1(q,t)$ is recognized as the Minkowski-form metric (Eq 11.9) with $r = 1$ and is commonly known as the "walk" or "city block" distance.

11.3.1.2 Histogram Euclidean Distance ($\mathcal{D}2$). The Euclidean distance between two color histograms $\mathbf{h}_{\mathrm{q}}$ and $\mathbf{h}_{\mathrm{t}}$ is a Minkowski-form metric Eq (11.9) with $r = 2$, defined by

$$\mathcal{D}2(q,t) = D2^2 = (\mathbf{h}_{\mathrm{q}} - \mathbf{h}_{\mathrm{t}})^T(\mathbf{h}_{\mathrm{q}} - \mathbf{h}_{\mathrm{t}}) = \sum_{m=0}^{M-1} [h_q(m) - h_t(m)]^2. \tag{11.13}$$

The Euclidean distance metric can be decomposed as follows

$$\mathcal{D}2(q,t) = \mathbf{h}_{\mathrm{q}}^T\mathbf{h}_{\mathrm{q}} + \mathbf{h}_{\mathrm{t}}^T\mathbf{h}_{\mathrm{t}} - 2\mathbf{h}_{\mathrm{q}}^T\mathbf{h}_{\mathrm{t}}. \tag{11.14}$$

Given the following normalization of the histograms, $\|\mathbf{h}_{\mathrm{q}}\| = \mathbf{h}_{\mathrm{q}}^T\mathbf{h}_{\mathrm{q}} = 1$ and $\|\mathbf{h}_{\mathrm{t}}\| = \mathbf{h}_{\mathrm{t}}^T\mathbf{h}_{\mathrm{t}} = 1$, the Euclidean distance is given by

$$\mathcal{D}2(q,t) = 2 - 2\mathbf{h}_{\mathrm{q}}^T\mathbf{h}_{\mathrm{t}}. \tag{11.15}$$

Given this formulation, $\mathcal{D}2$ can be derived from the inner product of the query $\mathbf{h}_{\mathrm{q}}$ and the target color histograms $\mathbf{h}_{\mathrm{t}}$. This formulation reduces the cost of distance computation from $3M$ to $2M + 1$ operations and allows efficient computation of approximate queries [33].

11.3.1.3 Binary Set Hamming Distance ($\mathcal{D}3$). A compact representation of color histograms using binary sets was investigated by Smith [25]. Binary sets count the number of colors with a frequency of occurrence within the image exceeding a predefined threshold T. As a result, binary sets indicate the presence of each color but do not indicate an accurate degree of presence. More formally, a binary set $\mathbf{s}$ is an M-dimensional binary vector with an i-th entry equal to 1 if the i-th entry of the color histogram $\mathbf{h}$ exceeds T and equal to zero otherwise.

The binary set Hamming distance ($\mathcal{D}3$) between $\mathbf{s}_q$ and $\mathbf{s}_t$ is given by

$$\mathcal{D}3(q,t) = \frac{|\mathbf{s}_q - \mathbf{s}_t|}{|\mathbf{s}_q||\mathbf{s}_t|}, \tag{11.16}$$

where, again, $|\cdot|$ denotes the sum of the elements of the vector. As the vectors $\mathbf{s}_q$ and $\mathbf{s}_t$ are binary, the Hamming distance can be determined by the bit difference between the binary vectors. Therefore, $\mathcal{D}3$ can be efficiently computed using an exclusive OR operator ($\odot$), which sets a one in each bit position where its operands have different bit values, and a zero where they are the same, as follows:

$$\mathcal{D}3(q, t)|\mathbf{s}_q||\mathbf{s}_t| = \mathbf{s}_q \odot \mathbf{s}_t. \tag{11.17}$$

The binary set metric $\mathcal{D}3$ is efficient to compute, and this property justifies exploring its use in large image-database applications.

11.3.2 Quadratic-Form Metrics

To address the shortcomings of Minkowski-form metrics in comparing only "like" bins, quadratic-form metrics consider the cross-relation of the bins. As shown in Figure 11.5, the quadratic-form metrics compare all bins and weight the inter-element distance by pairwise weighting factors.

11.3.2.1 Histogram Quadratic Distance Measures ($\mathcal{D}4$). The IBM QBIC system developed a quadratic-form metric for color histogram–based image retrieval [2]. Reference [34] reports that the quadratic-form metric between color histograms provides more desirable results than "like-color"-only comparisons. The quadratic-form distance between color histograms $\mathbf{h}_q$ and $\mathbf{h}_t$ is given by:

$$\mathcal{D}4(q, t) = D4^2 = (\mathbf{h}_q - \mathbf{h}_t)^T \mathbf{A}(\mathbf{h}_q - \mathbf{h}_t), \tag{11.18}$$

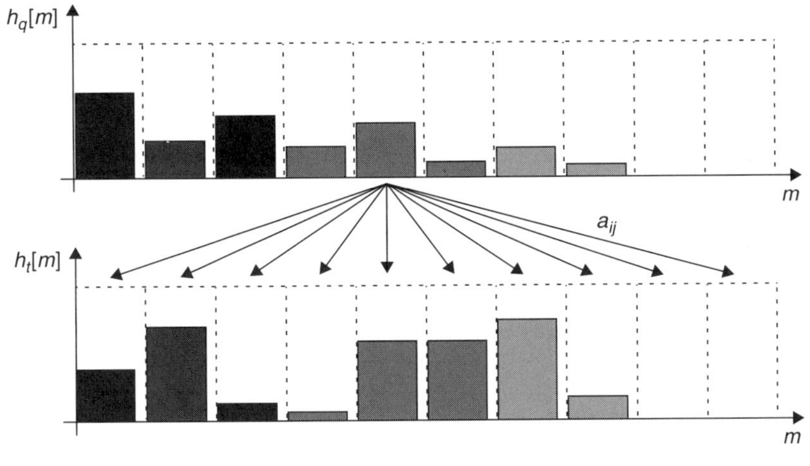

Figure 11.5. Quadratic-form metrics compare multiple bins between the color histograms using a similarity matrix $A = [a_{ij}]$, which can take into account color similarity or color covariance.

where $\mathbf{A} = [a_{ij}]$, and a_{ij} denotes the dissimilarity between histogram bins with indices i and j. The quadratic-form metric is a true-distance metric when the matrix $\mathbf{A}$ is positive definite ($a_{ij} = a_{ji}$ (symmetry) and $a_{ii} = 1$).

In a naive implementation, the color histogram quadratic distance is computationally more expensive than Minkowski-form metrics because it computes the cross-similarity between all elements. Smith proposed a strategy to decompose quadratic-form metrics in a manner similar to that described for the $\mathcal{D}2$ metric (see Eq (11.15)) to improve computational efficiency and allows approximate matching [25]. By precomputing $\mu_t = \mathbf{h}_{\mathrm{t}}^T\mathbf{A}\mathbf{h}_{\mathrm{t}}$, $\mu_q = \mathbf{h}_{\mathrm{q}}^T\mathbf{A}\mathbf{h}_{\mathrm{q}}$, and $\rho_t = \mathbf{A}\mathbf{h}_{\mathrm{t}}$, the quadratic metric can be formulated as follows:

$$\mathcal{D}4 - \mu_q = \mu_t - 2\mathbf{h}_{\mathrm{q}}^T \boldsymbol{\rho}_t. \tag{11.19}$$

Let $\mathcal{M}_s$ be a permutation matrix that sorts $\mathbf{h}_{\mathrm{q}}$ on the order of the largest element. Applying this permutation also to $\boldsymbol{\rho}_t$ gives, where $\mathbf{f}_q = \mathcal{M}_s\mathbf{h}_{\mathrm{q}}$ and $\boldsymbol{\theta}_t = \mathcal{M}_s\boldsymbol{\rho}_t$,

$$\mathcal{D}4 - \mu_q = \mu_t - 2\mathbf{f}_q^T\boldsymbol{\theta}_t, \tag{11.20}$$

In this way, by first sorting the query color histogram, the bins of ρ_t are accessed on the order of decreasing importance to the query. It is simple to precompute ρ_t from the $\mathbf{h}_{\mathrm{t}}$ for the color image database. This gives the following expression for computing $\mathcal{D}4^{M-1}$, where M is the dimensionality of the histograms,

$$\mathcal{D}4^{M-1} = \mathcal{D}4 - \mu_q = \mu_t - 2\sum_{m=0}^{M-1} f_q[m]\theta_t[m]. \tag{11.21}$$

By stopping the summation at a value $k < M - 1$, an approximation of $\mathcal{D}4^{M-1}$ is given, which satisfies

$$\mathcal{D}4^k \leq \mathcal{D}4^{k+1} \leq \ldots \leq \mathcal{D}4^{M-1}. \tag{11.22}$$

By virtue of this property, $\mathcal{D}4^k$ can be used in a process of bounding the approximation of the distance in which the approximation of $\mathcal{D}4^k$ to the $\mathcal{D}4^{M-1}$ can be made arbitrarily close and can be determined by the system or the user, based on the application. This technique provides for a reduction of complexity in computing $\mathcal{D}4$ and allows for lossy but effective matching. Smith showed in [25] that, for a database of 3,100 color images, nearly 80 percent of image color histogram energy is contained in the $k \approx 10$ most significant colors. When only the most significant p colors are used, the complexity of matching is reduced to $\mathcal{O}(M \log M + kN + N)$. Here, $M \log M$ operations are required to sort the query color histogram and N is the size of the database.

11.3.2.2 Binary Set Quadratic Distance ($\mathcal{D}5$). The quadratic-form metric can also be used to measure the distance between binary sets. The quadratic form between two binary descriptor sets $\mathbf{s}_q$ and $\mathbf{s}_t$ is given by

$$\mathcal{D}5(q,t) = D5^2 = (\mathbf{s}_q - \mathbf{s}_t)^T\mathbf{A}(\mathbf{s}_q - \mathbf{s}_t). \tag{11.23}$$

Similar to the histogram quadratic metric, by defining $\mu_q = \mathbf{s}_q^T \mathbf{A} \mathbf{s}_q$, $\mu_t = \mathbf{s}_t^T \mathbf{A} \mathbf{s}_t$, and $\mathbf{r}_t = \mathbf{A}\mathbf{s}_t$, and because $\mathbf{A}$ is symmetric, the quadratic-form binary set distance metric can be formulated as follows:

$$\mathcal{D}5(q, t) = \mu_q + \mu_t - 2\mathbf{s}_q^T \mathbf{r}_t. \tag{11.24}$$

11.3.2.3 Histogram Mahalanobis Distance ($\mathcal{D}6$). The Mahalanobis distance is a special case of the quadratic-form metric in which the transform matrix $\mathbf{A}$ is given by the covariance matrix obtained from a training set of color histograms, that is, $\mathbf{A} = \mathbf{\Sigma}^{-1}$. The Mahalanobis distance can take into account the variance and covariance of colors as they appear across sample images. Hence, colors that are widely prevalent across all images, and not likely to help in discriminating among different images, can be correctly ignored by the metric. In order to apply the Mahalanobis distance, the color histogram descriptor vectors are treated as random variables $\mathbf{X} = [x_0, x_1, \cdots, x_{M-1}]$. Then, the *correlation* matrix is given by $R = [r_{ij}]$, where $r_{ij} = \mathbf{E}\{x_i x_j\}$. In this notation, $\mathbf{E}\{Y\}$ denotes the expected value of the random variable Y. The *covariance* matrix is given by $\mathbf{\Sigma} = [\sigma_{ij}^2]$, where $\sigma_{ij}^2 = r_{ij} - \mathbf{E}\{x_i\}\mathbf{E}\{x_j\}$.

The Mahalanobis distance between color histograms is obtained by letting $\mathbf{X}_q = \mathbf{h}_\mathrm{q}$ and $\mathbf{X}_t = \mathbf{h}_\mathrm{t}$, which gives

$$\mathcal{D}6(q, t) = D6^2 = (\mathbf{X}_q - \mathbf{X}_t)^T \mathbf{\Sigma}^{-1} (\mathbf{X}_q - \mathbf{X}_t). \tag{11.25}$$

In the special case when the bins of the color histogram, x_i, are uncorrelated, that is, when all the covariances $r_{ij} = 0$ when $i \neq j$, $\mathbf{\Sigma}$ is a diagonal matrix [35]:

$$\mathbf{\Sigma} = \begin{bmatrix} \sigma_0^2 & & & 0 \\ & \sigma_1^2 & & \\ & & \ddots & \\ 0 & & & \sigma_{M-1}^2 \end{bmatrix} \tag{11.26}$$

In this case, the Mahalanobis distance reduces to

$$\mathcal{D}6(q, t) = \sum_{m=0}^{M-1} \left[\frac{x_q(m) - x_t(m)}{\sigma_m} \right]^2, \tag{11.27}$$

which is a weighted Euclidean distance. When the x_i are not uncorrelated, it is possible to rotate the reference system to produce uncorrelated coordinates. The rotation of the coordinate system is identified using standard techniques such as singular value decomposition (SVD) or principal component analysis (PCA). The transformation maps a vector x into a rotated vector y, within the same space. The m-th coordinate of y has now variance λ_m[3] then, the Mahalanobis distance

[3] SVD produces the *eigenvectors* $\boldsymbol{\phi}_m$ and the *eigenvalues* λ_m of the covariance matrix $\mathbf{\Sigma}$. Eigenvectors and eigenvalues are solutions of the equation $\lambda\boldsymbol{\phi} = \mathbf{\Sigma}\boldsymbol{\phi}$. The rotation from x to y is the transformation satisfying the equation $\boldsymbol{\phi}_m y = x[m]$ for $m = 1, \ldots, M$. In the rotated reference frame, the m-th coordinate of y has variance equal to λ_m.

is given by

$$\mathcal{D}6(q,t) = \sum_{m=0}^{M-1} \frac{[y_q(m) - y_t(m)]^2}{\lambda_m}. \tag{11.28}$$

11.3.3 Color Channel Metrics

It is possible to define descriptors that parameterize the color histograms of the color channels of the images. By treating each color channel histogram as a distribution, the mean, variance, and other higher moments can be used for matching.

11.3.3.1 Mean Color Distance ($\mathcal{D}7$). The mean color distance ($\mathcal{D}7$) is computed from the mean of the color histogram of each of the color channels. The image mean color descriptor can be represented by a color vector $\mathbf{v} = (\bar{r}, \bar{g}, \bar{b})$, which is extracted by measuring the mean color in each of the three color channels (r, g, b) of the color image. A suitable distance metric between the mean color vectors $\mathbf{v}_q$ and $\mathbf{v}_t$ is given by the Euclidean distance, as follows:

$$\mathcal{D}7 = (\mathbf{v}_q - \mathbf{v}_t)^T(\mathbf{v}_q - \mathbf{v}_t). \tag{11.29}$$

As each bin in a color histogram $\mathbf{h}$ refers to a point (r, g, b) in the 3-D RGB color space, $\mathbf{v}$ can be computed from $\mathbf{h}$ by $\mathbf{v} = \mathbf{Ch}$, where $\mathbf{C}$ has size $M \times 3$, and $C[i]$ gives the (r, g, b) triple corresponding to color histogram bin i. In general, for K feature channels and M color histogram bins, $\mathbf{C}$ has size $K \times M$. This allows the formulation of the mean color distance of Eq. [11.29] as

$$\mathcal{D}7(q,t) = (\mathbf{h}_\mathrm{q} - \mathbf{h}_\mathrm{t})^T\mathbf{C}^T\mathbf{C}(\mathbf{h}_\mathrm{q} - \mathbf{h}_\mathrm{t}). \tag{11.30}$$

11.3.3.2 Color Moment Distance ($\mathcal{D}8$). Other color channel moments besides the mean can be used for measuring the dissimilarity of color images. The variance and the skewness are typical examples of such moments. Stricker and Orengo explored the use of color moments for retrieving images from large color image databases [14]. The color moment descriptor based on variance can be represented by a color vector $\boldsymbol{\sigma}^2 = (\sigma_r^2, \sigma_g^2, \sigma_b^2)$, which can be extracted by measuring the variance of each of the three color channels (r, g, b) of the color image. A suitable distance metric between the color moment vectors $\boldsymbol{\sigma}_q^2$ and $\boldsymbol{\sigma}_t^2$ is given by the Euclidean distance, as follows:

$$\mathcal{D}8 = (\boldsymbol{\sigma}_q^2 - \boldsymbol{\sigma}_t^2)^T(\boldsymbol{\sigma}_q^2 - \boldsymbol{\sigma}_t^2). \tag{11.31}$$

11.4 RETRIEVAL EVALUATION

Color descriptor metrics are evaluated by performing retrieval experiments that carry out content-based query-by-color on a color image database. Consider the following test bed consisting of

1. A collection of $N = 3,100$ color photographs depicting a variety of subjects that include animals, sports, scenery, people, and so forth.
2. A set of four benchmark queries, referring to images depicting sunsets, flowers, nature, and lions.
3. The assessment of the ground-truth relevance score to each image for each benchmark query. Each target image in the collection was assigned a relevance score as follows: 1 if it belonged to the same class as the query image, 0.5 if partially relevant to the query image, and 0 otherwise.

A common practice in information retrieval for evaluating retrieval effectiveness is as follows: a benchmark query is issued to the system, the system retrieves the images in rank order, then, for each cutoff value k, the following values are computed, where $V_n \in \{0, 1\}$ is the relevance of the document with rank n, where $n, k = [1, \ldots, N]$ range over the N images:

- $A_k = \sum_{n=1}^{k} V_n$, is the number of relevant results returned among the top k,
- $B_k = \sum_{n=1}^{k}(1 - V_n)$, is the number of irrelevant results returned among the top k,
- $C_k = \sum_{n=k+1}^{N} V_n$, is the number of relevant results not returned among the top k,
- $D_k = \sum_{n=k+1}^{N}(1 - V_n)$, is the number of irrelevant results not returned among the top k.

From these values, the following quantitative retrieval effectiveness measures can be computed:

- Recall: $R_k = \dfrac{A_k}{A_k + C_k}$ indicates the proportion of desired results that are returned among the k best matches;
- Precision: $P_k = \dfrac{A_k}{A_k + B_k}$ measures the efficiency with which the relevant items are returned among the best k matches;
- Fallout: $F_k = \dfrac{B_k}{B_k + D_k}$ measures the efficiency of rejecting nonrelevant items.

On the basis of precision and recall, the retrieval effectiveness can be evaluated and compared to other systems. A more effective retrieval method shows a higher precision for all values of recall. The average retrieval effectiveness is evaluated by plotting the average precision as a function of the average recall for each of the four benchmark queries using each of the color descriptor metrics. In each query experiment, the distance between each relevant image (with relevance = 1) and all images in the database is measured using one of the color descriptor metrics ($\mathcal{D}1$–$\mathcal{D}8$). The images are then sorted on the order of lowest distance to the query image. In this order, recall and precision are measured for each image. The process was repeated for all the relevant images and an overall average retrieval effectiveness was computed for each of the distance metric and each of the query example. The overall average precision and recall at each rank n was computed by averaging the individual values of precision and recall at each rank n using each of the query images. These trials were summarized by the average recall versus precision curve (i.e., curve $\mathcal{D}1$ in Fig. 11.6) over the relevant query images. These experiments were repeated for different distance metrics, each generating a different plot.

11.4.1 Color Retrieval

The results of the retrieval experiments using content-based query-by-color are given for the following classes of images: (*1*) sunsets, (*2*) pink flowers, (*3*) nature scenes with blue skies, and (*4*) lions.

11.4.1.1 Query 1: Sunsets. In Query 1, the goal was to retrieve images of sunsets. Before the trials, the 3,100 images were viewed, and 23 were designated to be relevant (to depict sunsets). Each of these images was used in turn to query the image database. This was repeated for each distance metric. Examples of the retrieved images and plots of the retrieval effectiveness are shown in Figures 11.6 and 11.7. The metrics were fairly successful in retrieving sunset images, except for $\mathcal{D}7$. Simply using the mean of each color channel did not sufficiently capture color information in the images.

Table 11.2 compares the retrieval effectiveness at several operational values. The quadratic-form metrics $\mathcal{D}4$ and $\mathcal{D}6$ performed well in Query 1. However, the retrieval effectiveness for $\mathcal{D}1$ was slightly better. Contrary to the report in [34], Query 1 does not show that the quadratic-form color histogram metrics improve performance substantially over the Minkowski-form metrics.

11.4.1.2 Query 2: Flowers. The goal of Query 2 was to retrieve images of pink flowers. Before the trials, the 3,100 images were viewed, and 21 were designated to be relevant (to depict pink flowers). Table 11.3 compares the retrieval effectiveness at several operational values. The performance of metrics $\mathcal{D}1$, $\mathcal{D}2$, $\mathcal{D}4$, and $\mathcal{D}6$ was similar in providing good image retrieval results, returning, on average, seven pink flower images among the first ten retrieved. The binary set Hamming distance metric $\mathcal{D}3$ produced a substantial drop in retrieval effectiveness. However, the binary set quadratic-form metric $\mathcal{D}5$ improved the retrieval effectiveness over $\mathcal{D}3$.

11.4.1.3 Query 3: Nature. The goal of Query 3 was to retrieve images of nature depicting a blue sky. Before the trials, the 3,100 images were viewed, and 42 were designated to be relevant (to depict nature with blue sky). Query 3 was the most difficult of the color image queries because the test set contained many images with blue colors that did not come from blue skies. Only the fraction

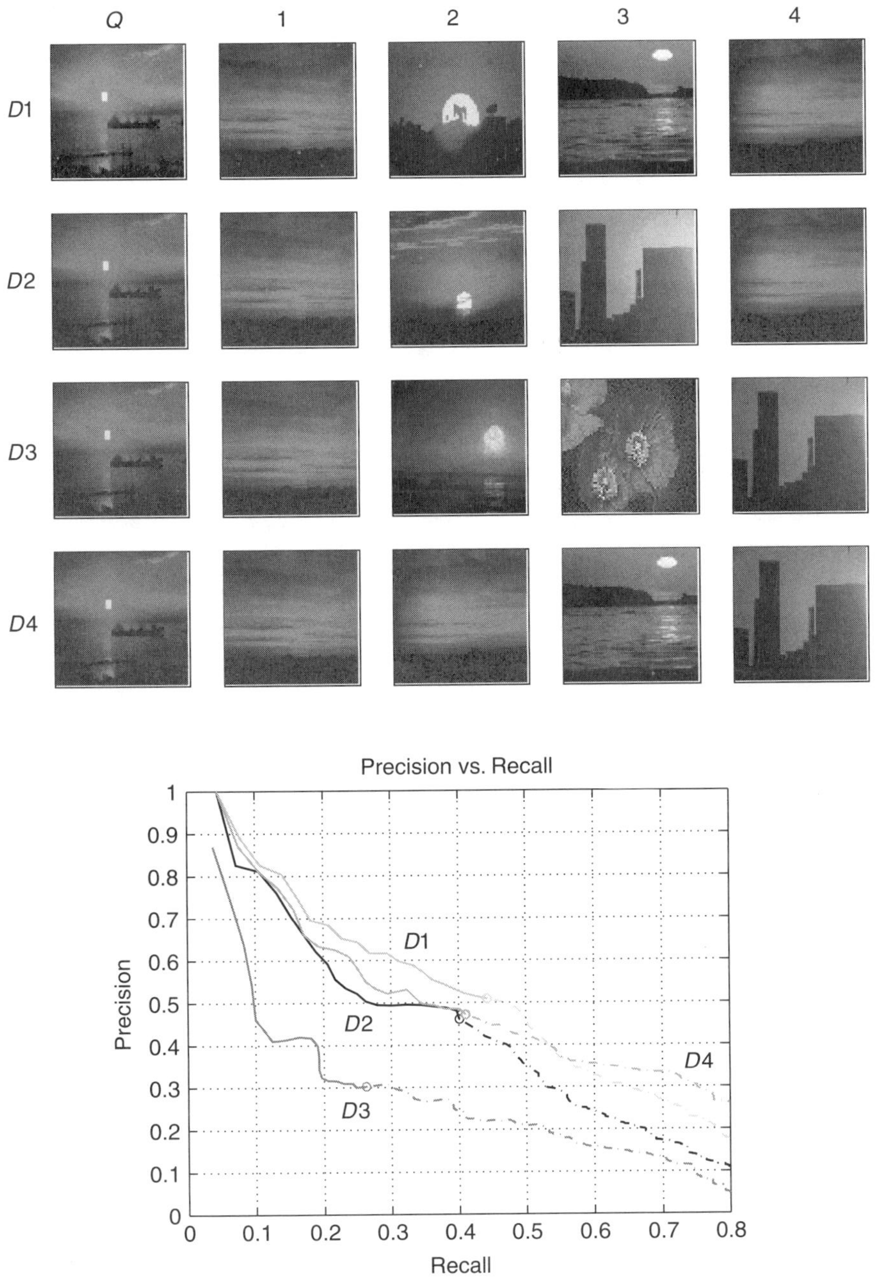

Figure 11.6. Query 1(**a**). Average retrieval effectiveness for 23 queries for sunset images (distances $\mathcal{D}1$, $\mathcal{D}2$, $\mathcal{D}3$, $\mathcal{D}4$). A color version of this figure can be downloaded from *ftp://wiley.com/public/sci_tech_med/image_databases*.

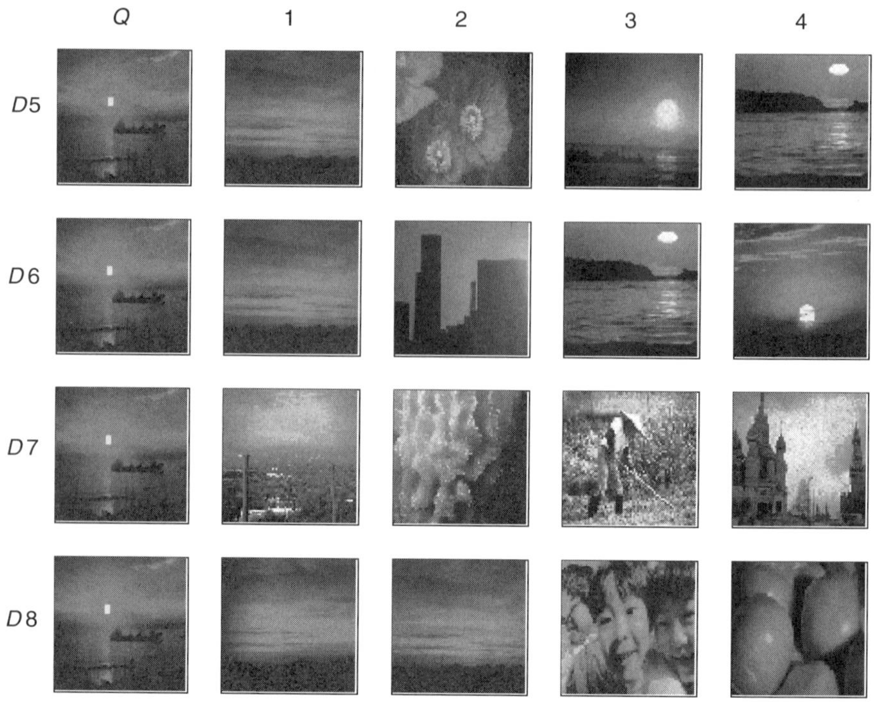

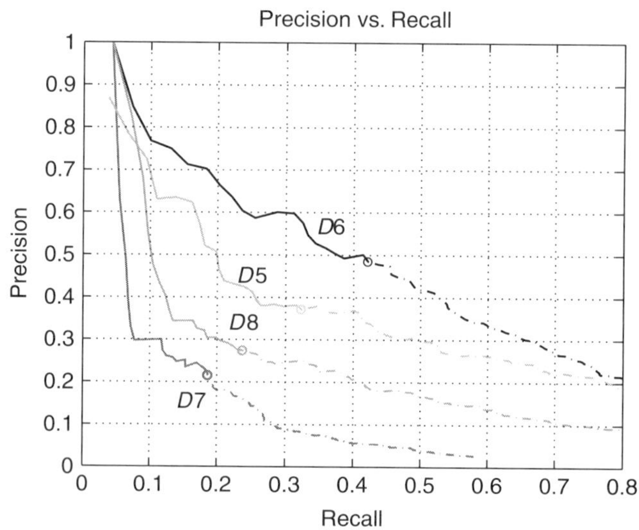

Figure 11.7. Query 1(**b**). Average retrieval effectiveness for 23 queries for sunset images (distances $\mathcal{D}5$, $\mathcal{D}6$, $\mathcal{D}7$, $\mathcal{D}8$). A color version of this figure can be downloaded from *ftp://wiley.com/public/sci_tech_med/image_databases*.

Table 11.2. Query 1: Sunsets — Comparison of Eight Distance Metrics

21 Pink Flower Images	$\mathcal{D}1$	$\mathcal{D}2$	$\mathcal{D}3$	$\mathcal{D}4$	$\mathcal{D}5$	$\mathcal{D}6$	$\mathcal{D}7$	$\mathcal{D}8$
# Relevant in Top 10 (20)	6(10)	5(9)	4(6)	5(9)	4(7)	5(9)	2(4)	3(5)
# Retrieved to Obtain 5 (10) Relevant Ones	8(20)	9(24)	16(46)	9(22)	12(32)	8(21)	29(186)	18(56)

Table 11.3. Query 2: Flowers — Comparison of Eight Distance Metrics

23 Sunset Images	$\mathcal{D}1$	$\mathcal{D}2$	$\mathcal{D}3$	$\mathcal{D}4$	$\mathcal{D}5$	$\mathcal{D}6$	$\mathcal{D}7$	$\mathcal{D}8$
# Relevant in Top 10 (20)	6(9)	6(9)	5(6)	6(9)	5(8)	7(10)	2(3)	3(3)
# Retrieved to Obtain 5 (10) Relevant Ones	7(21)	7(24)	10(62)	7(21)	8(34)	7(18)	48(291)	43(185)

of images depicting blue skies were deemed relevant. The other blue images retrieved in the experiment were considered false alarms.

Query 3 was representative of typical queries for unconstrained color photographs. The color information provides only a partial filter of the semantic content of the actual image. However, the color query methods provide varied but reasonable performance in retrieving the images of semantic interest even in this difficult image query. Table 11.4 compares the retrieval effectiveness at several operational values. The performance of metrics $\mathcal{D}1$, $\mathcal{D}2$, $\mathcal{D}4$, and $\mathcal{D}6$ was similar. These required, on average, retrieval of approximately 25 images in order to obtain ten images that depict blue skies. The binary set Hamming distance metric $\mathcal{D}3$ again provided a substantial drop in retrieval effectiveness, which was improved only slightly in the binary set quadratic-form metric $\mathcal{D}5$.

11.4.1.4 Query 4: Lions. The goal of Query 4 was to retrieve images of lions. Before the trials, the 3,100 images were viewed, and 41 were designated to be relevant (to depict lions). Examples of the retrieved images and plots of the

Table 11.4. Query 3: Nature with Blue Sky — Comparison of Eight Distance Metrics

42 Nature Images	$\mathcal{D}1$	$\mathcal{D}2$	$\mathcal{D}3$	$\mathcal{D}4$	$\mathcal{D}5$	$\mathcal{D}6$	$\mathcal{D}7$	$\mathcal{D}8$
# Relevant in Top 10 (20)	5(8)	5(8)	3(4)	5(8)	3(5)	5(9)	1(1)	2(3)
# Retrieved to Obtain 5 (10) Relevant Ones	10(25)	10(26)	27(76)	10(26)	20(62)	9(23)	148(462)	33(108)

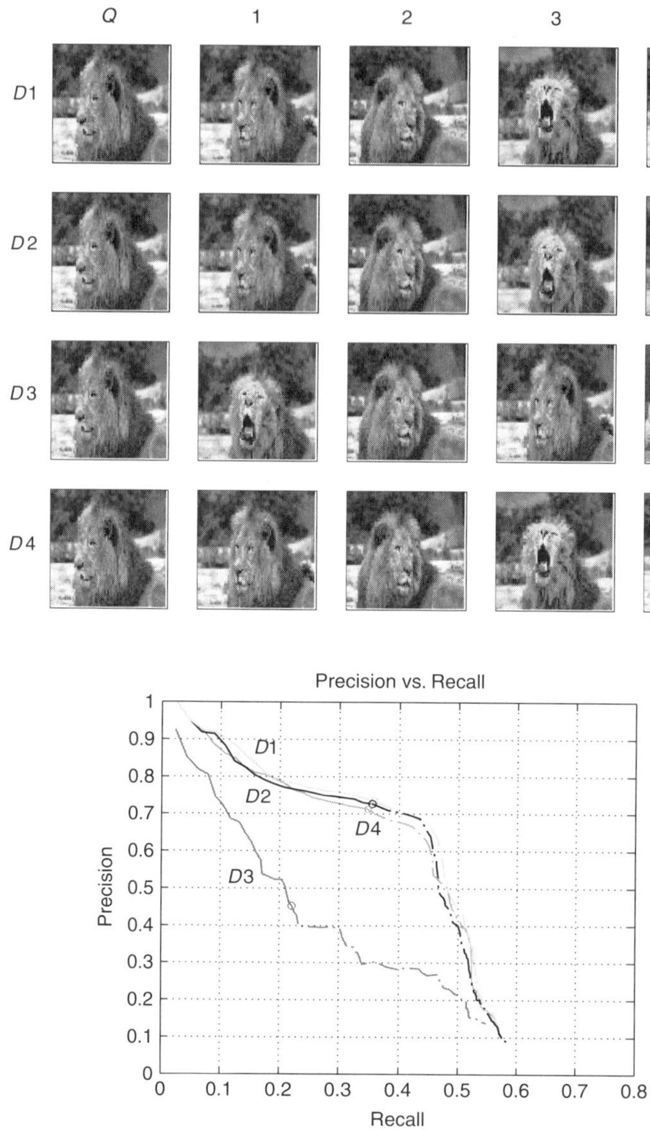

Figure 11.8. Query 4(**a**). Average retrieval effectiveness for 41 queries for lion images (distances $\mathcal{D}1$, $\mathcal{D}2$, $\mathcal{D}3$, $\mathcal{D}4$). A color version of this figure can be downloaded from *ftp://wiley.com/public/sci_tech_med/image_databases*.

retrieval effectiveness are shown in Figures 11.8 and 11.9. Table 11.5 compares the retrieval effectiveness at several operational values. The performance of metrics $\mathcal{D}1$, $\mathcal{D}2$, $\mathcal{D}4$, and $\mathcal{D}6$ was found to be excellent. Using these metrics, on average, only 13 to 14 images needed to be retrieved in order to obtain images of ten lions. With $\mathcal{D}3$ and $\mathcal{D}5$, over twenty images needed to be retrieved.

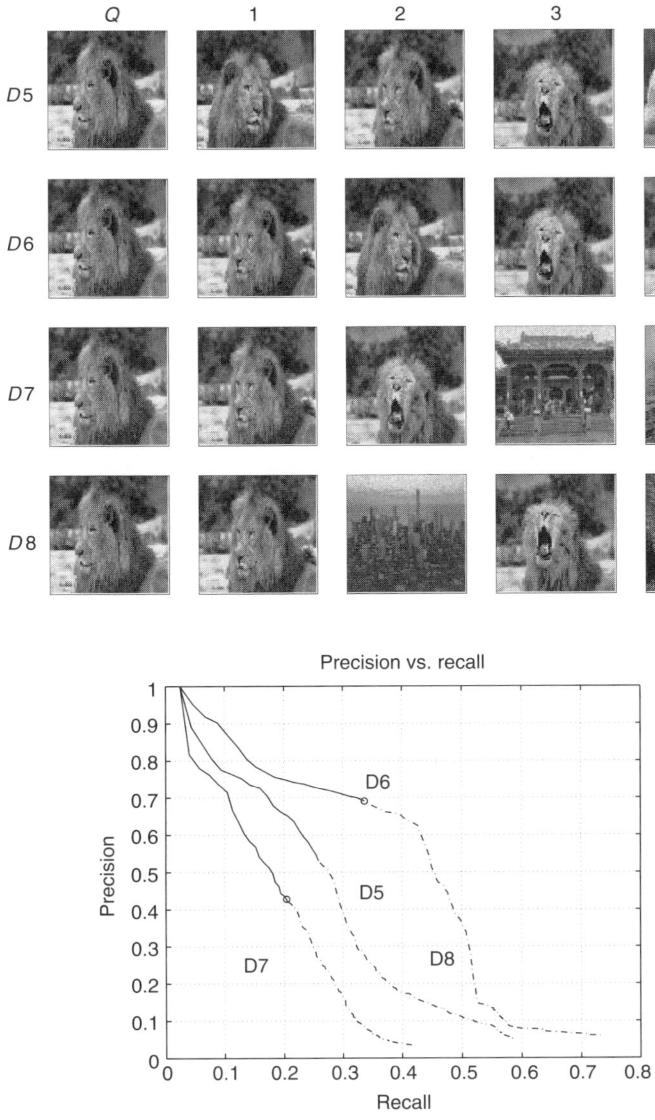

Figure 11.9. Query 4(**b**). Average retrieval effectiveness for 41 queries for lion images (distances $\mathcal{D}5$, $\mathcal{D}6$, $\mathcal{D}7$, $\mathcal{D}8$). A color version of this figure can be downloaded from *ftp://wiley.com/public/sci_tech_med/image_databases*.

Table 11.5. Query 4: Lions — Comparison of Eight Distance Metrics

41 Lion Images	$\mathcal{D}1$	$\mathcal{D}2$	$\mathcal{D}3$	$\mathcal{D}4$	$\mathcal{D}5$	$\mathcal{D}6$	$\mathcal{D}7$	$\mathcal{D}8$
# Relevant in Top 10 (20)	7(14)	7(14)	6(9)	7(14)	6(9)	7(13)	5(8)	7(10)
# Retrieved to Obtain 5 (10) Relevant Ones	6(13)	6(14)	8(26)	6(14)	7(22)	6(14)	8(32)	7(18)

11.4.1.5 Assessment. Overall, as shown in the experimental results in Tables 11.2–11.5, the color histogram metrics of $\mathcal{D}1$, $\mathcal{D}2$, $\mathcal{D}4$, and $\mathcal{D}6$ were found to be more effective than that of $\mathcal{D}3$, $\mathcal{D}5$, $\mathcal{D}7$, and $\mathcal{D}8$ in content-based query-by-color of image databases. The results showed that the simple descriptors and metrics based on average color ($\mathcal{D}7$) and color moments ($\mathcal{D}8$) were not effective for content-based query-by-color. In addition, retrieval effectiveness performance was poor for binary color sets, regardless of whether the metrics were based on Hamming distance ($\mathcal{D}3$) or quadratic distance ($\mathcal{D}5$). The performance of the remaining color histogram metrics, $\mathcal{D}1$, $\mathcal{D}2$, $\mathcal{D}4$, and $\mathcal{D}6$, was approximately the same.

One important consequence of this result is that the experiments do not show any quantifiable gain in retrieval effectiveness by using the more complex quadratic distance metrics $\mathcal{D}4$ or $\mathcal{D}6$. Furthermore, the added step of training to produce the covariance matrix in $\mathcal{D}6$ provided little, if any, gain. A slight improvement was found only for Query 2. Overall, looking at the retrieved images in Figure 11.6–11.9, the simple metrics based on histogram intersection ($\mathcal{D}1$) and Euclidean distance ($\mathcal{D}2$), appear to work quite well for efficient and effective content-based query-by-color of image databases.

11.5 SUMMARY

Advances in feature extraction and image-content analysis are enabling new functionalities for searching, filtering, and accessing images in image databases, based on perceptual features of the images such as color, texture, shape, and spatial composition. Color is one important dimension of human visual perception that allows discrimination and recognition of visual information. As a result, color features have been found to be effective for indexing and searching of color images in image databases.

A number of different color descriptors have been widely studied for content-based query-by-color of image databases in which images retrieved have color features that are most similar to the color features of a query image. The process of designing methods for content-based query-by-color involves the design of compact, effective color feature descriptors and of metrics for comparing them. Overall, the design space, involving specification of the color space, its partitioning, the color feature descriptors, and feature metrics, is extremely large.

This chapter studied the design of color descriptors. A number of different linear and nonlinear color spaces were presented and studied. We also examined the problem of color space quantization, which is necessary for producing color descriptors such as color histograms. We described the extraction of color histograms from images and metrics for matching. Image-retrieval experiments were used to evaluate eight different metrics for color histogram descriptors by comparing the results for content-based query-by-color to known ground truth for four benchmark queries. The results showed color histograms to be effective for retrieving similar color images from image databases. Also, the experiments showed that simple "walk" and "Euclidean" distance measures result in good matching performance.

New directions for improving content-based query include the integration of multiple features for better characterizing the images. Development of automatic preclassifiers for sorting images into classes such as indoor versus outdoor scenes, and city versus landscape, combined with other methods for detecting faces, people, and embedded text, has recently begun to show promise. As a result, content-based query effectiveness will be enhanced by retrieving similar images within a semantic class, rather than across semantic classes in which its performance is lacking. Finally, MPEG-7 is being developed to enable interoperable content-based searching and filtering by standardizing a set of descriptors. Images will be more self-describing of their content by carrying the MPEG-7 annotations, enabling richer descriptions of features, structure, and semantic information.

REFERENCES

1. W.F. Cody et al., Querying multimedia data from multiple repositories by content: the Garlic project, *Visual Database Systems 3: Visual Information Management*, Chapman & Hall, New York 1995, pp. 17–35.
2. M. Flickner et al., Query by image and video content: The QBIC system, *IEEE Comput.* **28**(9), 23 –32 (1995).
3. M.J. Swain and D.H. Ballard, Color indexing, *Int. J. Comput. Vis.*, **7**(1) (1991).
4. W.Y. Ma and B.S. Manjunath, Texture-based pattern retrieval from image databases. *Multimedia Tools Appl.* **1**(2), 35–51 (1996).
5. A. Pentland, R.W. Picard, and S. Sclaroff, Photobook: Tools for content-based manipulation of image databases, *Storage and Retrieval for Still Image and Video Databases II, Proc. SPIE 2185. IS&T/SPIE*, February 1994.
6. H.V. Jagadish, A retrieval technique for similar shapes, *ACM Proc. Int. Conf. Manag. Data (SIGMOD)*, (1991).
7. J.R. Smith and S.-F. Chang, Integrated spatial and feature image query, *Multimedia Syst.* **7**(2), 129–140 (1999).
8. W. Niblack, et al., The QBIC project: Querying images by content using color, texture, and shape, *IBM Res. J.* **9203**(81511), (1993).
9. J. Hafner, et al., Efficient color histogram indexing for quadratic form distance functions, *IEEE Trans. Pattern Anal. Machine Intell.* **17**(7), 729 –736 (1995).
10. J.R. Smith and S.-F. Chang, VisualSEEk: a fully automated content-based image query system, *Proceedings of ACM International Conference Multimedia (ACMMM)*, Boston, Mass., November 1996.
11. J.R. Smith and S.-F. Chang, Visually searching the Web for content, *IEEE Multimedia Mag.* **4**(3), 12 –20 (1997).
12. S. Sclaroff, L. Taycher, and M. La Cascia, ImageRover: A content-based image browser for the World Wide Web, *Proceedings of IEEE Workshop on Content-based Access of Image and Video Libraries*, June 1997.
13. J.R. Smith, A. Puri, and M. Tekalp, MPEG-7 multimedia content description standard. *IEEE Intl. Conf. on Multimedia and Expo (ICME)*, New York, July 2000.

14. M. Stricker and M. Orengo, Similarity of color images: Storage and Retrieval for Image and Video Databases III, SPIE **2420**, (1995).
15. M. Stricker and A. Dimai, Color indexing with weak spatial constraints, in Symposium on Electronic Imaging: Science and Technology — Storage & Retrieval for Image and Video Databases IV, *Proc. SPIE* **2670** IS&T/SPIE, (1996).
16. Y. Rui, T.S. Huang, M. Ortega, and S. Mehrotra, Relevance feedback: A power tool for interactive content-based image retrieval, *IEEE Trans. Circuits Syst. Video Technol.*, **8**(5), 644–655 (1998).
17. H. Nieman, *Pattern Analysis and Understanding*, 2nd ed., Springer Series in Information Sciences, Springer-Verlag, 1990.
18. G. Wyszecki and W.S. Stiles, Color science: concepts and methods, quantitative data and formulae, 2nd ed., The Wiley series in pure and applied optics, Wiley & Sons, New York, 1982.
19. K.R. Rao and J.J. Hwang, *Techniques and Standards for Image, Video, and Audio Coding*, Prentice-Hall, New York 1996.
20. A.N. Netravali and B.G. Haskell, Digital Pictures; representation and compression. *Applications of Communications Theory*, Plenum Press, New York, 1988.
21. A.H. Munsell, *A Color Notation: An Illustrated System Defining All Colors and Their Relations By Measured Scales of Hue, Value and Saturation*, Munsell Color Company. 1905.
22. A.H. Munsell. *Munsell Book of Color*, Munsell Color Company, 1942.
23. M. Miyahara and Y. Yoshida, Mathematical transform of (R, G, B) color data to Munsell (H, V, C) color data, *SPIE Vis. Commun. Image Process.* **1001**, (1988).
24. A.R. Robertson, Historical development of CIE recommended color difference equations, *COLOR Res. Appl.* **15**(3), (1990).
25. J.R. Smith, Integrated Spatial and Feature Image Systems:, *Retrieval Analysis and Compression*, PhD thesis, Graduate School of Arts and Sciences, Columbia University, New York 1997.
26. R.W.G. Hunt, *Measuring Color*, Ellis Horwood series in applied science and industrial technology, Halsted Press, New York, 1989.
27. ISO/IEC JTC 1/SC 29/WG 11. *Information Technology — Multimedia Content Description Interface–Part 3: Visual*, committee draft edition, October 2000.
28. A. Gersho and R.M. Gray, *Vector quantization and signal compression*, Kluwer international series in engineering and computer science, Kluwer Academic Publishers, Norwell, Mass. 1992.
29. J.R. Smith and S.-F. Chang, Tools and techniques for color image retrieval, IS&T/SPIE Symposium on Electronic Imaging: Science and Technology–Storage & Retrieval for Image and Video Databases IV, San Jose, Calif, February 1996.
30. W. Hsu, T.S. Chua, and H.K. Pung, An integrated color-spatial approach to content-based image retrieval, *Proc. ACM Intern. Conf. Multimedia (ACMMM)*, (1995).
31. C.E. Jacobs, A. Finkelstein, and D.H. Salesin, Fast multiresolution image querying, *ACM SIGGRAPH, Computer Graphics Proceedings, Annual Conference Series*, Los Angeles, Calif., 1995, pp. 277–286.
32. J.R. Smith and S.-F. Chang, Single color extraction and image query, *IEEE Proceedings of International Conference Image Processing (ICIP)*, Washington, D.C., October 1995.

33. J.R. Smith, Query vector projection access method, *IS&T/SPIE Symposium on Electronic Imaging: Science and Technology–Storage & Retrieval for Image and Video Databases VII*, San Jose, Calif., January 1999.
34. W. Niblack, et al., The QBIC project: Querying images by content using color, texture, and shape, *Storage and Retrieval for Image and Video Databases*, SPIE **1908**, (1993).
35. H. Van Trees, editor. *Detection, Estimation, and Modulation Theory; part I, Detection, Estimation and Linear Modulation Theory*, Wiley & Sons, New York 1968.

12 Texture Features for Image Retrieval

B.S. MANJUNATH

University of California at Santa Barbara, Santa Barbara, California

WEI-YING MA

Microsoft Research China, Beijing, China

12.1 INTRODUCTION

Pictures of water, grass, a bed of flowers, or a pattern on a fabric contain strong examples of image texture. Many natural and man-made objects are distinguished by their texture. Brodatz [1], in his introduction to *Textures: A photographic album*, states "The age of photography is likely to be an age of texture." His texture photographs, which range from man-made textures (woven aluminum wire, brick walls, handwoven rugs, etc.), to natural objects (water, clouds, sand, grass, lizard skin, etc.) are being used as a standard data set for image-texture analysis. Such textured objects are difficult to describe in qualitative terms, let alone creating quantitative descriptions required for machine analysis. The observed texture often depends on the lighting conditions, viewing angles and distance, may change over a period of time as in pictures of landscapes.

Texture is a property of image regions, as is evident from the examples. Texture has no universally accepted formal definition, although it is easy to visualize what one means by texture. One can think of a texture as consisting of some basic primitives (texels or Julesz's textons [2,3], also referred to as the micropatterns), whose spatial distribution in the image creates the appearance of a texture. Most man-made objects have such easily identifiable texels. The spatial distribution of texels could be regular (or periodic) or random. In Figure 12.1a, "brick" is a micropattern in which particular distribution in a "brick-wall" image constitutes a structured pattern. The individual primitives need not be of the same size and shape, as illustrated by the bricks and pebbles textures (Fig. 12.1b). Well-defined micropatterns may not exist in many cases, such as pictures of sand on the beach, water, and clouds. Some examples of textured images are shown in Figure 12.1. Detection of the micropatterns, if they exist, and their spatial arrangement offers important depth cues to the human visual system (see Fig. 12.2.)

Image Databases: Search and Retrieval of Digital Imagery, Edited by Vittorio Castelli and Lawrence D. Bergman.
ISBN 0-471-32116-8

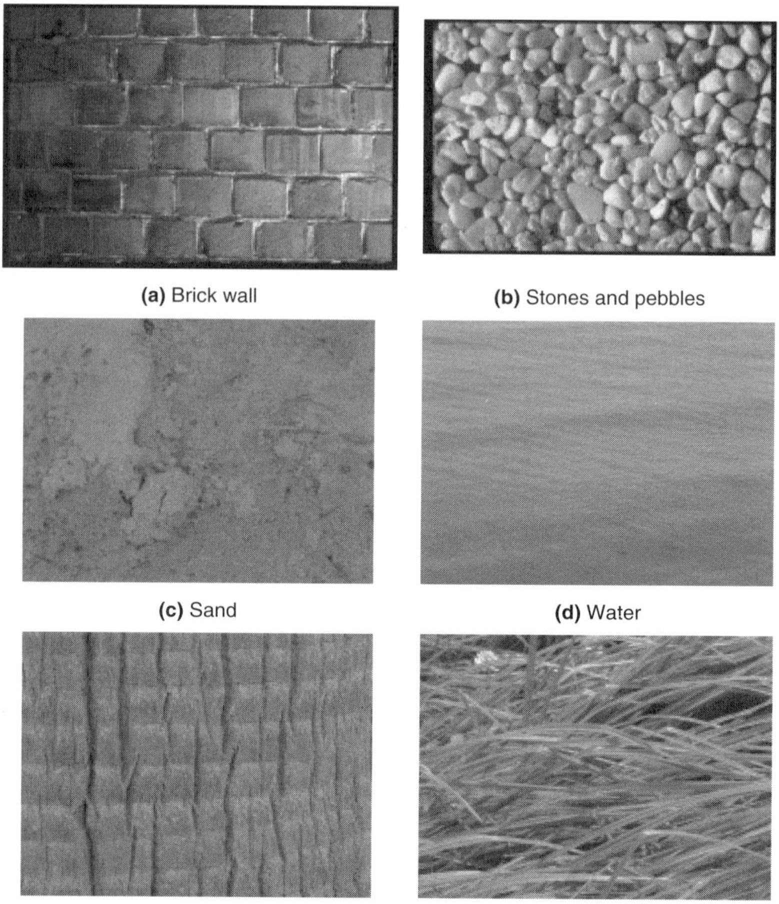

(a) Brick wall **(b)** Stones and pebbles

(c) Sand **(d)** Water

(c) Tree bark **(f)** Grass

Figure 12.1. Examples of some textured images.

Image-texture analysis during the past three decades has primarily focused on texture classification, texture segmentation, and texture synthesis. In texture classification the objective is to assign a unique label to each homogeneous region. For example, regions in a satellite picture may be classified into ice, water, forest, agricultural areas, and so on. In medical image analysis, texture is used to classify magnetic resonance (MR) images of the brain into gray and white matter or to detect cysts in X-ray computed tomography (CT) images of the kidneys. If the images are preprocesed to extract homogeneous-textured regions, then the pixel data within these regions can be used for classifying the regions. In doing so we associate each pixel in the image to a corresponding *class label*, the label of the region to which that particular pixel belongs. An excellent overview of some of the early methods for texture classification can be found in an overview paper by Haralick [4].

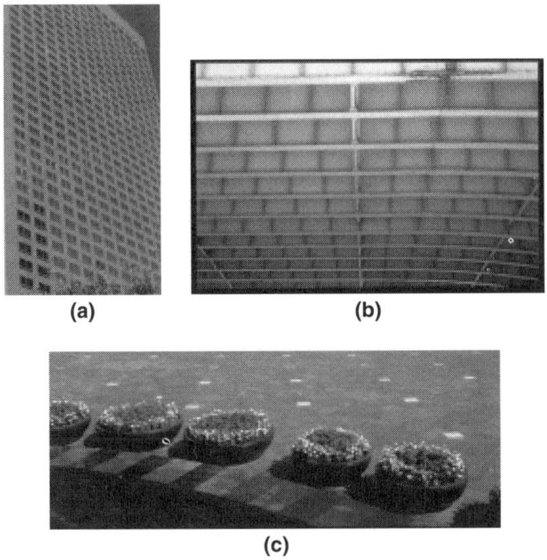

Figure 12.2. Texture is useful in depth perception and image segmentation. Picture of **(a)** a building, **(b)** a ceiling, and **(c)** a scene consisting of multiple textures.

Texture, together with color and shape, helps distinguish objects in a scene. Figure 12.2c shows a scene consisting of multiple textures. *Texture segmentation* refers to computing a partitioning of the image, each of the partitions being homogeneous in some sense. Note that homogeneity in color and texture may not ensure segmenting the image into semantically meaningful objects. Typically, segmentation results in an overpartitioning of the objects of interest. Segmentation and classification often go together — classifying the individual pixels in the image produces a segmentation. However, to obtain a good classification, one needs homogeneous-textured regions, that is, one must segment the image first.

Texture adds realism to synthesized images. The objective of *texture synthesis* is to generate texture that is perceptually indistinguishable from that of a provided example. Such synthesized textures can then be used in applications such as *texture mapping*. In computer graphics, texture mapping is used to generate surface details of synthesized objects. Texture mapping refers to mapping an image, usually a digitized image, onto a surface [5]. Generative models that can synthesize textures under varying imaging conditions would aid texture mapping and facilitate the creation of realistic scenes.

In addition, texture is considered as an important visual cue in the emerging application area of content-based access to multimedia data. One particular aspect that has received much attention in recent years is query by example. Given a query image, one is interested in finding visually similar images in the database. As a basic image feature, texture is very useful in similarity search. This is conceptually similar to the texture-classification problem in that we are interested in computing *texture descriptions* that allow us to make comparisons between different textured images in the database. Recall that in texture classification we compute a label for a given textured image. This label may have semantics associated with it, for example, water texture or cloud texture. If the textures in the database are similarly classified, their labels can then be used to retrieve other images containing the water or cloud texture. The requirements on similarity retrieval, however, are somewhat different. First, it may not be feasible to create an exhaustive class-label dictionary. Second, even if such class-label information is available, one is interested in finding the top N matches within that class that are visually similar to the given pattern. The database should store detailed texture descriptions to allow search and retrieval of similar texture patterns. The focus of this chapter is on the use of texture features for similarity search.

12.1.1 Organization of the Chapter

Our main focus will be on descriptors that are useful for texture representation for similarity search. We begin with an overview of image texture, emphasizing characteristics and properties that are useful for indexing and retrieving images using texture. In typical applications, a number of top matches with rank-ordered similarities to the query pattern will be retrieved. In presenting this overview, we will only be able to give an overview of the rich and diverse work in this area and strongly encourage the reader to follow-up on the numerous references provided.

An overview of texture features is given in the next section. For convenience, the existing texture descriptors are classified into three categories: features that are computed in the spatial domain (Section 12.3), features that are computed using random field models (Section 12.4), and features that are computed in a transform domain (Section 12.5). Section 12.6 contains a comparison of different texture descriptors in terms of image-retrieval performance. Section 12.7 describes the use of texture features in image segmentation and in constructing a texture thesaurus for browsing and searching an aerial image database. Ongoing work related to texture in the moving picture experts group (MPEG-7) standardization within the international standards organization (ISO) MPEG subcommittee has also been described briefly.

12.2 TEXTURE FEATURES

A feature is defined as a distinctive characteristic of an image and a descriptor is a representation of a feature [6]. A descriptor defines the syntax and the semantics of the feature representation. Thus, a texture feature captures one specific attribute of an image, such as coarseness, and a coarseness descriptor is used to represent that feature. In the image processing and computer-vision literature, however, the terms feature and descriptor (of a feature) are often used synonymously. We also drop this distinction and use these terms interchangeably in the following discussion.

Initial work on texture discrimination used various *image texture statistics*. For example, one can consider the gray level histogram as representing the first-order distribution of pixel intensities, and the mean and the standard deviation computed from these histograms can be used as texture descriptors for discriminating different textures. First-order statistics treat pixel-intensity values as independent random variables; hence, they ignore the dependencies between neighboring-pixel intensities and do not capture most textural properties well. One can use second-order or higher-order statistics to develop more effective descriptors. Consider the pixel value at position s, $I(s)$-l. Then, the joint distribution is specified by $P(l, m, \boldsymbol{r}) = \text{Prob } (I(s) = l \text{ and } I(s + \boldsymbol{r}) = m)$, where s and $\boldsymbol{r}$ denote 2D pixel coordinates. One of the popular second-order statistical features is the gray-level co-occurrence matrix, which is generated from the empirical version of $P(l, m, \boldsymbol{r})$ (obtained by counting how many pixels have value l and the pixel displaced by $\boldsymbol{r}$ has the value m). Many statistical features computed from co-occurrence matrices have been used in texture discrimination (for a detailed discussion refer to Ref. [7], Chapter 9). The popularity of this descriptor is due to Julesz, who first proposed the use of co-occurrence matrices for texture discrimination [8]. He was motivated by his conjecture that humans are not able to discriminate textures that have identical second-order statistics (this conjecture has since then proven to be false.)

During the 1970s the research mostly focused on statistical texture features for discrimination, and in the 1980s, there was considerable excitement and interest in generative models of textures. These models were used for both texture synthesis and texture classification. Numerous random field models for texture representation [9–12] were developed in this spirit and a review of some of the recent work can be found in Ref. [13]. Once the appropriate model features are computed, the problem of texture classification can be addressed using techniques from traditional pattern classification [14].

Multiresolution analysis and filtering has influenced many areas of image analysis, including texture, during the 1990s. We refer to these as spatial filtering–based methods in the following section. Some of these methods are motivated by seeking models that capture human texture discrimination. In particular, preattentive texture discrimination — the ability of humans to distinguish between textures in an image without any detailed scene analysis — has been extensively studied. Some of the early work in this field can be attributed to Julesz [2,3] for his theory of textons as basic textural elements. Spatial filtering approaches have been used by many researchers for detecting texture boundaries [15,16]. In these studies, texture discrimination is generally modeled as a sequence of filtering operations without any prior assumptions about the texture-generation process. Some of the recent work involves multiresolution filtering for both classification and segmentation [17,18].

12.2.1 Human Texture Perception

Texture, as one of the basic visual features, has been studied extensively by psychophysicists for over three decades. Texture helps in the studying and understanding of early visual mechanisms in human vision. In particular, Julesz and his colleagues [2,3,8,19] have studied texture in the context of preattentive vision. Julesz defines a "preattentive visual system" as one that "cannot process complex forms, yet can, almost instantaneously, without effort or scrutiny, detect differences in a few local conspicuous features, regardless of where they occur" (*quoted from* Ref. [3]). Julesz coined the word *textons* to describe such features that include elongated blobs (together with their color, orientation, length, and width), line terminations, and crossings of line-segments. Differences in textons or in their density can only be preattentively discriminated. The observations in Ref. [3] are mostly limited to line drawing patterns and do not include gray scale textures.

Julesz's work focused on low-level texture characterization using textons, whereas Rao and Lohse [20] addressed issues related to high-level features for texture perception. In contrast with preattentive perception, high-level features are concerned with *attentive* analysis. There are many applications, including some in image retrieval, that require such analysis. Examples include medical-image analysis (detection of skin cancer, analysis of mammograms, analysis of brain MR images for tissue classification and segmentation, to mention a few) and many process control applications. Rao and Lohse identify three features as being important in human texture perception: *repetition, orientation*, and *complexity*. Repetition refers to periodic patterns and is often associated with regularity. A brick wall is a repetitive pattern, whereas a picture of ocean water is nonrepetitive (and has no structure). Orientation refers to the presence or absence of directional textures. Directional textures have a flowlike pattern as in a picture of wood grain or waves [21]. Complexity refers to the descriptional complexity of the textures and, as the authors state in Ref. [20], "... if one had to describe the texture symbolically, it (complexity) indicates how complex the resulting description would be." Complexity is related to Tamura's *coarseness* feature (see Section 12.3.2).

12.3 TEXTURE FEATURES BASED ON SPATIAL-DOMAIN ANALYSIS

12.3.1 Co-occurrence Matrices

Texture manifests itself as variations of the image intensity within a given region. Following the early work on textons by Julesz [19] and his conjecture that human texture discrimination is based on the second-order statistics of image intensities, much attention was given to characterizing the spatial intensity distribution of textures. A popular descriptor that emerged is the co-occurrence matrix. Co-occurrence matrices [19, 22–26] are based on second-order statistics of pairs of intensity values of pixels in an image. A co-occurrence matrix counts how often pairs of grey levels of pixels, separated by a certain distance and lying along certain direction, occur in an image. Let $(x, y) \in \{1, \ldots, N\}$ be the intensity value of an image pixel at (x, y). Let $[(x_1 - x_2)^2 + (y_1 - y_2)^2]^{1/2} = d$ be the distance that separates two pixels at locations (x_1, y_1) and (x_2, y_2), respectively, and with intensities i and j, respectively. The co-occurrence matrices for a given

d are defined as follows:

$$c^{(d)} = [c(i, j)], i, j, \in \{l, \ldots, N\} \tag{12.1}$$

where $c(i, j)$ is the cardinality of the set of pixel pairs that satisfy $\boldsymbol{I}(x_1, y_1) = i$ and $I(x_2, y_2) = j$, and are separated by a distance d. Note that the direction between the pixel pairs can be used to further distinguish co-occurrence matrices for a given distance d. Haralick and coworkers [25] describe 14 texture features based on various statistical and information theoretic properties of the co-occurrence matrices. Some of them can be associated with texture properties such as homogeneity, coarseness, and periodicity. Despite the significant amount of work on this feature descriptor, it now appears that this characterization of texture is not very effective for classification and retrieval. In addition, these features are expensive to compute; hence, co-occurrence matrices are rarely used in image database applications.

12.3.2 Tamura's Features

One of the influential works on texture features that correspond to human texture perception is the paper by Tamura, Mori, and Yamawaki [27]. They characterized image texture along the dimensions of coarseness, contrast, directionality, line-likeness, regularity, and roughness.

12.3.2.1 Coarseness. Coarseness corresponds to the "scale" or image resolution. Consider two aerial pictures of Manhattan taken from two different heights: the one which is taken from a larger distance is said to be less coarse than the one taken from a shorter distance wherein the blocky appearance of the buildings is more evident. In this sense, coarseness also refers to the size of the underlying elements forming the texture. Note that an image with finer resolution will have a coarser texture. An estimator of this parameter would then be the best scale or resolution that captures the image texture. Many computational approaches to measure this texture property have been described in the literature. In general, these approaches try to measure the level of spatial rate of change in image intensity and therefore indicate the level of coarseness of the texture. The particular procedure proposed in Ref. [27] can be summarized as follows:

1. Compute moving averages in windows of size $2^k \times 2^k$ at each pixel (x, y), where $k = 0, 1, \ldots, 5$.
2. At each pixel, compute the difference $E_k(x, y)$ between pairs of nonoverlapping moving averages in the horizontal and vertical directions.
3. At each pixel, the value of k that maximizes $E_k(x, y)$ in either direction is used to set the best size: $S_{\text{best}}(x, y) = 2^k$.
4. The coarseness measure F_{crs} is then computed by averaging $S_{\text{best}}(x, y)$ over the entire image.

Instead of taking the average of S_{best}, an improved version of the coarseness feature can be obtained by using a histogram to characterize the distribution of S_{best}. This modified feature can be used to deal with a texture that has multiple coarseness properties.

12.3.2.2 ***Contrast.*** Contrast measures the amount of local intensity variation present in an image. Contrast also refers to the overall picture quality — a high-contrast picture is often considered to be of better quality than a low–contrast version. Dynamic range of the intensity values and sharpness of the edges in the image are two indicators of picture contrast. In Ref. [27], contrast is defined as

$$F_{\text{con}} = \sigma/(\alpha_4)^n \tag{12.2}$$

where n is a positive number, σ is the standard deviation of the gray-level probability distribution, and α_4 is the kurtosis, a measure of the polarization between black and white regions in the image. The kurtosis is defined as

$$\alpha_4 = \mu_4/\sigma^4 \tag{12.3}$$

where μ_4 is the fourth central moment of the gray-level probability distribution. In the experiments in [27], $n = 1/4$ resulted in the best texture-discrimination performance.

12.3.2.3 ***Directionality.*** Directionality is a global texture property. Directionality (or lack of it) is due to both the basic shape of the texture element and the placement rule used in creating the texture. Patterns can be highly directional (e.g., a brick wall) or may be nondirectional, as in the case of a picture of a cloud. The degree of directionality, measured on a scale of 0 to 1, can be used as a descriptor (for example, see Ref. [27]). Thus, two patterns, which differ only in their orientation, are considered to have the same degree of directionality. These descriptions can be computed either in the spatial domain or in the frequency domain. In [27], the oriented edge histogram (number of pixels in which edge strength in a certain direction exceeds a given threshold) is used to measure the degree of directionality. Edge strength and direction are computed using the Sobel edge detector [28]. A histogram $H(\phi)$ of direction values ϕ is then constructed by quantizing ϕ and counting the pixels with magnitude larger than a predefined threshold. This histogram exhibits strong peaks for highly directional images and is relatively flat for images without strong orientation. A quantitative measure of directionality can be computed from the sharpness of the peaks as follows:

$$F_{dir} = l - r \cdot n_p \cdot \sum_{p}^{p} \sum_{\phi \in w.p} (\phi - \phi_p)^2 \cdot H(\phi) \tag{12.4}$$

where n_p is the number of peaks and ϕ_p is the pth peak position of H. For each peak p, w_p is the set of bins distributed over it and r is the normalizing factor related to quantizing levels of ϕ.

In addition to the three components discussed earlier, Tamura and coworkers [27] also consider three other features, which they term line-likeness, regularity, and roughness. There appears to be a significant correlation between these three features and coarseness, contrast, and directionality. It is not clear that adding these additional dimensions enhances the effectiveness of the description. These additional dimensions will not be used in the comparison experiments described in Section 12.7.

Tamura's features capture the high-level perceptual attributes of a texture well and are useful for image browsing. However, they are not very effective for finer texture discrimination.

12.4 AUTOREGRESSIVE AND RANDOM FIELD TEXTURE MODELS

One can think of a textured image as a two-dimensional (2D) array of random numbers. Then, the pixel intensity at each location is a random variable. One can model the image as a function $f(r, \omega)$, where r is the position vector representing the pixel location in the 2D space and ω is a random parameter. For a given value of r, $f(r, \omega)$ is a random variable (because ω is a random variable). Once we select a specific texture ω, $f(r, \omega)$ is an image, namely, a function over the two-dimensional grid indexed by r. $f(r, \omega)$ is called a random field [29]. Thus, one can think of a texture-intensity distribution as a realization of a random field. Random field models (also referred to as spatial-interaction models) impose assumptions on the intensity distribution. One of the initial motivations for such model-based analysis of texture is that these models can be used for texture synthesis. There is a rich literature on random field models for texture analysis dating back to the early seventies and these models have found applications not only in texture synthesis but also in texture classification and segmentation [9,11,13,30–34].

A typical random field model is characterized by a set of neighbors (typically, a symmetric neighborhood around the pixel), a set of model coefficients, and a noise sequence with certain specified characteristics. Given an array of observations $\{y(s)\}$ of pixel-intensity values, it is natural to expect that the pixel values are locally correlated. This leads to the well known Markov model

$$P[y(s)|\text{all } y(r), r \neq s] = P[y(s)|\text{all } y(s+r), r \in N], \tag{12.5}$$

where N is a symmetric neighborhood set. For example, if the neighborhood is the four immediate neighbors of a pixel on a rectangular grid, then $N = \{(0, 1), (1, 0), (-1, 0), (0, -1)\}$.

We refer to Besag [35,36] for the constraints on the conditional probability density for the resulting random field to be Markov. If, in addition to being

Markov, $\{y(s)\}$ is also Gaussian, then, a pixel value at s, $y(s)$, can be written as a linear combination of the pixel values $y(s+r)$, $r \in N$, and an additive correlated noise (see Ref. [34]).

A special case of the Markov random field (MRF) that has received much attention in the image retrieval community is the simultaneous autoregressive model (SAR), given by

$$y(s) = \sum_{r \in N} \theta(r) y(s+r) + \sqrt{\beta} w(s), \tag{12.6}$$

where $\{y(s)\}$ are the observed pixel intensities, s is the indexing of spatial locations, N is a symmetric neighborhood set, and $w(s)$ is white noise with zero mean and unit variance. The parameters $(\{\theta(r), \beta\})$ characterize the texture observations $\{y(s)\}$ and can be estimated from those observations. The SAR and MRF models are related to each other in that, for every SAR there exists an equivalent MRF with second-order statistics that are identical to the SAR model. However, the converse is not true: given an MRF, there may not be an equivalent SAR.

The model parameters $(\{\theta(r)\}, \beta)$ form the texture feature vector that can be used for classification and similarity retrieval. The second-order neighborhood has been widely used and it consists of the 8-neighborhood of a pixel $N = \{(0, 1), (1, 0), (0, -1), (-1, 0), (1, 1)(1, -1), (-1, -1), (-1, 1)\}$. For a symmetric model $\theta(r) = \theta(-r)$; hence five parameters are needed to specify a symmetric second-order SAR model.

In order to define an appropriate SAR model, one has to determine the size of the neighborhood. This is a nontrivial problem, and often, a fixed-size neighborhood does not represent all texture variations very well. In order to address this issue, the multiresolution simultaneous autoregressive (MRSAR) model has been proposed [37,38]. The MRSAR model tries to account for the variability of texture primitives by defining the SAR model at different resolutions of a Gaussian pyramid. Thus, three levels of the Gaussian pyramid, together with a second-order symmetric model, requires $15 (3 \times 5)$ parameters to specify the texture.

12.4.1 Wold Model

Liu and Picard propose the Wold model for image retrieval application [39]. It is based on the Wold decomposition of stationary stochastic processes. In the Wold model, a 2D homogeneous random field is decomposed into three mutually orthogonal components, which approximately correspond to the three dimensions (periodicity, directionality, and complexity or randomness) identified by Rao and Lohse [20]. The construction of the Wold model proceeds as follows. First, the periodicity of the texture pattern is analyzed by considering the autocorrelation function of the image. Note that for periodic patterns, the autocorrelation function is also periodic. The corresponding Wold feature set consists of the frequencies and the magnitudes of the harmonic spectral peaks.

In the experiments in Ref. [39] the 10 largest peaks are kept for each image. The indeterministic (random) components of the texture image are modeled using the MRSAR process described in the preceding section. For similarity retrieval, two separate sets of ordered retrievals are computed, one using the *harmonic-peak matching* and the other using the distances between the MRSAR features. Then, a weighted ordering is computed using the confidence measure (the posterior probability) on the query pattern's regularity.

The experimental results in the Brodatz database, presented in Ref. [39], which shows that the Wold model provides perceptually better quality results than the MRSAR model. The comparative results shown in Ref. [39] also indicate that the Tamura features fare significantly worse than the MRSAR or Wold models.

12.5 SPATIAL FREQUENCY AND TRANSFORM DOMAIN FEATURES

Instead of computing the texture features in the spatial domain, an attractive alternative is to use transform domain features. The discrete Fourier transform (DFT), the discrete cosine transform (DCT), and the discrete wavelet transforms (DWT) have been quite extensively used for texture classification in the past. Some of the early work on the use of Fourier transform features in analyzing texture in satellite imagery can be found in Refs. [40–44]. The power spectrum computed from the DFT is used in the computation of texture features [45] and in analyzing texture properties such as periodicity and regularity [46]. In [46], the two spatial-frequencies, f_1 and f_2, that represent the periodicity of the texture primitives are first identified. If the texture is perfectly periodic, most of the energy is concentrated in the power spectrum at frequencies corresponding to $f = mf_1 + nf_2$ (m, n are integers). The corresponding spatial grid is overlaid on the original texture and the texture cell is defined by the grid cell. If the texture has a strong repetitive pattern, this method appears to work well in identifying the basic texture elements forming the repetitive pattern. In general, power spectrum–based features have not been very effective in texture classification and retrieval; this could primarily be a result of the manner in which the power spectrum is estimated. Laws [47] makes a strong case for computing local features using small windows instead of global texture features. Although some of the work in image retrieval has used block-based features (as in the DCT coefficients in 8×8 blocks of JPEG compressed images), detailed and systematic studies are not available on their performance at this time.

The last decade has seen significant progress in multiresolution analysis of images, and much work has been done on the use of multiresolution features to characterize image texture. Two of the more popular approaches have been reviewed, one based on orthogonal wavelet transforms and the other based on Gabor filtering, which appear very promising in the context of image retrieval. Conceptually, these features characterize the distribution of oriented edges in the image at multiple scales.

12.5.1 Wavelet Features

The wavelet transform [48,49] is a multiresolution approach that has been used quite frequently in image texture analysis and classification [17,50]. Wavelet transforms refer to the decomposition of a signal with a family of basis functions obtained through translation and dilation of a special function called the mother wavelet. The computation of 2D wavelet transforms involves recursive filtering and subsampling; and at each level, it decomposes a 2D signal into four subbands, which are often referred to as LL, LH, HL, and HH, according to their frequency characteristics (L = Low, H = High). Two types of wavelet transforms have been used for texture analysis, the pyramid-structured wavelet transform (PWT) and the tree-structured wavelet transform (TWT) (see Figure 12.3). The PWT recursively decomposes the LL band. However, for some textures the most important information often appears in the middle frequency channels and further decomposition just in the lower frequency band may not be sufficient for analyzing the texture. TWT has been suggested as an alternative in which the recursive decomposition is not restricted to the LL bands (see Figure 12.3). For more details, we refer the reader to Ref. [17].

A simple wavelet transform feature of an image can be constructed using the mean and standard deviation of the energy distribution in each of the subbands at each decomposition level. This in turn corresponds to the distribution of "edges" in the horizontal, vertical, and diagonal directions at different resolutions. For a three-level decomposition, PWT results in a feature vector of ($3 \times 3 \times 2 + 2 = 20$) components. As with TWT, the feature will depend on how subbands at each level are decomposed. A fixed decomposition tree can be obtained by sequentially decomposing the LL, LH, and HL bands, and thus results in a feature vector of 40×2 components. Note that, in this example, the feature obtained by PWT can be considered as a subset of the TWT features. The specific choice of basis functions of the wavelet does not seem to significantly impact the image-retrieval performance of the descriptors.

12.5.2 Gabor Features

The use of Gabor filters [18, 51–58] to extract image texture features has been motivated by many factors. The Gabor filters have been shown to be optimal

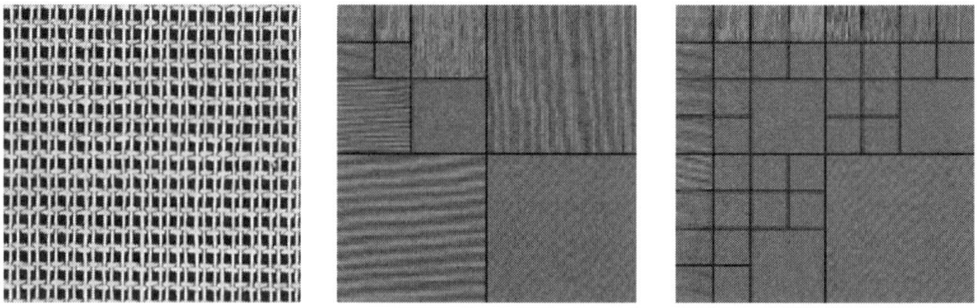

Figure 12.3. Wavelet transform: **(a)** original image, **(b)** PWT, and **(c)** TWT.

in the sense of minimizing the joint 2D uncertainty in space and frequency [52,59]. These filters can be considered as the orientation and scale-tunable edge and line (bar) detectors, and the statistics of these microfeatures in a homogeneous region are often used to characterize the underlying texture information. Gabor features have been used in several image-analysis applications, including texture classification and segmentation [51,60,61], image recognition [62,63], image registration, and motion tracking [57].

A 2D Gabor function is defined as

$$g(x, y) = \left(\frac{1}{2\pi\sigma_x\sigma_y}\right)\exp\left[-\frac{1}{2}\left(\frac{x^2}{\sigma_x^2}+\frac{y^2}{\sigma_y^2}\right)\right]\cdot\exp[2\pi jWx] \tag{12.7}$$

Figure 12.4 shows 3D profiles of the real (even) and imaginary (odd) components of such a Gabor function. A class of self-similar Gabor filters can be obtained by appropriate dilations and rotations of $g(x, y)$.

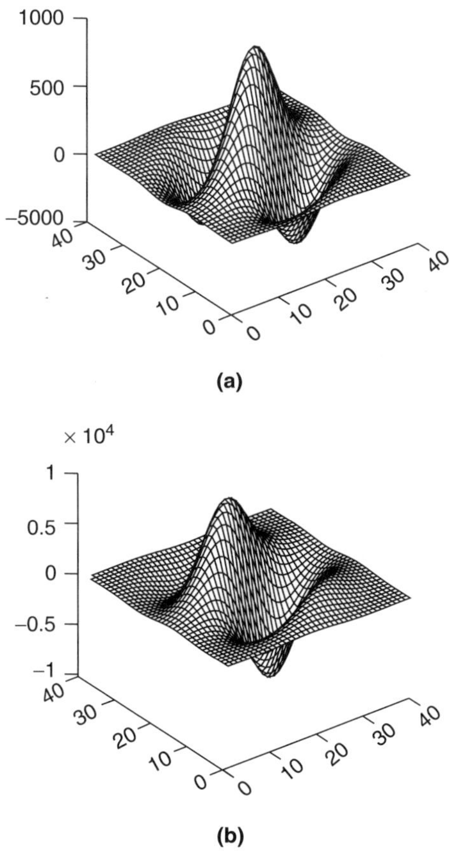

Figure 12.4. 3D profiles of **(a)** a Gabor function (real part) and **(b)** imaginary part.

To compute the Gabor texture feature vector, a given image $I(x,y)$ is first filtered with a set of scale- and orientation-tuned Gabor filters. Let m and n index the scale and orientation, respectively, of these Gabor filters. Let α_{mn} and β_{mn} denote the mean and the standard deviation, respectively, of the energy distribution, of the transform coefficients. If S is the total number of "scales" and K is the number of orientations, then the total number of filters used is SK. A texture feature can then be constructed as

$$\vec{f} = [\alpha_{00}\, \beta_{00}\, \alpha_{01}\, \beta_{01} \cdots \alpha_{(S-1)(K-1)}\beta_{(S-1)(K-1)}] \tag{12.8}$$

In the experiments described in the next section, $S = 6$ orientations and $K = 4$ scales are used to construct the texture feature vector of $6 \times 4 \times 2 = 48$ dimensions.

12.6 COMPARISON OF DIFFERENT TEXTURE FEATURES FOR IMAGE RETRIEVAL

12.6.1 Similarity Measures for Textures

We have presented several different texture descriptors that are useful for texture discrimination. As mentioned earlier, texture descriptors are quite useful in searching for similar patterns in a large database. In a typical "query-by-example" scenario, the user would be interested in retrieving several similar images and not just the best match. This requires comparing two descriptors to obtain a measure of similarity (or dissimilarity) between the two image patterns. Similarity judgments are perceptual and subjective; however, the computed similarity depends not only on the specific feature descriptors but also on the choice of metrics. It is generally assumed that the descriptors are in an Euclidean space (for a detailed discussion on similarity metrics see Ref. [64]). Some of the commonly used dissimilarity measures in listed are the following section (see Ref. [65].)

Let the descriptor be represented as an m-dimensional vector $\overline{f} = [f_1 \cdots f_m]^T$. Given two images I and J, let $D(I, J)$ be the distance between the two images as measured using the descriptors f_I and f_J.

Euclidean distance (squared) (also called the L-2 distance).

$$D(I, J) = \|f_I - f_J\| = (f_I - f_J)^T (f_I - f_J). \tag{12.9}$$

Mahalanobis distance.

$$D(I, J) = (f_I - f_J)^T \Sigma^{-1} (f_I - f_J), \tag{12.10}$$

where the covariance matrix

$$\Sigma = E[(f - \mu_f)(f - \mu_f)^T] \text{ and } \mu_f = E[f]. \tag{12.11}$$

L_1 distance.

$$D(I, J) = |f_i - f_j| = \sum_k |f_{k,I} - f_{k,J}| \tag{12.12}$$

In Ref. [58], a weighted L-1 norm is used:

$$D(I, J) = \sum_k \frac{|f_{k,I} - f_{k,J}|}{\sigma_k}, \tag{12.13}$$

where σ_k is the standard deviation of the kth feature component in the database.

L_∞ distance.

$$D(I, J) = \max_k |f_{k,I} - f_{k,J}| \tag{12.14}$$

Kullback-Leibler (K–L) divergence. If f is considered as a probability distribution (e.g., a normalized histogram), then

$$D(I, J) = \sum_k f_{k,I} \log \frac{f_{k,I}}{f_{k,J}}$$

denotes the "distance" between two distributions. In Information Theory it is commonly known as *relative entropy*. Note that this function is not symmetric and does not satisfy the triangle inequality. However, one can use a symmetric distance by taking the average of $D_{(I,J)}$ and $D_{(J,I)}$.

Reference [65] contains a systematic performance evaluation of different dissimilarity measures for texture retrieval. Performance is measured by precision, which is the percentage of relevant retrievals relative to the total number of retrieved images. The Gabor feature descriptor described in Section 12.5.2 is used in the comparisons. The weighted L_1 distance performs as well as some of the other distances for small sample sizes, whereas measures based on distributions such as the K-L divergence perform better for larger sample sizes. The authors conclude that no single measure achieves the best overall performance.

12.6.2 A Comparison of Texture Descriptors for Image Retrieval

In this section, experimental results intended to compare the effectiveness of several popular texture descriptors on a set of image retrieval tasks will be presented. The image database used consists of 19,800 *color natural images* from Corel photo galleries and 116 512 × 512 texture images from the Brodatz album [1] and the USC texture database [66].

Except for the MRSAR feature vector, the weighted L_1 distance is used in computing the dissimilarity between two texture descriptors. For the MRSAR, it is observed that the Mahalanobis distance gives the best retrieval performance [39]. Note that a covariance matrix for the feature vectors needs to be computed for this case, and using an image-dependent covariance matrix (one such matrix for each image pattern in the database) gives a better performance over using a global covariance matrix (one matrix for all the images in the database). In addition to the texture features described in the previous sections, we also used an edge histogram descriptor [67]. In constructing this histogram, we quantize the orientation into eight bins and use a predefined fixed threshold to remove weak edges. Each bin in the histogram represents the number of edges having a certain orientation.

Figure 12.5a shows the retrieval performance of different texture features using Corel photo galleries. The query and ground truth (relevant retrievals for a given query) are manually established. The performance is measured in terms of the average number of relevant retrievals as a function of the number of retrievals. The results are averaged over all the queries. The texture features with performance ordered from the best to the worst are: MRSAR (using image-dependent covariance), Gabor, TWT, PWT, MRSAR (using global covariance), modified Tamura coarseness histogram and directionality, Canny edge histogram, and traditional Tamura features. Note that using an image-dependent covariance matrix significantly increases the size of MRSAR features.

In addition to the Corel photo database, the Brodatz texture album was also used to evaluate the performance of texture features. This database has been widely used for research on texture classification and analysis, and therefore, is very appropriate for bench-marking texture features. Each 512×512 Brodatz texture image is divided into 16 nonoverlapping subimages, each 128×128 pixels in size. Thus, for each of the 16 subimages from a 512×512 texture image, there are 15 other subimages from the same texture. Having chosen any one subimage as the query, we would like to retrieve the remaining 15 other subimages from that texture as the top matched retrievals. The percentage of correct retrievals in the top 15 retrieved images is then used as a performance measure. Figure 12.5b shows the experimental results based on averaging the performance over all the database images. As can be seen, the features with performance ordered from the best to the worst are Gabor, MRSAR (using image-dependent covariance), TWT, PWT, modified Tamura, MRSAR (using global covariance), traditional Tamura, coarseness histogram, directionality, and Canny edge histogram. The results are similar to the ones shown in Figure 12.5(a) except that Gabor and traditional Tamura features show improved performance (for more details and discussions, see [58,68]). Note that, using the image class

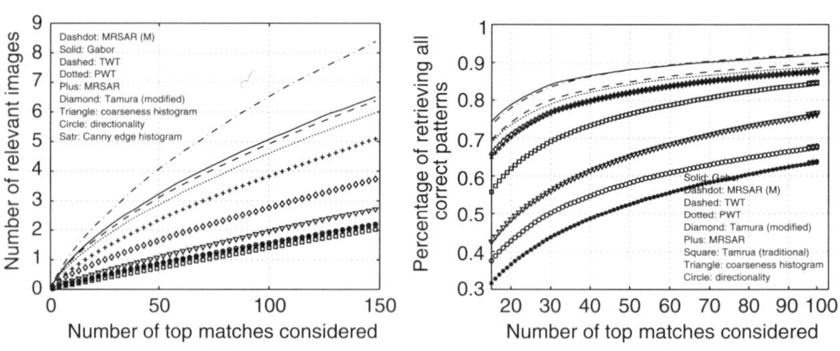

Figure 12.5. Retrieval performance of different texture features **(a)** for the Corel photo databases and **(b)** performance on the Brodatz texture image set.

information in evaluating the performance underestimates the effectiveness of the descriptors in that even if perceptually similar patterns are retrieved, they are not counted unless they belong to the same image class. The Brodatz album contains several pictures that are visually similar but are considered as belonging to different classes for the evaluation.

A more recent study by Li and coworkers [69] evaluated the performance of several texture descriptors using images of rock samples in applications related to oil exploration. They used descriptors computed using Gabor filters, DCT, and a spatial feature set that consists of *gray-level difference features* derived from histograms of gray-level directional differences. In their study, the Gabor descriptors proposed in Ref. [58] outperformed other texture descriptors. The performance was measured in terms of precision (percentage of retrieved images that are relevant, relevance is defined using ground truth) and recall (percentage of relevant results). In a related work using a satellite image database, Li and Castelli [70] note that the spatial feature set outperforms other descriptors.

Note that performance evaluation evaluates both feature extraction and similarity measures together. As the experiments with the MRSAR feature demonstrates, it is clear that different metrics for a given feature vector may result in a wide variance in performance. No detailed studies have been performed on the similarity measures that are best suited for the individual descriptors (except for the results presented in [65] for the Gabor feature descriptor.)

12.7 APPLICATIONS AND DISCUSSIONS

We conclude this chapter with a brief discussion of ongoing research on texture in a digital library project at UCSB. The UCSB Digital Library project [71] started in 1995 with the development of the Alexandria digital library (ADL, *http://www.alexandria.ucsb.edu*), a working digital library with collections of geographically referenced materials and services for accessing those collections. One of the primary objectives of the ADL project is to support collections related to research in Earth and social sciences. The ADL collections include satellite images such as *AVHRR* and *Landsat TM* images, digital elevation models, digital raster graphics (including digitized maps), and scanned aerial photographs. We are currently working on providing access to these image collections using visual primitives such as color and texture.

Texture features associated with salient geographic regions can be used to index the image data. For instance, a user browsing an aerial image database may want to identify all parking lots in an image collection. A parking lot with cars parked at regular intervals is an excellent example of a textured pattern. Similarly, agricultural areas and vegetation patches are other examples of textures commonly found in aerial imagery and satellite photographs. An example of a typical query that can be asked of such a content-based retrieval system could be “retrieve all Landsat images of Santa Barbara that have less than 20 percent cloud cover” or “Find a vegetation patch that looks like this region.” The size of the images (a typical aerial picture dimension is 6,000 × 6,000 pixels and requires about 80 MB of disk space) and the size of the descriptors (60-dimensional texture vectors, at 5 scales and 6 orientations) pose challenging image processing and database indexing issues. For the texture features to be effective, homogeneous texture regions need to be identified first. We have developed a novel segmentation scheme called *EdgeFlow* [60], which uses texture and color to partition a given image into regions having homogeneous color and texture. A texture thesaurus is developed for the aerial images to facilitate fast search and retrieval (for more details, see [72]).

12.7.1 EdgeFlow: Image Segmentation Using Texture

Traditionally, image boundaries are located at the local maxima of the gradient in an image feature space. In contrast, the detection and localization of boundaries are performed indirectly in the EdgeFlow method: first by identifying a direction at each pixel location — direction in which the edge vectors are eventually propagated — that points to the closest boundary; then by detecting locations at which two opposite directions of the propagated edge vectors meet. Because any of the image attributes, such as color, texture, or their combination, can be used to compute the edge energy and direction of flow, this scheme provides a general framework for integrating different image features for boundary detection.

The EdgeFlow method uses a predictive coding model to identify and integrate the direction of change in image attributes, such as color and texture, at each image location. To achieve this objective, the following values are estimated: $E(s, \theta)$, which measures the edge energy at pixel s along the orientation θ; $P(s, \theta)$, the probability of finding an edge in the direction of θ from s; and $P(s, \theta + \pi)$, the probability of finding an edge along $(\theta + \pi)$ from s. These edge energies and the associated probabilities can be estimated in any image feature space of interest, such as color or texture, and can be combined. From these measurements, an EdgeFlow vector $\vec{\mathbf{F}}(s)$ is computed. The magnitude of $\vec{\mathbf{F}}(s)$ represents the total edge energy and $\vec{\mathbf{F}}(s)$ points in the direction of the closest boundary pixel. The distribution of $\vec{\mathbf{F}}(s)$ in the image forms a flow field, which is allowed to propagate. At each pixel location, the flow is in the estimated direction of the boundary pixel. A boundary location is characterized by flows in opposing directions toward it.

Consider first the problem of estimating the flow vectors for intensity edges. Let $I_\sigma(x, y)$ be the smoothed image at scale σ obtained by filtering the original image $I(x, y)$ with a Gaussian $G_\sigma(x, y)$. The scale parameter controls both the edge energy computation and the estimation of local flow direction so that only edges larger than the specified scale are detected. The edge energy $E(s, \theta)$ at scale σ is defined to be the magnitude of the gradient of the smoothed image $I_\sigma(x, y)$ along the orientation θ:

$$E(s, \theta) = \left|\frac{\partial}{\partial \mathbf{n}} I_\sigma(x, y)\right| = \left|\frac{\partial}{\partial \mathbf{n}}[I(x, y) * G_\sigma(x, y)]\right| = \left|I(x, y) * \frac{\partial}{\partial \mathbf{n}} G_\sigma(x, y)\right| \tag{12.15}$$

where $s = (x, y)$ and $\mathbf{n}$ represents the unit vector in the θ direction. This edge energy indicates the strength of the intensity change. For a given $E(s, \theta)$, there are two possible flow directions: (θ) and $(\theta + \pi)$. The prediction error is used to estimate $P(s, \theta)$ as follows:

$$\begin{aligned} \text{Error}(s, \theta) &= |I_\sigma(x + d\cos\theta, y + d\sin\theta) - I_\sigma(x, y)| \\ &= |I(x, y) * DOOG_{\sigma,\theta}(x, y)| \end{aligned} \tag{12.16}$$

$$P(s, \theta) = \frac{\text{Error}(s, \theta)}{\text{Error}(s, \theta) + \text{Error}(s, \theta + \pi)} \tag{12.17}$$

where d is the offset distance in the prediction and is proportional to the scale at which the image is being analyzed. In the experiments we choose $d = 4\sigma$. The difference of offset Gaussians (DOOG) along the x-axis is defined as $DOOG_\sigma(x, y) = G_\sigma(x, y) - G_\sigma(x + d, y)$, and the difference of offset Gaussian functions along different orientations θ is denoted by $DOOG_{\sigma,\theta}(x, y)$. A large prediction error in a certain direction implies a higher probability of finding a boundary in that direction.

12.7.1.1 Texture Edges. The formulation for the intensity edges described in the preceding section can be easily extended to texture edges as well. The scale parameter σ determines the set of Gabor filters used in computing the texture features. In designing these filters, the lower cutoff frequency is set to $1/(4\sigma)$ cycles/pixel and the upper cutoff frequency is fixed at 0.45 cycles/pixel. Figure 12.6 shows the Fourier transforms of the Gabor filters, which are generated for different values of σ. The complex Gabor filtered images can be written as

$$O_i(x, y) = I(x, y) * g_i(x, y) = m_i(x, y)\exp[\phi_i(x, y)], \tag{12.18}$$

where $1 \leq i \leq N$, $N = S \cdot K$ is the total number of filters, $m(x, y)$ is the amplitude, and $\phi(x, y)$ is the phase. By taking the amplitude of the filtered output across different filters at the same location (x, y), we form a texture feature vector $\Phi(x, y) = [m_1(x, y), m_2(x, y), \ldots, m_N(x, y)]$, which characterizes the local spectral energies in different spatial frequency bands. The texture edge energy used to measure the change in local texture information is given by

$$E(s, \theta) = \sum_{1 \leq i \leq N} |m_i(x, y) * GD_{\sigma,\theta}(x, y)| \cdot w_i \tag{12.19}$$

where $w_i = 1/\Omega_i$, $\Omega_i = \sum_{x,y} m_i(x, y)$ is the total energy of the subband i, and $GD_{\sigma,\theta}$ is the first derivative of the Gaussian $G_\sigma(x, y)$ along the direction θ. The weighting coefficients w_i normalize the contribution of edge energy from the various frequency bands. Like the intensity edges, the direction of texture edge

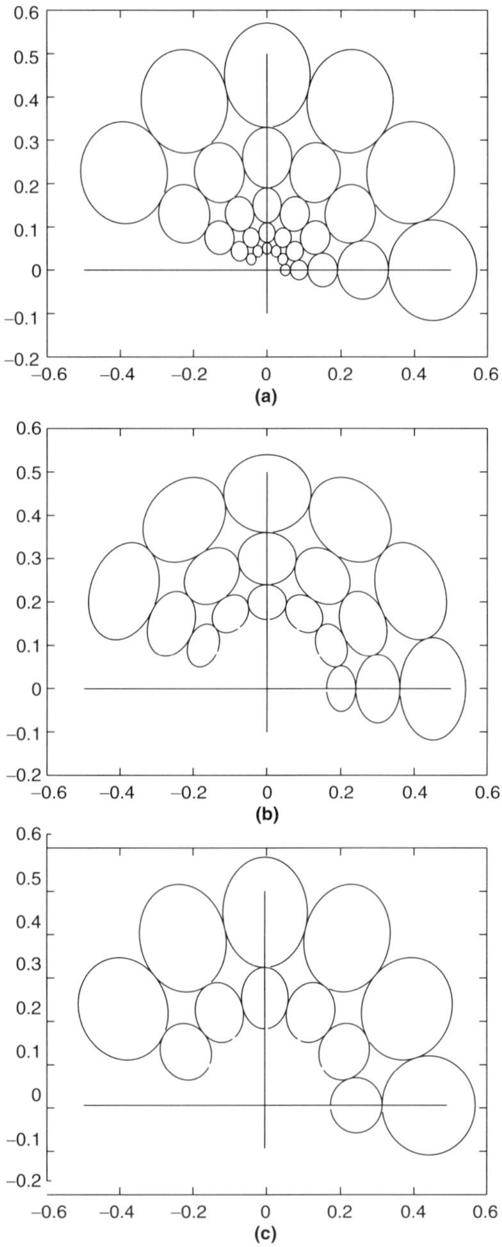

Figure 12.6. Fourier transforms of the Gabor filters used in computing the texture features. In the experiments, we use a fixed number of filter orientations, that is, $K = 6$. However, the number of filter scales S is dependent on the image smoothing scale σ. The three examples show the filter spectra for different S. **(a)** $\sigma = 5.0$ and $S = 5$, **(b)** $\sigma = 1.25$ and $S = 3$, and **(c)** $\sigma = 1.0$ and $S = 2$. Note that the contours indicate the half-peak magnitude of the filter response.

flow can be estimated from the texture prediction error at a given location:

$$\text{Error}(s,\theta) = \sum_{1\le i\le N} |m_i(x,y) * DOOG_{\sigma,\theta}(x,y)| \cdot w_i, \tag{12.20}$$

which is the weighted sum of prediction errors from each texture feature map. Thus, the probabilities $P(s,\theta)$ and $P(s,\theta+\pi)$ of the flow direction can be estimated using Eq. (12.17).

At each location $s = (x, y)$ in the image, we have $\{[E(s,\theta), P(s,\theta), P(s,\theta+\pi)]|_{0\le\theta<\pi}\}$. We first identify a continuous range of flow directions that maximizes the sum of probabilities in a corresponding half plane:

$$\Theta(s) = \operatorname*{argmax}_{\theta}\left\{\sum_{\theta\le\theta'<\theta+\pi} P(s,\theta')\right\} \tag{12.21}$$

The EdgeFlow vector is then defined to be the following vector sum:

$$\vec{\mathbf{F}}(s) = \sum_{\Theta(s)\le\theta<\Theta(s)+\pi} E(s,\theta)\cdot\exp(j\theta), \tag{12.22}$$

where $\vec{\mathbf{F}}(s)$ is a complex number, with its magnitude representing the resulting edge energy and angle representing the flow direction.

12.7.1.2 EdgeFlow Propagation and Boundary Detection. Boundary detection can be performed by propagating the EdgeFlow vector and identifying the locations where two opposite direction of flows encounter each other. At each location, the EdgeFlow energy is transmitted to its neighbor in the direction of flow if the neighbor also has a similar flow direction (the angle between them is less than 90 degrees). Once the EdgeFlow propagation reaches a stable state, we can detect the image boundaries by identifying the locations that have nonzero edge flows coming from two opposing directions.

Figure 12.7 shows an example of detecting boundaries using color and texture. Note that after the flow vector propagation step, the EdgeFlow vectors point at each other along the object boundaries (Figure 12.7(c)). After boundary detection, disjoint boundaries are connected to form closed contours and result in a number of image regions. A *region-merging algorithm* is used to merge similar regions. Regions are merged based on their color and texture similarity. We have applied this algorithm to segment about 2,500 images from the Corel color photo CDs (volume 7, *Nature*). Figure 12.8 shows some of the image segmentation results. The segmented image regions are used as query objects in a region-based image retrieval system. See *http:// maya.ece.ucsb.edu/Netra* for more segmentation results and a demonstration of the search and retrieval system.

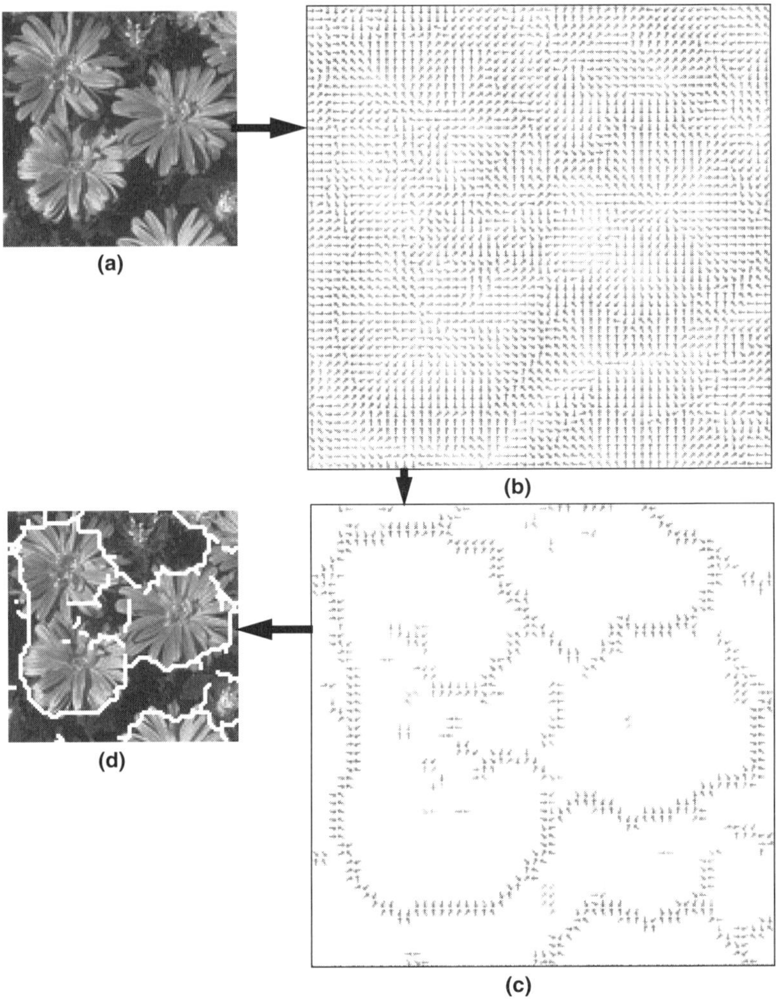

Figure 12.7. Different stages of image boundary detection based on EdgeFlow technique. **(a)** A flower image. **(b)** The edge flow field. **(c)** The result after edge flow propagation. **(d)** The result of boundary detection. Note that the scale parameter $\sigma = 6$ pixels, and only color information is used in computing the edge flow vectors.

12.7.2 A Texture Thesaurus

It is well known that traditional indexing structures such as B-trees or R-trees do not generalize well to more than 10 dimensions. In the database-indexing literature, this is often referred to as the curse of dimensionality. High-dimensional indexing is an active area of research in databases. There are three primary options: (*1*) Develop indexing structures that scale with the dimensions. Many such structures have been proposed and are being investigated, for example,

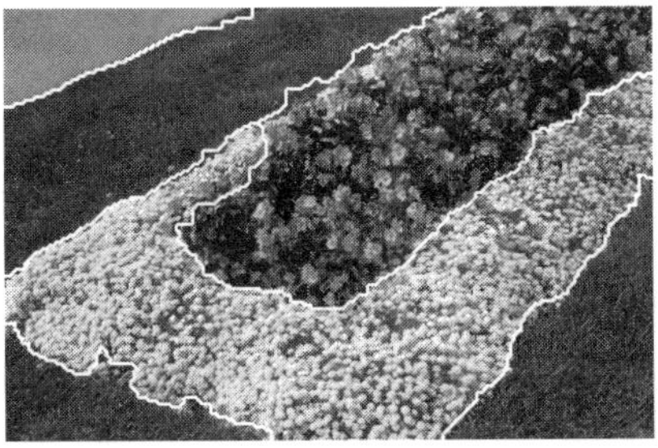

(a)

(b)

(c)

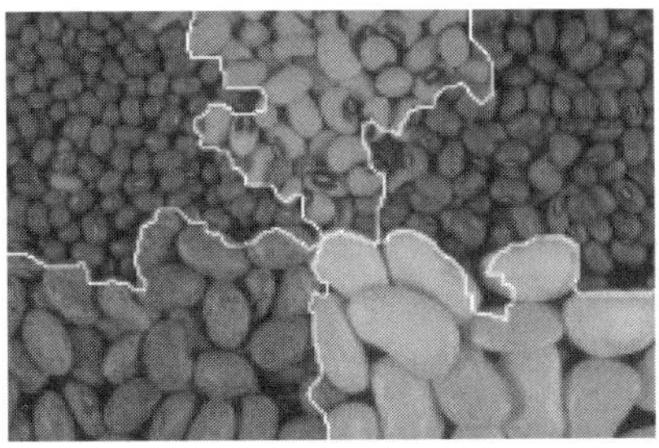

(d)

Figure 12.8. Segmentation results of natural images from the Corel photo CDs. Both color and texture are used in computing the EdgeFlow vectors and the segmentation.

the hybrid tree [73]; (*2*) Reduce the dimensionality of the feature vectors while preserving distance. Methods in this class include multidimensional scaling [74, 75], singular value decomposition [76–78], FastMap [79], and MetricMap [80]; (*3*) Use clustering to group the data such that the search space is restricted for a given query [81–85]. We proposed a novel solution in [72] for searching aerial pictures using 60-dimensional texture feature vectors. It is based on using self-organizing maps [86,87] to cluster the *texture feature vectors*. Experimental results on the Brodatz texture images demonstrate that with clustering the retrieval performance improves significantly [88]. We call the resulting structure a *texture thesaurus*.

In a texture thesaurus, information links are created among stored image data based on a collection of code words and sample patterns obtained from a training set. Similar to how the text documents can be parsed using a dictionary or thesaurus, the texture information computed from images can be classified and indexed with the help of a texture thesaurus. The construction of a texture thesaurus has two stages (Figure 12.9). The first stage uses Kohonen's self-organizing maps to create clusters, each of which contains visually similar patterns. A self-organizing map is typically a two-layered neural network in which the second layer — the output layer — is organized as a two- or three-dimensional lattice. The networks learn a mapping from a high-dimensional input feature space to this low-dimensional output space. In learning this mapping, the output

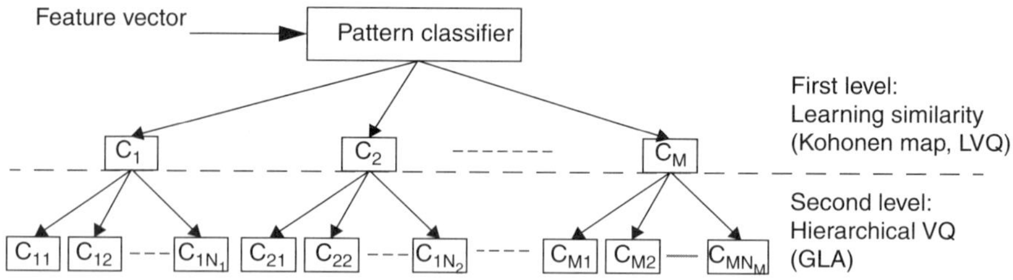

Figure 12.9. The construction of a texture thesaurus using learning similarity algorithm and a hierarchical vector quantization technique. The first level partitions the original feature space into many visually similar subspaces. Within each subspace, the second level of the tree further divides it into a set of smaller clusters.

units are ordered so that their spatial location is indicative of some statistical characteristics of the input patterns. The initial training of this network is based on a (manually) labeled set of training data. This is followed by a hierarchical vector-quantization technique to construct texture code words, each codeword representing a collection of texture patterns that are close to each other in the texture feature space. One can use a visual representation (image patterns in which texture descriptors are closest to the code words) of these code words as information samples to help users browse through the database. An iconic representation of these code words for the aerial image database is shown in Figure 12.10.

The number of code words depends on the number of distinct classes identified during the initial manual labelling and the number of texture patterns assigned to each of these classes. If a class has a large number of data points, it requires many code words to represent all its samples well. This results in an unbalanced tree structure for searching and indexing. An example of indexing 2D image

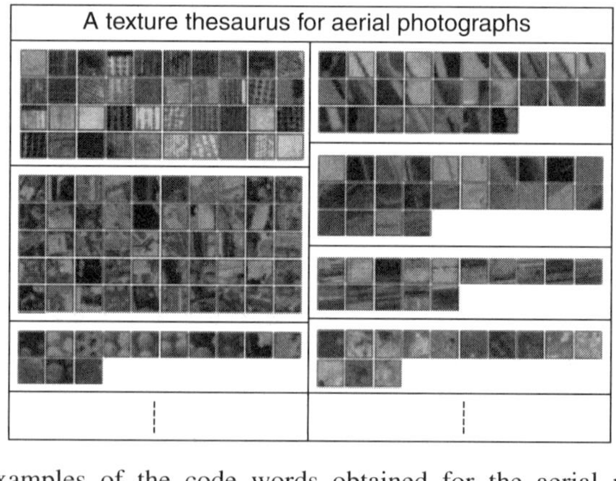

Figure 12.10. Examples of the code words obtained for the aerial photographs. The patterns inside each block belong to the same class.

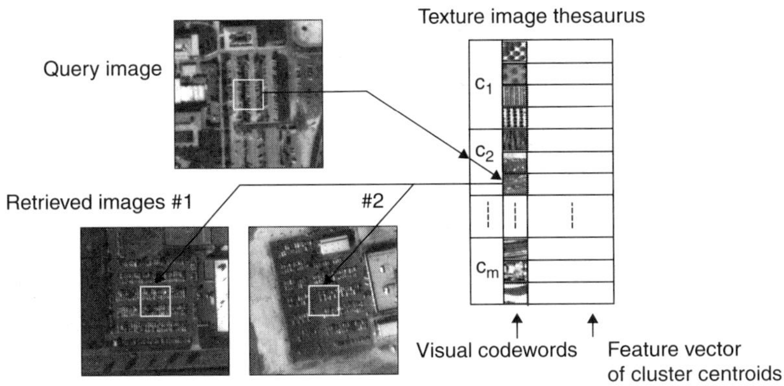

Figure 12.11. Using the texture thesaurus for content-based image retrieval. The image tiles shown here contain parking lots.

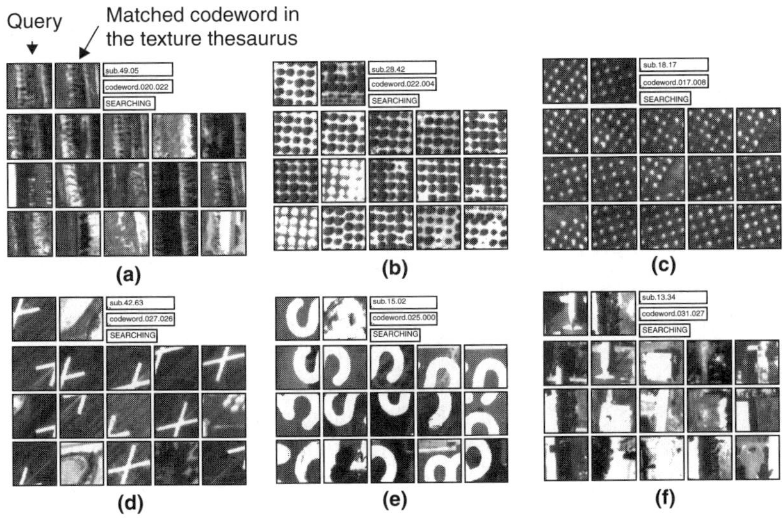

Figure 12.12. Examples of the tile-based search. **(a)**, **(b)**, and **(c)** are from the vegetation areas, **(d)** is the cross mark from the runway of an airport, **(e)** contains a portion of the marked letter 'S' in the image, **(f)** is an airplane. As can be seen, the top two matches also contain airplanes.

features is shown in Figure 12.11. As can be seen, the goal of the first level of the indexing tree is to identify a subspace within which the search and retrieval should be constrained in terms of pattern similarity. On the other hand, the second level of the indexing tree mainly focuses on exploring the data distribution (or density) within the subspace so that a set of the nearest neighbors (within the smaller cluster) can be quickly identified and retrieved.

Some retrieval examples are shown in Figure 12.12 and Figure 12.13. In Figure 12.12, the texture feature vectors are computed for nonoverlapping blocks

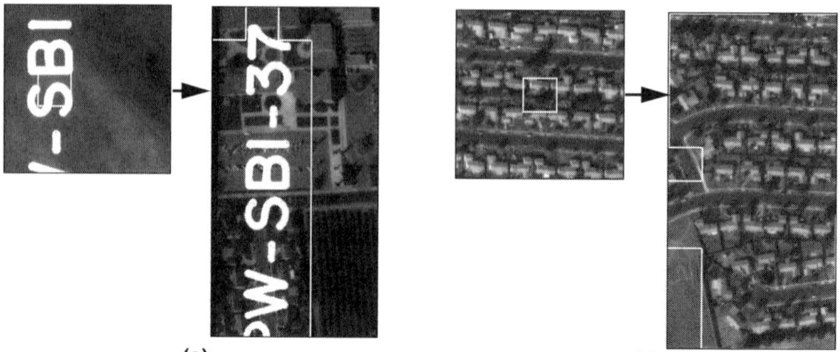

(a) (b)

Figure 12.13. Examples of the region-based search. (**a**) shows the region retrievals from areas containing an image identification number, (**b**) contains houses in residential areas.

of 64 × 64 pixels. The EdgeFlow segmentation method is then applied to these feature vectors (treating a 64 × 64 block as a single pixel, for computational reasons) to create uniform regions. Figure 12.13 shows some results on retrieving such segmented regions. A texture descriptor is computed by averaging the feature vectors of the 64 × 64 blocks belonging to each region.

12.7.3 MPEG-7 Texture Descriptors

MPEG-7 is an ISO/IEC standard developed by MPEG for multimedia content description (for current and up-to-date information on MPEG-7 and related activities, see *http:// www.mpeg.org*). The MPEG-7 standard is also referred to as the *multimedia content description interface standard* and is aimed at a broad range of applications, including content-based retrieval. At the time of writing this chapter, the committee draft (CD) of the MPEG-7 standard is in preparation. The CD is the final stabilized version of the standard, which is expected to be released in August 2001. The standardized descriptors for low level visual features include descriptors for color, texture, shape, and motion. Two texture descriptors are recommended for the current working draft — a *texture browsing descriptor* and a *homogeneous texture descriptor*. Computation of these two descriptors is based on filtering using scale- and orientation-selective Gabor kernels as described in Section 12.5.2. Together, the two descriptors provide a scalable solution to represent homogeneous texture regions in images.

12.7.3.1 Texture Browsing Descriptor. The texture browsing descriptor relates to a perceptual characterization of texture in terms of regularity, directionality, and coarseness (scale). This representation is useful for browsing applications and for coarse classification of textures. The browsing descriptor requires 12 bits (maximum) per texture. The computation of this descriptor proceeds as follows: first, the image is filtered with a bank of orientation- and scale-tuned filters (modeled using Gabor functions); from these filtered outputs, two dominant texture orientations are identified. Three bits are used to represent each of the dominant orientations. Then the filtered image projections along the dominant orientations are analyzed to determine the regularity (quantified to 2 bits) and coarseness (2 bits $\times$ 2). The second dominant orientation and second scale features are optional.

12.7.3.2 Homogeneous Texture Descriptor. The homogeneous texture descriptor provides a quantitative description that can be used for accurate search and retrieval. This descriptor uses 62 numbers (quantized to 8 bits each) per image or image region. The image is first filtered using Gabor filters. The first and the second moments of the energy in the frequency domain in the corresponding subbands are then used as the components of the texture descriptor. Note that the texture descriptor discussed in Section 12.5.2 is computed using the mean and standard deviations of the filtered outputs in the spatial domain. The number of filters used is $5 \times 6 = 30$, where 5 is the number of scales and 6 is the number of orientations in the multiresolution decomposition using Gabor functions. During the competitive phase of the MPEG-7 evaluation process, this descriptor was shown to outperform other texture descriptors. The performance evaluation was based on retrieval effectiveness on several different texture data sets and included scale and rotation invariant retrievals as well.

12.8 CONCLUSION

A very broad overview of various texture descriptors has been presented in this chapter. As low level descriptors of visual data, texture continues to play an important role in applications such as segmentation and image retrieval. The numerous references provide pointers to the rich and diverse literature on image texture for further exploration of this very interesting and exciting topic.

ACKNOWLEDGMENTS

The research work was supported in part by grants from NSF (UCSB Alexandria Digital Library Project award #IRI9411330 and IRI9704785) and by the Naval Air Warfare Center at China Lake (contract no. N68936-99-M1123).

REFERENCES

1. P. Brodatz, *Textures: A Photographic Album for Artists and Designers*, Dover Publications, New York, 1966.
2. B. Julesz, Textons, the elements of texture perception, and their interactions, *Nature* **290**(12), 91–97 (1981).
3. B. Julesz and J.R. Bergen, Textons, the fundamental elements in preattentive vision and perception of textures, *Bell Syst. Tech. J.* **62**(6), 1619–1645 (1983).

4. R.M. Haralick, Statistical and structural approaches to texture, *Proc. IEEE* **67**(5), 786–804 (1979).
5. J.D. Foley et al., *Introduction to Computer Graphics*, Addison-Wesley, Reading, Boston, Mass., 1993.
6. MPEG/ISO *Document N3349, MPEG-7 Overview*, Noordwijkerhout Netherlands, J. Martinez, ed., March 2000.
7. R.M. Haralick and L.G. Shapiro, *Computer and Robot Vision (Vol. I)*, Addison-Wesley, Reading, Boston, Mass., 1992.
8. B. Julesz, Visual pattern discrimination, *IRE Trans. Inf. Theory*, IT-8 84–92 (1961).
9. S. Chatterjee and R. Chellappa, Maximum likelihood texture segmentation using Gaussian Markov random field models, *Proceedings of IEEE International Conference on Computer Vision and Pattern Recognition*, San Francisco, Calif., June 1985.
10. F.S. Cohen and D.B. Cooper, Simple parallel hierarchical and relaxation algorithms for segmenting noncausal Markovian fields, *IEEE Trans. Pattern Anal. Machine Intell.* **9**, 195–219 (1987).
11. H. Derin and H. Elliott, Modeling and segmentation of noisy and textured images using Gibbs random fields, *IEEE Trans. Pattern Anal. Machine Intell.* **9**, 39–55 (1987).
12. C.W. Therrien, An estimation theoretic approach to terrain image segmentation, *Computer Vision, Graphics and Image processing* **22**, 313–326 (1983).
13. R. Chellappa, R.L. Kashyap, and B.S. Manjunath, Model-based texture segmentation and classification, in C.H. Chen, L.F. Pau and P.S.P. Wang, eds., *Handbook of Pattern Recognition and Computer Vision*, World Scientific Publishing, River Edge, N.J., 1993, pp. 279–310.
14. R.O. Duda and P.E. Hart, *Pattern Classification and Scene Analysis*, Wiley & Sons, New York, 1973.
15. J.R. Bergen and E.H. Adelson, Early vision and texture perception, *Nature* **333**, 363–364 (1988).
16. J. Malik and P. Perona, Preattentive texture discrimination with early vision mechanisms, *J. Opt. Soc. Am. A* **7**, 923–932 (1990).
17. T. Chang and C.-C. Jay Kuo, Texture analysis and classification with tree-structured wavelet transform, *IEEE Trans. Image Proc.* **2**(4), 429–441 (1993).
18. G. Haley and B.S. Manjunath, Rotation invariant texture classification using a complete space-frequency model, *IEEE Trans. Image Process.* **8**(2) 255–69 February (1999).
19. B. Julesz, Experiments in the visual perception of texture, *Sci. Am.* **232**(4), 2–11 (1975).
20. A.R. Rao and G.L.Lohse, Identifying high level features of texture perception, *CVGIP: Graphical Models Image Process.* **55**(3), 218–233 1993.
21. A.R. Rao, *A Taxonomy of texture description and identification*, Springer-Verlag, Berlin/New York, 1990.
22. F. Bello and R.I. Kitney, Co-occurrence based texture analysis using irregular tessellations, *Proceedings of IEEE International Conference on Pattern Recognition*, Vienna, Austria, August 1996, pp. 780–784.
23. L.S. Davis, S. Johns, and J.K. Aggarwal, Texture analysis using generalized co-occurrence matrices, *IEEE Trans. Pattern Anal. Machine Intell.* **1**(3), 251–259 (1979).

24. R. Haralick and R. Bosley, Texture features for image classification, *Third ERTS Symposium*, NASA SP-351, pp. 1219–28, 1973.
25. R.M. Haralick, K. Shanmugam, and I. Dinstein, Texture features for image classification, *IEEE Trans. Sys. Man, Cybernetics* **3**, 610–621 (1973).
26. J. Parkkinen, K. Selkainaho, and E. Oja, Detecting texture periodicity from the co-occurrence matrix, *Pattern Recog. Lett.* **11**, 43–50 (1990).
27. H. Tamura, S. Mori, and T. Yamawaki, Texture features corresponding to visual perception, *IEEE Trans. Sys. Man, and Cybernetics* **8**(6), 460–473 (1978).
28. W.K. Pratt, *Digital Image Processing*, Wiley & Sons, New York, 1978.
29. A. Rosenfeld and A.C. Kak, *Digital Picture Processing*, Academic Press, New York, 1982.
30. R. Chellappa and R.L. Kashyap, Texture synthesis using 2-D noncausal autoregressive models, *IEEE Trans. Acoust., Speech, Signal Proc.* **33**, 94–203 (1985).
31. A.L. Vickers and J.W. Modestino, A Maximum likelihood approach to texture classification, *IEEE Trans. Pattern Anal. Machine Intell.* **4**, 61–68 (January 1982).
32. R.L. Kashyap, R. Chellappa, and A. Khotanzad, Texture classification using features derived from random field models, *Pattern Recog. Lett. I* 43–50 (1982).
33. G.R. Cross and A.K. Jain, Markov random field texture models, *IEEE Trans. Pattern Anal. Machine Intell.* **5**, 25–39 (1983).
34. J.W. Woods, Two-dimensional discrete Markovian fields, *IEEE Trans. Information Theory* **18**, 32–240 (1972).
35. J. Besag, Spatial interaction and the statistical analysis of lattice systems, *J. Royal Stat. Soc. B* **36**, 192–236 (1973).
36. J. Besag, On the statistical analysis of dirty pictures, *J. Royal Stat. Soc. B* **48**, 259–302 (1986).
37. J. Mao and A.K. Jain, Texture classification and segmentation using multiresolution simultaneous autoregressive models, *Pattern Recog.* **25**(2), 173–188 (1992).
38. R.W. Picard, T. Kabir, and F. Liu, Real-time recognition with the entire Brodatz texture database, *Proceeding IEEE International Conference on Computer Vision and Pattern Recognition*, New York, June 1993, pp. 638–639.
39. F. Liu, R.W. Picard, Periodicity, directionality, and randomness: Wold features for image modeling and retrieval, *IEEE Trans. Pattern Anal. Machine Intell.* **18**(7), 722–733 (1996).
40. R. Bajcsy and L. Lieberman, Computer description of real outdoor scenes, *Proceedings 2nd International Joint Conference on Pattern Recognition*, Copenhagen, Denmark, August 1974, pp. 174–179.
41. N. Gramenopoulos, Terrain type recognition using ERTS-1 MSS images, in *Rec. Symp. Significant results obtained from the Earth research technology satellite*, NASA SP-327, 1229–1241, March 1973.
42. R.J. Horning and J.A. Smith, Application of Fourier analysis to multispectral/spatial recognition, presented at *Management and utilization of remote sensing data ASP symposium*, Sioux falls, S.Dak., October 1973.
43. L. Kirvida and G. Johnson, Automatic interpretation of ERTS data for forest management, *Rec. Symp. Significant results obtained from the Earth research technology satellite*, NASA SP-327, March (1973).

44. H. Maurer, Texture analysis with Fourier series, *Proceedings of the Ninth International Symposium on Remote Sensing of Environment*, April 1974, pp. 1411–1420.
45. R. Bajcsy, Computer description of textured surfaces, *Proc. 3rd IJCAI* 572–579 (1973).
46. T. Matsuyama, S. Miura and M. Nagao, Structural analysis of natural textures by Fourier transformation, *Comput. Vis., Graphics Image Process.* **24**, 347–362, (1983).
47. K. Laws, Textured image segmentation, Ph.D. thesis, University of Southern California, California, 1978.
48. I. Daubechies, The wavelet transform, time-frequency localization and signal analysis, *IEEE Trans. Inf. Theory* **36**, 961–1005 (1990).
49. S.G. Mallat, A theory for multiresolution signal decomposition: the wavelet representation, *IEEE Trans. Pattern Anal. Machine Intell.* **11**, 674–693 (1989).
50. A. Laine and J. Fan, Texture classification by wavelet packet signatures, *IEEE Trans. Pattern Anal. Machine Intell.* **15**(11), 1186–1191 (1993).
51. A.C. Bovic, M. Clark and W.S. Geisler, Multichannel texture analysis using localized spatial filters, *IEEE Trans. Pattern Anal. Machine Intell.* **12**, 55–73 (1990).
52. J.G. Daugman, Complete discrete 2-D Gabor transforms by neural networks for image analysis and compression, *IEEE Trans. Acoust., Speech, Signal Process.* **36**, 1169–1179 (1988).
53. D. Dunn, W.E. Higgins, and J. Wakeley, Texture segmentation using 2-D Gabor elementary functions, *IEEE Trans. Pattern Anal. Machine Intell.* **16**, 130–149 (1994).
54. D. Dunn, T.P. Weldon, and W.E. Higgins, Extracting halftones from printed documents using texture analysis, *Opt. Eng.* **36**(4), 1044–1052 (1997).
55. I. Fogel and D. Sagi, Gabor filters as texture discriminator, *Biol. Cybernetics* **61**, 103–113 (1989).
56. A.K. Jain and F. Farroknia, Unsupervised texture segmentation using Gabor filters, *Pattern Recog.* **24**(12), 1167–1186 (1991).
57. B.S. Manjunath, C. Shekhar, and R. Chellappa, A new approach to image feature detection with applications, *Pattern Recog.* **29**(4), 627–640 (1996).
58. B.S. Manjunath and W.Y. Ma, Texture features for browsing and retrieval of image data, *IEEE Trans. Pattern Anal. Machine Intell.* **18**(8), 837–842 (1996).
59. J.G. Daugman, Uncertainty relation for resolution in space, spatial frequency, and orientation optimized by two-dimensional visual cortical filters, *J. Opt. Soc. Am.* **2**(7), 1160–1169 (1985).
60. W.Y. Ma and B.S. Manjunath, Edge flow: a framework of boundary detection and image segmentation, *Proceedings of the IEEE International Conference on Computer Vision and Pattern Recognition*, Puerto Rico, June 1997, pp. 744–749.
61. B.S. Manjunath and R. Chellappa, A Unified approach to boundary detection, *IEEE Trans. Neural Networks* **4**(1), 96–108 (1993).
62. J.G. Daugman, High confidence visual recognition of persons by a test of statistical independence, *IEEE Trans. Pattern Anal. Machine Intell.* **15**(11), 1148–1161 (1993).
63. B.S. Manjunath and R. Chellappa, A feature based approach to face recognition, *Proceedings of IEEE International Conference on Computer Vision and Pattern Recognition*, Champaign, Il., June 1992, pp. 373–378.
64. S. Santini and R. Jain, Similarity Measures, *IEEE Trans. Pattern Anal. Machine Intell.* **21**(9), 871–883 (1999).

65. J. Puzicha, J.M. Buhmann, Y. Rubner, and C. Tomsai, Empirical evaluation of dissimilarity measures for color and texture, *Proceedings of IEEE International Conference on Computer Vision (ICCV'99)*, Kerkyra, Greece, September 1999, pp. 1165–1172.
66. A.G. Weber, The USC-SIPI Image Database Version 3, USC SIPI Report # 214, August 1992.
67. J. Canny, Computational approach to edge detection, *IEEE Trans. Pattern Analysis Machine Intelligence* **8**(6), 679–698 (1986).
68. W.Y. Ma and H.J. Zhang, Benchmarking of image features for content-based retrieval, *Proceedings of Asilomar Conference on Signals, Systems, and Computers*, Monterey, Calif., November 1998, pp. 253–257.
69. C.S. Li, J.R. Smith, V. Castelli, and L.D. Bergman, Comparing texture feature sets for retrieving core images in petroleum applications, *Proc. SPIE, Storage and Retrieval for Image and Video Databases VII* **3656**, 2–11 (1999).
70. C.S. Li and V. Castelli, Deriving texture feature set for content based retrieval of satellite image database, *Proceedings of the IEEE International Conference on Image Processing (ICIP'97)*, Santa Barbara, Calif., October 1997, pp. 576–579.
71. T.R. Smith, A digital library for geographically referenced materials, *IEEE Comput.* 54–60 (1996).
72. W.Y. Ma and B.S. Manjunath, A texture thesaurus for browsing large aerial photographs, *J. A. Soc. Inf. Sci.* **49**(7), 633–648 (1998).
73. K. Chakrabarti and S. Mehrotra, The hybrid tree: An index structure for high dimensional feature spaces, *Proceedings of the International Conference on Data Engineering (ICDE)* Sydney, Australia, March 1999, pp. 440–447.
74. J.W.Sammon, A nonlinear mapping for data analysis, *IEEE Trans. Comput.* **18**, 401–409 (1969).
75. R.N. Shepard, The analysis of proximities: Multidimensional scaling with an unknown distance function, *Psychometrika* **27**(2), 125–140 (1962).
76. H.C. Andrews and C.L. Patterson, Singular value decomposition (SVD) image, *IEEE Trans. Commun.* **24**(4), 425–432 (1976).
77. G.H. Golub and C.F. van Loan, *Matrix Computations*, John Hopkins University Press, Baltimori, Md., 1989.
78. K.V. Ravi Kanth, D. Agrawal, and A. Singh, Dimensionality reduction for similarity searching in dynamic databases *Proceedings of ACM SIGMOD International Conference on Management of Data*, Seattle, Wash., June 1998, pp. 166–176.
79. C. Faloutsos and K.-I. Lin, *Fast Map*, A fast algorithm for indexing, data mining and visualization of traditional and multimedia datasets, *Proceedings of ACM SIGMOD International Conference on Management of Data*, San Jose, Calif., May 1995, pp. 163–174.
80. J. Wang et al., Evaluating a class of distance mapping algorithms for data mining and clustering, *Proceedings of ACM SIGKDD International Conference on Knowledge Discovery and Data Mining*, San Diego, Calif., August 1999, pp. 307–311.
81. S. Blott and R. Weber, A simple vector-approximation file for similarity in high-dimensional vector spaces, Technical report No. 19, ESPRIT project HERMES (no. 9141), 1997.

82. R. Weber, H. Schek, and S. Blott, A quantitative analysis and performance study for similarity-search methods in high-dimensional spaces, *Proceedings of International Conference on Very Large Databases* (VLDB), New York, August 1998, pp. 194–205.
83. A. Gionis, P. Indyk, and R. Motwani, Similarity search in high dimensions via hashing, *Proceedings of International Conference on Very Large Databases* (VLDB), Edinburgh, U.K., September 1999, pp. 518–529.
84. V. Ganti et al., *Clustering large datasets in arbitrary metric spaces*, *Proceedings of International Conference on Data Engineering*, Sydney, Australia, March 1999, pp. 502–511.
85. T. Zhang, R. Ramakrishnan, and M. Livny, BIRCH: A new data clustering algorithm and its applications, *Data Mining Knowledge Discovery J.* **1**(2), 141–182 (1997).
86. T. Kohonen, Self-organized formation of topologically correct feature maps, *Biol. Cybernetics* **43**, 59–69 (1982).
87. T. Kohonen, The self-organizing map, *Proc. IEEE* **78**(9), 1464–1480 (1990).
88. W.Y. Ma and B.S. Manjunath, Texture features and learning similarity, *Proceedings of IEEE International Conference on Computer Vision and Pattern Recognition* San Francisco, Calif., June 1996, pp. 425–430.
89. M.M. Galloway, Texture analysis using gray level run lengths, *Comput. Graphics Image Process.* **4**, 172–179 (1975).
90. S. Geman and D. Geman, Stochastic relaxation, Gibbs distributions, and the Bayesian restoration of images, *IEEE Trans. Pattern Anal. Machine Intell.* **6**(6), 721–741 (1984).
91. C.C. Gotlieb and H.E. Kreyszig, Texture descriptors based on co-occurrence matrices, *CVGIP* **51**(1), 70–84 (1990).
92. W.Y. Ma and B.S. Manjunath, NeTra: A toolbox for navigating large image databases, *ACM Multimedia Syst.* **7**, 184–198 (1999).
93. B.S. Manjunath and R. Chellappa, A note on unsupervised texture segmentation, *IEEE Trans. Pattern Anal. Machine Intell.* **13**, 472–483 (1991).
94. S.R. Yhann and T.Y. Young, Boundary localization in texture segmentation, *IEEE Trans. Pattern Anal. Machine Intell.* **4**, 849–855 (1995).

13 Shape Representation for Image Retrieval

BENJAMIN B. KIMIA
Brown University, Providence, Rhode Island

13.1 INTRODUCTION

The human–machine interface is evolving at an incredible pace, surpassing the traditional text-based boundaries. A driving force motivating this development is the need to endow computers with capabilities that parallel our perceptual abilities. Vision is arguably our most significant sense, giving rise to efforts to empower computers to represent, process, understand, and act on visual imagery. As a result, *images* are being generated at a mind-boggling pace from a variety of sources. Terabytes of data are being generated in the form of aerial imagery, surveillance images, mug shots, fingerprints, trademarks and logos, graphic illustrations, engineering line drawings, documents, manuals, medical images, images from sports events, documentation of environmental resources in the form of images, and entertainment industry photos and videos [1–7]. Clearly, the management of such databases must rely on the perceptual and cognitive dimensions of the visual space, namely, color, texture, shape, and so on. The basic premise is that there exists qualitative aspects of images that can be used to retrieve images without fully specifying them.

The use of *shape* as a cue is less developed than the use of color or texture, mainly because of the inherent complexity of representing it. Yet, retrieval-by-shape has the potential of being the most effective search technique in many application fields. This chapter reviews and discusses the representation of shape as a cue for indexing image databases. The central question is how complete or partial information regarding a shape in an image can be represented so that it can be easily extracted, matched, and retrieved. Specifically, five key items must be addressed:

Image and Query Preparation. How are shapes extracted from images? The segregation of figure from ground is rather straightforward in images that

Image Databases: Search and Retrieval of Digital Imagery, Edited by Vittorio Castelli and Lawrence D. Bergman.
ISBN 0-471-32116-8

are binary or have a bi-level histogram, but usually difficult otherwise. As a consequence, a wide spectrum of shape-extraction techniques have been developed, ranging from segmenting the image to extracting related lower-level features, such as edges, that yield a partial representation of shape. Query formulation and shape extraction are therefore inherently related. The query-specification mechanism provided by the user interface (sketch drawing, query-by-example, query-by-keyword, spatial-layout specification, and so on) must closely match the shape extraction process, and, in particular, emphasize the specific representation of shape used during the search.

Shape Representation. How is shape represented? Is there "invariance" to a class of transformations? Is the representation contour-based or region-based? Is it based on local features or global attributes? Do parts play a role? Is the spatial relationship among parts or features represented explicitly? Is the representation multiscale?

Shape Similarity and Matching. How are the query and database items matched? Is the matching based on geometric hashing, graph matching, energy minimization, probabilistic formulation, and so on? How is the similarity between two objects represented?

Indexing and Retrieval. How is the database organized? Are prototypes or categories used? Do models guide the retrieval process?

Validation. How well does each approach perform in terms of accuracy and precision? How efficient is the retrieval?

This chapter focuses on the second question, namely, the issue of shape representation, although this necessarily requires a discussion of the remaining items. We will begin by citing some examples in which indexing by shape content is used, followed by a discussion on how the database of shapes and the related image queries are prepared. Next, we will discuss the main issues pertaining to shape representation. This is followed by a brief discussion of matching and shape similarity as it pertains to the nature of the underlying representation.

13.2 WHERE IS INDEXING BY SHAPE RELEVANT?

Although it is inherently difficult to characterize and manipulate, shape is a significant cue for describing objects. Despite the difficulty of capturing a computational notion of shape, an increasing number of applications have used it as a primary cue for indexing, (illustrated in Fig. 13.1) a few of which are now briefly reviewed.

Trademarks and logos are often distinguished by their specific shapes. Patent application offices must avoid duplication partly by checking the similarity in shape with previously used forms. ARTISAN is an example of a system that uses shape to retrieve trademarks [8–10]. Numerous shape-representation techniques (described in Section 13.4) have been applied to

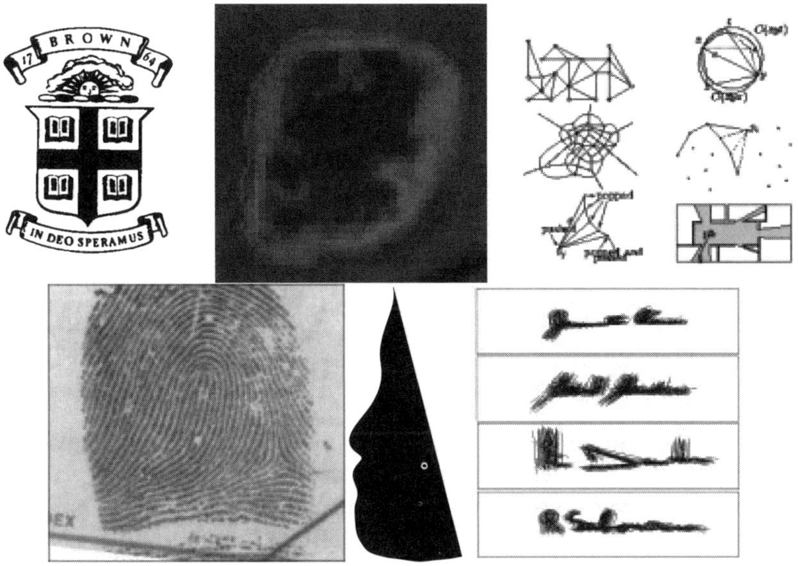

Figure 13.1. Examples of shapes for indexing into a database: trademarks and logos, medical structures, drawings, fingerprints, face profiles, and signatures.

trademark and logo retrieval, including geometric invariant signatures [11], string matching of the contour chain code [12], and combinations of moment invariants and Fourier descriptors [13,14].

In the *medical domain*, shape is used as a cue to describe the similarity of medical scans. Applications include detecting emphysema in high-resolution CT scans of the lung [15,16], classifying deformations arising from pathological changes as evident in dental radiographs (e.g., for periapical disease), and retrieving tumors [17]. Several image query systems supporting retrieval-by-shape have been developed [18,19].

Shape also plays a key role in the management of *document databases*. Sample applications include the retrieval of architectural drawings, computer-generated technical drawings [20], character bitmaps (e.g., Chinese characters) [21], technical drawing of machine parts (e.g., aircraft parts), clipart, and graphics.

Law-enforcement and security is another application area for retrieval of images by shape. Fingerprint matching [22] is used in automatic personal identification for criminal identification by law-enforcement agencies, access control to restricted facilities, credit card user identification, and other applications. The size of a fingerprint database is often very large, on the order of hundreds of million fingerprint codes, and requires indexing into terabytes of data.

Earth Science applications of retrieval-by-shape include indexing databases of auroras [23].

Other applications include *art* and art history [24], *electronic shopping*, multimedia systems for *museums and archaeology*, *defense*, *entertainment*, and so on.

13.3 IMAGE PREPARATION AND QUERY FORMULATION

The question of how images must be prepared prior to storage in a database, and how queries can be formulated are both intimately connected with how shape is used as an indexing mechanism.

In principle, a complete representation of a two-dimensional shape is provided by its contour. The contour is a continuous curve in the plane, and can specified by a large number of points. Clearly, such a voluminous representation of shape cannot be effectively used for similarity retrieval, and partial representations capturing its salient aspects are used in practice. These partial representations range from very simple (for example, a shape can be approximated by an ellipse and represented just by its elongation) to very complex (for example, the contour could be approximated by a piecewise polynomial representation). The specific application imposes requirements on the richness of the representation.

When a complete description of shape is used in the indexing scheme, the image must be segmented and entire shapes must be stored. This process is quite straightforward when images contain binary or nearly binary shapes, such as trademarks, logos, bitmaps of characters, signatures, clip art, designs, drawings, graphics, and so on. In general, however, the task of figure-ground segregation is formidable, as is evident from the relatively large "segmentation" literature in computer vision and image processing. Nevertheless, in certain domains automatic segmentation has been used. For example, Gunsel and Tekalp [25] address the segmentation, or figure background separation problem, by a combination of methods. A color histogram intersection method [26] is used to eliminate database objects with significantly different color from the query object. Boundaries are estimated using either the Canny edge detector [27] or the graduated nonconvexity (GNC) algorithm [28,29].

As a result of the difficulty of figure-ground segregation, partial representations are often used when application requirements permit. The most common methods rely on edge content, which is indicative of shape boundary. A brief historical sequence that samples these methods is presented here.

Hirata and Kato [30,31] performed a pixel-by-pixel edge-content comparison of a query and shifted image blocks and used the resulting "edge similarity score" to find the best match. Gray [32] evaluated this approach and concluded that its fundamental weakness is the "pixel-by-pixel" nature of the comparison, which produces multiple false matches. DelBimbo [33] introduced the notion of flexible matching for indexing, which allows for significant deviations of the sketch from the edge map. Rectangular regions of interest are identified for images containing well-delineated objects, and a gradient-descent method detects object boundaries from edge maps. Chan and coworkers [34] extend the pixel-by-pixel approach to correlation of "curvelets" by grouping edge pixels into edge elements using the Hough transform, by modeling grouped edges as curvelets using implicit polynomial (IP) models [35], and by computing the similarity between a pair of IP curvelets.

Other approaches augment the edge content by making the relative spatial arrangement of edges explicit. This evolution from local models of edge content to those that incorporate more of the global geometry, namely, deformable templates, curves, and the inclusion of relative spatial arrangement, indicates a move toward more complete descriptors of shape. Query formulation must closely match the underlying shape representation: a query shape specified by a user is necessarily an approximation of the shape the user is trying to communicate. Thus, a neighborhood of shapes is implicitly being presented to the system for a match, as determined by the underlying representation of the query. The requirement of indexing robustness with variations in the underlying representation of shape motivates the use of identical representations for the query and for the indexing mechanism.

13.4 REPRESENTATION OF SHAPE

As mentioned in the previous section, only approximate representations of shape are practically usable for image retrieval. There is clearly a trade-off between the complexity of the representation and its ability to capture different aspects of shape. However, the elusive nature of shape makes it almost impossible to formally analyze this trade-off. As a consequence, shape has been represented using a variety of descriptors such as moments, Fourier descriptors (FD), geometric and algebraic invariants, polygons, polynomials, splines, strings, deformable templates, skeletons, and so on, for both object recognition and for indexing of image databases.

Each of these representations aims at capturing specific perceptually salient dimensions of the qualitative aspects of shape. Because of the heterogeneous nature of the aspects captured, it is not possible to compare different descriptors outside the context of very specific applications.

Shape comparison is also a very difficult problem. It is well established that neither mathematical descriptions based on differential geometry [36], mathematical morphology [37], or statistics [38], nor formal metrics for shape comparison [39,40], fully capture the salient aspects of shape. The key observation is that shape, a construct of the projected object that is a *perceptual* invariant of the object, is multifaceted.

Existing approaches can be organized according to the particular facets that have been targeted in the representation. We specifically analyze several dimensions; we distinguish first between methods that describe the boundary and methods that describe the interior; we then contrast global and local representations; we differentiate between composition-based and deformation-based approaches; we discuss representations of shape at multiple scale; we categorize shape representation by their completeness; and finally, we distinguish between the descriptions of isolated shapes and of shape arrangements.

13.4.1 Boundary Versus Interior

Two large categories of shape descriptors can be identified: those capturing the *boundary* (or contour appearance) and those characterizing the *interior* region. Boundary representations emphasize the closed curve that surrounds the shape. This curve has been described by numerous models, including chain codes [41], polygons [42–46], circular arcs [9], splines [47–49], explicit and implicit polynomials [35,50], and boundary Fourier descriptors. Alternately, a boundary can be described by its features, for example, curvature extrema and inflection points [51,52].

Interior descriptions of shape, on the other hand, emphasize the "material" within the closed boundary. The interior has been modeled in a variety of ways, including collections of primitives [53] (rectangles, disks, superquadrics, etc.), deformable templates [54–56], by modes of resonance, skeletal models, or simply as a set of points (as in mathematical morphology).

Each description, whether boundary-based or region-based, is intuitively appealing and corresponds to a perceptually meaningful dimension. Clearly, each representation is complete, and can be used as a basis to compute the other, that is, by filling in the interior region or by tracing the boundary. Although the two representations are interchangeable in the sense of information content, the issue of which aspects of shape have been made explicit matters to the subsequent phases of the computation. For example, in boundary-based models, features such as curvature and arc length are immediately available; in region-based methods, the explicit features are quite different and include spatial relationship among shape features (for example, the shortest regional distance used in determining a neck). Shape features that are represented explicitly will generally permit more efficient retrieval when these particular features are queried. Because both contours and interiors correspond to meaningful perceptual dimensions, an ideal representation would include both, enabling a full range of queries. We now consider examples utilizing either contours, interiors, or both, in their representation of shape.

13.4.1.1 Boundary Representations of Shape. Grosky and Mehrotra [6,57] represent shape as an ordered set of boundary features, encoded as a polygonal approximation. Shape similarity is the distance between two boundary feature vectors. Eakins and coworkers [8–10] represent boundaries with circular polyarcs and discontinuities. In the query-by-visual example (QVE) system [30] a boundary-based approach is followed: edges are extracted, thinned, binarized, and stored in a 64×64 binary-edge map. A user query, which is formulated as a sketch, is similarly represented but viewed as a collection of 64 blocks (8×8). The sketch is correlated with the edge map in each block, allowing for one to four pixel horizontal and vertical shifts, thus effectively building some tolerance against deformation and warping.

The approach in DelBimbo and coworkers [48] is one of matching user sketches, which represent the boundaries of the object of interest. They argue that straightforward correlation measures, such as those used in QVE [30], produce good matches only when sketches are drawn exactly. In QVE, the lack of an exact match between a sketch and a set of image edges is tolerated only to some extent by allowing for limited horizontal and vertical shifts. In Ref. [48], the approach relies on a different measure of similarity in which the sketches are allowed to elastically deform. The sketch is deformed to adjust to the shape of target models; the extent of the final match and the elastic deformation energy are used as a measure of shape similarity. Specifically, the one-dimensional sketched template is modeled by a second-order spline and parameterized by arc length. The sketch is then allowed to act as an active contour (or snake) [58], namely, it is allowed to deform to maximize the edge strength integral along the curve, at the same time minimizing the strain and bending energies. These energies are typically modeled by integrals of the first and second derivatives of the deformation along the curve. Shape similarity is then measured as a combination of strain and bending energy, edge strength function along the curve, curve complexity, and correlation between certain functions classified by a back-propagation neural network subject to appropriate training (Fig. 13.2). This approach is translation-invariant, but requires template scaling and rotation.

Kliot and Rivlin [11] represent a binary shape via the local multivalued invariant signatures of its boundary. First, edge contours are traced and described as a set of geometric entities, such as circles, ellipses, and straight lines. Then, the relative position of these geometric entities is described via a containment tree in which each directed edge points to a curve contained in the current curves. Finally, each curve is represented by an invariant signature, which is essentially the derivative of the curve in a transform-invariant parameterization [60,61].

The shape representation by Gunsel and Tekalp [25] uses edge features obtained by either the Canny edge detector [27] or the graduated nonconvexity (GNC) algorithm [28]. If boundaries are closed, the method organizes the edges as B-splines [49,62]; otherwise, it represents them as a set of feature points. The advantages of the B-spline representation are the reduction of data volume to a small number of control points, affine invariance, and robustness to noise because of inherent smoothing.

Figure 13.2. This figure from Ref. [59] illustrates the use of deformable models in matching user-drawn sketches to shapes in images.

Jain and Vailaya [63] represent edge directions in a histogram, which is used as a shape feature. An alternate representation of shape boundary is a series of 2D strings, as presented in Refs. [64–66].

13.4.1.2 ***Interior Representations of Shape.*** Jaggadish [67] represents a shape by a fixed number of largest rectangles covering the shape. This allows a shape to be represented by a finite number of numeric parameters, which are mapped to a point in a multidimensional space, and indexed by a point-access method (PAM, Chapter 14).

Pentland and Sclaroff propose a physically motivated modal representation in which the low-order vibration modes of a shape are used as its representation [68–70]. For a related approach, see Ref. [71].

A class of rather intuitive representations of shape relies on the axis of symmetry between a pair of boundaries. The earliest use of this representation is by Blum [72], who defined the *medial axis* as a locus of inscribed circles that are maximal in size. The trace of this representation, typically known as a *skeleton*, is usually represented by a graph and used in Refs. [73,74].

The *symmetry set* is the locus of bitangent circles; its definition is identical to that of the medial axis minus the maximality condition. Thus, the medial axis is a subset of the symmetry set. However, although it appears that the symmetry set contains more information than the medial axis, the additional branches of the symmetry set are in fact redundant. Furthermore, their presence creates numerous difficulties for indexing when shapes undergo slight perturbations.

The *shock set* is another variant of the medial axis and is based on the notion of propagation from boundaries, much like a "grassfire" initiated from the boundaries of a field. Shocks are singularities that form from the collision of fronts. These shocks flow along with the wave-front itself [39,75–77]. This addition of a sense of flow or *dynamics* to each point of the medial axis and grouping of monotonically flowing shocks into branches leads to a shock graph, which is analogous to a skeletal graph, but is a finer partition of the medial axis. The shock graph has been used for indexing and recognition of shapes [74,78–84].

13.4.2 Local Versus Global

Shape can also be viewed either from a *local* or from a *global* perspective. Many early models in indexing by shape content used features such as moments, eccentricity, area, and so on, which are typically based on the entire shape and are thus global. Similarly, Fourier descriptors of two-dimensional shape are global descriptors. On the other hand, local representations restrict computations to small neighborhoods of the shape. For example, a representation based on curvature extrema and inflection points of the boundary is local.

Purely global representations are affected by variations, such as partial occlusion and articulation, whereas purely local representations are sensitive to noise. Ideally, our ability to focus on either facet implies that both must be emphasized in the representation for successful and intuitive indexing by shape.

The *binary edge map* used in the query by image content system (QBIC) [4,85] is an example of global shape representation. Here, edges are extracted (either manually or automatically) and represented as a binary edge map from which twenty-two global features are extracted (area, circularity, eccentricity, the major axis, and a set of associated algebraic moments up to degree 8). A Karhunen Loeve (KL) transform reduces the dimensionality of the feature space.

Transform-based methods are also typically global: Fourier descriptors [86,87], frequency subband decomposition, coefficients of 2D Discrete Wavelet transform (DFT) [88], Wavelet Transform [89], Karhunen-Loeve Transform [19], and others all encode global measures.

Orientation radiograms [90] project an image onto an axis by integrating image intensities along lines orthogonal to that axis. This results in a histogram for each of the four or eight orientations of the axis used. This is a global representation because local variations are not explicitly captured onto a profile and are thus global.

Grosky and Mehrotra represent boundary features by a property vector, which is matched using a string edit-distance similarity measure [6]. They use an m-way search tree-based index structure to organize boundary features.

A few approaches cannot be easily characterized as either global or local. These include local differential invariants [91] and semidifferential invariants [61,92,93].

Shyu and coworkers [94] discuss and compare the utility of local and global features in the context of a medical application [15].

Wang and coworkers [95] note the limited discrimination capability of global features, on the one hand, and the noise sensitivity of local features, on the other. They propose combining both and use two global features (shape elongation and compactness) as a filter to eliminate the most dissimilar images to the query template and then use local features to refine the search. Recall that *elongation* of a shape is the ratio of the eigenvalues of the covariance matrix of the contour points coordinates and compactness is the ratio of perimeter squared to area. Both measures are invariant under Euclidean (i.e., rotation plus translation) and scaling transformations. Wang and coworkers define a set of local features, referred to as *interest points*, which are a small subset of the contour points derived by a pairwise growing algorithm. First, a pair of contour points with maximal distance from each other are selected. Then a second pair farthest from the line connecting the first pair is chosen. The latter part of this process is repeated for each adjacent pair of points until a sufficient number of interest points have been obtained. Finally, the coordinates of the interest points are converted through a normalized affine-invariant transformation [96].

13.4.3 Composition of Parts Versus Deformation

Shape can also be viewed either as the composition of simpler, elementary parts, or as the deformation of simpler shapes.

In the "part-based view," shapes are composed of simple components; for example, a tennis racket is easily described as an elliptical head attached to a rectangular handle, and a hand is seen as four fingers and one thumb attached to a palm. *Superquadrics* [53] represent a rich space of shape primitives from which to choose [97].

The partitioning can be based on either global fit or local evidence. An example of global fit is the minimum description length (MDL) approach. Here, a shape is represented as a combination of primitives selected from a collection; for each combination, two quantities are computed: the fitting error, and the encoding cost. The encoding cost (expressed in "bits") is called *description length*, and measures the complexity of describing the combination. The overall energy is defined as an increasing function of both, fit error, and description length (e.g., a weighted average). Shape representation with the lowest energy is selected. Representations with few simple parts have short-description length but can also have a poor fit; complex representations better approximate the shape but have long-description length. The method therefore selects one that optimizes a linear combination of fit and description length [98].

Shape can also be decomposed into parts based on "local" evidence. Properties of the boundary belong to this category. For example, the boundary can be decomposed into codons along negative minima of its curvature [51,99–101] or by taking into account regional properties, such as good continuation of tangents [102]. The latter approach has been shown to produce parts that are perceptually meaningful [103].

The "part-based" methodology is not universally applicable. Biological shapes, such as the corpus collosum boundary in the brain, leaves, animal limbs, and so on, are often best described as the deformation of a simpler shape. This *morph-based* view has given rise to deformable templates [55,104–106], modal representation [69], and so on.

Deformable templates are representations in which shape variability is captured by allowable transformations of a template. Generally, two forms of deformable shape models have been proposed, which differ, based on whether the model itself or the deformation of the model is parameterized.

Parameterized (geometric) models use an underlying representation that has a few variable parameters. For example, Yuille and coworkers [73] use conic curve segments as templates for the eyes and the mouth in face recognition. The parameters of the conic allow for shape variations. As another example, Staib and Duncan [107] use elliptical Fourier descriptors to represent boundary templates. Superquadrics provide yet another example of parameterized shape models [97].

Parametric-deformation approaches represent the object by fitting it to a fixed template, using a set of allowable parametric deformations. For example, Jain and coworkers [108] represent the template shape via a bitmap and impose a probability distribution (a Bayesian prior) on the admissible mappings. Matching then reduces to selecting the transformation that minimizes a Bayesian objective function.

This class of methods also contains approaches based on skeletons [21], deformable templates [47,48,108], the methods by Grenander and coworkers [109–115], Yuille and coworkers [73], Staib and Duncan [107], and Cootes and Taylor [116].

13.4.4 Scale: Coarse to Fine

Shape can be represented along a *range of scales* spanning *coarse* to *fine*. At a coarse level, that is, viewed from a distance, a tree may be described as a blobby top attached to an elongated bottom at coarse level. However, as one approaches the tree, large branches become visible, then smaller branches play a role, followed by leaves, and so on. Similarly, the view of a hand at a coarse level may be that of a "mitten," whereas by decreasing the scale (increasing the level of detail) fingers first become visible, then the various joints, followed by the nails, and so on [117]. If shape is to be used as an invariant indicator of the object in the scene in which the viewing distance is variable, a multiscale structure is necessary to relate various views, thereby making the representation invariant with respect to the viewing distance.

Whereas earlier methods, such as the pyramid approaches [118], equated scale with resolution, it has now become clear that coarse-level descriptions must be built structurally.

The first type of scale-spaces description of shape was based on linear operators, such as *Gaussian scale space* [119–121]. Mokhtarian and coworkers [52,122,123] represent shape by two vectors corresponding to boundary coordinates (x and y). Each vector is smoothed by Gaussian smoothing and the shape is reconstructed from the smoothed boundary coordinate vectors. "Curve shortening flow" is a geometric smoothing method in which each point of a curve moves along its normal proportional to the signed curvature [39,75]. This formally leads to smoother curves without producing self-intersections or singularities in the process [124].

As an alternative to these boundary-based scale-space representations of shape, the mathematical morphology framework considers shape as a set of (interior) points that are simplified by "closing"and "opening" operations. Kimia and coworkers [125] described a geometric curve-based view of mathematical morphology operations based on which a combined view, the entropy scale-space [126,127], emerged. In this approach, a shape is modified by a combination of curvature-based flow (diffusion) and a pair of forward and backward flows (reaction). This combines the morphological and Gaussian scale spaces approaches to representing shapes across different scales. Other schemes smooth shapes by pruning the medial axis representation of a shape [128–130]. For a comprehensive review of nonlinear scale spaces, see Ref. [131].

Although at first glance the local and global distinction may seem identical to the coarse and fine distinction, these two axes are quite different: on the one hand, coarse-scale distinctive shape characteristics can be highly localized, for example, as in the corners of a rectangle with a rather noisy boundary; on the other hand, fine-scale distinctive properties need not be local, for example, Fourier coefficients at the first level of description.

13.4.5 Partial or Complete

Shape representations can be partial or complete. Complete representation of shape retains all the information necessary to reconstruct the shape. Partial representation of shape retains only those features that are most useful for distinguishing a pair of shapes in a database of interest and ignores other features. For example, in a database consisting of images of rectangular resistors and circular capacitors, low-order moments are sufficient to classify the object of interest. For some examples of these *feature-based* approaches, see Refs. [6,30,85]. The use of invariants [21,132,133], semi-differential invariants [60,61,92,130,134], and affine invariance [11,135] are other examples.

Experience has shown that, except under controlled conditions, shapes undergo unexpected transformations that unpredictably effect shape descriptors, because of occlusion, highlights, shadows, and other visual effects. For example, an occluded elongated rectangle may be similar to a circular blob in a moment-based description of shape. The range of variation in shapes because of visual transformations argues in favor of representations that are as complete as possible. Ideally, a shape, or at least its qualitative aspects, must be reconstructible from the representation.

13.4.6 Coverage and Denseness

The completeness of a representation can be measured not only in terms of its ability to perfectly reproduce shapes, but also in terms of coverage and density. *Coverage* is the extent to which a representation describes arbitrary shapes, that is, it is a measure of the size of the class of shapes perfectly captured by the representation. For example, a representation that only generates convex shapes has a small coverage.

A *dense* representation closely approximates every shape to any desired accuracy. The space of polygons with ten vertices, for example, covers a wide range of shapes, but it cannot approximate complex shapes in an arbitrarily close fashion (although it might be sufficient for many applications).

Denseness and coverage are distinct concepts: a representation may be dense for representing convex shapes, but its coverage is limited. On the other hand, ten-vertex polygons cover a broad range of shapes, but do not represent a dense sampling of the shape space. Questions of coverage and denseness are application related and must be addressed based on the variability of shapes in the database.

13.4.7 Isolated Shape and Shape Arrangements

A shape representation can focus on individual objects independently, or it can also include their spatial arrangement. For example, a polygonal model can represent a single biological cell examined under a microscope. However, as the cell splits, the representation can no longer effectively represent both cells! The polygonal representation needs to be enhanced in order to incorporate topological changes (splits and merges), for example, by allowing for multiple polygons to represent the split cells, which requires that such events be explicitly detected. This approach, however, ignores the issue of representing the relative spatial arrangement of split cells. Because the notion that arrangement of shapes is a key component of shape representation is not yet widely accepted, few representations are capable of capturing this notion, although there is some activity in this direction [64,65,136–143].

13.5 MATCHING, SHAPE SIMILARITY, AND VALIDATION

The type of shape representation used in an indexing scheme has significant implications for the matching process, and vice-versa. A poor representation, namely, one in which relevant variations in shape do not translate to variations in the representation, relegates much of the effort of accounting for variation to the matching process, whereas a rich representation allows for robust comparison with relatively less effort. Ideally, the representation should map each shape to a vector of numbers in such a way that the Euclidean distance between pairs of vectors indicates shape dissimilarity. Unfortunately, shape comparison is inherently complex and current representations do not allow for such a mapping. Thus, the role of the matching process is to define such a metric.

Boundary-based and region-based representations inherently lead to different matching procedures. Boundary-based techniques are typically accompanied by curve-based comparisons. In these approaches two curves are compared based on their properties, such as curvature, resulting in a single similarity measure. For example, Cohen and coworkers [144] and Younes [145] match high-curvature points while maintaining a smooth displacement field elsewhere. Gdalyahu and coworkers [146] use line primitives to describe the curve and use the length and absolute orientation of the primitives to measure curve similarity. Sebastian and coworkers [147,148] have proposed a recent approach to measuring curve similarity based on an initial alignment.

Alternatively, region-based representations typically involve trees and have relied on such methods as graph-tree matching [149], string edit distance [6], graduated assignment [79,150,151], tree edit distance [78], eigenvalue decomposition [80], Bayesian matching [137,152,153], containment tree matching [11], and so on. Other region-based techniques, such as modal matching and deformable prototypes [68,69,154], allow for a global to local ordering of shape deformations.

Geometric hashing is an example of a powerful feature-based matching technique [21,132,155–162]. A drawback of geometric hashing is that it requires large memory to store shape indices, thus is not well suited for very large databases. Other matching techniques rely on an explicit measurement of shape similarity [1,40,64,163–167].

Much more can be said about the various matching methods, but we simply note that they share the need to adapt the matching process to the constraints of the shape representation. Finally, although we have not discussed issues of performance, presentation, and evaluation of results and validation for comparing the representation and the matching process, these also play a significant role in the choice of shape representations [139,154,168–170] but are beyond the scope of this chapter.

ACKNOWLEDGMENT

The support of NSF grant IIS-0083231 is gratefully acknowledged.

REFERENCES

1. V.N. Gudivada and V.V. Raghavan, Content-based image retrieval systems, *IEEE Comput.* **28**, 18–22 (1995).
2. R. Mehrotra and J.E. Gary, Similar shape retrieval in shape data management, *Comput.* **28**(9), 57–62 (1995).
3. V.E. Ogle and M. Stonebraker, Chabot: retrieval from a relational database of images, *Comput.* **28**(9), 40–48 (1995).
4. M. Flicknet et al., Query by image and video contact: the QBIC system, *Computer* **28**(9), 23–31 (1995).
5. A.D. Narasimhalu, M.S. Kankanhali, and J. Wu, Benchmarking multimedia databases, *Multimedia Tools Appl.* **3**(4), 333–355 (1997).
6. W.I. Groski and R. Mehrota, Index-based object recognition in pictorial data management, *Comput. Vis. Graphics, Image Process.* **52**, 416–436 (1990).
7. A. Ralescu and R. Jain, Special issue on advances in visual information management systems, *J. Intell. Inf. Syst.* **3** (1994).
8. J.P. Eakins, Retrieval of trade-mark images by shape feature, *Proceedings of First International Conference on Electronic Library and Visual Information Research*, DeMontfort University, Milton Keynes, May 3–5 1994.
9. J.P. Eakins, K. Shields, and J. Boardman, ARTISAN — a shape retrieval system based on boundary family indexing, *Proc. SPIE* **2670**, 17–28 (1996).
10. K. Shields, J.P. Eakins, and J.M. Boardman, Automatic image retrieval using shape features, *New Rev. Doc. Text Manage.* **1**, 183–198 (1995).
11. M. Kliot and E. Rivlin, Shape retrieval in pictorial databases via geometric features, Technical Report CIS9701, Technion, Israel, 1997.
12. G. Cortelazzo et al., Trademark shapes description by string-matching techniques, *Pattern Recog.* **27**(8), 1005–1018 (1994).
13. J. Wu et al., STAR-A multimedia database system for trademark registration, *Proceedings of First International Conference*, ADB, **819**, 109–122 (1994).
14. C. Lam, J. Wu, and B. Methre, STAR-A system for trademark archival and retrieval, *Second Asian Conference on Computer Vision*, Singapore, pages III–214–III–217, December 1995.
15. C.-R. Shyu, A. Kak, C. Brodley, and L. Broderick, Testing for perpetual categories in a physician-in-a-loop CBIR system for medical imaging, *IEEE Workshop on Content-Based Access of Image and Video Libraries*, Fort Collins, Colorado, June 22, 1999 pp. 102–108.

16. W. Zhang et al., A shape-based indexing in a medical image database, *IEEE Workshop on Biomedical Image Analysis*, Santa Barbara, Calif., June 1998, pp. 221–230.
17. F. Korn et al., Fast and effective retrieval of medical tumor shapes, *IEEE Trans. Knowledge Data Eng.* **10**(6), 889–904 (1998).
18. D. Cheung, C.-H. Lee, and V. Ng, A content-based search engine on medical images for telemedicine, CBAIVL1998 Santa Barbara, Calif., June 21, 1998.
19. G. Bucci, S. Cagnoni, and R.D. Dominicis, Integrating content-based retrieval in a medical image reference database, *Comput. Med. Imaging Graphics* **20**(4) 231–241 (1996).
20. S.D. Cohen and L.J. Guibas, Shape-based illustration indexing and retrieval: some first steps, *Proceedings of the ARPA Image Understanding Workshop*, New Orleans, La.,February 1996, pp. 1209–1212.
21. S.D. Cohen and L.J. Guibas, Shape-based image retrieval using geometric hashing, *ARPA Image Understanding Workshop*, New Orleans, La., May 1997, pp. 669–674.
22. N.K. Ratha, K. Karu, S. Chen, and A.K. Jain, A real-time matching system for large fingerprint databases, *IEEE Trans. Pattern Analysis and Machine Intell.* **18**(8), 799–813 (1996).
23. R. Samadari, C. Han, and L.K. Katragadda, Content-based even selection from satellite images from the aurora, *Proc. SPIE Conf. on Storage and Retrieval for Image Video Databases*, **1908**, 50–59 (April 1993).
24. B. Holt and L. Hartwick, Visual image retrieval for applications in art and art history, *Proc. SPIE Storage and Retrieval for Image and Video Databases* **2185**, 70–81 (1994).
25. B. Gunsel and A.M. Tekalp, Shape similarity matching for query by example, *PR* **31**(7), 931–944 (1998).
26. M. Swain and D. Ballard, Color indexing, *Int. J. Comput. Vis.* **7**(1), 11–32 (1991).
27. J. Canny, A computational approach to edge detection, *IEEE Trans. Pattern Anal. and Machine Intell.* **8**, 679–698 (1986).
28. A. Blake and A. Zisserman, *Visual Reconstruction*, MIT Press, Cambridge, Mass. 1987.
29. L. Liu and S. Sclaroff, Deformable shape detection and description via model-based region grouping, *CVPR1999 IEEE Computer Society Conference on Computer Vision and Pattern Recognition*, IEEE Computer Society Press, Fort Collins, colo., 1999, pp. II:21–27.
30. K. Hirata and T. Kato, Query by visual example — content based image retrieval, *Adv. Database Technol.* **580**, 56–71 (March 1992).
31. T. Kato, T. Kurita, N. Otsu, and K. Hirata, A sketch retrieval method for full color image databases, *International Conference on Pattern Recognition*, Computer Society Press, The Hague, Netherlands, August 30–September 3, 1992, pp. 530–533.
32. R.S. Gray, Content-based image retrieval: Color and edges, *Proceedings of the Dartmouth Institute for Advanced Graduate Studies: Electronic Publishing and information Superhighway*, 1995, pp. 77–90.
33. A. DelBimbo, P. Pala, and S. Santini, Image retrieval by elastic matching of shapes and image patterns, *Proceedings of IEEE Conference on Multimedia Computing and Systems*, Hiroshima, Japan, 1996.

34. Z. Lei, Y. Chan, and D. Lopresti, Curvelet feature extraction and matching for content-based image retrieval, *1997 IEEE International Conference on Image Processing*, Santa Barbara, Calif., October 1997.
35. Z. Lei and D. Cooper, Interactive shape modeling, *First IEEE Workshop on Multimedia Signal Processing*, Princeton, N.J., June 1997.
36. M.P. do Carmo, *Differential Geometry of Curves and Surfaces*, Prentice-Hall, New Jersey, 1976.
37. J. Serra, ed. *Image Analysis and Mathematical Morphology*, Academic Press, New York, 1982.
38. I. Dryden and K. Mardia, *Statistical Analysis of Shape*, Wiley and Sons, New York, 1998.
39. B.B. Kimia, A.R. Tannenbaum, and S.W. Zucker, Shapes, shocks, and deformations, I: The components of shape and the reaction-diffusion space *IJCV* **15**, 189–224 (1995).
40. D. Mumford, Mathematical theories of shape: Do they model perception? *SPIE* **1570**, 2–10 (1991).
41. H. Freeman, Computer processing of line drawing images, *Comput. Surveys*, **6**(1), 57–98 (1974).
42. U. Ramer, An iterative procedure for the polygonal approximation of plane curves, *Comput. Vis. Graphics Image Process.* **1**(3), 244–256 (1972).
43. S.D. Cohen and L.J. Guibas, Partial matching of planar polylines under similarity transformation, *Proceedings of the Eighth Annual ACM-SIAM Symposium on Discrete Algorithms*, New Orleans, January 1997, pp. 777–786.
44. D. Eu and G. Toussaint, An approximating polygonal curves in two and three dimensions, *GMIP* **56**, 231–246 (1994).
45. W. Chan and F. Chin, Approximation of polygonal curves with minimum number of line segments or minimum errors, *Int. J. Comput. Geometry Appl.* **6**(1), 59–77 (1996).
46. H. Imai and M. Iri, Polygonal approximations of a curve-formulations and algorithms, G.T. Toussaint, in ed., *Computational Morphology: A computational geometric approach to the analysis of form*, Elsevier Science, New York, 1988, pp. 71–86.
47. A. DelBimbo, P. Pala, and S. Santini, Visual image retrieval by elastic deformation of shapes, *Proceedings of IEEE VL'94, International Symposium on Visual Languages*, New York, 1994.
48. A. DelBimbo and P. Pala, Visual image retrieval by elastic matching of user sketches, *IEEE Trans. Pattern Anal. Machine Intell.* **19**(2), 121–132 (1997).
49. F.S. Cohen, Z. Huang, and Z. Yang, Invariant matching and identification of curves using B-splines curve representation, *IEEE Trans. Image Process.* **1**(4), 1–17 (1995).
50. D. Keren, D.B. Cooper, and J. Subrahmonia, Describing Complicated Objects by Implicit Polynomials, *IEEE Trans. Pattern Anal. Machine Intell.* **16**, 38–54 (1994).
51. W. Richards and D. D. Hoffman, Codon constraints on closed 2d shapes, *Comput. Vis. Graphics Image Process.* **31**(2), 265–281 (1985).
52. F. Mokhtarian and A. Mackworth, Scale-based description of planar curves and two-dimensional shapes, *PAMI* **8**, 34–43 (1986).
53. A. Barr, Superquadrics and angle-preserving transformations, *IEEE CGA* **1**(1), 11–23 (1981).

54. D. Terzopoulos and D. Metaxas, Dynamic 3D models with local and global deformations: Deformable superquadrics, *IEEE Trans. Pattern Anal. Machine Intell.* **13**(7), 703–714 (1991).
55. D. DeCarlo, D. Metaxas, Shape evolution with structural and topological changes using blending, *IEEE Trans. Pattern Anal. Machine Intell.* **20**(11), 1186–1205, (1998).
56. G.E. Christensen, R.D. Rabbitt, and M.I. Miller, Deformable templates using large deformation kinematics, *IEEE Trans. Image Process.* **10**, 1435–1447 (1996).
57. R. Mehrotra, F. Kung, and W. Grosky, Industrial part recognition using a component index, *Image Vis. Comput.* **3**, 225–231 (1990).
58. M. Kass, A. Witkin, and D. Terzopoulos, Snakes: Active contour models, *Int. J. Comput. Vis.* **1**, 321–331 (1988).
59. A. DelBimbo and P. Pala, Visual image retrieval by elastic matching of user sketches, *IEEE Trans. Pattern Anal. Machine Intell.* **19**(2), 121–132 (1997).
60. A. Bruckstein, J. Holt, A. Netravali, and T. Richardson, Invariant signatures for planar shape recognition under partial occlusion, *Comput. Vis. Image Understanding* **58**, 49–65 (1993).
61. T. Moons, E. Pawels, L.V. Gool, and A. Oosterlinck, Recognition of planar shapes under affine distortion, *Int. J. Comput. Vis.* **14**, 49–65 (1995).
62. E. Saber and A.M. Tikalp, Region-based affine shape matching for automatic image annotation and query by example, *JVCIR* **8**(1), 3–20 (1997).
63. A.K. Jain and A. Vailaya, Image retrieval using color and shape, *Pattern Recog.* **29**(8), 1233–1244 (1996).
64. S.K. Chang, Q.Y. Shi, and C.W. Yan, Iconic indexing by 2D strings, *IEEE Trans. Pattern Anal. Machine Intell.* **9**(3), 413–428 (1987).
65. S. Lee and F. Hsu, Spatial reasoning and similarity retrieval of images using 2D C-string knowledge representation, *Pattern Recog.* **25**(3), 305–318 (1992).
66. P. Huang, Indexing pictures by key objects for large-scale image databases, *Pattern Recog.* **30**(7), 1229–1237 (1997).
67. H. Jagadish, A retrieval technique for similar shapes, *ACM SIGMOD Conference: Management of data*, pp. 208–217, Denver, Colo., May 1991.
68. A. Pentland and S. Sclaroff, Closed-form solutions for physically based shape modeling and recognition, *IEEE Trans. Pattern Analysis and Machine Intell.* **13**(7), 715–729 (1991).
69. S. Sclaroff and A. Pentland, Modal matching for correspondence and recognition, *IEEE Trans. Pattern Anal. Machine Intell.* **17**(6), 545–561 (1995).
70. L.S. Shapiro and J.M. Brady, Feature-based correspondence: an eigenvector approach, *Image Vis. Comput.* **10**(5), 283–288 (1992).
71. G. Lu and A. Sajjanhar, Region-based shape representation and similarity measure suitable for content-based image retrieval, *Multimedia Syst.* **7**(2), 165–174 (1999).
72. H. Blum, Biological shape and visual science, *J. Theor. Biol.* **38**, 205–287 (1973).
73. S.C. Zhu and A.L. Yuille, FORMS: A flexible object recognition and modeling system, *Int. J. Comput. Vis.* **20**(3), 187–212 (1996).
74. T. Liu and D. Geiger, Approximate tree matching and shape similarity, in *ICCV1999 ICCV'99 Seventh International Conference on Computer Vision*, IEEE Computer Society Press, Kerkyra, Greece, September 20–25, 1999, pp. 456–462.

75. B.B. Kimia, Conservation laws and a theory of shape, Ph.D. dissertation, McGill Center for Intelligent Machines, McGill University, Montreal, Canada 1990.
76. H. Tek and B.B. Kimia. Symmetry maps of free-form curve segments via wave propagation, in ICCV1999 *Seventh International Conference on Computer Vision*, IEEE Computer Society Press, Kerkyra, Greece, September 20–25, 1999 pp. 362–369.
77. H. Tek and B.B. Kimia, Symmetry map and symmetry transforms, CVPR1999 *IEEE Computer Society Conference on Computer Vision and Pattern Recognition*, IEEE Computer Society Press, Fort Collins, colo. June 23–25, 1999 pp. 471–477.
78. S. Tirthapura, D. Sharvit, P. Klein, and B.B. Kimia, Indexing based on edit-distance matching of shape graphs, *SPIE International Symposium on Voice, Video, and Data Communications*, Boston, Mass., November 1998, pp. 25–36.
79. D. Sharvit, J. Chan, H. Tek, and B. B. Kimia, Symmetry-based indexing of image databases, *J. Vis. Commun. Image Representation* **9**(4), 366–380 (1998).
80. K. Siddiqi, A. Shokoufandeh, S. Dickinson, and S. Zucker, Shock graphs and shape matching, *ICCV1998 Sixth International Conference on Computer Vision*, IEEE Computer Society Press, Bombay, India 1998, pp. 222–229.
81. K. Siddiqi, A. Shokoufandeh, S. Dickinson, and S. Zucker, Shock graphs and shape matching, *Int. J. Comput. Vis.* **35**(1), 13–32 (1999).
82. M. Pelillo, K. Siddiqi, and S. Zucker, Matching hierarchical structures using association graphs. *PAMI* **21**(11), 1105–1120 (1999).
83. P. Klein, S. Tirthapura, D. Sharvit, and B. Kimia, A tree-edit distance algorithm for comparing simple, closed shapes, Tenth Annual ACM-SIAM Symposium on Discrete Algorithms (SODA), San Francisco, California, January 9–11 2000, pp. 696–704.
84. P. Klein, T. Sebastian, and B. Kimia, Shape matching using edit-distance: an implementation, Twelfth Annual ACM-SIAM Symposium on Discrete Algorithms (SODA), Washington, D.C., January 7–9 2001, pp. 781–790.
85. W. Niblack et al., The QBIC project: Querying images by content using color texture and shape, in *Proc. SPIE, Storage and Retrieval for Image and Video Databases* **1908**, 173–187 (1993).
86. Y. Rui, A. She, and T. Huang, Modified Fourier descriptors for shape representation, *First International Workshop on Image Databases and Multimedia Search*, Amsterdam, The Netherlands, August 1996.
87. H.S. Stone, Content-based image retrieval — research issues, *Multimedia Technol. Appl.* 282–322 (1998).
88. Y. Mallet, D. Coomans, J. Kautsky, and O. DeVel, Classification using adaptive wavelets for feature-extraction, *PAMI* **19**(10), 1058–1066 (1997).
89. C.E. Jacobs, A. Finkelstein, and D.H. Salesin, *Fast multiresolution image querying*, SIGGRAPH, August 1995, pp. 277–286.
90. J. Bigun, S. Bhattacharjee, and S. Michel. Orientation radiograms for image retrieval: An alternative to segmentation, *Proceedings of 13th International Conference on Pattern Recognition*, Vienna, Austria, August 1996.
91. E. Rivlin and I. Weiss, Local invariants for recognition, *IEEE Trans. Pattern Anal. Machine Intell.* **17**(3), 226–238 (1995).
92. T. Moons, E. Pawels, L. V. Gool, and A. Oosterlinck, Foundations of semi-differential invariants, *Int. J. Comput. Vis.* **14**, 25–47 (1995).

93. I. Weiss, *Geometric invariants and object recognition* Center for automation research, University of Maryland, U.S. 1992.
94. C.R. Shyu et al., Local vs global features for content-based image retrieval, CBAIVL1998 Santa Barbara, Calif., June 21, 1998.
95. J. Wang, W.-J. Yang, and R. Acharya, Efficient access to and retrieval from shape image database, CBAIVL1998 Santa Barbare, Calif., June 21, 1998 pp. 63–67.
96. J. Wang and R. Acharya, A vertex-based shape encoding approach for similar shape retrieval, *ACM Symposium on Applied Computing*, Atlanta, Georgia, February 1998, pp. 520–524.
97. A. Pentland, Automatic extraction of deformable part models, *Int. J. Comput. Vis.* **4**(2), 107–126 (1990).
98. Y.G. Leclerc, Constructing simple stable descriptions for image partitioning, *Int. J. Comput. Vis.* **3**, 73–102 (1989).
99. A. Pentland, Part segmentation for object recognition, *Neural Comput.* **1**, 82–91 (1989).
100. M. Fischler and R. Bolles, Perceptual organization and curve partitioning, *IEEE Trans. Pattern Anal. Machine Intell.* **8**, 100–105 (1986).
101. M. Fischler and H.C. Wolf, Locating perceptually salient points on planar curves, *IEEE Trans. Pattern Anal. Machine Intell.* **16**, 113–129 (1994).
102. K. Siddiqi and B.B. Kimia, Parts of visual form: Computational aspects, *IEEE Trans. Pattern Anal. Machine Intell.* **17**(3), 239–251 (1995).
103. K. Siddiqi, K.J. Tresness, and B.B. Kimia, Parts of visual form: Ecological and psychophysical aspects, *Perception* **25**, 399–424 (1996).
104. T. Cootes and C. Taylor, *Active shape models — "smart snakes", Proceedings of British Machine Vision Conference*, Leeds, U.K., September 1992, pp. 266–275.
105. T. Cootes, C. Taylor, D. Cooper, and J. Graham. *Training models of shape from sets of examples*, *Proceedings of British Machine Vision Conference*, 1992, pp. 9–18.
106. T. Cootes, A. Hill, C. Taylor, and J. Haslam, The use of active shape models for locating structures in medical images, *Image Vis. Comput.* **12**(6) 355–365 (July–August 1994).
107. L. Staib and J. Duncan, Boundary finding with parametrically deformable models, *PAMI* **14**(11), 1061–1075 (November 1992).
108. A. Jain, Y. Zhong, and S. Lakshmanan, Object matching using deformable templates, *IEEE Trans. Pattern Anal. Machine Intell.* **18**(3), 267–278 (1996).
109. U. Grenander and D. Keenan, Towards automated image understanding in K.V. Mardia and G.K. Kanji, eds., *Advances in Applied Statistics: Statistics and Images*, **1**, Carfax Publishing, 1993, pp. 89–103.
110. U. Grenander and M. Miller, Representations of knowledge in complex systems, *J. Royal Statistical Society* **56**(4), 569–603 (1994).
111. U. Grenander and M. Miller, Computational anatomy: An emerging discipline, *Quarterly of Applied Mathematics* **LVI**(4), 617–694, (1998).
112. Y. Amit, V. Grenander, and M. Piccioni, Structural image restoration through deformable templates, *J. Am. Statistical Association* **86**(414), 376–387 (1991).
113. Y. Chow, U. Grenander, and D. Keenan, *HANDS: A pattern-theoretic study of biological shapes*, Springer Verlag, New York, 1991.

114. M.I. Miller, Y. Amit, G.E. Christensen, and U. Grenander, Mathematical textbook of deformable neuroanatomies, *Proc. National Acad. Sci.* **90**(24), 11944–11948 (1993).
115. S.C. Joshi et al., Hierarchial brain mapping via a generalized Dirichlet solution for mapping brain manifolds, *Proceedings of SPIE's 1995 International Symposium on Optical Science, Engineering and Instrumentation*, August 1995, pp. 278–289.
116. T. Cootes, C. Taylor, and A. Laritis, *Active shape models: Evaluation of a multiresolution method for improving image search, Proc. British Machine Vis. Conf.* **1**, 327–336 (1994).
117. D. Marr, *Vision*, W.H. Freeman, San Fransisco (1982).
118. P. Burt and E. Adelson, The laplacian pyramid as a compact image code, *T-COMM* **31**(4), 532–540 (1983).
119. A.P. Witkin, Scale-space filtering, *Proceedings of the 8th International Joint Conference on Artificial Intelligence*, Karlsruhe, West Germany, August 1983, pp. 1019–1022.
120. J.J. Koenderink, Scale-time, *Biol. Cybern.* **58**, 159–162 (1988).
121. J.J. Koenderink, The structure of images, *Biol. Cybern.* **50**, 363–370 (1984).
122. F. Mokhtarian and A. Mackworth, Convergence properties of curvature and torsion scale space representations, Technical Report 90–14, The University of British Columbia, Department of Computer Science, May 1990.
123. F. Mokhtarian and A. Mackworth, A theory of multiscale, curvature-based shape representation for planar curves, *PAMI* **14**(8), 789–805 (1992).
124. S.J. Altschuler and M.A. Grayson, Shortening space curves and flow through singularities, *J. Diff. Geometry* **35**, 283–298 (1992).
125. A. Arehart, L. Vincent, and B.B. Kimia, Mathematical morphology: The Hamilton-Jacobi connection, *Proceedings of the Fourth International Conference on Computer Vision (Berlin, Germany, May 11–13, 1993)*, IEEE Computer Society Press, Washington, D.C. 1993, pp. 215–219.
126. B.B. Kimia, A.R. Tannenbaum, and S.W. Zucker, *Entropy scale-space, Proceedings of the International Workshop on Visual Form*, Plenum Press, Capri, Italy, May 1991.
127. K. Siddiqi and B.B. Kimia, A shock grammar for recognition, *Proceedings of the Conference on Computer Vision and Pattern Recognition*, New York, 1996, pp. 507–513.
128. H. Tek and B.B. Kimia, Boundary smoothing via symmetry transforms, *Journal of Mathematical Imaging and Vision* **14**(3), 211–223 (2001).
129. R.L. Ogniewicz. *Discrete Voronoi Skeletons*. Hartung-Gorre Kontanz, Germany, 1993.
130. D. Shaked and A. Bruckstein, On symmetry axes and boundary curves, *Proceedings of the International Workshop on Visual Form*, pp. 497–506, May 1994.
131. B.M. ter Haar Romeny, ed., *Geometry-Driven Diffusion in Computer Vision*, Kluwer, Dordrecht, The Netherlands, September (1994).
132. Y. Lamdan and H. Wolfson, Geometric hashing: a general and efficient model-based recognition scheme, *Second International Conference on Computer Vision* (Tampa,, FL, December 5–8, 1988), IEEE Computer Society Press, Washington, D.C. 1988, pp. 238–249.
133. T.K. Leung, M.C. Burl, and P. Perona, Probabilistic affine invariants for recognition, *Proceedings of the IEEE Computer Society Conference on Computer Vision*

and Pattern Recognition, IEEE Computer Society Press, Santa Barbara, Calif. June 23–25 1998, pp. 678–684.

134. L. VanGool, P. Kempenaers, and A. Oosterlinck, Recognition and semi-differential invariants, CVPR1991 *IEEE Computer Society Conference on Computer Vision and Patten Recognition*, IEEE Computer Society Press, Maui, Hawaii June 1991, pp. 55–60.
135. D. Shen, W.-H. Wang, and H.H. Ip, Affine-invariant image retrieval by correspondence matching of shapes, *IVC17* **17**, 489–499 (1999).
136. N. Thacker, P. Ricreux, and R. Yates, Assessing the completeness properties of pair wise geometric histories, *IVC* **13**, 423–429 (1994).
137. B. Huet and E.R. Hancock, Retrieval of histographs for shape indexing, ICCV1998 *Sixth International Conference on Computer Vision*, IEEE Computer Society Press, Bombay, India, 1998, pp. 563–569.
138. M.S. Costa and L. Shapiro, Scene analysis using appearance based models and relational indexing, *ISCV95 IEEE international Symposium on Computer Vision, Coral Gables, Fla.*, November 20–22 1995.
139. K. Sengupta and K. Boyer, Organizing large structural databases, *IEEE Trans. Pattern Analysis and Machine Intell.* **17**(4), 321–332 (1995).
140. H.D. Tagare, F. Vos, C. C. Jaffe, and J.S. Duncan, Arrangement: A qualitative spatial relation between parts, *IEEE Trans. Pattern Anal. Machine Intell.* **17**(9), 880–893 (1995).
141. S.F. Chang and J.R. Smith, Extracting multi-dimensional signal features for content-based visual query, *Proc. SPIE Symposium on Visual Communications and Signal Processing*, **2501**, 995–1006 (May 1995).
142. T. Hou, A. Hsu, P. Liu, and M. Chiu, A content-based indexing technique using relative geometry features, *Proc. SPIE Image Storage Retrieval Syst.*, (1992) 59–68.
143. T. Hou, P. Liu, A. Hsu, and M. Chiu, Medical image retrieval by spatial features, *Proc. IEEE Int. Conf. Syst. Man, and Cybernetics*, pp. 1364–1369 1992.
144. I. Cohen, N. Ayache, and P. Sulger, *Tracking points on deformable objects using curvature information, Proceedings of the European Conference on Computer Vision*, Santa Margherita, Ligure, Italy 1992, pp. 458–466.
145. L. Younes, Computable elastic distance between shapes, *SIAM J. Appl. Math.* **58**, 565–586 (1996).
146. Y. Gdalyahu and D. Weinshall, Flexible syntactic matching of curves and its application to automatic hierarchical classification of silhouettes, *IEEE Trans. Pattern Anal. Machine Intell.* **21**(12), 1312–1328 (1999).
147. T.B. Sebastian, J.J. Crisco, P.N. Klein, and B.B. Kimia, Constructing 2D curve atlases, *Proceedings of Mathematical Methods in Biomedical Image Analysis*, pp. 70–77 Hilton Head, S.C., June 2000.
148. T.B. Sebastian, P.N. Klein, and B.B. Kimia, Alignment-based recognition of shape outlines, *IWVF*, Springer-Verlag, Capri, Italy, May 2001, pp. 606–618.
149. A. Kitamoto, C. Zhou, and M. Takagi, Similarity retrieval of NOAA satellite imagery by graph matching, *SPIE* **1908**, 60–72 (1993).
150. S. Gold, A. Rangarajan, and E. Mjolsness, Learning with preknowledge:clustering with point and graph matching distance measures, *Neural Comput.* **8**(4), 787–804 (1996).

151. S. Gold and A. Rangarajan, A graduated assignment algorithm for graph matching, *IEEE Trans. Pattern Anal. Machine Intell.* **18**(4), 377–388 (1996).
152. B. Huet and E.R. Hancock, *Inexact graph retrieval*, In CBAIVL1998 Santa Barbara, Calif., June 21, 1998, pp. 40–44.
153. R. Wilson and E.R. Hancock, Structural matching by discrete relaxation, *IEEE Trans. Pattern Anal. Machine Intell.* **19**, 634–648 (1997).
154. S. Sclaroff, Deformable prototypes for encoding shape categories in image databases, *Pattern Recog.* **30**(4), 627–641 (1997).
155. A. Beinglass and H. Wolfson, Articulated object recognition, or, how to generalize the Generalized Hough transform, Institute of Computer Sciences Tel Aviv University, 1990.
156. D. Clemens and D. Jacobs, Model group indexing for recognition, *CVPR91* 4–9 Maui, Hawaii, June 1991.
157. D. Clemens and D. Jacobs, Space and time bounds on indexing 3D models from 2D images. *IEEE Trans. Pattern Anal. Machine Intell.*, **13**(10), 1007–1017 (1991).
158. A. Califano and R. Mohan, Multidimensional indexing for recognizing visual shapes, *IEEE Trans. Pattern Anal. Machine Intell.* **16**(6), 373–392 (1994).
159. F. Stein and G. Medioni, TOSS — a system for efficient three dimensional object recognition, *DARPAIUW* (1989), Pittsburgh, Pa., September 1990.
160. F. Stein and G. Medioni, Structural indexing: Efficient 2D object recognition, *IEEE Trans. Pattern Anal. Machine Intell.* **14**(12), 1198–1204 (1992).
161. F. Stein and G. Medioni, Structural indexing: efficient 3D object recognition, *IEEE Trans. Pattern Anal. Machine Intell.* **14**(2), 125–145 (1992).
162. L. Creive and A.C. Kak, Interactive learning of a multiattributed hash table classifies for fast object recognition, *CVIU* **61**(3), 387–416 (1995).
163. B. Moghaddam, C. Nastar, and A. Pentland, A Bayesian similarity measure for direct image matching, Technical Report 393, M.I.T Media Lab, Boston, Mass., 1996.
164. V. Gudivada and V. Raghavan, Design and evaluation of algorithms for image retrieval by spatial similarity, *ACM Tran. Inf. Syst.* **13**(2), 115–144 (1995).
165. D.A. White and R. Jain, Similarity indexing with the SS-tree, *Proceedings of the Twelfth International Conference on Data Engineering*, New Orleans, LA, pp. 516–523 1996.
166. B. Bhanu, J. Peng, and S. Qirs, *Learning feature relevance and similarity metrics in image databases*, CBAIVL1998, Santa Barbarra, Calif., June 21, 1998, pp. 14–18.
167. S. Santini and R. Jain, Similarity measures, *IEEE Trans. Pattern Anal. Machine Intell.* **9**(21), 871–883 (1999).
168. B. Scassellati, S. Alexopoulos, and M. Flickner, Retrieving images by 2D shape: comparison of computation methods with human perceptual judgments, *Proc. SPIE Conf. on storage and retrieval of image and video databases II*, San Jose, Calif., Vol. 2185, February 1994, pp. 2–14.
169. C.-S. Li, J. Turek, and E. Feig, Progressive template matching for content-based retrieval in Earth observing satellite image database, *Proc. of SPIE, Digital Image Storage and Archiving Systems*, November 1995.
170. L. Prasad and R.L. Rao, Object recognition by multiresolutional template matching, *Proceedings of SPIE, Digital Image Storage and Archiving Systems*, Philadelphia, Pa., October 1995.

171. Virage engine, *http://www.virage.com/*.

172. Application briefs: Computer graphics in the detective business, *Comput. Graphics Appl.* **5**(4), 14–17 (1985).

173. P. Arigrain, H. Zhang, and D. Petrovic, Content based representations and retrieval of visual media: a state-of-the-art review, *Multimedia Tools Appl.* **3**, 124–150 (1988).

174. S. Arya, et al., An optimal algorithm for approximate nearest neighbor searching, *Proceedings of the Fifth Annual ACM-SIAM Symposium on Discrete Algorithms*, Arlington, Va., January 1994, pp. 573–582.

175. F.G. Ashby and N.A. Perrin, Towards a unified theory of similarity and recognition, *Psychol. Rev.* **95**(1), 124–150 (1988).

176. F. Attneave, Dimensions of similarity, *Am. J. Psychol.* **63**, 516–556 (1950).

177. D. Ballard, Generalizing the Hough transform to detect arbitrary shapes, *Pattern Recog.* **13**(2), 111–122 (1981).

178. M. Baroni and G. Barletta, Digital curvature estimation for left ventricular shape analysis, *IVC* **10**(7), 485–494 (1992).

179. R. Basri, L. Costa, D. Geiger, and D. Jacobs, Determining the similarity of deformable shapes, *Vis. Res.* **38**, 2365–2385 (1998).

180. J. Beis, Indexing without invariants in model-based object recognition, PhD thesis, University of British Columbia, June 1997.

181. J. Beis and D. Lowe, Shape indexing using approximate nearest-neighbor search in high-dimensional spaces, *Proceedings of the IEEE Computer Society Conference on Computer Vision and Pattern Recognition*, IEEE Computer Society Press, Puerto Rico, June 15–16, 1997, pp. 1000–1006.

182. S.O. Belkasim, M. Shridhar, and M. Ahmadi, Pattern recognition with moment invariants: a comparative study and new results, *Pattern Recog.* **24**(12), 1117–1138 (1991).

183. J. Blue, et al., Evaluation of pattern classifiers for fingerprint and OCR applications. *Pattern Recog.* **27**(4), 482–501 (1994).

184. S. Brin, Nearest neighbor search in large metric spaces, *Proceedings of VLDB'95 21st International Conference on Very Large Databases*, Zurich, Switzerland, September 1995, pp. 574–584.

185. J.W. Bruce and P.J. Giblin, Growth, motion and 1-parameter families of symmetry sets, *Proceedings of the Royal Society of Edinburgh* **104A**, 179–204 (1986).

186. Y. Chan and S.Y. Kung, A hierarchical algorithms for image retrieval by sketch, *IEEE*, First Workshop Multimedia Signs, Princeton, N.J., June 1997, pp. 565–569.

187. Z. Chen and S. Ho, Computer vision for robust 3D aircraft recognition with fast library search, *Pattern Recog.* **24**(5), 375–390 (1991).

188. C.C. Chu and J.K. Aggarwal, The integration of image segmentation maps using region and edge information, *IEEE Trans. Pattern Anal. Machine Intell.* **15**, 1241–1252 (1993).

189. I. Cohen, N. Ayache, and P. Sulger, Tracking points on deformable objects, Technical Report 1595, INRIA, Rocquencourt, France, 1992.

190. S.D. Cohen and L.J. Guibas, Partial matching of planar polylines under similarity transformations, *Eighth Annual ACM-SIAM Symposium on Discrete Algorithms*, New Orleans, La., 1997, pp. 777–786.

191. T. Cootes, D. Cooper, C. Taylor, and J. Graham, Trainable method of parametric shape description, *IVC* **5**(10), 289–294 (1992).

192. A. DelBimbo and E. Vicario, Using weighted spatial relationships in retrieval by visual contents, *CBAIVL9*, Santa Barbara, Calif., June 1998, pp. 35–39.

193. S. Dickinson, A. Pentland, and A. Rosenfeld, 3D shape recovery using distributed aspect matching, *IEEE Trans. Pattern Anal. Machine Intell.* **14**(2), 174–198 (1992).

194. S. Dickinson, A. Pentland, and A. Rosenfeld, From volumes to views: An approach to object recognition, *CVGIP: Image Understanding* **55**(2), 130–154 (1992).

195. C. Dorai and A.K. Jain, COSMOS — a representation scheme for free-form surfaces, *ICCV95 Fifth International Conference on Computer Vision*, IEE Computer Society Press, Boston, Mass., June 1995.

196. C. Dorai and A.K. Jain, View organization and matching of free-form objects, *ISCV95 IEEE International Symposium on Computer Vision*, Coral Gable, Fla., November 20–22, 1995.

197. J.P. Eakins, Design criteria for a shape retrieval system, *Comput. Ind.* **21**, 167–184 (1993).

198. S. Edelman, Representation of similarity in three-dimensional object discrimination, *Neural Comput.* **7**, 408–423 (1995).

199. D.M. Ennis, J.J. Palen, and K. Mullen, A multidimensional stochastic theory of similarity, *J. Math. Psychol.* **33**, 449–465 (1988).

200. M.A. Eshera and K.S. Fu, A similarity measure between attributed relational graphs for image analysis, *IEEE Trans. Pattern Anal. Machine Intell.* Montreal, Canada, July 1984, pp. 75–77.

201. A. Etemadi, *Robust segmentation of edge data, Proceedings of the IEEE International Conference on Image Processing*, IEEE Computer Society Press, Singapore, September 1992, pp. 311–314.

202. C. Faloutsos, R. Barber, M. Flickner, J. Hafner, W. Niblack, D. Petrkovic, and W. Equitz, Efficient and effective querying by image content, *J. Intell. Inf. Syst.* **3**, 231–262 (1994).

203. D. Forsyth, J. Mundy, A. Zisserman, and C. Brown, *Invariance: A new framework for vision*, ICCV1990, Third International Conferences on Computer Vision, IEEE Computer Society Press, Washington, D.C., 1990. pages 598–605.

204. B. Furht, S.W. Smoliar, and H. Zhang, *Image and video indexing and retrieval techniques*, Kluwer Academic Publishers, Norwell, Mass., 1995.

205. P. Gamba and L. Lombardi, in Shape analysis by means of the boundary integral resonant mode expansion method, C. Arcelli, ed., *Proceedings of the International Workshop on Visual Form*, World Scientific, Capri, Italy, 1997, pp. 227–236.

206. D. Geiger, T.-L. Liu, and R.V. Kohn, *representation and self-similarity of shapes.* In ICCV1998 Sixth International Conference on Computer Vision, IEEE Computer Society Press, Bombay, India, 1998.

207. R.S. Gray, Content based image retrieval: Color and edges, *Proceedings of 1995 Dartmouth Institute for Advanced Graduate Studies: Electroning Publishing and the Information Superhighway*, Hanover, N.H., 1995, pp. 77–90.

208. W.E.L. Grimson, On the recognition of parameterized 2D objects, *IJCV* **2**(4), 353–372 (1989).

209. W.E.L. Grimson, *Object recognition by computer: the role of geometric mass. constraints*, MIT press, Cambridge, Mass., 1990.

210. W.E.L. Grimson and D. Huttenlocher, On the sensitivity of geometric hashing, *ICCV1990 Third International Conference Vision*, IEEE Computer Society Press, Washington, D.C., pages 334–338.

211. B. Gunsel and A.M. Tekalp, Similarity analysis for shape retrieval by example, *International Conference on Pattern Recognition*, Computer Society Press, Vienna, Austria, 1996, pages 330–334.

212. J.F. Haddon and J.F. Boyce, Image segmentation by unifying region and boundary information, *IEEE trans. Pattern Anal. Mach. Intell.* **12**, 929–948 (1990).

213. M. Han and D. Jang, The use of maximum curvature points for the recognition of partially occluded objects, *Pattern Recog.* **23**(1–2), 21–33 (1990).

214. Y. Hara, K. Hirata, H. Takaru, and S. Kawagaki, Hypermedia navigation and content-based retrieval for distributed multimedia databases, *Proceedings of the 6th NEC Research Symposium on Multimedia Computing*, Tokyo, Japan, June 1995.

215. C. Hsu, W. Chu, and R. Taira, A knowledge-based approach for retrieving images by content, *IEEE Trans. Knowledge and Date Eng.* **8**(4), 522–532 (1996).

216. P. Huang and Y. Jean, Using 2D C^{+}-strings as spatial knowledge representation for image database systems, *Pattern Recog.* **27**(9), 1249–1257 (1994).

217. D.P. Huttenlocher, G.A. Klanderman, and W.J. Rucklidge, Comparing images using the Hausdorff distance, *IEEE Trans. Pattern Anal. Machine Intell.* **15**, 850–863 (1993).

218. M. Ireton and C. Xydeas, Classification of shape for content retrieval of images in a multimedia database, *6th Int. Conf. on Digital Processing of Signals in Communication*, pp. 111–116, Loughborough, U.K., September 1990.

219. D. Isenor and S. Zaky, Fingerprint identification using graph matching, *Pattern Recog.* **19**(2), 113–122 (1986).

220. A. Kalvin, E. Schonberg, J. Schwartz, and M. Charir, Two-dimensional model-based boundary matching using footprints, *Int. J. Robotic Res.* **5**(4), 38–55 (1986).

221. B. Kamgar-Parsi, A. Margalit, and A. Rosenfeld, Matching general polygonal arcs, *CVIU*, **53**(2), 227–234 (1991).

222. C.V.K. Kao and K. Black, Type classification of fingerprints, *IEEE Trans. Pattern Anal. Machine Intell.* **2**(31), 223–231 (1980).

223. K. Karu and A. Jain, Fingerprint classification, *Pattern Recog.* **29**(3), 389–404 (1996).

224. M. Kawagoe and A. Tojo, Fingerprint pattern classification, *Pattern Recog.* **17**(3), 295–303 (1984).

225. P.M. Kelly, T.M. Cannon, and D.R. Hush, Query by image example: The CANDID approach, *SPIE Storage and retrieval for image and video databases III* **2420**, 238–248 (1995).

226. C.P. Kolovson and M. Stonebreaker, Segment indexes: Dynamic indexing techniques for multi-dimensional interval data, *ACM*, Denver, Col., June 1991, pp. 138–147.

227. C.L. Krumhansl, Concerning the applicability of geometric models to similarity data: the interrelationship between similarity and spatial density, *Psych. Rev.* **85**, 445–463 (1978).

228. Y. Lamdan, J. Schwartz, and H. Wolfson, Affine invariant model-based object recognition, *IEEE Trans. Robotics Automation* **6**(5), 578–589 (1990).

229. A. Lee and R. Gaensslen, *Advances in Fingerprint Technology*, Elsevier, New York (1991).

230. H.C. Lee and D.R. Cok, Detecting boundaries in vector field, *IEEE Trans. Signal Proc.* **SP-39**, 1181–1194 (1991).

231. S.Z. Li, Matching: Invariant to translations, rotations and scale changes, *Pattern Recog.* **25**(6), 583–594 (1992).

232. Y.W. Lim and S.V. Lee, On the color image segmentation algorithm based on the thresholding and fuzzy C-means techniques, *Pattern Recog.* **9**(23), 935–952 (1990).

233. S.W. Link, The wave theory of difference and similarity, *Scientific Psychology Series*, Lawrence Elbrum Associates, New Jersey 1992.

234. F. Liu and R.W. Picard, Periodicity, directionality, randomness: Wold features for image modeling and retrieval, *IEEE Trans. Pattern Anal. Machine Intell.* **18**(7), 722–733 (1996).

235. D.G. Lowe, Similarity metric learning for a variable-kernel classifier, *Neural Computation* **7**, 72–85 (1994).

236. S. Mallot A theory of multiresolution signal decomposition: The wavelet representation, *IEEE Trans. Pattern Anal. Machine Intell.* **11**(7), 674–693 (1989).

237. F. Mokhtarian, S. Abbasi, and J. Kittler, Efficient and robust retrieval by shape content through curvature scale space, *First International Workshop on Image Databases and Multimedia Search*, Amsterdam, The Netherlands, August 1996, pp. 35–42.

238. S. Moss and E.R. Hancock, Multiple line-template matching with the EM algorithm, *Pattern Recog. Lett.* **18**(11–13), 1283–1292 (1997).

239. H. Murase and S. Nayar, Visual learning and recognition of 3D objects from appearance *Int. J. Comput. Vis.* **14**(1), 5–24 (1995).

240. C. Nastar. The image shape spectrum for image retrieval. Technical Report No. RR-3206, INRIA, 1997.

241. R. Nelson and A. Selinger, Large-scale tests of a keyed, appearance-based 3D object recognition system, *Vis. Res.* **38**(15), 2469–2488 (1998).

242. W. Niblack, et al., The QBIC project: Querying images by content using color texture and shape. Technical Report 9203, IBM Research Division, 1993.

243. R.R. Olson and F. Attreave, What variables produce similarity grouping? *Am. J. Psychol.* **83**, 1–21 (1970).

244. T. Pavlidis and Y.T. Liow, Integrating region growing and edge detection, *IEEE Trans. Pattern Anal. Mach. Intell.* **12**, 225–233 (1990).

245. M. Pelillo and A. Jagota, Feasible and infeasible maxima in a quadratic program for maximum clique, *J. Artif. Neural Networks* **2**(4), 411–420 (1995).

246. A. Pentland, R.W. Picard, and S. Sclaroff. Photobook: Tools for content-based manipulation of image databases. Technical Report 255, MIT, Media lab, Boston, Mass., 1993.

247. A. Pentland, R.W. Picard, and S. Sclaroff, Photobook: Tools for content-based manipulation of image databases, *Proceedings SPIE, Storage and Retrieval for Image and Video Databases II* **2185**, 34–47 1994.

248. K.E. Price, Relaxation matching techniques-a comparison, *IEEE Trans. Pattern Anal. Machine Intell.* **7**(5), 617–621 (1985).

249. A. Rangarajan, A novel optimizing network architecture with applications, *Neural Comput.* **8**, 1041–1060 (1996).

250. A. Rangarajan, H. Chiu, and F.L. Bookstein, The softassign procrustes matching algorithm, *Inf. Process. Med. Imaging* **1310**, 29–42 (1997).

251. A. Rattarangsi and R. Chin, Scale-based detection of corners of planar curves, *IEEE Trans. Pattern Anal. Machine Intell.* **14**(4), 430–449 (1992).

252. G. Robinson, H. Tagare, J. Duncan, and C. Jaffe, Medical image collection indexing: Shape-based retrieval using KD-tree, *Comput. Med. Imaging Graphics* **20**(4), 209–217 (1996).

253. E. Rosh, Cognitive reference points, *Cognitive Psychol.* **7**, 532–547 (1975).

254. P.L. Rosin and G.A. West, Nonparametric segmentation of curves into various representations, *IEEE Trans. Pattern Anal. Machine Intell.* **17**(12), 1140–1153 (1995).

255. C. Rothwell, A. Zisserman, J. Mundy, and D. Forsyth, Efficient model library access by projectively invariant indexing functions *Proceedings of Computer Vision and Pattern Recognition '92*, Champaign, Ill., June 1992, pp. 109–144.

256. E. Saber and A. Tekalp, Integration of color, edge, shape, and texture features for automatic region-based image annotation and retrieval, *Electron. Imaging* **7**(3), 592–604 (1998).

257. E. Saber and A.M. Tekalp, Region-based shape matching for automatic image annotation and query-by-example, *JVCIR* **8**(1), 3–20 (March 1997).

258. E. Saber, A.M. Tekalp, and G. Bozdagi, Fusion of color and edge information for improved segmentation and edge linking, *Image Vis. Comput.* **15**(10), 769–780 (1997).

259. S. Santini and R. Jain, Similarity queries in image databases, *Proceedings of the IEEE Computer Society Conference on Computer Vision and Pattern Recognition*, IEEE Computer Society Press, San Francisco, Calif., June 1996. 646–651.

260. S. Santini and R. Jain, The use of psychophysical similarity measure for queries in image databases, *Visual Computing Lab*, University of California San Diego (1996).

261. S. Santini and R. Jain, Similarity is a geometer, *Multimedia tools Appl.* **3**(5), 277–306 (1997).

262. B. Scassellati, S. Alexopolous, and M. Flickner, Retrieving images by 2D shape: a comparison of computation methods with human perceptual judgements, *SPIE* **2185**, 2–14 (1994).

263. B. Scassellati, S. Alexopolous, and M. Flickner, Retrieving images by 2D shape: a comparison of computation methods with human perceptual judgements, *SPIE* **2185**, 2–14 (1994).

264. B. Schiele and J. Crowley, Object recognition using multi-dimensional receptive field histograms, *Proc. Fourth European Conf. Computer Vision*, Cambridge, U.K., April 1996, pp. 610–619.

265. C. Schmid and R. Mohr, Local grayvalue invariants for image retrieval, *IEEE Trans. Pattern Anal. and Machine Intell.* **19**(5), 530–534(1997).

266. S. Sclaroff, Deformable prototypes for encoding shape categories in image databases, Technical Report CS TR 95-017, Boston University, 1995.

267. R.N. Shepard, Toward a universal law of generalization for psychological science, *Science*, **237**, 1317–1323 (1987).

268. I. Shimshoni and J. Ponce, Probabilistic 3D object recognition, *ICCV95 Fifth International Conference on Computer Vision*, IEEE Computer Society Press, Boston, Mass., June 1995. pp. 488–493.

269. J.R. Smith and S.F. Change An image and video search engine for the world-wide web, *Proc. SPIE V*, San Jose, Calif., Feburary 1997, pp. 84–95.

270. S. Smoliar and H. Zhang, Content based video indexing and retrieval, *IEEE Multimedia* **1**(2), 62–72 (1994).

271. V.S. Srinivasan and N.N. Murthy, Detection of singular points in fingerprint images, *Pattern Recog.* **25**(2), 139–153 (1992).

272. D.L. Swets and J. Weng, Using discriminate eigenfeatures for image retrieval, *IEEE Trans. Pattern Anal. Machine Intell.* **18**(8), 831–836 (1996).

273. H. Tagare, D. O'Shea, and A. Rangarajan, A geometric correspondence for shape-based non-rigid correspondence, *Proceedings of the Fifth International Conference on Computer Vision*, Boston, Mass., June 1995, pp. 434–439.

274. H.D. Tagare, Increasing retrieval efficiency by index tree adaption, *Proc. IEEE Workshop on Content-Based Access of Image and Video*, San Diego, Calif., December (1997) pp. 28–35.

275. H.D. Tagare, Efficient retrieval without a metric, *Vis. 97* (1997).

276. L. Thurstone, A law of comparative judgment, *Psychol. Rev.* **34**, 273–286 (1927).

277. J. Ton and A. Jain, Registering lansat images by point matching, *Trans. Geoscience Remote Sensing* **27**(5), 642–651 (1989).

278. D. Tsai and M. Chen, Curve fitting approach for tangent angle and curvature measurements, *Pattern Recog.* **27**(5), 699–711 (1994).

279. A. Tversky and I. Gati, Similarity, separability, and the triangle inequality, *Psychol. Rev.* (89), 123–154 (1982).

280. P. Tversky and D. Krantz, The dimensional representation and the metric structure of similarity data, *J. Math. Psychol.* **7**, 572–597 (1970).

281. P. Wayner, Efficiently using invariant theory for model-based matching, CVPR1991 *IEEE Computer Society Conference on Computer Vision and Pattern Recognition*, IEEE Computer Society Press, Maui, Hawaii, June 3–6, 1991, pp. 473–478.

282. Y. Wegstein, An automated fingerprint identification system, Technical Report 500-89, National Bureau of Standards, Bethesda, Maryland, 1982.

283. P.N. Yianilos, Data structures and algorithms for nearest neighbor search in general metric spaces, *Proceedings of the Fourth Annual ACM-SIAM Symposium on Discrete Algorithms (SODA)*, Austin, Tex., January 1993, pp. 311–321.

284. S.-S. Yu and W.-H. Tsai, Relaxation by the Hopfield neural network, *Pattern Recog.* **25**(2), 197–209 (1992).

285. A. Yuille, Statistical physics algorithms that converge, *Neural Comput.* **6**, 341–356 (1994).

286. A.L. Yuille, P. Stolorz, and J. Utans, Statistical physics, mixtures of distributions, and the EM algorithm, *Neural Computation* **6**(2) 334–340 (1974).

287. A. Zisserman, et al., 3D object recognition using invariance, *Artificial Intell.* **78**, 239–288 (1994).

14 Multidimensional Indexing Structures for Content-Based Retrieval

VITTORIO CASTELLI
IBM T.J. Watson Research Center, Yorktown Heights, New York

14.1 INTRODUCTION

Indexing plays a fundamental role in supporting efficient retrieval of sequences of images, of individual images, and of selected subimages from multimedia repositories.

Three categories of information are extracted and indexed in image databases: metadata, objects and features, and relations between objects [1]. This chapter is devoted to indexing structures for objects and features.

Content-based retrieval (CBR) of imagery has become synonymous with retrieval based on low-level descriptors such as texture, color, and shape. Similar images map to high-dimensional feature vectors that are close to each other in terms of Euclidean distance. A large body of literature exists on the topic and different aspects have been extensively studied, including the selection of appropriate metrics, the inclusion of the user in the retrieval process, and, particularly, indexing structures to support query-by-similarity.

Indexing of metadata and relations between objects are not covered here because their scope far exceeds image databases. Metadata indexing is a complex application-dependent problem. Active research areas include automatic extraction of information from unstructured textual description, definition of standards (e.g., for remotely sensed images), and translation between different standards (such as in medicine). The techniques required to store and retrieve spatial relations from images are analogous to those used in geographic information systems (GIS), and the topic has been extensively studied in this context.

This chapter is organized as follows. The current section is concluded by a paragraph on notation. Section 14.2 is devoted to background information

Image Databases: Search and Retrieval of Digital Imagery, Edited by Vittorio Castelli and Lawrence D. Bergman.
ISBN 0-471-32116-8

on representing images using low-level features. Section 14.3 introduces three taxonomies of indexing methods, two of which are used to provide primary and secondary structure to Section 14.4.1, which deals with vector-space methods, and Section 14.4.2, which describes metric-space approaches. Section 14.5 contains a discussion on how to select from among different indexing structures. Conclusions and future directions are in Section 14.6. The Appendix contains a description of numerous methods introduced in Section 14.4.

The bibliography that concludes the chapter also contains numerous references not directly cited in the text.

14.1.1 Notation

A database or a database table $\mathcal{X}$ is a collection of n items that can be represented in a d-dimensional real space, denoted by $\mathbb{R}^d$. Individual items that have a spatial extent are often approximated by a minimum bounding rectangle (MBR) or by some other representation. The other items, such as vectors of features, are represented as points in the space. Points in a d-dimensional space are in $1:1$ correspondence with vectors centered at the origin, and therefore the words vector, point, and database item are used interchangeably. A vector is denoted by a lower-case bold face letter, as in x, and the individual components are identified using the square bracket notation; thus $\mathrm{x}[i]$ is the ith component of the vector x. Upper case bold letters are used to identify matrices; for instance, $\mathbf{I}$ is the identity matrix. Sets are denoted by curly brackets enclosing their content, as in $\{A, B, C\}$. The desired number of nearest neighbors in a query is always denoted by k. The maximum depth of a tree is denoted by L, whereas the dummy variable for level is ℓ.

A significant body of research is devoted to retrieval of images based on low-level features (such as shape, color, and texture) represented by descriptors — numerical quantities, computed from the image, that try to capture specific visual characteristics. For example, the color histogram and the color moments are descriptors of the color feature. In the literature, the terms "feature" and "descriptor" are almost invariably used as synonyms, hence they will also be used interchangeably.

14.2 FEATURE-LEVEL IMAGE REPRESENTATION

In this section, several different aspects of feature-level image representation are discussed. First, full image match and subimage match are contrasted, and the corresponding feature extraction methodologies are discussed. A taxonomy of query types used in content-based retrieval systems is then described. Next, the concept of distance function as a means of computing similarity between images, represented as high-dimensional vectors of features, is discussed. When dealing with high-dimensional spaces, geometric intuition is extremely misleading. The familiar, good properties of low-dimensional spaces do not carry over to high-dimensional spaces and a class of phenomena arises, known as the "curse of dimensionality," to which a section is devoted. A way of coping with the curse of dimensionality is to reduce the dimensionality of the search space, and appropriate techniques are discussed in Section 14.2.5.

14.2.1 Full Match, Subimage Match, and Image Segmentation

Similarity retrieval can be divided into *whole image match*, in which the query template is an entire image and is matched against entire images in the repository, and *subimage match*, in which the query template is a portion of an image and the results are portions of images from the database. A particular case of subimage match consists of retrieving portions of images, containing desired objects.

Whole match is the most commonly used approach to retrieve photographic images. A single vector of features, which are represented as numeric quantities, is extracted from each image and used for indexing purposes. Early content-based retrieval systems, such as QBIC [2] adopt this framework.

Subimage match is more important in scientific data sets, such as remotely sensed images, medical images, or seismic data for the oil industry, in which the individual images are extremely large (several hundred megabytes or larger) and the user is generally interested in subsets of the data (e.g., regions showing beach erosion, portions of the body surrounding a particular lesion, etc.).

Most existing systems support subimage retrieval by segmenting the images at database ingestion time and associating a feature vector with each interesting portion. Segmentation can be data-independent (windowed or block-based) or data-dependent (adaptive).

Data-independent segmentation commonly consists of dividing an image into overlapping or nonoverlapping fixed-size sliding rectangular regions of equal stride and extracting and indexing a feature vector from each such region [3,4]. The selection of the window size and stride is application-dependent. For example, in Ref. [3], texture features are extracted from satellite images, using nonoverlapping square windows of size 32×32, whereas, in Ref. [5], texture is extracted from well bore images acquired with the formation microscanner imager, which are 192 pixel wide and tens-to-hundreds of thousands of pixels high. Here the extraction windows have a size of 24×32, have a horizontal stride of 24, and have a vertical stride of 2.

Numerous approaches to data-dependent feature extraction have been proposed. The *blobworld* representation [6] (in which images are segmented, simultaneously using color and texture features by an Expectation–Maximization (EM) algorithm [7]) is well-tailored toward identifying objects in photographic images, provided that they stand out from the background. Each object is efficiently represented by replacing it with a "blob"—an ellipse identified by its centroid and its scatter matrix. The mean texture and the two dominant colors are extracted and associated with each blob. The *EdgeFlow* algorithm [8,9] is designed to produce an exact segmentation of an image by using a smoothed texture field and predictive coding to identify points where edges exist with high probability. The *MMAP* algorithm [10] divides the image into overlapping rectangular regions, extracts from each region a feature vector, quantizes it, constructs a cluster index map by representing each window with the label produced by the quantizer, and applies a simple random field model to smooth the cluster index map. Connected regions having the same cluster label are then indexed by the label.

Adaptive feature extraction produces a much smaller feature volume than data-independent block-based extraction, and the ensuing segmentation can be used for automatic semantic labeling of image components. It is typically less flexible than image-independent extraction because images are partitioned at ingestion time. Block-based feature extraction yields a larger number of feature vectors per image and can allow very flexible, query-dependent segmentation of the data (this is not surprising, because often a block-based algorithm is the first step of an adaptive one). An example is presented in Refs. [5,11], in which the system retrieves subimages that contain objects are defined by the user at query specification time and constructed during the execution of the query, using finely-gridded feature data.

14.2.2 Types of Content-Based Queries

In this section, the different types of queries typically used for content-based search are discussed.

The search methods used for image databases differ from those of traditional databases. Exact queries are only of moderate interest and, when they apply, are usually based on metadata managed by a traditional database management system (DBMS). The quintessential query method for multimedia databases is *retrieval-by-similarity*. The user search, expressed through one of a number of possible user interfaces, is translated into a query on the feature table or tables. Similarity queries are grouped into three main classes:

1. *Range Search.* Find all images in which feature 1 is within range r_1, feature 2 is within range r_2, and ..., and feature n is within range r_n. Example: *Find all images showing a tumor of size between* $size_{\min}$ *and* $size_{\max}$ *within a given region.*
2. *k-Nearest-Neighbor Search.* Find the k most similar images to the template. Example: *Find the 20 tumors that are most similar to a specified example, in which similarity is defined in terms of location, shape, and size, and return the corresponding images.*
3. *Within-Distance (or α-cut).* Find all images with a similarity score better than α with respect to a template, or find all images at distance less than d from a template. Example: *Find all the images containing tumors with similarity scores larger than* α_0 *with respect to an example provided.*

This categorization is the fundamental taxonomy used in this chapter.

Note that nearest-neighbor queries are required to return at least k results, possibly more in case of ties, no matter how similar the results are to the query, whereas within-distance queries do not have an upper bound on the number of returned results but are allowed to return an empty set. A query of type 1 requires a complex interface or a complex query language, such as SQL. Queries of type 2 and 3 can, in their simplest incarnations, be expressed through the use of simple, intuitive interfaces that support query-by-example.

Nearest-neighbor queries (type 2) rely on the definition of a *similarity function*. Section 14.2.3 is devoted to the use of distance functions for measuring similarity. Nearest-neighbor search problems have wide applicability beyond information retrieval and GIS data management. There is a vast literature dealing with nearest-neighbor problems in the fields of pattern recognition, supervised learning, machine learning, and statistical classification [12–15], as well as in the areas of unsupervised learning, clustering, and vector quantization [16–18].

α-Cut queries (type 3) rely on a distance or *scoring function*. A scoring function is nonnegative and bounded from above, and assigns higher values to better matches. For example, a scoring function might order the database records by how well they match the query and then use the record rank as the score. The last record, which is the one that best satisfies the query, has the highest score. Scoring functions are commonly normalized between zero and one.

In the discussion, it has been implicitly assumed that query processing has three properties[1]:

Exhaustiveness. Query processing is exhaustive if it retrieves all the database items satisfying it. A database item that satisfies the query and does not belong to the result set is called a *miss*. Nonexhaustive range-query processing fails to return points that lie within the query range. Nonexhaustive α-cut query processing fails to return points that are closer than α to the query template. Nonexhaustive k-nearest-neighbor query processing either returns fewer than k results or returns results that are not correct.

Correctness. Query processing is correct if all the returned items satisfy the query. A database item that belongs to the result set and does not satisfy the query is called a *false hit*. Noncorrect range query processing returns points outside the specified range. Noncorrect α-cut-query processing returns points that are farther than α from the template. Noncorrect k-nearest-neighbor query processing misses some of the desired results, and therefore is also nonexhaustive.

[1] In this chapter the emphasis is on properties of indexing structures. The content-based retrieval community has concentrated mostly on properties of the image-representation: as discussed in other chapters, numerous studies have investigated how well different feature-descriptor sets perform by comparing results selected by human subjects with results retrieved using features. Different feature sets produce different numbers of misses and different numbers of false hits, and have different effects on the result rankings. In this chapter the emphasis is not on the performance of feature descriptors: an indexing structure that is guaranteed to return exactly the k-nearest feature vectors of every query, is, for the purpose of this chapter, exhaustive, correct, and deterministic. This same indexing structure, used in conjunction with a specific feature set, might yield query results that a human would judge as misses, false hits, or incorrectly ranked.

Determinism. Query processing is deterministic if it returns the same results every time a query is issued and for every construction of the index[2]. It is possible to have nondeterministic range, α-cut, and k-nearest-neighbor queries.

The term *exactness* is used to denote the combination of exhaustiveness and correctness. It is very difficult to construct indexing structures that have all three properties and are at the same time efficient (namely, that perform better than brute-force sequential scan), as the dimensionality of the data set grows. Much can be gained, however, if one or more of the assumptions are relaxed.

Relaxing Exhaustiveness. Relaxing exhaustiveness alone means allowing misses but not false hits, and retaining determinism. There is a widely used class of nonexhaustive methods that do not modify the other properties. These methods support fixed-radius queries, namely, they return only results that have a distance smaller than r from the query point. The radius r is either fixed at index construction time, or specified at query time. Fixed-radius k-nearest-neighbor queries are allowed to return less than k results if less than k database points lie within distance r of the query sample.

Relaxing Exactness. It is impossible to give up correctness in nearest-neighbor queries and retain exhaustiveness, and an awareness of methods that achieve this goal for α-cut and range queries is lacking. There are two main approaches to relax exactness.

- $1 + \varepsilon$ *queries* return results in which distance is guaranteed to be less than $1 + \varepsilon$ times the distance of the exact result.
- *Approximate queries* operate on an approximation of the search space obtained, for instance, through dimensionality reduction (Section 14.2.5).

Approximate queries usually constrain the average error, whereas $1 + \varepsilon$ queries limit the maximum error. Note that it is possible to combine the approaches, for instance, by first reducing the dimensionality of the search space and indexing the result with a method supporting $1 + \varepsilon$ queries.

Relaxing Determinism. There are three main categories of algorithms, yielding nondeterministic indexes, in which the lack of determinism is due to a randomization step in the index construction [19,20].

- Methods, which yield indexes that relax exhaustiveness or correctness and are slightly different every time the index is constructed — repeatedly reindexing the same database produces indexes with very similar but not identical retrieval characteristics.
- Methods, yielding "good" indexes (e.g., both exhaustive and correct) with arbitrarily high probability and poor indexes with low

[2] Although this definition may appear cryptic, it will soon be clear that numerous approaches exist that yield nondeterministic queries.

probability — repeatedly reindexing the same database yields mostly indexes with the desired characteristics and very rarely an index that performs poorly.

- Methods with indexes that perform well (e.g., are both exhaustive and correct) on the vast majority of queries and poorly on the remaining — if queries are generated "at random," the results will be accurate with high probability.

A few nondeterministic methods rely on a randomization step during the query execution — the same query on the same index might not return the same results.

Exhaustiveness, exactness, and determinism can be individually relaxed for all three main categories of queries. It is also possible to relax any combination of these properties: for example, CSVD (described in Appendix A.2.1) supports nearest-neighbor searches that are both nondeterministic and approximate.

14.2.3 Image Representation and Similarity Measures

In general, systems supporting k-nearest-neighbor and α-cut queries rely on the following assumption:

> *Images (or image portions) can be represented as points in an appropriate metric space where dissimilar images are distant from each other, similar images are close to each other, and where the distance function captures well the user's concept of similarity.*

Because query-by-example has been the main approach to content-based search, substantial literature exists on how to support nearest-neighbor and α-cut searches, both of which rely on the concept of distance (a score is usually directly derived from a distance). A *distance function* (or *metric*) $D(\cdot, \cdot)$ is by definition nonnegative, symmetric, satisfies the triangular inequality, and has the property that $D(x, y) = 0$ if and only if $x = y$. A metric space is a pair of items: a set $\mathcal{X}$, the elements of which are called points, and a distance function defined on pairs of elements of $\mathcal{X}$.

The problem of finding a universal metric that acceptably captures photographic image similarity as perceived by human beings is unsolved and indeed ill-posed because subjectivity plays a major role in determining similarities and dissimilarities. In specific areas, however, objective definitions of similarity can be provided by experts, and in these cases it might be possible to find specific metrics that solve the problem accurately.

When images or portions of images are represented, by a collection of d features $\mathbf{x}[1], \ldots, \mathbf{x}[d]$ (containing texture, shape, color descriptors, or combinations thereof), it seems natural to aggregate the features into a vector (or, equivalently, a point) in the d-dimensional space $\mathbb{R}^d$ by making each feature correspond to a different coordinate axis. Some specific features, such as the color histogram, can be interpreted both as point and as probability distributions.

Within the vector representation of the query space, executing a range query is equivalent to retrieving all the points lying within a hyperrectangle aligned with the coordinate axes. To support nearest-neighbor and α-cut queries, however, the space must be equipped with a metric or a dissimilarity measure. Note that, although the dissimilarity between statistical distributions can be measured with the same metrics used for vectors, there are also dissimilarity measures that were specifically developed for distributions.

We now describe the most common dissimilarity measures, provide their mathematical form, discuss their computational complexity, and mention when they are specific to probability distributions.

Euclidean or $D^{(2)}$. Computationally simple (O(d) operations) and invariant with respect to rotations of the reference system, the Euclidean distance is defined as

$$D^{(2)}(\mathbf{x}, \mathbf{y}) = \sqrt{\sum_{i=1}^{d} (\mathbf{x}[i] - \mathbf{y}[i])^2}. \tag{14.1}$$

Rotational invariance is important in dimensionality reduction, as discussed in Section 14.2.5. The Euclidean distance is the only rotationally invariant metric in this list (the rotationally invariant correlation coefficient described later is not a distance). The set of vectors of length d having real entries, endowed with the Euclidean metric, is called the d-dimensional Euclidean space. When d is a small number, the most expensive operation is the square root. Hence, the square of the Euclidean distance is also commonly used to measure similarity.

Chebychev or $D^{(\infty)}$. Less computationally expensive than the Euclidean distance (but still requiring O(d) operations), it is defined as

$$D^{(\infty)}(x, y) = \max_{i=1}^{d} |\mathbf{x}[i] - \mathbf{y}[i]|. \tag{14.2}$$

Manhattan or $D^{(1)}$ or city-block. As computationally expensive as a squared Euclidean distance, this distance is defined as

$$D^{(1)}(\mathbf{x}, \mathbf{y}) = \sum_{i=1}^{d} |\mathbf{x}[i] - \mathbf{y}[i]|. \tag{14.3}$$

Minkowsky or $D^{(p)}$. This is really a family of distance functions parameterized by p. The three previous distances belong to this family, and correspond to $p = 2$, $p = \infty$ (interpreted as $\lim_{p\to\infty} D^p$), and $p = 1$, respectively.

$$D^{(p)}(\mathbf{x}, \mathbf{y}) = \left[\sum_{i=1}^{d} |\mathbf{x}[i] - \mathbf{y}[i]|^p \right]^{\frac{1}{p}}. \tag{14.4}$$

Minkowsky distances have the same number of additions and subtractions as the Euclidean distance. With the exception of D^1, D^2, and D^∞, the main computational cost is due to computing the power functions. Often Minkowsky distances between functions are also called L_p distances, and Minkowsky distances between finite or infinite sequences of numbers are called l_p distances.

Weighted Minkowsky. Again, this is a family of distance functions parameterized by p, in which the individual dimensions can be weighted differently using nonnegative weights w_i. Their mathematical form is

$$D^{(p)}_{\underline{\mathrm{f}}w}(\mathbf{x}, \mathbf{y}) = \left[\sum_{i=1}^{d} w_i |\mathbf{x}[i] - \mathbf{y}[i]|^p \right]^{\frac{1}{p}}. \tag{14.5}$$

The weighted Minkowsky distances require d more multiplications than their unweighted counterpart.

Mahalanobis. A computationally expensive generalization of the Euclidean distance, it is defined in terms of a covariance matrix $\mathbf{C}$

$$D(\mathbf{x}, \mathbf{y}) = |\det \mathbf{C}|^{1/d} (\mathbf{x} - \mathbf{y})^T \mathbf{C}^{-1} (\mathbf{x} - \mathbf{y}), \tag{14.6}$$

where det is the determinant, $\mathbf{C}^{-1}$ is the matrix inverse of $\mathbf{C}$, and the superscript T denotes transpose. If $\mathbf{C}$ is the identity matrix $\mathbf{I}$, the Mahalanobis distance reduces to the Euclidean distance squared, otherwise, the entry $\mathbf{C}[i, j]$ can be interpreted as the joint contribution of the ith and jth feature to the overall dissimilarity. In general, the Mahalanobis distance requires $O(d^2)$ operations. This metric is also commonly used to measure the distance between probability distributions.

Generalized Euclidean or quadratic. This is a generalization of the Mahalanobis distance, where the matrix $\mathbf{K}$ is positive definite but not necessarily a covariance matrix, and the multiplicative factor is omitted:

$$D(\mathbf{x}, \mathbf{y}) = (\mathbf{x} - \mathbf{y})^T \mathbf{K} (\mathbf{x} - \mathbf{y}). \tag{14.7}$$

It requires $O(d^2)$ operations.

Correlation Coefficient. Defined as

$$\rho(\mathbf{x}, \mathbf{y}) = \frac{\sum_{i=1}^{d} (\mathbf{x}[i] - \overline{x}[i])(\mathbf{y}[i] - \overline{x}[i])}{\sqrt{\sum_{i=1}^{d} (\mathbf{x}[i] - \overline{x}[i])^2 \sum_{i=1}^{d} (\mathbf{y}[i] - \overline{x}[i])^2}}, \tag{14.8}$$

(where $\overline{x} = [\overline{x}[1], \ldots, \overline{x}[d]]$ is the average of all the vectors in the database), the correlation coefficient is not a distance. However, if the points $\mathbf{x}$ and $\mathbf{y}$ are projected onto the sphere of unit radius centered at $\overline{\mathbf{x}}$, then the quantity $2 - 2\rho(\mathbf{x}, \mathbf{y})$ is exactly the Euclidean distance between the projections. The correlation coefficient is invariant with respect to rotations and scaling of the search space. It requires $O(d)$ operations. This measure of similarity is used in statistics to characterize the joint behavior of pairs of random variables.

Relative Entropy or Kullback-Leibler Divergence. This information-theoretical quantity is defined, only for probability distributions, as

$$D(\mathbf{x}\|\mathbf{y}) = \sum_{i=1}^{d} \mathbf{x}[i] \log \frac{\mathbf{x}[i]}{\mathbf{y}[i]}. \tag{14.9}$$

It is meaningful only if the entries of $\mathbf{x}$ and $\mathbf{y}$ are nonnegative and $\sum_{i=1}^{d} \mathbf{x}[i] = \sum_{i=1}^{d} \mathbf{y}[i] = 1$. Its computational cost is $O(d)$, however, it requires $O(d)$ divisions and $O(d)$ logarithm computations. It is not a distance as it is not symmetric, and it does not satisfy a triangle inequality. When used for retrieval purposes, the first argument should be the query vector and the second argument should be the database vector. It is also known as Kullback-Leibler distance, Kullback-Leibler cross-entropy, or just as cross-entropy.

$\mathcal{X}^2$-Distance. Defined, only for probability distributions, as

$$D_{\chi^2}(\mathbf{x}, \mathbf{y}) = \sum_{i=1}^{d} \frac{\mathbf{x}^2[i] - \mathbf{y}^2[i]}{\mathbf{y}[i]}. \tag{14.10}$$

It lends itself to a natural interpretation only if the entries of $\mathbf{x}$ and $\mathbf{y}$ are nonnegative and $\sum_{i=1}^{d} \mathbf{x}[i] = \sum_{i=1}^{d} \mathbf{y}[i] = 1$. Computationally, it requires $O(d)$ operations, the most expensive of which is the division. It is not a distance because it is not symmetric.

It is difficult to convey an intuitive notion of the difference between distances. Concepts derived from geometry can assist in this task. As in topology, where the structure of a topological space is completely determined by its open sets, the structure of a metric space is completely determined by its balls. A ball centered at $\mathbf{x}$ having radius r is the set of points having distance r from $\mathbf{x}$. The Euclidean distance is the starting point of our discussion as it can be measured using a ruler. Balls in Euclidean spaces are the familiar spherical surfaces (Figure 14.1). A ball in D^∞ is a hypersquare aligned with the coordinate axes, inscribing the corresponding Euclidean ball. A ball in D^1 is a hypersquare, having vertices on the coordinate axes and inscribed in the corresponding Euclidean ball. A ball in D^p, for $p > 2$, looks like a "fat sphere" that lies between the D^2 and D^∞ balls, whereas for $1 < p < 2$, lies between the D^1 and D^2 balls and looks like a "slender sphere." It is immediately possible to draw several conclusions. Consider the distance between two points $\mathbf{x}$ and $\mathbf{y}$ and look at the absolute values of the differences $d_i = |\mathbf{x}[i] - \mathbf{y}[i]|$.

- The Minkowsky distances differ in the way they combine the contributions of the d_i's. All the d_i's contribute equally to $D^1(\mathbf{x}, \mathbf{y})$, irrespective of their values. However, as p grows, the value $D^p(\mathbf{x}, \mathbf{y})$ is increasingly determined by the maximum of the d_i, whereas the overall contribution of all the other differences becomes less and less relevant. In the limit, $D^\infty(\mathbf{x}, \mathbf{y})$ is uniquely determined by the maximum of the differences d_i, whereas all the other values are ignored.

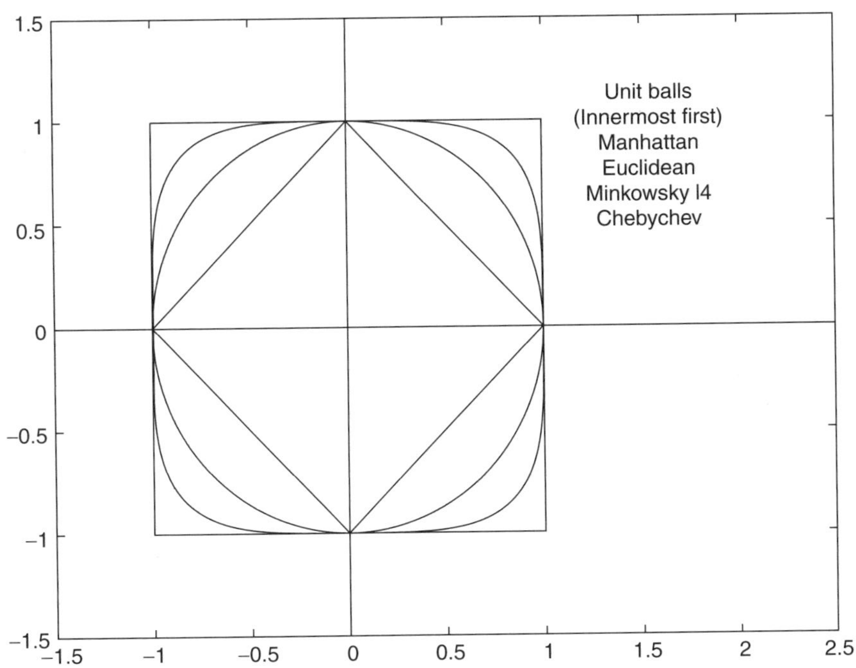

Figure 14.1. The unit spheres under Chebychev, Euclidean, $D^{(4)}$, and Manhattan distance.

- If two points have distance D^p equal to zero for some $p \in [1, \infty]$, then they have distance D^q equal to zero for all $q \in [1, \infty]$. Hence, one cannot distinguish points that have, say, Euclidean distance equal to zero by selecting a different Minkowsky metric.
- If $1 \leq p < q \leq \infty$, the ratio $D^p(\mathbf{x}, \mathbf{y})/D^q(\mathbf{x}, \mathbf{y})$ is bounded from above $K_{p,q}$ and from below by 1. The constant $K_{p,q}$ is never larger than 2^d and depends only on p and q, but not on $\mathbf{x}$ and $\mathbf{y}$. This property is called *equivalence* of distances. Hence, there are limits on how much the metric structure of the space can be modified by the choice of Minkowsky distance.
- Minkowsky distances do not take into account combinations of d_i's. In particular, if two features are highly correlated, differences between the values of the first feature are likely to be reflected in distances between the values of the second feature. The Minkowsky distance combines the contribution of both differences and can overestimate visual dissimilarities.

We argue that Minkowsky distances are substantially similar to each other from the viewpoint of information retrieval and that there are very few theoretical arguments supporting the selection of one over the others. Computational cost and rotational invariance are probably more important considerations in the selection.

If the covariance matrix $\mathbf{C}$ and the matrix $\mathbf{K}$ have full rank and the weights w_i are all positive, then the Mahalanobis distance, the generalized Euclidean distance, and the unweighted and weighted Minkowsky distances are equivalent.

Weighted $D^{(p)}$ distances are useful when different features have different ranges. For instance, if a vector of features contains both the fractal dimension (which takes values between two and three) and the variance of the gray scale histogram (which takes values between 0 and 2^{14} for an 8-bit image), the latter will be by far the main factor in determining the $D^{(p)}$ distance between different images. This problem is commonly corrected by selecting an appropriate weighted $D^{(p)}$ distance. Often each weight is the reciprocal of the standard deviation of the corresponding feature computed across the entire database.

The Mahalanobis distance solves a different problem. If two features i and j have significant correlation, then $|\mathbf{x}[i] - \mathbf{y}[i]|$ and $|\mathbf{x}[j] - \mathbf{y}[j]|$ are correlated: if $\mathbf{x}$ and $\mathbf{y}$ differ significantly in the ith dimension, they are likely to differ significantly in the jth dimension, and if they are similar in one dimension, they are likely to be similar in the other dimension. This means that the two features capture very similar characteristics of the image. When both features are used in a regular or weighted Euclidean distance, the same dissimilarities are essentially counted twice. The Mahalanobis distance offers a solution, consisting of correcting for correlations and differences in dispersion around the mean. A common use of this distance is in classification applications, in which the distributions of the classes are assumed to be Gaussian. Both Mahalanobis distance and generalized Euclidean distances have unit spheres shaped as ellipsoids, aligned with the eigenvectors of the weights matrices.

The characteristics of the problem being solved should suggest the selection of a distance metric. In general, the Minkowsky distance considers only the dimension in which **x** and **y** differ the most, the Euclidean distance captures our geometric notion of distance, and the Manhattan distance combines the contributions of all dimensions in which **x** and **y** are different. Mahalanobis distances and generalized Euclidean distances consider joint contributions of different features.

Empirical approaches exist, typically consisting of constructing a set of queries for which the correct answer is determined manually and comparing different distances in terms of efficiency and accuracy. Efficiency and accuracy are often measured using the information-retrieval quantities *precision* and *recall*, defined as follows. Let $\mathbb{D}$ be the set of desired (correct) results of a query, usually manually selected by a user, and $\mathbb{A}$ be the set of actual query results. We require that $|\mathbb{A}|$ be larger than $|\mathbb{D}|$. Some of the results in $\mathbb{A}$ will be correct and form a set $\mathbb{C}$. Precision and recall for individual queries are then respectively defined as

$$
\begin{aligned}
P &= \frac{|\mathbb{C}|}{|\mathbb{A}|} = \text{fraction of returned results that are correct;} \\
R &= \frac{|\mathbb{C}|}{|\mathbb{D}|} = \text{fraction of correct results that are returned.}
\end{aligned}
\tag{14.11}
$$

For the approach to be reliable, the database size should be very large, and precision and recall should be averaged over a large number of queries.

Smith [21] observed that on a medium-sized and diverse photographic image database and for a heterogeneous set of queries, precision and recall vary only slightly with the choice of (Minkowsky or weighted Minkowsky) metric when retrieval is based on color histogram or on texture.

14.2.4 The "Curse of Dimensionality"

The operations required to perform content-based search are computationally expensive. Indexing schemes are therefore commonly used to speed up the queries.

Indexing multimedia databases is a much more complex and difficult problem than indexing traditional databases. The main difficulty stems from using longfeature vectors to represent the data. This is especially troublesome in systems supporting only whole image matches in which individual images are represented using extremely long feature vectors.

Our geometric intuition (based on experience with the three-dimensional world in which we live) leads us to believe that numerous geometric properties hold in high-dimensional spaces, whereas in reality they cease to be true very early on as the number of dimensions grows. For example, in two dimensions a circle is well-approximated by the minimum bounding square; the ratio of the areas is $4/\pi$. However, in 100 dimensions the ratio of the volumes becomes approximately $4.2 \cdot 10^{39}$: most of the volume of a 100-dimensional hypercube is outside the largest inscribed sphere — hypercubes are poor approximations of hyperspheres and a majority of indexing structures partition the space into hypercubes or hyperrectangles.

Two classes of problems then arise. The first is algorithmic: indexing schemes that rely on properties of low-dimensionality spaces do not perform well in high-dimensional spaces because the assumptions on which they are based do not hold there. For example, R-trees are extremely inefficient for performing α-cut queries using the Euclidean distance as they execute the search by transforming it into the range query defined by the minimum bounding rectangle of the desired search region, which is a sphere centered on the template point, and by checking whether the retrieved results satisfy the query. In high dimensions, the R-trees retrieve mostly irrelevant points that lie within the hyperrectangle but outside the hypersphere.

The second class of difficulties, called the "curse of dimensionality," is intrinsic in the geometry of high-dimensional hyperspaces, which entirely lack the "nice" properties of low-dimensional spaces.

One of the characteristics of high-dimensional spaces is that points randomly sampled from the same distribution appear uniformly far from each other and each point sees itself as an outlier (see Refs. [22–26] for formal discussions of the problem). More specifically, a randomly selected database point does not perceive itself as surrounded by the other database points; on the contrary, the vast majority of the other database vector appears to be almost at the same distance and to be located in the direction of the center. Note that, although the semantics of range queries are unaffected by the curse of dimensionality, the meaning of nearest-neighbor and α-cut queries is now in question.

Consider the following simple example: let a database be composed of 20,000 independent 100-dimensional vectors, with the features of each vector independently distributed as standard Normal random (i.e., Gaussian) variables. Normal distributions are very concentrated: the tails decay extremely fast and the probability of sampling observations far from the mean is negligible. A large Gaussian sample in three-dimensional space resembles a tight, well concentrated cloud, a nice "cluster." This is not the case in 100 dimensions. In fact, sampling an independent query template according to the same 100-dimensional standard Normal, and computing the histogram of the distances between this query point and the points in the database, yields the result shown in Figure 14.2. In the data used for the figure, the minimum distance between the query and a database point is 10.1997 and the maximum distance is 18.3019. There are no "close" points to the query or "far" points from the query. α-cut queries become very sensitive to the choice of the threshold. With a threshold smaller than 10, no result is returned; with a threshold of 12.5, the query returns 5.3 percent of the database; the threshold is barely increased to 13, when almost three times as many results, 14 percent of the database, are returned.

14.2.5 Dimensionality Reduction

If the high-dimensional representation of images actually behaved as described in the previous section, queries of type 2 and 3 would be essentially meaningless.

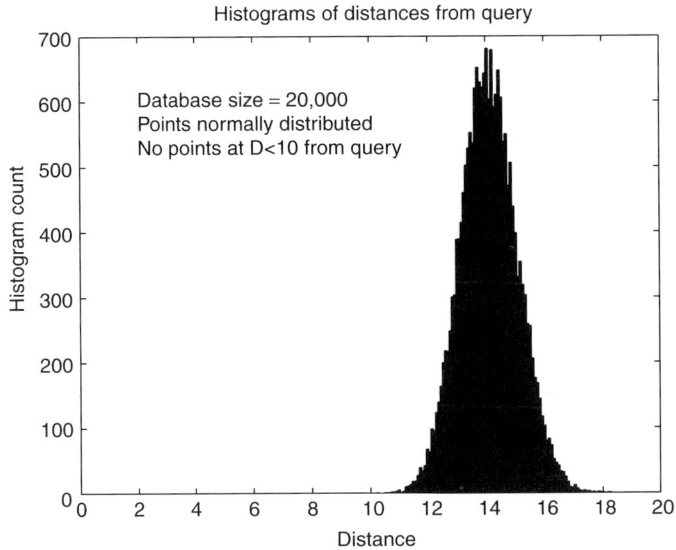

Figure 14.2. Distances between a query point and database points. Database size = 20,000 points, in 100 dimensions.

Luckily, two properties come to the rescue. The first, noted in Ref. [23] and, from a different perspective, in [27,28], is that the feature space often has a local structure, thanks to which query images have, in fact, close neighbors. Therefore, nearest-neighbor and α-cut searches can be meaningful. The second is that the features used to represent the images are usually not independent and are often highly correlated: the feature vectors in the database can be well-approximated by their "projections" onto a lower-dimensionality space, where classical indexing schemes work well. Pagel, Korn, and Faloutsos [29] propose a method for measuring the intrinsic dimensionality of data sets in terms of their fractal dimensions. By observing that the distribution of real data often displays self-similarity at different scales, they express the average distance of the kth nearest neighbor of a query sample in terms of two quantities, called the Haussdorff and the Correlation fractal dimension, which are usually significantly smaller than the number of dimensions of the feature space and effectively deflate the curse of dimensionality.

The mapping from a higher-dimensional to a lower-dimensional space, called *dimensionality reduction*, is normally accomplished through one of three classes of methods: variable-subset selection (possibly following a linear transformation of the space), multidimensional scaling, and geometric hashing.

14.2.5.1 Variable-Subset Selection. Variable-subset selection consists of retaining some of the dimensions of the feature space and discarding the remaining ones. This class of methods is often used in statistics or in machine learning [30]. In CBIR systems, where the goal is to minimize the error induced by approximating the original vectors with their lower-dimensionality projections, variable-subset selection is often preceded by a linear transformation of the feature space. Almost universally, the linear transformation (a combination of translation and rotation) is chosen so that the rotated features are uncorrelated, or, equivalently, so that the covariance matrix of the transformed data set is diagonal. Depending on the perspective of the author and on the framework, the method is called Karhunen-Loève transform (KLT) [13,31], singular value decomposition (SVD) [32], or principal component analysis (PCA) [33,34] (although the setup and numerical algorithms might differ, all the above methods are essentially equivalent). A variable-subset selection step then discards the dimensions having smaller variance. The rotation of the feature space induced by these methods is optimal in the sense that it minimizes the mean squared error of the approximation, resulting from discarding the d' dimensions with smaller variance for every d'. This implies that, on an average, the original vectors are closer (in Euclidean distance) to their projections when the rotation decorrelates the features than with any other rotation.

PCA, KLT, and SVD are data-dependent transformations and are computationally expensive. They are therefore poorly suited for dynamic databases in which items are added and removed on a regular basis. To address this problem Ravi Kanth, Agrawal, and Singh [35] proposed an efficient method for updating the SVD of a data set and devised strategies to schedule and trigger the update.

14.2.5.2 Multidimensional Scaling. Nonlinear methods can reduce the dimensionality of the feature space. Numerous authors advocate the use of *multidimensional scaling* [36] for content-based retrieval applications. Multidimensional scaling comes in different flavors, hence it lacks a precise definition. The approach described in [37] consists of remapping the space $\mathbb{R}^n$ into $\mathbb{R}^m$ $(m < n)$ using m transformations, each of which is a linear combination of appropriate radial basis functions. This method was adopted in Ref. [38] for database image retrieval. The *metric* version of multidimensional scaling [39] starts from the collection of all pairwise distances between the objects of a set and tries to find the smallest-dimensionality Euclidean space, in which the objects can be represented as points with Euclidean distances "close enough" to the original input distances. Numerous other variants of the method exist.

Faloutsos and Lin [40] proposed an efficient solution to the metric problem, called *FastMap*. The gist of this approach is pretending that the objects are indeed points in an n-dimensional space (where n is large and unknown) and trying to project these unknown points onto a small number of orthogonal directions.

In general, multidimensional-scaling algorithms can provide better dimensionality reduction than linear methods but are computationally much more expensive and modify the metric structure of the space in a fashion that depends on the specific data set, and are poorly suited for dynamic databases.

14.2.5.3 Geometric Hashing. *Geometric hashing* [41,42] consists of hashing from a high-dimensional space to a very low-dimensional space (the real line or the plane). In general, hashing functions are not data-dependent. The metric properties of the hashed space can be significantly different from those of the original space. Additionally, an ideal hashing function should spread the database uniformly across the range of the low-dimensionality space, but the design of such a function becomes increasingly complex with the dimensionality of the original space. Hence, geometric hashing can be applied to image database indexing only when the original space has low-dimensionality and when only local properties of the metric space need to be maintained.

A few approaches that do not fall in any of the three classes described above have been proposed. An example is the indexing scheme called *Clustering and Singular Value Decomposition* (CSVD) [27,28], in which the index preparation step includes recursively partitioning the observation space into nonoverlapping clusters and applying SVD and variable-subset selection independently to each cluster. Similar approaches have since appeared in the literature, confirming the conclusions. Aggarwal and coworkers in Refs. [43,44] describe an efficient method for combining the clustering step with the dimensionality reduction, but the paper does not contain applications to indexing. A different decomposition algorithm is described in Ref. [44], in which the empirical results on indexing performance and behavior are in remarkable agreement with those in Refs. [27,28].

14.2.5.4 Some Considerations. Dimensionality reduction allows the use of efficient indexing structures. However, the search is now no longer performed on the original data.

The main downside of dimensionality reduction is that it affects the metric structure of the search space in at least two ways. First, all the mentioned approaches introduce an approximation, which might affect the ranks of the query results. The results of type 2 or type 3 queries executed in the original space and in the reduced-dimensionality space need not be the same. This approximation might or might not negatively affect the retrieval performance: as feature-based search is in itself approximate and because dimensionality reduction partially mitigates the "curse of dimensionality," improvement rather than deterioration is possible. To quantify this effect, experiments measuring precision and recall of the search can be used, in which users compare the results retrieved from the original- and the reduced-dimensionality space. Alternatively, the original space can be used as the reference (in other words, the query results in the original space are used as baseline), and the difference in retrieval behavior can be measured [27].

The second type of alteration of the search space metric structure depends on the individual algorithm. Linear methods, such as SVD (and the nonlinear CSVD), use rotations of the feature space. If the same non-rotationally-invariant distance function is used before and after the linear transformation, then the distances between points in the original and in the rotated space will be different even without accounting for the variable-subset selection step (for instance, when using $D^{(\infty)}$, the distances could vary by a factor of $\sqrt{d}$). However, this problem does not exist when a rotationally invariant distance or similarity index is used. When nonlinear multidimensional scaling is used, the metric structure of the search space is modified in a position-dependent fashion and the problem cannot be mitigated by an appropriate choice of metric.

The methods that can be used to quantify this effect are the same ones proposed to quantify the approximation induced by dimensionality reduction. In practice, distinguishing between the contributions of the two discussed effects is very difficult and probably of minor interest, and as a consequence, a single set of experiments is used to determine the overall combined influence on retrieval performance.

14.3 TAXONOMIES OF INDEXING STRUCTURES

After feature selection and dimensionality reduction, the third step in the construction of an index for an image database is the selection of an appropriate indexing structure, a data structure that simplifies the retrieval task. The literature on the topic is immense and an exhaustive overview would require an entire book.

Here, we will quickly review the main classes of indexing structures, describe their salient characteristics, and discuss how well they can support queries of the three main classes and four categories defined in Section 14.2.2. The appendix describes in detail the different indexes and compares their variations. This section describes different ways of categorizing indexing structures. A taxonomy of spatial access methods can also be found in Ref. [45], which also contains historical perspective of the evolution of spatial access methods, a description of several indexing methods, and references to comparative studies.

A first distinction, adopted in the rest of the chapter, is between *vector space indexes* and *metric space indexes*. The former represent objects and feature vectors as sets or points in a d-dimensional vector space. For example, two-dimensional objects can be represented as regions of the $x-y$ plane and color histograms can be represented as points in high-dimensional space, where each coordinate corresponds to a different bin of the histogram. After embedding the representations in an appropriate space, a convenient distance function is adopted, and indexing structures to support the different types of queries are constructed accordingly. Metric space indexes start from the opposite end of the problem: given the pairwise distances between objects in a set, an appropriate indexing structure is constructed for these distances. The actual representation of the individual objects is immaterial; the index tries to capture the metric structure of the search space.

A second division is algorithmic. We can distinguish between nonhierarchical, recursive partitioning, projection-based, and miscellaneous methods. *Nonhierarchical* schemes divide the search space into regions having the property that the region to which a query point belongs can be identified in a constant number of operations. *Recursive partitioning* methods organize the search space in a way that is well-captured by a tree and try to capitalize on the resulting search efficiency. *Projection-based* approaches, usually well-suited for approximate or probabilistic queries, rely on clever algorithms that perform searches on the projections of database points onto a set of directions.

We can also take an orthogonal approach and divide the indexing schemes into *spatial access methods* (SAM) that index spatial objects (lines, polygons, surfaces, solids, etc.), and *point access methods* (PAM) that index points in multidimensional spaces. Spatial data structures are extensively analyzed in Ref. [46]. Point access methods have been used in pattern-recognition applications, especially for nearest-neighbor searches [15]. The distinction between SAMs and PAMs, is somewhat fuzzy. On the one hand, numerous schemes exist that can be used as either SAMs or PAMs, with very minor changes. On the other, many authors have mapped spatial objects (especially hyperrectangles) into points in higher dimensional spaces, called parameter space [47–51], and used PAMs to index the parameter space. For example, a d-dimensional hyperrectangle aligned with the coordinate axes is uniquely identified by its two vertices lying on its main diagonal, that is, by $2d$ numbers.

14.4 THE MAIN CLASSES OF MULTIDIMENSIONAL INDEXING STRUCTURES

This section contains a high-level overview of the main classes of multidimensional indexes. They are organized taxonomically, dividing them into vector-space methods and metric-space methods and further subdividing each category. The appendix contains detailed descriptions, discusses individual methods belonging to each subcategory, compares methods within each class, and provides references to available literature.

14.4.1 Vector-Space Methods

Vector-space approaches are divided into nonhierarchical methods, recursive decomposition approaches, projection-based algorithms, and miscellaneous indexing structures.

14.4.1.1 Nonhierarchical Methods. Nonhierarchical methods constitute a wide class of indexing structures. Ignoring the brute-force approach (namely, the sequential scan of the database table), they are divided into two classes.

The first group (described in detail in Appendix A.1.1.1) maps the d-dimensional spaces onto the real line by means of a space-filling curve (such as the Peano curve, the z-order, and the Hilbert curve) and indexes the mapped records, using a one-dimensional indexing structure. Because space-filling curves tend to map nearby points in the original space into nearby points on the real line, range queries, nearest-neighbor queries, and α-cut queries can be reasonably approximated by executing them in the projected space.

The second group of methods partitions the search space into a predefined number of nonoverlapping fixed-size regions that do not depend on the actual data contained in the database.

14.4.1.2 Recursive Partitioning Methods. Recursive partitioning methods (see also Appendix A.1.2) recursively divide the search space into progressively smaller regions that depend on the data set being indexed. The resulting hierarchical decomposition can be well-represented by a tree.

The three most commonly used categories of recursive partitioning methods are quad-trees, k-d-trees, and R-trees.

Quad-trees divide a d-dimensional space into 2^d regions by simultaneously splitting all axes into two parts. Each nonterminal node has therefore 2^d children, and, as in the other two classes of methods, corresponds to hyperrectangles aligned with the coordinate axes. Figure 14.3 shows a typical quad-tree decomposition in a two-dimensional space.

K-d-trees divide the space using $(d-1)$-dimensional hyperplanes perpendicular to a specific coordinate axis. Each nonterminal node has therefore at least two children. The coordinate axis can be selected using a round-robin criterion or as a function of the properties of the data indexed by the node. Points are stored at the leaves, and, in some variations of the method, at internal nodes. Figure 14.4 is an example of a k-d-tree decomposition of the same data set used in Figure 14.3.

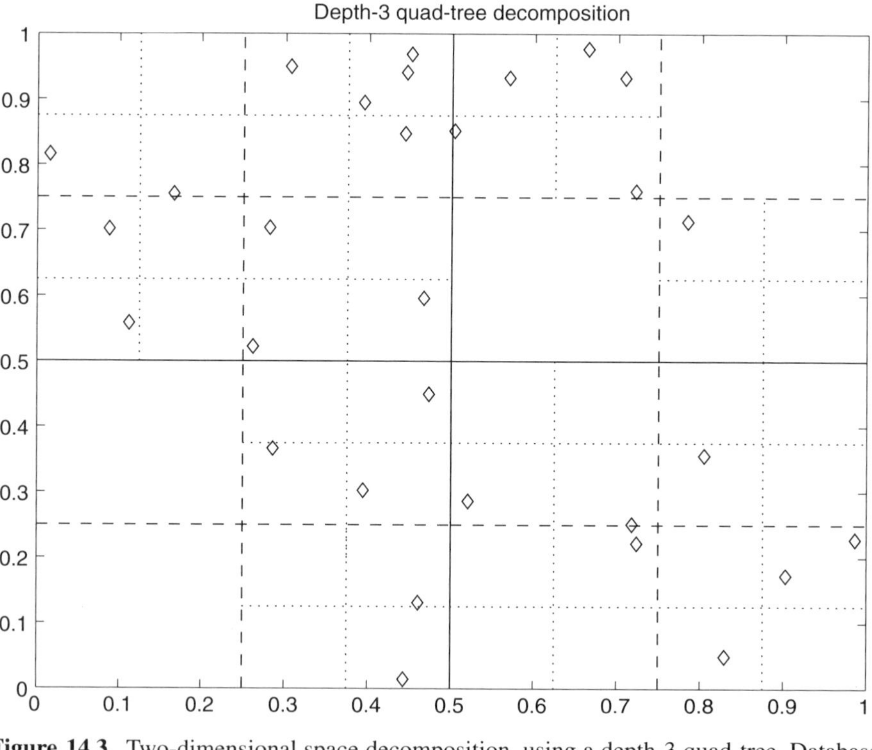

Figure 14.3. Two-dimensional space decomposition, using a depth-3 quad-tree. Database vectors are represented as diamonds. Different line types correspond to different levels of the tree. Starting from the root, these line types are solid, dashed, and dotted.

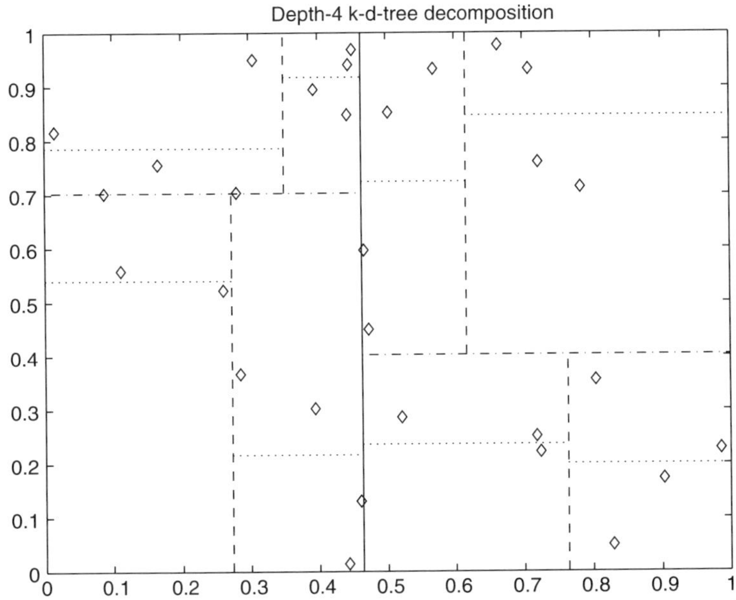

Figure 14.4. Two-dimensional space decomposition, using a depth-4 k-d-b-tree, a variation of the k-d-tree characterized by binary splits. Database vectors are denoted by diamonds. Different line types correspond to different levels of the tree. Starting from the root, these line types are solid, dash-dot, dashed, and dotted. The data set is identical to that of Figure 14.3.

R-trees divide the space into a collection of possibly overlapping hyperrectangles. Each internal node corresponds to a hyperrectangular region of the search space, which generally contains the hyperrectangular regions of the children. The indexed data is stored at the leaf nodes of the tree. Figure 14.5 shows an example of R-tree decomposition of the same data set used in Figures 14.3 and 14.4. From the figure, it is immediately clear that the hyperrectangles of different nodes need not be disjoint. This adds a further complication that was not present in the previous two classes of recursive decomposition methods.

Variations of the three types of methods exist that use hyperplanes (or hyperrectangles) having arbitrary orientations or nonlinear surfaces (such as spheres or polygons) as partitioning elements.

Although these methods were originally conceived to support point queries and range queries in low-dimensional spaces, they also support efficient algorithms for α-cut and nearest-neighbor queries (described in the Appendix).

Recursive-decomposition algorithms have good performance even in 10-dimensional spaces and can occasionally be useful to index up to 20 dimensions.

14.4.1.3 ***Projection-Based methods.*** Projection-based methods are indexing structures that support approximate nearest-neighbor queries. They can be

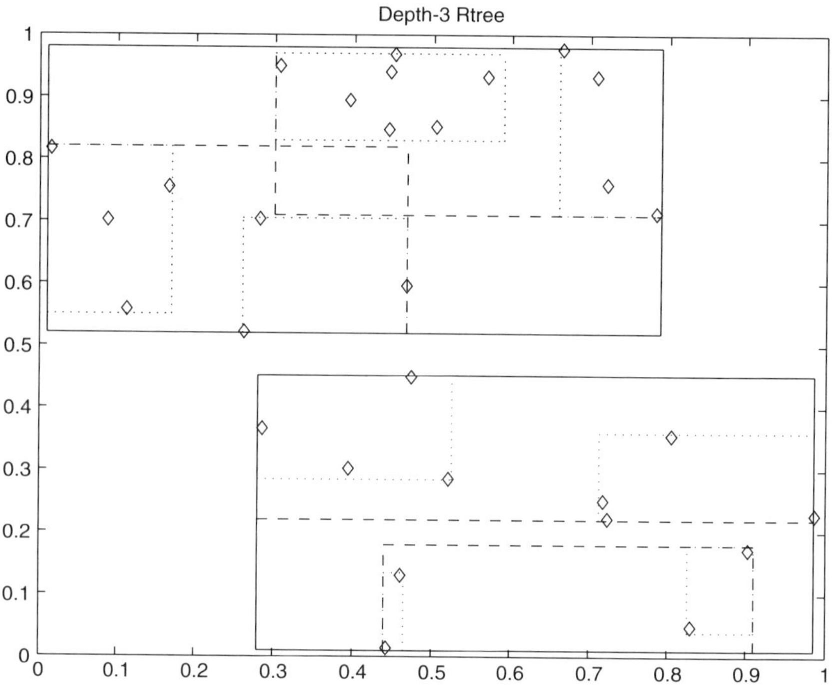

Figure 14.5. Two-dimensional space decomposition, using a depth-3 R-tree. The data set is identical to that of Figure 14.3. Database vectors are represented as diamonds. Different line types correspond to different levels of the tree. Starting from the root, these line types are solid, dashed, and dotted.

further divided into two categories, corresponding to the type of approximation performed.

The first subcategory, described in Appendix A.1.3.1, supports fixed-radius queries. Several methods project the database onto the coordinate axes, maintain a list for each collection of projections, and use the list to quickly identify a region of the search space containing a hypersphere of radius r centered on the query point. Other methods project the database onto appropriate $(d + 1)$-dimensional hyperplanes and find nearest neighbors by tracing an appropriate line[3] through the query point and finding its intersection with the hyperspaces.

The second subcategory, described in Appendix A.1.3.2, supports $(1 + \varepsilon)$-nearest-neighbor queries and contains methods that project high-dimensional databases onto appropriately selected or randomly generated lines and index the projections. Although probabilistic and approximate in nature, these algorithms support queries, the cost for which grows only linearly in the dimensionality of the search space, and are therefore well-suited for high-dimensional spaces.

[3] Details on what constitutes an appropriate line are contained in Appendix A.1.3.2.

14.4.1.4 Miscellaneous Partitioning Methods. There are several methods that do not fall into any of the previous categories. Appendix A.2 describes three of these: CSVD, the Onion index, and Berchtold's, Böhm's, and Kriegel's Pyramid (not to be confused with the homonymous quad-tree-like method described in Appendix A.1.2.1).

CSVD recursively partitions the space into "clusters" and independently reduces the dimensionality of each, using SVD. Branch-and-bound algorithms exist to perform approximate nearest-neighbor and α-cut queries. Medium- to high-dimensional natural data, such as texture vectors, appear to be well-indexed by CSVD.

The Onion index indexes a database by recursively constructing the convex hull of its points and "peeling it off." The data is hence divided into nested layers, each of which consist of the convex hull of the contained points. The Onion index is well-suited for search problems, in which the database items are scored using a convex scoring function (for instance, a linear function of the feature values) and the user wishes to retrieve the k items with highest score or all the items with a score exceeding a threshold. We immediately note a similarity with k-nearest-neighbor and α-cut queries; the difference is that k-nearest-neighbor and α-cut queries usually seek to maximize a concave rather than a convex scoring function.

The Pyramid divides the d-dimensional space into $2d$ pyramids centered at the origin and with heights aligned with the coordinate axes. Each pyramid is then sliced by $(d - 1)$-dimensional equidistant hyperplanes perpendicular to the coordinate axes. Algorithms exist to perform range queries.

14.4.2 Metric-Space Methods

Metric-space methods index the distances between database items rather than the individual database items. They are useful when the distances are provided with the data set (for example, as a result of psychological experiments) or when the selected metric is too computationally complex for interactive retrieval (and therefore it is more convenient to compute pairwise distances when adding items to the database).

Most metric-space methods are tailored toward solving nearest-neighbor queries and are not well-suited for α-cut queries. Few metric-space methods have been specifically developed to support α-cut queries but are not well-suited for nearest-neighbor searches. In general, metric-space indexes do not support range queries[4].

We can distinguish two main classes of approaches: those that index the metric structure of the search space and those that rely on vantage points.

14.4.2.1 Indexing the Metric Structure of a Space. There are two main ways of indexing the metric structure of a space to perform nearest-neighbor queries. The

[4] It is worth recalling that algorithms exist to perform all the three main similarity query types on each of the main recursive-partitioning vector-space indexes.

first is applicable when the distance function is known and consists of *indexing the Voronoi regions* of each database item. Given a database, each point of the feature space can be associated with the closest database item. The collection of feature space points associated with a database item is called its Voronoi region. Different distance functions produce different sets of Voronoi regions. An example of this class of indexes is the *cell* method [52] (Appendix A.3.1), which approximates Voronoi regions by means of their minimum-bounding rectangles (MBR) and indexes the MBRs with an X-tree [53] (Appendix A.1.2.3).

The second approach is viable when all the pairwise distances between database items are given. In principle, then, it is possible to associate with each database item an *ordered list* of all the other items, sorted in ascending order of distance. Nearest-neighbor queries are then reduced to a point query followed by the analysis of the list associated with the returned database item. Methods of this category are variations of this basic scheme, and try to reduce the complexity of constructing and maintaining the index.

14.4.2.2 Vantage-Point Methods. Vantage-point methods (Appendix A.3.2) rely on a tree structure to search the space. The vp-tree is a typical example of this class of methods. Each internal node indexes a disjoint subset of the database, has two children, and is associated with a database item called the *vantage point*. The items indexed by an internal node are sorted in increasing distance from the vantage point, the median distance is computed, and the items closer to the vantage point than the median distance are associated with the left subtree and the remaining ones with the right subtree. The indexing structure is well-suited for fixed-radius nearest-neighbor queries.

14.5 CHOOSING AN APPROPRIATE INDEXING STRUCTURE

It is very difficult to select an appropriate method for a specific application. There is currently no recipe to decide which indexing structure to adopt. In this section, we provide very general data-centric guidelines to narrow the decision to a few categories of methods.

The characteristics of the data and the metric used dictate whether it is most convenient to represent the database items as points in a vector space or to index the metric structure of the space.

The *useful dimensionality* is the other essential characteristic of the data. If we require exact answers, the useful dimensionality is the same as the original dimensionality of the data set. If approximate answers are allowed and dimensionality-reduction techniques can be used, then the useful dimensionality depends on the specific database and on the tolerance to approximations (specified, for example, as the allowed region in the precision-recall space). Here, we (somewhat arbitrarily) distinguish between low-dimensional spaces (with two or three dimensions), medium-dimensional spaces (with 4 to 20 dimensions), and high-dimensional spaces, and use this categorization to guide our selection criterion.

Finally, a category of methods that supports the desired type of query (range, α-cut, or nearest-neighbor) is selected.

Figure 14.6 provides rough guidelines to selecting vector-space methods, given the dimensionality of the search space and the type of query. Nonhierarchical methods are in general well-suited for low-dimensionality spaces, and algorithms exist to perform the three main types of queries. In general, their performance decays very quickly with the number of dimensions. Recursive-partitioning indexes perform well in low- and medium-dimensionality spaces. They are designed for point and range queries, and the Appendix describes algorithms to perform nearest-neighbor queries, which can also be adapted to α-cut queries. CSVD can often capture well the distribution of natural data and can be used for nearest-neighbor and α-cut queries in up to 100 dimensions, but not for range queries. The Pyramid technique can be used to cover this gap, although it does not gracefully support nearest-neighbor and α-cut queries in high dimensions. The Onion index supports a special case of α-cut queries (wherein the score is computed using a convex function). Projection-based methods are well-suited for nearest-neighbor queries in high-dimensional spaces, however, their complexity does not make them competitive with recursive-partitioning indexes in less than 20 dimensions.

Figure 14.7 guides the selection of metric-space methods, the vast majority of which support nearest-neighbor searches. A specific method, called the

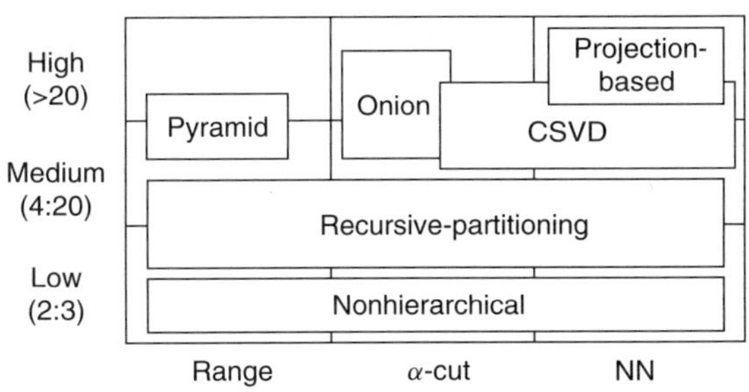

Figure 14.6. Selecting vector-space methods by dimensionality of the search space and query type.

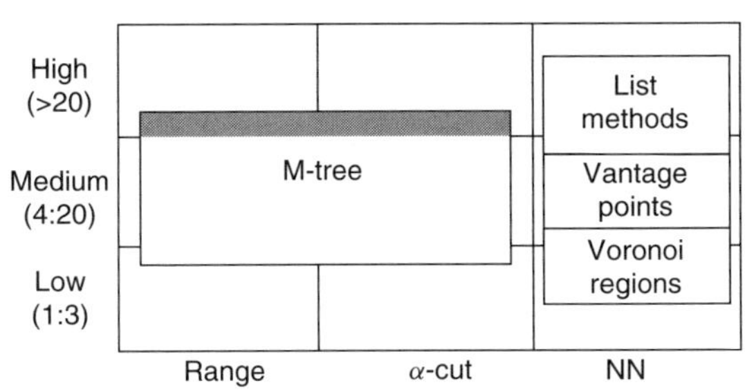

Figure 14.7. Selecting metric-space methods by dimensionality of the search space and type of query.

M-tree (Appendix A.3.4) can support range and α-cut searches in low- and medium-dimensionality spaces but is a poor choice for high-dimensional spaces. The remaining methods are only useful for nearest-neighbor searches. List methods can be used in medium-to-high-dimensional spaces, but their complexity precludes their use in low-dimensional spaces. Indexing Voronoi regions is a good solution to the 1-nearest-neighbor search problem, except in high-dimensionality spaces. Vantage point methods are well-suited for medium-dimensionality spaces.

Once a few large classes of candidate indexing structures have been identified, the other constraints of the problem can be used to further narrow the selection. We can ask whether probabilistic queries are allowed, whether there are space requirements, limits on the preprocessing cost, constraint on dynamically updating the database, and so on. The appendix details this information for numerous specific indexing schemes.

The class of recursive-partitioning methods is especially large. Often structures and algorithms have been developed to suit specific characteristics of the data sets, which are difficult to summarize, but are described in detail in the appendix.

14.5.1 A Caveat

Comparing indexing methods based on experiments is always extremely difficult. The main problem is of course the data. Almost invariably, the performance of an indexing method on real data is significantly different from the performance on synthetic data, sometimes by almost an order of magnitude. Extending conclusions obtained on synthetic data to real data is therefore questionable. On the other hand, because of the lack of an established collection of benchmarks for multidimensional indexes, each author performs experiments on data at hand, which makes it difficult to generalize the conclusions. Theoretical analysis is often tailored toward worst-case performance or probabilistic worst-case performance and rarely to average performance. Unfortunately, it also appears that some of the most commonly used methods are extremely difficult to analyze theoretically.

14.6 FUTURE DIRECTIONS

Despite of the large body of literature, the field of multidimensional indexing appears to still be very active. Aside from the everlasting quest for newer, better indexing structures, there appear to be at least three new directions for research, which are especially important for image databases.

In image databases, the search often is based on a combination of heterogeneous types of features (i.e., both numeric and categorical) specified at query-formulation time. Traditional multidimensional indexes do not readily support this type of query.

Iterative refinement is an increasingly popular way of dealing with the approximate nature of query specification in multimedia databases. The indexing structures described in this chapter are not well-suited to support iterative refinements, except when a query-rewrite strategy is used, namely, when the system does not keep a history of the previous refinement iterations.

Finally, it is interesting to note that the vast majority of multidimensional indexing structures are designed and optimized for obsolete computer architectures. There seems to be a consensus that most of the index should reside on disk and that only a part of it should be cached in main memory. This view made sense in the mid-1980s when a typical 1 MIPS machine would have 64–128 KB of RAM (almost as fast as the processor). In the meantime, several changes have occurred: the speed of the processor has increased by three orders of magnitude (and dual-processor PC-class machines are very common), the amount of RAM has increased by four orders of magnitude, and the size of disks has increased by five or six orders of magnitude. At the same time, the gap in the speed of the processor and the RAM has become increasingly wide, prompting the need for multiple levels of cache, while the speed of disks has barely tripled. Accessing a disk is essentially as expensive today as it was 15 years ago. However, if we think of accessing a processor register as opening a drawer of our desk to get an item, accessing a disk is the equivalent of going from New York to Sydney to retrieve the same information (though latency-hiding techniques exist in multitasking environments). Systems, supporting multimedia databases, are now sized in such a way that the indexes can comfortably reside in main memory, whereas the disks contain the bulk of the data (images, video clips, and so on.) Hence, metrics such as the average number of pages accessed during a query are nowadays of lesser importance. The concept of a page itself is not well-suited to current computer architectures, with the performance being strictly related to how well the memory hierarchy is used. Cache-savvy algorithms can potentially be significantly faster than similar methods that are oblivious to memory hierarchy.

APPENDIX

A.1 Vector-Space Methods

In this appendix we describe nonhierarchical methods, recursive decomposition approaches, projection-based algorithms, and several miscellaneous indexing structures.

A.1.1 Nonhierarchical Methods. A significant body of work exists on nonhierarchical indexing methods. The brute-force approach (*sequential scan*), in which each record is analyzed in response to a query, belongs to this class of methods. The *inverted list* of Knuth [54] is another simple method, consisting of separately indexing each coordinate in the database. One coordinate is then selected (e.g., the first) and the index is used to identify a set of candidates, which is then exhaustively searched.

We describe in detail two classes of approaches. The first maps a d-dimensional space onto the real line through a space-filling curve, the second partitions the space into nonoverlapping cells of known size.

Both methods are well-suited to index low-dimensional spaces, where $d \leq 10$, but their efficiency decays exponentially when $d > 20$. Between these two values, the characteristics of the specific data sets determine the suitability of the methods. Numerous other methods exist, such as the BANG file [55], but are not analyzed in detail here.

A.1.1.1 Mapping High-Dimensional Spaces onto the Real Line. A class of method exists that addresses multidimensional-indexing by mapping the search space onto the real line and then using one-dimensional-indexing techniques. The most common approach consists of ordering the database using the positions of the individual items on a space-filling curve [56], such as the *Hilbert* or *Peano-Hilbert curve* [57] or the *z-ordering*, also known as *Morton ordering* [58–63]. We describe the algorithms introduced in Ref. [47] that rely on the z-ordering, as representative. For a description of the *zkdb-tree*, the interested reader is referred to the paper by Orenstein and Merret [62].

The z-ordering works as follows. Consider a database $\mathcal{X}$ and partition the data into two parts by splitting along the x axis according to a predefined rule (e.g., by dividing positive and negative values of x). The left partition will be identified by the number 0 and the right by the number 1. Recursively split each partition into two parts, identifying the left part by a 0 and the right part by a 1. This process can be represented as a binary tree, the branches of which are labeled with zeros and ones. Each individual subset obtained through s recursive steps is a strip perpendicular to the x axis and is uniquely defined by a string of s zeros or ones, corresponding to the path from the root of the binary tree to the node associated with this subset. Now, partition the same database by recursively splitting along the y axis. In this case, a partition is a strip perpendicular to the y axis. We can then represent the intersection of two partitions (one obtained by splitting the x axis and the other obtained by splitting the y axis) by interleaving the corresponding strings of zeros and ones. Note that, if the search space is two-dimensional, this intersection is a rectangle, whereas in d dimensions the intersection is a $(d-2)$-dimensional cylinder (that is, a hyperrectangle that is unbounded in $d-2$ dimensions) with an axis that is perpendicular to the x-y plane and a rectangular intersection with the x-y plane. The z-ordering has several interesting properties. If a rectangle is identified by a string s, it contains all the rectangles whose strings have s as a prefix. Additionally, rectangles whose strings are close in lexicographic order are usually close in the original space, which allows one to perform range and nearest-neighbor queries, as well as spatial joins.

The *HG-tree* of Cha and Chung [64–66] also belongs to this class. It relies on the Hilbert Curve to map n-dimensional points onto the real line. The indexing structure is similar to a B*-tree [67]. The directory is constructed and maintained using algorithms that keep the directory coverage to a minimum and control the correlation between storage utilization and directory coverage.

When the tree is modified, the occupancy of the individual nodes is kept above a minimum, selected to meet requirements on the worst-case performance. Internal nodes consist of pairs (*minimum bounding interval, pointer to child*), in which minimum bounding intervals are similar to minimum bounding rectangles, but are not allowed to overlap. In experiments on synthetically generated four-dimensional data sets containing 100,000 objects, the HG-tree shows improvements on the number of accessed pages of 4 to 25 percent more than the Buddy-Tree [68] on range queries, whereas on nearest-neighbor queries the best result was a 15 percent improvement and the worst a 25 percent degradation.

A.1.1.2 Multidimensional-Hashing and Grid Files. *Grid files* [51,69–74] are extensions of the *fixed-grid method* [54]. The fixed-grid method partitions the search space into hypercubes of known fixed size and groups all the records contained in the same hypercube into a bucket. These characteristics make it very easy to identify (for instance, via a table lookup) and search the hypercube that contains a query vector. Well-suited for range queries in small dimensions, fixed grids suffer from poor space utilization in high-dimensional spaces, where most buckets are empty. Grid files attempt to overcome this limitation by relaxing the requirement that the cells be fixed-size hypercubes and by allowing multiple blocks to share the same bucket, provided that their union is a hyperrectangle.

The index for the grid file is very simple: it consists of d one-dimensional arrays, called *linear scales*, each of which contains all the splitting points along a specific dimension and a set of pointers to the buckets, one for each grid block. The grid file is constructed using a top-down approach by inserting one record at a time. Split and merge operations are possible during construction and index maintenance. There are two types of split: overflowed buckets are split, usually without any influence on the underlying grid; the grid can also be refined by defining a new splitting point when an overflowed bucket contains a single grid cell. Merges are possible when a bucket becomes underutilized.

To identify the grid block to which a query point belongs, the linear scales are searched and the one-dimensional partitions to which an attribute belongs are found. The index of the pointer is then immediately computed and the resulting bucket exhaustively searched. Algorithms for range queries are rather simple and are based on the same principle. Nievergelt, Hinterberger, and Sevcik [51] showed how to index spatial objects, using grid files, by transforming the d-dimensional minimum bounding rectangle into a $2d$-dimensional point. The cost of identifying a specific bucket is $O(d \log n)$ and the size of the directory is linear in the number of dimensions and (in general) superlinear in the database size.

As the directory size is linear in the number of grid cells, nonuniform distributions that result in most cells being empty adversely affect the space requirement of the index. A solution is to use a hashing function to map data points into their corresponding bucket. *Extendible hashing*, introduced by Fagin, Nievergelt, Pippenger, and Strong [75], is a commonly used and widely studied approach [63,76–78]. Here we describe a variant due to Otoo [74] (the *BMEH-tree*), suited for higher-dimensional spaces. The index contains a directory and a set of pages. A directory entry corresponds to an individual page and consists of a pointer to the page, a collection of *local depths*, one per dimension, describing the length of the common prefix of all the entries in the page along the corresponding dimension, and a value specifying the dimension along which the directory was last expanded. Given a key, a d-dimensional index is quickly constructed that uniquely identifies, through a mapping function, a unique directory entry. The corresponding page can then be searched. A hierarchical directory can be used to mitigate the negative effects of nonuniform data distributions.

G-trees [79,80] combine B^+-trees [67] with grid-files. The search space is partitioned using a grid of variable size partitions, individual cells are uniquely identified by a string describing the splitting history, and the strings are stored in a B^+-tree. Exact queries and range queries are supported. Experiments in Ref. [80] show that when the dimensionality of the search space is moderate (<16) and the query returns a significant portion of the database, the method is significantly superior to the Buddy Hash Tree [81], the BANG file [55], the hB-tree [50] (Section A.1.2.2), and the 2-level grid file [82]. Its performance is somewhat worse when the number of retrieved items is small.

A.1.2 Recursive Partitioning Methods. As the name implies, recursive partitioning methods recursively divide the search space into progressively smaller regions, usually mapped into nodes of trees or tries[1], until a termination criterion is satisfied. Most of these methods were originally developed as SAM or PAM to execute point or range queries in low-dimensionality spaces (typically, for images, geographic information systems applications, and volumetric data) and have subsequently been extended to higher-dimensional spaces. In more recent times, algorithms have been proposed to perform nearest-neighbor using several of these indexes. In this section, we describe three main classes of indexes: quad-trees, k-d-trees, and R-trees, which differ in the partitioning step. In each section, we first describe the original method from which all the indexes in the class were derived, then we discuss its limitations and how different variants try to overcome them. For k-d-trees and R-trees, a separate subsection is devoted to how nearest-neighbor searches should be performed.

We do not describe in detail numerous other similar indexing structures such as the *range tree* [83] and the *priority search tree* [84].

Note, finally, that recursive partitioning methods were originally developed for low-dimensionality search spaces. It is therefore unsurprising that they all suffer from the curse-of-dimensionality and generally become ineffective when $d > 20$, except in rare cases in which the data sets have a peculiar structure.

A.1.2.1 Quad-Trees and Extensions. *Quad-Trees* [85] are a large class of hierarchical indexing structures that perform recursive decomposition of the search space. Originally devised to index two-dimensional data, they have been extended to multidimensional spaces. Three-dimensional quad-trees are called *octrees*; there is no commonly used name for the d-dimensional extension. We will refer to them simply as quad-trees. Quad-trees are extremely popular in Geographic

[1] With an abuse of terminology, we will not make explicit distinctions between tries and trees, both to simplify the discussion and because the distinction is actually rarely made in the literature.

Information System (GIS) applications, in which they are used to index points, lines, and objects.

Typically, quad-trees are trees of degree 2^d, where d is the dimension of the sample space; hence, each nonterminal node has 2^d children. Each step of the decomposition consists of identifying d splitting points (one along each dimension) and partitioning the space by means of $(d - 1)$-dimensional hyperplanes passing through the splitting point and orthogonal to the splitting point coordinate axis. Splitting a node of a d-quad-tree consists of dividing each dimension into two parts, thus defining 2^d hyperrectangles. A detailed analysis of the retrieval performance of quad-trees can be found in Ref. [78].

The various flavors of these indexing structures correspond to the type of data indexed (i.e., points or regions), to specific splitting rules (i.e., strategies for selecting the splitting points) and tree-construction methods, to different search algorithms, and to where the data pointers are contained (just at the leaves or also at intermediate nodes).

The *region quad-tree* [87] decomposes the space into squares aligned with the axes and is well-suited to represent regions. A full-region quad-tree is also commonly known as a *pyramid.*

The *point quad-tree* introduced by Finkel and Bentley [88] uses an adaptive decomposition in which the splitting points depend on the distribution of the data and is well-suited to represent points.

Although the implementations of region quad-trees and linear quad-trees rely on pointers, more efficient representations are possible. The key observation is that individual nodes of a quad-tree can be uniquely identified by strings, called *location codes*, of four symbols, representing the four quadrants (NE, NW, SW, SE). Linear quad-trees [61,89] rely on location codes to represent the quad-tree as an array of nodes, without using pointers.

Extensions to spatiotemporal indexing include the segment indexes of Kolovson and Stonebraker [90] (that are really general extensions of multidimensional-indexing techniques) and the overlapping linear Quad-Trees [91].

Point queries (exact searches) using quad-trees are trivial and are executed by descending the tree until the result is found. Because of the geometry of the space partition, which relies on hyperplanes aligned with the axes, the quad-tree can be easily used to perform range queries. In low-dimensionality spaces, fast algorithms for range queries exist for quad-trees and pyramids [92].

Quad-Trees, however, are not especially well-suited for high-dimensional indexing. Their main drawback is that each split node has always 2^d children, irrespective of the splitting rule. Thus, even in search spaces that are of small dimensions for image database applications, for instance $d = 20$, the quad-tree is in general very sparse, that is, most of its nodes are empty. Faloutsos and coworkers [93] derived the average number of blocks that need to be visited to satisfy a range query, under the assumption that the conditional distribution of the query hyperrectangle given its dimensions is uniform over the allowable range, and showed that it grows exponentially in the number of dimensions. Quad-trees

Experiments on a database containing 160,000 60-dimensional texture feature vectors show that when performing 20-nearest-neighbor queries, CSVD using 32 clusters, is 100 times faster than sequential scan if the desired recall is .985 and 140 times faster if the desired recall is .97.

A.2.2 ***The Onion Index.*** Although most queries belong to the three main categories described in Section 14.2.2, sometimes the user wants to retrieve from the databases, records that maximize a particular scoring function.

The Onion technique [144] retrieves from a database the points maximizing a linear- or convex-scoring function. The main property on which the method relies is that points maximizing a convex function belong to the convex hull of the database. The index is then constructed by iteratively computing the convex hull of the data set and removing all its points. The database is therefore "peeled" in layers like an onion, hence the name. Points belonging to each layer are stored in a separate list. Figure 14A.2 contains an example.

A query is specified by providing a scoring function and the number of desired results. If the function is linear, only the coefficients associated with each dimension are required. The search starts by sequentially searching the outermost layer, proceeds toward the center, and maintains a list of current results. The search

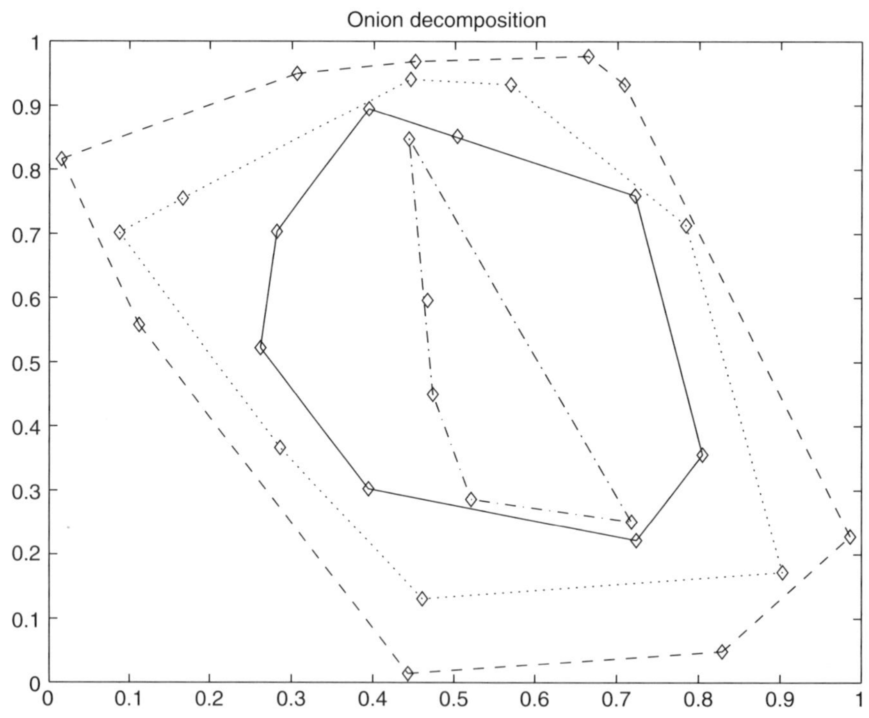

Figure 14A.2. Two-dimensional space indexing, using the onion data structure. Database vectors are denoted by diamonds. The data set is identical to that of Figure 14.3.

are also rather inefficient for exact α-cut and nearest-neighbor queries because hyperspheres are not well-approximated by hyperrectangles (see Section 14.2.4).

Quad-Trees can be used in image databases to index objects segmented from images and to index features in low-dimensionality spaces. Despite their simplicity, quad-trees are rarely used for high-dimensional feature-indexing because of their poor performance in high-dimensional spaces.

A.1.2.2 K-Dimensional Trees. The k-dimensional tree, known as *k-d tree* [94,95], is another commonly used hierarchical indexing structure.

The original version, Bentley's, operates by recursively subdividing the search space one dimension at a time, using a round-robin approach. Each splitting step is essentially identical to that of a binary search tree [54]. Points are stored at both internal nodes and leaves, somewhat complicating the deletion process. In its original incarnation, the tree is constructed by inserting one point at a time and the splitting hyperplanes are constrained to pass through one of the points. A subsequent version [83], called *adaptive k-d-tree*, selects splitting points that divide the number of points in the node into two equal sets.

A dynamic version, called *k-d-b-tree*, supporting efficient insertion and deletion of points was proposed by Robinson [96]. K-d-b-trees consist of collections of pages: region pages, which correspond to disjoint regions of the search space, and point pages, which contain collections of points. The leaves of the tree are point pages and the internal nodes are region pages. Several splitting strategies and algorithms for efficient insertion, deletion, and reorganization are described in [144]. The method is quite elegant and is amenable to very efficient and compact implementations. As a consequence, it is still commonly used and is often one of the reference methods in experiments.

A limitation of the k-d-tree is that, in some cases, the index and data nodes cannot be efficiently split and the result is a significant utilization imbalance. The *hB-trees* (holey brick trees) [50] address this problem by allowing nodes to represent hyperrectangular regions with hyperrectangular holes. This last property makes them also a multidimensional extension of the DL*-tree [97]. The shape of the holey hyperrectangles indexed by an internal node is described by a k-d-tree called *local k-d-tree*. Several mechanisms for constructing and maintaining the data structure are derived from the one-dimensional B+-tree [67]. Node-splitting during construction is a distinguishing feature of hB-trees: corner splits remove a quadrant from a hyperrectangle or a holey hyperrectangle. Most of the complexity associated with the data structure is concentrated in the splitting algorithms, guaranteeing robustness in worst cases. This index supports both exact and range queries.

Although most k-d-tree variations split the space along one coordinate at a time and the partitioning hyperplanes at adjacent levels are perpendicular or parallel, this restriction can be relaxed. For example, the *BSP-tree (Binary Space Partition Tree)* [98–100] uses general partitioning hyperplanes.

NEAREST-NEIGHBOR QUERIES USING K-D-TREES. K-d-trees and variations are well-suited for nearest-neighbor searches when the number of indexed dimensions is moderate.

Kim and Park [101] proposed an indexing structure, called *ordered partition*, which can be considered a variation of the k-d-tree. The database is recursively divided across individual dimensions, in a round-robin fashion, and the split points are selected to produce subsets of equal size. The recursive decomposition can be represented as a tree, in which a node at level ℓ corresponds to a region that is unbounded in the last $d - \ell + 1$ dimensions and bounded between a pair of hyperplanes parallel to the first $\ell - 1$ dimensions. A branch-and-bound search strategy [102,103] is used to retrieve the k-nearest points (in Euclidean distance) to the query sample. First, the node to which the query sample belongs (primary node) is identified by descending the tree and exhaustively searched, thus producing a current k-nearest-neighbor set. The distance of the kth neighbor becomes the bound B. The distances between the query sample and the hyperrectangles of the siblings of the primary node are then computed and a candidate set that includes all nodes at distance less than B is created. The candidate nodes are exhaustively searched on the order of increasing distance from the query. The bound B and the candidate set are updated at the end of every exhaustive search. When all candidates have been visited, a backtracking step is taken by considering the siblings of the parent of the primary node and applying the same algorithm recursively. The search terminates when the root is reached. If the Euclidean distance is used, distance computations can be performed during the traversal of the tree and require only one subtraction, one multiplication, and one addition per node. The method is also suited for general Minkowsky and weighted Minkowsky distances. The authors suggest a fan-out equal to the (average) number of points stored at the leaves. The approach is extremely simple to implement in a very efficient fashion and produces very good results in few dimensions. However, for synthetic data, the number of visited terminal and nonterminal nodes appears to grow exponentially in the number of dimensions. For real data, the method significantly benefits from a rotation (using SVD) of the feature spaces into uncorrelated coordinates ordered by descending eigenvalues. A similar method was proposed by Niemann and Goppert [104]. The main difference lies in the partitioning algorithm, which is not recursive, and divides each dimension into a fixed number of intervals. A matrix containing the split points along each coordinate is maintained and used during the search. Niemann's approach seems to be twice as fast as previous versions [103].

A data structure that combines properties of quad-trees and of k-d-trees is the *balanced quad-tree* [105–107], which can be used to efficiently perform approximate nearest-neighbor queries provided the allowed approximation is large. A balanced quad-tree, like a k-d-tree, is a binary tree. Coordinates are split in a round-robin fashion as in the case of the construction of the region quad-tree, and in the same spirit, splits divide the hyperrectangle of inner nodes into two hyperrectangles of equal size. To efficiently process nearest-neighbor queries on a database $\mathcal{X}$, a set of vectors $\{\mathbf{v}_j\}$ is considered and a balanced quad-tree is

Table 14A.1. Comparsion of $(1+\varepsilon)$ Nearest-Neighbors (see Section 14.2.2 for the Definition of This Type of Queries), Relying on Balanced Quad-Trees

Author and Ref.	Nr. of Vectors	Vector Selection	Value of ε	Search Time	Construction Time
Bern [105]	$\sqrt{d}$	Deterministic	2^d	$d \cdot 2^d \cdot \log n$	$d \cdot 8^d \cdot n \cdot \log n$
Bern [105][a]	$t \cdot \log n$	Randomized	$d^{3/2}$		
Chan [106,107]	d	Deterministic	$4d^{\frac{3}{2}} + 4d^{\frac{1}{2}} + 1$	$d^2 \log n$	

[a] Bern's second algorithm depends on the parameter t: this parameter determines the probability that the algorithm actually finds $(1+\varepsilon)$-neighbors (which is equal to $1 - O(1/n^t)$) and the number of vectors used in the construction of the index. *Note*: As described in the text, this type of search is supported by constructing a set of vectors, adding each vector to all the database records, and constructing a balanced quad-tree. Hence, the index is composed of one balanced quad-tree for each vector in the set. The methods summarized differ in the number of required vectors and in the procedure used to select them. These parameters determine the magnitude of the approximation (ε), the construction time, and the search time. Time values are $O(\cdot)$-order costs; ε and the number of vectors are actual values.

constructed for each translated version $\mathcal{X} + \mathbf{v}_j$ of the database. Several algorithms belonging to this class have been proposed and are summarized in Table 14A.1. They differ on the number of representative vectors and on the selection criterion for the vectors. They yield different approximations (the ε), and have different index construction and search costs.

The *BBD-tree* (balanced-box-decomposition) of Arya and coworkers [108,109] is an extension that supports $(1+\varepsilon)$-approximate nearest-neighbor. The recursive decomposition associates nodes with individual *cells*, each of which is either a hyperrectangle aligned with the axes or the set-theoretic difference between two such nested hyperrectangles. Each leaf contains a single database item. As is often the case, the tricky part of the tree-construction algorithm is the splitting of nodes: here a decision must be made on whether to use a hyperplane perpendicular to one of the coordinate axes or an inner box (called *shrinking box*). Searching a BBD-tree consists of first finding the cell that contains the query point, computing the distances from the other cells, and finally searching the terminal cells ordered by increasing distance. A list of current results is maintained during the search. The algorithm terminates when the closest unsearched cell is at a distance larger than $(1-\varepsilon)$ times the distance of the farthest current result. The search is therefore approximate as cells that could contain exact neighbors can be discarded. The decomposition into cells achieves exponential decrease in the number of points and in the volume of the space searched while the tree is visited, and in this sense, the BBD-tree combines properties of the optimized k-d-tree and of quad-trees with bounded aspect ratio. Theoretical analysis shows that the number of boxes intersected by a sphere of radius r is $O(r^d)$, thus it grows exponentially in the number of dimensions. The number of leaf cells visited by a k-nearest-neighbor search is $O(k + d^d)$ for any Minkowsky metric, wherein k is the desired number of neighbors. Experimental results on synthetic data sets containing 100,000 points in 15 dimensions show that, depending on the distribution, the BBD-tree can perform from slightly better than the optimized k-d-tree up to 100 times faster. Additionally, the quality of the search is apparently very good despite the approximation and the number of missed nearest-neighbors is small. Search times, space requirements, and construction times for this method and for subsequent improvements are reported in Table 14.A.2.

A.1.2.3 R-Trees and Derived Methods. The R-tree [112] and its numerous variations (such as [113]) are probably the most-studied multidimensional indexing structures, hence we devote a long section to their description. The distinctive feature of the R-tree is the use of hyperrectangles, rather than hyperplanes, to partition the search space. The hyperrectangle associated with a particular node contains all the hyperrectangles of the children.

The most important properties for R-tree performance are overlap, space utilization, rectangle elongation, and coverage.

- *Overlap* between k nodes is the area (or volume) contained in at least two of the rectangles associated with the nodes. Overlap for a level is the overlap of all the nodes at that level. If multiple overlapping nodes intersect a query region, they need to be visited even though only one might contain relevant data.
- *Utilization.* Nodes in an R-tree contain a predefined number of items, often selected to ensure that the size of the node is a multiple of the unit of storage on disk. The utilization of a node is the ratio of the actual number of

Table 14A.2. The Table Compares the Costs of Different Algorithms to Perform $1 + \varepsilon$ Approximate Nearest-Neighbor Queries, Using BBD-Trees

Author	1-nn search time	k-nn search time	Space requirement	Construction time
Arya et al. [108,109]	$d \cdot \left(\frac{d}{\varepsilon}\right)^d \cdot \log n$	$d \cdot \left(\frac{d}{\varepsilon}\right)^d + k \cdot d \cdot \log n$	$d \cdot n$	$d \cdot n \cdot \log n$
Clarkson [110]	$\varepsilon^{\frac{1-d}{2}} \cdot \log n$	—	$\varepsilon^{\frac{1-d}{2}} \cdot n \cdot \log \rho$	$\varepsilon^{1-d} \cdot n^2 \cdot \log \frac{1}{\varepsilon}$
Chan[106,107]	$\varepsilon^{\frac{1-d}{2}} \cdot \log n$	—	$\varepsilon^{\frac{1-d}{2}} \cdot n \cdot \log n$	$\varepsilon^{\frac{1-d}{2}} \cdot n \cdot \log n$

Note: The values reported are the search times for 1 and k nearest-neighbor queries, the space requirement for the index, and the preprocessing time. The reported values describe the $O(\cdot)$-order costs. Recall that d is the number of dimensions, n is the database size, and k is the number of desired neighbors. Clarkson's algorithm is a probabilistic method (guarantees results with high probability) that relies on results in Ref. [111]. The quantity ρ is the ratio of the distance between the two furthest points and the distance between the two closest points in the database.

contained items to its maximum value. Poor utilization affects performance. If numerous nodes have a small number of descendants, the size of the tree grows, and consequently, the number of nodes to be visited during searches becomes large. Another effect, relevant when the index is paged on disk and only a maximum number of nodes is cached, is the increase in the I/O cost.

- *Node elongation* is the ratio of the lengths of the longest and the shortest sides of the associated hyperrectangle. Bounding rectangles that are very elongated in some directions, whereas thin in others, are visited fruitlessly more often than rectangles that are close to squares (or hypercubes). A measure of skewness or elongation is the ratio of surface area to volume, which is minimized by hypercubes.
- *Coverage* is defined for each level of the tree as the total area (or volume) of the rectangles associated with the level. Excessive coverage is a small problem in low dimensions, but it can become significant in high dimensions, where the data set is sparser and a large part of the covered space is, in fact, empty (dead space).

Because the tree is constructed by inserting one item at a time, the result is highly dependent on the order in which the data is inserted. Different orders of the same data can produce highly optimized trees or very poorly organized trees.

Although some authors, for instance, Faloutsos [114], have reported that the R-tree shows some robustness with respect to the curse-of-dimensionality, being efficient in up to 20 dimensions, over the years there have been numerous extensions of the basic scheme that attempt to minimize the different causes of inefficiency.

The first class of extensions retain most of the characteristics of the original R-tree. In particular, the partitioning element is a hyperrectangle, data is stored at the leaves, and each data point is indexed by a unique leaf.

R^+-trees [115] address the problem of minimizing overlap. They are constructed in a top-down fashion using splitting rules that generate nonoverlapping rectangles. The rectangle associated with each node is constrained to strictly contain the rectangles of its children, if the children are internal nodes, and can overlap the rectangles of its children only if the children are leaves. Copies of a spatial object are stored in each leaf it overlaps. The similarity with k-b-d-trees is not accidental: R^+-trees can, in fact, be thought of as extensions of k-b-d-trees that add two properties: the ability to index spatial objects (rather than points in k-dimensional spaces) and an improvement in coverage as the coverage of the children of a node need not be equal to the coverage of their parent and can be significantly smaller. The search algorithms are essentially identical to those used for regular R-trees. The insertion algorithm is a derivation of the downward split used in the k-b-d-trees. Splitting when a node overflow occurs involves a partitioning and a packing step, which maintain the desired properties of the tree. The R^+-tree shows significant performance improvement over R-trees, especially for large database sizes.

R-trees* [116] are an attempt to optimize the tree with respect to all four main causes of performance degradation described above. The node selection procedure of the insertion algorithm selects the node that results in smaller overlap enlargement and resolve ties by minimizing area enlargement. Alternatively, to reduce the high computational cost of the procedure, the nodes are first sorted in increasing value of area enlargement and the selection algorithm is applied to the first p nodes of the list. When splitting a node, different algorithms can be used that minimize the overall volume increase (area in 2-d), the overall surface area (perimeter in 2-d), the overall overlap, and combinations of the above. A forced reinsertion algorithm is also proposed to mitigate the dependence of the tree on the order in which the data are inserted: during the insertion of a new item, when a split occurs at a particular level, the node is reorganized by selecting an appropriate subset of its children, removing them from the node, and reinserting them from the top. Note that the procedure could induce new splits at the same level from which it was initiated. Forced reinsertion is applied at most once per level during each insertion of a new item. In experiments reported in Ref. [116] based on a database containing 100,000 points, the R*-tree outperforms the original R-tree by a factor of 1.7 to 4 and Greene's version [113] by a factor of 1.2 to 2.

Packed R-trees are a family of methods that attempt to improve space utilization. The strategy proposed by Roussopoulos and Leifker [117] consists of sorting the data on one of the coordinates of a selected corner of the minimum-bounding rectangle, representing the objects. Let n be the maximum number of objects that a leaf of an R-tree can contain. Then the first n items in the sorted list are assigned to the first leaf of the R-tree, the following n to the second leaf, and so on. The resulting leaves correspond to rectangles that are elongated in one direction and rather thin in the other. Experimental results suggest that in two dimensions, the approach outperforms quadratic split R-trees and R*-trees for point queries on point data but not on range queries or for spatial data represented as rectangles. Kamel and Faloutsos introduced a different packed R-tree [118], which overcomes these limitations. Instead of ordering the data according to a chosen dimension, they use a space-filling curve and select the Hilbert curve over the z-ordering [47] and the Gray-code [119]. Results in Ref. [120] show that it achieves better clustering than the other two methods. The Hilbert curve induces an ordering on the k-dimensional grid; several methods that rely on this ordering are described to assign a unique numeric index to each of the minimum-bounding rectangle (MBR) of the objects. The R-tree is then constructed by first filling the leaves and then building higher-level nodes. The first leaf (leaf no i) contains the first n items in the Hilbert order, the second leaf contains the next n items, and so on. Higher-level nodes are generated by grouping nodes from the previous level on the order of their creation. For instance, the first node at level 1, which corresponds to a set of L leaves, will contain pointers to leaves $1, 2, \ldots, L$. In experiments on two-dimensional real and synthetic data, the number of pages touched by Kamel's and Faloutsos' packed R-tree during range queries is between 1/4 and 1/2 of those touched by Roussopoulos' and

Leifker's version and always outperforms (by a factor of up to 2) the R*-trees and the quadratic split R-tree. The *Hilbert R-tree* [121] is a further development characterized by sorting hyperrectangles by the Hilbert ordering of their centers and having intermediate nodes contain information on the Hilbert values of the items stored at its descendant leaves. The Hilbert R-tree has also improved index management properties.

A different approach to minimizing overlap is used in the *X-tree* [53]. Three types of nodes are used: the first two are the data nodes (corresponding to a set of objects and containing for each of these, an MBR and a pointer) and the directory nodes (containing for each child, an MBR and a pointer) that have fixed size and are essentially identical to those of a traditional R-tree. The third type of nodes are called supernodes, which contain large directories and have variable size. They are used to avoid splits that would produce inefficient directory structures. Appropriate construction and management algorithms ensure that the X-tree maintains minimum node overlap. Experimental comparisons, using real data in 2 to 16 dimensions, show that insertion is up to 10 times faster than with R*-trees. When performing nearest-neighbor queries on synthetic data, the R*-trees require up to twice the CPU of the X-trees and access up to 6 times more leaf nodes. When operating on real data, the X-trees are up to 250 times faster than the corresponding R*-trees. When performing point queries on a database of 25,000 synthetically generated data points in up to 10 dimensions, the X-tree is essentially equivalent to the TV-tree [122] (described in the following sections) but becomes significantly faster in more than 10 dimensions. Berchtold [123] also proposed a parallel version of the X-tree, in which the search space is recursively decomposed into quadrants and a graph-coloring algorithm is used to assign different portions of the database to different disks for storage and to different processors during nearest-neighbor search. Experimental results, on 8 to 15 dimensional real and artificial data, show that declustering using the Hilbert curve [124] (a well-known competitive approach) is slower than the parallel X-tree, typically by a factor of $a(n_{\text{disks}} - 2) + b$, where n_{disks} is the number of available disks, b varies between 1 and 2, and a is between .3 and .6.

The *VAMSplit R-Tree* [125] optimizes the R-tree construction by employing techniques derived from the k-d-tree. The main gist of this top-down approach is the recursive partitioning of the data space using a hyperplane perpendicular to the coordinate along which the variance of the data is maximum. The split-point selection algorithm minimizes the number of disk blocks required to store the information. In the experiments, it appears to outperform both SStrees and R*-trees.

The *S-Tree* [126] (skew tree) is a data structure for range queries and point queries that tries to minimize the number of pages touched during the search. It combines the properties of the R-tree and of the B-Tree [67]. Leaves and internal nodes are identical to the data and directory nodes of the R-tree. Each internal node has a fan-out exactly equal to its maximum value, except for the "penultimate" nodes, whose children are all leaves. Two parameters of the index are the skew factor p, taking values between 0 and 1/2, and the maximum allowed overlap. Given any pair of sibling nodes and calling $N1$ and $N2$ the number of leaves in the subtrees rooted at these nodes, the index construction and maintenance try to minimize the total coverage while guaranteeing that $p \leq N1/N2 \leq p^{-1}$ and that the allowable overlap is not exceeded. The index construction time is $O(d \cdot n \cdot \log n)$, where d is the number of dimensions and n is the database size. Experiments on two-dimensional synthetic data showed that the method performs better than Hilbert R-tree, but the results in higher dimensions are not known.

NEAREST-NEIGHBOR QUERIES USING R-TREES. Although range queries (both for overlap and for containment) are easily performed using R-trees and spatial joins can be performed by transforming them into containment queries [127], the first method for nearest-neighbor queries was proposed by Roussopoulos, Kelley, and Vincent [128]. The search relies on two metrics defined in Table 14A.3 called MINDIST and MINMAXDIST, which measure the distance between a point $\mathbf{x}$ and a hyperrectangle R by using the two vertices on the main diagonal, $\mathbf{s}$ and $\mathbf{t}$. MBRs with MINDIST larger than the distance to the farthest current result will be pruned and MBRs with MINMAXDIST smaller than the distance to the farthest current result will be visited.

Methods Derived from the R-Tree. We now devote the rest of the section to indexing structures that, although derived from the R-tree, significantly depart from its basic paradigm by using partitioning elements other than hyperrectangles, by storing pointers to database elements in internal nodes, or by allowing multiple pointers to the same database elements. These methods are often tailored to specific types of queries.

Some data types are not well-suited for indexing with R-trees or for multidimensional indexing structures based on recursive decomposition. These are typically objects, with a bounding box that is significantly more elongated in one dimension than in another. An example is segments aligned with the coordinate axes. A paradigm was introduced by Kolovson and Stonebraker [90], aimed at solving this difficulty. The resulting class of indexing approaches, called *Segment Indexes*, can be used to modify other existing techniques. When the methodology is applied to an R-tree, the resulting structure is called a *Segment R-tree* or a *SR-tree*. SR-trees can store data items at different levels, not only at leaves. If a segment spans the rectangles of several nodes, it is stored in the one closest to the root. If necessary, the end portions of the segment are stored in the other nodes. A variation of the index is the *Skeleton SR-tree*, in which the data domain is recursively partitioned into nonoverlapping rectangles, using the distribution of the entire database, and items are subsequently inserted in any order. The resulting tessellation of the search space resembles more closely that of a nonbalanced quad-tree than that of an R-tree. Experimental results in two dimensions show that the SR-tree has essentially the same performance as the R-tree, whereas 10-fold gains can be obtained using the Skeleton version.

When the restriction that the hyperplanes defining a hyperrectangle be perpendicular to one of the Cartesian coordinate axes is removed, a bounding polyhedron can be used as the base shape of an indexing scheme. Examples are the

Table 14A.3. Definition of the Metrics MINDIST and MINMAXDIST Used by Branch-and-Bound Nearest-Neighbor Search Algorithms, Using R-trees

Let **x** be the query point and R be a hyperrectangle. Let **s** and **t** be the vertices on the main diagonal of R, with the convention that $\mathbf{s}[i] \leq \mathbf{t}[i], \forall i$.

$$\text{MINDIST}(\mathbf{x}, R) \triangleq \sum_{i=1}^{d} (\mathbf{x}[i] - \mathbf{r}[i])^2,$$

$$\text{MINMAXDIST}(\mathbf{x}, R) \triangleq \min_k \left\{ (\mathbf{x}[k] - \mathbf{rm}[k])^2 + \sum_{i=1, i \neq k}^{d} (\mathbf{x}[i] - \mathbf{rM}[i])^2 \right\},$$

where

$$\begin{aligned}
\mathbf{r}[i] &= \mathbf{x}[i] \text{ if } \mathbf{s}[i] \leq \mathbf{x}[i] \leq \mathbf{t}[i], \\
&= \mathbf{s}[i] \text{ if } \mathbf{x}[i] \leq \mathbf{s}[i], \\
&= \mathbf{t}[i] \text{ if } \mathbf{x}[i] \geq \mathbf{t}[i]. \\
\mathbf{rm}[k] &= \mathbf{s}[k] \text{ if } \mathbf{x}[k] \leq (\mathbf{s}[k] + \mathbf{t}[k])/2, \\
&= \mathbf{t}[k] \text{ otherwise.} \\
\mathbf{rM}[i] &= \mathbf{s}[i] \text{ if } \mathbf{x}[i] \geq (\mathbf{s}[k] + \mathbf{t}[k])/2, \\
&= \mathbf{t}[i] \text{ otherwise.}
\end{aligned}$$

cell-tree [84], and the P-tree [130]. In the *Polyhedron-tree* or *P-tree*, a set of vectors V, of size larger than the number of dimensions of the space, is fixed, and bounding hyperplanes are constrained to be orthogonal to these vectors. The constraint significantly simplifies the index construction, maintenance, and search operations over the case in which arbitrary bounding hyperplanes are allowed, while yielding tighter bounding polyhedra than the traditional R-tree. Two properties are the foundations of the approach. First, one can map any convex polyhedron having n faces into an m-dimensional hyperrectangle in which $m \leq n \leq 2m$. The corresponding m-dimensional space is called orientation space. Thus, if the number of vectors in V is m and the constraint on the hyperplanes is enforced, any bounding polyhedron can be mapped into a m-dimensional hyperrectangle, and indexing methods that efficiently deal with rectangles can then be applied. The second property is that the intersection of bounding polyhedra in feature space (again assuming that the constraint is satisfied) is equivalent to the intersection of the corresponding hyperrectangles in orientation space. A P-tree

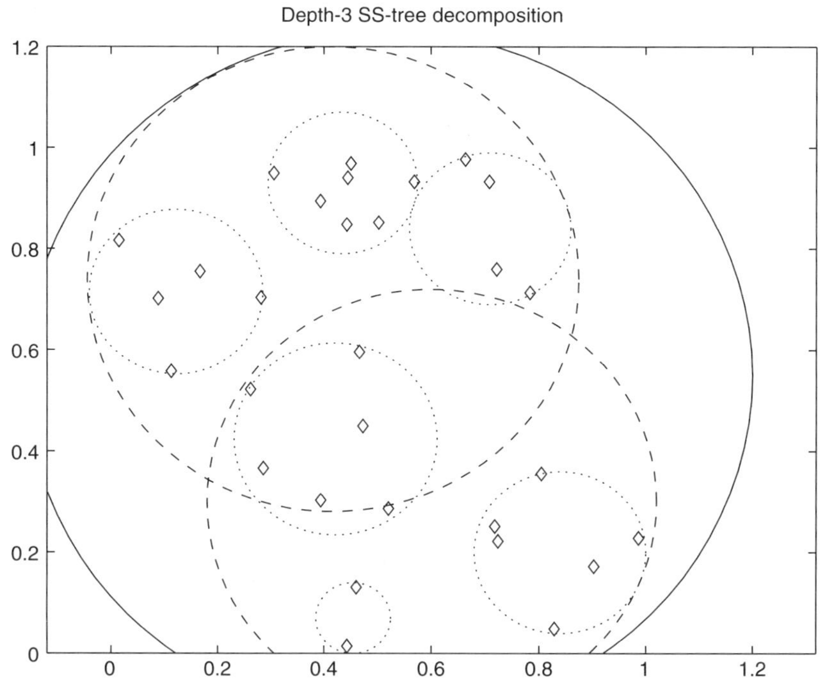

Figure 14A.1. Two-dimensional space decomposition using a depth-3 SS-tree. Database vectors are denoted by diamonds. Different line types correspond to different levels of the tree. Starting from the root, these line types are: solid, dash-dot, dashed, and dotted. The data set is identical to that of Figure 14.3.

is a data structure based on a set of orientation axes, defining a mapping to an orientation space and an R-tree that indexes hyperrectangles in orientation space. Compared to a traditional R-tree, the P-tree trades off dimensionality of the query space, resulting in "curse of dimensionality" type of inefficiencies, for (potentially significantly) better coverage, resulting in better discrimination of the data structure. Algorithms exist to select the appropriate axes and to manage the data structure. Variations of the scheme rely on different variants of the R-tree and one could conceivably construct P^+-trees, P^*-trees, P^X-trees (using X-trees), and so on. Because of the higher dimensionality of the orientation space, the P-tree is better suited to representing two- or three-dimensional objects (for instance, in GIS applications) than high-dimensional features.

When used for nearest-neighbor queries, R-tree-like structures suffer from the fact that hyperrectangles are poor approximations of high-dimensional Minkowsky balls (except for $D^{(\infty)}$), and, in particular, of Euclidean balls. The *similarity search tree* or *SS-tree* (Fig. 14A.1) [131] is a variation of the R^*-tree that partitions the search space into hyperspheres rather than hyperrectangles. The nearest-neighbor search algorithm adopted is the one previously mentioned [128]. On 2- to 10-dimensional synthetic data sets, containing 100,000 points (normally and uniformly distributed), the SS-tree has a storage utilization of about 85 percent, compared with the 70 to 75 percent achieved by the R*-tree. The index construction also requires 10 percent to 20 percent CPU time. During searches, when $d > 5$, the SS-tree is almost invariably faster than the R*-tree, although it appears to suffer from a similar performance degradation as the dimensionality of the search space increases.

Hyperrectangles are not particularly well-suited to represent Minkowsky balls, and hyperspheres do not pack particularly well and cover too much volume. These considerations were used by Katayama and Satoh [132] to develop the *Sphere-Rectangle Tree*, also called *SR-tree* (not to be confused with the SR-tree in [90]). The partitioning elements are the intersection of a bounding rectangle with a bounding sphere. Pointers to the data items are contained in the leaves, and intermediate nodes contain children descriptors, each consisting of a bounding rectangle, a bounding sphere, and the number of points indexed by the subtree rooted at the child. The insertion algorithm is similar to that of the SS-tree, except that here both the bounding sphere and the bounding rectangle must be updated. The center of the bounding sphere of a node is the centroid of all the database elements indexed by the subtree rooted at the node. To determine the radius of the bounding spheres, two values are computed: the first is the radius of the sphere containing all the bounding spheres of the children nodes, the second is the radius of the sphere containing the bounding rectangles of the children. The radius of the bounding sphere is defined as the minimum of these values. The space refinement approach is similar in spirit to that of the P-tree [130]. The tree construction is less CPU-intensive than the R*-tree and the SS-tree, however, the number of required disk accesses is larger. During nearest-neighbor search, the method outperforms the SS-tree as it requires up to 33 percent less CPU time and 32 percent fewer disk accesses, and visits a smaller number of leaves. Only smaller gains are observed over the VAMSplit R-tree, and only for certain data sets, whereas for other data sets the SR-tree can be significantly worse.

All the variants of the R-tree examined so far partition the space, using all the dimensions simultaneously. The *Telescopic-Vector tree* or *TV-tree* [122] is a variant of the R*-tree that attempts to address the curse of dimensionality by indexing only a selected subset of dimensions at the root and increasing the dimensionality of the indexed space at intermediate nodes whenever further discrimination is needed. Each internal node of the tree considers a specified number of active dimensions, α, and corresponds to an α-cylinder, that is, to an infinite region of the search space, in which projection on the subspace of the active dimensions is a sphere. The number of active dimensions is not fixed, but changes with the distance from the root. In general, higher levels of the tree will use fewer dimensions, whereas lower levels use more dimensions to achieve a desired discrimination ability. The tree need not be balanced, and different nodes at the same level generally have different active dimensions. The strategy proposed in the original paper to select the active dimensions consists of sorting the coordinates of the search space in increasing order of discriminatory ability through a transformation (such as the Karhunen-Loève transform, the discrete cosine transform [133], or the wavelet transform [134]) and specifying the number of active coordinates, α at each node. The α of most discriminatory coordinates are then used. The search algorithm relies on the branch-and-bound algorithm of Fukunaga and Narendra [102]. Experiments on a database, in which words are represented as 27-dimensional histograms of letter counts, show that the scheme scales very well with the database size. In the experiments, the best value of α appears to be 2. The TV-tree accesses 1/3 to 1/4 of the leaves accessed by the R*-tree for exact match queries.

A.1.3 Projection-Based Methods. Projection-based indexing methods (Table 14A.4) support nearest-neighbor searches. We can divide them into at least two classes: indexing structures returning results that lie within a prespecified radius of the query point and methods supporting approximate $(1+\varepsilon)$ queries.

A.1.3.1 Approaches Supporting Fixed-Radius Nearest-Neighbor Searches. The first category is specifically tailored to fixed-radius searches and was originally

Table 14A.4. Comparison of Projection-Based Methods. All the Values Are Order $O(\cdot)$ Results

Author and Reference	k-nn Search Time	Space Requirement	Construction Time	Query Type
Friedman et al. [135]	ndr	nd	$dn \log n$	Fixed radius (r)
Yunck [136]	ndr	—	—	Fixed radius
Nene and Shree[a] [137,138]	$nd + n\dfrac{1-r^d}{1-r}$	nd	$dn \log n$	Fixed radius (r)
Agarwal[b] and Matoušek [139]	$n \log^3 nm^{-1/\lceil d/2\rceil}$ $+k \log^2 n$	$m^{1+\delta}$	$m^{1+\delta}$	Ray tracing: Exact
Meiser [140]	$d^5 \log n$	$n^{d+\delta}$	—	Exact
Kleinberg [20]	$(d \log^2 d)$ $\cdot(d+\log n)$	$n \cdot (d \log^2 d \cdot n^2)^d$ $+(d \cdot \log^2 d \cdot n^2)^{d+1}$	$n \cdot (d \log d)^2$	$1+\varepsilon$, Probabilistic
Kleinberg [20][c]	$n + d \cdot \log^3 n$	$d^2 \cdot n \cdot p(n)$	$d^2 \cdot n \cdot p(n)$	Probabilistic
Indyk and[d] Motwani [25]	$d \cdot n^{1/\varepsilon}$ $+\mathrm{Pl}(n)$	$n\mathrm{Pl}(n)$	$n^{1+1/\varepsilon} + d \cdot n$ $+\mathrm{Pl}(n)$	$1+\varepsilon$
Indyk and Motwani [25]	$d + \mathrm{Pl}(n)$[e]	$n \cdot \mathrm{Pl}(n)$	$[n + \mathrm{Pl}(n)]$ $\cdot(1/\varepsilon)^d$	$1+\varepsilon$, $(0<\varepsilon<1)$

a The expression for Nene and Shree's search time assumes that the database points are uniformly distributed in the unit d-dimensional hypercube.

b The expressions for Agarwal and Matoušek results hold for each $m \in [n, n^{\lceil d/2\rceil}]$; δ is an arbitrarily small but fixed value.

c In the second method by Kleinberg, $p(n)$ is a polynomial in n.

d The term "Pl(n)" denotes a polynomial in log(n).

e The method works for D^p distances, $p \in [1,2]$.

introduced by Friedman, Baskett, and Shustek [135]. Friedman's algorithm projects the database points onto the individual coordinate axes and produces d sorted lists, one per dimension. In response to a query, the algorithm retrieves from each list the points with coordinates within r of the corresponding coordinate of the query point. The resulting d sets of candidate points are finally searched exhaustively. If the data points are uniformly distributed, the complexity of the search is approximately $O(ndr)$. An improvement to the technique was proposed by Yunck [136], but the overall complexity of the search is still $O(ndr)$.

In the same spirit as Friedman [135], Nene and Shree [137,138] order the database points according to their values along individual coordinates, and for each ordered list maintain a forward mapping from the database to the list and a backward mapping from the list to the database. In response to a nearest-neighbor query, the first list is searched for points whose first coordinate lies within r of the 1st coordinate of the query point. This candidate set is then pruned in $d - 1$ steps. At the ith iteration, the ith forward map is used to remove those points whose ith coordinate does not lie within r of the ith coordinate of the query. The procedure returns a set of points that lie within a hypercube of side $2r$ centered at the query point, which are then searched exhaustively. The selection of the parameter r is critical: if it is too small, the result set will be empty most of the times, and if it is too large, the scheme does not perform significantly better than Friedman's. Two selection strategies are suggested. The first finds the smallest hypersphere that will contain at least one point with high (prespecified) probability and uses the radius of the hypersphere as the value of r. As discussed in Section 14.2.4 the drawback of the approach is that the hypercube returned by the search procedure quickly becomes too large as the number of dimensions increases. The second approach directly finds the smallest hypercube that contains at least a point with high, prespecified probability. Experiments on a synthetic data set containing 30,000 points show that the proposed algorithm is comparable to or is slightly better than the k-d-tree for $d < 10$ and is significantly better in higher dimensionality spaces. For $d = 15$, where the k-d-tree has the same efficiency as a linear scan, the proposed method is approximately eight times faster. Interestingly, for $d \in [5,25]$ the difference in search time between exhaustive search and the proposed method does not vary significantly. As the database size grows to 100,000, the k-d-tree appears to perform better for $d \leq 12$ when the data are uniformly distributed and for $d \leq 17$ for normally distributed data. Beyond these points k-d-tree performance quickly deteriorates and the method becomes slower than exhaustive search. Nene's method, however, remains better than exhaustive search over the entire range of analyzed dimensions. The approach appears to be better suited for pattern recognition and classification than for similarity search in feature space, in which an empty result set would often be returned.

A substantially different projection method was proposed by Agarwal and Matoušek [139]. Their algorithm maps d-dimensional database points $\mathbf{x}$ into $(d+1)$-dimensional hyperplanes through the functions

$$h_{\mathbf{x}}(\mathbf{t}) = 2\mathbf{t}[1]\mathbf{x}[1] + \cdots + 2\mathbf{t}[d]\mathbf{x}[d] - (\mathbf{x}[1]^2 + \cdots + \mathbf{x}[d]^2).$$

The approach relies on a result from Ref. [141], which says that $\mathbf{x}$ is closest point in the database $\mathcal{X}$ to the query $\mathbf{q}$ if and only if

$$h_{\mathbf{x}}(\mathbf{q}) = \max_{\mathbf{y} \in \mathcal{X}} h_{\mathbf{y}}(\mathbf{q}).$$

Then, nearest-neighbor searching is equivalent to finding the first hyperplane in the upper envelope of the database hit by the line parallel to the $(d+1)$st coordinate axis and passing through the augmented point $[\mathbf{q}[1], \ldots, \mathbf{q}[d], \infty]$. The actual algorithms rely on results from Ref. [142]. Another algorithm based on hyperplanes is described by Meiser [140].

A.1.3.2 Approaches Supporting (1 + ε) Nearest-Neighbor Searches. Data structures based on projecting the database onto random lines passing through the origin are extremely interesting members of this class. A random line is defined as follows: Let d be the dimensionality of the search space, let $\mathcal{B}_0$ be the unit radius ball centered on the origin, and $\mathcal{S}$ be its surface. Endow $\mathcal{S}$ with the uniform distribution and sample a point accordingly. Then a random line is defined as the line that passes through the random point and the origin of the space. The fundamental property on which methods of this class rely is that, *if a point* $\mathbf{x}$ *is closer in Euclidean distance to* $\mathbf{y}$ *than to* $\mathbf{z}$*, then, with probability greater than 1/2, its projection* x' *on a random line is closer to the projection* y' *than to the projection* z'. Given ε and an acceptable probability of error, the index is built by independently sampling L vectors $\{v_\ell\}$ from the uniform distribution on the sphere $\mathcal{S}$. L is chosen to be on the of order $d \log^2 d$, in which the multiplicative constants depend on ε and the probability of error. If $\mathbf{x}_1, \ldots, \mathbf{x}_N$ are the points in the database, the collection of midpoints $\{\mathbf{x}_{ij} = (\mathbf{x}_i + \mathbf{x}_j)/2 | 1 \le i, j \le N\}$ is then generated. For each random vector v_ℓ, the $\mathbf{x}_{ij}$ are ordered by the value of their inner product with v_ℓ, thus producing L lists $S_i, \ldots, S_\ell$. A pair of entries in a list is called an *interval*, a pair of adjacent entries is a *primitive interval*, and a sequence of L primitive intervals, one from each list, is called a trace. A trace is realizable if there exists a point in $\mathbb{R}^d$ such that its inner product with the ℓth vector v_ℓ lies in the ℓth primitive interval of the trace for all values of ℓ. For each realizable trace, build a complete directed graph on the database with an edge from $\mathbf{x}_i$ to $\mathbf{x}_j$ if $\mathbf{x}_i$ dominates $\mathbf{x}_j$ in more than $L/2$ lists and from $\mathbf{x}_j$ to $\mathbf{x}_i$ otherwise. $\mathbf{x}_i$ dominates $\mathbf{x}_j$ in list S_ℓ with respect to a trace, if, in S_ℓ, p_{ij} lies between the ℓth primitive interval of the trace and the point p_{jj} (equal to p_j). The nodes of the directed graph are ordered in such a way that there is a path of length at most 2 from each node to any of the ones following it in the ordering (called an apex ordering). Each realizable trace σ is stored together with the corresponding apex ordering S_σ^*. Note that there are $O(n \log d)^{2d}$ realizable traces. Index construction requires the computation of nL inner products in d dimensions, enumerating the realizable traces (which requires $O(L^d n^{2d})$ operations [60], computing the corresponding digraph $[O(Ln^2)]$, and storing the derived sorted list $[O(n)]$. Note the exponential dependencies on the number of dimensions. To search for neighbors of the query point q, for each ℓ, the inner product $v_\ell \cdot q$ is computed and its position in the list S_ℓ is found by binary search. The primitive interval σ_ℓ^q of S_ℓ in which $v_\ell \cdot q$ falls is determined and the trace $\sigma_1^q \ldots \sigma_L^q$ is constructed. The corresponding apex ordering S_σ^* is then retrieved and its first k elements are returned. Thus, a query involves computing L ($O(d \log^2 d)$) inner products in d dimensions, performing L binary searches on n items, a lookup in a large table, and reading the first k entries of a list; thus, the query time is $O((d \log d^2)(d + \log n))$. The query processing is deterministic. The index construction, however, is based on the selection of L random vectors. One can show that, with probability that can be made arbitrarily small, the set of vectors can lead to an erroneous index. If the set of vectors is correct, all the resulting retrievals will be exact.

Kleinberg [20] proposes a probabilistic method to find $(1 + \varepsilon)$ nearest-neighbors, using random projections.

Kleinberg [20] also proposes a randomized algorithm that removes the exponential dependence of the preprocessing in the number of dimensions and relies on a randomization step in the query processing. The method is, however, less efficient while processing a query.

Indyk and Motwani [25] introduced the *ring-cover trees*. Nearest-neighbor queries are reduced to point location in equal balls: given a database $\mathcal{X} = \{\mathbf{x}_1, \ldots, \mathbf{x}_n\}$, fix a radius r, consider the balls $\mathcal{B}_{\mathbf{x}_1}(r), \ldots, \mathcal{B}_{\mathbf{x}_n}(r)$, and construct a data structure that returns $\mathbf{x}_i$ if a query point q belongs to any $\mathcal{B}_{\mathbf{x}_i}(r)$ and returns a FAILURE otherwise. The ε-approximation of the problem consists of returning $\mathbf{x}_i'$ rather than $\mathbf{x}_i$ if $q \in \mathcal{B}_{\mathbf{x}_i}(r)$, where $\mathbf{x}_i'$ is such that $q \in \mathcal{B}_{\mathbf{x}_i'}(r + \varepsilon)$. To describe the Ring-Cover Tree, the following definitions are needed. A *ring* $R(\mathbf{x}, r1, r2)$ where $r1 < r2$ is the difference $\mathcal{B}_{\mathbf{x}}(r2) - \mathcal{B}_{\mathbf{x}}(r1)$. A ring $R(\mathbf{x}, r1, r2)$ is $(\alpha_1, \alpha_2, \beta)$*-ring separator* for the database $\mathcal{X}$ if $|\mathcal{X} \bigcap \mathcal{B}_{\mathbf{x}}(r_1)| \geq \alpha_1 |\mathcal{X}|$ and $|\mathcal{X} \backslash \mathcal{B}_{bfx}(r_2)| \geq \alpha_2 |\mathcal{X}|$. A set $S \subset \mathcal{X}$ is a (γ, δ)*-cluster* if for each $\mathbf{x} \in S$, $|\mathcal{X} \bigcap \mathcal{B}_{\gamma\rho(S)}(\mathbf{x})| \leq \delta \mathcal{X}$, where $\rho(S)$ is the maximum distance between the farthest points in S. A sequence $S_1, \ldots, S_l$ of subsets of $\mathcal{X}$ is a *(b,c,d)-cover* for $S \subset \mathcal{X}$ if there exists $r > d \cdot \rho(\bigcup_i S_i)$, such that $S \subset \bigcup_i S_i$, $|\mathcal{X} \bigcap (\bigcup_{\mathbf{x} \in S_i} \mathcal{B}_r(\mathbf{x}))| \leq b \cdot |S_i|$ and $|S_i| \leq c \cdot |\mathcal{X}|$. The ring cover tree is constructed by recursively decomposing the database $\mathcal{X}$ (which corresponds to the root) into smaller sets $S_1, \ldots, S_l$, which become nodes of the tree. There are two cases: either a nonleaf node has an (α, α, β)- ring separator, in which case the node is a ring node and is split into its intersection and its difference with the outer ball of the ring; or the node has a (b, α, d)-cover, in which case it is called a *cover node* and is split into $l + 1$ nodes, the first l of which corresponds to its intersections with $\bigcup_{\mathbf{x} \in S_i} \mathcal{B}_r(\mathbf{x})$, $(1, \ldots, l)$ and the last contains all the remaining items (residual node). Ring nodes and cover nodes also contain different information on how their descendants are obtained. Searching a ring node corresponds to checking whether the query is inside the outer sphere of the separator and searching for the appropriate child. Searching a cover node is performed by identifying the set S_i to which the query belongs (i.e., the query is within a sphere of appropriate radius, centered at one of the elements of S_i). If such a set is identified, then the corresponding subtree is searched. If no such S_i exists, but the query is close to S_j, then both S_j and the residual set are searched and the closest of the two results is returned. Otherwise, the residual set is searched. Two algorithms are proposed to index cover nodes; the first is based on bucketing and is similar to the Elias algorithm described in Ref. [143]; the second is based on *locality-sensitive hashing*. The search algorithm for the ring cover tree is polynomial in $\log(n)$ and in d.

A.2 Miscellaneous Partitioning Methods

In this section, we describe three recent partitioning methods that attempt to reduce the curse-of-dimensionality in different ways: CSVD, the Onion index, and the pyramid of Berchtold, Böhm, and Kriegel. All these methods are specifically designed to support a particular class of queries.

A.2.1 Clustering with Singular Value Decomposition: CSVD. Most dimensionality reduction approaches are either computationally intensive (multidimensional scaling) or rely on the properties of the entire database (SVD followed by variable-subset selection). To efficiently capture the local structure of a database without incurring the high costs of multidimensional scaling, *CSVD* [27,28] first partitions the data into homogeneous groups, or clusters, and then separately reduces the dimensionality of each group. Clustering is accomplished either with optimal methods, such as LBG [16], or with faster suboptimal schemes, such as tree-structured vector quantizers [17]. Dimensionality reduction of each individual cluster is performed using SVD followed by variable-subset selection. Data points are then represented by their projection on the subspace associated with the cluster they belong to. The scheme can be recursively applied.

The index is represented as a tree. Each node contains the centroid of the cluster, its radius (defined as the distance between the centroid and the farthest point of the cluster), and the dimensionality reduction information, namely, the projection matrix and the number of retained dimensions. Nonleaf nodes contain the partitioning information used to assign a query vector to its corresponding cluster and pointers to the children, each of which represents a separate cluster. Terminal nodes contain an indexing scheme supporting nearest-neighbor queries, such as the ordered partition [101].

Nearest-neighbor queries are executed by descending the tree and identifying the terminal cluster to which the query point belongs, called the primary cluster. The query point is projected onto the subspace of the primary cluster, the within-cluster index is searched, and an initial set of results is retrieved. The Pythagorean theorem is used to account for the distance between the query point and the subspace of the primary cluster. Then, a branch-and-bound algorithm is applied to identify other candidate nodes. The radii are used to discard clusters that cannot contain any of the k-nearest-neighbors and the other clusters are visited on the order of the distance between centroids and query point.

The method yields exact point queries and approximate k-nearest-neighbor queries. The number of the cluster is selected empirically. Different algorithms guide the dimensionality reduction. The user can either specify the desired average number of dimensions to retain, a desired normalized mean-squared error of the approximation, or a desired precision and recall target.

terminates when the list of current results is not modified while searching a layer. Index maintenance algorithms exist, but the index usually must be recomputed after a large number of insertions or deletions.

A.2.3 The Pyramid Technique. All the described recursive decomposition methods are affected by the curse of dimensionality. Berchtold, Böhm, and Kriegel [145] propose a method, the *pyramid technique*, which partitions the space into a number of regions that grow linearly in the number of dimensions. The d-dimensional search space is partitioned into $2d$ pyramids having vertices at the origin and height aligned with one of the coordinate axis. Each pyramid is then cut into slices parallel to the base, which correspond to a page in the index. The slices of each pyramid can then be indexed using a B^+-tree.

Insertions are very simple and so are point queries performed by identifying the appropriate pyramid, using the B^+-tree to find the right slice and exhaustively searching the corresponding page. Range queries, however, are computationally complex because they entail identifying which pyramids intersect the query rectangle.

Experimental results, carried out on one million uniformly distributed synthetic data in up to 100 dimensions, compare the pyramid technique to the X-tree. For cubic query regions, the pyramid is about 2,500 times faster than the X-tree in 100 dimensions (where the X-tree is probably significantly slower than linear scan). When the query box is a hyperrectangle restricted in n' dimensions and fully extended in $d - n'$ dimensions, the pyramid is still faster than linear scan. For example, for $d = 100$ and $n' = 13$, the pyramid is about 10 times faster than sequential scan.

A.3 Metric Space Methods

This section describes metric space indexes, the second main class of indexing methods. The defining characteristic is that the space itself is indexed, rather than the individual database elements.

A.3.1 The Cell Method. Berchtold and coworkers [52] precalculate an index for the 1-nearest-neighbor *search space* rather than for the points in the space. Given a database $\mathcal{X}$, solving the nearest-neighbor problem is equivalent to computing a tessellation of the search space into Voronoi regions [146] and identifying the region to which a query vector belongs. In general, Voronoi regions are complex polyhedra, which are difficult to represent in a compact form and to store in a database. The solution proposed in Ref. [52] consists of approximating the Voronoi regions by their minimum-bounding hyperrectangle (MBH) and storing the MBHs in an X-tree. As the computation of the exact MBH can be quite time consuming, a slightly suboptimal linear programming method is suggested: to construct the Voronoi region of a particular point, the method uses only those database elements that lie within a prespecified distance and in which the MBHs intersect, and the nearest neighbors in each of the coordinate directions.

As MBHs of neighboring points overlap, a decomposition technique is proposed that yields a better approximation of the actual Voronoi regions, thus reducing the overlap. Each MBH is successively "carved out" in a different dimension.

Experimental results on 10,000 4- to 16-dimensional synthetically generated uniform data points show that this technique is between 1.01 and 3.5 times faster than the R*-tree and up to 2 times faster than the X-tree. On eight-dimensional real data, the method is four times faster than the X-tree alone.

A.3.2 Vantage Point Methods. Vantage point methods are a relatively recent class of approaches, although their origins could be found as early as in Ref. [147]. Yianilos introduced the *Vantage Point Tree* or *vp-tree* in 1986–87, apparently as a development of the work in Ref. [148]. An analogous data structure was developed by Uhlmann and called *Metric Tree* [149,150]. A *vp-tree* [151] relies on pseudometrics. First, the distance function is remapped to the range [0,1] by either scaling (if the distance is bounded) or through the well-known formula $\overline{D}(\mathbf{x}, \mathbf{y}) = D(\mathbf{x}, \mathbf{y})/[1 + D(\mathbf{x}, \mathbf{y})]$. Then a point $\mathbf{v}$ (*vantage point*) is selected. To construct the index, the database points are then sorted according to their scaled distance from $\mathbf{v}$ (i.e., in ascending order of $\overline{D}(\cdot, \mathbf{v})$), the median scaled distance is computed, and the points having scaled distance smaller than the median are assigned to the *left subspace* of $\mathbf{v}$, whereas the remaining ones are assigned to the *right subspace*. The procedure is recursively applied to the left and right subspace. Different selection and termination criteria define different versions of the indexing structures. The simplest vp-tree relies on simple operations to select the appropriate vantage point among a random subset of the points associated with each node of the tree. Enhanced versions use a pseudometric, defined as $D_{\mathbf{v}}(\mathbf{x}, \mathbf{y}) = |\overline{D}(\mathbf{x}, \mathbf{v}) - \overline{D}(\mathbf{y}, \mathbf{v})|$, the key property of which is that $D_{\mathbf{v}}(\mathbf{x}, \mathbf{y}) \leq \overline{D}(\mathbf{x}, \mathbf{y})$, to map the original space into a lower-dimensional Euclidean space, each coordinate of which corresponds to a different node in the path between the root and a leaf.

The algorithm returns fixed-radius nearest-neighbors, where the radius ρ is determined at query time. The search is performed using a branch-and-bound method, which discards subtrees whose distance to the query point is larger than that of the current result or than the radius. Theoretical arguments suggest that search is possible in $O(d \log n)$ time. Experiments show that on synthetic data with limited structure, vp-trees have very similar performances to k-d-trees in up to 15 dimensions. When the space has a structure, and, in particular, when the intrinsic dimensionality is much smaller than the actual dimensionality, the vp-trees are 1 to 2 orders of magnitude faster than the k-d-trees for $d > 10$ and the gap appears to increase with the dimensionality. When applied to image snippet retrieval, on a database of about one million images of size 32×32, the vp-tree appears to visit on an average only 5 percent of the nodes.

A.3.3 M(S,Q) and D(S). Clarkson [152] considers the following problem: given a set $\mathcal{X}$ (the universe), an appropriate distance function on pairs of elements of $\mathcal{X}$, and a database $S \subset \mathcal{X}$, build a data structure on S that returns efficiently the closest element of S to any query point $q \in \mathcal{X}$.

$M(S, Q)$ is a fast, approximate data structure, which supports probabilistic queries. $M(S, Q)$ is constructed using a set Q of representative query points, which can be provided a-priori or constructed at query time using user input. For each point (or site) p_j in S, $M(S, Q)$ maintains a list of other points $\mathcal{D}_j$. $\mathcal{D}_j$ is built as follows: consider a subset R of the database, construct a random ordering of its points, and let R_i be the collection of the first i points according to this ordering. Consider a sequence Q_i of randomly selected subsets of Q, having size $(K \cdot i)$. If p_k is the nearest element of R_{i-1} to $q \in Q_i$ and p_j is a $(1+\varepsilon)$-neighbor of q, then p_j is added to $\mathcal{D}_i$. Searching $M(S, Q)$ consists of starting at point p_1, walking $\mathcal{D}_1$ and until a site closer to the query than p_1 is found, repeating recursively the same operation on the list of the newly found point until a list $\mathcal{D}^*$ is found that does not contain closer elements to the query than its corresponding point p^*. By fine-tuning the parameters of the algorithm and selecting ε appropriately, one can show that the probability of failure to return the nearest neighbor of the query point is $O(\log n^2/K)$.

A different structure, called $D(S)$, is also proposed. The index construction is recursive and proceeds as follows. Select a random subset R of S. Associate with each element y of R an initially empty list, L_y, and two initially empty sets, S_y^1 and S_y^3. The list L_y contains the other elements of R sorted in nondecreasing distance from y. For each element x of $S \backslash R$ (i.e., belonging to S but not to R), find its nearest neighbor in R, say y, and add x to the set S_y^1. For each element x of S_y^1, compute its 3-nearest neighbors among the points of R. Add x to the sets S_y^3, belonging to its three nearest neighbors. Recursively construct $D(R)$ and $D(S_y^3)$ for each y. Recursion terminates either when a predefined depth is reached or when the number of elements is below a threshold. Leaves consists of a list of sites.

To find the nearest neighbor of a query point $\mathbf{q}$, recursively search $D(R)$ to find its nearest neighbor x within R. Walk the list L_x and retrieve the three closest points to $\mathbf{q}$ in R. Recursively search the structures $D(S_y^3)$ of the found neighbors and return the nearest point to the query among the sites found by each search. When a leaf node is reached, perform a sequential scan of the list. If $\Upsilon(S)$ is the ratio of the largest distance between distinct points of S to the smallest distance between distinct points of S, then the preprocessing time is $O(n(\log n)^{O(\log\log \Upsilon(S))})$ and the query time is $(\log n)^{O(\log\log \Upsilon(S))}$.

A.3.4 The M-Tree. α-cut queries can also be executed in metric spaces, and can be supported by indexing structures, of which the *M-tree* [153–156] is an example. Internal nodes of an M-tree contain a collection of routing objects, whereas the database objects are stored in groups at the leaves. The description of a routing object consists of the object itself, of its covering radius, defined as the maximum distance between the routing object and the objects stored at the leaves of its subtree (covering tree), the distance between the covering object and the covering object of its parent node, and a pointer to the root. The description of a database object stored within a leaf consists of the object itself, an identifier, and the distance between the object and the covering object of its parent. The tree is constructed sequentially by adding new items to the most suitable leaf, which is either the unique leaf covering the object or, in case of overlap, the leaf whose parent covering object is closest to the item. When leaves (or internal nodes) are full, they are split, the original covering object is discarded, and a new covering object is created for each of the new leaves. The basic algorithm consists of selecting new covering objects so that the corresponding regions have minimum overlap and minimum covering volume. Numerous routing object selection policies are proposed by the authors, including random selection, which incidentally is not significantly worse than other policies.

An α-cut query that returns all the database entries at distance less than r from the query q starts at the root node and recursively traverses the tree. At each node, the covering objects whose covering tree might intersect the search region are identified and recursively searched, and the remaining covering objects are pruned. When a leaf is reached, it is scanned sequentially. The pruning algorithm uses $D(q, R_p)$, the distance between the query and the routing node of the parent, $D(R_n, R_p)$, the distance between the routing node being analyzed and the routing node of its parent, r and r_n, and the covering radius of the current node. A subtree is selected if $|D(q, R_p) - D(R_n, R_p)| \leq r + r_n$.

The average number of distance computations and of I/O operations during a search appears to grow linearly in the dimensionality of the search space.

Compared to a R* in terms of I/O cost for building the index and for performing square range queries, covering 1% of the indexed space, the M-tree yields gains that increase approximately linearly with the number of dimensions. In terms of distance selectivity, the M-tree appears to be better than the R* by a constant factor in databases with up to 50 dimensions.

The M-Tree can also be used for k-nearest-neighbor queries, in which it also outperforms the R*.

REFERENCES

1. Y. Niu, M.T. Özsu, and X. Li, 2D-h trees: an indexing scheme for content-based retrieval of images in multimedia systems, *Proceedings of 1997 International Conference on Intelligent Processing Systems*, Beijin, China, October 28–31, 1997, pp. 1717–1715.
2. W. Niblack et al., The QBIC project: Querying images by content using color texture, and shape, *Storage and Retrieval for Image and Video Databases*, *Proc. SPIE*, **1908**, San Jose, Calif., 1993, pp. 173–187.
3. C.-S. Li and V. Castelli, Deriving texture feature set for content-based retrieval of satellite image database, *Proceedings of IEEE International Conference Image Processing, ICIP'97*, Santa Barbara, Calif., October 26–29, 1997, pp. 567–579.
4. C.-S. Li et al., Comparing texture feature sets for retrieving core images in petroleum applications, *Proc. SPIE Storage Retrieval Image Video Database VII* **3656**, San Jose, Calif., 1999, pp. 2–11.
5. L.D. Bergman et al., PetroSPIRE: A multi-modal content-based retrieval system for petroleum applications, *Proc. SPIE Multimedia Storage Arch. Syst. IV* **3846**, Boston, Mass., 1999.

6. C. Carson, et al., Region-based image query, *Proceedings of IEEE CVPR '97 Workshop on Content-Based Access of Image and Video Libraries*, Santa Barbara, Calif., June 20, 1997.
7. A.P. Dempster, N.M. Laird, and D.B. Rubin, Maximum likelihood from incomplete data via the algorithm, *J. Royal Stat. Soc. B* **39**(1), 1–38 (1977).
8. B.S. Manjunath, Image processing in the Alexandria digital library project, *Proceedings of IEEE ADL* 80–87 Santa Barbara, Calif., April 21–22, 1998.
9. W.Y. Ma and B.S. Manjunath, Edge flow: a framework of boundary detection and image segmentation, *Proceedings IEEE Computer Vision and Pattern Recognition, CVPR'97*, 1997, pp. 744–749.
10. N. Strobel, C.-S. Li, and V. Castelli, Texture-based image segmentation and MMAP for digital libraries, *Proceedings of IEEE International Conference Image Processing, ICIP'97*, vol. I, Santa Barbara, Calif., October 26–29 1997, pp. 196–199.
11. L.D. Bergman and V. Castelli, The match score image: A visualization tool for image query refinement, *Proc. SPIE Vis. Data Explor. Anal. V* **3298**, 172–183 (1998).
12. T.M. Cover and P. Hart, Nearest neighbor pattern classification, *IEEE Trans. Inf. Theory* **IT-13**(1), 21–27 (1967).
13. R.O. Duda and P.E. Hart, *Pattern Classification and Scene Analysis*, Wiley & Sons, New York, 1973.
14. L. Devroye, L. Györfi, and G. Lugosi, *A probabilistic theory of pattern recognition*, Springer Publishing, New York, 1996.
15. B.V. Dasarathy, ed., *Nearest Neighbor Pattern Classification Techniques*, IEEE Computer Society, Los Alamitos, Calif., 1991.
16. Y. Linde, A. Buzo, and R.M. Gray, An algorithm for vector quantizer design, *IEEE Trans. Commun.* **COM-28**(1), 84–95 (1980).
17. L.M. Po and C.K. Chan, Tree search structures for image vector quantization, *Proceedings of International Symposium on Signal Processing and Applications ISSPA 90*, Australia, August 1990, pp. 527–530.
18. V. Ramasubramanian and K.K. Paliwal, Fast k-dimensional tree algorithms for nearest neighbor search with applications to vector quantization encoding, *IEEE Trans. Signal Process.* **40**(3), 518–530 (1992).
19. K. Clarkson, A randomized algorithm for closed-point queries, *SIAM J. Comput.*, 1988, pp. 160–164.
20. J.M Kleinberg, Two algorithms for nearest-neighbor search in high dimensions, *Proceedings of 29th ACM Symposium on Theory of Computing (STOC)*, El Paso, Tex., 1997, pp. 599–607.
21. J.R. Smith, Integrated spatial and feature image systems: Retrieval analysis and compression, Ph.D. Dissertation, Columbia University, New York, 1997.
22. V.S. Cherkassky, J.H. Friedman, and H. surWechsler, *From Statistics To Neural Networks: Theory and Pattern Recognition Applications*, Springer-Verlag, New York, 1993.
23. K. Beyer et al., When is "nearest neighbor" meaningful? *Proceedings of International Conference on Database Theory (ICDT'99)*, Jerusalem, Israel, 1999, 217–235.
24. A. Borodin, R. Ostrovsky, and Y. Rabani, Lower bounds for high dimensional nearest neighbor search and related problems, *Proceedings of 31st ACM Symposium on Theory of Computing (STOC)*, Atlanta, Georgia, May 1–10, 1999, 312–321.

25. P. Indyk and R. Motwani, Approximate nearest neighbors: towards removing the curse of dimensionality, *Proceedings of 30th ACM Symposium on Theory of Computing on (STOC)*, Dallas, Tex., 1998, pp. 604–613.
26. J. Friedman, On bias, variance, 0/1 — loss and the curse of dimensionality, *J. Data Mining Knowledge Discovery* **1**(55) (1997).
27. A. Thomasian, V. Castelli, and C.-S. Li, Clustering and singular value decomposition for approximate indexing in high dimensional spaces, *Proceedings of 7th International Conference on Information and Knowledge Management CIKM '98*, Bethesda, Md., November 3–7, 1998, pp. 201–207.
28. A. Thomasian, V. Castelli, and C.-S. Li, Approximate nearest neighbor searching in high-dimensionality spaces the clustering and singular value decomposition method, *Proceedings SPIE Multimedia Storage and Archiving Systems III*, Boston, Mass., November 2–4, 1998, pp. 144–154.
29. B.-U. Pagel, F. Korn, and C. Faloutsos, Deflating the dimensionality curse using multiple fractal dimensions, *Proceedings of 16th International Conference on Data Engineering*, San Diego, Calif., 2000, pp. 589–598.
30. B.V. Bonnlander and A.S. Weigend, Selecting input variables using mutual information and nonparametric density estimation. *Proceedings of International Symposium on Artificial Neural Networks, ISANN94*, Tainan, Taiwan, December 15–17, 1994, 312–321.
31. K. Fukunaga, *Introduction to Statistical Pattern Recognition*, 2nd ed., Academic Press, New York, 1990.
32. R.A. Horn and C.R. Johnson, *Matrix Analysis*, Cambridge University Press, New York, 1992.
33. I.T. Jolliffe, *Principal Component Analysis*, Springer-Verlag, New York, 1986.
34. R. Ng and A. Sedighian, Evaluating multi-dimensional indexing structures for images transformed by principal component analysis, *Proceedings of SPIE, Storage and Retrieval for Still Image Video Databases*, San Jose, Calif., USA, February 1996, pp. 50–61.
35. K.V. RaviKanth, D. Agrawal, and A.D. Singh, Dimensionality reduction for similarity searching in dynamic databases, *Proceedings of 1998 ACM SIGMOD International Conference on Management of Data*, 1998, pp. 166–176.
36. J.B. Kruskal, Multidimensional scaling, *Psychometrika* **29**(1), 1–27 (1964).
37. Andrew R. Webb, Multidimensional scaling by iterative majorization using radial basis functions, *Pattern Recog.* **28**(5), 753–759 (1995).
38. M. Beatty and B.S. Manjunath, Dimensionality reduction using multidimensional scaling for content-based retrieval, *Proceedings of IEEE International Conference Image Processing, ICIP '97* Santa Barbara, Calif., October 1997, pp. 835–838.
39. W.S. Torgerson, Multidimensional scaling: I, theory and method, *Psychometrika* **17**, 401–419 (1952).
40. C. Faloutsos and K.-I. Lin, FastMap: a fast algorithm for indexing, data-mining, and visualization of traditional and multimedia data sets, *Proceedings of 1995 ACM SIGMOD International Conference on Management of Data*, San Jose, Calif., May 1995, pp. 163–174.
41. A. Califano and R. Mohan, Multidimensional indexing for recognizing visual shapes, *Proceedings of IEEE Computer Vision and Pattern Recognition, CVPR '91*, June 1991, pp. 28–34.

42. H. Wolfson, Model-based object recognition by geometric hashing, *Proceedings of 1st European Conference Computer Vision*, April 1990, Antibes, France, pp. 526–536.
43. C.C. Aggarwal et al., Fast algorithms for projected clustering, *Proceedings of 1999 ACM SIGMOD International Conference on Management of Data*, Philadelphia, Pa., June 1999, pp. 61–72.
44. K. Chakrabarti and S. Mehrotra, Local dimensionality reduction: A new approach to indexing high dimensional spaces, *Proceedings of 26th International Conference on Very Large Data Bases VLDB '98*, Cairo, Egypt, September 2000, pp. 89–100.
45. V. Gaede and O. Günther, Multidimensional access methods, *ACM Comput. Surveys* **30**(2) 170–231 (1998).
46. Hanan Samet, *The design and analysis of spatial data structures*, Addison-Wesley, Reading, Mass., 1990.
47. J. Orenstein, Spatial query processing in an object-oriented database system, *Proc. 1986 ACM SIGMOD Int. Conf. Manage. Data*, 326–336 (1986).
48. J. Orenstein, A comparison of spatial query processing techniques for native and parameter spaces, *Proceedings of 1990 ACM SIGMOD International Conference on Management of Data*, ACM Press Atlantic City, N.J., May 23–25, 1990, pp. 343–352.
49. D. Lomet and B. Salzberg, A robust multiattribute search structure, *Proceedings of 5th International Conference on Data Engineering*, Los Angeles, Calif., February 6–10, 1989, pp. 296–304.
50. D. Lomet and B. Salzberg, The hB-tree: a multiattribute indexing method with good guaranteed performance, *ACM Trans. Database Syst. (TODS)* **15**(4), 625–658 (1990).
51. J. Nievergelt, H. Hinterberger, and K.C. Sevcik, The grid file, and adaptible, symmetric multi-key file structure, *ACM Trans. Database Syst. (TODS)* **9**, 38–71 (1984).
52. S. Berchtold et al., Fast nearest neighbor search in high-dimensional space, *Proc. 14th Int. Conf. Data Eng.* 209–218, (1998).
53. S. Berchtold, D.A. Keim, and H.-P. Kriegel, The X-tree: An index structure for high-dimensional data, *Proceedings 19th International Conference on Very Large Data Bases VLDB'93*, Bombay, India, September 1996, pp. 28–39.
54. D.E. Knuth, Sorting and searching, *The Art of Computer Programming*, 2nd ed., vol. 3, Addison Wesley, Reading, Mass., 1973.
55. Michael Freeston, The BANG file, a new kind of grid file, *Proceedings 1987 ACM SIGMOD International Conference on Management of Data*, May 1987, San Francisco, Calif., pp. 260–269.
56. M.F. Goodchild and A.W. Grandfield, Optimizing raster storage, an examination of four alternatives, *Proc. Auto-Carto 6*, vol. 1, Ottawa, Canada, October 1983, pp. 400–407.
57. D. Hilbert, Uber die stetige abbildung einer linie auf ein flachenstuck, *Math. Ann.* **38**, (1891).
58. G.M. Morton, A computer-oriented geodetic data base and a new technique infile sequencing, Technical report, IBM Ltd., Ottawa, Canada, 1966.
59. D.J. Abel and J.L. Smith, A data structure and algorithm based on a linear key for a rectangle retrieval problem, *Comput. Vis. Graphics Image Process.* **27**(1), 1983.

60. W.A. Burkhard, Interpolation-based index maintenance, *Proceedings of 2nd ACM SIGACT-SIGMOD Symp. Principles Database Syst.* 76–89 (1983).
61. I. Gargantini, An effective way to represent quadtrees, *Commun. ACM* **25**(12), 905–910 (1982).
62. J. Orenstein and T.H. Merret, A class of data structures for associative searching, *Proc. 3rd ACM SIGACT-SIGMOD Symp. Principles Database Syst.* 181–190 (1984).
63. M. Ouksel and P. Scheuermann, Storage mapping for multidimensional linear dynamic hashing, *Proc. 2nd ACM SIGACT-SIGMOD Symp. Principles Database Syst.* 90–105 (1983).
64. G.-H. Cha and C.-W. Chung, H-G tree: and index structure for multimedia database, *Proceedings 3rd IEEE International Conference Multimedia Computing and Systems*, June 1996, pp. 449–452.
65. G.-H. Cha and C.-W. Chung, Multi-mode indices for effective image retrieval in multimedia systems, *Proceedings IEEE International Conference Multimedia Computing and Systems*, Austin, 28 June–1 July 1998, pp. 152–158.
66. G.-H. Cha and C.-W. Chung, A new indexing scheme for content-based image retrieval, *Multimedia Tools Appl.* **6**(3), 263–288 (1998).
67. D. Comer, The ubiquitous B-tree, *ACM Comput. Surveys* **11**(2), 121–137 (1979).
68. B. Seeger and H.-P. Kriegel, The buddy-tree: an efficient and robust method for spatial data base systems, *Proc. 16th Int. Conf. Very Large Data Bases VLDB'92*, 590–601, (1990).
69. M. Tamminen, The extendible cell method for closest point problems, *BIT* **22**, 24–41 (1982).
70. K. Hinrichs and J. Nievergelt, The grid file: a data structure to support proximity queries on spatial objects, *Proc. Int. Workshop Graph Theoretic Concepts Comput. Sci.* 100–113 (1983).
71. E.J. Otoo, A mapping function for the directory of a multidimensional extendible hashing, *Proceedings 10th International Conference on Very Large Data Bases VLDB'84*, Singapore, 1984, pp. 493–506.
72. M. Ouksel, The interpolation-based grid file, *Proceedings 4th ACM SIGACT-SIGMOD Symposium on Principles of Database Systems*, Portland, Ore., 1985, pp. 20–27.
73. M. Regnier, Analysis of the grid file algorithm, *BIT* **25**, 335–357 (1985).
74. E.J. Otoo, Balanced multidimensional extendible hash tree, *5th ACM SIGACT-SIGMOD Symp. Principles Database Syst.* 100–113 (1986).
75. R. Fagin et al., Extendible hashing a fast access method for dynamic files, *ACM Trans. Database Syst. (TODS)* **4**(3), 315–344 (1979).
76. H. Mendelson, Analysis of extendible hashing, *IEEE Trans. Software Eng.* **SE-8**(6), 611–619 (1982).
77. P. Flajolet, On the performance evaluation of extendible hashing and trie searching, *Acta Inf.* **20**, 345–369 (1983).
78. W.A. Burkhard, Index maintenance for non-uniform record distribution, *Proceedings of 3rd ACM SIGACT-SIGMOD Symposium on Principles of Database Systems*, Waterloo, Canada, 1984, pp. 173–180.
79. A. Kumar, G-tree: a new data structure for organizing multidimensional data, *IEEE Trans. Knowledge Data Eng.* **6**(2), 341–347 (1994).

80. C. Liu et al., Performance evaluation of G-tree and its application in fuzzy databases, *Proc. 5th Int. Conf. Information and Knowledge Management CIKM'98*, Rockville, Md., 1996, pp. 235–242.
81. H.P. Kriegel et al., Performance comparison of point and spatial access methods, *Proc. 1st Symp. Design Large Spatial Databases*, **49**, 89–114 (1989).
82. K. Hinrichs, Implementation of the grid file: design, concepts and experiences, *BIT* **25**, 569–592 (1985).
83. J.L. Bentley and J.H. Friedman, Data structures for range searching, *ACM Comput. Surveys* **11**(4), 397–409 (1997).
84. E.M. McCreight, Priority search trees, *SIAM J. Comput.* **18**(2), 257–276 (1985).
85. H. Samet, Quadtree and related hierarchical data structures, *ACM Comput. Surveys* **16**(2), 187–260 (1984).
86. P. Flajolet et al., The analysis of multidimensional searching in quad-trees, *Proc. 2nd ACM-SIAM Symp. Discrete algorithms*, 1991, 100–109.
87. A. Klinger, Pattern and search statistics, in J.S. Rustagi, ed., *Optimizing Methods in Statistics*, Academic Press, New York, 1971, pp. 303–337.
88. R.A. Finkel and L.J. Bentley, Quad trees, a data structure for retrieval on composite keys, *Acta Inf.*, **4**(1), 1–9 (1974).
89. W.G. Aref and H. Samet, Optimization strategies for spatial query processing, *Proceedings of 17th International Conference on Very Large Data Bases VLDB'92*, Vancouver British Columbia, Canada September 1991, pp. 81–90.
90. C.P. Kolovson and M. Stonebraker, Segment indexes: dynamic indexing techniques for multi-dimensional interval data, *Proc. 1991 ACM SIGMOD Int. Conf. Manage. Data* 138–147 (1991).
91. T. Tzouramanis, M. Vassilakopoulos, and Y. Manolopoulos., Overlapping linear quadtrees: a spatio-temporal access method, *Proc. 6th Int. Symp. Adv. Geographic Inf. Syst.*, 1–7 (1998).
92. W.G. Aref and H. Samet, Efficient processing of window queries in the pyramid data structure, *Proc. ninth ACM SIGACT-SIGMOD-SIGART Symp. Principles Database Syst.* 265–272, (1990).
93. C. Faloutsos, H.V. Jagadish, and Y. Manolopoulos, Analysis of the n-dimensional quadtree decomposition for arbitrary hyperrectangles, *IEEE Trans. Knowledge Data Eng.* **9**(3), 373–383 (1997).
94. J.L. Bentley, Multidimensional binary search trees used for associative searching, *Commun. ACM* **18**(9), 509–517 (1975).
95. J.L. Bentley, Multidimensional binary search in database applications, *IEEE Trans. Software Eng.* **4**(5), 333–340 (1979).
96. J.T. Robinson, The k-d-b-tree: A search structure for large multidimensional dynamic indexes, *Proceedings of 1981 ACM SIGMOD International Conference on Management of Data*, May 1981, pp. 10–18.
97. D. Lomet, DL* trees, Research Report RC 10860, IBM T.J. Watson Research Center, Yorktown Heights, N.Y., 1984.
98. H. Fuchs, G.D. Abram, and B.F. Naylor, On visible surface generation by a priori tree structure, *In 7th ACM Annual Conference on Computer Graphics SIGGRAPH'80*, Boston, Mass., USA, 1980.

99. H. Fuchs, G.D. Abram, and B.F. Naylor, On visible surface generation by a priori tre structure, *Comput. Graphics* **14**(3), 124–133 (1980).
100. W.C. Thibault and B.F. Naylor, Set operations on polyhedra using binary space partitioning trees, *Comput. Graphics* **21**(4), 153–162 (1987).
101. B.S. Kim and S.B. Park, A fast k nearest neighbor finding algorithm based on the ordered partition, *IEEE Trans. Pattern Anal. Machine Intell.* **PAMI-8**(6), 761–766 (1986).
102. K. Fukunaga and P.M. Narendra, A branch and bound algorithm for computing k-nearest neighbors, *IEEE Trans. Comput.* **C-24**, 750–753 (1975).
103. B. Kamgar-Parsi and L. Kanal, An improved branch and bound algorithm for computing k-nearest neighbors, *Pattern Recog. Lett.* **3**, 7–12 (1985).
104. H. Niemann and R. Goppert, An efficient branch-and-bound nearest neighbor classifier, *Pattern Recog. Lett.* **7**, 67–72 (1988).
105. M. Bern, Approximate closest-point queries in high dimensions, *Inf. Proc. Lett.* **45**, 95–99 (1993).
106. T.M. Chan, Approximate nearest neighbor queries revisited, *Proc. 13th ACM Symp. Comput. Geometry* 352–358 (1997).
107. T.M. Chan, Approximate nearest neighbor queries revisited, *Discrete Comput. Geometry* **20**, 359–373 (1998).
108. S. Arya et al., An optimal algorithm for approximate nearest neighbor searches, *Proceedings 5th Annual ACM-SIAM Symposium on Discrete Algorithms*, Chapter 63, ACM, New York, 1994, pp. 572–582.
109. S. Arya et al., An optimal algorithm for approximate nearest neighbor searching in fixed dimensions, *J. ACM* **45**(6), 891–923 (1988).
110. K.L. Clarkson, An algorithm for approximate closest-point queries, *Proc. 10th Annu. Symp. Comput. Geometry* 160–164 (1994).
111. S. Arya and D.M. Mount, Approximate nearest neighbor queries in fixed dimensions, *Proceedings 4th Annual ACM-SIAM Symposium on Discrete Algorithms*, ACM, New York, 1993, pp. 271–280.
112. A. Guttman, R-Trees: a dynamic index structure for spatial searching, *ACM SIGMOD Rec.* **14**(2), 47–57 (1984).
113. D. Greene, An implementation and performance analysis of spatial access data methods, *Proceedings 5th International Conference on Data Engineering*, Los Angeles, Calif., February 6–10, 1989, pp. 606–615.
114. C. Faloutsos et al., Efficent and effective querying by image content, *J. Intell. Inf. Syst.* **3**(3/4), 231–262 (1994).
115. T. Sellis, N. Roussopoulos, and C. Faloutsos, The R+-tree: A dynamic index for multi-dimensional objects, *Proceedings 13th International Conference on Very Large Data Bases VLDB'87*, Brighton, England, September 1987, pp. 507–518.
116. N. Beckmann et al., The R* tree: an efficient and robust access method for points and rectangles, *Proceedings 1990 ACM SIGMOD International Conference on Management of Data*, Atlantic City, N.J., May 23–25 1990, pp. 322–331.
117. N. Roussopoulos and D. Leifker, Direct spatial search on pictorial databases using packed R-trees, *Proceedings 1985 ACM SIGMOD International Conference on Management of Data*, Austin, Tex., May 28–31, 1985, pp. 17–31.

118. I. Kamel and C. Faloutsos, On packing r-trees, *Proceedings 3rd International Conference Information and Knowledge Management CIKM'93*, Washington, D.C., November 1–5, 1993, pp. 490–499.

119. C. Faloutsos, Gray codes for partial match and range queries, *IEEE Trans. Software Eng.* **14**(10), 1381–1393 (1988).

120. C. Faloutsos and S. Roseman, Fractals for secondary key retrieval, *Proceedings of 8th ACM ACM SIGACT-SIGMOD-SIGART Symposium on Principles of Database Systems, PODS'89*, Philadelphia, Pa, March 29–31 1989, pp. 247–252.

121. I. Kamel and C. Faloutsos, Hilbert R-tree: An improved R-tree using fractals, *Proceedings of 20th International Conference on Very Large Data Bases VLDB'94*, Santiago, Chile, September 12–15 1994, pp. 500–509.

122. K.-I. Lin, H.V. Jagadish, and C. Faloutsos, The TV-tree: and index structure for high-dimensional data, *VLDB J.* **3**(4), 517–542 (1994).

123. S. Berchtold et al., Fast parallel similarity search in multimedia databases, *Proceedings of 1997 ACM SIGMOD International Conference on Management of Data*, Tucson, Ariz., May 12–15, 1997, pp. 1–12.

124. C. Faloutsos and P. Bhagwat, Declustering using fractals, *PDIS J. Parallel Distrib. Inf. Syst.* 18–25 (1993).

125. D.A. White and R. Jain, Similarity indexing: Algorithms and performance. *Proceedings of SPIE, Storage and Retrieval for Still Image Video Databases*, vol. 2670, San Diego, Calif., January 1996 pp. 62–73.

126. C. Aggarwal et al., The S-Tree: an efficient index for multidimensional objects, *Proceedings of Symposium on Large Spatial Databases (SSD)*, Vol.1262, Lecture Notes in Computer Science, Springer Berlin, Germany, 1997, pp. 350–373.

127. T. Brinkhoff, H.-P. Kriegel, and B. Seeger, Efficient processing of spatial joins using R-trees, *Proc. 1993 ACM SIGMOD Int. Conf. on Management of Data*, San Jose, Calif., May 23–26, 1983, pp. 237–246.

128. N. Roussopoulos, S. Kelley, and F. Vincent, Nearest neighbor queries, *Proceedings of 1995 ACM SIGMOD International Conference on Management of Data*, San Jose, Calif., May 1995, pp. 71–79.

129. O. Günther and E. Wong, A dual-space representation for geometric data, *Proceedings of 13th International Conference on Very Large Data Bases VLDB'87*, Brighton, U.K., September 1987, pp. 501–506.

130. H.V. Jagadish, Spatial search with polyhedra, *Proceedings of 6th International Conference on Data Engineering*, February 1990, pp. 311–319.

131. D.A. White and R. Jain, Similarity indexing with the SS-Tree. *Proceedings of 12th International Conference on Data Engineering*, New Orleans, Louisiana, February 1996, pp. 516–523.

132. N. Katayama and S. Satoh, The SR-tree: an index structure for high-dimensional nearest neighbor query, *Proceedings of 1997 ACM SIGMOD International Conference on Management of Data*, Tucson, Ariz, 12–15 May 1997, pp. 369–380.

133. W. Pennebaker and J.L. Mitchell, *JPEG Still Image Data Compression Standard*, Van Nostrand Reinhold, New York, 1993.

134. I. Daubechies, *Ten Lectures on Wavelets*, Society for Industrial and Applied Mathematics, Philadelphia, Pa, 1992.

135. J.H. Friedman, F. Baskett, and L.J. Shustek, An algorithm for finding nearest neighbors, *IEEE Trans. Comput.* **C-24**, 1000–1006 (1975).

136. T.P. Yunck, A technique to identify nearest neighbors, *IEEE Trans. Syst., Man Cybern.* **6**(10), 678–683 (1976).

137. S.A. Nene and S.K. Nayar, Closest point search in high dimensions, *Proceedings of IEEE Computer Vision and Pattern Recognition, CVPR'96*, San Francisco, Calif., Jun. 18–20 1996, 859–865.

138. S.A. Nene and S.K. Nayar, A simple algorithm for nearest neighbor search in high dimensions, *IEEE Trans. Pattern Anal. Machine Intell.* **19**(9), 989–1003 (1997).

139. P.K. Agarwal and J. Matouvsek, Ray shooting and parametric search, *Proc. 24th ACM Symp. Theory Comput. (STOC)*, ACM Press Victoria, BC, Canada, 517–526, (1992).

140. S. Meiser, Point location in arrangements of hyperplanes, *Inf. Comput.* **106**, 286–303 (1993).

141. H. Edelsbrunner, *Algorithms in Combinatorial Geometry*, Springer-Verlag, New York, 1987.

142. J. Matouvsek, Reporting points in halfspaces, *Comput. Geometry: Theory Appl.* **2**, 169–186 (1992).

143. T. Welch, Bounds on the information retrieval efficiency of static file structures, Technical Report88, MIT press, Cambridge, Mass., 1971.

144. Y.-C. Chang et al., The onion technique: Indexing for linear optimization queries, *Proc. 2000 ACM SIGMOD Int. Conf. Manage. Data*, SIGMOD Record **29**(2) 391–402 2000.

145. S. Berchtold, C. Böhm and H.-P. Kriegel, The pyramid-tree: Breaking the curse of dimensionality, *Proc. 1998 ACM SIGMOD Int. Conf. Manage. Data*, 142–153 (1998).

146. F. Aurenhammer, Voronoi diagrams — a survey of fundamental geometric data structures, *ACM Comput. Surveys* **23**(3), 345–405 (1991).

147. W.A. Burkhard and R.M. Keller, Some approaches to best-match file searching, *Commun. ACM* **16**, 230–236 (1973).

148. P.N. Yianilos, A dedicated comparator matches symbol strings fast and intelligently, *Electronics Magazine (Cover Story)*, December 1983.

149. J.K. Uhlmann, Satisfying general proximity/similarity queries with metric trees, *Inf. Processing Lett.* **40**, 175–179 (1991).

150. J.K. Uhlmann, Metric trees, *Appl. Math. Lett.*, **4**(5) 1991.

151. P.N. Yianilos, Data structures and algorithms for nearest neighbor search in general metric spaces. *Proc. Proc 2nd Annu. ACM-SIAM Symp. Discrete Algorithms* 311–321 (1993).

152. K.L. Clarkson, Nearest neighbor queries in metric spaces. *Proc. 29th Symp. Theory Comput.* pp. 609–617 (1997).

153. P. Ciaccia, M. Patella, and P. Zezula, M-tree, an efficient access method for similarity search in metric spaces, *Proceedings of 23rd International Conference on Very Large Data Bases VLDB '97*, Athens, Greece, 1997, pp. 426–435.

154. P. Ciaccia et al., Indexing metric spaces with M-tree, *SEBD*, 1997, pp. 67–86.

155. P. Zezula et al., Processing M-trees with parallel resources, *Proc. 7th Int. Workshop Res. Iss. Data Eng.* 147–154 (1997).

156. P. Ciaccia, A. Nanni, and M. Patella, A query-sensitive cost model for similarity queries with M-tree, *Australasian Database Conf.* 65–76 (1999).

157. K. Bennett, U. Fayyad, and Geiger D, Density-based indexing for approximate nearest-neighbor queries, *Proceedings of 5th ACM SIGKDD International Conference Knowledge Discovery & Data Mining*, San Diego, Calif., August 15–18 1999, pp. 233–243.

158. S. Berchtold and H.-P. Kriegel, S3: Similarity search in cad database systems, *Proceedings of 1997 ACM SIGMOD International Conference on Management of Data*, Tucson, Ariz., May 12–15 1997, pp. 564–567.

159. T. Bozkaya and M. Ozsoyoglu, Indexing large metric spaces for similarity search queries, *ACM Trans. Database Syst. (TODS)* **24**(3), 361–404 (1999).

160. T. Brinkhoff et al., GeneSys: a system for efficient spatial query processing, *Proc. 1994 ACM SIGMOD Int. Conf. Manage. Data*, SIGMOD Record **23**(2), 519 (1994).

161. T. Brinkhoff, H.-P. Kriegel, and B. Seeger, Parallel processing of spatial joins using R-trees, *Proceedings of 12th Int. Conf. on Data Engineering* 258–265 (1996).

162. C. Buckley et al., New information retrieval approaches using SMART, *Proceedings of 4th Text Retrieval Conference*, National Institute of Standards and Technology, NIST Spec. Publ. 500–236, 1995.

163. A. Chakrabarti et al., A lower bound on the complexity of approximate nearest neighbor searching on the hamming cube, *Proceedings of 31st ACM Symposium on Theory of Computing (STOC)*, Atlanta, May 1–10 1999, pp. 305–311.

164. O. Günther and J. Bilmes, Tree based access methods for spatial databases: Implementation and performance evaluation, *IEEE Trans. Knowledge Data Eng.* **3**(3), 342–356 (1991).

165. G.R. Hjaltason and H. Samet, Distance browsing in spatial databases, *ACM Trans. Database Syst. (TODS)* **24**(2), 265–318 (1999).

166. A. Hutflesz, H.-W. Six, and P. Widmayer, Twin grid files: space optimizing access schemes, *Proceedings of 1988 ACM SIGMOD International Conference on Management of Data*, Chicago, Ill, June 1988, pp. 183–190.

167. A. Moffat and J. Zobel, Index organization for multimedia database systems, *ACM Comput. Surveys* **27**(4), 607–609 (1995).

168. B.-U. Pagel and H.-W. Six, Are window queries representative for arbitrary range queries?, *Proceedings of 15th ACM ACM Symposium on Principles of Database Systems, PODS'96*, Montreal, Quebec, Canada, 1996, pp. 150–160.

169. B. Seeger and H.-P. Kriegel, Techniques for design and implementation of efficient spatial access methods, *Proceedings of 14th International Conference on Very Large Data Bases VLDB'88*, Los Angeles, Calif., 1997, pp. 360–371.

170. K. Shim, R. Srikant, and R. Agrawal, High-dimensional similarity joins, *Proc. 13th Int. Conf. on Data Engineering*, Birmingham, UK, 7–11 April 1997, pp. 301–311.

171. Q. Yang, A. Vellaikal, and S. Dao, Mb^+ -tree: a new index structure for multimedia databases, *Proc. IEEE Int. Workshop Multi-Media Database Management Systems*, Blue Mountain Lake, N.Y., 28–30 August 1995. 151–158.

172. N. Yazdani, M. Ozsoyoglu, and G. Ozsoyoglu, A framework for feature-based indexing for spatial databases, *Proceedings of 7th International Working Conf Scientific and Statistical Database Management*, Charlottesville, September, 28–30 1994, pp. 259–269.

15 Multimedia Indexing

CHRISTOS FALOUTSOS
Carnegie Mellon University, Pittsburgh, Pennsylvania

15.1 INTRODUCTION

In this chapter we focus on the design of methods for rapidly searching a database of multimedia objects, allowing us to locate objects that match a query object, exactly or approximately. We want a method that is general and that can handle any type of multimedia objects. Objects can be two-dimensional (2D) color images, gray scale medical images in two-dimensional or three-dimensional (3D) (e.g., MRI brain scans), one-dimensional (1D) time series, digitized voice or music, video clips, and so on. A typical query-by-content is "*in a collection of color photographs, find ones with the same color distribution as a sample sunset photograph.*"

Specific applications include the following:

- Image databases [1] in which we would like to support queries on color (Chapter 11), shape (Chapter 13), and texture (Chapter 12).
- Video databases [2,3].
- Financial, marketing, and production time series, such as stock prices, sales numbers and so on. In such databases, typical queries would be "*find companies whose stock prices move similarly,*" or "*find other companies that have sales patterns similar to our company,*" or "*find cases in the past that resemble last month's sales pattern of our product*"[4].
- Scientific databases (Chapters 3 and 5), with collections of sensor data. In this case, the objects are time series, or, more general, *vector fields*, that is, tuples of the form, $< x, y, z, t, pressure, temperature, \ldots >$. For example, in weather data [5], geologic, environmental, and astrophysics databases, and so on, we want to ask queries of the form "*find previous days in which the solar magnetic wind showed patterns similar to today's pattern*" to help in predictions of the Earth's magnetic field [6].

Image Databases: Search and Retrieval of Digital Imagery, Edited by Vittorio Castelli and Lawrence D. Bergman.
ISBN 0-471-32116-8

- Multimedia databases, with audio (voice, music), video, and so on [7]. Users might want to retrieve, for example, music scores or video clips that are similar to provided examples.
- Medical databases (Chapter 4) in which 1D objects (e.g., ECGs), 2D images (e.g., X rays), and 3D images (e.g., MRI brain scans) are stored. Ability to rapidly retrieve past cases with similar symptoms would be valuable for diagnosis and for medical and research purposes [8,9].
- Text and photographic archives [10], digital libraries [11,12] containing ASCII text, bitmaps, gray scale, and color images.
- DNA databases [13] containing large collections of long strings (hundred or thousand characters long) from a four-letter alphabet (A,G,C,T); a new string has to be matched against the old strings to find the best candidates.

Searching for similar patterns in databases such as these are essential because it helps in predictions, computer-aided medical diagnosis and teaching, hypothesis testing and, in general, in "data mining" [14–16] and rule discovery.

Of course, the dissimilarity between two objects has to be quantified. Dissimilarity is measured as a distance between feature vectors, extracted from the objects to be compared. We rely on a domain expert to supply such a distance function $\mathcal{D}()$:

Definition 1. The distance (= dissimilarity) between two objects O_1 and O_2 is denoted by

$$\mathcal{D}(O_1, O_2). \tag{15.1}$$

For example, if the objects are two (equal length) time series, the distance $\mathcal{D}()$ could be their Euclidean distance (sum of squared differences), whereas for DNA sequences, the editing distance (smallest number of insertions, deletions, and substitutions that are needed to transform the first string to the second) is customarily used.

Similarity queries can been classified into two categories:

Whole Match. Given a collection of N objects $O_1, O_2, \ldots, O_N$ and a query object Q, we want to find those data objects that are within distance ε from Q. Notice that the query and the objects are of the same type: for example, if the objects are 512×512 gray scale images, so is the query.

Subpattern Match. Here, the query is allowed to return only part of the objects being searched. Specifically, given N data objects (e.g., images) $O_1, O_2, \ldots, O_N$, a query object Q and a tolerance ε, we want to identify the parts of the data objects that match the query. If the objects are, for example, 512×512 gray scale images (such as medical X-rays), the query might be a 16×16 subpattern (e.g., a typical X-ray of a tumor).

Additional types of queries include "*nearest neighbors*" queries (e.g., "*find the five most similar stocks to IBM's stock*") and "*all pairs*" queries or "*spatial joins*" (e.g., "*report all the pairs of stocks that are within distance* ε *from each other*"). Both these types of queries can be supported by our approach: As we shall see, we can reduce the problem into searching for multidimensional points that will be organized into R-trees; in this case, nearest-neighbor search can be handled with a branch-and-bound algorithm [17,18] and the spatial-join query can be handled with recently developed, finely tuned algorithms [19].

For both "whole match" and "subpattern match," the ideal method should fulfill the following requirements:

- It should be *fast*. Sequential scanning and computing distances for each and every object can be too slow for large databases.
- It should be *correct*. In other words, it should return all the qualifying objects without missing any (i.e., no "false dismissals"). Notice that "false alarms" are acceptable because they can be discarded easily through a post-processing step.
- The ideal method should require a small amount of additional memory.
- The method should be dynamic. It should be easy to insert, delete, and update objects.

The remainder of the chapter is organized as follows. Section 15.2 describes the main ideas for "GEMINI," a generic approach to indexing multimedia objects. Section 15.3 shows the application of the approach for 1D time series indexing. Section 15.4 focuses on indexing methods for shape, texture, and particularly, color. Section 15.5 shows how to extend the ideas to handle subpattern matching. Section 15.6 summarizes the chapter and lists problems for future research. Appendix 15.6 gives some background material on past-related work, on image indexing, and on spatial access methods (SAMs).

15.2 GEMINI: FUNDAMENTALS

To illustrate the basic concepts of indexing, we shall focus on "whole match" queries. The problem is defined as follows:

- We have a collection of N objects: $O_1, O_2, \ldots, O_N$;
- The distance and dissimilarity between two objects (O_i, O_j) is given by the function $\mathcal{D}(O_i, O_j)$
- The user specifies a query object Q and a tolerance ε.

Our goal is to find the objects in the collection that are within distance ε of the query object. An obvious solution is to apply sequential scanning: for each and every object $O_i (1 \leq i \leq N)$, we can compute its distance from Q and report the objects with distance $\mathcal{D}(Q, O_i) \leq \varepsilon$.

However, sequential scanning may be slow, for two reasons:

1. The distance computation might be expensive. For example, the editing distance in DNA strings requires a dynamic-programming algorithm, which

grows with the product of the string lengths (typically, in the hundreds or thousands, for DNA databases);

2. The database size N might be huge.

Thus, we look for a faster alternative. The "GEMINI" (GEneric Multimedia object INdexIng) approach is based on two ideas, each of which tries to avoid the two disadvantages of sequential scanning:

- a "quick-and-dirty" test, to discard quickly the vast majority of nonqualifying objects (possibly, allowing some false alarms);
- the use of SAM, to achieve faster-than-sequential searching, as suggested by Jagadish [20].

This is best illustrated with an example. Consider a database of time series, such as yearly stock price movements, with one price per day. Assume that the distance function between two such series S and Q is the Euclidean distance

$$\mathcal{D}(S, Q) \equiv \left(\sum_{i=1}^{365} (S[i] - Q[i])^2 \right)^{1/2}, \qquad (15.2)$$

where $S[i]$ stands for the value of stock S on the i-th day. Clearly, computing the distance between two stocks will take 365 subtractions and 365 squarings.

The idea behind the "quick-and-dirty" test is to characterize a sequence with a single number, which will help us discard many nonqualifying sequences. Such a number could be, for example, the average stock price over the year. Clearly, if two stocks differ in their averages by a large margin, they cannot be similar. The converse is not true, which is exactly the reason we may have false alarms. Numbers that contain some information about a sequence (or a multimedia object, in general), will be referred to as "*features*" for the rest of this paper. A good feature (such as the "average" in the stock prices example) will allow us to perform a quick test, which will discard many items, using a single numerical comparison for each.

If using a single feature is good, using two or more features might be even better because they may reduce the number of false alarms, at the cost of making the "quick-and-dirty" test a bit more elaborate and expensive. In our stock prices example, additional features might include the standard deviation or some of the discrete Fourier transform (DFT) coefficients, as we shall see in Section 15.3.

By using f features, we can map each object into a point in f-dimensional (f-d) space. We shall refer to this mapping as $F()$:

Definition 2. Let $F()$ be the mapping of objects to f-d points, that is, $F(O)$ will be the f-d point that corresponds to object O.

This mapping provides the key to improving on the second drawback of sequential scanning: by organizing these f-d points into a SAM, we can cluster them in a

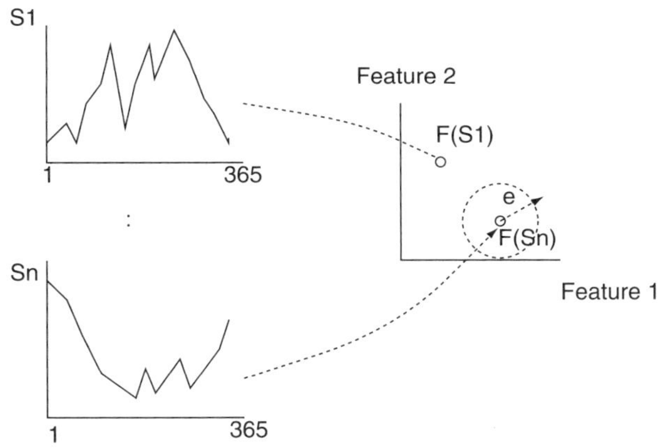

Figure 15.1. Illustration of the basic idea: a database of sequences S1, ... Sn; each sequence is mapped to a point in feature space; a query with tolerance ε becomes a sphere of radius ε.

hierarchical structure, for example, an R*-tree. In processing a query, we use the R*-tree to prune out large portions of the database that are not promising. Such a structure will be referred to as an *F-index* (for "Feature index"). By using an F-index, we do not even have to do the "quick-and-dirty" test on all of the f-d points!

Figure 15.1 illustrates the basic idea: Objects (e.g., time series that are 365-points long) are mapped into 2D points (e.g., using the average and standard deviation as features). Consider the "whole-match" query that requires all the objects that are similar to S_n within tolerance ε: this query becomes an f-d sphere in feature space, centered on the image $F(S_n)$ of S_n. Such queries on multidimensional points is exactly what R-trees and other SAMs are designed to answer efficiently. More specifically, the search algorithm for a whole-match query is as follows:

Algorithm 1. Search an F-index:

1. Map the query object Q into a point $F(Q)$ in feature space;
2. Using the SAM, retrieve all points within the desired tolerance ε from $F(Q)$;
3. Retrieve the corresponding objects, compute their actual distance from Q, and discard the false alarms.

Intuitively, an F-index has the potential to relieve both problems of the sequential scan, presumably resulting in much faster searches.

However, the mapping $F()$ from objects to f-d points must not distort the distances. More specifically, let $\mathcal{D}()$ be the distance function between two objects and $\mathcal{D}_{\text{feature}}()$ be the distance between the corresponding feature vectors. Ideally, the mapping $F()$ should preserve the distances exactly, in which case the SAM will have neither false alarms nor false dismissals. However, preserving distances exactly might be very difficult: for example, it is not obvious which features can be used to match the editing distance between two DNA strings. Even if the features are obvious, there might be practical problems: for example, we could treat every stock price sequence as a 365-dimensional vector. Although in theory a SAM can support an arbitrary number of dimensions, in practice they all suffer from the "dimensionality curse" discussed in the survey appendix.

The crucial observation is that we can avoid false dismissals completely in the "F-index" method if the distance in feature space never overestimates the distance between two objects. Intuitively, this means that our mapping $F()$ from objects to points should make things look closer. Mathematically, let O_1 and O_2 be two objects (e.g., same-length sequences) with distance function $\mathcal{D}()$ (e.g., the Euclidean distance) and $F(O_1)$, $F(O_2)$ be their feature vectors (e.g., their first few Fourier coefficients), with distance function $\mathcal{D}_{\text{feature}}()$ (e.g., the Euclidean distance, again). Then we have:

Lemma 1. To guarantee no false dismissals for whole-match queries, the feature extraction function $F()$ should satisfy the following formula:

$$\mathcal{D}_{\text{feature}}[F(O_1), F(O_2)] \leq \mathcal{D}(O_1, O_2) \tag{15.3}$$

Proof. Let Q be the query object, O be a qualifying object, and ε be the tolerance. We want to prove that if the object O qualifies for the query, then it will be retrieved when we issue a range query on the feature space. That is, we want to prove that

$$\mathcal{D}(Q, O) \leq \varepsilon \Rightarrow \mathcal{D}_{\text{feature}}[F(Q), F(O)] \leq \varepsilon \tag{15.4}$$

However, this is obvious, because

$$\mathcal{D}_{\text{feature}}[F(Q), F(O)] \leq \mathcal{D}(Q, O) \leq \varepsilon \tag{15.5}$$

QED.

Notice that we can still guarantee no false dismissals, if

$$K\mathcal{D}_{\text{feature}}[F(O_1), F(O_2)] \leq \mathcal{D}(O_1, O_2) \tag{15.6}$$

where K is a constant. In this case, the only modification is that the query in feature space should have a radius of ε/K. We shall need this generalization in Section 15.4.

In conclusion, the approach to indexing multimedia objects for fast similarity searching is as follows:

Algorithm 2. "GEMINI" approach:

1. Determine the distance function $\mathcal{D}()$ between two objects;

2. Find one or more numerical feature-extraction functions, to provide a "quick-and-dirty" test;
3. Prove that the distance in feature space *lower-bounds* the actual distance $\mathcal{D}()$, to guarantee correctness
4. Choose a SAM and use it to manage the f-d feature vectors.

In the next sections we show two case studies of applying this approach to 2D color images and to 1D time series. We shall see that the philosophy of the "quick-and-dirty" filter, in conjunction with the lower-bounding lemma, can lead to solutions to two problems:

- The dimensionality curse (time series)
- The "cross talk" of features (color images)

For each case study we (*1*) describe the objects and the distance function, (*2*) show how to apply the lower-bounding lemma, and (*3*) give experimental results, on real or realistic data.

15.3 1D TIME SERIES

Here the goal is to search a collection of (equal length) time series to find the ones that are similar to a desired series. For example, in a collection of yearly stock price movements, we want to find the ones that are similar to IBM. For the rest of the paper, we shall use the following notational conventions: If S and Q are two sequences, then:

- $Len(S)$ denotes the length of S;
- $S[i : j]$ denotes the subsequence that includes entries in positions i through j;
- $S[i]$ denotes the ith entry of sequence S;
- $\mathcal{D}(S, Q)$ denotes the distance of the two (equal length) sequences S and Q.

15.3.1 Distance Function

The first step in the GEMINI algorithm is to determine the distance measure between two time series. This is clearly application-dependent. Several measures have been proposed for 1D and 2D signals. In a recent survey for images (2D signals), Brown [21] mentions that one of the typical similarity measures is the cross-correlation (which reduces to the Euclidean distance, plus some additive and multiplicative constants).

We chose the Euclidean distance because (*1*) it is useful in many cases and (*2*) other similarity measures often can be expressed as the Euclidean distance between feature vectors after some appropriate transformation [22]. As in Ref. [23], we choose the Euclidean distance because it is generally applicable, and because other similarity measures can often be expressed as the Euclidean distance between appropriately transformed feature vectors [22].

We denote the Euclidean distance between two sequences S and Q by $\mathcal{D}(S, Q)$.

Additional and more elaborate distance functions, such as time-warping [24], can also be handled [4] as long as we are able to extract appropriate features from the time series.

15.3.2 Feature Extraction and Lower-Bounding

Having decided on the Euclidean distance as the dissimilarity measure, the next step is to find some features that can lower-bound it. We would like a set of features that preserve or lower-bound the distance and carry enough information about the corresponding time series to limit the number of false alarms. The second requirement suggests that we use "good" features, namely, features with more discriminatory power. In the stock price example, a "bad" feature would be, for example, the value during the first day: two stocks might have similar first-day values, yet they may differ significantly from then on. Conversely, two otherwise similar sequences, may agree everywhere, except for the first day's values.

A natural feature to use is the average. Additional features might include the average of the first half, of the second half, of the first quarter, and so on. These features resemble the first coefficients of the Hadamard transform [25]. In signal processing, the most well-known transform is the Fourier transform, and, for our case, the discrete Fourier transform (DFT). Before we describe the desirable features of the DFT, we proceed with its definition and some of its properties.

15.3.3 Introduction to DFT

The n-point DFT [26,27] of a signal $\vec{x} = [x_i]$, $i = 0, \ldots, n-1$ is defined to be a sequence $\vec{X}$ of n complex numbers X_F, $F = 0, \ldots, n-1$, given by

$$X_F = 1/\sqrt{n} \sum_{i=0}^{n-1} x_i \exp(-j2\pi Fi/n) \quad F = 0, 1, \ldots, n-1, \tag{15.7}$$

where j is the imaginary unit $j = \sqrt{-1}$. The signal $\vec{x}$ can be recovered by the inverse transform:

$$x_i = 1/\sqrt{n} \sum_{F=0}^{n-1} X_F \exp(j2\pi Fi/n) \quad i = 0, 1, \ldots, n-1, \tag{15.8}$$

where X_F is a complex number (with the exception of X_0, which is a real, if the signal $\vec{x}$ is real). The *energy* $E(\vec{x})$ of a sequence $\vec{x}$ is defined as the sum of energies (squares of the amplitude $|x_i|$) at every point of the sequence:

$$E(\vec{x}) \equiv \|\vec{x}\|^2 \equiv \sum_{i=0}^{n-1} |x_i|^2. \tag{15.9}$$

A fundamental theorem for the correctness of our method is Parseval's theorem [27], which states that the DFT preserves the energy of a signal:

Theorem (Parseval). Let $\vec{X}$ be the DFT of the sequence $\vec{x}$. Then:

$$\sum_{i=0}^{n-1} |x_i|^2 = \sum_{F=0}^{n-1} |X_F|^2 \tag{15.10}$$

Because the DFT is a linear transformation [27] and the Euclidean distance between two signals $\vec{x}$ and $\vec{y}$ is the Euclidean norm of their difference, Parseval's theorem implies that the DFT preserves the Euclidean distance also:

$$\mathcal{D}(\vec{x}, \vec{y}) = \mathcal{D}(\vec{X},\ \vec{Y}). \tag{15.11}$$

where $\vec{X}$ and $\vec{Y}$ are Fourier transforms of $\vec{x}$ and $\vec{y}$, respectively.

Thus, if we keep the first f coefficients of the DFT as the features, we have

$$\begin{aligned} \mathcal{D}_{\text{feature}}(F(\vec{x}), F(\vec{y})) &= \sum_{F=0}^{f-1} |X_F - Y_F|^2 \leq \sum_{F=0}^{n-1} |X_F - Y_F|^2 \\ &= \sum_{i=0}^{n-1} |x_i - y_i|^2 \equiv \mathcal{D}(\vec{x},\ \vec{y}), \end{aligned} \tag{15.12}$$

that is, the resulting distance in the f-d feature space will clearly underestimate the distance of two sequences. Thus, according to Lemma 1, there will be no false dismissals.

Note that the F-index approach can be applied with any orthonormal transform, such as, the discrete cosine transform (DCT) [28], the wavelet transform [29], and so on, because they all preserve the distance between the original and the transformed space. In fact, our response time will improve with the ability of the transform to concentrate the energy: the fewer the coefficients that contain most of the energy, the fewer the false alarms, and the faster our response time. Thus, the performance results presented next are pessimistic bounds; better transforms will achieve even better response times.

We have chosen the DFT because it is the most well known, its code is readily available (e.g., in the *Mathematica* package [30] or in "C" [31]), and it does a good job of concentrating the energy in the first few coefficients. In addition, the DFT has the attractive property that the *amplitude* of the Fourier coefficients is invariant under time shifts. Thus, using the DFT for feature extraction allows us to extend our technique to finding similar sequences, while ignoring shifts.

15.3.4 Energy-Concentrating Properties of DFT

Having proved that keeping the first few DFT coefficients lower-bounds the actual distance, we address the question of how good DFT is, that is, whether it produces few false alarms. To achieve that, we have to argue that the first few DFT coefficients will usually contain most of the information about the signal.

The worst-case signal for the method is *white noise*, in which each value x_i is completely independent of its neighbors x_{i-1} and x_{i+1}. The energy spectrum of white noise follows $O(F^0)$ [32], that is, it has the same energy in every frequency. This is bad for the F-index because it implies that all the frequencies are equally important. However, many real signals have a skewed energy spectrum. For example, *random walks* (also known as *brown noise* or *brownian walks*) exhibit an energy spectrum of $O(F^{-2})$ [32] and therefore an amplitude spectrum of $O(F^{-1})$. Random walks follow the formula

$$x_i = x_{i-1} + z_i, \tag{15.13}$$

where z_i is noise, that is, a random variable. Stock movements and exchange rates have been successfully modeled as random walks [33,34].

Figure 15.2 plots the movement of the exchange rate between the Swiss franc and the U.S. dollar from August 7, 1990 to April 18, 1991 (30,000 measurements). This data set is available through *ftp* from *sfi.santafe.edu*. Figure 15.3 shows the amplitude of the Fourier coefficients and the $1/F$ line, in a doubly logarithmic plot. Notice that, because it is a random walk, the amplitude of the Fourier coefficients follow the $1/F$ line.

The mathematical argument for keeping the first few Fourier coefficients agrees with the intuitive argument of the Dow Jones theory for stock price

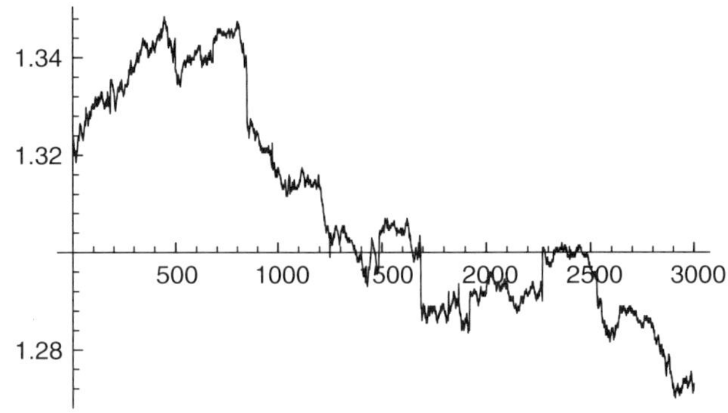

Figure 15.2. The Swiss franc exchange rate; August 7, 1990 to April 18, 1991 (first 3,000 values).

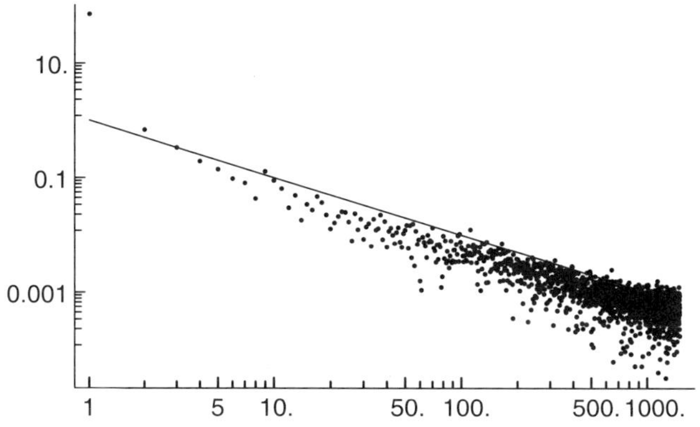

Figure 15.3. (Log-log) amplitude of the Fourier transform of the Swiss franc exchange rate, along with the $1/F$ line.

movement [35]. This theory tries to detect *primary* and *secondary* trends in the stock market movement and ignores *minor* trends.

Primary trends are defined as changes that are larger than 20 percent, typically lasting more than a year; secondary trends show 1/3 to 2/3 relative change over primary trends, with a typical duration of a few months; minor trends last approximately for a week. From the foregoing definitions, we conclude that primary and secondary trends correspond to strong, low-frequency signals, whereas minor trends correspond to weak, high-frequency signals. Thus, the primary and secondary trends are exactly the ones that our method will automatically choose for indexing.

In addition to the signals mentioned earlier, there is another group of signals, called *black noise* [32]. Their energy spectrum follows $O(F^{-b})$, $b > 2$, which is even more skewed than the spectrum of the brown noise. Such signals model successfully, for example, the water level of rivers as they vary over time [34].

In addition to stock price movements and exchange rates, it is believed that several families of real signals belong to the family of "colored noises," with skewed spectra. For example, 2D signals, like photographs, are far from white noise, exhibiting a few strong coefficients in the lower-spatial frequencies. The JPEG image-compression standard [28] exploits this phenomenon, effectively ignoring the high-frequency components of the DCT, (which is closely related to the Fourier transform). If the image consisted of white noise, no compression would be possible at all. Birkhoff's theory [32] claims that "*interesting*" signals, such as musical scores and other works of art, consist of *pink noise*, whose energy spectrum follows $O(F^{-1})$. The theory argues that white noise with $O(F^0)$ energy spectrum is completely unpredictable, whereas brown noise with $O(F^{-2})$ energy spectrum is too predictable and therefore uninteresting, and so is black noise. The energy spectrum of pink noise lies inbetween. Signals with pink noise also have their energy concentrated in the first few frequencies (but not as few as in the random walk).

15.3.5 Experiments

To determine the effectiveness of the *F-index* method, we compare it to a *sequential-scanning* method.

Experiments in Ref. [23] used an R*-tree and showed that the response time has a (rather flat) minimum when we retain $f = 2$ or 3 features. For the rest of the experiments, we kept $f = 2$ Fourier coefficients for indexing, resulting in a four-dimensional (4D) R^*-tree (two real numbers for each complex DFT coefficient). The sequences were artificially generated random walks, with length $n = 1024$; their number N varied from 50 to 400. Figure 15.4 shows the response time for the two methods (F-index and sequential scan), as a function of the number of sequences N. Clearly, the F-index method outperforms sequential scanning.

The major conclusions from applying the F-index method to time series are the following:

1. The F-index approach can be successfully applied to time series, and specifically to ones that behave like "colored noises" (stock prices movements, currency exchange rates, water level in rivers, and etc.);
2. For signals with skewed spectra, the minimum response time is achieved for a small number of Fourier coefficients ($f = 1 - 3$). Moreover, the minimum is rather flat, which implies that a suboptimal choice for f will give a search time that is close to the minimum. Thus, with the help of the lower-bounding lemma and the energy-concentrating properties of the DFT, we avoid the "dimensionality curse";
3. The success in 1D series suggests that the F-index method seems promising for 2D or higher-dimensionality signals if those signals also have skewed spectrum. The success of JPEG (using DCT) indicates that real images indeed have a skewed spectrum.

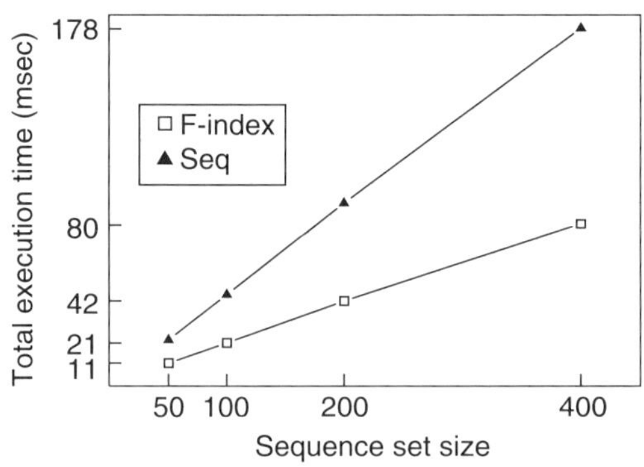

Figure 15.4. Search time per query versus number N of sequences, for whole-match queries; F-index method (black line) and sequential scanning (gray line).

15.4 2D COLOR IMAGES

One of the earliest systems for content search in large image databases was query by-image content (QBIC) [36]. The QBIC project studies methods to query large on-line image databases using image content as the basis for the queries. Types of content include color, texture, shape, position, and dominant edges of image items and regions. Potential applications include medical ("*Give me other images that contain a tumor with a texture like this one*") and photojournalism ("*Give me images that have blue at the top and red at the bottom*"), as well as art, fashion, cataloging, retailing, and industry.

In this section, we give an overview of the indexing aspects of QBIC, specifically the distance functions and application of the lower-bounding lemma. More details about the algorithms and the implementation are in Refs. [1,37].

We restrict the discussion to databases of still images, with two main data types: "images" (≡ "scenes") and "items." A scene is an (color) image; an item is a part of a scene, for example, a person, a piece of outlined texture, or an apple. Each scene has zero or more items. The identification and extraction of items is beyond the scope of this paper [1].

Given that semantic features are outside the capability of current machine vision technology, QBIC uses (in addition to text key words) the properties of *color*, *texture*, *shape*, *location*, and overall *sketch-like* appearance as the basis for retrieval. These properties are computable (to a greater or lesser degree), and have broad, intuitive applicability. For either a scene or an item, the user may query on any or a combination of the above properties. All queries are "approximate" or "similarity" queries, and the system ranks the images, based on the selected similarity function.

As an example, a user interested in retrieving a beach scene needs to map the query into the available parameters offered by QBIC: for instance the color distribution would be set to 35 percent white and 65 percent blue, and the texture to "sand texture." QBIC will retrieve and display images with these properties ranked by the selected similarity measure. The result will include beach scenes and false alarms (images that happened to have similar color and texture distribution). The user is then given an opportunity to select items of interest and discard unwanted information, thereby guiding the retrieval process.

QBIC supports two ways of specifying a query:

1. "Direct query," in which the user specifies the desired color, shape, texture, or sketch directly, through methods such as picking colors from a palette on the screen or drawing a freehand shape with the mouse.
2. "Query-by-example," closely related to the concept of relevance feedback [38], in which the user chooses a displayed image or item (say, the result of a previous query) and asks for additional, similar images or items.

The two modes of query may be used interchangeably within the same query session.

15.4.1 Image Features and Distance Functions

In this section, we describe the feature sets used to characterize images and items, and the associated distance functions that try to capture the similarity that a human perceives. The features are computed once during image ingest, whereas the matching functions are applied at query time using those features. We focus mainly on color features because color presents an interesting problem (namely, the "*cross talk*" between features), which can be resolved by the GEMINI algorithm 2.

Color. A typical method for representing color is to compute a k-element color histogram for each item and scene. Conceptually, k can be as high as 16×10^6 colors, with each individual color being denoted by a point in a 3D color space. In practice, we can cluster similar colors together using an agglomerative clustering technique [25], divide the color space into nonoverlapping buckets (called "color bins"), and choose one representative color for each color bin. In the experiments reported later, the number of clusters was $k = 256$ and $k = 64$. Each component in the color histogram is the fraction of pixels that are most similar to the corresponding representative color. For such a histogram of a fictitious photograph of a sunset, there are many red, pink, orange, and purple pixels, but few white and green ones (Fig 15.5).

Determining the similarity of two images now reduces to the problem of measuring the distance between their color histograms. One such method ($k \times 1$ vectors) $\vec{x}$ and $\vec{y}$ is given by

$$d_{hist}^2(\vec{x}, \vec{y}) = (\vec{x} - \vec{y})^t A(\vec{x} - \vec{y}) = \sum_i^k \sum_j^k a_{ij}(x_i - y_i)(x_j - y_j), \qquad (15.14)$$

where the superscript t indicates matrix transposition and the color-to-color similarity matrix A has entries a_{ij} that describe the similarity between color i and color j. This formulation was proposed in Ref. [39], and results in good retrieval performance.

This measure correctly accounts for color similarity (an orange image is similar to a red one) and color distribution (a half red–half blue image is different from an all-purple one).

Shape Features. Shape similarity has proven to be a difficult problem [40,41] in model-based vision applications and the problem remains difficult in content-based image retrieval. Typical features are the area, circularity, eccentricity, major axis orientation, and a set of algebraic moment invariants.

The distance between two shape vectors is the (weighted) Euclidean distance in which the weights reflect the importance of each feature.

Texture Features. Our texture features are modifications of the coarseness, contrast, and directionality features proposed in Ref. [42]. See Ref. [37] for

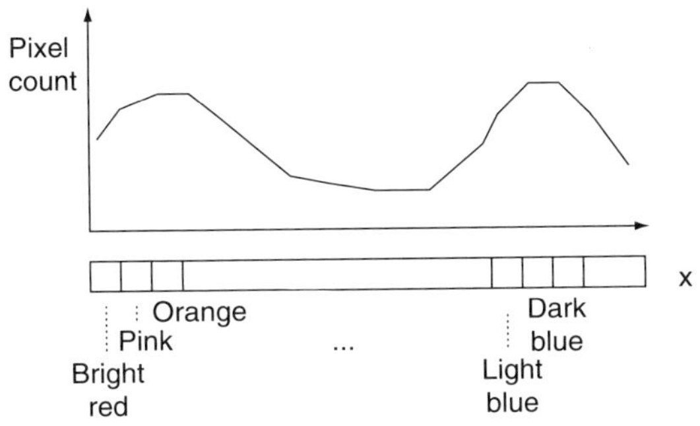

Figure 15.5. An example of a color histogram of a fictitious sunset photograph: Many red, pink, orange, purple, and bluish pixels; few yellow, white, and green ones.

more details on our implementation of texture features, including descriptions of how we improved the robustness and efficiency of these measures. The distance function is the (weighted) Euclidean distance in the 3D texture space. Because indexing points in the 3D texture space is straightforward, we do not discuss texture further.

Sketch. The system supports the image retrieval method described in Refs. [43,44] that allows images to be retrieved based on a rough user sketch. A Canny edge operator is applied to the luminance of each data image, transforming it to a black-and-white sketch ("edge-map"), and the user's sketch is compared with each edge map in order to retrieve the similar ones. Because of the complexity of the matching function, the current implementation uses sequential scanning. Applying the lower-bounding lemma for faster indexing is the topic of future research.

15.4.2 Lower-Bounding

As mentioned earlier, we focus on indexing color; the texture creates no indexing problems, whereas shapes present only the "dimensionality curse" ($f \approx 20$ features), which can be resolved with an energy-concentrating transformation: we can use the Karhunen-Loeve (K-L) transform [25]. Experiments on a collection of 1,000 and 10,000 shapes showed that an R^*-tree with the first $f = 2$ K-L coefficients gives the best overall response time [45].

There are two obstacles in applying the F-index method for color indexing: (*1*) the "*dimensionality curse*" (see Chapter 14): because the histogram can have numerous bins, for instance 64 or 256; and, most importantly, (2) the *quadratic nature of the distance function*: the distance function in the feature space involves "cross talk" among the features (see Eq. 15.14), and it is thus a full quadratic form involving all cross terms. Not only is such a function much more expensive to compute than a Euclidean (or any L_p) distance, but it also precludes efficient implementation of commonly used multikey indexing methods. Figure 15.6 illustrates the situation: to compute the distance between the two color histograms

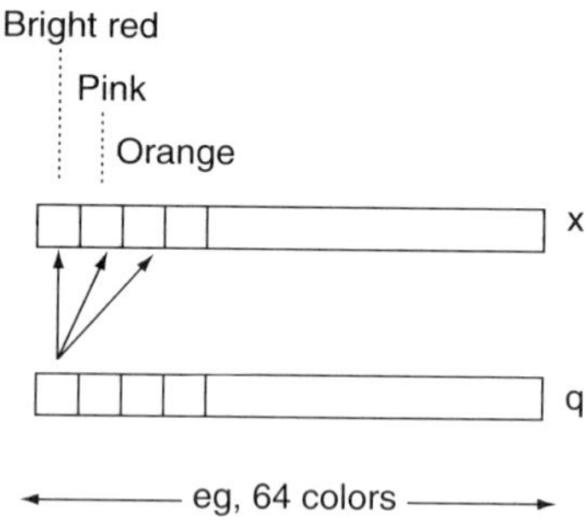

Figure 15.6. Illustration of the "cross talk" between two color histograms.

x and **q**, the bright-red component of **x** has to be compared not only to the bright-red component of **q**, but also to the pink, orange, and other components of **q**.

To resolve the cross talk problem, we try to apply GEMINI (algorithm 2). As we shall see, this algorithm simultaneously solves both the dimensionality curse and the cross talk problems. The first step of the algorithm, computing the distance function between two color images, is given by Eq. 15.14: $\mathcal{D}() = d_{\text{hist}}()$. The next step is to find one or more numerical features, in which the Euclidean distance lower-bounds $d_{\text{hist}}()$. Intuitively, the question is again:

> If we are allowed to use only one numerical feature to describe each color image, what should this feature be?

Taking a cue from the previous section on time series, we can consider some average value, or the first few 2D DFT coefficients. Because we have three color components (e.g., red, green, and blue), we could consider the average amount of red, green, and blue in a given color image.

Note that the algorithm does not depend on the color space, and the conclusions, albeit derived for the RGB case, are general. In our discussion, the color of an individual pixel is described by the triplet (R,G,B) (for 'R'ed, 'G'reen, 'B'lue). The average color of an image or item $\overline{x} = (R_{\text{avg}}, G_{\text{avg}}, B_{\text{avg}})^t$ is defined in the obvious way:

$$R_{\text{avg}} = (1/N) \sum_{p=1}^{N} R(p),\ G_{\text{avg}} = (1/N) \sum_{p=1}^{N} G(p),\ B_{\text{avg}} = (1/N) \sum_{p=1}^{N} B(p), \tag{15.15}$$

where there are N pixels in the item and $R(p)$, $G(p)$, and $B(p)$ are the red, green, and blue components (intensities, typically in the range 0–255), respectively, of the pth pixel. Given the average colors $\overline{x}$ and $\overline{y}$ of two items, we define $d_{\text{avg}}()$ as the simple Euclidean distance between the 3D average color vectors,

$$d_{\text{avg}}^2(\overline{x}, \overline{y}) = (\overline{x} - \overline{y})^t (\overline{x} - \overline{y}). \tag{15.16}$$

The next step of algorithm 2 is to prove that our simplified distance $d_{\text{avg}}()$ lower-bounds the actual distance $d_{\text{hist}}()$. Indeed, this is true as an application of the so-called *QDB* — "Quadratic Distance Bounding" Theorem; here, we provide a simplified version, whereas the exact theorem and its proof are in Ref. [46].

Theorem 1 (QDB — "Quadratic Distance Bounding"). Let $d_{\text{hist}}()$ be defined by equation 15.13 applied to the color-quantized image, and $d_{\text{avg}}()$ by 15.14. Then,

$$d_{hist}^2() \geq \lambda_1 d_{\text{avg}}^2(),$$

where λ_1 is a constant, depending on the matrix A.

Notice that the constant λ_1 depends only on the way we have created the k colors (that is, it depends only on the color-to-color similarity matrix A). The result is that, given a color query, our retrieval proceeds by first filtering the set of images based on their average (R, G, B) color, then doing a final, more accurate matching using their full k-element histogram. The resulting speedup is discussed in the following section.

15.4.3 Experiments

In Ref. [45] we report experiments on color, using the bounding theorem, to illustrate the efficiency gains of the GEMINI methodology. These experiments compared the relative performance (in terms of CPU time and disk accesses) between (*1*) simple sequential evaluation of d_{hist} for all database vectors (referred to as *"naive"*) and (*2*) filtering using d_{avg} followed by evaluation of d_{hist} only on those records that pass through the filter (referred to as *"filtered"*).

These experiments focused on the total time and on the CPU time required by the methods, by performing simulations on a database of $N = 924$ color image histograms, each of $k = 256$ colors, extracted from assorted natural images.

Results are shown in Figure 15.7, which presents the total response time as a function of the selectivity (ratio of actual hits over the database size N). The figure also shows the CPU time for each method. We note that, even for a selectivity of 5 percent (which would return ≈ 50 images to the user), the GEMINI method is much faster than the straightforward, sequential computation of histogram distances. Specifically, it requires from a fraction of a second up to approximately four seconds, whereas the "naive" method consistently requires about ten seconds. Moreover, notice that for larger databases, the "naive" method will have a linearly increasing response time. Notice further that the "naive" method is CPU bound, which is almost 80 percent of the total time.

The conclusions are the following:

- The idea of extracting some features for a quick-and-dirty test motivated the development of a fast method, using the average RGB distance; it also

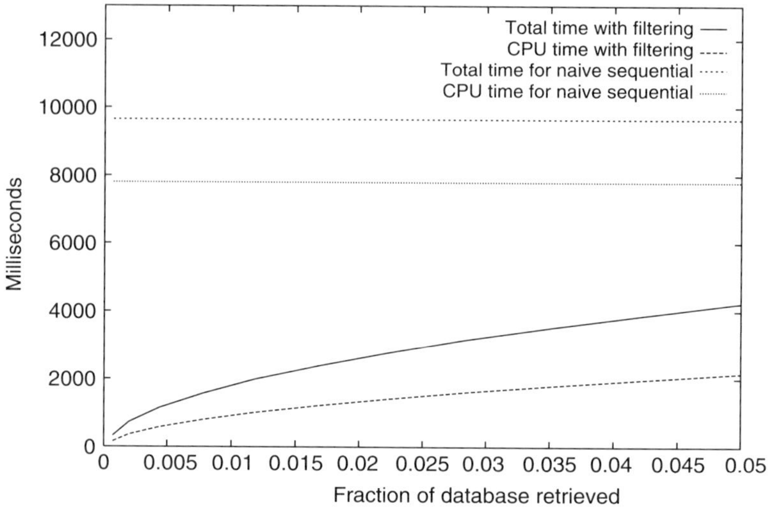

Figure 15.7. Time spent with sequential retrieval versus filtered retrieval.

motivated formulation of a strong theorem (Theorem 1), which guarantees correctness in our case.

- Resolving the cross talk problem has several benefits:
  — it allows indexing with SAMs
  — it solves the "dimensionality curse" problem, and
  — it saves CPU time, because $d_{\text{hist}}()$ is quadratic on the number of colors ($O(k^2)$).

15.5 EXTENSION: SUBPATTERN MATCHING

In this chapter, we have examined the "whole-match" case. We now address the question: *Could we extend the GEMINI approach so that we can handle subpattern matching queries?*

We will use 1D time series to illustrate the problem and the solution more clearly. The problem is defined as follows:

- We are given a collection of N sequences of real numbers S_1, S_2, S_N, each one of potentially different length.
- The user specifies a query subsequence Q of length $Len(Q)$ (which may vary) and a tolerance ε, that is, the maximum acceptable dissimilarity (= distance).
- We want to quickly find all the sequences S_i ($1 \leq i \leq N$), along with the correct offsets k, such that the subsequence $S_i[k : k + Len - 1]$ matches the query sequence: $\mathcal{D}(Q, S_i[k : k + Len(Q) - 1]) \leq \varepsilon$.

As in Section 15.3, we use the Euclidean distance as the dissimilarity measure. The brute-force solution is to sequentially examine every possible subsequence of the data sequences for a match. We shall refer to this method as the *SequentialScan* method. Next, we describe a method that achieves order of magnitude savings over the SequentialScan method, at the cost of a small increment in storage.

15.5.1 Sketch of the Approach — ST-index

Without loss of generality, we denote the application-dependent minimum query length by w. For example, in stock price databases, analysts are interested in weekly or monthly patterns because shorter patterns are susceptible to noise [35]. Notice that we never lose the ability to answer queries shorter than w because we can always resort to sequential scanning.

Generalizing the reasoning of the method for "whole matching," we use a *sliding window* of size w and place it at every possible position (offset), on every data sequence. For each such placement of the window, we extract the features of the subsequence inside the window. Thus, a data sequence of length $Len(S)$ is mapped to a trail in feature space, consisting of $Len(S) - w + 1$ points: one point for each possible offset of the sliding window. Figure 15.8 gives an example of a trail: Consider the sequence S_1, and assume that we keep the first $f = 2$ features (e.g., the amplitude of the first and second coefficient of the w-point DFT). When the window of length w is placed at offset = 0 on S_1, we obtain the first point of the trail; as the window slides over S_1, we obtain the rest of the points of the trail. Figure 15.12 gives an example of trails, using a real-time series (stock price movements).

The straightforward way to index these trails would be to keep track of the individual points of each trail, storing them in a SAM. We call this method ***I-naive***, where "I" stands for "Index" (as opposed to sequential scanning). However, storing the individual points of the trail in an R^*-tree is inefficient, both in

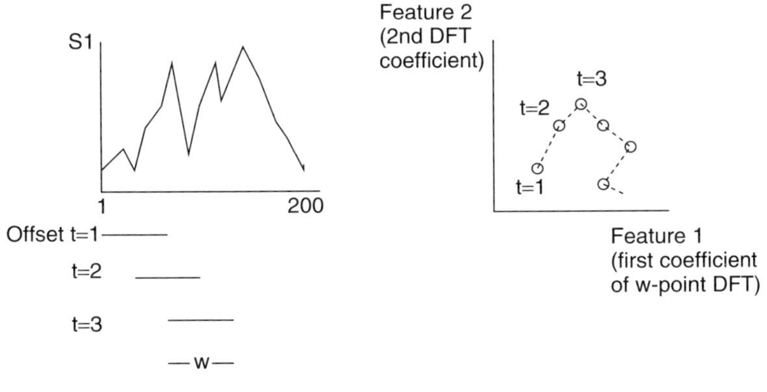

Figure 15.8. Illustration of the way trails are created in feature space.

terms of space and search speed. The reason is that almost every point in a data sequence will correspond to a point in the f-dimensional feature space, leading to an index with a $1 : f$ increase in storage requirements. Moreover, the search performance will also suffer because the R^*-tree will become tall and slow. In experiments [47], the I-naive method was almost twice as slow as the SequentialScan. Thus, we want to improve the I-naive method, by making the representation of the trails more compact.

Here is where the idea of a "quick-and-dirty" test leads to a solution. Instead of laboriously keeping track of each and every point of a trail in feature space, we can exploit the fact that successive points of the trail are likely to be similar because the contents of the sliding window in nearby offsets are similar. We can divide the trail of a given data sequence into subtrails and represent each of them with its *minimum bounding (hyper)-rectangle (MBR)*. Thus, instead of storing thousands of points of a given trail, we store only a few MBRs. More importantly, at the same time we still guarantee "no false dismissals": when a query arrives, we retrieve all the MBRs that intersect the query region; thus, we retrieve all the qualifying subtrails plus some false alarms (subtrails that do not intersect the query region, whereas their MBR does).

Figure 15.9a gives an illustration of the approach. Two trails are drawn; the first curve, labeled $C1$, has been divided into three subtrails (and MBRs), whereas the second one, labeled $C2$, has been divided into five subtrails. Notice that MBRs belonging to the same trail may overlap, as $C2$ illustrates.

Thus, we map a data sequence into a *set of rectangles* in feature space. This yields significant improvements with respect to space, and with respect to response time, as we shall see in Section 15.5.2. Each MBR corresponds to a whole subtrail, that is, to points in feature space that correspond to successive positionings of the sliding window on the data sequences.

These MBRs can be stored in a SAM. We have used R*-trees [48], in which case the MBRs are recursively grouped into parent MBRs, grandparent MBRs, and so on. Figure 15.9b shows how the eight leaf-level MBRs of Figure 15.9a are

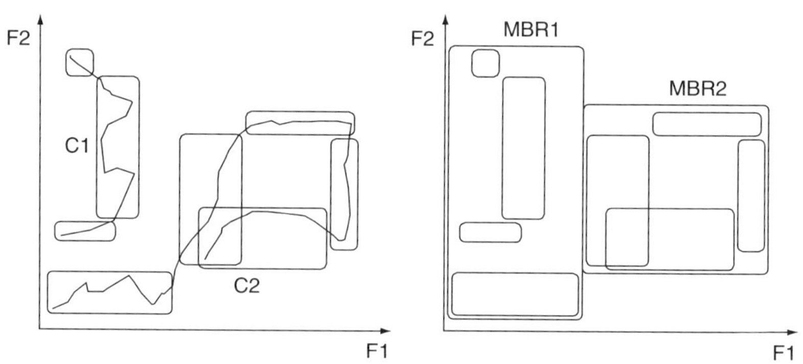

Figure 15.9. Example of (**a**) dividing trails into subtrails and MBRs, and (**b**) grouping of MBRs into larger ones.

grouped to form two MBRs at the next higher level, assuming a fanout of 4 (i.e., at most 4 items per nonleaf node). Note that the higher-level MBRs may contain leaf-level MBRs from different data sequences. For example, in Figure 15.9b, we note that MBR1 contains a part of the curve C2.

This completes the sketch of the index structure. We shall refer to it by ***ST-index***, for "Sub-trail index." There are two issues that we have to address to complete the description of the method—how to handle insertions and how to handle queries.

Insertions. When a new data sequence is inserted, what is a good way to divide its trail in feature space into subtrails? We propose [47] using an adaptive, heuristic algorithm, which breaks the trail into subtrails, so that the resulting MBRs of the subtrails have small volume (and, therefore, result in few disk accesses on search).

Queries. How do we handle queries, especially ones that are longer than w? Figure 15.10 shows how to handle queries of length w: the query subsequence is translated into a point Q in feature space; all the MBRs that are within radius ε from Q are retrieved. Searching for longer queries is handled by the following algorithm:

- Break the query subsequence into p disjoint pieces of length w each (ignoring the last piece if it is shorter than w);
- Search for each piece, with tolerance $\varepsilon/\sqrt{p}$;
- Compute the union of the results and discard false alarms.

Figure 15.11 illustrates the algorithm: the query sequence is broken into $p = 2$ pieces, each of length w; each piece gives rise to a range query in feature space. Justifications and correctness proofs for the above algorithms are in Ref. [47].

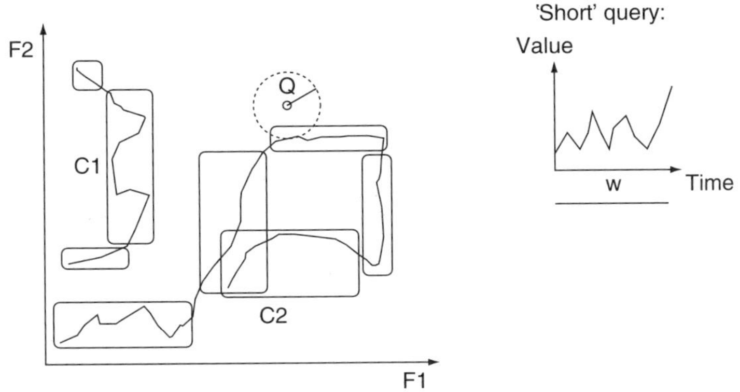

Figure 15.10. Illustration of the search algorithm for minimum-length queries. The query becomes a sphere of radius ε in feature space.

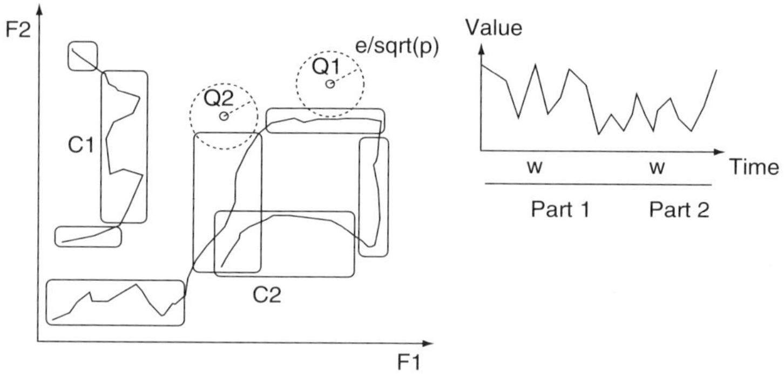

Figure 15.11. Illustration of the search algorithm for a longer query. The query is divided in $p = 2$ pieces of length w each, giving rise to p range queries in feature space.

15.5.2 Experiments

We report experimental results on the *ST-index* method from Ref. [47]. The test bed was a stock prices database containing 329,000 points (obtained from *sfi.santafe.edu*). Figure 15.12a shows a sample of 250 points of such a stock price sequence. The experiments used only the first three frequencies of the DFT; thus the feature space has $f = 6$ dimensions (real and imaginary parts of each retained DFT coefficient). Figure 15.12b illustrates a trail in feature space: it is a 2 "phase" plot of the amplitude of the zeroth DFT coefficient versus the amplitude of the first DFT coefficient. Figure 15.12c similarly plots the amplitudes of the first and second DFT coefficients. For both figures the window size w was 512 points. The smooth evolution of both curves justifies the method of grouping successive points of the feature space into MBRs. An R*-tree [48] was used to store the MBRs of each subtrail in feature space.

Figure 5.13 gives the relative response time of the sequential-scanning method (T_s) over our index-assisted method (T_r, where r stands for 'R^*-tree') by counting the actual wallclock time for each method. The queries had length equal to the window size [$Len(Q) = w = 512$]. The horizontal axis is the selectivity; both axes are in logarithmic scales. The query selectivity varies up to 10 percent, which is fairly large in comparison with our 329,000 points time series database. We see that the *ST-index* method achieves from 3 up to 100 times better response time for selectivities in the range 10^{-4} to 10^{-1}.

Similar experiments for longer queries ($Len(Q) > w$) revealed similar trends. The conclusions are the following:

- The idea of using a "quick-and-dirty" filter pays off again. Every sequence is represented *coarsely* by a set of MBRs in feature space; despite the loss of information, these MBRs provide the basis for quick filtering, which eventually achieves large savings over sequential scanning.
- The method can be easily generalized for subpattern matching in 2D (and, in general, n-dimensional) signals. The idea is best illustrated in 2D: Consider,

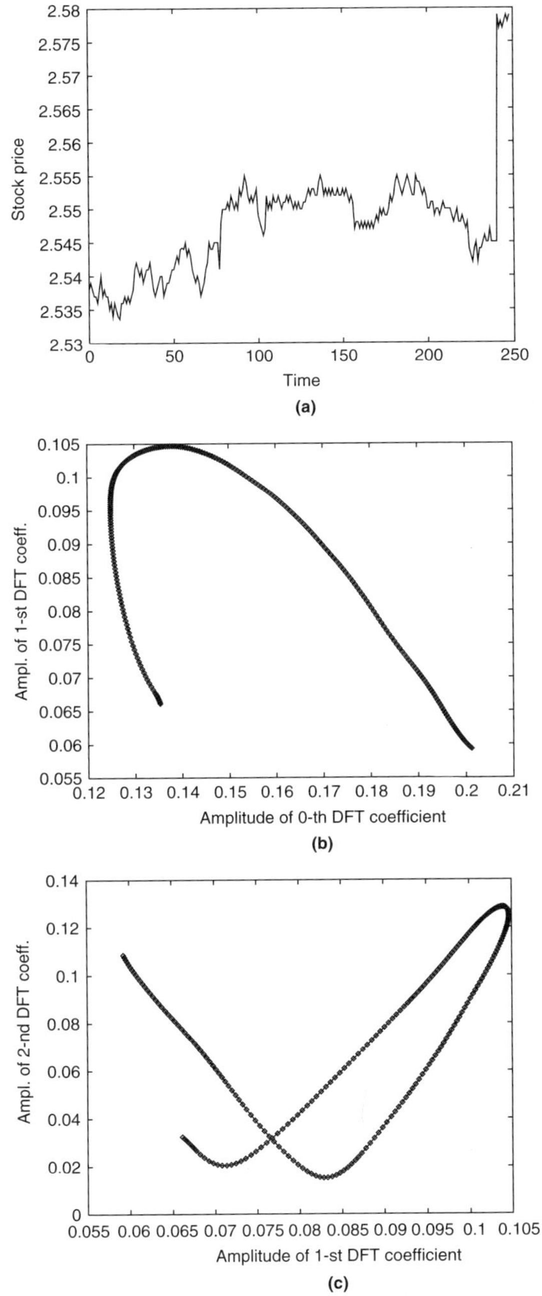

Figure 15.12. (**a**) Sample stock price sequence; (**b**) its trail in the feature space of the zeroth and first DFT coefficients; and (**c**) the equivalent trail of the first and second DFT coefficients.

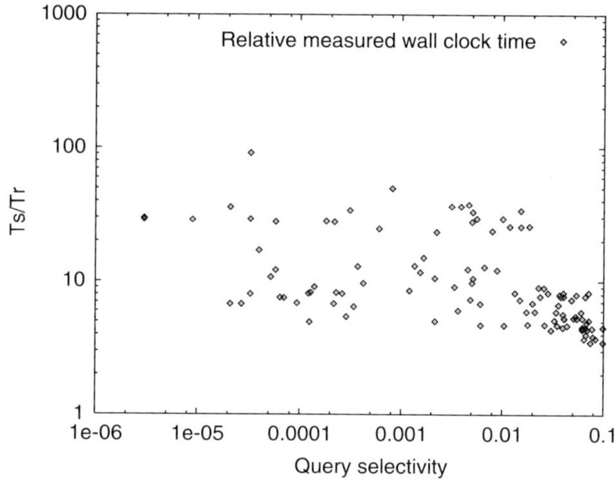

Figure 15.13. Relative wallclock time [sequential (T_s) over F-index with R^*-tree (T_r)] versus selectivity in log–log scale [$Len(Q) = w = 512$ points].

for example, a gray scale image; it can be transformed into a trail in feature space as follows: We can use a sliding window of dimensions $w \times w$, which will move over all the possible positions on the image, using a scanning pattern (e.g., row-wise scanning, or, even better, the Hilbert curve [49,50]); for each position of the window, we compute the features (e.g., the first f 2D DFT coefficients). Thus, the image has become a trail in f-dimensional space; the rest of the *ST-index* method applies with no changes.

15.6 CONCLUSION

We have presented a general method (the *GEMINI* algorithm) to accelerate queries by content on arbitrary, multimedia databases. We presented two case studies, namely image databases and time-sequence databases. Target queries are of the form "*find images with a color distribution of a sunset photograph*" or "*find companies whose stock price moves similarly to a given company's stock.*"

The method expects a distance function $\mathcal{D}()$ (provided by domain experts), which should measure the dissimilarity between two objects O_1 and O_2. We mainly focus on *whole-match* queries (that is, *queries by example*, where the user specifies the ideal object and asks for all objects that are within distance ε from the ideal object).

The "*GEMINI*" approach combines two ideas:

- The first is to devise a "*quick-and-dirty*" test, which eliminates several nonqualifying objects. To achieve that we should extract f numerical features from each object, which should somehow describe the object (for example, the first few DFT coefficients for a time sequence or for a gray scale image).

- The second idea is to further accelerate the search by organizing these f-dimensional points using state-of-the-art SAMs, such as R^*-trees. These methods typically group neighboring points together, thus managing to discard large unpromising portions of the address space early.

The two foregoing ideas achieve fast searching. We went further and considered conditions under which the foregoing method will not only be fast, but also *correct*, in the sense that it will not miss any qualifying object (false alarms are acceptable because they can be simply discarded). Specifically, we proved the *lower-bounding* lemma, which intuitively states that the mapping of objects to f-d points should *make things look closer*.

The rest of the paper shows how to apply the method to a variety of applications, including 2D color images and 1D time sequences. These applications are specifically chosen because they give rise to the "cross talk" and the "dimensionality curse" problems, respectively. The philosophy of the "quick-and-dirty" filter, together with the "lower-bounding" lemma, provided solutions to both problems. Experimental results on real or realistic data confirmed both the correctness and the speedup that our approach provides.

Finally, we described how to extend the method to handle subpattern matching. Again, the idea is to provide an approximate and inexpensive description of each object (in this case, a set of MBRs that cover the trail of the time sequence in feature space), which may allow false alarms but no false dismissal. The approach can be generalized for subpattern matching in 2D signals (and, in general, in n-dimensional vector fields).

Future work involves (*1*) the comparison of GEMINI with other alternatives, such as the "metric trees" of Chapter 4 [M-trees [51], with many earlier versions [51–54], and several newer variations [55,56], (*2*) the incorporation of multimedia indexing methods into commercial, object-relational DBMSs, and (*3*) the application of the GEMINI method to data mining in multimedia databases. The goal is to determine rules, clusters, and outliers, in a collection of multimedia objects.

APPENDIX: SURVEY

Our method maps objects into points in f-d space and uses multiattribute access methods (also referred to as *SAMs*) to cluster them and to search for them.

A fundamental requirement is a distance function $\mathcal{D}()$ that measures the dissimilarity between two objects. We briefly discuss distance functions and previous work on query-by-image content in color image databases. A survey on SAMs is in Chapter 14.

Querying image databases by their image content is an active area of research. In terms of features to use, it benefits from the large body of work in machine vision on feature extraction and similarity measures [25,57].

In terms of methods and systems for image retrieval, examples of recent work include Refs. [58] and [59], which consider methods to retrieve images of line drawings and engineering diagrams; Refs. [60–63], which assume known objects have been identified in images and define and use 2D- and 2D-C strings to perform image retrieval, based on the relative position of combinations of these known objects; Ref. [43], which presents a method for "query by sketch" in which a rough user sketch of overall scene layout is used as the basis of a query; Refs. [20,64–69], which give methods for retrieving and indexing, based on shapes of objects in images; and Refs. [39,70,71], which present retrieval methods based on the colors in a scene.

Many references emphasize the vision aspects of the problem [39,43,64,70], or the indexing issues [20,72]. Several papers such as Refs. [7,73,74] comment on the need for communication between the vision and the database communities. This has led to a number of research efforts that bridge this gap, for example Refs. [2,36,75,76].

REFERENCES

1. W. Niblack, et al., The QBIC project: Querying images by content using color, texture and shape, *Proceedings of SPIE International Symposium Electronic Imaging: Science and Technology, Conf. 1908, Storage and Retrieval for Image and Video Databases*, February 1993; Computer Science, IBM Research Report RJ 9203 (81511), February. 1, 1993.
2. D. Howard et al., Lessons learned from building a terabyte digital video library, *IEEE Comput.* **32**(2), 66–73, (1999).
3. S.-F. Chang, Videoq- an automatic content-based video search system using visual cues, *ACM Multimedia Conference*, Seattle, Wash., November 1997; Columbia University/CTR Technical Report, CTR-TR # 478-97-12.
4. B.K. Yi, H.V. Jagadish, and C. Faloutsos, Efficient retrieval of similar time sequences under time warping, *Proc. 14th Int. Conf. Data Eng.*, 201–208, (1998).
5. Committee on Physical, Mathematical and Engineering Sciences, NSF, *Grand Challenges: High Performance Computing and Communications*, The FY 1992 U.S. Research and Development Program, National Science Foundation, 1992.
6. D. Vassiliadis, The input-state space approach to the prediction of auroral geomagnetic activity from solar wind variables, *Int. Workshop on Applications of Artificial Intelligence in Solar Terrestrial Physics*, Lund, Sweden, September 22–24, 1993.
7. A.D. Narasimhalu and S. Christodoulakis, Multimedia information systems: The unfolding of a reality, *IEEE Comput.* **24**(10), 6–8 (1991).
8. M. Arya et al., QBISM: Extending a DBMS to support 3D medical images, *Proc. 10th Int. Conf. Data Eng.*, February 14–18 (1994).
9. F. Korn, et al., Fast and effective similarity search in medical tumor databases using morphology, *Proceedings of SPIE*, Boston, Mass., November 1996.
10. P.J. Nofel, 40 million hits on optical disk, *Modern Office Technol.*, 84–88 (1986).
11. G.R. Thoma et al., A prototype system for the electronic storage and retrieval of document images, *ACM TOOIS* **3**(3), (1985).

12. D. Harman, The second text retrieval conference (TREC-2). Special Publication 500–215, National Institute of Standards and Technology, Gaithersburg, Md., 1994
13. S.F. Altschul, et al., A basic local alignment search tool. *J. Mol. Biol.*, **215**(3), 403–410, (1990).
14. R. Agrawal, et al., An interval classifier for database mining applications, *Proceedings of 18th International Conference on Very Large Data Bases VLDB '92*, August 23–27 1992, pp. 560–573.
15. R. Agrawal, T. Imielinski, and A. Swami, Mining association rules between sets of items in large databases, *Proceedings of 1983 ACM SIGMOD International Conference on Management of Data*, Washington, D.C., May 26–28, 1993, pp. 207–216.
16. R. Agrawal and R. Srikant, Fast algorithms for mining association rules in large databases, *Proceedings of 20th International Conference on Very Large Data Bases VLDB '94*, pp. 487–499, Santiago, Chile, September 12–15, 1994.
17. K. Fukunaga and P.M. Narendra, A branch and bound algorithm for computing k-nearest neighbors, *IEEE Trans. Comput.* **C-24**(7),750–753 (1975).
18. J.L. Bentley, Multidimensional binary search trees used for associative searching, *Commun. ACM*, **18**(9), 509–517 (1975).
19. T. Brinkhoff, H.P. Kriegel, R. Schneider, and B. Seeger, Multistep processing of spatial joins, *Proceedings of 1994 ACM SIGMOD International Conference on Management of Data*, May 24–27, 1994, pp. 197–208.
20. H.V. Jagadish, A retrieval technique for similar shapes, *International Conference on Management of Data, SIGMOD 91*, ACM, Denver, Co., May 1991, pp. 208–217.
21. L.G. Brown, A survey of image registration techniques, *ACM Comput. Surveys*, **24**(4), 325–376 (1992).
22. J.S.N. Jean, New distance measure for binary images, *Proc. IEEE ICASSP '90*, **4** 3–6 (1990); paper#: M5.19.
23. R. Agrawal, C. Faloutsos, and A. Swami, Efficient similarity search in sequence databases, *Fourth International Conference on Foundations of Data Organization and Algorithms (FODO)*, October 13–15 1993, pp. 69–84; also available through anonymous ftp, from *olympos.cs.umd.edu: ftp/pub/TechReports/fodo.ps.*
24. D. Sankoff and J.B. Kruskal, *Time warps, string edits and macromolecules: The theory and practice of sequence comparisons*, Addison-Wesley, Reading, Mass., 1983.
25. R.O. Duda and P.E. Hart, *Pattern Classification and Scene Analysis*, Wiley, New York, 1973.
26. R.W.Hamming, *Digital Filters*, Prentice Hall Signal Processing Series, Englewood Cliffs, N.J., 1977.
27. A.V. Oppenheim, and R.W. Schafer, *Digital Signal Processing*, Prentice Hall, Englewood Cliffs, N.J., 1975.
28. G.K. Wallace, The JPEG still picture compression standard, *Commun. ACM* **34**(4), 31–44 (1991).
29. M.B. Ruskai et al., *Wavelets and Their Applications*, Jones and Bartlett Publishers, Boston, Mass., 1992.
30. S. Wolfram, *Mathematica*, 2nd ed., Addison-Wesley, Reading, Mass., 1991.
31. W.H. Press et al., *Numerical Recipes in C*, Cambridge University Press, New York, 1988.

32. M. Schroeder, *Fractals, Chaos, Power Laws: Minutes from an Infinite Paradise*, W.H. Freeman and Company, New York, 1991.

33. C. Chatfield, *The Analysis of Time Series: An Introduction*, 3rd ed., Chapman and Hall, London & New York, 1984.

34. B. Mandelbrot, *Fractal Geometry of Nature*, W.H. Freeman, New York, 1977.

35. R.D. Edwards and J. Magee, *Technical Analysis of Stock Trends*, 5th ed., John Magee, Springfield, Mass., 1966.

36. M. Flickner et al., Query by image and video content: The QBIC system, *IEEE Comput.* **28**(9), 23–32 (1995).

37. W. Equitz, Retrieving images from a database using texture — algorithms from the QBIC system, Research report, IBM Almaden Research Center, San Jose, Calif., 1993.

38. G. Salton and M.J. McGill. *Introduction to Modern Information Retrieval*, New York McGraw-Hill, 1983.

39. M. Ioka, A method of defining the similarity of images on the basis of color information, Technical report RT-0030, IBM Tokyo Research Lab, 1989.

40. D. Mumford, Mathematical theories of shape: Do they model perception? *Geometric Meth. Comput. Vis.* **1570**, 2–10 (1991).

41. D. Mumford, The problem with robust shape descriptions, First International Conference on Computer Vision, IEEE, London, England, June 1987, pp. 602–606.

42. H. Tamura, S. Mori, and T. Yamawaki, Texture features corresponding to visual perception, *IEEE Trans. Syst., Man, and Cybern.* SMC-**8**(6); 460–473 (1978).

43. K. Hirata and T. Kato, Query by visual example, Advances in Database Technology EDBT'92, *Third International Conference on Extending Database Technology*, Springer-Verlag, Vienna, Austria, March 1992.

44. T. Kato, T. Kurita, N. Otsu, and K. Hirata, *A* sketch retrieval method for full color image database, *International Conference on Pattern Recognition (ICPR)*, IAPR, The Hague, The Netherlands, September 1992, pp. 530–533.

45. C. Faloutsos et al., Efficient and effective querying by image content, *J. Intell. Inf. Syst.* **3**(3/4); 231–262 (1994).

46. J. Hafner et al., Efficient color histogram indexing for quadratic form distance functions, *IEEE Trans. Pattern Anal. Machine Intell.* **17**(7), 729–736, (1995).

47. C. Faloutsos, M. Ranganathan, and Y. Manolopoulos, Fast subsequence matching in time-series databases, *Proceedings of 1994 ACM SIGMOD International Conference on Management of Data*, pp. 419–429, Minneapolis, Minn., May 25–27, 1994; 'Best Paper' award; CS-TR-3190, UMIACS-TR-93-131, ISR TR-93-86.

48. N. Beckmann, H.-P. Kriegel, R. Schneider, and B. Seeger, The R*-tree: An efficient and robust access method for points and rectangles, *Proceedings of 1990 ACM SIGMOD International Conference on Management of Data*, May 23–25, 1990, pp. 322–331.

49. C. Faloutsos and S. Roseman, Fractals for secondary key retrieval, *Proceedings of 8th ACM ACM SIGACT-SIGMOD-SIGART Symposium Principles of Database Systems, PODS '89*, Philadelphia, Pa., March 29–31, 1989, pp. 247–252; UMIACS-TR-89-47 and CS-TR-2242.

50. H.V. Jagadish, Linear clustering of objects with multiple attributes, *Proceedings of 1990 ACM SIGMOD International Conference on Management of Data*, May 23–25, 1990, pp. 332–342.
51. P. Ciaccia, M. Patella, and P. Zezula, M-tree: An efficient access method for similarity search in metric spaces, *Proc. 23rd Int. Conf. on Very Large Data Bases VLDB '97*, pp. 426–435, 1997.
52. A. Ricardo, Proximity matching using fixed queries trees, in M. Crochemore and D. Gusfield, eds., *5th Combinatorial Pattern Matching, LNCS 807*, Springer-Verlag, Asilomar, Calif., 1994, pp. 198–212.
53. T. Bozkaya and Z.M. Ozsoyoglu, Distance-based indexing for high-dimensional metric spaces, *Proceedings of 1997 ACM SIGMOD International Conference on Management of Data*, pp. 357–368, 1997.
54. S. Brin, Near neighbor search in large metric spaces, *Proceedings 21st International Conference on Very Large Data Bases VLDB '95*, Zurich, Switzerland, September 11–15, 1995, pp. 574–584.
55. C. Traina, A.J.M. Traina, B. Seeger, and C. Faloutsos, Slim-trees: High performance metric trees minimizing overlap between nodes, *EDBT* 51–65 (2000).
56. R.F.S. Filho, A. Traina, C. Traina, and C. Faloutsos, Similarity search without tears: the OMNI family of all-purpose access methods, *Proceedings 16th International Conference on Data Engineering*, 2001, in press.
57. D. Ballard and C. Brown., *Computer Vision*, Prentice Hall, New York 1982.
58. S. Tanaka, M. Shima, J. Shibayama, and A. Maeda, Retrieval method for an image database based on topological structure, *Appl. Digital Image Process.* **1153**, 318–327. (1989).
59. K. Wakimoto, M. Shima, S. Tanaka, and A. Maeda, An intelligent user interface to an image database using a figure interpretation method, *9th Int. Conf. Pattern Recog.* **2**, 516–991 (1990).
60. C.C. Chang and S.Y. Lee, Retrieval of similar pictures on pictorial databases, *Pattern Recog.* **24**(7), 675–680 (1991).
61. C.C. Chang and T.C. Wu, Retrieving the most similar symbolic pictures from pictorial databases, *Inf. Process. Manage.* **28**(5),581–588 (1992).
62. S.Y. Lee and F.J. Hsu, 2D c-string: A new spatial knowledge representation for image database systems, *Pattern Recog.*, **23**(10), 1077–1087 (1990).
63. S.Y. Lee and F.J. Hsu Spatial reasoning and similarity retrieval of images using 2D c-string knowledge representation, *Pattern Recog.*, **25**(3), 305–318 (1992).
64. M.A. Ireton and C. S. Xydeas, Classification of shape for content retrieval of images in a multimedia database, *Sixth International Conference on Digital Processing of Signals in Communications*, IEE, Loughborough, U.K., 2–6 September, 1990, pp. 111–116.
65. T. Kato et al., A cognitive approach to visual interaction, *International Conference of Multimedia Information Systems, MIS'91*, ACM and National University of Singapore, January 1991, pp. 109–120.
66. Z. Chen and S.Y. Ho, Computer vision for robust 3D aircraft recognition with fast library search, *Pattern Recog.* **24**(5), 375–390 (1991).

67. R. Mehrotra and W.I. Grosky, Shape matching utilizing indexed hypotheses generation and testing, *IEEE Trans. Robotics Automat.* **5**(1), 70–77 (1989).

68. W.I. Grosky, P. Neo, and R. Mehrotra, A pictorial index mechanism for model-based matching, *Data Knowledge Eng.*, **8**, 309–327 (1992).

69. Y. Lamdan and H.J. Wolfson, Geometric hashing: A general and efficient model-based recognition scheme, *2nd International Conference on Computer Vision (ICCV)*, IEEE, Tampa, Fla., 1988, pp. 238–249.

70. E. Binaghi, I. Gagliardi, and R. Schettini, Indexing and fuzzy logic-based retrieval of color images, *Visual Database Systems, II, IFIP Transactions A-7*, Elsevier Science Publishers, New York, 1992, pp. 79–92.

71. M.J. Swain and D.H. Ballard, Color indexing, *Int. J. Comput. Vis.*, **7**(1), 11–32 (1991).

72. M. Vassilakopoulos and Y. Manolopoulos, Dynamic inverted quadtree: a structure for pictorial databases, *Inf. Syst.*, 1995, in press.

73. ACM SIGIR, *Proceedings of International Conference on Multimedia Information Systems*, Singapore, 1991.

74. R. Jain and W. Niblack, NSF workshop on visual information management, February 1992

75. N. Katayama and S. Satoh, The SR-tree: An index structure for high-dimensional nearest neighbor queries, *Proceedings of 1997 ACM SIGMOD International Conference on Management of Data*, 1997, pp. 369–380.

76. A. Natsev, R. Rastogi, and K. Shim, WALRUS: A similarity retrieval algorithm for image databases, *Proceedings of 1999 ACM SIGMOD International Conference on Management of Data*, Philadelphia, Pa., 1999, pp. 395–406.

16 Compressed or Progressive Image Search

SETHURAMAN PANCHANATHAN
Arizona State University, Tempe, Arizona

16.1 INTRODUCTION

The explosive growth of multimedia data, both on the Internet and in domain-specific applications, has produced a pressing need for techniques that support efficient storage, transmission, and retrieval of such information. Indexing (Chapters 7, 14, and 15) and compression (Chapter 8) are complementary methods that facilitate storage, search, retrieval and transmission of imagery, and other multimedia data types.

The voluminous nature of visual information requires the use of compression techniques, in particular, of lossy methods. Several compression schemes have been developed to reduce the inherent redundancy present in visual data. Recently, the International Standards Organization and CCITT have proposed a variety of standards for still image and video compression. These include JPEG, MPEG-1, MPEG-2, H.261, and H.263. In addition, compression standards for high-resolution images, content-based coding, and manipulation of visual information, such as JPEG 2000 and MPEG-4, have been recently defined. These standardization efforts highlight the growing importance of image compression.

Typically, indexing and compression are pursued independently (Fig. 16.1), and the features used for indexing are extracted directly from the pixels of the original image. Many of the current techniques for indexing and navigating repositories containing compressed images require the decompression of all the data in order to locate the information of interest. If the features were directly extracted in the compressed domain, the need to decompress the visual data and to apply pixel-domain-indexing techniques would be obviated. Compressed-domain indexing (CDI) techniques are therefore important for retrieving visual data stored in compressed format [1,2].

As the principal objectives of both compression and indexing are extraction and compact representation of information, it seems obvious to exploit the

Image Databases: Search and Retrieval of Digital Imagery, Edited by Vittorio Castelli and Lawrence D. Bergman.
ISBN 0-471-32116-8

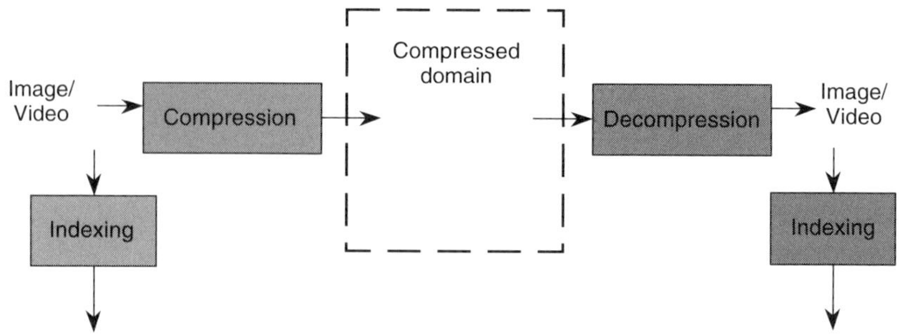

Figure 16.1. Pixel domain indexing and compression system.

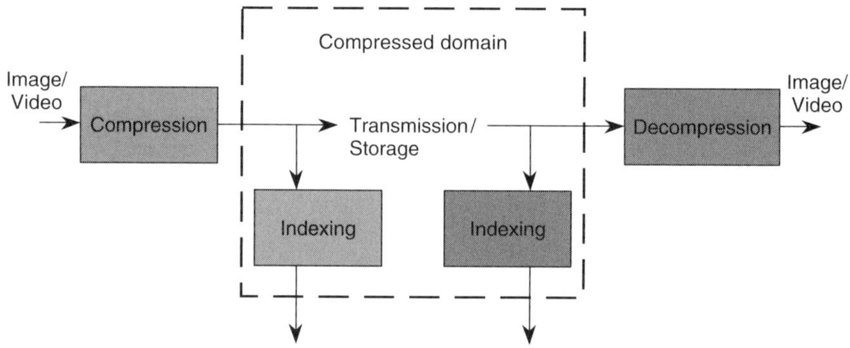

Figure 16.2. Compressed domain indexing system.

commonalties between the two approaches. CDI has the inherent advantage of efficiency and reduced complexity. A straightforward approach to CDI (Fig. 16.2) is to apply existing compression techniques and to use compression parameters and derived features as indices.

The focus of this chapter is indexing of image data. These techniques can often be applied to video indexing as well. A variety of video-indexing approaches have been proposed, in which the spatial (i.e., within-frame) content is indexed using image-indexing methods and the temporal content (e.g., motion and camera operations) is indexed using other techniques.

The following section analyzes and compares image-indexing techniques for compression based on the discrete Fourier transform (DFT), the Karhunen-Loeve transform (KLT), the discrete cosine transform (DCT), wavelet and subband coding transforms, vector quantization, fractal compression, and hybrid compression.

16.2 IMAGE INDEXING IN THE COMPRESSED DOMAIN

CDI techniques (summarized in Table 16.1) can be broadly classified into two categories: transform-domain and spatial-domain methods. Transform-domain techniques are generally based on DFT, KLT, DCT, subband, or wavelet transforms. Spatial-domain techniques include vector quantization (VQ) and fractal-based methods. We now present the details of the various compressed-domain image-indexing techniques along with derived approaches.

Table 16.1. Compressed Domain Indexing Approaches

Technique	Characteristics/Advantages	Disadvantages	References
	Transform Domain		
Discrete Fourier transform	Uses complex exponentials as basis functions. The magnitudes of the coefficients are translation invariant. Spatial domain correlation can be computed by the product of the transforms.	Lower compression efficiency.	[3,4]
Discrete cosine transform	Uses real sinusoidal basis functions Has energy compaction efficiency close to optimal KLT.	Block DCT produces blocking artifacts.	[5,6]
Karhunen-Loeve transform	Employs the 2nd order statistical properties of an image for coding. Provides maximum energy compaction among linear transformations. It minimizes the mean-square error for any image among linear transformations.	Is data dependent: basis images for each subimage has to be obtained, and hence has high computational cost.	[7]
Discrete wavelet transform	Numerous basis functions exist. There is no blocking of data as in DCT. Yields, as by-product, a multiresolution pyramid. Better adaptation to nonstationary signals. High decorrelation and energy compaction.	Chip-sets for real-time implementation is not readily available.	[8,9]

(*Continued overleaf*)

Table 16.1. (*Continued*)

Technique	Characteristics/Advantages	Disadvantages	References
	Spatial Domain		
Vector quantization	Fast decoding. Reduced decoder hardware requirements makes it attractive for low power applications. Asymptotically optimum for stationary signals.	A codebook has to be available at both the encoder and decoder, or has to be transmitted along with the image. Encoding and codebook generation are highly complex.	[10]
Fractals	Exploits self-similarity to achieve compression. Potential for high compression.	Computationally intensive, hence hinders real-time implementation.	[11]

16.2.1 Discrete Fourier Transform

The Fourier transform is an important tool in signal and image processing [3,4,7]. Its basis functions are complex exponentials. Fast algorithms to compute its discrete version (DFT) can be easily implemented in hardware and software. From the viewpoint of image compression, the DFT yields a reasonable coding performance, because of its good energy-compaction properties.

Several properties of the DFT are useful in indexing and pattern matching. First, the magnitudes of the DFT coefficients are translation-invariant. Second, the cross-correlation of two images can be efficiently computed by taking the product of the DFTs and inverting the transform.

16.2.1.1 Using the Magnitude and Phase of the Coefficients as Index Key. A straightforward image-indexing approach is to use the magnitude of the Fourier coefficients as an index key. The Fourier coefficients are scanned in a zigzag fashion and normalized with respect to the size of the corresponding image. In order to enable fast retrieval, only a subset of the coefficients (approximately 100) from the zigzag scan is used as a feature vector (index). The index of the query image is compared with the corresponding indices of the target images stored in the database, and the retrieved results are ranked in decreasing order of similarity. The most commonly used similarity metrics are the mean absolute difference (MAD) and the mean square error (MSE).

We now evaluate the retrieval performance of this technique using a test database containing 500 images of wildlife, vegetation, natural scenery, birds, buildings, airplanes, and so forth. When the database is assembled, the target images undergo a Fourier transform, and the coefficients are stored along with the image data. When a query is submitted, the Fourier transform of the template image is also computed, and the required coefficients extracted. Figure 16.3 shows the retrieval results corresponding to a query (top) image using the first 100 coefficients and the MAD error criterion. The 12 highest ranked images are arranged from left to right and top to bottom. It can be seen that the first and second ranked images are similar to the query image, as expected. However, it is immediately clear that a human would rank the 12 images returned by the system quite differently.

Note that in the example of Figure 16.3, the feature vector is composed of low-frequency Fourier coefficients. Consequently, images having similar average intensity values are considered similar by the system. However, if edge information is relevant, higher frequency coefficients and features derived from them should be used. Additionally, the direction and angle information is embedded in the phase component of the Fourier transform, rather than in its magnitude. The phase component and the high-frequency coefficients are therefore useful in retrieving images that have similar edge content. Figure 16.4 is the result of a query on a database in which indexing relies on directional features extracted from the DFT. Note that the retrieved images either contain a boat, such as the query image, or depict scenes with directional content similar to that of the query image. The union of results based on these low and high frequency component features has the potential for good overall retrieval performance.

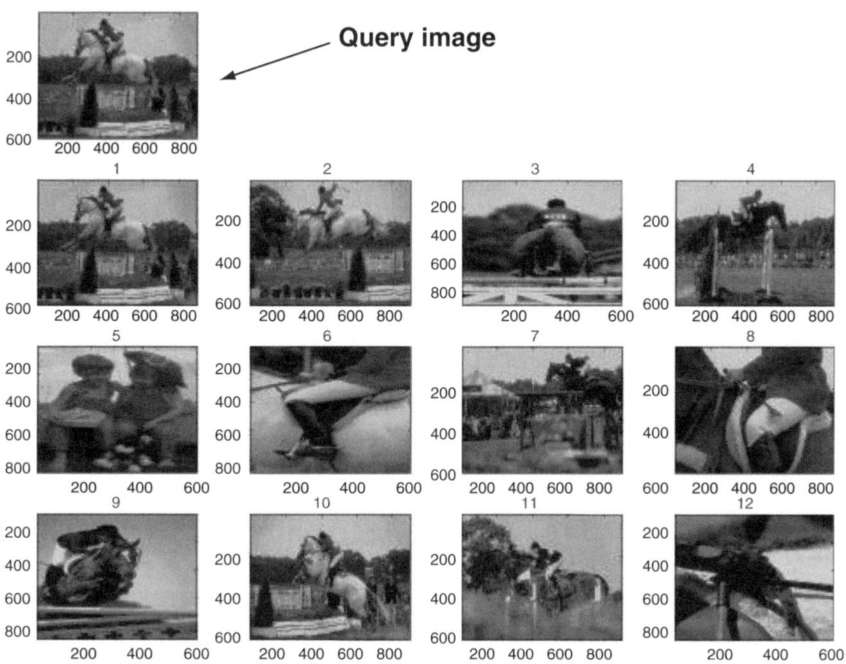

Figure 16.3. Query results when the indexing key is the amplitude of the Fourier coefficients. The query image is shown at the top. The top 12 matches are sorted by similarity score and displayed in left-to-right, top-to-bottom order.

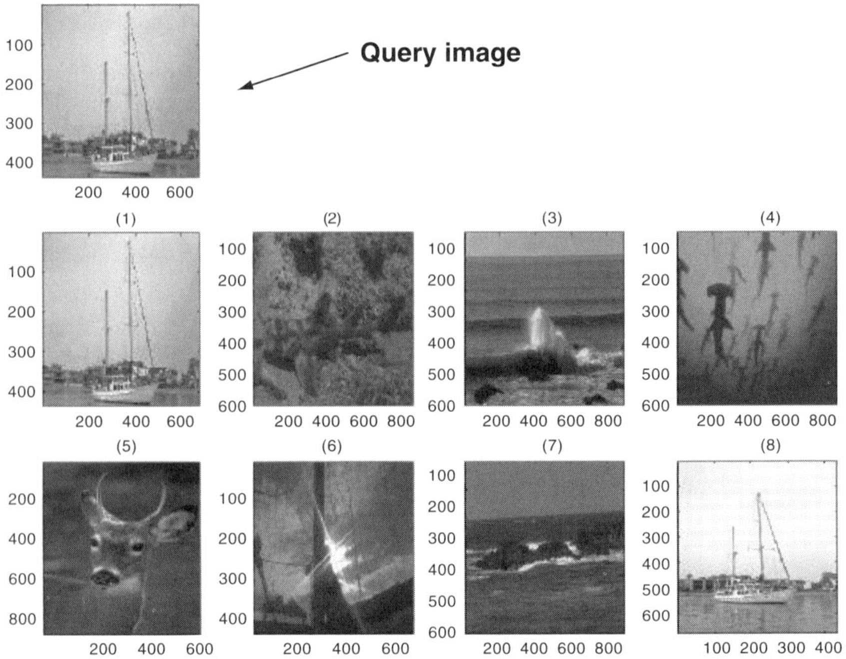

Figure 16.4. Query example based on the angular information of the Fourier coefficients.

16.2.1.2 Template Matching Using Cross-Correlation. Template matching can be performed by computing the two-dimensional cross-correlation between a query template and a database target, and analyzing the value of the peaks. A high value of a cross-correlation denotes a good match. Although cross-correlation is an expensive operation in the pixel domain, it can be efficiently performed in the Fourier domain, where it corresponds to a product of the transforms. This property has been used as the basis for image indexing schemes. For example, Ref. [12] discusses an algorithm in which the threshold used for matching based on intensity and texture is computed. This threshold is derived using the cross-correlation of Fourier coefficients in the transform domain.

16.2.1.3 Texture Features Derived from the Fourier Transform. Several texture descriptors based on FT have been proposed. Augusteijn, Clemens, and Shaw [13] evaluated their effectiveness in classifying satellite images. The statistical measures include the maximum coefficient magnitude, the average coefficient magnitude, the energy of the magnitude, and the variance of the magnitude of Fourier coefficients. In addition, the authors investigated the retrieval performance based on the radial and angular distribution of Fourier coefficients. They observed that the radial and angular measures provide good classification performance when a few dominant frequencies are present. The statistical measures provide a satisfactory performance in the absence of dominant frequencies. Note that the radial distribution is sensitive to texture coarseness, whereas the angular distribution is sensitive to the directionality of textures. The performance of the angular distribution of Fourier coefficients for image indexing has been evaluated in Ref. [14]. Here, the images are first preprocessed with a low-pass filter, the FFT is calculated, and the FFT spectrum is then scanned by a revolving vector exploring a 180° range at fixed angular increments. The angular histogram is finally calculated by computing, for each angle, the sum of the image-component contributions. While calculating the sum, only the middle-frequency range is considered, as it represents visually important image characteristics. The angular histogram is used as an indexing key. This feature vector is invariant with respect to translations in the pixel domain, but not to rotations in the pixel domain, which correspond to circular shifts of the histogram.

There have been numerous other applications of the Fourier transform to indexing. The earlier-mentioned techniques demonstrate the potential for combining compression and indexing for images using FT.

16.2.2 Karhunen-Loeve Transform (KLT)

The Karhunen-Loeve transform (principal component analysis) uses the eigenvectors of the autocorrelation matrix of the image as basis functions. If appropriate assumptions on the statistical properties of the image are satisfied, the KLT provides the maximum energy compaction of all invertible transformations. Moreover, the KLT always yields the maximum energy compaction of all invertible *linear* transformations. Because the KLT basis functions are not fixed but image-dependent, an efficient indexing scheme consists of projecting the images onto the K-L space and comparing the KLT coefficients.

KLT is at the heart of a face-recognition algorithm described in Ref. [15]. The basis images, called *eigenfaces*, are created from a randomly sampled set of face images. To construct the index, each database image is projected onto each of the eigenfaces by computing their inner product. The result is a set of numerical coefficients, interpreted as the coordinates of the image in the eigenface-reference system. Hence, each image is represented as a point in a high-dimensional Euclidean space. Similarity between images is measured by the Euclidean distance between their representative points.

During query processing, the coordinates of the query image are computed, the closest indexed representative points are retrieved, and the corresponding images returned to the user. The user can also specify a distance threshold to control the allowed dissimilarity between the query image and the results.

It is customary to arrange the eigen-images in decreasing order of the magnitude of the corresponding eigenvalue. Intuitively, this means that the first eigenimage is the direction along which the images in the database vary the most, whereas the last eigenimage is the direction along which the images in the database vary the least. Hence, the first few KLT coefficients capture the most salient characteristics of the images. These coefficients are the *most expressive features* (MEFs) of an image, and can be used as index keys. The database designer should be aware of several limitations in this approach. First, eigenfeatures may represent aspects that are unrelated to recognition, such as the direction of illumination. Second, using a larger number of eigenfeatures does not necessarily lead to better retrieval performances. To address this last issue, a discriminant Karhunen-Loeve (DKL) projection has been proposed in Ref. [16]. Here, the images are grouped into semantic classes, and KLT coefficients are selected to simultaneously maximize between-class scatter and minimize within-class scatter. DKL yields a set of *most discriminating features* (MDFs). Experiments suggest that DKL results in an improvement of 10 to 30 percent over KLT on a typical database.

16.2.2.1 Dimensionality Reduction Using KLT. KLT has also been applied to reduce the dimensionality of texture features for classification purposes, as described, for instance, in Ref. [17]. Note that KLT is generally not used in traditional image coding (i.e., compression) because it has much higher complexity than competitive approaches. However, it has been used to analyze and encode multispectral images Ref. [18], and it might be used for indexing in targeted application domains, such as remote sensing.

16.2.3 Discrete Cosine Transform

DCT, a derivative of DFT, employs real sinusoids as basis functions, and, when applied to natural images, has energy compaction efficiency close to the optimal KL Transform. Owing to this property and to the existence of efficient algorithms, most of the international image and video compression standards, such as JPEG, MPEG-1, and MPEG-2, rely on DCT for image compression.

Because block-DCT is one of the steps of the JPEG standard and as most photographic images are in fact stored in JPEG format, it seems natural to index the DCT parameters. Numerous such approaches have been proposed in the literature. In the rest of this section, we present in detail the most representative DCT-based indexing techniques and briefly describe several related schemes.

16.2.3.1 Histogram of DC Coefficients. This technique uses the histogram of the DC image parameters as the indexing key. The construction of the DC image is illustrated in Figure 16.5. Each image is partitioned into nonoverlapping blocks of 8×8 pixels, and each block is transformed using the two-dimensional DCT. Each resulting 8×8 block of coefficients consists of a DC value, which is the lowest frequency coefficient and represents the local average intensity, and of 63 AC values, capturing frequency contents at different orientations and wavelengths. The collection of the DC values of all the blocks is called the DC image. The DC image looks like a smaller version of the original, with each dimension reduced by a factor of 8. Consequently, the DC image also serves as a thumbnail version of the original and can be used for rapid browsing through a catalog.

The histogram of the DC image, which is used as a feature vector, is computed by quantizing the DC values into N bins and counting the number of coefficients

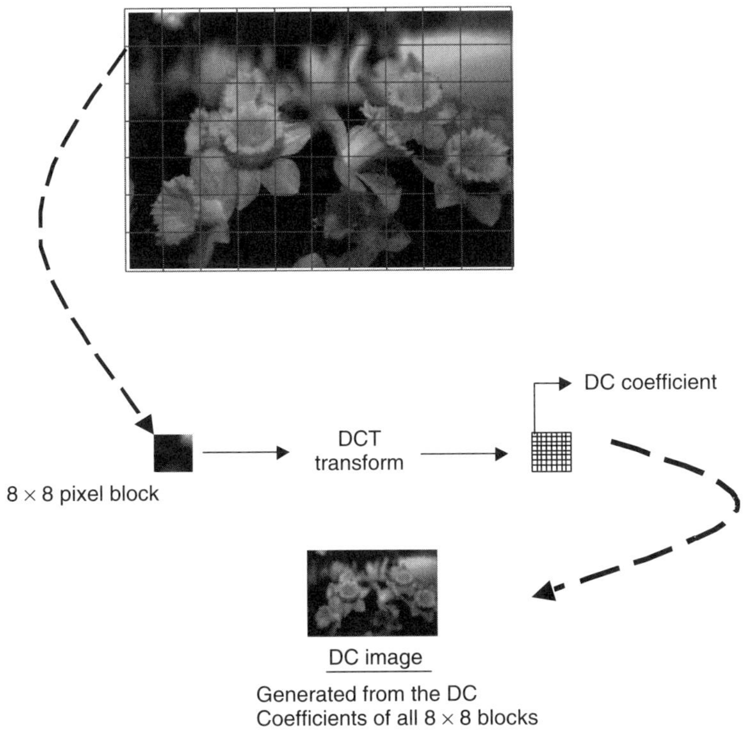

Figure 16.5. DC image derived from the original image through the DCT transform.

that fall within each bin. It is then stored and indexed in the database. In the example shown in Figure 16.6, 15 bins have been used to represent the color spectrum of the DC image. These values are normalized in order to make the feature vectors invariant to scaling.

When a query is issued, the quantized histogram of the DC image is extracted from the query image and compared with the corresponding feature vectors of all the target images in the database. Similarity is typically computed using the histogram intersection method (see Chapter 11) or the weighted distance between the color histograms [19]. The best matches are then displayed to the user as shown in Figure 16.7. As histograms are invariant to rotation and have been normalized, this method is invariant to both rotation and scaling.

16.2.3.2 Indexing with the Variance of the AC Coefficients. A feature vector of length 63 can be constructed by computing the variance of the individual AC coefficients across all the 8×8 DCT blocks of the image. Because natural images contain mostly low spatial frequencies, most high-frequency variances will be small and play a minor role in the retrieval. In practice, good retrieval performance can be achieved by relying just on the variances of the first eight AC coefficients. This eight-component feature vector represents the overall texture of

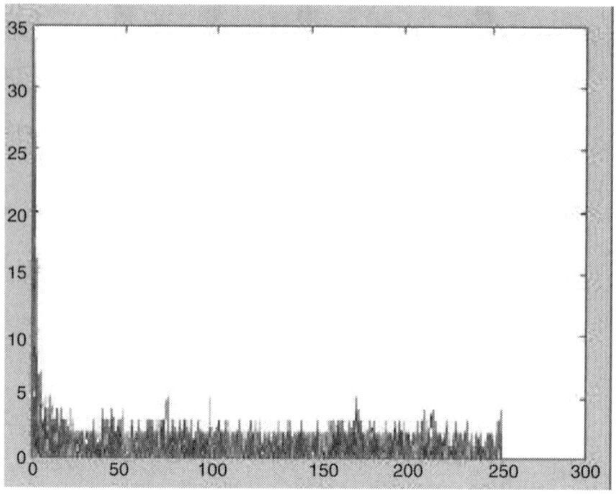

(a)

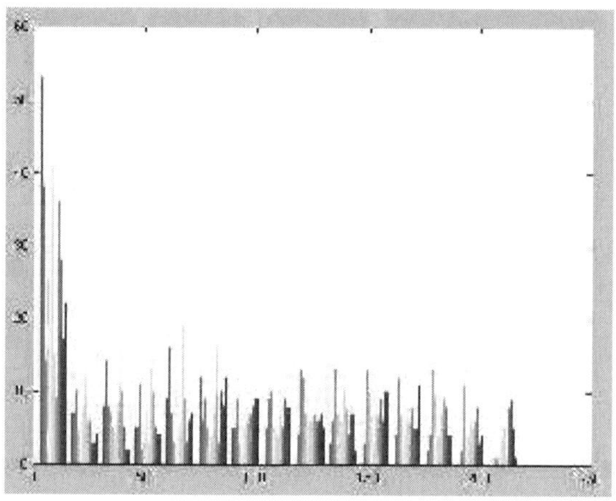

(b)

Figure 16.6. **(a)** Histogram of DC image; **(b)** Binwise quantized DC image.

the entire image. Figure 16.8 shows some retrieval results using this approach. It is worthwhile noting that the runtime complexity of this technique is smaller than that of traditional transform features used for texture classification and image discrimination, as reported in Ref. [20].

16.2.3.3 Indexing with the Mean and Variance of the Coefficients. A variety of other DCT-based indexing approaches have appeared in recent literature. A method based on the DCT transform of 4×4 blocks, which produces 16 coefficients per block, is described in Ref. [20]. The variance and the mean of the absolute values of each coefficient are calculated over the blocks spanning the entire image. This 32-component feature vector represents the texture of

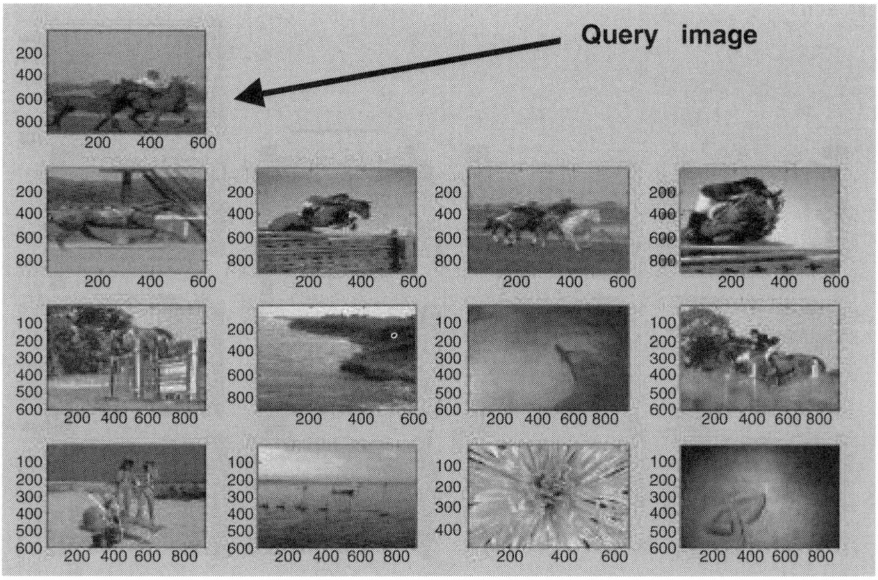

Figure 16.7. Image retrieval based on the histogram of DC image.

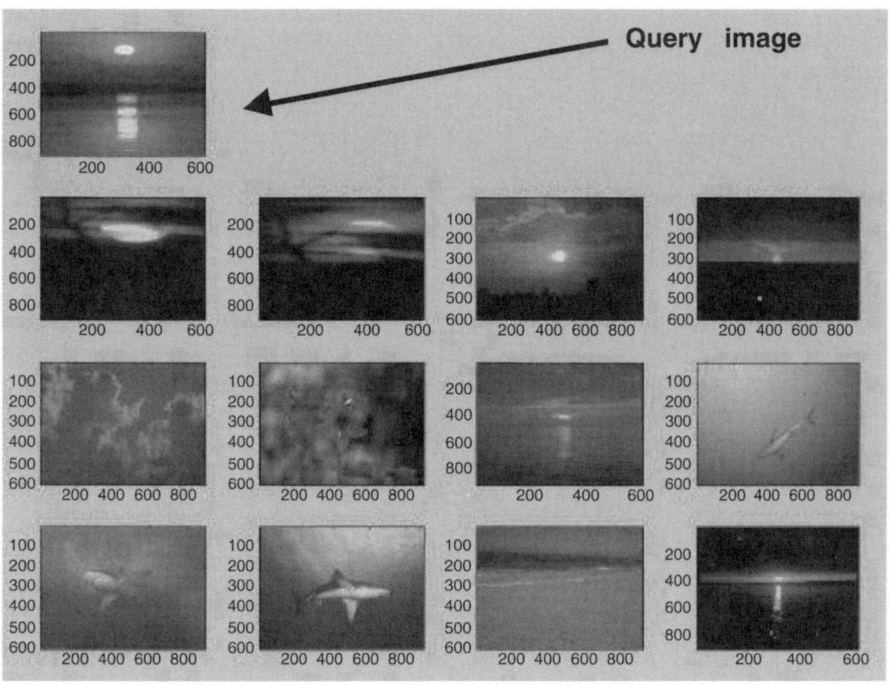

Figure 16.8. Retrieval based on the variance of the first eight AC coefficients of images.

the whole image. A Fisher discriminant analysis (FDA) is used to reduce the dimensionality of the feature vector, which is then used for indexing.

16.2.3.4 ***Combining DCT Coefficients with Spatial Information.*** A technique for image retrieval using JPEG has been detailed in Ref. [21]. This technique is based on the mutual relationship between the DCT coefficients of unconnected regions in both the query image and the target image. The image spatial plane is divided into 2 K windows; the size of the windows is a function of the size of the image and is selected to be the smallest multiple of 8 that is less than the initial window size. These windows are randomly paired into K pairs. The average of each DCT coefficient from all the 8×8 JPEG blocks in each window is computed. The DCT coefficients of the windows in the same pair are compared. If the DCT coefficient in one window is greater than the corresponding one in the other window, a "1" is assigned, otherwise a "0" is assigned. Each window pair yields 64 binary values, and therefore each image is represented by a binary feature vector of length 64^*K. The similarity of the query and target images can be determined by employing the Hamming Distance of their binary feature vectors.

16.2.3.5 ***Comparing Edges Using DCT.*** Many content-based indexing and retrieval methods rely on the discriminating power of edge information: similar images often have similar edge content. A technique to detect oriented line features using DCT coefficients has been presented in Ref. [22]. This technique is based on the observation that predominantly horizontal, vertical, and diagonal features produce large values of DCT coefficients in vertical, horizontal, and diagonal directions, respectively. It has been noted that a straight line of slope m in the spatial domain generates a straight line with a slope of approximately $1/m$ in the DCT domain. The technique can be extended to search for more complex features composed of straight-line segments. A DCT-based approach to detect edges in regions of interest within an image has been discussed in Ref. [23]. Here the *edge orientation, edge offset from center*, and *edge strength* are estimated from the DCT coefficients of an 8×8 block. The orientations are horizontal, vertical, diagonal, vertical-dominant, and horizontal-dominant. Experimental results presented in [23] demonstrate that the DCT-based edge detection provides a performance comparable to the Sobel edge-detection operator (see the chapter on Image Analysis and Computer Vision in [7]).

16.2.4 Subbands/Wavelets/Gabor Transform

Recently, subband coding and the discrete wavelet transforms (DWT) have become popular in image compression and indexing applications [8,24] (Chapter 8 describes in detail the DWT and its use for compression). These techniques recursively pass an image through a pair of filters (one low pass and the other high pass), and decimate the filter outputs (i.e., discard every other sample) in order to maintain the same data rate as the input signal. As the length of the filter outputs is halved after each iteration, this decomposition is often called dyadic. Two-dimensional signals (images) are commonly encoded with separable filters. This means that one step of the decomposition (the combination of filtering and downsampling) is performed independently on each row of the image, and then the same step is performed on each column of the transformed-rows matrix. This process produces four subbands, labeled LL, LH, HL, and HH, respectively, to denote which filters (L = low pass, H = high pass) were applied in the row and column directions. If more levels are desired, separable filtering is applied to the subband obtained by low-pass filtering both rows and columns. An interesting feature of these transforms is that they are applied to the entire image, rather than to blocks as in JPEG. Consequently, there are no blocking artifacts in images that undergo lossy compression with wavelets or subband coding (see Chapter 8 for a discussion of artifacts introduced by lossy compression schemes and of the advantages of DWT over the previously mentioned schemes).

The difference between DWT, subband coding, and the wavelet-packets transform lies in the recursive application of the combination of filtering and downsampling. The DWT recursively decomposes only the LL subband; subband filtering recursively decomposes all four subbands; the wavelet-packets transform lies in the middle and adaptively applies the decomposition to subbands where it yields better compression. An example image along with the corresponding two level wavelet transform is shown in Figure 16.9.

The Gabor transform (described also in Chapter 12) is similar to the wavelet transform, but its basis functions are complex Gaussians, and hence have optimal time-frequency localization [9]. Unlike the wavelet transform, which uses a complete set of basis functions (i.e., the number of coefficients of the transform is the same as the number of pixels in the image, and the transform is invertible), the Gabor transform is in general overcomplete, that is, redundant. Several indexing approaches based on Subband, Wavelet, and Gabor transforms have appeared in recent literature.

Figure 16.9. Original lena image and the corresponding two-level wavelet decomposed image.

16.2.4.1 Direct Comparison of Wavelet Coefficients. An indexing technique based on direct comparison of DWT coefficients is presented in Ref. [25]. Here, all images are rescaled to 128 × 128 pixels, and transformed. The average color, the sign (positive or negative), and the positions of the M DWT coefficients having the largest magnitude (the authors have used $M = 40$ to 60) are calculated for each image and become the index key. Good indexing performance has been reported. However, the index is dependent on the location of DWT coefficients. Hence, translated or rotated versions of the query image may not be retrieved using this technique.

16.2.4.2 Indexing on the Lowest-Resolution Subbands. A technique similar to that of Ref. [25] has been detailed in Ref. [26]. All the images are rescaled to 128 × 128 pixels and transformed with a four-level DWT. Only the four lowest-resolution subbands (having size 8 × 8 pixels), denoted by S_L (low pass), S_H (horizontal band), S_V (vertical band), and S_D (diagonal band), as shown in Figure 16.10 are considered for indexing. Image matching is then performed using a three-step procedure. In the first stage, 20 percent of the images are retrieved using the variance of the S_L band. In the second stage, pruning is performed using the difference between the S_L coefficients of the query and of the target images. Finally, the differences between the S_L, S_H, S_V, and S_D coefficients of the query and target images are used to select the query results. For color images, this procedure is repeated on all three-color channels. The complexity of this technique is small due to its hierarchical nature. Although it provides a performance improvement over the techniques detailed in Ref. [26], this indexing scheme is still not robust to translation and rotation.

16.2.4.3 Histogram of the Wavelet Transform. This section describes a wavelet-based indexing technique that relies on the histogram of the wavelet transform, called the wavelet histogram technique (WHT). To motivate the approach, we note that comparing histograms in the pixel domain may result in rather erroneous retrievals. As an example, consider Fig. 16.11, which shows two images, one of a lady and the other of an owl. The spatial histograms of these images are very similar. A wavelet histogram, however, uses the wavelet coefficients of the high-pass bands, which contain discriminative textural properties such as directionality.

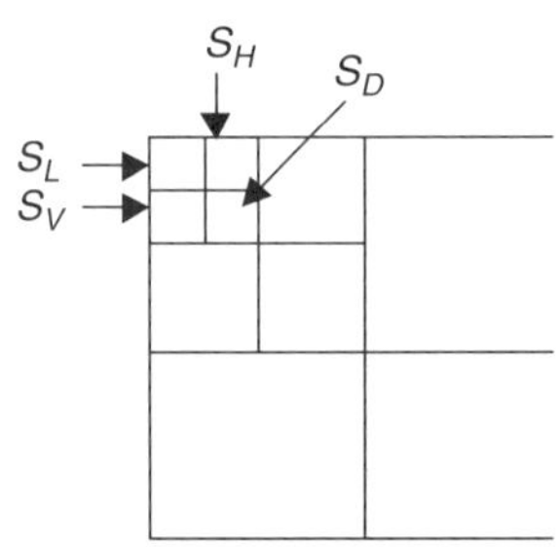

Figure 16.10. Four-stage wavelet decomposition showing S_L, S_H, S_V, and S_D.

Lady

Owl

Figure 16.11. Images with similar histograms.

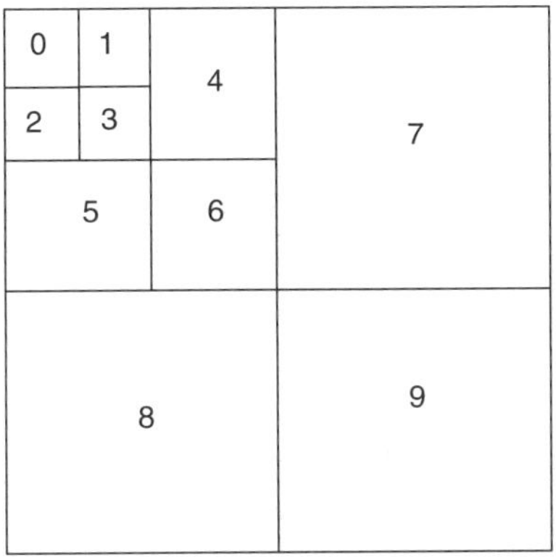

Figure 16.12. Three-stage wavelet decomposition showing the nine high-pass bands.

In the WHT technique, a three-level wavelet transform of the image is computed as shown in Figure 16.12 (which has 10 subbands), and a 512-bin histogram is generated from the coefficients in the nine high-pass subbands.

It is known that when a texture image is transformed into the wavelet domain, most of the energy characterizing the texture is compacted into the high frequency subbands. The WHT is therefore used to discriminate among different global textures for it captures the energy content in the higher frequency subbands. Queries are executed by comparing the histograms of the query image with those of the images in the database. The wavelet histogram technique yields better retrieval performance than techniques relying on pixel-domain histograms. The only drawback of this method is that it may not be well suited for natural images that contain large objects as these objects tend to have the same textural properties at the global level.

Figure 16.13 compares the histogram of the wavelet coefficients of the two images shown in Figure 16.11. It is immediately apparent that the histograms are rather different and that the corresponding images would not have been declared similar by a WHT-based matching technique.

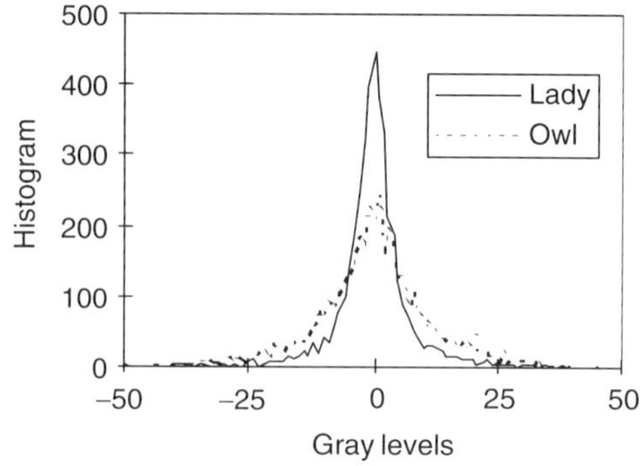

Figure 16.13. Wavelet histogram of the images in Fig. 16.11.

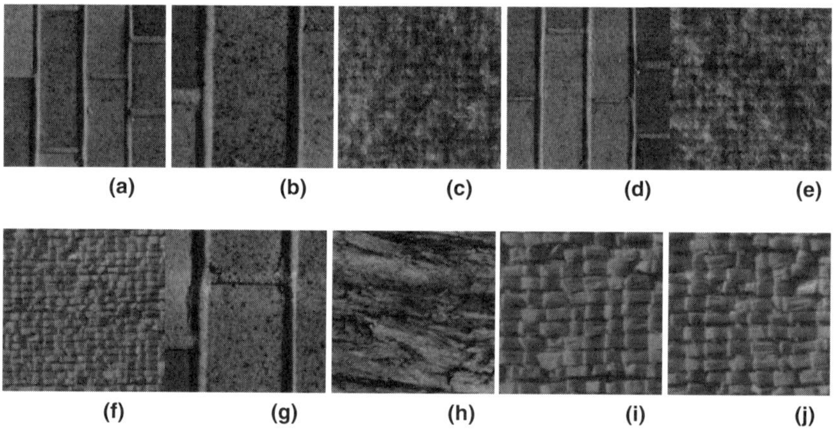

Figure 16.14. Images retrieved using WHT: **(a)** query image, **(b)**–**(j)** retrieved images in monotonically increasing order of distance.

An example of texture retrieval using WHT is shown in Figure 16.14. Here, a brick texture (Fig. 16.14a) is used as the query image. The database contains seven other similar brick textures (three of them have the same scale and four of them have a lower scale). The nine retrieved images (Fig. 16.14b to j) contain one brick texture with the same scale (Fig. 16.14d) and two brick textures with a lower scale (Fig. 16.14b and Fig. 16.14g).

Generating the wavelet histogram is a computationally demanding process. All high-pass bands must be upsampled and filtered using wavelet synthesis filters (the filters for the direct DWT are called "analysis filters," whereas those for the inverse DWT are called "synthesis filters"; in general, analysis and synthesis filters are different) to produce an image of the same size as the original, before the histogram can be computed. The process is repeated for each of the subbands. Also, comparing large histograms (with 512 bins) is an expensive operation to perform at query-execution time. Comparing features derived from the histograms, such as moments, can achieve a substantial reduction in the complexity of WHT.

16.2.4.4 Combining Wavelet and Pixel-Domain Features. A joint moment and wavelet indexing technique, using the Legendre moments of the original image histogram along with the shape and variance parameters of the wavelet subimages, has been presented in Ref. [27]. Substantial reduction in complexity can be achieved by comparing moments instead of directly comparing histograms. This indexing technique combining moments and wavelets provides a 4 percent improvement over the technique that uses only the Legendre moments.

16.2.4.5 Comparing the Histograms of Individual Subbands. Similar images have similar directional information. Directionality is preserved under translation and small rotations: for example, pictures of the same scene obtained from similar viewing angles have similar directional content. A technique that captures directionality by relying on the wavelet transform has been presented in Ref. [28]. The different subbands of the wavelet transform capture different directional content. In a one-level transform, LL, HL, LH, and HH denote the four subbands, where the first letter refers to the filter used to transform the individual rows, and the second letter refers to the filter used to transform the columns (L = low pass, H = high pass). The HL subband captures vertical lines, the LH subband captures horizontal lines, and the HH subband captures diagonal lines. When the transform has multiple levels, each subband captures directional information at a different scale. Although different images might have similar overall wavelet histograms, they might have different subband statistics.

The complexity of directly comparing the histograms of all the subbands is high and can be substantially reduced by comparing parameters extracted from the histograms. The histograms of high-pass wavelet subbands can be modeled using generalized Gaussian density (GGD) functions [29], which are expressed in terms of two parameters — σ (standard deviation) and γ (shape parameter). If the target and query images are different, the two parameters are likely to be different. The "distance" between two images f and g can be expressed in terms of standard deviations and shape parameters as

$$d(f,g) = \sum_{k=1}^{Q} B_k(\gamma_{f_k} - \gamma_{g_k})^2 + \sum_{k=1}^{Q} A_k(\sigma_{f_k} - \sigma_{g_k})^2, \tag{16.1}$$

where Q is the number of wavelet bands used for comparison and A_k and B_k are appropriate weights that are empirically determined to optimize the retrieval performance.

16.2.4.6 Rotationally Invariant Wavelet Transforms. A complex wavelet transform, in which the magnitude of the DWT coefficients is invariant under rotation, has been presented in Ref. [30]. The mother wavelet, which is the basic wavelet not subjected to any scaling or translation, is defined in polar coordinates. An experiment on a set of English character images shows that this technique performs better than complex Zernike moments [31,32], the magnitude of which is rotation invariant.

Nonlinear wavelet transforms that are invariant under scale, rotation, and shift (SRS) transformations have been described in Ref. [33]. The paper also contains an algorithm that adaptively changes the mother function according to the input signal to provide SRS invariance. This technique of changing the basis function is called dilation. The concept of *super wavelets* has also been introduced in the same paper, using a linear combination of adaptive wavelets that is subjected to dilation, thereby handling the scale changes in the signal.

16.2.4.7 Separating Edges and Texture Information. An image coding technique that separates edge information from texture information has been detailed in Ref. [9]. Edges at different levels of decomposition, also called multiscale edges, along the main directions (horizontal, vertical, or diagonal) are detected from the local maxima of the wavelet transform subbands. The image is reconstructed from the wavelet subbands using synthesis filters and an error image is computed by subtracting the reconstructed image from the original image. The error image thus obtained provides a significant amount of texture information. The textures are coded with a standard orthogonal wavelet transform. The multiscale edges have the potential to provide a good indexing performance.

16.2.4.8 Texture Indexing Using Irregular Tree Decomposition. A texture analysis scheme using an irregular tree decomposition, in which the middle resolution subband coefficients are used for texture matching, has been presented in Ref. [34]. In this scheme, a J dimensional feature vector is generated consisting of the energy of J subbands that contain most of the energy. Indexing is done by matching the feature vector of the query image with those of the target images in a database. For texture classification, superior performance can be obtained by training the algorithm. Such a method of classification is called *supervised classification*. Here, for each representative class of textures that is known a priori, the training process finds the most important subbands in terms of energy content. A query image can then be categorized into one of the texture classes by employing a suitable distance measure between the feature vectors of the query image and the representative classes.

16.2.4.9 Describing Texture Using the Subband Energy. In Ref. [20] the global texture properties of images are described using the energy of DWT subbands. Images are transformed with a five-level DWT, producing 16 subbands, and the variance and mean absolute value within each subband are computed. The result is a 32-dimensional texture vector. The method was compared to three alternatives, namely, straight subband coding with 16 subbands, Mandala DCT [35,36] (standard block DCT in which the coefficients are rearranged into blocks having the same frequency content), and straight blocking in the pixel domain.

Comparison of the four methods was performed on images from the Brodatz set, which are examples of uniform textures. The goal of the experiment was to determine which feature set is better for texture classification. Dimensionality reduction was performed using standard Fisher Discriminant Analysis, and dissimilarity between images was measured in terms of the Mahalanobis distance (see Chapter 14.2.3) between the feature vectors. The experiments in Ref. [20] showed that wavelet- and subband-coding-derived features perform significantly better than Mandala DCT and spatial domain blocking. More recent results [37,38], however, show that, at least for scientific data sets, features derived from the Gabor wavelets and texture features computed from the gray scale levels of the images significantly outperform this method.

16.2.4.10 Combining Wavelet and Hidden Markov Models. A two-stage, rotation- and gray scale transformation-invariant texture recognition technique that combines wavelets and hidden Markov models (HMM) has been discussed in Ref. [39]. In the first stage, gray scale transformation-invariant features are extracted from each subband. In the second stage, the sequence of subbands is modeled as an HMM. Texture is represented by a set of texture classes. Each texture class is associated with a specific HMM. The HMM is used to model the statistical dependence among these subbands and is able to capture changes caused by rotation. During recognition, the unknown texture is matched against all the models in a fixed collection and the model with the best match identifies the texture class.

16.2.4.11 Robustness to Illumination Changes Using Wavelet Histograms. Most of the indexing algorithms presented in the literature assume that the illumination levels of the images are similar. The indexing performance may substantially degrade if this is not the case.

A technique that is robust to changes in illumination and relies on the histogram of the wavelet transform is discussed in Ref. [40]. Changes in illumination level are estimated using scale-invariant moments of the wavelet histogram. The parameters s and g of each subband (Section 16.2.4.5) of the target image are modified to account for illumination changes. Matching can then be carried out using Eq. (16.1).

16.2.4.12 Describing Textures Using Gabor Wavelets. An indexing technique using Gabor wavelets (Chapter 12) is detailed in Ref. [41]. Each image is decomposed into four scales and six orientations. A feature vector, of dimension 48, is then formed using the mean and standard deviation within each subband. The similarity between the query image and a target image is determined by the similarity of their feature vectors. Gabor wavelets capture directionality better than separable wavelets, which describe only vertical, horizontal, and diagonal (45 degrees) directions. However, the Gabor transform is computationally much more expensive than the dyadic, separable decomposition.

16.2.4.13 Computing Cross-Correlation in the Subband Domain. A correlation-based pattern matching approach operating in the subband domain is discussed in Ref. [42]. Cross-correlation between two images can be expressed in terms of cross-correlations of the corresponding subbands. Consider two one-dimensional signals $x(n)$ and $w(n)$, having z-transforms $W(z)$ and $X(z)$. It is well known, from elementary signal processing, that the cross-correlation of the signals can be expressed in the z-transform domain as $\widetilde{W}(z)X(z)$, where the tilde operator denotes the complex conjugate. Let the low-pass and high-pass analysis filters be $H_0(z)$ and $H_1(z)$, respectively. Denoting the decompositions of $x(n)$ and $w(n)$ into two subbands by $\{y_0(n), y_1(n)\}$ and $\{z_0(n), z_1(n)\}$, we can obtain the cross-correlation of $x(n)$ and $w(n)$ as:

$$\widetilde{W}(z)X(z) = \sum_{i,j=0}^{1} F_{ij}(z)\widetilde{Z}_i(z^2)Y_j(z^2) \tag{16.2}$$

where $F_{ij}(z) = H_i(z)\tilde{H}_j(z)$, $i, j = 0, 1$.

Eq. (16.2) shows that the cross-correlation of two signals equals the weighted sum of the cross-correlations of their corresponding subbands. Although Eq. (16.2) can still be computationally expensive, it was conjectured in Ref. [42] that a reasonable estimate of the correlation peaks can be obtained by just considering the subbands with highest energy. A characteristic of this technique is that the location of cross-correlation maxima (that correspond to matches) can be immediately derived from Eq. (16.2). This is an advantage over Fourier–Transform-based methods in which cross-correlation is very efficiently computed by coefficient-wise multiplication of the transforms but the inverse transform of this product must be computed to retrieve the locations and the values of the maxima.

16.2.4.14 Combining Image Coding and Indexing. A joint wavelet-based image representation and description system has been presented in Ref. [43]. In this system, images are compressed with a wavelet-coding technique and indexed using color, texture, and shape descriptions generated in the wavelet domain during the encoding process. All the features (texture, color, and shape) are based on the most significant wavelet coefficients and their energy distribution across subbands and decomposition levels. As the images are compressed and indexed at the same time, the image database management problem can be greatly simplified.

16.2.4.15 Remarks. In summary, wavelets are being increasingly considered as the leading candidates for compression in standards such as JPEG 2000 and

MPEG 4 due to their superior coding. Wavelet-based techniques serve the joint purposes of compression and indexing of visual content.

16.2.5 Vector Quantization (VQ)

Vector quantization (VQ) is an efficient technique for low bit rate image and video compression [44]. VQ pushes most of the complexity into the compressor, to allow for very efficient and simple decompression. It is possible to write very fast and efficient software decoders for VQ, which makes this scheme appealing for general-purpose computers. It is also possible to build simple and small hardware decoders, which makes VQ attractive for low-power applications such as portable video-on-demand over wireless networks.

VQ uses for compression a codebook containing $K = 2^{NR}$ code words. The codebook could be defined a priori, in which case it could be known to both the encoder and the decoder and would not need to be stored with the compressed data or constructed adaptively for each image, in which case it must be stored with the image. Each code word is an L-dimensional vector and has a unique label. The number L, N, and R are parameters of the algorithm, discussed later.

During compression, the image is first decomposed into nonoverlapping regular tiles containing L pixels each, which are represented as L-dimensional vectors. For example, the image can be tiled into 2×2 nonoverlapping blocks, and the pixels of each block arranged in a 4-dimensional vector. In a gray scale image in which the luminance is described by 8 bits, there are 2^{8L} possible such vectors. It is customary to write this number as 2^N, where N $(= 8L$ in this example) is the number of bits required to describe each possible vector. Each input vector is mapped onto the label of the closest code word as shown in Figure 16.15, using, for instance, the nearest-neighbor rule. Because there are 2^{NR} distinct code words, we need NR bits to represent each label, whereas to represent the original tile we need N bits. Hence, the number $1/R$ is the compression ratio

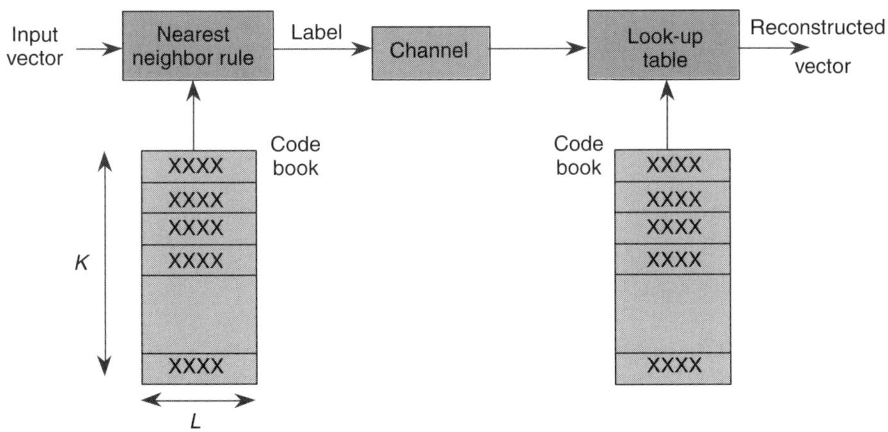

Figure 16.15. Compression and decompression using vector quantization (VQ).

(expressed as the ratio of the original image size to the compressed size), and R is called the *rate* of the quantizer.

Thus, after encoding, the image has been replaced by a sequence of code word labels, one per tile. Image reconstruction is implemented as a simple table lookup procedure: the code word label is used as an index into a table containing the code words; the corresponding code word is retrieved and written into the appropriate image tile.

For a fixed value of L, a larger codebook yields a lower compression ratio, makes encoding more computationally expensive, but provides on average smaller differences between the original and the reconstructed image. Note that the length L of the vector should also be carefully selected. Larger values of L correspond to larger block sizes: images are then divided in a smaller number of blocks, and hence more quickly decompressed; at the same time, larger codebooks are needed to yield the desired reconstruction performance, which complicates the codebook generation and the image encoding and, if the codebook is stored with the image, reduces the compression ratio.

The coding performance of VQ for different vector dimensions and code word sizes corresponding to two different compression ratios is shown in Figure 16.16.

VQ can also be used to construct a lower-resolution version of the original image. The set of tile labels can be represented as an image, called the "label map," and each label can be assigned an appropriate gray level (for example, the average of the entries of the corresponding code word) so that the label map resembles a scaled version of the original image. The effect of appropriately selecting labels for similar code words can be seen in the label map of Figure 16.17b, which looks like a scaled version of the original.

A sampling of VQ-based indexing techniques is now presented.

16.2.5.1 Indexing with the Histogram of the Label Map. In this technique the images are compressed using VQ, and the labels of the tiles are stored in the database [10]. The histogram of the labels serves as an index to the image. The histogram of the labels of an image is a K-dimensional vector (where $K = 2^{NR}$

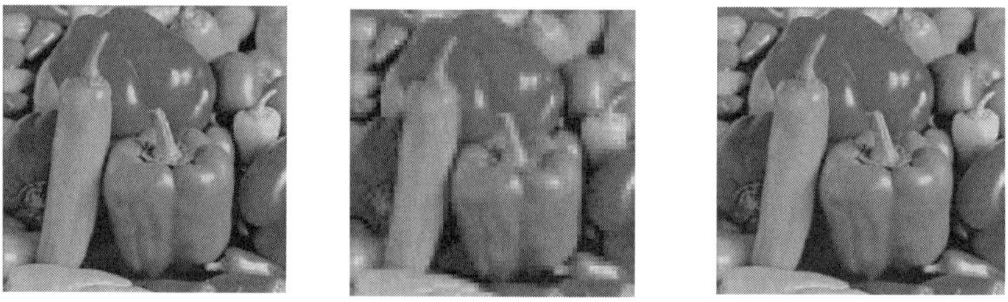

(a) (b) (c)

Figure 16.16. **(a)** Original image, **(b)** Reconstructed image at a compression ratio 128:1, Block size: 8 by 8 pixels (64-D vector), codebook size: 16 code words, **(c)** Reconstructed image at a compression ratio 14:1 Block size: 4 by 4 pixels (16-D vector), Codebook size: 512 code words.

(a) Original image (b) Label map

Figure 16.17. Images and their label maps using ordered codebook VQ.

Figure 16.18. Retrieval using the histogram of labels approach in VQ compressed domain. The image at the top is the query image, and the results are arranged from left to right in decreasing matching score.

is the number of code words in the codebook), the ith entry of which contains number of tiles having label i. The similarity between two images is measured using the histogram intersection (INTR) or the Euclidean (EUCL) distance metric. The retrieval results for a query image from a database of 3000 images are shown in Figure 16.18.

For an image of size $X \times Y$ pixels, the computation of the gray-level histogram in the pixel domain has a complexity of $O(XY)$, whereas the computation of label histogram has a lower complexity of $O(XY/L)$ where L is the dimension of the code words.

16.2.5.2 The Universal Quantizer Usage Map as an Indexing Key. This technique is based on adaptive VQ using a large universal codebook [45]. Here, a map of the used code words is generated for each image and is stored along with the image in the database. To illustrate this, let us say the image to be coded is tiled and represented as a collection of L-dimensional vectors, which are then translated into labels by the quantizer. If the universal codebook is very large, the image will use only a subset of the available labels (in fact, if the image has size $X \times Y$ pixels, it can use at most $X \times Y/L$ different code words). A usage map, indicating which code words have been used, can then be associated with the image. Although the usage map could be just a list of the used code words, more commonly it consists of a bit-array of length K, containing a "1" in the positions corresponding to used code words and a "0" everywhere else. The usage map defines a reduced codebook containing only the code words used. The labels assigned by the quantizer to the image tiles are used to index the reduced codebook rather than the large, universal codebook. Hence, if the image uses only k code words, each compressed tile can be represented by $\log(k)$ bits, instead of the $\log(K)$ bits required to use the entire large codebook. A reduced codebook constructed with the bit-array method is shown in Figure 16.19.

Usage maps reduce the quantizer bit rate. With this method, the compressed representation of an image consists of the labels and of the usage map (since the codebook is universal, it is assumed that both encoder and decoder have a copy of it). This technique requires only K bits to represent the used code words, where again K is the universal codebook size.

The universal quantizer usage map can be used as an index. The key observation is that similar images have in general similar reduced codebooks. The usage map corresponding to an image constitutes a feature vector, which is used as an index to store and retrieve the image. If the usage maps are stored as bit vectors, the dissimilarity between two images can be computed by taking the bitwise exclusive OR of the corresponding usage maps, which produces a bit vector wherein code words that belong to only one of the reduced codebooks are marked with a "1." The number of bits that are "1" in the bit vector is then used as a measure of dissimilarity. Mathematically, the similarity between two images f_m and f_n is measured using the following equation:

$$S(f_m, f_n) = \sum_{i=0}^{N-1} [u(f_m, i) \oplus u(f_n, i)] \tag{16.3}$$

where $\oplus$ is the XOR operation.

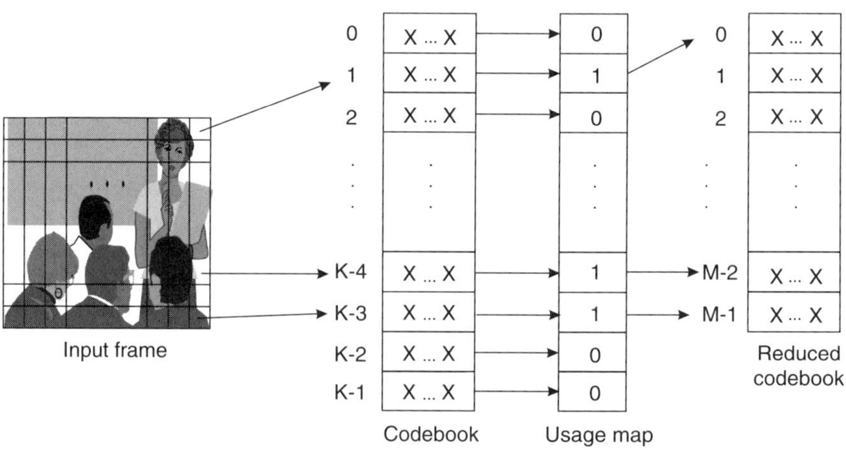

Figure 16.19. Usage map generation.

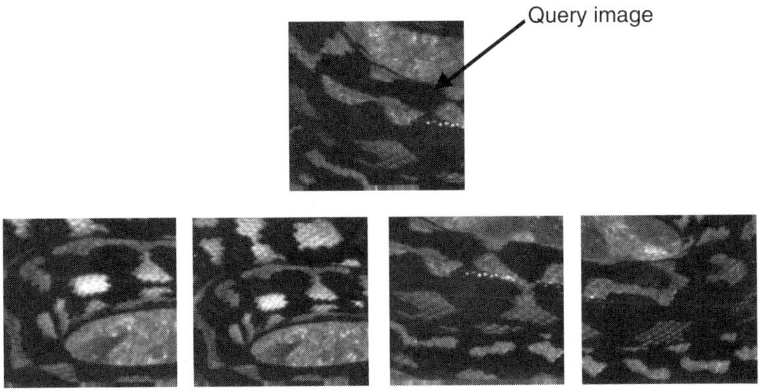

Figure 16.20. Retrieval results based on usage map in VQ compressed domain.

As the usage map is constructed while encoding the image, the described technique does not have a preprocessing cost. The cost of storing the index keys is $O(K)$ bits per image. Searching also requires $O(K)$ operations per target image. A downside of the technique is the coding complexity, which grows with the size of the codebook: for large values of the tile size L, compressing an image of size $X \times Y$ pixels can require $O(XYK)$ operations (which can be reduced to $O(XY \log(K))$ with tree-structured vector quantizers).

The retrieval results corresponding to this technique are shown in Figure 16.20.

16.2.5.3 Content-Based Retrieval of Remotely Sensed Images. A VQ indexing technique for content-based retrieval of remotely sensed images is discussed in Ref. [46]. Assignment of code words for image blocks involves minimization of a weighted error that incorporates a distortion measure. Various distortion measures have been proposed in an effort to enhance the performance of the VQ code words as content descriptors. Two types of query, query-by-class and query-by-value, have been tested with this technique. Query-by-class involves classification of each pixel in an image into predefined classes, whereas query-by-value involves matching on the basis of distribution of intensity values in various bands of a multispectral remotely sensed image. Query-by-value makes optimum use of VQ code words as these code words are directly indicative of the multispectral intensity distributions in the image. Query-by-class, on the other hand, performs some transformations so that VQ code words can be used to answer the queries. As a result of this, it has been found that query-by-value outperforms query-by-class for this VQ indexing technique.

16.2.6 Fractals/Affine Transform

Fractals are irregular patterns made up of parts that are in some way similar to the whole pattern, for example, twigs and tree branches. This property is called self-similarity or self-symmetry. Fractal image compression [11] uses the concepts of fractal geometry to encode natural images through a small set of parameters. Natural images often display fractal characteristics and portions of images can be well approximated by an appropriate fractal image.

In block-fractal coding, an image is partitioned into a collection of nonoverlapping regions known as *range blocks*. The coding process uses a collection of *domain blocks*, which form a dictionary, and a set of parametric fractal transformations known as *fractal codes*. Each range block is transformed with one of the transformations and the result is compared with all domain blocks. The transformation and mapping steps are repeated for all fractal codes and the best match is found. The range block is associated with the best matching domain block and with the fractal code that produced the match. The block is then encoded by replacing it with the parameters of the best fractal code, and thus the compressed image is a collection of fractal parameters. The size of the compressed image is the product of the number of bits required to describe the fractal parameters of a fractal code times the number of range blocks contained in the image. For a fixed family of fractal codes, larger range blocks yield higher compression ratio, but potentially worse fidelity to the original.

16.2.6.1 Matching Fractal Codes. A texture-based image retrieval technique by which image similarity is detected by matching fractal codes has been presented in Ref. [47]. Here, each database image is decomposed into blocks, each of which is encoded using fractal codes. The collection of the fractal codes of a query image is used as a key and matched with the fractal codes of the images in a database.

16.2.6.2 Indexing Based on Matching Domain Blocks. A comparison of the performance of wavelet and fractals in image retrieval is presented in Ref. [48]. In the wavelet domain, the mean absolute value and variance of different subbands are used as image features. In the fractal domain, fractal coding of the query and target images (denoted by M_1 and M_2 respectively) is performed jointly, with the best matching domain blocks for range blocks of image M_1 searched in both M_1 and M_2. The similarity between M_1 and M_2 is measured as the ratio of the number of matching domain blocks found in M_1 and M_2. Simulation results indicate that wavelets are more effective for images in which texture is predominant, whereas fractals performs relatively well over a variety of images.

16.2.7 Hybrid Schemes

Hybrid schemes are a combination of two or more basic coding techniques [8,49]. Their goal is to exploit the advantages of the associated compression techniques in order to provide a superior coding performance. The indices can therefore be a combination of features derived from the individual coding techniques. This section contains a brief description of several hybrid schemes.

16.2.7.1 Combining Wavelets and VQ. A wavelet-based indexing technique using vector quantization has been described in Ref. [50]. Here, the images are first decomposed using the wavelet transform, and the transform subbands are then encoded using vector quantization. The collection of codebook labels of each image forms the feature vector used to index the database.

16.2.7.2 Combining Wavelets and Tree-Structured Vector Quantizers. A representation methodology for large databases of pulsed radar returns from naval vessels, which economizes memory and minimizes search time, is presented in Ref. [51]. This technique uses a hierarchical representation by developing clustering schemes based on wavelet representations of these signals. Additionally, a sophisticated version of vector quantization called *tree structured* VQ (TSVQ) is used to further cluster and compress the wavelet representations of the radar signals in a way that permits a hierarchical search across resolutions.

16.2.7.3 Combining Spatial Segmentation, DWT, and VQ. Another technique combining vector quantization, spatial segmentation, and discrete wavelet transform, has been proposed [52] to develop a coding scheme for content-based retrieval. When an image is inserted in the database, it is first decomposed into 8×8 nonoverlapping blocks. Next, a segmentation algorithm is applied to the image to define *image regions* and *objects*. Image regions and objects denote entities of interest in a given image database. Each segmented region in the image is then covered with the smallest possible rectangular collection of the previously defined 8×8 blocks. This collection is called a superblock. The next step consists of applying a wavelet transform to each superblock. The number of levels of decomposition depends on the size of the superblock. The wavelet transform is applied until the lowest frequency subband is of size 8×8. Finally, a coding scheme that incorporates Vector Quantization is applied to map the wavelet transform subbands of the superblocks to finite codebooks.

User-defined queries, in the form of sample images, are provided as input to the wavelet transform. The resulting subbands are mapped to find the appropriate VQ code words for retrieval. The file headers of the image files contain information in terms of a coarse-to-fine discriminant structure. A technique of *progressive refinement retrieval* is adopted to successively reduce the number of files searched at each level of coarseness as more bits are read from the headers.

16.2.7.4 Combining DCT and VQ. A VQ-based face-recognition technique in the DCT domain has been detailed in Ref. [53]. When the database is first created, a set of training images is selected, their block-DCTs are computed, and a k-means quantizer [7] is trained on the vector of DCT coefficients in order to produce a database codebook. When an image is inserted in the database, its block-DCT is quantized using the trained quantizer. Similarity between the query and database images is determined by maximizing a cost function. The retrieval performance has been evaluated based on feature selection, codebook size, and feature dimensionality. For feature selection, transform-based techniques are compared with pixel-intensity techniques, both of which operate on blocks.

It is observed that block-based transform techniques are better in terms of performance efficiency than block-based pixel-intensity techniques. In terms of feature dimension, transform-based techniques show the same performance results as pixel-intensity-based techniques for lower dimensions of feature vectors. Increasing the codebook size also appears to yield better performance.

16.3 CONCLUSION

The success of compressed domain indexing greatly depends on how well the compression or coding technique represents the discriminative features in images. It is generally difficult to compare the performance of the various techniques. KLT, though statistically optimal (if the process is Gaussian), is computationally intensive and requires the basis images to be stored in the database, which yields poor overall compression rates unless the database size is large. Block-DCT in JPEG provides a good coding and indexing performance; nevertheless, the block structure was not originally intended for indexing and can have negative effects. Wavelet-based techniques are promising for indexing applications because of their inherent multiresolution capability, of the simplicity of edge and shape detection, and of the availability of information. However, they have been known to perform well only on images that contain significant textural information. Vector quantization produces the indexing keys while compressing the image but suffers from the additional overhead and approximations involved in codebook generation. Although fractals have a potential to provide good coding performance, they are image-dependent. Finally, the complexity of both VQ and fractal coding is highly asymmetric, namely, coding is computationally intensive, while decoding is fast.

16.4 SUMMARY

In this chapter, we have discussed a variety of compressed-domain indexing approaches and presented examples of techniques derived from each approach. Existing compressed-domain indexing techniques are primarily oriented toward extracting low-level features from the compression parameters. There are extensive similarities between the processes of compression and indexing. For example, the goal of lossy compression is to minimize a cost function that combines distortion, bit rate, and complexity, whereas the purpose of indexing is to compactly represent the visual content in an image or video sequence to facilitate fast retrieval. As both compression and indexing rely on efficient extraction of visual content, they can be addressed jointly. Future research will not only involve investigations of how to use existing compression parameters for indexing, but also explore the possibility of employing the spatio-temporal indexing parameters for compression. Furthermore, novel joint compression indexing schemes will need to be devised that yield very low data rate with high retrieval performance.

ACKNOWLEDGMENTS

The author would like to acknowledge Dr. Mrinal Mandal, Dr. Fayez Idris, Mr. Mohammed Zubair V, Mr. Jayank Bhalod, and Mr. Madhusudhana Gargesha for their valuable help in writing this chapter.

REFERENCES

1. M. O'Docherty and C. Daskalakis, Multimedia information systems: the management and semantic retrieval of all electronic datatypes, *Comput. J.* **34**(3), 225–238 (1991).
2. V.N. Gudivada and V.V. Raghavan, Content based image retrieval systems, *IEEE Comput.* **28**(9), 18–22 (1995).
3. J.D. Villasenor, Full-frame compression of tomographic images using the discrete Fourier transform, *Data Compression Conference*, 195–203 (1993).
4. G.M. Binge and E. Micheli-Tzanakou, Fourier compression-reconstruction technique (MRI application), *Proc. Annu. Int. Conf. IEEE Eng.* **2**, 524–525 (1989).
5. N. Ahmed, T. Natarajan, and K.R. Rao, Discrete Cosine Transform, *IEEE Trans. Comput.* **23**, 90–93 (1974).
6. K.R. Rao and P. Yip, *Discrete Cosine Transforms—Algorithms, Advantages, Applications*, Academic Press, New York, 1990.
7. A.K. Jain, *Fundamentals of Digital Image Processing*, Prentice Hall, Englewood Cliffs, New Jersey, 1989.
8. M. Antonini et al., Image coding using wavelet transform, *IEEE Trans. Image Process.* **1**(2), 205–220 (1992).
9. J. Froment and S. Mallat, in Second generation compact image coding with wavelets, C.K. Chui, ed., *Wavelets: A Tutorial in Theory and Applications*, Academic Press, New York, 1992.
10. F. Idris and S. Panchanathan, Image indexing using vector quantization, *Proc. SPIE: Storage and Retrieval for Image and Video Databases III* **2420**, 373–380 (1995).
11. M.F. Barnsley and L.P. Hurd, *Fractal Image Compression*, AK Peters Ltd., Wellesley, Mass., 1993.
12. H.S. Stone, C.S. Li, Image matching by means of intensity and texture matching in the fourier domain, *Proc. SPIE* **2670**, 337–349 (1996).
13. M. Augusteijn, L.E. Clemens, and K.A. Shaw, Performance evaluation of texture measures for ground cover identification in satellite images by means of a neural network classifier, *IEEE Trans. Geosci. Remote Sensing* **33**(3), 616–626 (1995).
14. A. Celentano and V.D. Lecce, A FFT based technique for image signature generation, *Proc. SPIE: Storage and Retrieval for Image and Video Databases V* **3022**, 457–466 (1997).
15. A. Pentland, R.W. Picard, and S. Sclaroff, Photobook: tools for content-based manipulation of image databases, *Proc. SPIE: Storage and Retrieval for Image and Video Databases II* **2185**, 34–47 (1994).
16. D.L. Swets and J. Weng, Using discriminant eigenfeatures for image retrieval, *IEEE Trans. Pattern Anal. Machine Intell.* **18**(8), 831–836 (1996).

17. X. Tang and W.K. Stewart, Texture classification using principal-component analysis techniques, *Proc. SPIE* **2315**, 22–35 (1994).
18. J.A. Saghri, A.G. Tescher, and J.T. Reagan, Practical transform coding of multispectral imagery, *IEEE Signal Process. Mag.* **12**(1), 33–43 (1995).
19. J. Hafner et al., Efficient color histogram indexing for quadratic form distance function, *IEEE Trans. Pattern Anal. Mach. Intell.* **17**(7), 729–736 (1995).
20. J.R. Smith and S.-F. Chang, Transform features for texture classification and discrimination in large image databases, *Proc. IEEE Int. Conf. Image Process.* **3**, 407–411 (1994).
21. M. Shneier and M.A. Mottaleb, Exploiting the JPEG Compression Scheme for Image Retrieval, *IEEE Trans. Pattern Anal. Machine. Intell.* **18**(8), 849–853 (1996).
22. A.A. Abdel-Malek and J.E. Hershey, Feature cueing in the discrete cosine domain, *J. Electron. Imaging* **3**, 71–80 (1994).
23. B. Shen and I.K. Sethi, Direct feature extraction from compressed images, *Proc. SPIE* **2670**, 404–414 (1996).
24. S.G. Mallat, A Theory for multiresolution signal representation: the wavelet decomposition, *IEEE Trans. Pattern Anal. Machine. Intell.* **11**(7), 674–693 (1989).
25. C.E. Jacobs, A. Finkelstein, and D.H. Salesin, Fast multiresolution image querying, *Proc. ACM SIGGRAPH Conference on Computer Graphics and Interactive Techniques*, Los Angeles, Calif. August, 1995.
26. J.Z. Wang et al., Wavelet-based image indexing techniques with partial sketch retrieval capability, *Proceedings of the Forum on Research and Technology Advances in Digital Libraries*, Washington, DC, 13–24 (1997).
27. M.K. Mandal, S. Panchanathan, and T. Aboulnasr, Image indexing using translation and scale-invariant moments and wavelets, *Proc. SPIE: Storage and Retrieval for Image and Video Databases V* **3022**, 380–389 (1997).
28. M.K. Mandal, T. Aboulnasr and S. Panchanathan, Image indexing using moments and wavelets, *IEEE Trans. Consumer Electron.* **42**(3), 557–565 (1996).
29. K.A. Birney and T.R. Fischer, On the modeling of DCT and subband image data for compression, *IEEE Trans. Image Process.* **4**(2), 186–193 (1995).
30. F. Qi, D. Shen and L. Quan, Wavelet transform based rotation invariant feature extraction in object recognition, *Proc. Int. Symp. Inform. Theory Appl.* 221–224, (1994).
31. R.J. Prokop and A.P. Reeves, A survey of moment-based techniques for unoccluded object representation and recognition, *CVGIP: Graphical Models and Image Process.* **54**, 438–460 (1992).
32. M.R. Teague, Image Analysis via the General Theory of Moments, *J. Opt. Soc. Am.* **70**, 920–930 (1990).
33. P. Rashkovskiy and L. Sadovnik, Scale, rotation and shift invariant wavelet transform, *Proc. SPIE: Optical Pattern Recognition V* **2237**, 390–401 (1994).
34. T. Chang and C.C.J. Kuo, Texture analysis and classification with tree-structured wavelet transform, *IEEE Trans. Image Process.* **2**(4), 429–441 (1993).
35. J.S. Lee, R.C. Kim, and S.U. Lee, Transformed entropy-constrained vector quantizers employing mandala block for image coding, *Signal-Process. Image-Commun. J.* **7**, 75–92 (1995).

36. J.S. Lee, R.C. Kim, and S.U. Lee, Entropy-constrained vector quantization of images in the transform domain, *Proc. SPIE* **2308**, 434–445 (1994).

37. C.S. Li et al., Comparing texture feature sets for retrieving core images in petroleum applications, *Proc. SPIE: Storage and Retrieval for Image and Video Databases* **3665**, 2–11 (1999).

38. C.S. Li and V. Castelli, Deriving texture feature sets for content-based retrieval of satellite image databases, Calif. Santa Barbara, October 26–29, 1997.

39. J.L. Chen and A. Kundu, Rotation and gray scale invariant texture identification using wavelet decomposition and hidden markov model, *IEEE Trans. Pattern Anal. Machine Intell.* **16**(2), 208–214 (1994).

40. M.K. Mandal, S. Panchanathan, and T. Aboulnasr, Image indexing using translation and scale-invariant moments and wavelets, *Proc. SPIE: Storage and Retrieval for Image and Video Databases V* **3022**, 380–389 (1997).

41. B.S. Manjunath and W.Y. Ma, Texture features for browsing and retrieval of image data, *IEEE Trans. Pattern Anal. Machine Intell.* **18**(8), 837–841 (1996).

42. H. Wang and S.-F. Chang, Adaptive image matching in the subband domain, *Proc. of SPIE: VCIP* **2727**, 885–896 (1996).

43. K.-C. Liang and C.-C. Jay Kuo, WaveGuide: A joint wavelet-based image representation and description system, *IEEE Trans. Image Process.* **8**(11), 1619–1629 (1999).

44. F. Idris and S. Panchanathan, Video compression using frame adaptive vector quantization, *J. Vis. Commun. Image Represent.* **9**(2), 107–118 (1998).

45. F. Idris and S. Panchanathan, Storage and retrieval of compressed images, *IEEE Trans. Consumer Electron.* **41**, 937–941 (1995).

46. A. Vellaikal, C.C.J. Kuo, and S. Dao, Content-based retrieval of remote-sensed images using vector quantization, *Proc. SPIE* **2488**, 178–189 (1995).

47. A. Zhang, B. Cheng, and R.S. Acharya, Approach to query-by-texture in image database systems, *Proc. SPIE: Digital Image Storage and Archiving Systems* **2606**, 338–349 (1995).

48. A. Zhang et al., Comparison of wavelet transforms and fractal coding in texture-based image retrieval, *Proc. SPIE: Visual Data Exploration and Anal. III* **2656**, 116–125 (1996).

49. J. Li, Hybrid wavelet-fractal image compression based on a rate-distortion criterion, *Proc. SPIE: Visual Commun. Image Process.* **3024**, 1014–1025 (1997).

50. F. Idris and S. Panchanathan, Image indexing using wavelet vector quantization, *Proc. SPIE: Digital Image Storage Archiving Systems* **2606**, 269–275 (1995).

51. J.S. Barbas and S.I. Wolk, Efficient organization of large ship radar databases using wavelets and structured vector quantization, *Proc. Asilomar Conf. Signals, Syst. Comput.* **1**, 491–498 (1993).

52. M.D. Swanson, S. Hosur, and A.H. Tewfik, Image coding for content-based retrieval, *Proc. SPIE: VCIP* **2727**, 4–15 (1996).

53. C. Podilchuk and X. Zhang, Face recognition using DCT-based feature vectors, *Proc. IEEE Int. Conf. Acoustics, Speech Signal Process.* **4**, 2144–2147 (1996).

17 Concepts and Techniques for Indexing Visual Semantics

ALEJANDRO JAIMES and SHIH-FU CHANG
Columbia University, New York, New York

17.1 INTRODUCTION

In the previous chapters, several techniques to handle visual information have been presented, primarily in reference to *syntax*: the visual elements that appear in an image[1] (e.g., color, texture, and so on). In this chapter, the focus is on *semantics*: the interpretation of those visual elements (e.g., objects, scenes, and so on).

The continuing increase in the amount of visual information available in digital form has created a strong interest in the development of new techniques that allow efficient and accurate access to that information. One crucial aspect is the creation of indexes (e.g., labels or classifications) that facilitate such access. In traditional approaches, textual annotations are used for indexing — a cataloger manually assigns a set of key words or expressions to describe an image. Users can then perform text-based *queries* or *browse* through manually assigned categories. In contrast to text-based approaches, recent techniques in content-based image retrieval (CBIR) [1–4] have focused on automatic indexing of images on the basis of their visual content. The data in the images and video is indexed, and users can perform *queries-by-example* (e.g., images that look like this one) or *user-sketch* (e.g., images that look like this sketch). Traditional query-by-example and query-by-sketch techniques are usually based on low-level features (color, texture, and so on), thus concentrating on the form of the visual information (*syntax*: color, texture, and so on) rather than on the meaning (*semantics*: objects, events, and so on). Users, however, are generally interested in semantics. Moreover, even when syntax is a necessary part of the query, the user frequently wishes it to be subordinate to semantics — the query "show me all the images

[1] We will use the general term *image* to refer to visual information (photograph, illustration, video, and so on).

Image Databases: Search and Retrieval of Digital Imagery, Edited by Vittorio Castelli and Lawrence D. Bergman.
ISBN 0-471-32116-8

that contain green apples" is more likely than the query "show me all the green areas that are apples." Although useful, low-level features are often unsuitable at the semantic level: meaningful queries-by-sketch are difficult to formulate and example-based queries often do not express semantic-level distinctions.

One crucial aspect of building a CBIR system is understanding the data that will be included in the system so that it can be appropriately indexed. Appropriate indexing of visual information is a challenging task because there is a large amount of information present in a single image (e.g., *what* to index?), and different levels of description are possible (e.g., *how* to index?). Consider, for example, a portrait of a man wearing a suit. It would be possible to label the image with the terms "suit" or "man." The term *man*, in turn, could carry information at multiple levels: *conceptual* (e.g., definition of man in the dictionary), *physical* (size, weight), and *visual* (hair color, clothing), among others. A category label implies explicit (e.g., the person in the image is a man, not a woman) and implicit or undefined information (e.g., from that term alone, it is not possible to know what the man is wearing).

In addition to issues regarding the complexity of visual information, there are issues related to users and their subjectivity while searching or browsing. It is well understood that different users search for information in different ways and that their search criteria change over time [5,6].

In the first part of the chapter, a conceptual framework for indexing visual information is discussed [7]. The framework is used to stresses differences between syntax and semantics and highlights the issues that arise in the indexing of images. We show that indexing can occur at multiple levels and present structures to accommodate these different levels. This discussion stresses that different techniques are useful for different purposes and that the level of indexing depends on the application. For example, it makes no sense to look for pictures of Bill Clinton, using texture. Similarly, there are many instances in medical imaging in which textual search is not nearly as powerful as query-by-example.

In the second part of the chapter, the framework is used to place state-of-the-art CBIR techniques in perspective. In particular, we emphasize the differences between the query-formulation paradigm[2] (e.g., query-by-example or similarity) and the indexing technique (e.g., placing items in semantic categories or indexing using low-level features). We discuss the main CBIR interface paradigms, outlining their advantages and disadvantages with respect to semantics, and recent interactive techniques (e.g., relevance feedback) that aim to enhance those interfaces. Our discussion shows that most of the current CBIR techniques operate at the syntactic level. We then focus on automatic semantic classification and present a brief overview of some Object Recognition approaches from the Computer Vision literature. We then highlight the relationship between CBIR and object-recognition techniques, emphasizing the differences between the two and outlining the new challenges for object recognition if it is to be applied to

[2] We will use the terms *query formulation* and *interface* interchangeably.

CBIR. That part of the chapter is motivated by the conceptual framework, which suggests the importance of objects in indexing semantics.

One of the limitations of most object-recognition approaches is that the algorithms are manually constructed and their application is constrained to very specific domains. One way to enhance the capability of such systems is to construct flexible frameworks that use machine-learning techniques. In the last part of the chapter, we discuss one such framework, the *Visual Apprentice* [8], in which users are able to build classifiers by providing training examples based on their specific interests. The framework is discussed in some detail, aiming to highlight some of the issues that arise when machine-learning techniques are used to automatically detect objects. The discussion also includes some of the issues that arise when a CBIR system that uses learning is applied in a real-world application (e.g., baseball). The advantages and disadvantages of using such techniques are discussed.

17.1.1 Related Work

Discourses on imagery have arisen in many different academic fields. Studies in *art* have focused on interpretation and perception [9,10], aesthetics and formal analysis [11], visual communication [12], levels of meaning [13], and so on. Studies in *cognitive psychology* have dealt with issues such as perception [14–16], visual similarity [17], mental categories (i.e., concepts) [18], distinctions between perceptual and conceptual category structure [19–21], internal category structure (i.e., levels of categorization) [22–26], and so on. In the field of *information sciences*, work has been performed on analyzing the subject of an image [27–30], indexing [31–34], the attributes that can be used to describe images [35,36], classification [32,37], query analysis [38,39], and indexing schemes [40–43], among others.

There have also been many efforts related to the organization of multimedia data. Some of that work includes Refs. [44–49]. In addition, the development of the MPEG-7 standard[3] has triggered a large number of proposals to describe and structure multimedia information [50]. Some of the work presented in Section 17.2 has been proposed to MPEG-7 [51–53] (also see most recent draft on MPEG-7 description schemes [54]).

17.1.2 Outline

In Section 17.2, conceptual structures that identify important issues in content-based retrieval are discussed. This work demonstrates the difficulties of image indexing and similarity matching. In Section 17.3, we place CBIR techniques in perspective, using the framework of Section 17.2. We also give a brief overview of object-recognition approaches and relate them to CBIR. In Section 17.4, we present an interactive framework to build *Visual Object Detectors*. Finally, we summarize future directions in Section 17.5.

[3] MPEG-7 aims to standardize a set of descriptors for multimedia information.

17.2 INDEXING VISUAL INFORMATION AT MULTIPLE LEVELS

In this section, we focus on the problem of multiple levels of description while indexing visual information. We discuss a conceptual framework [7], which draws on concepts from the literature in diverse fields such as cognitive psychology, library sciences, art, and content-based retrieval. We distinguish between *visual* and *nonvisual* information and provide the appropriate structures. We describe a 10-level *visual* structure, which provides a systematic way of indexing images based on syntax (e.g., color, texture, and so on) and semantics (e.g., objects, events, and so on) and includes distinctions between *general concepts* and *visual concepts*. We define different types of relations (e.g., syntactic, semantic) at different levels of the visual structure and also use a *semantic information table* to summarize the important aspects of an image.

This structure places state-of-the art content-based retrieval techniques in perspective, relating them to real user-needs and research in other fields. Using these structures is beneficial not only in terms of understanding the users and their interests, but also in characterizing the content-based retrieval problem according to the levels of description used to access visual information.

17.2.1 Basic Definitions

17.2.1.1 Percept vs. Concept. Images are multidimensional representations of information, but at the most basic level they simply cause a response to light (tonal light or absence of light) [12]. At the most complex level, images represent abstract ideas that depend largely on individual knowledge, experience, and even a particular mood. We can make distinctions between *percept* and *concept* [9]. The percept refers to what our senses perceive, which, in the visual system, is light. These patterns of light produce the perception of different elements such as texture and color. No interpretation process takes place when we refer to the percept: no knowledge is required. A concept[4], on the other hand, refers to a representation, an abstract or generic idea, generalized from particular instances. As such, it implies the use of background knowledge and an inherent interpretation of what is perceived. Concepts, which can be described in different ways (e.g., using attributes as in Section 17.2.1.3), can be very abstract and subjective in the sense that they depend on an individual's knowledge and interpretation.

17.2.1.2 Syntax vs. Semantics. Whereas a percept refers to what we perceive through our senses (e.g., visual elements), *syntax* refers to the visual elements themselves and the way in which they are arranged. When referring to syntax, no consideration is given to the meaning of the elements or to the meaning of their arrangements. *Semantics*, on the other hand, deals with the meaning

[4] Definition from Merriam-Webster dictionary.

of those elements and the meaning of their arrangements. As will be shown in the discussion that follows, syntax can refer to several perceptual levels — from simple global color and texture to local geometric forms, such as lines and circles. Semantics can also be treated at different levels.

17.2.1.3 ***General vs. Visual Concepts.*** In this section we wish to emphasize that *general concepts* and *visual concepts* are different, and that these may vary among individuals. A visual concept includes only visual attributes, whereas a general concept can include any kind of attribute. We use a ball as an example. One possible general concept describes a ball as a round mass[4]. A volleyball player, however, may have a different general concept of a ball than a baseball player because, as described earlier, a concept implies background knowledge and interpretation. Naturally, different individuals have very different interpretations of ideas (or in this case concrete objects). In Figure 17.1, we see that the attributes[5] used for the general and visual concepts of a ball can differ. Each box represents a universe of attributes, and each circle, the set of attributes observers A and B choose to describe a ball. Attributes outside the circles are not chosen by the observers to describe this particular concept. Observer A is a volleyball player, and when asked to give the general *attributes* of a ball, she chooses soft, yellow, round, leather, and light weight. Observer B is a baseball player and when asked to give the general attributes of a ball, she chooses hard, heavy, white, round, and leather. Note that, naturally, there is also a correlation between some general and visual attributes (e.g., big).

These basic definitions are useful because they point out a very important issue in content-based retrieval: different users have different concepts (of even simple objects) and even simple objects can be seen at different conceptual levels. Specifically, there is an important distinction between *general concept* (i.e., helps answer the question: what is it?) and *visual concept* (i.e., helps answer the question: what does it look like?). We apply these ideas to the construction of our

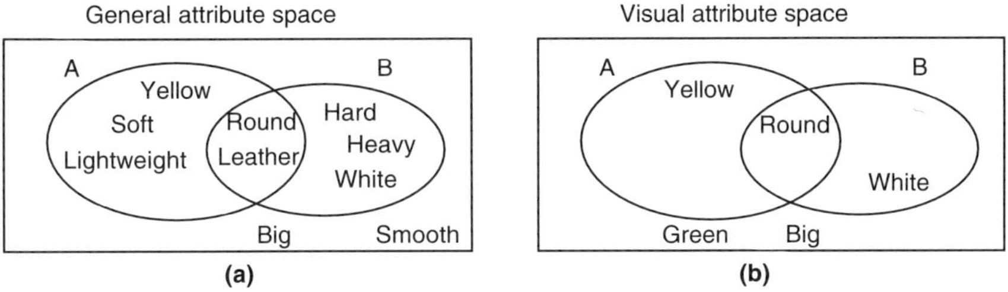

Figure 17.1. We divide attributes into those that are general **(a)** and those that are visual **(b)**. Attributes in each set (A, B) are used by different individuals to describe the same object in this example (a ball).

[5] In this section, we use the word *attribute* to refer to a characteristic or quality of an object (e.g, blue, big, and heavy). We do not make a distinction between attribute name and attribute type (e.g., color: blue).

conceptual indexing structures and to the development of techniques for automatically learning visual object detectors (discussed in Section 17.4).

17.2.2 Visual and Nonvisual Content

The first step in creating conceptual indexing structures is to make a distinction between *visual* and *nonvisual* content. The visual content of an image corresponds to what is directly perceived when the image is observed (the lines, shapes, colors, objects, and so on). The nonvisual content corresponds to information that is closely related to the image, but that is not present in the image. In a painting, for example, the price, current owner, and so on, belong to the nonvisual category. Next, we present an indexing structure for the visual content of the image and we follow with a structure for *nonvisual* content.

17.2.2.1 Visual Content. Our visual structure contains 10 levels, all of which are obtained from the image alone: the first four refer to syntax and the remaining six refer to semantics. In addition, levels one to four are directly related to percept and levels 5 through 10 to visual concept. Although some of these divisions may not be strict, they should be considered because they have a direct impact on understanding *what* users are searching for and *how* they try to find it. They also emphasize the limitations of different indexing techniques (manual and automatic) in terms of the knowledge required. An overview of the structure is given in Figure 17.2.

The width of each layer of the pyramid represents the amount of knowledge required for operating at that level — more knowledge is necessary to recognize a specific scene (e.g., Central Park in New York City) than to recognize a generic scene (e.g., park). Note that there may be exceptions — an average observer may not be able to determine the technique or materials (e.g., oil, watercolor) that were used to produce a painting, but an expert would.

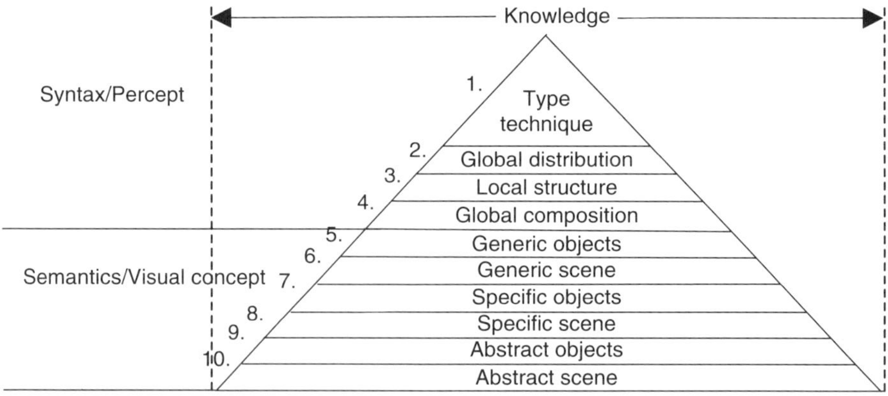

Figure 17.2. The indexing structure is represented by a pyramid.

Each level is explained in the sections that follow and experimental results in the application of the pyramid are discussed in Section 17.2.3. Note that different operations can be performed with the content at different levels. For example, an image can be searched on the basis of similarity at the type and technique level or classified on the basis of its generic objects. In other words, features from an image can be classified at different levels of the pyramid and therefore the image itself can be classified and searched for at different levels. It is important to keep in mind that the levels chosen for a particular application will depend on the data being indexed and on the way it is used. Similarly, indexing techniques that perform well at one level (e.g., color histogram) may not be adequate at other levels and such choices must be made carefully. These issues are discussed further in Section 17.3.

17.2.2.2 Type and Technique. At the most basic level, we are interested in the general visual characteristics of the image or the video sequence. Descriptions of the type of image or video sequence or the technique used to produce it are very general, but prove to be of great importance. Images, for example, may be placed in categories such as painting, black and white photograph, color photograph, and drawing. Related classification schemes at this level have been developed conceptually in Refs. [45,47] and automatically in WebSEEk [55].

In the case of digital photographs, the two main categories could be color and gray scale, with additional categories and descriptions such as number of colors, compression scheme, resolution, and so on. We note that some of these may have some overlap with the nonvisual indexing aspects described in Section 17.2.2.13. Figure 17.3a shows an interesting example.

17.2.2.3 Global Distribution. The *type* and *technique* in the previous level gives general information about the visual characteristics of the image or the video

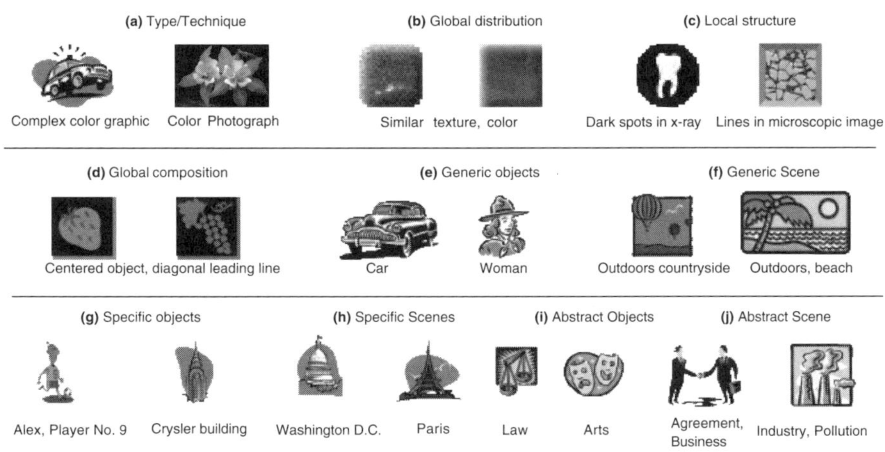

Figure 17.3. Example images for each level of the *Visual* structure presented.

sequence, but gives little information about the visual content. An image (or video sequence) is characterized at the *global distribution* level using low-level perceptual features such as spectral sensitivity (color) and frequency sensitivity (texture). Individual components of the content are not processed at this level: the low-level perceptual features are extracted from the image as a whole. Global distribution features may include global color (measured, for instance, as dominant color, average color, or color histogram), global texture (using one of the descriptors analyzed in Chapter 12, such as coarseness, directionality, contrast), and global shape (e.g., aspect ratio), and, for video data, global motion (e.g., speed, acceleration, and trajectory), camera motion, global deformation (e.g., growing speed), and temporal and spatial dimensions (e.g., spatial area and temporal dimension), among others. The example in Figure 17.3b shows images of two buttons that have similar texture and color. Note that the global distribution attributes of the example could be quite useful for retrieving visually similar images, but they would probably be useless for retrieving images containing specific objects (see Section 17.3.1.2).

Although some global measures are less intuitive than others (e.g., it is difficult for a human to imagine what the color histogram of an image looks like), these global low-level features have been successfully used in various content-based retrieval systems to perform query-by-example (QBIC [56], WebSEEk [55], Virage [57]) and to organize the contents of a database for browsing (see discussions in Ref. [2]). An interesting comparison of human and machine assessments of image similarity based on global features at this level can be found in Ref. [58].

17.2.2.4 Local Structure. *Local structure* is concerned with image components. At the most basic level, these components result from low-level processing and include elements, such as *dots, lines, tone, color*, and *texture*, extracted from the images. In visual literacy literature [12], some of these are referred to as the "*basic elements*" of visual communication and are regarded as the *basic syntax symbols*. Other examples of local structure attributes are temporal and spatial position, local color, local motion, local deformation, local shape, and two-dimensional (2D) geometry. Figure 17.3c shows images in which attributes of this type may be of importance. In the X-ray image of a tooth, the shape and location of a cavity are of great importance. Likewise, identification of local components in microscopic images can be more important than the image as a whole.

Such elements have also been used in content-based retrieval systems, mainly in query-by-user sketch interfaces such as those in Refs. [59–62]. The concern here is not with objects but rather with the basic elements that represent them and with combinations of such elements: four lines, for example, form a square. In that sense, we can include here some "basic shapes" such as a circle, an ellipse, and a polygon.

17.2.2.5 Global Composition. Local structure is characterized by basic elements. *Global composition* refers to the arrangement or spatial layout of these basic elements. Traditional analysis in art describes composition concepts such as balance, symmetry, center of interest (e.g., center of attention or focus), leading line, viewing angle, and so on [9]. At this level, however, there is no notion of specific objects; only basic elements (i.e., dot, line, etc.) or groups of basic elements are considered. In that sense, the view of an image is simplified to an entity that contains only basic syntax symbols: an image is represented by a structured set of lines, circles, squares, and so on. Figure 17.3d presents images with similar composition (both images have objects in the center and the leading line is diagonal). The composition of the images in Figure 17.3e is also similar in that the leading line is horizontal. A composition similarity-search was implemented in Virage [57].

17.2.2.6 Generic Objects. In the first four levels, the emphasis is on the perceptual aspects of the image, and hence, no knowledge of actual objects is required (i.e., recognition is not necessary) to perform indexing, and automatic techniques rely only on low-level processing. Although this is an advantage for automatic indexing and classification, studies have demonstrated that humans mainly use higher-level attributes to describe, classify, and search for images [35–37]. Objects are of particular interest and they can also be placed in categories at different levels: an apple can be classified as a fruit, as an apple, or as a Macintosh apple.

While referring to *generic objects*, we are interested in what Rosch [24] calls the *basic level categories*: the level at which there are attributes common to all or most members of a category — the highest level of abstraction at which clusters of features are assigned to categories. In other words, it is the level at which there are attributes common to all or most members of a category. In the study of art, this level corresponds to *pre-iconography* [13], and in information sciences [29], it is called the *generic of* level. Only general everyday knowledge is necessary to recognize the objects at this level. When viewed as a generic object, a Macintosh apple would be classified as an apple: that is, the level at which the object's attributes are common to all or most members of the category. In the experiments reported in Ref. [24], for example, the authors found that a large number of features were listed as common to most elements of a basic category such as "apple," whereas few features, if any, were listed as common to elements in a superordinate category one level higher, such as "fruit." The general guideline is that only everyday knowledge is required at this level. Techniques to automatically detect objects at this level include a significant amount of work in object recognition (see Section 17.3.2) and techniques in CBIR (e.g., Refs. [8,63]).

A possible difference between our definition and the definitions in Refs. [13,24,29] is that our generic objects may differ from traditional objects. The sky or the ocean would perhaps not be considered objects under the traditional definition, but correspond to our generic objects (as well as traditional ones such as a car, a house, and so on). Examples of the generic objects "car" and "woman" are shown in Figure 17.3. Figure 17.3g shows a "building," but note that in that figure the name of the building is used; hence that particular attribute is a specific object attribute.

17.2.2.7 Generic Scene. Just as an image can be indexed according to the individual objects that appear in it, it can also be indexed as a whole, based on the set of all the objects it contains (i.e., what the image is of). Examples of scene classes include city, landscape, indoor, outdoor, still life, portrait, and so on. Some work in automatic scene classification has been performed by [64–66], and studies in basic scene categories include [22,25].

The guideline for this level is that only general knowledge is required. It is not necessary to know a specific street or building name in order to determine that it is a city scene or to know the name of an individual to know that it is a portrait. Figure 17.3f shows two images with attributes that correspond to a generic scene. Other generic scene attributes for the same pair of images could be "mountain scene," "beach," and so on.

17.2.2.8 Specific Objects. *Specific Objects* can be identified and named. Shatford refers to this level as *specific of* Ref. [29]. Specific knowledge of the objects in the image is required and such knowledge is usually objective because it relies on known facts. Examples include individual persons (e.g., Ana and Alex in Fig. 17.7) and objects (e.g., "Alex" and "Chrysler building" in Fig. 17.3g). In Ref. [67], automatic indexing at this level is performed: names in captions are mapped to faces detected automatically.

When observing the difference between the generic and specific levels, it is important to note that there are issues of indexing consistency that should be taken into account. For example, assume that we have an image of a Siamese cat named Fluffy. Indexer A may decide to label this object as "generic object cat" and "specific object Siamese cat." Indexer B may decide to label this object as "generic object cat" and "specific object Fluffy." Indexer C, on the other hand, may decide to label the object as "generic object Siamese cat" and "specific object Fluffy." All three approaches are correct because the *relationship* between the generic and specific labels is maintained: the specific description is more specific than the generic one in all three cases. The level of specificity chosen, then, depends on the application. In many indexing systems in information sciences, issues of indexer consistency are addressed by the use of templates (e.g., indexers fill in the fields of a template specially designed for the application or type of data) and vocabularies (e.g., indexers can only use certain words). Despite these

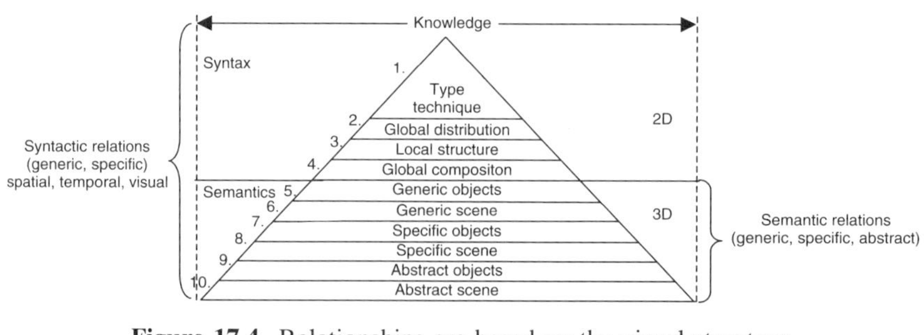

Figure 17.4. Relationships are based on the visual structure.

mechanisms, however, indexer consistency is always an issue that should be addressed. In Section 17.2.3 we discuss some experiments comparing the use of the pyramid with the use of a template developed specifically for indexing images.

17.2.2.9 Specific Scene. This level is analogous to a *generic scene*, but specific knowledge about the scene is used. A picture that clearly shows the Eiffel Tower, for example, can be classified as a scene of Paris (see Fig. 17.3h). The other image in the same figure shows a similar example for Washington D.C.

17.2.2.10 Abstract Objects. At this level, specialized or interpretative knowledge about what the objects *represent* is applied. This is related to *Iconology* in art [13] or the *about* level presented in Ref. [29] (i.e., what the object is about). This is the most difficult indexing level because it is completely subjective, and assessments among different users vary greatly. The importance of this level was shown in experiments [36] in which viewers used abstract attributes to describe images. For example, a woman in a picture may represent anger to one observer but pensiveness to another observer. Other examples of abstract object descriptions appear in Figure 17.3i as "arts" and "law."

17.2.2.11 Abstract Scene. The *abstract scene* level refers to what the image as a whole *represents* (i.e., what the image is about). It was shown in Ref. [36], for example, that users sometimes describe images in affective (e.g., emotional) or abstract (e.g., atmospheric, thematic) terms. Examples at the abstract scene level include sadness, happiness, power, heaven, and paradise. Examples of abstract scene descriptions for the images in Figure 17.3j are "Agreement" and "Industry."

17.2.2.12 Visual Content Relationships. As shown in Figure 17.4, the structure presented can be used to accommodate elements[6] within each level according to two types of relationships: *syntactic* (i.e., related to perception) and *semantic*

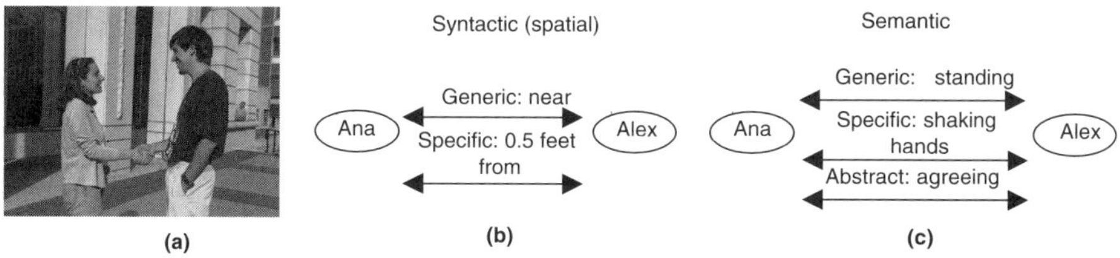

Figure 17.5. Syntactic (spatial) **(a)** and semantic **(b)** relationships that could describe this image.

[6] We use the word *element* here to refer to any image component (e.g., dot, line, object, etc.), depending on the level of analysis used.

(i.e., related to meaning). Syntactic relationships can occur between elements at any of the levels of the pyramid shown in Figure 17.3 but semantic relationships occur only between elements of levels 5 through 10. Semantic relationships between syntactic components could be determined (e.g., a specific combination of colors can be described as warm [68]), but we do not include them in our analysis.

Syntactic relationships include *spatial* (e.g., next to), *temporal* (e.g., before), and *visual* (e.g., darker than) relationships. Elements at the semantic levels (e.g., objects) of the pyramid can have both syntactic and semantic relationships (e.g., two people are next to each other and they are friends). Additionally, each relationship can be described at different levels (*generic, specific*, and *abstract*). In Figure 17.5, we see an example of how relationships at different levels can be used to describe an image — relationships between objects can be expressed at the syntactic and semantic levels.

We note that relationships that take place between the syntactic levels of the visual structure can only occur in 2D space[7] because no knowledge of the objects exist (i.e., relationships in three-dimensional (3D) space cannot be determined). At the *local structure* level, for example, only the basic elements of visual literacy are considered, so relationships at that level are only described between such elements. Relationships between elements of levels 5 through 10, however, can be described in terms of 2D or 3D. We divide *spatial relationships* into the following classes [69]: (*1*) *topological* (i.e., how the boundaries of elements relate) and (*2*) *orientational* (i.e., where the elements are placed relative to each other). Topological relationships include near, far, touching, and so on, and orientation relationships include diagonal to, in front of, and so on.

Temporal relationships connect elements with respect to time (e.g., in video, these include before, after, between, and so on), whereas *visual relationships* refer only to visual features (e.g., bluer, darker, and so on). A more detailed explanation of relationships is provided in Ref. [51].

17.2.2.13 Nonvisual Content. *Nonvisual information* (Fig. 17.6) refers to information that is not depicted directly in the image but is associated with

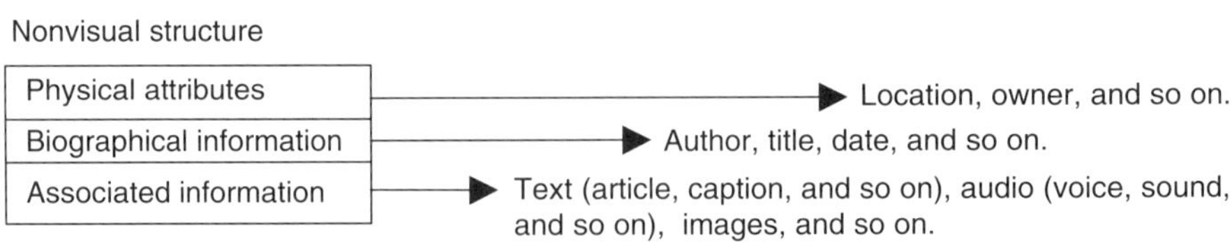

Figure 17.6. Nonvisual information.

[7] In some cases, we could have depth information associated with each pixel, without having knowledge of the objects. Here, we make the assumption that depth information is not available.

it in some way. Although it is possible for nonvisual information to consist of sound, text, hyperlinked text, and so on, our goal here is to present a simple structure that gives general guidelines for indexing.

Often there is *biographical information* including author, date, title, material, and so on. This information may relate to the image as a whole or to any of the items contained within the image.

Associated Information is directly related to the image in some way and may include a caption, article, a sound recording, and so on. *Physical attributes* simply refer to those that have to do with the image as a physical object. These include location of the image, location of the original source, storage (e.g., size, compression), and so on. As an alternative to our division of nonvisual attributes, similar attributes in Ref. [70] were divided into biographical and relationship attributes.

17.2.2.14 Semantic Information Table. We define a *Semantic Information Table* to gather high-level information about the image [29] (Fig. 17.7). The table can be used for individual objects, groups of objects, the entire image, or parts of the image. In most cases, both visual (i.e., levels 5 through 10 in Fig. 17.2) and nonvisual information (i.e., associated information in Fig. 17.6) contribute to populating the table. Although the way in which visual and nonvisual content contribute to populate the fields in the semantic table may vary depending on the specific image, the table does help answer questions such as: "What is the subject (person, object, and so on)? What is the subject doing? Where is the subject? When? How? Why?"

Although the table provides a compact representation for some information related to the image, it does not replace the indexing structures presented in previous sections.

17.2.3 Experiments

Several experiments have been performed [71,72] to evaluate the application of the pyramid presented in this section. First, descriptions were generated manually using the pyramid and an image-indexing template developed independently over several years of research in image indexing [42]. The descriptions were generated by individuals trained in indexing (i.e., with an information sciences background) and also by individuals without any prior indexing experience (i.e., naïve users). Experiments were performed to answer several questions: (*1*) How well can the

	Specific	Generic	Abstract
Who	A. Jaimes, A.B. Benitez	Man, woman	Happy
What action	Discussing MPEG-7	Meeting	Research
What object	Video Monitor VR3230	Video Monitor	Hi-tech
Where	Image Lab, Columbia U.	Indoors	University
When	February 3, 2000	Daytime	Winter
Why	Proposal deadline	Academic work	?

Figure 17.7. Visual and nonvisual information can be used to semantically characterize an image or its parts.

pyramid classify terms, describing image attributes generated by naïve users for retrieval? (*2*) How well can the Pyramid classify the attributes that result from a structured approach to indexing? (*3*) How well can the Pyramid guide the process of generating and assigning a full range of indexing attributes to images? (*4*) How well can the Pyramid classify varying conceptual levels of information (specific, generic, and abstract)? These experiments, reported in detail in Ref. [71], suggest that the Pyramid is conceptually complete (i.e., can accommodate a full range of attributes) and can be used to organize visual content for retrieval. It can be used to guide the indexing process and classify descriptions generated manually. In a related set of experiments (reported in detail in Ref. [73]), it was shown that using the pyramid for retrieval tasks was more effective than using key word search alone. This improvement occurs because a search in which the level of the pyramid is specified helps eliminate ambiguity results. For example, a query with the word "blue" could refer to the color (a syntactic level attribute) or to the emotion (a semantic level attribute). A simple "blue" query can easily return the wrong results if the user is interested in the semantic blue and not in the syntactic blue. In Ref. [73], 29 key words were examined from the descriptions generated by different individuals for 850 images, and it was found that using the pyramid resulted in improvements in precision between 5 and 80 percent.

17.2.4 Summary

In this section, we have discussed a conceptual framework for indexing visual information at multiple levels [7]. The structures are suitable for syntactic and semantic, as well as perceptual and conceptual distinctions. Visual concepts and general concepts have been distinguished, and a structure (the semantic information table) that represents semantic information extracted from visual and nonvisual data has been discussed. These structures allow indexing of visual information at multiple levels and include descriptions of relationships at multiple levels.

Although different indexing levels are more or less useful, depending on the application, a complete content-based retrieval system would index the images and videos according to each level of the structure. In the next section, we examine in more detail how current CBIR techniques relate to this conceptual framework and emphasize that most existing systems operate at syntactic levels.

17.3 CONTENT-BASED TECHNIQUES AND OBJECT RECOGNITION

17.3.1 Content-Based Techniques to Express Semantics: Benefits and Limitations

In this section, we analyze current CBIR techniques in terms of the conceptual structure described in the previous section. We make a distinction between the interface and the indexing process.

The Interface. When users perform searches, they interact with a system to express what they are looking for (Fig. 17.8). Typically, users look for concepts (Section 17.2.1.3) and use an interface to express their search. This is done by

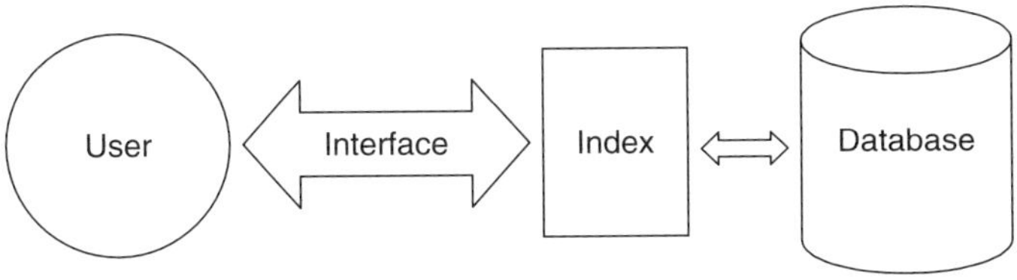

Figure 17.8. A CBIR system consists of three basic components: the *database* (e.g., images), the *indexing information* (e.g., color histograms), and the *interface* (e.g., query-by-example).

providing the system with a representation for a query. The system must then interpret the query and, using the database's indexing information, return relevant images to the user. In some cases, the query representation is fairly straightforward because the interface allows the user and the system to "speak the same language." In other words, the interface lets the users express exactly what they want to express and the index contains enough information to represent a user's interests. For example, a user looks for any image that contains a horizontal line and performs a query by drawing a sketch of a horizontal line. The system can then return images that have a horizontal line. For this query to be successful it is necessary for the user to be able to express his request unambiguously, using the interface, and for the index to have enough information to satisfy that query. Note that in most cases, the interface is used to *represent* a query. In other words, in this particular case, the representation used for the query (i.e., the straight line) matches the query itself very well because the user is actually searching for a straight line. When the user is looking for semantics, however, (levels 5 through 10 in Fig. 17.2), it might be difficult for the system to interpret the representation used to specify the query. The line in the example may represent the surface of the ocean or a landscape.

The interface serves as the *language*[8] between the user and the system: it is the mechanism by which the user and system communicate. Two important aspects of the language used to perform the query are its *expressive power* and its *ease of use*. By expressive power we mean *what* can be expressed using the language. The second aspect refers to *how* difficult it is for the users to formulate the desired query using the language. Of course, such language should be common to system and user, otherwise misunderstandings will occur — in other words, the index must represent information that is not different from what the user expresses using the query. For example, it is common for CBIR systems to use color histograms. When a user performs a query like "show me all the images similar to this sunset," the user may be thinking of a semantic scene query (i.e., level 6 in Fig. 17.2). The index information (color histogram in this example), however, provides access to the images only at the syntactic global distribution level (i.e., level 2 in Fig. 17.2). In this example there is a clear

[8] Note that the strict definition of language requires the existence of symbols, syntax, and semantics.

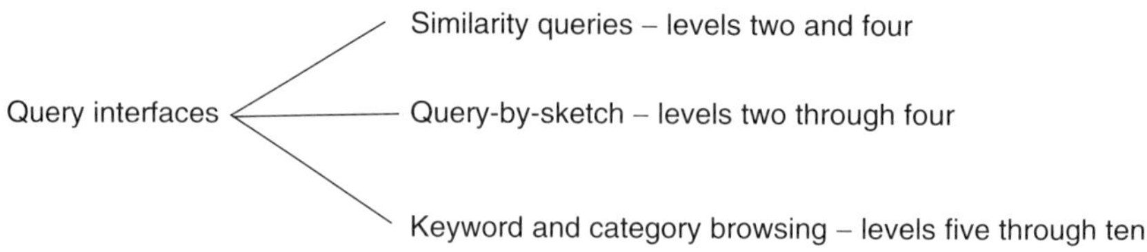

Figure 17.9. Types of query interfaces and relation to the levels of the conceptual structure in Figure 17.2.

mismatch between what the user is expressing and what the system is interpreting. In Figure 17.9 we classify the different interface modalities available in most *existing* CBIR systems[9] and show how they relate to the conceptual structure of Section 17.2.

As the previous example suggests, it is important when designing CBIR systems to be aware of the way in which indexing structures represent information (i.e., structures in Section 17.2). Similarly, query interface modalities play an important role. Each of these interface modalities will be further explained in Section 17.3.1.1.

Indexing

The interface is the language through which the user and the system communicate. The index, on the other hand, is data that provides the access point to the information in the database. Different modalities to index visual content provide access to images at different levels. As depicted in Figure 17.10, indexing techniques in most current content-based retrieval can be approximately divided into two groups, depending on the types of features they use: (*1*) local and global syntax features; and (*2*) local and global semantics.

In the first modality, indexing is usually performed automatically, using color, texture, and other features, at levels two through four of the pyramid of Section 17.2 (Fig. 17.2). In the second one, images are classified according to the objects they contain or according to the scene they represent (e.g., indoor or outdoor). Manual annotation is mostly used at levels 5 through 10 of Figure 17.2, but it can be used at any level, whereas automatic indexing (classification) of semantic features currently occurs only at levels five and six.

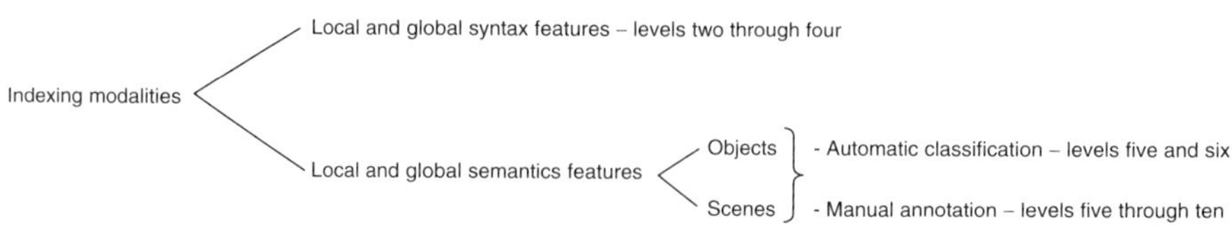

Figure 17.10. Content-based retrieval indexing modalities and their relation to the structure in Figure 17.2.

[9] We use the terms *similarity query* and *query-by-example* interchangeably.

In the sections that follow, we analyze different interface and indexing modalities, stressing the advantages and limitations of each technique.

17.3.1.1 Query Interface Modalities. In this section, we describe the three different interface modalities of Figure 17.9: query-by-example, query-by-sketch, and key word and category browsing. Then we discuss interactive techniques (relevance feedback, learning, and assisting query-by-sketch) and indexing (Section 17.3.1.2).

Query-by-Example. In query-by-example (similarity query) interfaces, the user selects one or more images (or portions of them as in the SPIRE system [74]) and queries the system for images that are similar. Typically, low-level features (e.g., color, texture, and so on) are used to represent the example images and to perform the query. Although this approach is very useful for certain types of databases (e.g., textile fabrics, wall paper, and so on), it suffers from major disadvantages when users are interested in semantic content. This is because low-level features used by current systems do not capture the semantics of the query image and because the concept of similarity is particularly complex with visual information. Although this type of interface is *easy to use*, the *expressive power* of such queries is limited. In certain cases, however, it is possible to use query-by-example interfaces to search for semantics. In the SPIRE system [74], for instance, higher-level objects can be constructed from portions of images. Similarly, in QBIC [56], semantically meaningful regions are manually selected when the database is populated. For example, if the image is from an on-line catalog and represents a person wearing a sweater, only the region corresponding to the sweater would be indexed and the rest of the image would be ignored. When a user performs a query-by-example using an image or a portion of an image, semantic information (e.g., the region from the sweater) is used to search for meaningful results.

As shown by the structures in Section 17.2, semantics can be considered at many different levels. Images (a) and (b) in Figure 17.11, for example, could be considered similar because they show a complete object at some distance. Images (c) and (d) in the same figure are similar because they are close-ups of objects. At the same time, we could say that images (a) and (c) are very similar

(a) (b) (c) (d)

Figure 17.11. An example of images that could be considered similar or dissimilar, depending on the basis used to measure similarity (photographs courtesy of A. Jaimes).

because they contain the same object. They are dissimilar, however, in terms of colors and composition (syntactic attributes).

Many systems allow the user to select the features that are more relevant to each query (e.g., find images that look like this with respect to shape, color, and so on). The functionality of current systems in this respect, however, is not sufficient to allow users to express similarity in terms of syntax or semantics when complex images are used (e.g., photographs in Fig. 17.11).

The concept of similarity depends largely on the index used to represent the images (e.g., the features used) and on the metric used to measure similarity. In most cases, the judgment of similarity varies depending on the context. For example, an observer given three circles and two squares is asked to group the most similar items. If she uses shape, the three circles would be in one group and the squares in a different group. If the size feature is used, however, two small squares and a small circle would be grouped together. Note that "small" depends on how objects are compared, in other words, on the metric used to measure similarity. Another alternative would be to group the elements based on overall similarity (in which shape and size are equally weighted). This is shown in Figure 17.12.

It is apparent from the figure that the similarity of objects depends on the context. If A and B were the only elements, there could be little doubt about placing them in the same group. The work presented in Ref. [75] is based on a similar principle: the meaning of an image can only be defined in the context of a query (e.g., similarity of images in Fig. 17.11). In that work, an exploratory interface is implemented, in which browsing and searching are mixed so that the user explores the database rather than query it. The authors propose the use of the decision cycle model [76,77] to build the interface. The basic idea is that the user should have a global view of the database and should be able to manipulate its environment in a simple way. In the implementation presented by the authors, users can view a set of 100 to 300 images at a time and are able to move the images so that similar ones are closer to each other. Based on the manipulations, the database engine (in this case El Niño [78,79]) creates a new similarity criterion to reorganize the entire collection in the database and present new results to the user. Note that the interface paradigm and the database engine

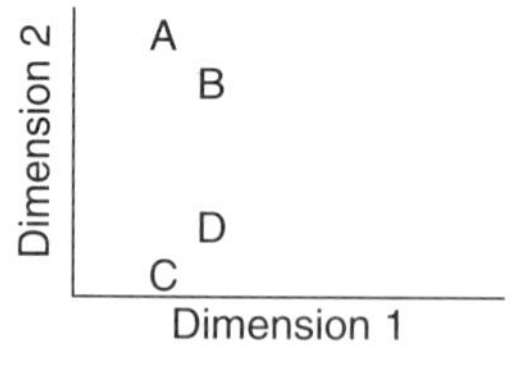

Figure 17.12. An example from Ref. [26] of how four elements can be grouped, depending on the feature used to determine similarity. If we consider overall similarity (measured, in the example, by the Euclidean distance between representative points), reasonable groups would be AB and CD. If we consider dimension 1, the groups would be AC and BD. Considering dimension 2, the groups would be AB and CD.

are separate, but the database engine in this case must satisfy two requirements: it must understand the manipulations performed by the user and it must be able to create similarity criteria as the user interacts with the system.

An important advantage of the query-by-example paradigm is its ease of use. A serious disadvantage of this type of query, however, is the difficulty for the system to understand or know what kind of similarity the user seeks when providing the example (e.g., images of Fig. 17.11 and example of Fig. 17.12). In other words, current similarity queries lack expressive power. A possible approach to improving query-by-example queries is placing the user in a loop so that the system can obtain feedback as the user interacts with the system. This is discussed in the section on interactive techniques below.

Query-by-Sketch. In query-by-sketch systems, users typically draw a sketch corresponding to the image or video they are interested in (Fig. 17.13). In addition to drawing a sketch, the user is usually required to determine the features that are important for each query (e.g., color, texture).

A sketch is a good way of making a precise request to a system because the user has total freedom in arranging different components when creating the sketch. In theory, any image could be retrieved using a sketch query as the user could potentially draw an exact replica of the image of interest. Despite its expressive power, this technique suffers from two major disadvantages when users are searching at the semantic level: (*1*) the queries are difficult to formulate and (*2*) queries are performed in terms of low-level features. Drawing is a

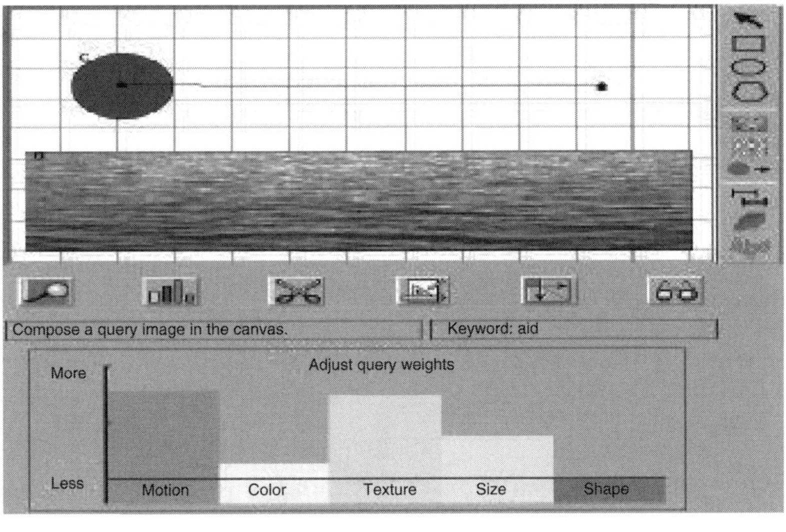

Figure 17.13. A query-by-sketch example from *VideoQ* [60]. In this example, the user has drawn a sketch to represent a water skier. The user has given the water a particular texture and has placed the most importance on motion (indicated by the horizontal line in the sketch) and texture features (followed by size, color, and shape, which is unimportant in this query).

difficult task, particularly for people without any training in drawing or art. The task is simpler for individuals with some training or practice in drawing, but even then, using a computer interface to draw is usually unnatural. Although it is likely that interface devices will continue to improve (e.g., light pens, touch screens, and so on), there are human factors that place inherent limitations on this type of system (e.g., the ability of humans to accurately remember what they are searching for and to draw it).

Regardless of whether the user is able to draw a "good" example to perform the query, the success of the system will depend on how the query is interpreted. In Figure 17.13, the user drew a circle to represent a skier. Similarly, in Figure 17.14, a naive user performs a sketch query, hoping to retrieve an image of a person standing in front of a building. As shown in this illustration, the drawing itself is simply a way of conveying a concept to the system. The sketch does not quite correspond to what the image being searched for actually looks like. In this figure, the photograph on the right is conceptually similar to the sketch but very different in terms of the drawing itself. Current query-by-sketch approaches focus on the form of the sketch (i.e., syntax) and not on what the sketch may represent (i.e., semantics). In that respect, syntax-level techniques (e.g., those in Refs. [59,60]) to interpret sketch queries are insufficient at the semantic level because they do not consider the sketch to be a representation of a concept. Their expressive power is limited to syntax — the language used by the system expresses only syntax. When a user creates a drawing, she usually attaches a semantic meaning to the drawing. For the system, however, the drawing is just a collection of low-level features.

Despite that limitation, users who understand such systems well and have enough practice and ability in drawing their queries can use query-by-sketch systems effectively. Although unsuitable at the semantic level, this approach supports queries that retrieve images based on local structure (i.e., level 3 of Fig. 17.2). In Figure 17.14, a more accurate sketch could be effective in retrieving the desired image, but note that users must know exactly what they are looking for and have exceptional visual memory to remember important details (e.g., size, location, 3D perspective, and so on).

Keyword and Category Browsing. Early image database systems used text as their only interface mechanism, and many new systems still provide this functionality. Although text provides an excellent way to communicate with the system at

Figure 17.14. A sketch used to represent a concept (a person in front of a building), and the image the user may actually want to retrieve.

levels 5 through 10 of the structure of Figure 17.2 (particularly at the abstract levels), it is well known that there are serious limitations to the use of text alone.

Some information is easily accessible using text. A query for a "car" is easily formulated by typing in that key word or browsing in that category. In some applications (e.g., medical systems), some of the information can only be accessed using text: it would be difficult to find a particular patient's X ray otherwise. Text annotations can also carry important image content information that would be difficult to find using a different mechanism (e.g., a medical term to explain an anomaly in an X-ray image). One of the problems, however, is that in most cases there is not enough textual information associated with the images.

However, even when sufficient text information is available, users may still want alternatives to key word search because text alone does not fully express the desired visual content. For example, a radiologist could ask for all mammograms, containing calcifications similar in location and texture to those being analyzed. Although images with calcifications in the desired location could be retrieved using the associated radiological report, textural similarity would be very difficult to express using text. Query-by-example techniques in this type of application would most likely yield much better results than key word and category browsing.

Interactive Techniques. Several techniques have been developed to reduce the limitations of sketch and similarity interfaces. The main goal of such techniques is to increase the expressive power and ease of use of those interfaces. In this section, we discuss approaches in which the results obtained with query interfaces (query-by-example and query-by-sketch) are utilized in a feedback loop by the user.

Relevance Feedback. In *Relevance Feedback* [80,81] a user performs an initial query and the system returns the best matches. (The user can then label those images that are most similar to the ones in which she is interested as positive matches and the ones most dissimilar as negative matches.) The system then performs a new search utilizing the user's feedback. The process repeats as many times as needed as the user continues the search.

Many different relevance feedback approaches have been proposed [55,80,82–85]. In particular, feedback can be *categorical* (i.e., the user indicates what items are in the same category as the target,) or *relative* (i.e., item A is more relevant than item B) [82]. For example, in Ref. [80] the user marks each returned image with one of the following labels: *highly relevant, relevant, no-opinion, nonrelevant*, or *highly nonrelevant*. In Ref. [82], however, the user simply selects the images that are closer to the target concept than the unselected images.

In the PicHunter system [82], for example, a user selects one or more images as examples. A query is performed using those images and the results returned are labeled by the user (images that are most similar to the target are selected). A new query is performed based on the feedback and the process is repeated until the user is satisfied with the results. In PicHunter, the performance of the relevance feedback algorithm is measured in terms of the feedback (number of iterations) required for a user to retrieve a particular item from the database. The feedback loop ends when the user finds the desired image.

The main advantage of relevance feedback is that the search is guided by the user. A drawback of these techniques, however, is that it is assumed that the database is rich enough to return "good matches" that can guide the search process. This may not always be the case. In addition, the problems (and benefits) associated with different types of interfaces outlined in the sections on Query by Example, Query by Sketch, and Keyword and Category Browsing should still be considered (e.g., ways to express similarity, and so on).

Learning. An alternative to performing relevance feedback at the time of the query is to learn what the users want, allowing them to assign class labels to the objects and image classes in which they are interested. In other words, the user may label some image regions with a name such as "sky" and others with a name such as "not sky." The system can then use that information to learn the concept in which the user is interested (e.g., sky) and construct a classifier — a program that, given an input (e.g., a region), makes a decision to determine the class of that input (e.g., sky, not sky). The classifier learned can then be used to automatically label content (e.g., indoor, outdoor image). Once the content is labeled, it can be accessed using the key word and category browsing approach discussed in the Keyword and Category Browsing section. The learning of classifiers is closely related to indexing and classification (Section 17.3.1.2), to object recognition (Section 17.3.2), and to learning object detectors (Section 17.4). The process of learning from the user, however, often requires some form of user interaction, which is related to the other techniques discussed in this section.

In the FourEyes approach [5], for example, the system begins by creating groupings[10] of data, using different features (regions are grouped based on color, texture, and so on). The way in which features are extracted, in turn, depends on different models (e.g., texture features can be extracted using MSAR texture [6] or other models). The user then creates semantically meaningful groupings by labeling regions in images, and the system learns to select and combine existing groupings of the data (generated automatically or constructed manually) in accordance with the input provided by the user. This way, different features can be used for forming different semantically meaningful groupings (e.g., skies are grouped by color features, trees are grouped by texture features). For example, blue skies could easily be grouped using color and texture but other objects (e.g., cars) may be better grouped using shape information. The underlying principles in the system are that models (i.e., used to extract the features used to form groupings) are data-dependent, groupings may vary across users and groupings may also change depending on the task (e.g., the same user may want to group regions differently at different times). Therefore, the system aims to form groupings in many different ways (based on user input) and combine the appropriate groupings so that they represent semantically meaningful concepts (e.g., sky).

---

[10] A grouping in FourEyes is a "set of image regions (patches) that are associated in some way" [5].

FourEyes receives as input a set of images to be labeled by the user. In the first stage, within-image groupings are formed automatically, resulting in a hierarchical set of image regions for each image and for each model. For example, if image A contains trees and a house, the first stage may place all tree pixels in the same group and similarly for the house pixels; thus two different models are used, one for trees and one for houses. Pixels that were used in the tree grouping may also be used in a grouping of leaves (thus resulting in a hierarchical set of regions for each image). In the second stage, the groupings obtained in the first stage are grouped, but this time across the images of the database. In other words, for a given image, the groupings of the first stage are themselves grouped in the second stage with similar groupings of other images. For instance, trees from different images would be grouped together and houses from different images would also be grouped together.

The first two stages in FourEyes are performed off-line. The third stage corresponds to the actual learning process in which the user labels image regions as positive (e.g., sky) and negative examples (not sky) of a concept. The system then tries to select or combine the existing groupings into compound groupings that cover all of the positive examples but none of the negative examples labeled by the user. The selection and combination of existing groupings constitute the learning stage of the system for the goal is actually to find (and combine) the models or features that group the regions according to the labels provided by the user. The groupings learned by the system that cover the positive (and none of the negative) examples labeled by the user are utilized to classify new regions. Regions that have not been labeled by the user are then automatically labeled by the system according to the examples the user has provided (according to the groupings, the systems has found to be adequate). In this stage (when the system labels new regions based on what it has learned) the user can correct the labels assigned by the system in an interactive process. The system then uses this information to modify the groupings it had learned, making learning incremental — the system learns constantly from user input as opposed to learning in a single training session (referred to as *batch learning* [86]).

The approach taken in FourEyes has several advantages: (*1*) several models are incorporated; (*2*) user feedback is allowed; and (*3*) user subjectivity [87] is considered. Inclusion of several models is important, as is evident from the discussion in Refs. [5,6] that no single model is best for all tasks (e.g., different ways of extracting texture features may be useful for different types of texture). User feedback and subjectivity are also very important, for as shown by the discussion in Section 17.2, multiple levels of indexing can be performed. This, however, can be a drawback in the FourEyes system: finding the right concept, given the groupings provided by the user and those generated automatically, can be difficult. The system performs grouping based solely on low-level features, whereas the groupings (examples) provided by the user may be based on higher-level semantic attributes. One way to improve this is to acquire more structured examples (i.e., not just regions, but hierarchies) and to constrain the application domain so that only appropriate features are used in the different grouping stages. Similar issues in a related framework are discussed in Section 17.4.

Assisting Query-by-Sketch. One of the advantages of query-by-sketch techniques is that they allow the user to make very specific queries. A query, however, is used to represent a concept (see introduction of Section 17.3.1). Two disadvantages of this approach, therefore, are that a single sketch query usually retrieves images that are very specific to the sketch, and as discussed in the section on Query by Sketch, it is difficult for the user to formulate the query. For example, if the user draws a sunset with the sun on the left side, only sunsets with the sun in that position will be retrieved[11]. This query will therefore fail to return most sunset images. Hence, for the user to be able to retrieve all of the sunsets, several sketches would have to be drawn. One possible way to expand the coverage of each query is to help the users generate different sketches to represent the concept they are interested in. This approach was taken in the generation of *Semantic Visual Templates* presented in Ref. [88], and described next.

The goal of Semantic Visual Templates (SVT) is to semiautomatically generate sketches that correspond to a concept, using an interaction loop between the system and the user. For example, the user draws an initial sunset query and the system helps the user create other sketch queries to cover different sunsets. This is done by automatically generating other sketch queries and obtaining feedback from the user.

In the SVT work, the *VideoQ* [60] system is used: a user first formulates a sketch query for the desired concept. The initial query is formulated as a set of objects (represented by low-level drawing primitives, such as squares or circles; Fig. 17.13) with spatial and temporal constraints, specified using the interface (e.g., in Fig. 17.13 the horizontal line connected to the circle indicates that the object will move from left to right). During the initial query specification, the user assigns weights to each of the features (e.g., color, motion, and so on) for each of the objects in the query. The system then generates "variations" of each object (to automatically construct new sketches), using the weights specified by the user to quantize the feature space. A low feature weight, for example, indicates that a coarse quantization of the feature space is sufficient. A high feature weight, on the other hand, indicates that the feature is very important — small variations of this feature for the object may impact the retrieval results significantly. In this case, a finer quantization of the feature space is performed. The quantization is used to generate feature variations that are used to construct new sketch queries.

For example, a user wishing to find slalom skiers may perform an initial query that has an object (e.g., the skier represented by a circle) and its motion trajectory. The system automatically generates variations in the features (e.g., generates different colors and motion trajectories for the skier object). The user

[11] We use this as an example. In practice, the user can usually place weights on different features. In this case, it could be possible for the user to indicate that the horizontal position of the sun object is unimportant to his query. However, the sketch query is quite specific and would return only a small percentage of the sunsets in the database.

then selects the plausible feature variations (e.g., the colors that may be possible for the skier and the possible motion trajectories). The system then performs a join on the set of feature variations selected by the user and utilizes the results to generate a set of sketch queries. The sketch queries, in turn, are employed by the user in a relevance-feedback loop that determines the best sketch queries for the concept of interest. In the slalom example, if the user selects four colors and three motion trails, then 12 "sketch queries" are generated. This set is used to perform queries, and with the assistance of relevance feedback, the best sketches (i.e. the SVT) are saved to represent the skier concept.

This technique provides a partial solution to the mapping of syntax to semantics and aids the user in formulating the difficult sketch queries. Its disadvantage, however, is that if the original sketch provided by the user is not successful, the generated templates will also fail. In addition, generation of the templates is a difficult problem because of the large number of possibilities for each component of the sketch. Significant user input is required in formulating the initial query, selecting low-level features (often a difficult task), and providing relevance feedback. In selecting feature variations, an assumption is made that these features are independent, although this may not always be the case.

Although in this approach the queries (syntax) are mapped to concepts (semantics), the queries themselves suffer from the same limitations as regular sketch queries. Syntax (i.e., the sketch) must be used to express semantics (e.g., concepts) (Fig. 17.14). The approach, however, represents an important step toward mechanisms that help the system understand what the user is looking for, and at the same time, employ user feedback to improve performance.

17.3.1.2 Indexing. In this section, we go back to the indexing modalities of Figure 17.10. As mentioned earlier, the interface used to perform a query and the indexing scheme to access the data are tightly linked (Fig. 17.8). With the exception of text-based interfaces (Section 17.3.1.1), in most existing systems, indexing for similarity and sketch queries is performed using low-level features.

Low-level features, however, are not suitable at the semantic level. For example, Figure 17.15 shows two images having very different color histograms but very similar semantic content. In many cases, users perform queries (either sketch or similarity) hoping to retrieve images that are visually and semantically

Figure 17.15. Two images having very distinct color histograms but identical subject matter (photographs courtesy of A. Jaimes). A color version of this figure can be downloaded from *ftp://wiley.com/public/sci_tech_med/image_databases*.

similar but instead obtain images that are similar only in terms of their low-level features.

In low-level feature-indexing, the features themselves are the access points to the visual information. Instead, each image could be classified and assigned one or more labels, which are collections of one or more key words. The labels can be used to access the elements in the database by using key words to perform the queries or through browsing (Section 17.3.1.1).

In this section we outline different techniques to perform indexing, with particular attention to semantic level classification — levels 5 through 10 of the structure in Figure 17.2. In particular, we focus on automatic classification, which provides semantic access points to the contents of the database.

Classification. *Classification* seeks to place images into specific semantic categories (i.e., a *classifier* is a function that, given an input, assigns it to one of k classes). Typically, this is performed at the scene level (e.g., indoor, outdoor, and so on) and the object level (e.g., objects in the image are labeled or the image is labeled with the names of objects it contains). Techniques that automatically perform classification can be approximately placed into three categories: methods using *visual features only*; methods using *textual features only*; and methods using *both visual and textual features.*

In many classification approaches, a training set is used to build the classifier. For example, a training set for an indoor and outdoor scene classifier would consist of a set of indoor images and a set of outdoor images. Each of the approaches described below uses training sets in different ways.

Visual Features. Content-based classification using visual features can be *scene-based* (e.g., using global low-level features [64,89], region configuration-based [90–92]) or *object-based* (e.g., detection of faces in Ref. [93], naked people and horses in Ref. [63], objects defined by the user in Ref. [8]).

Scene Classification. In scene-based classification, the image as a whole is given a semantic label. Examples include indoor-outdoor [64], city-landscape [65,89,94], beach, sunsets [90,91], and so on.

In the particular approach presented in Ref. [64], the image is first divided into a 4×4 grid of 16 blocks. Low-level features are then computed for each block and for the whole image. Features for color (Otha color histogram [95]) and texture (multiresolution simultaneous autoregressive model [96] and DCT coefficients) are computed for each image and for each block. Using a multistage classification approach, the blocks are classified independently and the results are used to classify the images. More specifically, for each image, each of the 16 blocks is classified using a nearest-neighbor classifier [97]. The classification results of each block for each image are concatenated into a feature vector. In the second classification stage, a majority vote classifier is applied to the vectors, yielding a final result for the image.

The division of the image into blocks is useful because it tends to capture the spatial characteristics of images belonging to the same class. For example, in outdoor images, the sky appears at the top, whereas in indoor images, sections of the wall are common in the upper part of the images. Features, such as color and texture, also capture the characteristics of images in each class. Indoor images tend to have textures that are formed mostly by horizontal and vertical edges. The colors and texture of elements that appear in outdoor images are quite different from those in indoor images.

Other approaches similar to the one in Ref. [64] have been developed to classify images. In Ref. [65], for example, images are divided into 10×10 sub-blocks for classification. Features such as edge direction histograms are used to discriminate between city and landscape images.

Approaches to perform scene-level classification can be very effective and thus demonstrate that semantic classification can be achieved using low-level features. Building such classifiers usually requires little user input (e.g., only labeling of the images at the scene level). The accuracy of these techniques, however, is limited by how well the selected features can be used to discriminate between the classes of interest. Additionally, the test sets (if a training set is required) and the size and nature of the training directly affect the accuracy.

The following example shows that the same approach to discriminate between indoor and outdoor scenes yields very inconsistent results, depending on how it is actually applied. In the original work [64], the approach yielded an error rate of 9.7 percent (namely, 90.3 percent of the images were correctly classified), when evaluated on a set of approximately 1,300 consumer photographs. The same approach applied on a different database of 1,675 news images resulted in a 25.8 percent error rate [66]. Balancing the number of indoor and outdoor images in the training set, using the same set of news images, improved the performance of the approach in Ref. [64] to an error rate of 18.89 percent from an error rate of 25.8 percent [66]. One explanation for the initial increase in the error rate (from 9.7 to 25.8 percent reported in Ref. [66]) is that in the particular set of consumer photographs used in Ref. [64], adjacent photographs (in each roll of film) contained similar content; hence, images in the training and test sets were more similar. Placing a restriction to ensure that consumer images in the same film would not be at the same time part of the training and test sets resulted in an error rate of 15 percent, using the approach presented in Ref. [64] (reported in Ref. [66]).

These results show the importance of correctly selecting training and testing sets for a particular application and the importance of paying close attention to the data that is used when evaluating a system or an approach. The appearance of similar images in the same roll of film in that work had an impact on the evaluation of the system. In the work presented in Ref. [98], repetition (i.e., *Recurrent Visual Semantics* of Section 17.4.1) is used to organize the images in rolls of film and help the user create digital albums. In particular, the sequence information in rolls of film is used in conjunction with visual similarity to semiautomatically cluster images together for a user. This is an example of how a characteristic of the data can cause a problem in one application but have a positive impact in a different application, if correctly used. It is important to keep in mind the structure of the data and the way in which it is used.

Object Classification. Several approaches have been devised to perform object-level classification[12]. In the Body-plans approach presented in Ref. [63], specialized filters (e.g., skin for humans, hide for horses) are first applied to the image to detect naked people or horses. Once the filters detect the presence of skin or hide, the extraction of cylinder-like primitives occurs and their configurations are matched against a Body-plan. A Body-plan is a sequence of groups constructed to mirror the layout of body segments in people and animals. For example, a horse has four legs, a trunk, a neck, a head, and so on. To detect a person or a horse, the system tries to construct a sequence of groups according to the Body-plan. In the case of a horse, it would try to collect body, neck, and leg segments. Then, it would try to construct body-neck or body-leg pairs, and so on. Note that each model representation includes a combination of constraints on color, and texture and constraints on geometric properties, such as the structure of individual parts and the relationships between parts. Each segment (e.g., body, neck) is found by a classifier (which, in this case, is a routine that decides if a segment is present or not). The naked-people Body-plan is built manually, and although a learning component is used in the horse classifier, its topology is given in advance. Learning is achieved by constructing an augmented feature-vector that all classifiers (for the segments) use for training. Once individual classifiers are learned, their decisions are used to obtain subclassifiers.

One disadvantage of this approach is that various components of the models are built manually. The filters for skin and hide, for example, are very specific to the naked people or horses application, and applying the same techniques to other classes would require building new filters. Another drawback of this approach is that it is based on cylinder-like primitives — detecting them is often a difficult task due to occlusion, changes in lighting, and so on. (see Section 17.3.2.4). The Body-plans technique, however, demonstrates that models for object recognition can be effectively used in content-based retrieval applications. It also stresses the importance of including real-world constraints on the models (e.g., body-leg pairs) and the possibility of combining manually constructed components with automatic ones. In Section 4, we discuss another approach that addresses some of the disadvantages of the Body-plans technique.

Other approaches (e.g., detection of faces in Ref. [99]) have been successfully applied to content-based retrieval. The WebSeer system [93], for example, uses the face-detection technique developed in Ref. [100] to index images collected from the World Wide Web. In Section 17.3.2.4, we explore the area of object recognition and discuss how it relates to CBIR.

Textual Features. Some existing CBIR systems use manually assigned text terms for indexing [57] in addition to providing access by content (e.g., using color histograms). Other systems, however, automatically use text surrounding the image for automatic classification. In WebSEEk [55], for example, a spider

---

[12] In some cases, we will use the word *detection*. *Classification* assigns an object to a category, whereas *detection* determines the presence of an object.

program [101] automatically collects images and videos from the World Wide Web. From the image URL, terms are extracted (e.g., image-location directory name and file name) and the images are indexed and placed in semantic categories according to the terms. For example, if a web page contains a link such as *http://www.ee.columbia.edu/students/peter.jpg*, the terms "students" and "peter" are automatically extracted and used to index that particular image and to place that image in the semantic category "people." Users that perform text queries using the word "students" or browsing in the "people" category would be able to find this particular image. Additionally, the type of each image (e.g., color photograph, or color graphic) is automatically determined by using visual features and Fisher discriminant analysis (see [102], Chapter 3).

In many cases the WebSEEk approach successfully indexed the images but, as expected, several errors occurred mainly because of unreliability of the text associated with those images. In one particular case, for example, 22 of 23 images under the Ferrari Sports car category were correctly classified. The error occurred because the system found an image with the file name ferrari.jpg, which was not the image of a car but of a person with that last name.

The main drawback of this approach is that it assumes a strong correlation between the content of the image and the related text, but text can often be unreliable. For certain sources, however (e.g., newspapers, newsgroups, and medical images), the associated text is a valuable source of information and can be used effectively for classification (see the next section).

Visual and Textual Features. Some work has been performed on classifying images using a combination of visual and textual features. In some approaches, classification is done using textual and visual features separately. In Ref. [90], for example, images are classified using text, and images that cannot be successfully classified using text are then classified using visual features based on *Composite Region Templates (CRT)*. The basic idea in *CRTs* is that images that belong to the same semantic class show a similar configuration of regions. For example, in a beach scene, the top region is blue (sky), with a yellow region (sand) beneath it. Initially, a string is generated that represents the configuration of regions in an image in a vertical scan (e.g., blue followed by yellow, and so on). Instead of directly comparing the strings, region configurations called *Composite Region Templates* are created. A *CRT* is a relative ordering of M symbols from the string (e.g., "blue yellow" for M = 2). For example, suppose we have two strings that represent two images and their respective regions: $S_a = s_0s_1s_2s_3$ and $S_b = s_0s_1s_3$. The *CRT* $T = s_0s_3$ occurs once in each image. Note that if regions s_0 and s_3 are important for that semantic class (e.g., sky and sand in a beach class), they will be accounted for in S_a and S_b, regardless of other regions in the image (such as s_1 and s_2) that would be taken into account if the strings were compared directly. The system classifies images by first extracting regions and generating a *CRT*. A decision is then made based on the frequencies of the image's CRT with respect to the training set (e.g., the probability that the image is a beach scene, given that there is a blue patch followed by a yellow patch). The use of *CRTs* is similar to the work presented in Ref. [91], in which region configurations are also used to perform scene classification.

Another method for combining textual and visual features is to perform the classification using one of the modalities and to augment the classification using the other modality. For example, in the work presented in Ref. [67], visual features are used to automatically detect faces, and textual features are automatically extracted from image captions. Names extracted from the captions are then automatically linked to the faces detected.

The approach presented in Ref. [66] proposes scene classification of images into the indoor and outdoor categories, integrating visual and textual features. The text information accompanying the image is used to compute a TF*IDF score. For a single caption, a word's TF (term frequency) is the number of times the word appears in the caption. The word's IDF (inverse document frequency) is computed from a training set (e.g., a set of captions for indoor images) as the log of the ratio of the total number of captions to the number of captions in the training set that contains the word. The TF*IDF scores are computed for the caption of each image to be classified. In addition, the TF*IDF scores for all captions associated with each class (indoor, outdoor) are computed. An image receives a score, based on the caption, by computing the dot product of the TF*IDF score obtained for the caption and the score of each of the classes in question.

In an analogous manner, an OF*IIF (object frequency, inverse image frequency) score is computed for each image (and the training set), based on visual features instead of text. Each image is divided into a set of regions (i.e., objects), and the frequencies of those regions are used to calculate the scores for each class. An image is classified by computing dot products of TF*IDF and OF*IIF vectors. For indoor and outdoor classes, integration of the two scores resulted in an error rate of 13.8 percent. Results in Ref. [66] showed an improvement of approximately 12 percent over other image classifiers based on visual information alone. Integration also showed a 3 percent increase in classification accuracy over the TF*IDF approach alone and a 4 percent improvement over OF*IIF alone. These results demonstrate that better performance can be achieved by integrating textual and visual features.

The three approaches discussed in this section show possible ways in which textual and visual information can be combined. In Ref. [90], text classification is performed first, followed by classification using visual features. In Ref. [67], textual information augments the result of visual classification (face detection). Lastly, in Ref. [66], the benefits of combining visual and textual features are explored.

In addition to improving performance, text can help in indexing images at higher semantic levels (i.e., levels 5 through 10 in Fig. 17.2). One of the common problems, however, is that the use of both modalities is not always possible because text is not always available. When it is available, it can often be unreliable (e.g., text accompanying web documents in Ref. [90]). Additionally, it may come from different sources and have strong variations in style and quality.

Despite some of the technical difficulties associated with the use of features from different modalities (e.g., visual and textual), their use is of extreme importance for indexing visual content in terms of semantics (see the news application in Ref. [103]). Research in this direction is likely to increase and continue to contribute to better retrieval systems.

Manual Annotation. Manual annotation continues to be of great importance for indexing visual information (for searching and browsing as discussed in Section 17.3.1.1). One reason for this is that often a great deal of knowledge is required to identify certain aspects of images. In the medical domain, for example, a simple annotation can be a powerful index to an image that exhibits certain characteristics. For example, it is worth remembering that the radiologist does *not* make the diagnosis: it is the appropriate specialist that combines the radiological report with other data (such as the results of laboratory tests and the case history) to produce a diagnosis. Such annotations are of extreme importance and although it is conceptually possible to assign some of them automatically, with the current state of the art, no automatic system is able to replace human annotation in many scenarios.

In other domains, emotive attributes (e.g., sad or happy) can be manually assigned to the images. In the work presented in Ref. [36], for example, it was shown that users employ emotive attributes to describe and access images. Although some attempts have been made to automatically index images at those levels (e.g., Ref. [68]), manual annotation continues and is likely to continue to be crucial in many CBIR systems.

In the future, we envision systems that facilitate manual annotation of visual information and allow users to exploit that information when searching.

17.3.1.3 Content-Based Retrieval Techniques in Context. In this section, we place the main content-based retrieval techniques in the context of the visual indexing structure presented in Section 17.2. Rather than attempting to be exhaustive in citing techniques in CBIR (for surveys, see [3,4,104], among others), the goal of this classification is to give the reader an understanding of where each technique fits in a framework that describes the multiple levels of visual information. The diagram in Figure 17.16 shows the level of indexing that each technique covers. The classification used in this diagram is by no means exhaustive (a list of recent commercial and prototype systems can be found in Ref. [1]) — a particular work may very well fit into more than one level of the pyramid. For example, the Chabot [105] system uses a combination of textual and visual features for integrated image queries, thus spanning several levels of the pyramid.

As the diagram suggests, little work in CBIR has been done to index images at the object and scene levels. The discussion in Section 17.2, however, underlined the importance of object-level indexing. Because object-recognition has been an active research area within computer vision for over 30 years, we outline some of the main techniques in that area and relate that work to CBIR, in the following section.

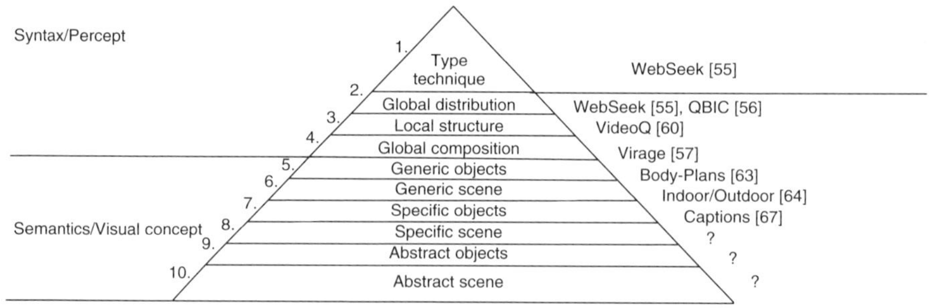

Figure 17.16. Examples of current content-based retrieval placed next to some of the levels of the pyramid at which they provide functionality. There are many more systems for levels one through four, but very few systems for levels 5 through 10 (marked by a question).

17.3.2 Object Recognition

Object recognition is perhaps the largest area within computer vision. In this section, we give a brief overview of some techniques for two-dimensional object recognition. A complete review and classification of all the approaches would be a very difficult task. The goal here is to give the reader a general understanding of some of the main techniques. There are many ways in which different techniques can be grouped and the divisions below are presented to aid in the explanations rather than to classify different approaches. Extensive reviews can be found throughout the computer vision literature (e.g., [106,107]).

First, we give a brief overview of object recognition (model-based and classification approaches). Then, we outline important knowledge representation techniques and discuss the differences between object recognition and CBIR.

17.3.2.1 The Object Recognition Problem. The goal of object recognition is to determine *which* objects are present in a scene and *where* they are located [108].

There are many approaches to the object recognition problem in the computer vision literature. In general, however, recognition involves three basic components (Fig. 17.17): (*1*) the image, (*2*) the features extracted from the image (e.g., geometric features, and so on), and (*3*) a decision process based on those features. The features can be pixel intensity values or complex geometric representations, among others. The decision process depends not only on the features extracted from the image but also on the type of knowledge the system uses in making a

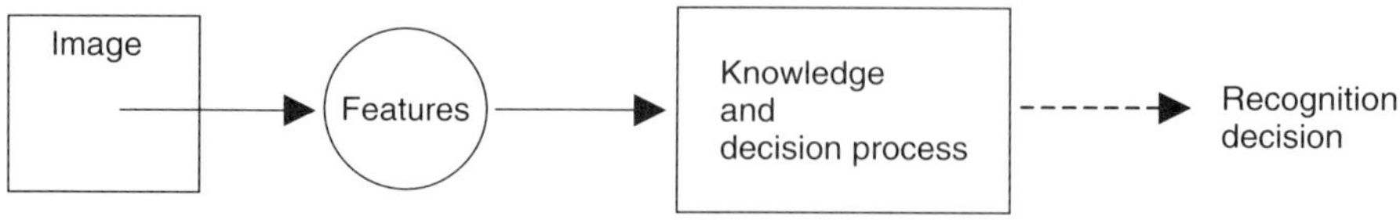

Figure 17.17. Basic components of an object recognition system.

decision. There are many variations in how a decision is made, what knowledge is included, and how such knowledge is represented internally.

One possible strategy for recognition is to have a detailed model (e.g., with detailed geometric constraints) for each object (or type of object) to be recognized and to try to match image features to each model. Traditionally, this approach is referred to as *model-based* recognition, described next.

Model-Based Recognition. A *model* is an internal representation for each object that is to be recognized. The recognition process consists of a search for correspondences between components of a model and observations in an image. For example, to recognize a square, using the simple model of a square in Figure 17.18, the object recognition process would entail finding two corners as determined by the model in the model database.

Given a set of models in a model database, the search strategy used to find a match between a model and the observed features can be classified into either *model-driven* or *data-driven* [109]. In the model-driven approach, a model is selected from the database and the image is searched in order to find components that match that model. In the data-driven approach, the system picks a component from the image (e.g., one of the lines) and tries to find the model that best matches that component. In both cases, recognition is complete when a correspondence is found between all of the components of a model and the observations in the image.

Regardless of whether the recognition strategy is model- or data-driven (or a combination of both), the recognition process can be formulated as having three stages [110]: *selection*, *indexing*, and *matching*. For example, in the work presented in Ref. [110], object recognition is performed by selecting a subset of the image data, indexing (i.e., searching) the object models from a model database, and matching the models and the image data. Many systems have followed this three-stage process.

As the number of models and the complexity of each model increases, the model indexing process becomes more complex, requiring the use of special structures and techniques for efficient recognition. Efficient indexing of the models is important in supporting scalability of model-based approaches. One technique, the data-driven indexed-hypotheses technique [109], provides a data structure for model-related data so that during recognition, models can be

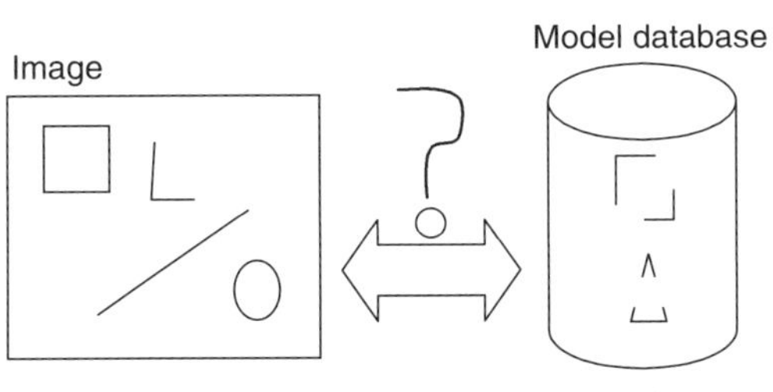

Figure 17.18. An image and a database of models.

efficiently added to a database and the search for a model component that best matches a given image feature can be efficiently performed.

In general, many techniques use *hypothesize-and-test* algorithms to find correspondence. A hypothesis is formed first (e.g., there is a square in the image). Then tests are performed to determine whether that hypothesis is correct or not (i.e., find a correspondence between the model and the elements in the image). As the example suggests, the features used to represent the image, the model used, and the decision process can be treated independently, although they are closely related.

Classification. The object recognition task can be characterized as a classification problem. In model-based recognition there is usually a search for correspondence between a *model* for a single object and the image *features*. When a distinction between classification and recognition is made[13], the former usually refers to types of objects (e.g., face, plane, boat), whereas the latter usually refers to specific instances (e.g., face of Bill Clinton, F-16 plane, and so on). Some researchers [111] have made such distinctions between generic objects[14] (e.g., chairs) and specific objects (e.g., a specific type of chair).

In Section 17.4, we will revisit the classification task and discuss how it can be applied to object recognition in the context of content-based retrieval.

17.3.2.2 Model Representation. The discussion in Section 17.3.2.1 emphasized that recognition implies the use of knowledge during the process (unknown objects cannot be recognized). In this section, we give a brief overview of some of the major knowledge representation techniques [112] used in object recognition [113]. We argue that although some of these techniques have not been widely used in object recognition and CBIR, their use and importance is likely to increase due to the significance of knowledge representation in future CBIR systems. This is specially likely in systems that integrate different types of data (audio, text, video, and so on).

Over the last few years, the number of ways in which models can be represented has grown significantly. Some of the earlier techniques discussed here have been applied to recognizing 2D and 3D objects, under different types of constraints and for different applications.

Template-Matching. One of the simplest ways to model an object is to have a template of a particular view of the object. During recognition, the template is simply swept over the image in an attempt to maximize cross-correlation (e.g., find the best match between the template and the image features). Template-matching tries to find the best embedding of a template subimage to an observed image, over all translations and rotations. In some cases, multiple two-dimensional views of the same object are stored as templates and the recognition

[13] This distinction is not strictly necessary. In fact, model-based approaches and classification approaches have similar components and can be used to recognize the same objects. The term *classification*, however, is commonly used in the field of machine learning, and recently in CBIR.

[14] Note that this distinction differs from the generic/specific distinctions of Section 17.2. Here, a generic object is a representation of a set of specific objects.

process tries to find the best pixel-level matches between the template and the image.

In the work presented in Ref. [114], template-matching was used to index news video (e.g., recognize news anchor scenes).

Template-matching is simple but can be computationally expensive, and it is very restrictive in the sense that the templates must closely match the observed objects.

Production Systems. In this paradigm, a model is represented by a set of production ("if-then") rules, which are usually constructed manually. During the recognition process, an if-then rule is executed only when the "if" part of the rule is matched. Using this mechanism, the designer of the system can control the way in which the rules are applied and thus search for correspondence between the models and the image components.

Production systems are very successful in the medical domain (text only), enabling diseases to be diagnosed based on a set of rules obtained from an expert. In the MYCIN system [112], for example, it was found that the production system could actually outperform experts in diagnostic tasks.

The same principle has been applied, less successfully, to recognizing objects in 2D images, in aerial image interpretation, and in other tasks. For example, in one of the earliest rule-based image analysis systems [95], semantic labels are assigned to regions in color images of outdoors scenes. The initial image is segmented and a symbolic top down analysis of the regions is performed using production rules — each region is labeled according to the set of rules. In this system, rules included the following relations: the sky touches the upper edge of the picture, the road touches the lower edge of the picture, and so on. The system is capable of recognizing four objects and four subobjects.

In another early rule-based system [115], a similar approach is used to recognize objects in aerial images. In this system, the number of rules is close to 500. This exemplifies one of the drawbacks of this technique: although rules in these systems are easily understood by humans, as the number of rules grows, maintenance and understanding of the rules becomes more complex. Generation of the rules is often a difficult task as well. The same authors present a set of tools for knowledge acquisition in that domain in Ref. [116]. Despite their disadvantages, rule-based systems can be powerful because they allow modularity, easy expansion, and natural expression (i.e., human readable rules).

Semantic Networks. Representing topological and inclusion relationships with rules tends to be very cumbersome. In contrast, semantic networks allow for richer representations of knowledge (an important advantage of semantic networks). A semantic network is a method of knowledge representation, using a graph made up of nodes and arcs, with the nodes representing objects (and their parts) and arcs representing the relationship between the objects [112]. Examples of relationships include part and subpart, specialization, and adjacency. Little work has been done in object recognition using semantic networks, but their use is likely to gain importance in CBIR systems.

Blackboard Systems. The goal of blackboard systems [86] is to integrate the knowledge of different "experts" (e.g., a sky recognizer, a grass recognizer) into a single framework. Each expert is called a knowledge source (*KS*), which is basically a procedural module, and the experts act independently but interact and exchange information by using a blackboard. A blackboard usually consists of an area in memory that the different experts can write to and read from. A separate entity, called the *scheduler* (usually a set of if-then rules), decides when to use each knowledge source. Examples of systems that use this paradigm include [117] and [118].

The main difference between production and blackboard systems is that production systems handle simple if-then declarative statements, whereas in blackboard systems, knowledge sources may be complex software modules. The drawbacks, however, are the same: manually constructed rules are difficult to generate and maintain.

An alternative that allows the combination of different experts is belief networks [119]. A belief network represents the joint probability distribution for a set of variables. This is represented by a directed graph in which nodes represent variables and arcs represent conditional dependency. Each variable (node) is associated with a conditional probability table that specifies the conditional distribution of the variable given its immediate parents in the graph. Belief networks can be used to represent causal dependence and to integrate the inputs of different classifiers (e.g., the value of a variable could be determined by a classifier). In the work presented in Ref. [120], different object detectors (i.e., experts) are combined to classify images. The probability that an image is an outdoor image, for example, is computed from the probability scores produced by different classifiers (for example, a classifier that detects sky, a classifier that detects vegetation, etc.). In this case, the "rules" correspond to a network of nodes and the directed arcs determine the order of evaluation. One of the advantages is that the network can, in principle, be learned automatically from the training set provided by the user. In other words, the network structure does not have to be manually constructed. In practice, however, this is not the case: finding an optimal network structure given a data set is an NP-complete problem, and suboptimal network structures often have very poor performance (in the example above, the learning algorithm could produce a network in which the outdoor and indoor variable is a precursor of both sky and vegetation nodes). The structure, then, is usually constructed manually, but the conditional probability tables associated with each node are computed automatically.

17.3.2.3 Transform Methods. As discussed earlier, we can characterize the object recognition problem as a classification problem. The majority of model-based systems have relied heavily on shape-based descriptions to represent the geometry of the objects. The goal in many of these systems is to recognize objects from any viewing angle, both in two- and three-dimensional scenarios.

A different set of techniques, however, has focused on *appearance matching*. Under this paradigm, object models are constructed as collections of images of the object in various positions, orientations, and lighting conditions. Features are extracted from the images in one domain (e.g., spatial) and in some cases transformed to other domains (e.g., frequency). A very successful technique consists of representing images using an eigen (function, image) decomposition and performing the classification using the decomposition coefficients. In many of these techniques, though, either good automatic segmentation results or the existence of a single object on a uniform, known background are assumed (e.g., [121,122]).

17.3.2.4 Object Recognition for Content-based Retrieval. Object recognition for content-based retrieval can be formulated the same way as the traditional object recognition problem: determining *which* objects appear in an image and *where* they appear.

Differences Between Object Recognition and CBIR. Although research in object recognition goes back to more than 30 years, most of the work in this area has focused on the recognition of simple isolated objects in highly constrained environments in which factors such as viewpoint, occlusion, scale, lighting, noise, and sensor quality (e.g., cameras, and so on), are carefully controlled. In content-based retrieval, however, a few of these constraints hold; many of the traditional object recognition techniques have limited applicability for CBIR.

Although most of the work on object recognition has focused on use of knowledge-based systems for finding correspondence (e.g., model-based recognition), the majority of content-based retrieval techniques have focused on similarity: images are searched or classified according to how similar they are to a set of examples. Although this is rapidly changing, little domain knowledge is usually included in CBIR systems.

In object recognition, the goal has often been to *precisely* determine which objects appear in a scene and where they are located. In an industrial inspection system or a robotics system, for example, there is a computable cost for errors in recognizing an object and its exact location, and requirements are often posed in terms of system accuracy. In contrast, in most content-based retrieval applications, the accuracy requirements vary widely and performance is measured differently (in terms of precision and recall).

Another major difference is the involvement of the user: in traditional object recognition, the goal is to build systems that work without user input. In CBIR, humans are the final users of the systems developed. This has many implications not only in terms of performance but also in terms of the subjectivity involved.

The New Challenges. Despite the recent advances in object recognition and the successful application of techniques in certain domains, all of the recognition systems developed to date[15] have serious limitations if they are to be applied to the general problem of content-based retrieval. Of course, the success of the techniques depends largely on the contents of the database, the user, and the purpose.

[15] This is rapidly changing. Many object recognition researchers are developing new techniques and applying previous ones that are specific to CBIR.

A database of simple objects with controlled lighting conditions and uncluttered background, for example, can benefit greatly from many of the traditional object recognition approaches.

Traditional object recognition techniques, however, face new challenges when applied in the context of content-based retrieval. We outline some of the major difficulties, which cannot usually be controlled in CBIR applications.

- Illumination: the appearance of objects can vary significantly under different lighting conditions.
- Extraneous features: shadows and specular reflections make feature extraction more difficult.
- Occlusion: parts of objects are often covered by other objects, complicating the recognition process.
- Viewpoint: large variations of viewpoint occur.
- Scale: objects and textures appear in many different sizes.
- Noise: color variations and other imperfections.
- Clutter: presence of numerous unmodeled objects in the scene.
- Background: foreground-background separation is nontrivial.
- Types of objects: rigid, deformable, and flexible objects. Existence of nontraditional objects, such as the sky, water, and trees.
- Types of models: geometric models typically used in object recognition do not necessarily coincide with "models" used by humans. For example, a car jack is usually thought of in terms of its function, not its geometric characteristics. Novel model representations may be necessary.
- Ability to adapt: there is a large number of objects in realistic scenes, therefore it is desirable to have systems that can learn to detect new objects (instead of having an expert construct a detector for each object), and easily adapt to variations in realistic scenes (lighting, and so on).

For object recognition approaches to be applicable to general content-based retrieval (face detection is a good example), they must more closely resemble general vision systems [107]. They should be able to adapt to different conditions (e.g., lighting, occlusion, and so on), make more use of world knowledge, and be suitable for application under fewer constraints. These three aspects — *adaptability*, *knowledge*, and *constraints* — represent the major limitations of current systems. For example, most of the systems described in Ref. [107] "know" a limited set of objects: four objects and subobjects in outdoor scenes [95], area classes (vegetation, buildings, and so on) [123], airplanes [124], lamps, desks, and so on. These systems use limited sets of objects, follow top-down interpretation, and rely heavily on prediction. Although the inclusion of specific knowledge is beneficial, future systems for CBIR must be scalable in the number of objects they can recognize and must be easily adaptable to the many variations encountered in domains with few constraints. Therefore, knowledge representation (this section) and adaptability are likely to play an important role in future CBIR systems.

17.3.3 Summary

In this section, we analyzed current techniques in CBIR from the perspective of the conceptual framework of Section 17.2. In particular, we separated the CBIR problem into interface and indexing components. The interface of a CBIR system helps the user formulate the query, and indexing provides the access points to the information stored in the database. We discussed the major interface paradigms and their advantages and disadvantages.

We emphasized that when users are looking for semantics (i.e., levels 5 through 10 of the conceptual structure of Fig. 17.2), there is a significant gap between what users are looking for and what can be expressed through existing query-by-sketch and query-by-example interfaces. The interface is meant to provide a common language through which user and system can communicate. We identified difficulties in two areas: (*1*) lack of expressive power of the interface and (*2*) difficulties in formulating queries, using the language of the interface. Many query-by-example systems do not provide sufficient expressive power. Query-by-sketch systems prove difficult to use due to the user's inability to provide an accurate sketch. One option to help the user formulate the query in both cases is to employ relevance feedback mechanisms.

When searching for elements at the syntactic level, however, current interfaces allow an expressive power not provided by traditional text-based systems.

We discussed the major approaches to indexing in CBIR and related them to the different levels of the pyramid in Figure 17.2. We also emphasized the importance of text-based techniques and manual indexing of elements in a database. Our discussion argues that the majority of techniques work well at syntactic levels (levels 1 through 4 in Fig. 17.2) but not at semantic levels. We described how recent efforts in CBIR are moving toward indexing content at the semantic level. In particular, we discussed how classification is being used to index scenes and objects. We gave a brief overview of some object recognition techniques and discussed how these techniques relate to content-based retrieval. Many of the techniques used in traditional object recognition approaches are very useful. Indeed, the majority of CBIR techniques have their roots in traditional computer vision and pattern recognition. Perhaps one of the biggest challenges is to apply object recognition under looser sets of constraints. One possibility for widening the scope of object recognition techniques is to make them as flexible as possible by using learning techniques. In particular, we argued that one of the strongest limitations of current object recognition approaches is their lack of flexibility. In Section 17.4, we discuss an approach to content-based retrieval in which users can define their own models and in which object detectors are built by using machine learning.

17.4 LEARNING VISUAL OBJECT DETECTORS: THE VISUAL APPRENTICE

One of the main limitations of many CBIR systems that perform classification or detect objects is that many or all of their components are built manually. As the number of objects to be recognized grows, this approach becomes impractical. First, the algorithms used are *static* — an expert must manually perform all changes. Second, class definitions depend on the experts that build the systems, thus the concepts in the database may not match the concepts the user has in mind when searching. Although specialized algorithms can be very useful in some domains (e.g., face recognition), we argue that successful content-based retrieval systems should be *dynamic*. Algorithms should be as general as possible so that they can be applied in several domains, and they must exhibit enough flexibility to allow users to determine the classes in which they are interested.

One way to achieve flexibility is to use machine learning techniques [86,125] to build dynamic systems. This is the approach to CBIR discussed in this section. Before applying such techniques, however, it is important to identify *how* and *where* machine learning might be used in the context of content-based retrieval.

17.4.1 Recurrent Visual Semantics: Learning Opportunities

In Ref. [126], *Recurrent Visual Semantics* (*RVS*) was defined as the repetitive appearance of elements (e.g., objects, scenes, or shots) that are *visually similar* and have a common level of meaning within a specific context. Examples of domains in which RVS can be easily identified include news, consumer photography [98], and sports.

Baseball video provides a good example of RVS as a result of the fairly standard way in which cameras are placed in the broadcast of professional games, resulting in repetition of visually similar elements that have a common level of meaning. This repetition occurs at various levels: *objects* (e.g., players), *scenes* (e.g., the batting scene in Section 17.4.3), *shots* (e.g., the camera motion after a homerun occurs), and *shot sequences* (e.g., a homerun shot sequence often includes the batting scene, a scene of the player running, etc.).

The first step in deciding whether learning techniques are applicable (in the context of content-based retrieval) is to identify the existence of *RVS*. In other words, a domain is chosen and the repetitive elements (objects, shots, scenes) are identified. We can refer to these as the *basic repetitive elements*. Note that these elements can be similar at different levels (e.g., in terms of syntactic or semantic attributes). The main concern in this section, however, is with *visually similar* elements (i.e., visual concepts in Section 17.2.1.3 that are visually similar).

The existence of *RVS* motivates the approach of using learning techniques in content-based retrieval. Using this concept, we can identify domains in which learning techniques can be used to build automatic classifiers (for objects or scenes). The existence of repetition facilitates training, and the domain constrains future data inputs to the classifiers, thus decreasing the possibility of errors.

17.4.2 Visual Learning

Machine learning has been employed in CBIR in a number of different ways. Many systems have focused on performing automatic classification of visual content, particularly, *generic scene* classification (indoor-outdoor [64,66], city-landscape [89]), and object recognition (faces [93], naked people, and horses [63]. Other techniques, such as *Relevance Feedback* (Section 17.3.1.1), also use some machine learning concepts.

In Section 17.3.1.1, we described the FourEyes system, which deals with user subjectivity. The FourEyes system, however, does not allow the definition of complex objects that are divided into parts. In Section 17.3.1.2, we described the body-plans approach, which allows the definition of complex object models. The limitation of the latter technique is that many of the components of the system are built manually and require expert knowledge (e.g., the skin filter).

Learning in computer vision has also been a very active research area, with new developments in the last few years [111,127]. The main difference between the approach discussed in this section and previous work in object recognition is the role the user plays in defining objects and the lack of constraints imposed by the system (e.g., no constraints on lighting conditions, etc.). There are also many technical differences between the different approaches that incorporate machine learning. These differences range from the representation of the data (e.g., features used) to the learning algorithms and how they are applied. Other issues include the application domain, selection of training data, and operational requirements (e.g., speed, computational complexity).

Here, we discuss an approach toward content-based retrieval in which user subjectivity is considered but generic algorithms are used. In the *Visual Apprentice* (VA) [8], users define visual object models in terms of a multiple-level *object-definition hierarchy* that models a scene as a collection of objects, an object as a collection of object parts, and so on. As the user provides examples from images or video, different learning algorithms learn classifiers for different parts of the user-defined hierarchy. The resulting hierarchy of classifiers (a *Visual Object or Scene Detector* — VOD), automatically classifies images or videos based on the user's interests. This approach is flexible because each user can have a personal set of *detectors*, and framework components *dynamically* change according to the training data (i.e., different features and classifiers at each node of the hierarchy).

17.4.3 Overview of the Visual Apprentice Framework

As discussed in Section 17.2, users are often interested in objects and their parts. In the VA presented in Ref. [8], users can build automatic visual object detectors, using an object-definition hierarchy consisting of the following levels (Fig. 17.19): (*1*) *region*, (*2*) *perceptual*, (*3*) *object part*, (*4*) *object*, and (*5*) *scene*[16]. Using this

[16] A hierarchy such as this one could be recursive, meaning that an object could be infinitely divided into subparts. We have chosen the five levels presented because they provide an intuitive representation that is useful in practice.

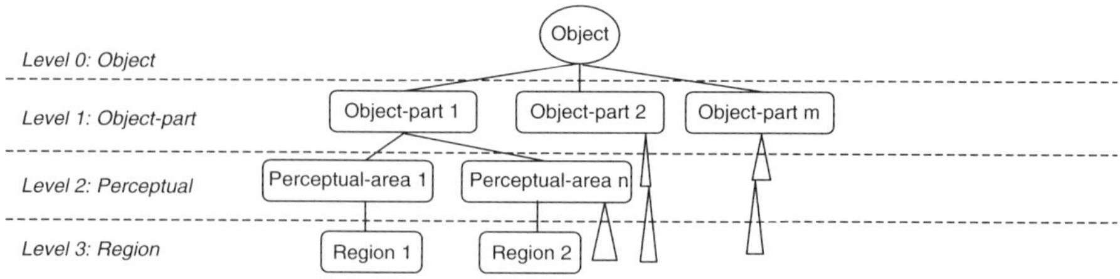

Figure 17.19. General object-definition hierarchy. Note that a scene (not shown in the figure) is a collection of objects and corresponds to the highest level.

basic framework, users can define hierarchies to model objects or scenes. In other words, the user explicitly decides how a scene should be modeled: what its objects are, their corresponding object parts, and so on. Instead of constructing the model manually (e.g., explicitly stating what the exact spatial relationships are), however, the user defines a structure similar to that of Figure 17.9 and labels training examples.

The VA is concerned with visual (i.e., visual concept) rather than conceptual (i.e., general concept) classification. This distinction is of great importance because, as mentioned in Section 17.2, a semantic label implies information at multiple levels. Interest is in the visual appearance of objects and, in particular, in letting users define classes in those terms.

Studies of cognition and human vision have shown that during visual recognition, humans perform grouping of features at different levels [128,129]. The highest level of grouping is semantic: areas that belong to an object are grouped together. An object, however, can be separated into object parts, which consist of perceptual areas: areas that we perceive categorically. Categorical perception (CP) is best described as a qualitative difference in how similar things look or sound, depending on whether or not they are in the same category [14]. The best example of categorical perception is color [130] (see also [131,132]): when observing an object, we often "group" similar colors (e.g., we say the jeans are blue, although they may have different shades of blue). Alternative models that represent objects and scenes in terms of their parts have also been proposed in the CBIR community (e.g., [133–135]). For example, the object definition hierarchy of the VA framework is similar to the definition of composite visual objects presented in Ref. [135], with the difference that classifiers in the VA are learned automatically.

The VA framework is based on classification and grouping at each level in Figure 17.19. An object definition hierarchy is defined as follows:

(5) *Scene*: structured[17] set of objects.

(4) *Object*: structured set of adjoining object parts.

[17] The word *structured* is used only to emphasize the importance of spatial relationships between elements in the particular set. Spatial locations of elements may be part of their attributes.

(3) *Object part*: structured set of perceptual areas.
(2) *Perceptual area*: set of regions that are contiguous to each other and homogeneous within the set.
(1) *Region*: set of connected[18] pixels.

To construct a VOD, the user begins by selecting training images and videos and defining an *object-definition hierarchy*. The hierarchy has two meanings: in the training phase, for each image, each node corresponds to a set of connected pixels in the image. Arcs between nodes (from top to bottom) indicate parent-child relationships, in which all descendants of a node are spatially contained in that node. For example, in Figure 17.19, object part1 is an area that contains n perceptual areas, each of which contains a number of regions. In the classification phase, each node of the hierarchy corresponds to a classifier that is automatically learned from the training set for that particular node. Note that every node has a conceptual meaning (e.g., pitcher in Fig. 17.20), corresponds to an image area in a training example (e.g., pitcher region), and corresponds to a classifier (e.g., pitcher object classifier). The user explicitly defines the hierarchy before the training begins (e.g., in Fig. 17.20, the user defines a hierarchy containing a field, a pitcher, a batter, and so on). Then the user explicitly labels each individual training example based on the hierarchy. As described in Ref. [8], the recognition strategy is based on automatic segmentation of training images and new images (see automatically segmented image in Fig. 17.20): during training, each image and video is automatically segmented, and regions are manually

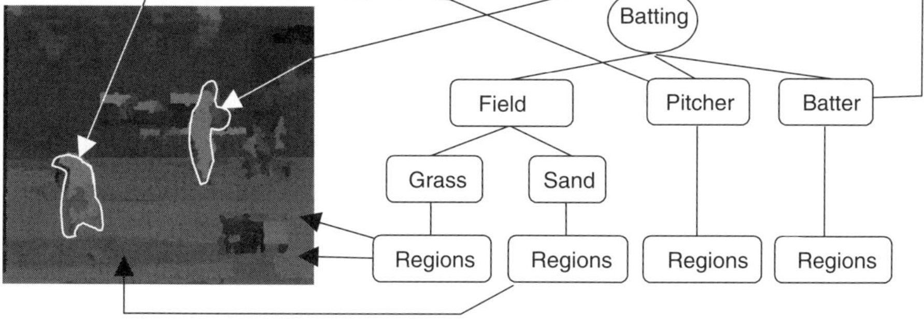

Figure 17.20. Automatically segmented baseball image. Every node in the hierarchy has a conceptual meaning (e.g., pitcher), but also corresponds to a set of connected pixels in the image. This example shows how a scene can be modeled using the *hierarchy*. The white outlines were drawn manually to illustrate how the regions map to the hierarchy. Note that although conceptually it is necessary to have all five levels of Figure 17.19, the choice is up to the user, who in this case modeled the scene using only four levels.

[18] Regions, which are at the lowest level of the hierarchy, constitute the basic units in the framework and can be extracted using any segmentation algorithm based on low-level features such as color, texture, or motion. The implementation from [136] is used for image and video segmentation.

labeled by the user according to the hierarchy defined. The labeled regions from all of the training examples are then used to compute the training set: features (color, texture, shape, spatial relationships, and so on) for each *node* of the *hierarchy* are automatically extracted and stored in a database. Since with the same training data, different algorithms will produce classifiers that will perform differently, it is important to use several algorithms so that the best classifiers can be chosen, depending on how well they perform. For each node, several classifiers are trained, and the classifier with the best performance is chosen automatically using cross-validation, as discussed in Section 17.4.5.2.

The VOD (a collection of classifiers organized in an object-definition hierarchy) performs automatic classification by first applying automatic segmentation and then combining classifiers and grouping at the levels of Figure 17.19: *regions* are classified first and combined to obtain *perceptual areas* that are used by *object part* classifiers. *Object parts*, in turn, are combined and passed to *object* classifiers.

The way in which object-definition hierarchies are built is subjective and may vary between users. This flexibility is an important advantage because it accommodates subjectivity, allowing users to build different models based on their individual preferences. Figure 17.21 shows three hierarchies for different object and scene detectors.

Although the user explicitly defines the hierarchy in VA, it would be possible to build a hierarchy automatically or semiautomatically. This is strongly related to research in which the goal is to automatically detect regions of interest (ROIs) — these are areas that would approximately correspond to nodes in an hierarchy (i.e., areas of the image that are more important than others). For example, see Ref. [137] for a comparison of ROIs obtained by different automatic algorithms and ROIs obtained from eye-tracking experiments (i.e., an individual's gaze is tracked as he observes an image). In Ref. [138], experiments were also reported in using eye-tracking results for automatic classification — potentially, this type of interaction could replace the current mode of interaction in the training stage of VA, which we describe next.

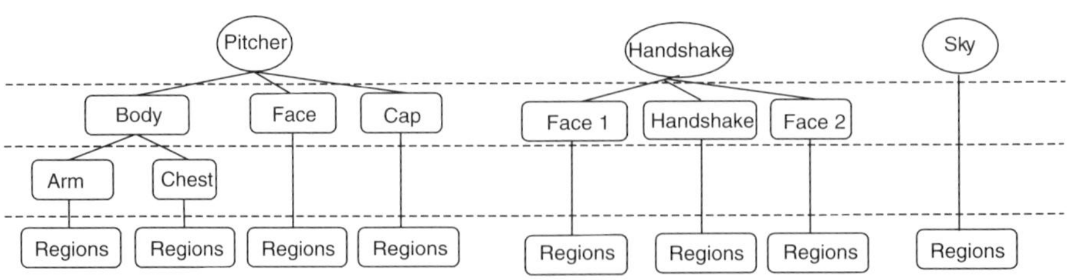

Figure 17.21. Example of object definition hierarchies. The first hierarchy was not used in experiments but shows how the close-up of a player could be modeled. The other two hierarchies were used in the experiments reported.

17.4.4 Training Phase

17.4.4.1 User Input. The first step is for the user to define an hierarchy and provide the system with the training examples so that classifiers can be built for each node of the hierarchy. The user is only required to define the set of labels for the nodes that are part of the hierarchy and to define how the nodes are connected (i.e., which node is connected to which node). In Figure 17.20, for example, there are 10 nodes, so the user must create 10 labels because each node in the hierarchy has a conceptual meaning (e.g., pitcher). Each training example labeled by the user corresponds to an area in an example image or video. The label "batter region of the batter in the batting scene," for example, clearly defines the connections between the batter region, the batter object part, and the batting object. Indeed, using the interface (Fig. 17.22), the user would not have to create a label that long. Instead, he would set the corresponding variables according to the label he would be assigning (e.g., the "object part" button would say "batter," the "scene" button would say batting, and so on). Once the labels are created during training, the user labels *regions*, *perceptual areas*, *object parts*, and *objects*, in each training image or video (by clicking on regions or outlining image of video areas). Regions that are not labeled are used by the system as negative examples (using the closed-world assumption [125]). Note that the user also has the option of including additional images and regions to be used as negative examples.

To build a batting video scene detector (Fig. 17.20), for example, the user would simply collect a set of training videos and label the first frame of each video. Only the first frame must be labeled because the segmentation algorithm from [136] is used, in which regions are automatically segmented and tracked in each video frame. On that first frame, the user identifies regions that correspond to each node in his object definition hierarchy: all the sand regions and sand perceptual areas, object parts, and so on. In most cases, it is only necessary to label individual regions (by clicking on them): once all the pitcher regions of Figure 17.20 have been labeled, the system automatically generates a pitcher object part region

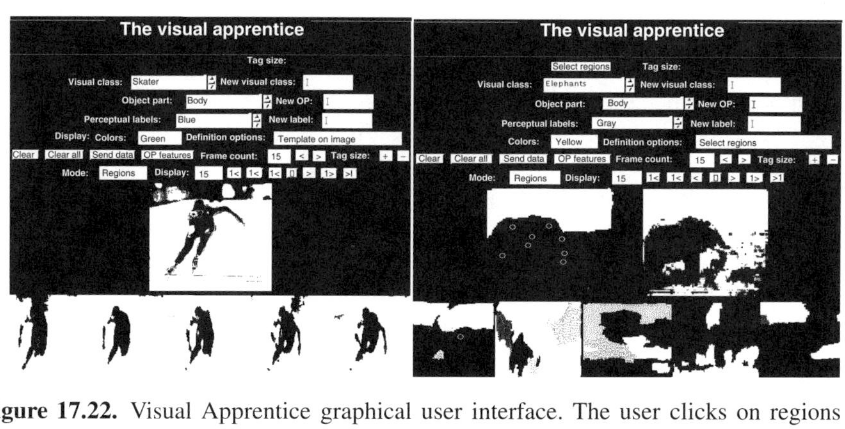

Figure 17.22. Visual Apprentice graphical user interface. The user clicks on regions to label them.

by grouping contiguous pitcher regions labeled by the user. For example, in Figure 17.20, the user labels all the pitcher regions with the name "pitcher region." Then the system automatically groups all contiguous "pitcher regions" (those that are connected) and labels that group "pitcher object" (because it is the parent of the label that was used, "pitcher regions"). Alternatively, the user can manually outline objects, object parts, or perceptual areas (note manual outline in white in Fig. 17.20). The difference between using the automatic grouping provided by the system and manually outlining components is that the automatic grouping may incorporate errors produced by the initial automatic segmentation. Again in Figure 17.20, notice that in the segmented image the pitcher region includes areas that belong to the background (not the actual pitcher). Manually outlining the pitcher eliminates that error because the user drew an outline that does not include any part of the background as part of the pitcher.

The main goal of this stage is to let the user construct a VOD, without any low-level knowledge about features or learning algorithms. Note that the hierarchy is defined when the user creates the labels and training is performed by labeling each of the training examples, so that labeling constitutes the only required user input (i.e., no input on features, classifiers, and so on). In some cases, however, additional input could be beneficial. For example, it may be beneficial to select parameters of the automatic segmentation algorithm according to the hierarchy defined by the user (e.g., segmentation parameters for a sky detector may be very different from segmentation parameters for a baseball scene). The best segmentation for a given class minimizes areas of internal regions that fall outside the boundaries of the objects of interest, while minimizing the number of regions inside those objects. In such cases, the parameters of the specific segmentation algorithm being used for the given class may be included as part of the training.

17.4.4.2 Feature Extraction. For each labeled element (e.g. region, object part, and so on), a feature vector is computed[19], which is a set of attribute-value pairs (e.g., x_location: 32) that represent the visual features of the element (e.g., color, shape, and so on). By computing feature vectors for each element, a training set is obtained for every node in the hierarchy.

Different nodes of the hierarchy may benefit from a different set of features. Therefore, a large number of features are computed for each training example, at each node of the object definition hierarchy defined by the user, and the best set for each node is selected automatically. First, a feature *superset* is extracted for each example. As part of the superset, the Visual Apprentice includes 43 features[20], which can be placed into five different groups.

- *Area and location*: area, bounding box center (x, and y), orientation, major axis length, major axis angle, minor axis length [139].

[19] Features are also extracted for regions obtained from the automatic segmentation that are not labeled by the user. Such regions are used by the learning algorithms as negative examples.

[20] Features that deal with spatial relationships between perceptual areas and between object parts are also used.

- *Color*: average L, U, and V, dominant L, U, and V (LUV quantized to 166 colors [62]).
- *Shape*: perimeter, form factor, roundness, bounding box aspect ratio, compactness, extent [139].
- *Texture*: mean maximum difference, mean minimum total variation (MTV), horizontal, vertical, diagonal, and antidiagonal mean local directed standard deviation (MLDSD), edge direction histogram (see [65,140]).
- *Motion*: motion trajectory, maximum and minimum horizontal and vertical displacement, absolute horizontal and vertical displacement, trajectory length, displacement distance, average motion angle, average horizontal and vertical speed and acceleration.

The feature extraction starts with the lowest level (i.e., regions) and proceeds upward through nodes of the hierarchy. As discussed in Section 17.4.4.1, grouping occurs (manually or automatically) between regions that are connected and have the same label (e.g., Pitcher regions of Fig. 17.20). This grouping is performed at the parent node of the region node in question (e.g., sand regions in Fig. 17.20 are grouped at the sand perceptual area node). For each image example, when the grouping is performed, a new area of the image is used for feature extraction. Again, in Figure 17.20, the area outlined in white would be used to compute features for the pitcher object part — in other words, the features of the regions of the pitcher are used at the pitcher region node, but at the parent node (pitcher object part in this case) a new set of features is computed for the image area that results from merging all connected pitcher regions together. The connected (labeled) pitcher regions then serve as a kind of mask that is used to extract new features for the parent node (again in Fig. 17.20, pitcher object part for pitcher regions, sand perceptual area for sand regions, and so on). Nodes that have more than one child, however (e.g., in Fig. 17.20 field object part and batting object), are treated differently in the sense that their features are characterized in terms of their components and the spatial relationships of those components instead of using raw features (i.e., the 43 features described earlier) extracted directly from the image. For example, in Figure 17.20, the feature vector for the field object part does not contain the 43 features discussed earlier. Instead, it contains the labels of its two children (i.e., grass, sand) and their spatial relationships. This is explained in further detail in the following text. During training, each feature vector corresponds to an example provided by the user. For instance, the following feature vectors could be obtained:

Grass region = {label = grass_region, color = green, texture = coarse, and so on} (i.e., a region and its 43 features from the set described earlier).

Field object part = {label = field_object_part, grass perceptual area next to sand perceptual area} (e.g., an object part in terms of its perceptual areas and their spatial relationships)

Spatial relationships between nodes at the same level that have the same parent are considered at the perceptual area, object part, and object levels. For example, an object part, by definition, may or may not contain more than one perceptual area. When only one perceptual area is present, it is equivalent to its corresponding parent object part; thus, perceptual area classification alone yields the result for the object part (as is the case with the pitcher object part). In cases wherein more than one perceptual area is present, spatial relationships between those areas must be considered. If they are ignored, two object parts having similar perceptual areas but very distinct spatial layout would be incorrectly placed in the same class. To represent the structural relationships between perceptual areas within object parts (or object parts within objects, and so on), *Attributed Relational Graphs (ARG)* [125,140] are constructed. Simple spatial relationships, such as above and below, right and left, and so on are used. In an *ARG*, each node represents an element and an arc between two nodes represents a relationship between them. Instead of using a relational representation (e.g., *ARG*) directly, each *ARG* is converted to an attribute-value representation: elements in the *ARG* are ordered and a feature vector is generated.

In a similar way in which feature vectors are used to learn classifiers for each individual component (e.g., region classifier), the feature vectors obtained by converting ARGs are used to construct classifiers that include lower levels of the hierarchy. In other words, for the example in Figure 17.20, a field object part learning algorithm receives feature vectors as input. These feature vectors are generated through the transformation of *ARGs*, which include sand and green perceptual labels but not the 43 features described earlier.

The process of learning structural relationships is repeated throughout the hierarchy when nodes have more than one child node. In other words, if object parts have more than one perceptual area and if objects have more than one object part, spatial relationships are considered. *ARGs* are converted to feature vectors.

The reason for having a large number of features in the feature-extraction stage is that it is difficult to determine in advance which features will be most useful for each situation. As in FourEyes (Section 17.3.1.1), the goal here is to include different features that may be useful in different scenarios.

17.4.5 Learning Classifiers and Feature Selection

A *classifier* is a function that, given an input, assigns it to one of k classes. A *learning algorithm* is a function that, given a set of examples and their classes, constructs a classifier [125].

These two definitions are of extreme importance in machine learning and in particular, in the framework of the VA because one of the main aspects of the approach is the selection of classifiers based on performance and not on the selection of learning algorithms. Using the labeled feature vectors, learning algorithms are applied at *each node* of the hierarchy to obtain classifiers. This is done at the five levels defined earlier: (*1*) region, (*2*) perceptual, (*3*) object part, (*4*) object, and (*5*) scene.

In the Visual Apprentice framework, feature subsets and classifiers are chosen automatically for each node of the object definition hierarchy [142]. In Figure 17.23, $D1$ represents the training set for a node and C_i represents

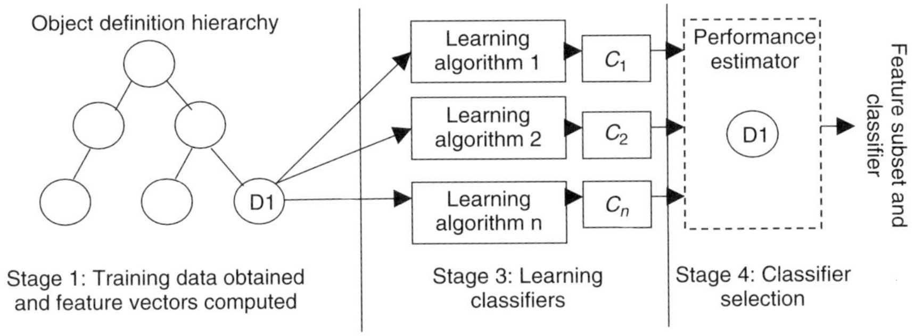

Figure 17.23. Overview of the learning process for each node in the hierarchy.

the classifiers built by each algorithm. As each algorithm is applied, the set of best features is selected from the initial superset (Section 17.4.5.1) because different features may be better for representing different concepts. For example, "good" features to represent grass (in Fig. 17.20) might be color and texture, but good features to represent the pitcher object part might be spatial location and aspect ratio. Additionally, different learning algorithms may produce different results for the same training data. Because of this, performance of classifiers is automatically compared and the best classifier for each node is selected.

Note that it would be possible to include other criteria in the selection of classifiers. For example, computational complexity, speed, requirements in terms of the number of training examples, and others, could be used. In cases in which there are very few examples, for instance, it could be beneficial to use a simpler classifier (e.g., nearest-neighbor) instead of a more complex one (e.g., a neural network) because the more complex classifier would be more likely to overfit the data than a simpler one. Issues of speed and availability of other resources (e.g., a nearest-neighbor classifier can be constructed more quickly than a neural network classifier, but it is slower at the classification stage) could also be used for making such decisions.

17.4.5.1 Learning Classifiers. The goal of the training stage is to obtain the best possible classifier (*not* learning algorithm) for each node. Because different learning algorithms may produce classifiers that perform differently on the same training data, the system simultaneously trains several algorithms from Ref. [143] (ID3, Naïve-Bayes, IB, MC4) and selects the classifier that produces the best results (see Appendix A, and [86,125] for more details on machine learning techniques). Note that the process of learning classifiers for each node of the hierarchy contrasts with the manual construction of domain-specific filters in the Body-Plans approach (Section 17.3.1.2). Although components built manually by experts may perform better in some domains, they do limit the flexibility of the system.

Feature Selection. The feature selection problem can be characterized as follows [144]: given a set of features A (e.g., the *superset* described in Section 17.4.4.2) with cardinality n, we wish to find a set B such that $B \subseteq A$ and where B is a better feature set than A. The criterion for any feature set S can be defined in terms of a function $C(S)$, which gives high values for better feature sets and lower values for worse feature sets. One possibility is to define a criterion function as $(1 - P_e)$, where P_e is the probability of error of the classifier. This measure is dependent on the learning algorithm, the *training* set, and *test* set used.

Feature subset selection is a search problem for which several strategies have been proposed [144] (in CBIR, see [145,146]). In many of them, the goal is to find the optimal feature subset without exhaustively searching all possibilities. Because the measure P_e is dependent on the learning algorithm *and* data used, the wrapper model [147] is used in the VA. In this model, feature selection is performed with respect to a particular classifier and data set. A learning algorithm is repeatedly run on the data set, using various feature subsets so that each run produces a classifier that uses a specific set of features. In the VA, best-first forward search [119] is used to find the best features, which does not guarantee the optimal feature subset but does not require exhaustive search. The performance of the classifiers learned using each feature set is measured (using k-fold cross-validation, described in the following section), and the best feature subset is chosen according to the performance. Once the features are chosen, the learning algorithm is used to construct a classifier using only those features.

Because we use more than one learning algorithm at each node of the hierarchy, the result of this process is a set of classifiers for each node as shown in Figure 17.23. We then select the best classifier for each node.

Automatic feature selection serves to shield the user from the difficulties inherent in deciding which features are more important for a specific task. Note that this is different from most approaches in which users determine the importance of features (e.g., query-by-sketch and query-by-example techniques in Section 17.3.1.1). One of the difficulties, however, is that automatic selection of features on small training sets is not always very accurate [144].

Feature selection, however, is beneficial, even with learning algorithms that incorporate some form of feature selection. The justification and benefits in performance of selecting features when using decision trees [148], for example, is given in Refs. [149,150]. Particular examples of beneficial feature selection for ID3 are given in Ref. [151].

17.4.5.2 Combining and Selecting Classifiers. In most studies in the machine-learning community, the goal is to compare different algorithms (e.g., [152]). The criterion in these cases is often the performance of the algorithms on standard data sets (e.g., UC Irvine repository [153]) or in a particular domain. Instead of trying to find the best algorithms for classifying visual information, the goals in the Visual Apprentice framework center on determining the best classifiers[21] for specific tasks (e.g., nodes of the object hierarchy).

[21] As defined at the beginning of Section 17.4.5, a *classifier* is a function that, given an input example, assigns that example to one of k classes. A *learning algorithm* is a function that, given a set of examples and their classes, constructs a classifier.

In order to select the best classifier, the performance of each classifier is measured using *k-fold cross-validation* [154] (see also [155]): the set of training examples is randomly split into k mutually exclusive sets (folds) of approximately equal size. The learning algorithm is trained and tested k times, each time it is tested on a fold and trained on the data set minus the fold. The *cross-validation* estimate of accuracy is the average of the estimated accuracies from the k folds. Accuracy can be measured in different ways, as long as the same accuracy estimate is used with all k folds. Accuracy is usually determined as the overall number of correct classifications divided by the number of instances in the data set. The process is repeated for each classifier that is being considered.

The best classifier is chosen according to its performance estimate given by the cross-validation accuracy: for each node, the classifier with the highest accuracy is selected. The process occurs for every node of the hierarchy defined by the user.

This stage basically chooses a classification scheme in a dynamic manner. Note that in some cases the specific application will place additional constraints on the type of learning algorithm that the system should use to produce classifiers. For example, if the user wants to build a very fast object detector, decision trees would be more appropriate than nearest-neighbor algorithms. In selecting the best classifiers, as with feature selection, there may be cases in which the number of training examples is too small for the system to make an accurate decision.

An alternative to selecting the best classifier is to combine all or some of the classifiers resulting from the cross-validation process. In Ref. [156], other ways in which classifiers can interact in the VA framework were presented (also see [120] for a different combination strategy in a different framework). For example, although the training stage yields different classifiers for each node, it is possible to combine their classification results to make each decision (e.g., different pitcher region classifiers vote on whether a region belongs to a pitcher or not).

17.4.6 Classification at Multiple Levels

The first step in the classification of a new image or video is its automatic segmentation. Classification then follows the bottom up order of the object definition hierarchy.

Once the input image or video has been segmented, a region-level classifier is applied. At every level of the hierarchy, it is possible to have classifiers that make hard decisions about their input (i.e., yes or no answers) or those that make soft decisions about the input (e.g., a region is not in the class, it is in the class, it is most likely in the class, and most likely not in the class). One possibility is to use *fuzzy classifiers* [157]. A classifier receives an input and assigns it to one of k classes. A *fuzzy classifier* performs the same function but instead of making a hard decision (e.g., the input belongs only to class k) yields a fuzzy set (e.g., the input may belong to different classes to different degrees). A fuzzy set is a set of elements, wherein each element has a degree of membership, often indicated by a number between zero and one, where zero indicates nonmembership and one indicates the highest level of membership. For example, for a class S, we can have the set $Ss = \{(a, 0), (b, 0.2), (c, 0.8), (d, 1)\}$, in which each pair represents an element and its membership in set S. Element a does not belong to the set, b is a "weak" member, c is a "strong" member, and d has the highest level of membership possible in the class S. Note that, using membership values allows us to add semantic labels, such as "strong" and "weak" to the membership of elements in each class.

In the Visual Apprentice, regions at the lowest level of the hierarchy of Figure 17.19 are generated automatically and merged to obtain the corresponding perceptual areas or object parts (depending on the hierarchy). In the training phase, regions that have the same label (e.g., "pitcher region") can be automatically grouped together to define the corresponding object part. The same process occurs during classification: regions are classified first and those that have the same label (e.g., "pitcher region") are automatically grouped together and passed on to the corresponding classifier at the next level of the hierarchy (e.g., pitcher object part in the example of Fig. 17.20). During classification, although an individual region may unlikely be a member of the current class in question (e.g., not a "pitcher region"), when grouped with other possible "pitcher regions," it may actually correspond to a higher-level node in the hierarchy (e.g., pitcher object part). As a result, making hard decisions about regions (i.e., the lowest level of the hierarchy) may eliminate some possible groups that could potentially belong to the class of the parent node in the hierarchy (e.g., pitcher object part). For this reason, fuzzy classifiers are used at the region level. For each region classifier, we use a fuzzy classifier that yields a fuzzy set [157] of candidate regions that belong to a particular *perceptual area*, *object part*, or *object*, depending on the specific hierarchy (i.e., depending on the parent node of the region classifier being applied). The regions selected by the fuzzy classifier as possible candidates are then used to form groups of adjoining regions that are used by the parent node classifier. In particular, an evolution program [158], explained next, is used to find suitable groups (e.g., a set of adjoining face regions may correspond to a face).

Perceptual Grouping, Search, and Evolution Programs. Depending on the object-definition hierarchy, groups of adjoining regions are formed corresponding to perceptual areas, object parts, or objects (see differences between direct ancestors of "pitcher" and "grass regions" in Fig. 17.20). Region classification then serves as an initial selection process similar to the one in Ref. [130]. Once candidate regions are found (as determined by the fuzzy region classifier), the system tries to find from the set of candidates, groups of regions that may match the parent node (e.g., "pitcher" object part or "grass" perceptual area in Fig. 17.20). In other words, the system searches the space of possible groups of adjoining regions to find groups that when taken as a whole will be selected by the classifier of the parent node that corresponds to the region classifier being applied. This is done using an Evolution Algorithm [158], which searches the space, treating each possible group of adjoining regions as an element in the population of possible solutions. Over several iterations, different groups are tested (using the classifier of the parent node in question as a fitness criterion) until a solution is found or the maximum number of iterations is reached. Other approaches to a search problem like this one are described in Refs. [110,119].

A final decision is made by the visual object detector (*VOD*), on the basis of decisions of all of its classifiers. In particular, all elements of the hierarchy must be present for a *VOD* to detect the object or scene. For the batting scene of Figure 17.20 to be found, all elements must be found (i.e., pitcher, field and its parts, and so on).

17.4.7 Experiments

In this section, we highlight some of the important issues that arise when using learning techniques in CBIR. As an example and to aid in the explanations, we describe the experimental setup and results reported in Ref. [142].

In the machine-learning community, common data repositories (e.g., Ref. [153] are often used to test algorithms. In content-based retrieval, however, different researchers use distinct sets of images and videos to test their approaches. As a result, selection of training and testing data sets in a particular domain is not a trivial issue. One of the difficulties is not knowing specifically what type of data will be used for training and how the resulting classifiers will be used. In the discussions that follow, we give some insights into the issues that were encountered in applying the techniques presented in this section and discuss some of the factors that must be considered when learning approaches are used in CBIR.

First we describe experiments using professional baseball video and then news images.

17.4.7.1 Baseball Video. In Ref. [142], several factors that influence the quality and visual appearance of baseball scenes from professional television broadcast were reported. Some factors were found to vary significantly within a single game but others remained constant. Weather, for example, can be very different in two segments of the same game, whereas lighting might remain constant if the game is played at night. Differences across games depend on the stadium in which the game is played (patterns on the natural grass or artificial grass; lighting in outdoor, indoor, or semicovered stadium fields, and so on), and team uniforms (a team usually has several uniforms), among others. It was surprising to find, for instance, that sometimes the variations in the quality of the signal were high within a game (mostly because of human error or noise). All of these factors show the difficulty of applying content-based techniques in real-world scenarios.

For humans, most of those factors have no impact on the ability to recognize different scenes. For a CBIR system, however, these changes can often mean significant feature-value variations (e.g., color). Most of these issues, however, are ignored in most of the experiments reported in content-based retrieval, mainly because in most cases the data used for training and testing comes from a single "collection" (e.g., a particular news source, and so on).

To select scenes for classification, the concept of *recurrent visual semantics* of Section 17.4.1 was used. The batting scene of Figure 17.20 was selected as the main object class[22] for which to build an automatic classifier, using the *visual apprentice*. This class was chosen because it marks a semantically meaningful event in Baseball.

For training and testing, innings from six different New York Mets games were digitized in MPEG1 format at 1.5 MBps (30 frames/sec). All scene cuts were obtained manually (alternatively, scene cuts could be detected automatically using Ref. [159]) and each shot was forced to a length of 30 frames. The final training and test set consisted of 376 baseball shots, each consisting of 30 frames. In order to build a somewhat robust classifier, the training set included natural grass and artificial turf for the field, natural light (day games), and artificial light (night games). In addition, the shots were selected from different television broadcasters. In selecting a training set for a specific classifier, it is important to consider the conditions under which it will be applied. In the baseball example, the goal was to build a batting scene detector that would work well when applied to professional baseball broadcasts, independent of location, time of the day, weather, and broadcast company.

Choices regarding the type of training data are then strongly linked to the way in which the classifiers will be used. Recall that in Section 17.3.1.2 we discussed the impact of using different training data with the same approach for classifying images into the indoor and outdoor categories (that of Ref. [64] as applied in Ref. [66]). At the same time, we highlighted how the structure of that type of data (similarity of contiguous images in the same roll of film) could be used to benefit a different application (album creation in Ref. [98]). This discussion is meant to highlight the importance of carefully selecting the data not only for the training stage but also for the testing stage and emphasizing that data selection is influenced by the specific technique being developed and its application.

Results. The training set consisted of 376 baseball video shots, out of which, 125 were shots of the batting scene of Figure 17.20. Out of the 125, 60 shots were employed by the user to train the system, on the basis of an object-definition hierarchy similar to the one depicted in Figure 17.20.

Feature and classifier selection were performed using only the training set provided by the user; hence, testing of the approach was performed on the remaining 316 shots. The following nodes were included in the hierarchy used in the experiments: pitcher, top grass (grass near the batter), mound (where the pitcher stands), bottom grass (near the pitcher), and batter.

In each of the experiments performed, the test sets were independent of the training sets (i.e., testing set was not used in training and vice versa). For the baseball batting scene classifier, 316 shots were used for testing. The

[22] An *object definition hierarchy* defines a class, which may correspond to a scene. See Figure 17.20 for the *definition hierarchy* of the class chosen.

test set included 65 batting scene shots, and, as mentioned earlier, an independent training set of 60 shots was used. An accuracy (overall percentage of correct classifications) of 92 percent was obtained (64 percent recall and 100 percent precision). A precision of 100 percent is not surprising because detection of a batting scene implies detection of each of the components, so all of the components of the object hierarchy must be present in each test shot in order for it to pass the classifier. The object detector for this scene is not likely to encounter false positives for all the components of the hierarchy within a single shot. It is also important to note that a change in the hierarchy (e.g., removing the sand node in the hierarchy of Fig. 17.20) implies changes in performance. Having more nodes in the hierarchy improves precision: fewer false alarms occur because all elements of the hierarchy must be present when the visual object detector decides that the object and scene in question are detected. At the same time, although recall is reduced, if an image contains all of the elements but there is an error in the segmentation such that the pitcher regions in Figure 17.20 are merged with the field regions, the image will be rejected. On the other hand, having fewer nodes in the hierarchy increases recall but reduces precision.

The number of training examples for this experiment (and the ones that follow) was chosen by the authors on the basis of their experience in CBIR and, in particular, with the Visual Apprentice system. Although it is possible to provide some insight into the number of examples required (on the basis of computational learning theory; see Ref. [125], among others), it is difficult to make general statements without having knowledge about the specific class that the system will learn. Issues, such as the size and complexity of the hypothesis space, desired accuracy of the classifiers, and features used, play an important role. Another factor that plays a role is the amount of time the user wants to spend labeling the data; in each of the experiments reported in this section (baseball, handshakes, skies) the amount of time required to complete the training stage was less than two hours. In most of the work in CBIR in which machine learning is used, the number of training examples is usually in the hundreds, at most. This is, in part, due to difficulties in obtaining training data and difficulties in storage and manipulation of the data. The number of training examples required for a particular classifier are strongly linked to the questions outlined earlier. Although it is difficult to provide general answers, computational learning theory does provide some tools that could be applied in the Visual Apprentice framework, as long as constraints could be placed on the types of classifiers being used, their expected performance, and so on. This could be done independently at each node for a particular object-definition hierarchy, making it possible to obtain theoretical bounds on the number of training examples required for a complete hierarchy. These could be computed on the basis of a number of parameters and presented to the user as general guidelines for the number of training examples required. This, however, would place an additional burden on the user of the system, because more information would have to be provided.

17.4.7.3 Handshakes and Skies. In addition to testing the approach on baseball, results were reported for handshake images (see object hierarchies for handshakes and skies in Fig. 17.21). For the handshake tests, 80 training images and an independent test set of 733 news images were used. Out of the 733 images, 85 were handshakes. An overall accuracy of 94 percent (94 percent of the set of 733 images were correctly classified) was achieved (74 percent recall and 70 percent precision), with 89 images automatically labeled as handshake by the system. Sky detection was performed on a set of 1,300 images that contained 128 skies (with an independent training set of 40 images, see Ref. [66]). An accuracy of 94 percent was achieved (50 percent recall, and 87 percent precision) in a set of 134 images retrieved.

Results. The results reported for the different types of hierarchies show that the Visual Apprentice framework is flexible, allowing the construction of different types of detectors. More importantly, performance in each case was similar to performance reported for similar classifiers using other techniques (overall accuracy around 90 percent and higher).

17.4.8 Summary

In this section we discussed the Visual Apprentice approach to classification for CBIR. In the Visual Apprentice, the user defines visual object models that depend on the classes in which he is interested, through a multiple-level object definition hierarchy (*region*, *perceptual area*, *object part*, *object*). As the user provides examples from images or video, visual features are extracted and classifiers are learned for each node of the hierarchy. At each node the best features and classifiers are selected on the basis of their performance, using k-fold cross-validation over the training set.

The concept of *recurrent visual semantics (RVS)* was also discussed. RVS is defined as the repetitive appearance of elements (e.g., objects, scenes, or shots) that are *visually similar* and have a common level of meaning within a specific context. Using that concept, it is possible to identify where and when learning techniques can be used in CBIR. For the particular examples shown, experimental results were presented in the detection of baseball scenes, handshake images, and skies.

The framework of the Visual Apprentice shows several desirable characteristics of CBIR systems. The system uses learning techniques to automatically build classifiers; thus, object detectors can easily be constructed without the need for any specialized algorithms. New classifiers can be constructed without the use of expert knowledge. However, because classifiers are built independently (for each node of the hierarchy), specialized algorithms can be easily incorporated. For example, in the handshake classifier, a face-recognition module could be used instead of the face classifiers. Similarly, a domain-specific segmentation algorithm could be used to improve performance.

Another major advantage of the framework is that users are allowed to construct their own classifiers, accommodating subjectivity across different users (and for a single user). In this process, users are not required to provide any input on difficult issues, such as the importance of low-level features. Similarly, decisions, such as which learning algorithms to use, are made automatically by the system.

Despite of the advantages of the framework, there are several issues that need to be addressed. Although the framework is suitable for building visual object detectors for objects that are visually similar, it is unsuitable for classes in which there is substantial variation in visual appearance or in which a well-defined structure is not easily identified. For example, in scene classes, such as indoor and outdoor, there is great variation in visual appearance. Additionally, it is difficult to clearly define what an indoor scene looks like: what is the structure of indoor scenes? One possibility is that there are many hierarchies that correspond to each of those classes. For example, different hierarchies could be built for different types of landscapes. Different classifiers would then be built for each class (e.g., different types of outdoor images as in Ref. [65]). In this case, however, techniques, such as those presented in Ref. [64,66,89], might be more suitable because they require less user input and yield promising results. The Visual Apprentice framework, however, performs classification on the basis of the local structure of the images. This is of great importance because different areas of the image can be labeled by the system according to how the object model was defined. Local information, then, is also indexed automatically (e.g., the Visual Apprentice could generate MEG-7 descriptors for the image and each of its components) — this cannot be done with approaches that perform scene-level classification only.

Another very important issue, which is common to approaches that use learning techniques, is the selection of the training set. The performance and scope of such systems depend strongly on how the training set is selected: what is the source of the training set? Which images should be used? How large should the training set be? These are important questions for which there are very few general answers — we emphasized that computational learning theory provides some tools to determine the number of training examples in a learning task but important constraints (e.g., desired system accuracy, type of learning algorithm, and so on.) have to be determined. Although the *RVS* concept helps to identify and restrict the domain of application of such techniques, it only serves as a general guideline. This issue is also related to the definition of the hierarchy, which, being subjective, may lead to different classification results.

The use of segmentation as a basis for this approach is an advantage but at the same time a disadvantage. It allows the use of nonspecialized algorithms, therefore bypassing the need for expert input. On the other hand, segmentation remains an open problem owing to difficulties in handling variations in lighting conditions, occlusion, and so on. In the Visual Apprentice framework, the problem is bypassed, because the training itself is based on segmentation. There is no doubt, however, that inaccurate segmentation places strong limitations on the VA's accuracy.

It is also important to point out that in some domains specialized algorithms may present better solutions than flexible frameworks, such as the Visual

Apprentice's. The large number of objects to be recognized in CBIR, however, suggests that domain-specific approaches may not always be adequate.

17.5 CONCLUSION AND FUTURE DIRECTIONS

In this chapter, we discussed content-based retrieval, emphasizing that visual information can be indexed at multiple levels. In particular, we discussed a conceptual framework to index visual content and analyzed different CBIR approaches from the perspective of the conceptual framework. A distinction was made between the interface and indexing components of CBIR systems, the advantages and limitations of different interface modalities were outlined, and the benefits of different indexing mechanisms were discussed. The discussion, which was carried out in the context of the conceptual framework for indexing visual information, showed the importance of object-level indexing techniques in CBIR. As a result, a brief overview of some of the major object-recognition strategies was presented, particularly in relation to CBIR.

We identified the differences between traditional object recognition and object recognition for CBIR and outlined the challenges that object-recognition techniques face if they are to be applied to the general CBIR problem. Following the discussion, we reviewed the specific framework of the Visual Apprentice in which users can build object detectors by constructing an object definition hierarchy and by providing training examples. Some of the issues encountered in the *VA* framework are common to many CBIR systems, particularly to those that use learning techniques. More specifically, we discussed some of the following issues: user subjectivity, feature and classifier selection, choice of training data, and problems that arise when applying such techniques in real-world scenarios.

The material in this chapter emphasized that, although many systems are used to retrieve content based on semantics, most of the current CBIR techniques actually focus on the syntactic aspects of visual information. Despite this limitation, the importance and advantages of the different techniques were emphasized.

In the future, we envision complex knowledge-intensive systems that incorporate human expertise and learning techniques that make them adaptive. When humans detect or classify objects, information and knowledge at different levels (e.g., domain-specific, spatial, functional, and so on) are used during the process. In addition, humans adapt easily to changing conditions — a desirable functionality in CBIR systems.

Because of the large number of levels at which visual information can be described, it is clear that classification based on visual features alone is unlikely to succeed in many real-world applications. The development of new technologies, and standards, such as MPEG-7, also suggests that a lot of information will be included with images and videos at origin (i.e., when they are created). Automatic indexing will increasingly make use of annotations generated at origin, so future content-based indexing systems are likely to rely on different sources and forms of information. Consequently, future content-based retrieval systems will contain a combination of approaches, such as the ones discussed in this chapter. Manual annotation at origin (and after creation) is likely to continue playing a very important part of CBIR. Therefore, we also envision a great deal of research to facilitate annotation tasks and management of multimedia data. In addition, future efforts will continue to tackle issues that deal with human aspects of CBIR, in particular, in gaining a better understanding of the data, the users, and the subjectivity that is inherent in indexing and retrieving visual information. As a result, researchers in the field of CBIR are likely to continue to use work from other fields (e.g., Computer Vision, Cognitive psychology, Information Retrieval, Human vision understanding, and so on) in the design and construction of CBIR systems.

ACKNOWLEDGMENTS

The author thank Efstathios Hadjidemetriou for his comments on the object recognition section, Sara Brock for revising the manuscript, and the editors for their guidance and insightful comments.

APPENDIX

The ID3 algorithm [125] constructs decision trees by ordering classification rules based on the attribute values present in the training data. The algorithm begins with an empty tree and uses a statistical test to determine which feature alone is best for classifying the training examples. For example, if one of the features is color, the algorithm will try to construct the tree by dividing the feature values so that each branch covers a different set of instances in the training set (e.g., if the color is blue, it is a sky, otherwise it is not). A descendant of that node[23] is then created for each possible value of that attribute and the training examples are sorted to the appropriate descendant node (e.g., if color is the parent node, texture could be one of the descendants). The process is repeated for the training examples of each node. Information gain can be used to determine how well a given attribute separates the training examples according to their target classification (e.g., how color separates positive sky examples from negative sky examples):

$$\text{Entropy}(S) \equiv -p_{\oplus} \log_2 p_{\oplus} - p_{\otimes} \log_2 p_{\otimes} \tag{7.1}$$

where S is a collection of positive and negative examples of a target concept (e.g., sky), $p_{\oplus}$ is the proportion of positive examples in S (e.g., skies), and $p_{\otimes}$ is the proportion of negative examples in S (e.g., areas that are not skies). Information gain is defined as follows:

$$\text{Gain}(S, A) \equiv \text{Entropy}(S) - \sum_{v \in \text{Values}(A)} \frac{|S_v|}{|S|} \text{Entropy}(S_v) \tag{7.2}$$

[23] Note that node here refers to node in the decision tree and not a node in the object-definition hierarchy defined earlier.

where *Values(A)* is the set of all possible values for attribute A, and S_v is the subset of S for which attribute A has value v.

REFERENCES

1. A. Del Bimbo, *Visual Information Retrieval*, Morgan Kaufmann Publishers, San Francisco, Calif., 1999.
2. S.-F. Chang, J.R. Smith, M. Beigi, and A. Benitez, Visual information retrieval from large distributed on-line repositories, *Commun. ACM* **40**(12), 63–71 (1997).
3. Y. Rui, T.S. Huang, and S.-F. Chang, Image retrieval: current directions, promising techniques, and open issues, *J. Vis. Commun. Image Represent.* **10**, 1–23, (1999).
4. A. Yoshitaka and T. Ichikawa, A survey on content-based retrieval for multimedia databases, *IEEE Trans. Knowledge Data Eng.* **11**(1), 81–93 (1999).
5. T. Minka and R. Picard, Interactive learning using a society of models, *Pattern Recog.* **30**(4), 565–581 (1997).
6. R.W. Picard, A society of models for video and image libraries, Technical Report, No. 360, MIT Media Laboratory Perceptual Computing Section, Cambridge, Mass., 1996.
7. A. Jaimes and S.-F. Chang, A conceptual framework for indexing visual information at multiple levels, *Proc. SPIE Internet Imaging 2000* **3964**, 2–15 (2000).
8. A. Jaimes and S.-F. Chang, Model-based classification of visual information for content-based retrieval, *Proc. SPIE Storage Retrieval Image Video Databases VII* **3656**, 402–414 (1999).
9. R. Arnheim, *Art and Visual Perception: A Psychology of the Creative Eye*, University of California Press, Berkeley, Calif., 1984.
10. G.T. Buswell, *How People Look at Pictures: A Study of the Psychology of Perception in Art*, University of Chicago press, Chicago, Ill, 1935.
11. S. Barnet, *A Short Guide to Writing About Art*, 5txsh ed., Logman, New York, 1997.
12. D.A. Dondis, *A Primer of Visual Literacy*, MIT Press, Cambridge, Mass., 1973.
13. E. Panofski, *Studies in Iconology*, Harper & Row, New York, 1962.
14. S. Harnad, ed., *Categorical Perception: The Groundwork of Cognition*, Cambridge University Press, New York, 1987.
15. W.R. Hendee and P.N.T. Wells, ed., *The Perception of Visual Information* 2nd ed., Springer Verlag, New York, 1997.
16. E.R. Tufte, *Visual Explanations: Images and Qualities, Evidence and Narrative*, Graphics press, Cheshire, Conn., 1997.
17. A. Tversky, Features of similarity, *Psychol. Rev.* **84**(4), 327–352 (1977).
18. S.L. Armstrong, L.R. Gleitman, and H. Gleitman, What some concepts might not be, *Cognition* **13**, 263–308 (1983).
19. B. Burns, ed., *Percepts, Concepts and Categories: The Representation and Processing of Information*, Elsvier Academic Publishers, New York, 1992.
20. B. Burns, Perceived similarity in perceptual and conceptual development: the influence of category information on perceptual organization, in B. Burns, ed., *Percepts, Concepts and Categories*, Elsvier Academic Publishers, New York, 1992, pp. 175–231.

21. L.B. Smith and D. Heise, Perceptual similarity and conceptual structure, in B. Burns, ed., *Percepts, Concepts and Categories*, Elsvier Academic Publishers, New York, 1992, pp. 233–272.
22. M.W. Morris and G.L. Murphy, Converging operations on a basic level in event taxonomies, *Memory Cogn.* **18**(4), 407–418 (1990).
23. A. Rifkin, Evidence for a basic level in event taxonomies, *Memory Cogn.* **13**(6), 538–556 (1985).
24. E. Rosch et al., Basic objects in natural categories, *Cogn. Psychol.* **8**, 382–439 (1976).
25. B. Tversky and K. Hemenway, Categories of environmental scenes, *Cogn. Psychol.* **15**, 121–149 (1983).
26. F.C. Keil and M.H. Kelly, Developmental changes in category structure, in S. Hanard, ed., *Categorical Perception: The Groundwork of Cognition*, Cambridge University Press, New York, 1987, pp. 491–510.
27. B.J. Jones, Variability and universality in human image processing, in F.T. Marchese, ed., *Understanding Images: Finding Meaning in Digital Imagery*, TELOS, Santa Clara, Calif. 1995.
28. H. Roberts, Do you have any pictures of subject access to works of art in visual collections and book reproductions, *Art Documentation*, **7**(3), 87–90 (1988).
29. S.S. Layne, Analyzing the subject of a picture: a theoretical approach, *Cataloguing Classification Q.* **6**(3), 39–62 (1986).
30. J. Turner, Determining the subject content of still and moving image documents for storage and retrieval: an experimental investigation, Ph.D. thesis, University of Toronto, Toronto, Canada, 1994.
31. R. Fidel, T.B. Hahn, E.M. Rasmussen, and P.J. Smith, eds., *Challenges in Indexing Electronic Text and Images*, ASIS Monograph Series, Learned Information, Inc., Medford, N.J. January 1994.
32. B. Orbach, So that others may see: tools for cataloguing still images, *Describing Archival Materials: The Use of the MARC AMC Format*, Haworth Press, Binghamton, N.Y., 1990, pp. 163–191.
33. E.M. Rasmussen, Indexing images, *Annu. Rev. Inf. Sci. Technol. (ARIST)* **32**, 169–196 (1997).
34. J. Turner, Cross-Language Transfer of Indexing Concepts for Storage and Retrieval of Moving Images: Preliminary Results, *Proceedings of ASIS 1996 Annual Conference*, Baltimore, Md., October 1996.
35. C. Jorgensen, Image attributes, *Ph.D. thesis*, Syracuse University, Syracuse, N.Y., 1995.
36. C. Jorgensen, Attributes of images in describing tasks, *Inf. Process. Manage.* **34**(2/3), 161–174 (1998).
37. C. Jorgensen, Classifying images: criteria for grouping as revealed in a sorting task, *Adv. Classification Res.* **6**, 45–64 (1995).
38. J.P. Eakins, Design criteria for a shape retrieval system, *Comput. Ind.* **21**(2), 167–184 (1993).
39. P.G.B. Enser, Query analysis in a visual information retrieval context, *J. Document Text Manage.* **1**(1), 25–39 (1993).

40. E.T. Davis, A Prototype item-level index to the civil war photographic collection of the Ohio Historical Society, Master of Library Science thesis, Kent State University, Kent, Ohio, August 1997.
41. K. Markey, Computer assisted construction of a thematic catalog of primary and secondary subject matter, *Vis. Resources* **3**, 16–49 (1983).
42. C. Jorgensen, Indexing Images: Testing an Image Description Template, *Proceedings of ASIS 1996 Annual Conference*, Baltimore, Md., October 1996.
43. E.B. Parker, LC Thesaurus for Graphic Materials: Topical Terms for Subject Access, Library of Congress, Washington, D.C., 1987.
44. A.B. Benitez et al., Object-based multimedia description schemes and applications for MPEG-7, *Image Commun. J.* **16**, 235–269 (1999).
45. R.S. Heller and C.D. Martin, A media taxonomy, *IEEE Multimedia Mag.* **2**(4), 36–45 (1995).
46. N. Hirzalla, B. Falchuk, and A. Karmouch, A temporal model for interactive multimedia scenarios, *IEEE Multimedia Mag.* **2**(3), 24–31 (1995).
47. G.L. Lohse, K. Biolsi, N. Walker, and H.H. Rueter, A classification of visual representation, *Commun. ACM* **37**(12); 36–49 (1994).
48. U. Srinivasan, C. Lindley, and B. Simpson-Young, A multi-model framework for video information systems, *Database Semantics: Issues in Multimedia Systems*, Kluwer Academic Publishers, Norwell, Mass., 1999, 85–108.
49. H. Purchase, Defining Multimedia, *IEEE Multimedia Mag.*, **5**(1),8–15 (1998).
50. MPEG Multimedia Description Scheme Group, Text of ISO/IEC CD 15938-5 Information technology — Multimedia content description interface: Multimedia description schemes, ISO/IEC JTC1/SC29/WG11 MPEG00/N3705, La Baule, France, October 2000 (see also MPEG-7 website: *http://drogo.cselt.stet.it*)
51. A.B. Benitez et al., Fundamental Entity-Relationship Models for the Generic Audo Visual DS, Contribution to *ISO/IEC JTC1/SC29/WG11 MPEG99/M4754*, Vancouver, Canada, July 1999.
52. A.B. Benitez, A. Jaimes, S. Paek, and S.-F. Chang, Fundamental Entity-Relation Models for a Multimedia Archive DS, Contribution to *ISO/IEC JTC1/SC29/WG11 MPEG99/M4755*, Vancouver, Canada, July 1999.
53. A. Jaimes, C. Jorgensen, A.B. Benitez, and S.-F. Chang, Multiple Level Classification of Visual Descriptors in the Generic AV DS, Contribution to *ISO/IEC JTC1/SC29/WG11 MPEG99/M5251*, Melbourne, Australia, October 1999.
54. MPEG-7, MMDS Group, MPEG-7 Multimedia Description Schemes (V6.0), *Doc. ISO/IEC JTC1/SC29/WG11 MPEG01/N3815*, Pisa, Italy, January, 2001.
55. J.R. Smith and S.-F. Chang, An Image and Video Search Engine for the World-Wide Web, *Proc. SPIE Storage Retrieval Image Video Databases V* **3022**, 84–95 (1997).
56. W. Niblack et al., The QBIC project: quering images by content using color, texture, and shape, *Proc. SPIE Storage Retrieval Image Video Databases* **1908**, 173–187 (1993).
57. J.R. Bach et al., The VIRAGE image search engine: an open framework for image management, *Proc. SPIE Storage Retrieval Still Image Video Databases IV*, **2670**, 76–87 (1996).

58. D.McG. Squire and T. Pun, A Comparison of Human and Machine Assessments of Image Similarity for the Organization of Image Databases, *Proceedings Scandinavian conference on Image Analysis*, Lappeenranta, Finland, June 9–11, 1997.
59. C.E. Jacobs, A. Finkelstein, and D.H. Salesin, Fast Multiresolution Image Querying, *Proceedings of ACM Conference on Computer Graphics (SIGGRAPH)*, Los Angeles, Calif., August 1995, pp. 277–286.
60. S.-F. Chang et al., A fully automatic content-based video search engine supporting multi-object spatio-temporal queries, *IEEE Trans. Circuits Syst. Video Technol., Special Issue on Image Video Process. Interact. Multimedia* **8**(5), 602–615, (1998).
61. R.K. Rajendran and S.-F. Chang, Visual search tools and their application in K-12 education, *ADVENT Project Technical Report*, Columbia University, New York May 1999.
62. J.R. Smith and S.-F. Chang, VisualSEEk: a fully automated content-based image query system, *Proceedings of the ACM Conference on Multimedia (ACM MM '96)*, Baston, Mass., November 1996, 87–98.
63. D.A. Forsyth and M. Fleck, Body Plans, *Proceedings of IEEE Computer Vision and Pattern Recognition (CVPR '97)*, San Juan, Puerto Rico, 1997, pp. 678–683.
64. M. Szummer and R.W. Picard, Indoor-Outdoor Image Classification, *Proceedings of IEEE International Workshop on Content-based Access of Image and Video Databases*, Bombay, India, 1998, pp. 42–51.
65. A. Vailaya, M. Figueiredo, A. Jain, and H.J. Zhang, Content-Based Hierarchical Classification of Vacation Images, *Proc. IEEE Multimedia Comput. Syst.* **1**, 518–523 (1999).
66. S. Paek et al., Integration of visual and text based approaches for the content labeling and classification of photographs, *Proceedings of ACM SIGIR '99 Workshop on Multimedia Indexing and Retrieval*, Berkeley, Calif., August, 1999.
67. R.K. Srihari, "Automatic Indexing and Content-Based Retrieval of Captioned Images," *IEEE Comput. Mag.* **28**(9), 49–56 (1995).
68. J.M. Corridoni, A. Del Bimbo, and P. Pala, Retrieval of paintings using effects induced by color features, *Proceedings of IEEE Workshop on Content-Based Access of Image and Video Databases*, Bombay, India, January 1998, pp. 2–11.
69. D. Hernandez, Qualitative representation of spatial knowledge, *Lecture Notes in Artificial Intelligence*, 804, Springer-Verlag, Berlin, Germany, 1994.
70. S.S. Layne, Some issues in the indexing of images, *J. Am. Soc. Inf. Sci.* **45**(8), 583–588 (1994).
71. C. Jorgensen, A. Jaimes, A.B. Benitez, and S.-F. Chang, A Conceptual Framework and Research for Classifying Visual Descriptors, invited paper, *J. Am. Soc. Inf. Sci. (JASIS), special issue on "Image Access: Bridging Multiple Needs and Multiple Perspectives*," Spring 2001 (to appear).
72. A. Jaimes, C. Jorgensen, A.B. Benitez, and S.-F. Chang, Experiments in indexing multimedia data at multiple levels, *ASIS& T Adv. Classification Res.* **11** (2001).
73. A. Benitez, A. Jaimes, C. Jorgensen, and S.-F. Chang, Report of CE on Multilevel Indexing Pyramid, contribution to *ISO/IEC JTC1/SC29/WG11 MPEG00/M6495*, La Baule, France, October 2000.
74. L.D. Bergman, V. Castelli, C.-S. Li, and J.R. Smith, SPIRE, a digital library for scientific information, *Int. J. Digital Libr., Special Issue On the Tradition of the Alexandrian Scholars*, **3**(1), 85–99 (2000).

75. S. Santini, A. Gupta, and R. Jain, A user interface for emergent semantics in image databases, *Proceedings of 8th IFIP Workshop on Database Semantics* (DS-8), Rotuva, New Zealand, January 1999.
76. D.A. Norman and S.D., eds., *User Centered System Design: New Perspectives on Human-Computer Interaction*, L. Erlbaum Associates, Hillsdale, N.J., 1986.
77. D. Kirsh, Interactivity and multimedia interface, *Instructional Sci.* **25**(2), 79–96 (1997).
78. S. Santini, Explorations in Image Databases, Ph.D. thesis, University of California, San Diego, Calif., 1998.
79. S. Santini and R. Jain, Beyond Query by Example, *Proceedings of the ACM International Conference on Multimedia 98*, Bristol, England, September 1998, pp. 345–350.
80. Y. Rui, T.S. Huang, M. Ortega, and S. Mehrotra, Relevance feedback: a power tool for interactive content-based image retrieval, *IEEE Trans. Circuits Video Technol.* **8**(5), 644–655 (1998).
81. J.J. Rocchio Jr., Relevance feedback in information retrieval, Gerard Slaton, ed., *The Smart Retrieval System: Experiments in Automatic Document Processing*, Prentice-Hall, Englewood Cliffs, N.J., 1971, pp. 313–323.
82. I.J. Cox, M.L. Mller, T.P. Minka, and P.N. Yianilos, An optimized interaction strategy for bayesian relevance feedback, *Proceedings IEEE Conference on Computer Vision and Pattern Recognition (CVPR '98)*, Santa Barbara, Calif., 1998, pp. 553–558.
83. C. Meilhac and C. Nastar, Relevance feedback and category search in image databases, *Proc. IEEE Int. Conf. Multimedia Comput. Syst.* **1**, 512–517 (1999).
84. T.-S. Chua, W.-C. Low, and C.-X. Chu, Relevance feedback techniques for color-based image retrieval, *Proceedings of IEEE Multimedia Modeling(MMM '98)*, 1998, pp. 24–31.
85. C.S. Lee, W.-Y. Ma, and H.J. Zhang, Information embedding based on user's relevance feedback for image retrieval, *Proc. SPIE Multimedia Storage Arch. Syst. IV* **3846**, 294–304 (1999).
86. G. Briscoe and T. Caelli, ed., *A Compendium of Machine Learning*, Ablex series in Artificial Intelligence, Norwood, N.J., 1996.
87. R.W. Picard, Computer learning of subjectivity, *ACM Comput. surveys* **27**(4), 621–623 (1995).
88. S.-F. Chang, B. Chen, and H. Sundaram, Semantic visual templates: linking visual features to semantics, *Proceedings of International Conference on Image Processing (ICIP'98), Workshop on Content Based Video Search and Retrieval*, Chicago, Ill., October 1998, pp. 531–535.
89. A. Vailaya, A. Jain, and H.J. Zhang, On image classification: city vs. landscape, *Proceedings of IEEE Workshop on Content-Based Access of Image and Video Libraries*, Santa Barbara, Calif., June 21, 1998, pp. 3–8.
90. J.R. Smith and S.-F. Chang, Multi-stage classification of images from features and related text, *Proceedings Fourth DELOS workshop*, Pisa, Italy, August, 1997.
91. P. Lipson, Context and configuration based scene classification, Ph.D. thesis, MIT Electrical and Computer Science Department, Cambridge, Mass., September 1996.

92. C. Carson, S. Belongie, H. Greenspan, and J. Malik, Region-based image querying, *Proceedings IEEE Workshop on Content-Based Access of Image and Video Libraries*, 1997, pp. 42–49.

93. C. Frankel, M.J. Swain and V. Athitsos, WebSeer: an image search engine for the world wide web, University of Chicago Technical Report TR-96-14, July 31, 1996.

94. M. Gorkani and R.W. Picard, Texture orientation for sorting photos at a glance, *Proc. IEEE Int. Conf. Pattern Recog. (ICPR '94)* **1**, 459–464 (1994).

95. Y.A. Otha, A region-oriented image-analysis system by computer, Ph.D. thesis, Kyoto University, Kyoto, Japan, March 1980.

96. J. Mao and A.K. Jain, Texture classification and segmentation using multiresolution simultaneous autoregressive models, *Pattern Recog.* **25**(2), 173–188 (1992).

97. D. Aha, ed., *Lazy Learning*, Kluwer Academic Publishers, The Netherlands, 1997.

98. A. Jaimes, A.B. Benitez, S.-F. Chang, and A.C. Loui, Discovering recurrent visual semantics in consumer photographs, invited paper, *International Conference on Image Processing (ICIP 2000), Special Session on Semantic Feature Extraction in Consumer Contents*, Vancouver, Canada, September 10–13, 2000.

99. H. Wang and S.-F. Chang, A highly efficient system for automatic face region detection in MPEG video, *IEEE Trans. Circuits Syst. Video Technol., Special issue on Multimedia Syst. Technol.* **7**(4), 615–628 (1997).

100. H.A. Rowley, S. Baluja, and T. Kanade, Human Face Detection in Visual Scenes, Carnigie Mellon University Technical Report CMU-CS-95, 158, 1995.

101. M. Koster, Robots in the web: threat or treat?, *Connexions* **9**(4), April 1995.

102. R.O. Duda, P.E. Hart, and D.G. Stork, *Pattern Classification*, Wiley & Sons, New York, 2001.

103. A.V. Aho et al., Columbia digital news system, an environment for briefing and search over multimedia information, *Proceedings IEEE International Conference on the Advances in Digital Libraries (ADL) International Forum on Advances in Research and Technology*, Washington, D.C., May 1997, pp. 82–94.

104. A.W.M. Smeulders et al., Content-Based Image Retrieval at the End of the Early Years, *IEEE Trans. Pattern Anal. Machine Intell. (PAMI)* **22**(12), 1349–1380, (2000).

105. V.E. Ogle and M. Stonebraker, Chabot: retrieval from a relational database of images, *IEEE Comput. Mag.* **28**(9), 40–48 (1995).

106. A. Rosenfeild, Survey, image analysis and computer vision: 1992, *Comput. Vis. Graphics, Image Process. (CVGIP): Image Understanding* **58**(1), 85–135, (1993).

107. T.O. Binford, Survey of model-based image analysis systems, *Int. J. Robotics Res.* **1**(1), 18–64 (1992).

108. D. Marr, *Vision: A Computational Investigation into the Human Representation and Processing of Visual Information*, W. H. Freeman and Company, San Francisco, Calif., 1982.

109. W.I. Grosky and R. Mehrotra, Index-based object recognition in pictoral data management, *Comput. Vis., Graphics, Image Process. (CVGIP)* **52**, 416–436 (1990).

110. W.E.L. Grimson, *Object Recognition by Computer: The Role of Geometric Constraints*, MIT Press, Cambridge, Mass., 1990.

111. K. Ikeuchi and M. Veloso, ed., *Symbolic Visual Learning*, Oxford University Press, New York, 1997.

112. J. Durkin, *Expert Systems: Design and Development*, Prentice Hall, New Jersey, 1994.

113. B.A. Draper, Learning object recognition strategies, Ph.D. thesis, Computer Science Department, University of Massachusetts, Massachusetts, 1993.

114. B. Gunsel, A.M. Ferman, and A.M. Tekalp, Temporal video segmentation using unsupervised clustering and semantic object tracking, *IS&T/SPIE J. Electron. Imaging* **7**(3), 592–604 (1998).

115. D.M. McKeown, Jr., W.A. Harvey, Jr., and J. McDermott, Rule-based interpretation of aerial imagery, *IEEE Trans. Pattern Anal. Machine Intell. (PAMI)* **7**(5), 570–585 (1985).

116. D.M. McKeown, Jr., W.A. Harvey, Jr., and L.E. Wixson, Automatic knowledge acquisition for aerial image interpretation, *Comput. Vis., Graphics, Image Process. (CVGIP)* **46**, 37–81 (1989).

117. A.R. Hanson and E.M. Riseman, VISIONS: a computer system for interpreting scenes, in Hanson and Riseman, ed., *Computer Vision Systems*, Academic Press, New York, 1978, pp. 303–333.

118. K.M. Andress and A.C. Kak, Evidence accumulation and flow of control in a hierarchical reasoning system, *Artif. Intell. Magazine* **9**(2), 75–94 (1988).

119. S.J. Russell and P. Norvig, *Artificial Intelligence: A Modern Approach*, Prentice Hall series in artificial intelligence, Prentice Hall, Englewood Cliffs, N.J., 1995.

120. S. Paek and S.-F. Chang, The case for image classification systems based on probabilistic reasoning, *Proceedings, IEEE International Conference on Multimedia and Expo (ICME 2000)*, New York City, July 2000.

121. M. Turk, and A. Pentland, "Eigenfaces for recognition," *J. Cogn. Neurosci.* **3**(1), 71–86 (1991).

122. H. Murase and S.K. Nayar, Visual learning and recognition of 3D objects from appearance, *Int. J. Comput. Vis.* **14**(1), 5–24 (1995).

123. M. Nagao and T. Matsuyama, *A Structural Analysis of Complex Aerial Photographs*, Plenum Press, New York, 1980.

124. R. Brooks, Symbolic reasoning among 3-dimensional models and 2-dimensional images, *Artif. Intell.* **17**, 285–349 (1981).

125. T. Mitchell, *Machine Learning*, McGraw-Hill, New York, 1997.

126. A. Jaimes and S.-F. Chang, Learning visual object filters and agents for on-line media, ADVENT Project Technical Report, Columbia University, June 1999.

127. S. Nayar and T. Poggio, ed., *Early Visual Learning*, Oxford University Press, New York, 1996.

128. D.G. Lowe, *Perceptual Organization and Visual Recognition*, Kluwer Academic Publishers, Boston, Mass., 1985.

129. A. Amir, and M. Lindenbaum, A generic grouping algorithm and its quantitative analysis, *IEEE Trans. Pattern Recog. Machine Intell. (PAMI)* **20**(2), 186–192 (1998).

130. T.F. Syeda-Mahmood, Data and Model-Driven Selection Using Color Regions, *Int. J. Comput. Vis.* **21**(1/2), 9–36 (1997).

131. D. Healey, Preattentive Processing in Visualization, *http://www.cs.berkeley.edu/~healey/PP/PP.shtml*

132. S. Santini and R. Jain, Gabor Space and the Development of Preattentive Similarity, *Proc. Int. Conf. Pattern Recogn. (ICPR'96)* **1**, 40–44, (1996).

133. R. Jain and A. Hampapur, Metadata in Video Databases, *SIGMOD Record, Special Issue on Metadata for Digital Media*, December, 1994.
134. Y. Tonomura, A. Akutsu, Y. Taniguchi, and G. Suzuki, Structured video computing, *IEEE Multimedia Mag.* **1**(3), 34–43 (1994).
135. G. Durand, C. Thienot, and P. Faudemay, Extraction of composite visual objects from audiovisual materials, *Proc. SPIE Multimedia Arch. Syst. IV* **3846**, 194–203 (1999).
136. D. Zhong and S.-F. Chang, Video object model and segmentation for content-based video indexing, *Proc. IEEE Int. Conf. Circuits Syst.*, Special session on Networked Multimedia Technology & Applications **2**, 1492–1495, (1997).
137. C.M. Privitera and L.W. Stark, Algorithms for Defining Visual Regions-of-Interest: Comparison with Eye Fixations, *IEEE Trans. Pattern Anal. Machine Intell. (PAMI)* **22**(9), 970–981, 2000.
138. A. Jaimes et al., Using human observers' eye movements in automatic image classifiers, *Proceedings of SPIE Human Vision and Electronic Imaging VI*, San Jose, 2001.
139. J. Russ, *The Image Processing Handbook*, 3rd ed., CRC Press, Boca Raton, Fla., 1999.
140. T.R. Reed and J.M. Hans Du Buf, A review of recent texture segmentation and feature extraction techniques, *Comput. Vis. Graphics, Image Process. (CVGIP): Image Understanding* **57**(3), 359–372 1993.
141. E.G.M. Petrakis and C. Faloutsos, Similarity searching in large image databases, University of Maryland Department of Computer Science, Technical Report, No. 94–88, College Park, Md., 1995.
142. A. Jaimes and S.-F. Chang, Automatic selection of visual features and classifiers, *Proc. SPIE Storage Retrieval Media Databases 2000* **3972**, 346–358, (2000).
143. R. Kohavi et al., MLC++: A machine learning library in C++, *Proceedings of Conference on Tools with Artificial Intelligence 94*, New Orleans, La., November 1994.
144. A. Jain and D. Zongker, Feature selection: evaluation, application, and small sample performance, *IEEE Trans. Patt. Anal. Machine Intell. (PAMI)* **19**(2), 153–158 (1997).
145. D.L. Swets and J.J. Weng, Efficient content-based image retrieval using automatic feature selection, *Proceedings of International Conference on Computer Vision (ICCV'95)*, Coral Gables, Fla. November 1995.
146. M. Das and E.M. Riseman, Feature selection for robust color image retrieval, *Proceedings of DARPA IUW*, New Orleans, La., 1997.
147. R. Kohavi, Feature subset selection using the wrapper model: overfitting and dynamic search space topology, *Proceedings of First International Conference on Knowledge Discovery and Data Mining*, Montreal, Canada, August 1995, pp. 192–197.
148. J.R. Quinlan, Induction of Decision Trees, *Machine Learning* **1**(1), 81–106 (1986).
149. A.Y. Ng, On feature selection: learning with exponentially many irrelevant features as training examples, *Proceedings of International Conference on Machine Learning (ICML)*, Madison, Wis., July 1998.
150. D. Koller and M. Sahami, Toward optimal feature selection, *Proceedings of 13th International Conference on Machine Learning (ICML)*, Bary, Italy, July 1996.

151. G.H. John, R. Kohavi, and K. Pfleger, Irrelevant features and the subset selection problem, *Proceedings of 11th International Conference on Machine Learning (ICML'94)*, 1994, pp. 121–129.

152. T.G. Dietterich, Proper statistical tests for comparing supervised classification learning algorithms, Technical Report, Department of Computer Science, Oregon State University, Corvallis, Ore., 1996.

153. P.M. Murphy, *UCI Repository of Machine Learning Databases- a machine-readable data repository*, Maintained at the department of Information and Computer Science, University of California, Irvine; Anonymous FTP from *ics.uci.edu* in the directory pub/machine-learning-databases, 1995.

154. R. Kohavi, A study of cross-validation and bootstrap for accuracy estimation and model selection, *Proceedings of the 14th International Joint Conference on Artificial Intelligence (JCAI'95)*, Morgan Kaufmann Publishers, I. 1995, pp. 1137–1143.

155. A.W. Moore and M.S. Lee, Efficient algorithms for minimizing cross validation error, *Proceedings of the 11th International Conference on Machine Learning*, Morgan Kaufmann, 1994.

156. A. Jaimes and S.-F. Chang, Integrating multiple classifiers in visual object detectors learned from user input, invited paper, session on Image and Video Databases, *4th Asian Conf. Comput. Vis. (ACCV 2000)* **1**, 376–381 (2000).

157. J.M. Keller, M.R. Gray, and J.A. Givens Jr., A fuzzy k-nearest neighbor algorithm, *IEEE Trans. Syst. Man, Cybern.* **15**(4), 580–585 (1985).

158. Z. Michalewicz, *Genetic Algorithms + Data Structures = Evolution Programs*, Springer-Verlag, New York, 1992.

159. J. Meng and S.-F. Chang, Tools for compressed-domain video indexing and editing, *Proc. SPIE Conf. Storage Retrieval Image Video Database* **2670**, 180–191 (1996).

160. E. Rosch and C.B. Mervis, Family resemblances: studies in the internal structure of categories, *Cogn. Psychol.* **7**, 573–605 (1975).

161. D.M. Bates and D.G. Watts, *Nonlinear Regression Analysis and its Applications*, Wiley & Sons, New York, 1988.

162. W. Cohen, Learning trees and rules with set-valued features, *Proceedings of Thirteenth National Conference on Artificial Intelligence (AAAI 1996)*, Portland, Oregon, August 1996.

163. S. Geman, D.F. Potter, and Z. Chi, Composition systems, *Technical Report Division of Applied Mathematics*, Brown University, 1998.

164. T. Hastie and D. Pregibon, Shrinking trees, *AT&T Bell Laboratories Technical Report*, 1990.

165. C.R. Hick, *Fundamental Concepts in the Design of Experiments*, Holt, Rinehart, and Wilson, New York, 1982.

166. Y.S. Ho and A. Gersho, Classified transform coding of images using vector quantization, *IEEE Int. Conf. Acoust. Signal Process. (ICASP'89)* **3**, 1890–1893 (1989).

167. A. Jaimes, and S.-F. Chang, Learning visual object detectors from user input, invited paper, *International Journal of Image and Graphics (IJIG), special issue on Image and Video Databases* (to appear).

168. R.A. Jarvis and E.A. Patrick, Clustering using similarity measure based on shared near neighbors, *IEEE Trans. Comput.* **22**(11), 1973.

169. R. Kasturi and R.C. Jain, ed., *Computer Vision: Principles*, IEEE Computer Society Press, 1991.

170. E. Lang, K.-U. Carstensen, and G. Simmons, Modelling spatial knowledge on a linguistic basis, *Lecture Notes in Artificial Intelligence*, 481, Springer-Verlag, Berlin, 1991.

171. F. Liu and R.W. Picard, Periodicity, directionality and randomness: wold features for image modeling and retrieval, *IEEE Trans. Pattern Anal. Machine Intell. (PAMI)* **18**(7), 722–733 (1996).

172. J. Novovicová, P. Pudil, and J. Kittler, Divergence based feature selection for multimodal class densities, *IEEE Trans. Pattern Anal. Machine Intell. (PAMI)* **18**(2), 218–223 (1996).

173. S. Paek, A.B. Benitez and S.-F. Chang, Self-describing schemes for interoperable MPEG-7 content descriptions, *Proc. SPIE Vis. Commun. Image Process.* **3653**, 1518–1530 (1999).

174. A. Pentland, R.W. Picard, and S. Sclaroff, Photobook: tools for content-based manipulation of image databases, *Proc. SPIE Storage Retrieval Image Video Databases II*, **2187**, 34–47, (1994).

175. G. Salton, *Automatic Text Processing: The Transformation, Analysis, and Retrieval of Information by Computer*, Addison-Wesley, Mass. 1989.

176. G. Salton and C. Buckley, Term weighting approaches in automatic text retrieval, *Inform. Process. Manage.* **25**(5), (1988).

177. S.L. Salzberg, On comparing classifiers: a critique of current research and methods, *Data Mining and Knowledge Discovery* **1**, 1–12 (1999).

178. T.J. Santner and D.E. Duffy, *The Statistical Analysis of Discrete Data*, Springer-Verlag, New York, 1989.

179. D.W. Scott, *Multivariate Density Estimation: Theory, Practice, and Visualization*, Wiley and Sons, New York, (1992).

180. J.R. Smith and S.-F. Chang, Transform features for texture classification and discrimination in large image databases, *IEEE Int. Conf. Image Process.* **3**, 407–411 (1994).

181. M.J. Swain and D.H. Ballard, Color indexing, *Int. J. Comput. Vis.* **7**(1), 11–12, (1991).

182. H. Tamura, S. Mori, and T. Yamawaki, Textural features corresponding to visual perception, *IEEE Trans. Syst. Man Cybern.* SMC-8:6, 1978.

183. A. Triesman, Preattentive processing in vision, *Comput. Vis. Graphics, Image Process. (CGVIP)* **31**, 156–177 (1985).

184. A. Vailaya, M. Figueiredo, A. Jain, and H.J. Zhang, Automatic orientation detection, *Proc. Int. Conf. Image Process. (ICIP'99)* **2**, 600–604 (1999).

185. N. Wacholder, Y. Ravin, and M. Choi, Disambiguation of proper names in text, *Proceedings of 5th Conference on Applied Natural Language Processing*, Washington, D.C., April 1997.

186. D. Zhong and S.-F. Chang, AMOS: an active system for Mpeg-4 video object segmentation, *Proc. Int. Conf. Image Process. (ICIP'98)* **2**, 647–651 (1998).

Index